PHP 5 Recipes

A Problem-Solution Approach

Lee Babin, Nathan A. Good,
Frank M. Kromann, Jon Stephens

 Apress®

PHP 5 Recipes: A Problem-Solution Approach
Copyright © 2005 by Lee Babin, Nathan A. Good, Frank M. Kromann, Jon Stephens

ISBN (pbk): 1-59059-509-2

Printed and bound in the United States of America 9 8 7 6 5 4 3 2 1

Trademarked names may appear in this book. Rather than use a trademark symbol with every occurrence of a trademarked name, we use the names only in an editorial fashion and to the benefit of the trademark owner, with no intention of infringement of the trademark.

Lead Editor: Chris Mills
Technical Reviewer: Rob Kunkle
Editorial Board: Steve Anglin, Dan Appleman, Ewan Buckingham, Gary Cornell, Tony Davis,
    Jason Gilmore, Jonathan Hassell, Chris Mills, Dominic Shakeshaft, Jim Sumser
Associate Publisher: Grace Wong
Project Manager: Kylie Johnston
Copy Edit Manager: Nicole LeClerc
Copy Editor: Kim Wimpsett
Assistant Production Director: Kari Brooks-Copony
Production Editor: Katie Stence
Compositor and Artist: Van Winkle Design Group
Proofreader: April Eddy
Indexer: Broccoli Information Management
Interior Designer: Van Winkle Design Group
Cover Designer: Kurt Krames
Manufacturing Manager: Tom Debolski

Distributed to the book trade worldwide by Springer-Verlag New York, Inc., 233 Spring Street, 6th Floor, New York, NY 10013. Phone 1-800-SPRINGER, fax 201-348-4505, e-mail orders-ny@springer-sbm.com, or visit http://www.springeronline.com.

For information on translations, please contact Apress directly at 2560 Ninth Street, Suite 219, Berkeley, CA 94710. Phone 510-549-5930, fax 510-549-5939, e-mail info@apress.com, or visit http://www.apress.com.

The source code for this book is available to readers at http://www.apress.com in the Source Code section.

Contents at a Glance

Contents

About the Authors

 **LEE BABIN** is a programmer based in Calgary, Alberta, where he serves as the chief programmer for an innovative development firm duly named The Code Shoppe. He has been developing complex web-driven applications since his graduation from DeVry University in early 2002 and has since worked on more than 50 custom websites and online applications. Lee is married to a beautiful woman, Dianne, who supports him in his rather full yet rewarding work schedule. He enjoys playing video games, working out, practicing martial arts, and traveling and can usually be found working online on one of his many fun web projects. While Lee has experience in a multitude of web programming languages, his preference has always been PHP. With the release of PHP 5, many of his wishes have been fulfilled.

 **NATHAN A. GOOD** is an author, software engineer, and system administrator in the Twin Cities in Minnesota. He fancies himself a regular Renaissance man but is known by his friends as having delusions of grandeur. His books include *Professional Red Hat Enterprise Linux 3* (Wrox, 2004), *Regular Expression Recipes: A Problem-Solution Approach* (Apress, 2005), and *Regular Expressions for Windows Developers: A Problem-Solution Approach* (Apress, 2005).

When Nathan is not working at a computer (which is rare), he spends time with his family, spends time at church, and during the three weeks of summer in Minnesota enjoys kayaking and biking.

 **FRANK M. KROMANN** is the senior software engineer at intelleFLEET, where he is responsible for software design and development as well as hardware integration. Most of this work is done as database-driven web applications and involves a combination of centralized Linux servers and decentralized Linux and Windows XP systems (touch-screen computers) for data acquisition.

Frank has been involved with PHP development since 1997; he has contributed several extensions to the project, has worked on countless others, and was responsible for the Windows version of PHP-GTK.

When he is not writing code, you can find him on a golf course in Southern California or having fun with his family.

 **▪JON STEPHENS** started in IT during the mid-1990s, teaching computers how to operate radio stations (and then teaching humans how to operate the computers). He has been working with and writing about web and open-source technologies since the turn of the century. A coauthor of *Professional JavaScript, Second Edition* (Wrox, 2001), *Constructing Usable Shopping Carts* (friends of ED, 2004), and most recently *Beginning MySQL Database Design and Optimization* (Apress, 2004), he's also a regular contributor to International PHP magazine.

Jon now works as a technical writer for MySQL AB, where he helps maintain the MySQL manual, hangs out in the MySQL user forums, and asks the MySQL developers questions about things he doesn't understand.

Having lived in most places where one can reasonably live in the United States, Jon migrated to Australia in 2002. He shares a house in Brisbane's South End with varying numbers of cats and computers. In his spare time, he likes going to the ocean, riding his bicycle, finding new and interesting places to drink coffee, reading the odd detective thriller, and watching *Bananas in Pyjamas* with his daughter, Eleanor.

About the Technical Reviewer

ROB KUNKLE has been a programmer and general computer enthusiast since he first got his index fingers on a Commodore 64. More recently, he makes a living as a consultant, both putting together applications and joyfully taking them apart. He loves a good airy discussion about subjects such as computational linguistics, dumb luck, artificial intelligence, or just wild speculation about the future.

He has a deep passion for photography; he enjoys trying to highlight the unspoken truths and converting beauty found in everyday events and otherwise overlooked things. If you ever happen to find yourself sitting in a cafe in the Inner Sunset district of San Francisco, be sure to sit by the window and daydream; he might just stroll by with his dog and snap your photo. You can see some of his images on `http://www.flickr.com` under the name "goodlux."

Introduction

As the Internet continues to evolve, so too does the necessity for a language that addresses the functionality needs of the Internet's web viewers. Over time, some programming languages have come and gone, and others have continued to evolve. Several languages have moved into the lead in the race for supremacy. Although languages such as ColdFusion, ASP.NET, and CGI certainly have their advantages, PHP seems to be the developer's choice for a versatile, open-source solution.

PHP has grown over the years and, thanks to its devotees, has continued to adopt the functionality most preferred by its user base. By actually listening to the developers to help guide PHP's development path, the PHP creators have introduced some impressive functionality over the years. However, PHP 4, while a sound developmental language and tool, was lacking on a few fronts. For instance, it had a means for developers to take an object-oriented approach, but several key pieces of functionality were not implemented, such as exception handling and session support (for objects).

PHP 5 has changed all that. No longer must developers write classes that are missing functionality. Available to PHP is a full set of object-oriented development tools. Of particular note in PHP 5 is the ability to protect class variables in several ways. In addition, inheritance difficulties are now a thing of the past, and exception handling has become a nice way of taking care of pesky errors and validation.

Thankfully, while PHP 5 has continued to develop, so too have the many extensions that work alongside it. Several key extensions are bundled with the download package; for instance, those who follow the MySQL database's continued evolution will be happy to find that the new `mysqli` extension contains a large set of functionality to help you work with queries in a much more object-oriented way and to help speed up the efficiency of database-driven web projects.

Further, the process of creating dynamic images has been improved; it is no longer difficult to install the GD2 library. Instead, it is bundled in PHP 5 from the start. All the bugs from recent incarnations of the GD library seem to have been dealt with, and creating images using the PHP 5 engine is simple and effective.

As web developers (and otherwise) continue to see XML as the be-all and end-all of portable data storage, PHP 5 has gracefully adopted such functionality in the form of Simple XML, which is a set of easy-to-use, custom-made, object-oriented methods for working with XML.

We could go on and on about the additions to PHP 5 that are getting rave reviews, but it is much more helpful to actually see such functionality at work. While advancements in technology take place every day, it is the actual implementation of such technology that brings forward movement to the world.

Therefore, to show you some of the new PHP 5 functionality in real-world situations, this book includes recipes that will allow you to simply drop code into your already custom-built applications. By covering the vast scope of web applications, this book's authors—with specialties in custom applications, database design, and Internet functionality—have devised a set of code-based snippets that will allow you to take your code and port it to the next level of PHP greatness.

We have considered everything from ease of use to migration (after all, many servers have not handled the PHP upgrade yet) so that you will be able to search this book and bring your code up to the cutting edge where it belongs. We hope you enjoy all that *PHP 5 Recipes* has to offer; by using the recipes in this book, you can put our extensive research and experience to work in your everyday coding conundrums.

Who This Book Is For

PHP 5 Recipes is for any PHP programmer looking for fast solutions to their coding problems and wanting to capitalize on PHP 5's new functionality. A basic knowledge of PHP is expected and will come in handy when using the recipes in this book. Ideally, any PHP programmer, from beginner to expert, will be likely to learn new things about PHP, especially PHP 5, and gain a cutting-edge script or three to add to their repertoire.

How This Book Is Structured

PHP 5 Recipes is essentially a cookbook of programming snippets. You will be able to search for the topic you are interested in and then find a sample you can integrate into your own projects. Each recipe has an overview, contains code listing, and is followed by an in-depth explanation of how the code works and where it might be applicable.

This book will guide you through the PHP 5 functionality set. In Chapter 1, you will start with the basics, including a complete overview of what makes the PHP language what it is. In Chapter 2, you will enter the world of object-oriented programming and see the advancements in PHP's fifth rendition.

In Chapter 3, you will learn how to take care of math issues (with an object-oriented approach, of course); in Chapter 4, you will enter the flexible and powerful world of arrays. One issue that can be a constant battle for programmers is dates and times. Therefore, Chapter 5 covers date and time–related functionality. Chapter 6 covers how to work with everyone's favorite virtual textile, strings.

Chapter 7 covers files and directories and explains in detail how PHP 5 can deal with a server's file structure. Once you have a good grasp of how to work with files and directories, you can then move into the rather amusing Chapter 8, which covers dynamic imaging; this chapter will teach you everything you need to know about creating images that can captivate the Internet and its audience.

Because working with regular expressions can be a difficult endeavor, Chapter 9 provides you with some custom expressions to help you improve your programming skills. Then you will return to the basics; Chapter 10 covers variables, and Chapter 11 explains functions. Don't be fooled, though—PHP 5 has added a lot of functionality that will make these two chapters interesting and informative.

We will then get away from the basic programming content and cover web basics. In Chapter 12, you will understand how to use some of the bells and whistles available in PHP 5. Forms will follow in Chapter 13, which contains a lot of functionality for providing a web interface to your potential development projects. Chapter 14 is on the cutting edge of technology in that it provides an in-depth listing of markup recipes.

Things will then wind down to Chapter 15, which covers MySQL and brings you up to speed on the technology associated with the new `mysqli` extension; these recipes use MySQL 4.1. Lastly, Chapter 16 provides an informative look at Internet services.

Prerequisites

For *PHP 5 Recipes*, it is recommended, naturally, that you upgrade your current version of PHP to the fifth incarnation. As this book goes to print, version 5.0.4 is the newest stable release. In fact, many code samples in this book will not work on the PHP 4 platform. With this in mind, you should also make sure to upgrade the server on which you are planning to host applications so that it supports PHP 5.*x*.

In addition, certain pieces of functionality within Chapter 16 will require MySQL 4.1. Of particular note is the `mysqli` extension, which requires MySQL 4.1 to run some of its functionality.

We tested all the code within this book on Apache server configurations within PC- and Linux-based operating systems. While most functionality should work on other popular server platforms, certain bugs may arise; of particular note is the newest version of IIS, which this book's code does not fully function on.

Downloading the Code

All the code featured in this book is available for download; just browse to `http://www.apress.com`, navigate to the Source Code section, and click this book's title. The sample code is compressed into a single ZIP file. Before you use the code, you'll need to uncompress it using a utility such as WinZip. Code is arranged in separate directories by chapter. Before using the code, refer to the accompanying `readme.txt` file for information about other prerequisites and considerations.

Customer Support

We always value hearing from our readers, and we want to know what you think about this book—what you liked, what you didn't like, and what you think we can do better next time. You can send us your comments by e-mail to `feedback@apress.com`. Please be sure to mention the book title in your message.

We've made every effort to ensure the text and code don't contain any errors. However, mistakes can happen. If you find an error in the book, such as a spelling mistake or a faulty piece of code, we would be grateful to hear about it. By sending in errata, you may save another reader hours of frustration, and you'll be helping to provide higher-quality information. Simply e-mail the problem to `support@apress.com`, where your information will be checked and posted on the errata page or used in subsequent editions of the book. You can view errata from the book's detail page.

■ ■ ■

CHAPTER 1

Overview of PHP Data Types and Concepts

PHP began life as a way to manage a small personal website and was imagined and realized by just one man, Ramsus Lerdorf. Originally dubbed Personal Home Page Tools, PHP quickly evolved over the years from the basic scripting engine for a personal website into a highly competitive, extremely robust code engine that is deployed on millions of websites across the globe. PHP's fast, effective engine; its widespread, open-source developer base; and its platform flexibility have all come together to create one of the world's most effective online scripting languages.

Throughout the years PHP has continued to improve on its foundations, providing increased functionality and scalability. Because of PHP's standard of listening to the community, fresh functionality is consistently added to every new release, allowing for more versatile code and upgrades to its already substantial library of built-in methods. For years, people have been using the PHP 4 series of code to create robust and powerful applications.

There is always room for improvement, however. Although PHP 4 is considered to be an object-oriented programming (OOP) language, the class functionality found within it was not entirely as flexible as some developers wanted it to be. Older OOP languages that have had more time to grow have some strong functionality that PHP simply was not able to roll out in its PHP 4 releases.

But that was then, and this is now. A very exciting occasion occurred for PHP developers everywhere on July 13, 2004: PHP released its long-anticipated version 5. Sporting a new object model powered by the already superb Zend II engine, PHP was ready to bring OOP to a new level with this release.

On top of new, more powerful class structures and functionality, PHP 5 has introduced many exciting features, some of which the community has been clamoring about for ages. Say "hello (world)" to proper exception handling; new, simple-to-implement XML support; more verbose Simple Object Access Protocol (SOAP) functionality for web services; and much, much more.

This book will provide you with highly versatile recipes for improving and expanding things with the new PHP 5 release. However, before we dive into that, in this chapter we will give you a simple overview of what PHP can do, what is new with PHP 5, and how you can apply these new concepts.

1-1. Variables

Variables in PHP are handled somewhat differently than in other similar programming languages. Rather than forcing the developer to assign a given variable a data type and then assign a value to it (as in languages such as C++ and Java), PHP automatically assigns a data type to a variable when a value is allocated to it. This makes PHP rather simple to use when declaring variables and inputting values into them.

PHP variables, of course, follow a certain set of rules. All variables must begin with $ and must be immediately followed by a letter or an underscore. Variables in PHP are indeed case-sensitive and can contain any number of letters, numbers, or underscores after the initial $ and first letter or underscore.

Although initially variables in PHP were always assigned by value, since the PHP 4 release (and including PHP 5), you can now assign variables by reference. This means you can create something of an alias to a variable that will change the original value if you modify the alias. This is quite different from value-assigned variables that are essentially copies of the original.

The following example shows a couple blocks of code to give you a good handle on PHP 5 variable functionality.

The Code

```php
<?php
  //sample1_1.php
  //A properly set-up PHP variable.
  $myvar = 0;
  //An improper PHP variable.
  //$1myvar = 0;

  $yourvar = "This is my value<br />";

  //An example of assigning variables by value.
  $myvar = $yourvar;
  //If we were to change it.
  $myvar = "This is now my value.<br />";
  echo $yourvar; //Echoes This is my value

  //An example of assigning a variable by reference.
  $myvar = &$yourvar;
  $myvar = "This is now my value.<br />";
  echo $yourvar; //Echoes This is now my value.<br />
?>
```

```
This is my value
This is now my value.
```

How It Works

Using superglobals has taken precedent while people slowly migrate their code from the old, variable-based method (which requires `register_globals` to be set to on in the `php.ini` file) to the new superglobal array method (which does not require `register_globals` to be set to on). Basically, rather than using the old method of gathering data from places such as cookies, sessions, and form variables, PHP 5 is moving its focus toward the concept of superglobals. A few custom PHP globals can gather information from different sources. By using these superglobals, a developer can keep order within a script by knowing and managing exactly where a variable has come from or will be going to. Considered largely more secure because you can build code to tell exactly where variables are coming from, rather than just accepting a variable at face value, superglobals are becoming the standard.

The default configuration for PHP 5 insists that the `register_globals` value be set to off. This means you have to put a little more thought into your code. Rather than just receiving a value and running with it, you must specify to PHP where the value is coming from and potentially where you are going to put it. The following is an example of some superglobals in action:

```php
<?php
  //Rather than accepting a value from a form like this:
  $formvar = $formvar;
  //Or like this:
  $formvar = $HTTP_POST_VARS['formvar'];

  //The new, way to receive a form var is as such:
  $formvar = $_POST['formvar'];
?>
```

Similarly, get variables, session variables, cookies, files, and a few others are now handled in much the same way. Consider this example with sessions that will check for a valid login:

```php
<?php
  if ($_SESSION['loggedin']){
    echo "Proper login";
  } else {
    echo "You are not logged in.";
  }
?>
```

By knowing exactly where your data has come from, you can prevent malicious people from inserting false code into your premade scripts through, say, the address bar.

To get a full understanding of PHP 5 and its variable system, please see Chapter 10 by Frank M. Kromann, where he will cover the wide world of variables in depth.

1-2. Numbers

As any good programming language should be able to, PHP is more than capable of taking care of any math problems you may have. PHP 5 is especially flexible when dealing with numbers because its variable accessing is so simple. That being said, you must exert a certain degree of caution while working with said variables in order to make sure you retain the proper data context. Luckily, PHP fully supports data typing; you just have to be careful when implementing it.

PHP also supports the full range of math functionality and even has a couple of math-related libraries to use. Everything from the basic math equations and operators, such as division or multiplication, all the way up to logarithms and exponents have a place to call home in PHP 5.

Basic math operations are quite simple in PHP 5, but you must exude a bit of extra caution when maintaining the integrity of the data and outputting the end result.

The Code

```php
<?php
  //sample1_2.php
  //You could assign an integer value this way:
  $myint = 10;
  //Then you could simply output it as so:
  echo $myint . "<br />";
  //But in order to MAKE SURE the value is an integer, it is more
  //practical to do it like this:
  echo (int) $myint . "<br />";
  //That way, when something like this occurs:
  $myint = 10 / 3;
  //You can still retain an integer value like this:
  echo (int) $myint . "<br />"; //echoes a 3.
?>
```

```
10
10
3
```

How It Works

The next important aspect to numbers in PHP that you may want to consider is how to output them. PHP 5 supports a couple of nice functions, including printf() and sprintf(), that allow you to output the display as you would like. By using either of these functions, you can format your output data in several ways. Consider the following example in which it is integral that the value be displayed as a dollar amount set to two decimal places:

```php
<?php
  //Let's say you live in Canada and want to add GST tax to your amount.
  $thenumber = 9.99 * 1.07;
  //If you simply outputted this, the value would be skewed.
  echo "$" . $thenumber . "<br />"; //Outputs $10.6893
  //In order to show the value as a dollar amount, you can do this:
  echo "$" . sprintf ("%.2f", $thenumber); //Outputs $10.69
?>
```

```
$10.6893
$10.69
```

Basically, you can manipulate numbers in PHP in much the same way as you handle them in most programming languages. Those familiar with a language such as C++ or JavaScript will not have many issues when piecing together equations for PHP 5. To get a more in-depth explanation of numbers and some helpful real-world examples (including a static math class), skip ahead to Frank M. Kromann's detailed explanation on PHP 5's number crunching in Chapter 3.

1-3. Arrays

One of PHP 5's major strengths resides in its rather powerful and verbose array processing capabilities. Those familiar with a programming language such as C++ will feel right at home, as PHP 5 has a truly formidable set of array functionality.

Many types of arrays are available to you in PHP 5, and you have many different ways to work with them. PHP 5 fully supports regular arrays, multidimensional arrays, and even the handy associative array. Unlike the string functions available to PHP, the array functions are actually rather well organized and follow fairly easy-to-use naming conventions that make it straightforward to work with them.

Setting up and assigning both associative arrays and regular arrays in PHP is easy. PHP arrays start the index at zero, as most programming languages do. Indexing arrays is just as easy; PHP 5 supports several methods to cycle through arrays and even has many built-in functions for performing all sorts of handy methods such as sorting, reversing, and searching.

The following is a simple example of how to set up an array in PHP 5.

The Code

```php
<?php
  //sample1_3.php

  //Set up a standard array.
  $myarray = array("1","2","3");
  //You can access values from the array as simply as this:
  echo $myarray[0]; //Would output "1".
  //Or with a for loop.
  for ($i = 0; $i < count ($myarray); $i++){
    echo $myarray[$i] . "<br />";
  }
```

```
   //Setting up an associative array is similarly easy.
   $myassocarray = array ("mykey" => 'myvalue', "another" => 'one');
   //And there is the handy while, each method for extracting info from
   //associative arrays.
   while ($element = each ($myassocarray)) {
    echo "Key - " . $element['key'] . " and Value - " . $element['value'] . "<br />";
   }
?>
```

```
11
2
3
Key - mykey and Value - myvalue
Key - another and Value - one
```

How It Works

Arrays are quite a powerful tool in PHP 5; you can use them in a myriad of ways. To take advantage of arrays in truly powerful ways, be sure to check out Jon Stephen's Chapter 4. Chapter 4 is chock-full of examples that will help you get the most from PHP 5's array functionality.

1-4. Strings

Strings within PHP have evolved in an interesting manner. Over time PHP has accumulated a fair amount of truly powerful timesaving functions that are included in any fresh install of PHP 5. Combine this with PHP's useful variable handling, and PHP 5 seems set to do anything you would like with strings.

Unfortunately, although the functionality for strings that PHP contains is both powerful and handy, it is also somewhat all over the place. Function naming conventions are rather skewed and do not make a whole lot of sense. You may need to do a fair bit of searching the PHP manual to utilize strings to their full potential.

String handling plays an important role in today's online software development. With the need for proper data validation and security constantly on the rise, so too must the developer's skill with string handling improve. By using some of the more powerful functions in the PHP language, you can make it so only the data you want gets put into your data storage agents and only the data you want to be visible makes its appearance on your web pages.

Setting up and working with both strings and substrings is effortless with PHP 5, as the following example demonstrates.

The Code

```php
<?php
  //sample1_4.php

  //Because PHP determines the data type when a value is assigned to a variable
  //setting up a string is as easy as this:
  $mystring = "Hello World!";
  //And naturally, outputting it is as easy as this:
  echo $mystring . "<br />";

  //Similarly, with the help of built-in functions like substr(), it is easy to work
  //with substrings as well.
  echo substr ($mystring,0,5), //Would output Hello.
?>
```

```
Hello World!
Hello
```

How It Works

Because working with strings is an important matter, to really get the most out of them make sure you visit Chapter 6 get an in-depth look at what is truly possible in PHP 5 by using strings. Not only will you get a good string explanation and plenty of examples, but you will also see PHP 5's class handling put to good use.

1-5. Regular Expressions

Regular expressions are interesting animals. Basically, a regular expression helps to validate against a certain pattern of characters. Regular expressions provide you with a means to give your script an example, if you will, to compare its variables against. By using PHP 5's regular expressions, you can create something of a variable map that you can then compare a value against to determine its validity.

There are no real barriers to using regular expressions in PHP 5; the library containing its important functions has been included in PHP since version 4.2. Those familiar with Perl's syntax for regular expressions will feel right at home working with them in PHP, as they share similar structures.

Basically, two major subcategories of functions for regular expressions exist: ereg() and preg_match(). Both of them allow you to set up a regular expression that you can then use to compare strings against.

Commonly, regular expressions are used to validate data before insertion into a database or some other form of data storage. When you need to ensure that an exact data string has been submitted, there is no better way to confirm this than with regular expressions. Common uses of regular expressions are to check Uniform Resource Locator (URL) or e-mail submissions, because they both follow a common set of rules. (In other words, all e-mail addresses will have a grouping of words, potentially divided by periods on either side of an @ character.)

The following is an example of a regular expression that will check to ensure that a properly formatting e-mail string has been submitted.

The Code

```php
<?php
 //sample1_5.php

 $email = "lee@babinplanet.ca";
 echo preg_match("/^([a-zA-Z0-9])+([.a-zA-Z0-9_-])*@([a-zA-Z0-9_-])+➡
(.[a-zA-Z0-9_-]+)+[a-zA-Z0-9_-]$/",$email); //Would return 1 (true).
 echo "<br />";
 $bademail = "leebabin.ca";
 echo preg_match("/^([a-zA-Z0-9])+([.a-zA-Z0-9_-])*@([a-zA-Z0-9_-])+➡
(.[a-zA-Z0-9_-]+)+[a-zA-Z0-9_-]$/",$bademail); //Would return 0 (false).

?>
```

```
1
0
```

How It Works

As you can see, regular expressions can be confusing and can quite easily get out of hand. Coding them requires a fair bit of trial and error and can quickly become overwhelming if you are not careful. On the plus side is that most regular expressions, once coded, never really need to be coded again, as they generally validate against strings that follow a rigid set of rules and rarely change.

With that in mind, please feel free to check out Nathan A. Good's Chapter 9 to experience a fair amount of regular expressions that will come in handy with your everyday code.

1-6. Functions

A staple to any good programming language is the ability to declare and then program functions. Basically, functions are blocks of code that can be called upon to produce a desired effect. Functions in PHP 5 can have values both passed to them and returned from them. By using functions effectively, you can clean up a lot of redundant code by placing commonly used functionality into a single method.

The way functions work has not changed all that drastically with the advent of PHP 5. You can still write functions however you want, you can still pass them values, and they can still return values. One new addition to PHP 5, however, is the ability to include functions in XSL Transformations (XSLT) stylesheets. While XML purists will no doubt have trouble with the removal of the portability of XML, those who strictly use PHP to access and maintain their XML will find it a godsend.

Functions follow the same sort of naming conventions that variables do, but $ is not required to precede the name of the function as it is with variables. The first character in a function name can similarly not be a number and can instead be any letter or an underscore. The following characters can then be any combination of letters, numbers, and underscores.

Class-embedded methods now have a few new features in PHP 5. You can now call parent methods from within a child class and set up the protection you want to implement on methods declared within classes. By doing this, you can set up methods that can be called from any object instance or strictly allow only child classes or internal methods to take advantage of certain methods.

The following example shows how to build and then call a function; it is a simple process that will look familiar to those fluent in other programming languages.

The Code

```php
<?php
//sample1_6.php

  //Here we create and then call a simple function that outputs something.
  function helloworld (){
     echo "Hello World!<br />";
  }
  //We call it as easy as this:
  helloworld();

  //Creating and calling a function that accepts arguments is just as easy.
  function saysomething ($something){
     echo $something . "<br />";
  }
  Saysomething ("Hello World!"); //This would output "Hello World!"

  //And of course we can have our function return something as well.
  function addvalues ($firstvalue, $secondvalue){
     return $firstvalue + $secondvalue;
  }
  $newvalue = addvalues (1,3);
  echo $newvalue; //Would echo "4".
?>
```

```
Hello World!
Hello World!
4
```

How It Works

Obviously, as you can imagine, functions can get complicated but can generate some powerful results. As you go through this book, you will find plenty of worthy functions that may come in handy during your application development. Feel free to skip ahead to Chapter 11 to get a more in-depth explanation on what is truly possible in the world of PHP 5 functions.

1-7. Project: Finding the Data Type of a Value

Because of the (potentially) constantly changing data types in a variable, PHP can sometimes be a little too lenient. Sometimes keeping constant control over a variable's data type is not only required but is essential. Thankfully, while PHP variables can and will change data types on the fly, ways still exist to force a variable to retain a certain data type. PHP supports both typecasting and methods that can force a variable into a certain data type. Table 1-1 lists PHP 5's data types.

Table 1-1. *PHP 5 Data Types*

Data Type	Description
Boolean	Stores either a `true` or `false` value
Integer	Stores a numeric value that is a whole number
Double	Stores a numeric value that can contain a number of decimal places (commonly called a *float*)
String	Stores a chain of characters
Array	Stores an indexed container of values
Object	Stores an instance of a defined class
Resource	Holds a reference to an external source
NULL	Represents a variable that has no value

Two all-inclusive functions in PHP both get and set the value of a variable. Aptly titled `gettype()` and `settype()`, they do exactly what you would assume they would. The `gettype()` function returns a string containing the (current) data type of a variable. The `settype()` function sets the variable supplied to it with the data type also supplied to it. The prototypes for these two functions are as follows:

```
bool settype ( mixed &var, string type )
string gettype ( mixed var )
```

Both of these variables may not be the best way to get things done, however. Although `gettype()` will tell you what the data type of a variable is, you should already have a good idea of what the variable probably is. More often than not, if you are checking on the data type of a variable, you are attempting to confirm that it is the type that you need it to be, quite often for validation. In this case, each data type corresponds to a function that begins with `is_` (see Table 1-2). If you are completely clueless as to what the data type of a variable is, then either you are not paying enough attention to what is going on in your script or you are using it for some extremely heavy debugging.

Table 1-2. *PHP* is_ *Functions*

Data Type	Return Type	Function
Boolean	bool	is_bool (mixed var)
Integer	bool	is_int (mixed var)
Double	bool	is_float (mixed var)
String	bool	is_string (mixed var)
Array	bool	is_array (mixed var)
Object	bool	is_object (mixed var)
Resource	bool	is_resource (mixed var)
NULL	bool	is_null (mixed var)

In the following example, the script illustrates how to use an is_ function to determine a proper data type and then work with it if necessary.

The Code

```php
<?php
 //sample1_7.php

 //Here is a variable. It is pretty easy to see it is a string.
 $unknownvar = "Hello World";
 echo gettype ($unknownvar) . "<br />"; //Will output string.
 //The gettype is quite slow; the better way to do this is:
 if (is_string ($unknownvar)){
   //Then do something with the variable.
   echo "Is a string<br />";
 }
?>
```

```
String
Is a string
```

How It Works

As you can see in the previous example, although the gettype() function will tell you that you have a string, in most cases of validation the is_ functions will do a far superior job. Not only are the is_ functions more efficient from a processing point of view, but by using them at all times to validate the data type of a variable, you get around the real possibility that a PHP variable will have its type changed again somewhere else within the script.

Similar to getting the data type of a variable, it is not always best to use settype() to assign a data type to a variable. PHP supports the concept of data typing, which will allow you to force a variable into a specific data type. Not only is this fast and efficient, but you can use it much more cleanly in scripts. For example:

```php
<?php
  //Let's say we start with a double value.
  $mynumber = "1.03";
  //And let's say we want an integer.
  //We could do this:
  $mynumber = settype ($mynumber ,"integer");
  echo $mynumber . "<br />"; //Would output 1.
  //But it is better and looks far cleaner like this:
  echo (int) $mynumber;
?>
```

Sometimes PHP is almost a little too simple to set up and maintain, which can lead to obvious mistakes. Thankfully, for the careful programmer, you can easily control the type of your variables and ensure a successful, highly functional application.

1-8. Project: Discovering What Variables, Constants, Functions, Classes, and Interfaces Are Available

While running scripts in PHP, it may become necessary from time to time to check whether an instance of a method, function, class, variable, or interface exists. PHP 5 has all your bases covered in this case and contains some built-in functions to provide your script with the answers it truly requires.

PHP provides you with a set called the _exists function line-up. Through four of these functions you can determine if a function exists, whether an interface or method exists, and even whether a class exists. The prototypes for function_exists(), method_exists(), class_exists(), and interface_exists() are as follows:

```php
bool function_exists ( string function_name )
bool method_exists ( object object, string method_name )
bool class_exists ( string class_name [, bool autoload] )
bool interface_exists ( string interface_name [, bool autoload] )
```

These functions can come in handy when preparing your scripts for use. Validation is always key when programming large-scale applications, and the more massive in size they become, the more important validation such as this becomes. The following example shows how to use these functions for validation.

The Code

```php
<?php
  //sample1_8.php

  //Let's say you had a script that for a long time
  //called a function called isemail().
  //Like this, for instance:
  /*
  if (isemail($email)){ //This will generate an error.
    //Insert e-mail address into the database.
  } else {
```

```
  //Perform validation.
  echo "Not a valid e-mail address.";
}
*/
//Now, if someone went ahead and changed the name of isemail(), your script
//would crash.
//Now, try something like this instead:
if (function_exists($isemail)){
  if (isemail($email)){
    //Insert e-mail address into the database.
  } else {
    //Perform validation.
    echo "Not a valid e-mail address.";
  }
} else {
  //Handle the error by sending you an e-mail telling you the issues.
  echo "Function does not exist.<br />";
}
?>
```

```
Function does not exist.
```

How It Works

As you can see, the second part of the previous script will take care of things in a much more
professional manner. As we mentioned, this sort of thing may not be an issue with smaller
applications, but as application size increases and the number of members on your team
upgrades substantially, issues such as this quickly become valid.

Especially important is this sort of validation within classes. Using class_exists(),
method_exists(), and interface_exists() can be a lifesaver within real-world, large-scale
applications that have a significantly sized team attending to them. An example of some
serious validation is as follows:

```
<?php
  //First off, before we extend any class, we should confirm it exists.
  if (class_exists (myparent)){
    class anyclass extends myparent {
      public $somemember;
      public function dosomething (){
        //Here we ensure that the parent method exists.
        if (method_exists (parent,"parentmethod")){
          //Then we can proceed.
        } else {
          //Mail us a warning.
        }
      }
```

```
    }
  } else {
    //Mail us a warning.
    echo "Class does not exist.<br />";
  }
?>
```

Class does not exist.

Lastly, and most commonly, sometimes you will want to test to see whether a variable exists. Likely, this will come about from user- or script-submitted values that will determine whether a script will perform an action. By using the isset() function, your script can determine whether a variable has been set up. Consider the following example, which will help you determine whether a search variable has been posted from a search engine:

```
<?php
  //We are looking to receive a value from a "post" form before we search.
  if (isset ($_POST['searchterm'])){
    //Then we would perform our search algorithm here.
  } else {
    //Or else, we generate an error.
    echo "You must submit a search term. Please click the Back button.";
  }
?>
```

You must submit a search term. Please click the Back button.

1-9. Getting Information About the Current Script

Sometimes while developing it can be prudent to find out information about the environment you are developing in and also where certain aspects of the script stand. For an all-encompassing look at everything you would ever need to know about your version of PHP (but were afraid to ask), you could do worse than calling the function phpinfo(). The function phpinfo() lists pretty much every applicable variable in the PHP configuration as well as general interesting facts such as the version number and when it was last compiled.

You can even display a table detailing the masterminds behind this wonderful language by using the phpcredits() function; this is really nothing more than a curiosity, but it is there should you require it.

To output all this fancy information, you need to make a quick function call or two, as shown in the following example.

The Code

```php
<?php
  //sample1_9.php
  //Yes, that is it…
  phpinfo();
  //And credits if you so wish to see:
  phpcredits();
?>
```

Figure 1-1 shows some output of the phpinfo() function, and Figure 1-2 shows some output of the phpcredits() function.

PHP Version 5.0.3

System	Windows NT BABINZ-CODEZ 5.1 build 2600
Build Date	Dec 15 2004 08:06:41
Configure Command	cscript /nologo configure.js "--enable-snapshot-build" "--with-gd=shared"
Server API	Apache 2.0 Handler
Virtual Directory Support	enabled
Configuration File (php.ini) Path	C:\WINDOWS\php.ini
PHP API	20031224
PHP Extension	20041030
Zend Extension	220040412
Debug Build	no
Thread Safety	enabled
IPv6 Support	enabled
Registered PHP Streams	php, file, http, ftp, compress.zlib
Registered Stream Socket Transports	tcp, udp

This program makes use of the Zend Scripting Language Engine:
Zend Engine v2.0.3, Copyright (c) 1998-2004 Zend Technologies

Powered By

Figure 1-1. *Example output of the* phpinfo() *function*

PHP Credits

PHP Group
Thies C. Arntzen, Stig Bakken, Shane Caraveo, Andi Gutmans, Rasmus Lerdorf, Sam Ruby, Sascha Schumann, Zeev Suraski, Jim Winstead, Andrei Zmievski

Language Design & Concept
Andi Gutmans, Rasmus Lerdorf, Zeev Suraski

PHP 5 Authors	
Contribution	Authors
Zend Scripting Language Engine	Andi Gutmans, Zeev Suraski
Extension Module API	Andi Gutmans, Zeev Suraski, Andrei Zmievski
UNIX Build and Modularization	Stig Bakken, Sascha Schumann
Win32 Port	Shane Caraveo, Zeev Suraski
Server API (SAPI) Abstraction Layer	Andi Gutmans, Shane Caraveo, Zeev Suraski
Streams Abstraction Layer	Wez Furlong

SAPI Modules	
Contribution	Authors
ActiveScript	Wez Furlong
AOLserver	Sascha Schumann
Apache 1.3 (apache_hooks)	Rasmus Lerdorf, Zeev Suraski, Stig Bakken, David Sklar, George Schlossnagle, Lukas Schroeder
Apache 1.3	Rasmus Lerdorf, Zeev Suraski, Stig Bakken, David Sklar
Apache 2.0 Filter	Sascha Schumann, Aaron Bannert
Apache 2.0 Handler	Ian Holsman, Justin Erenkrantz (based on Apache 2.0 Filter code)

Figure 1-2. *Example output of the* phpcredits() *function*

How It Works

You can also get little tidbits of information to display to your screen without outputting the overwhelming mass of information that phpinfo() or phpcredits() create for you by using a more specific function such as phpversion(). This function is just as easy to use as phpinfo():

```php
<?php
  echo phpversion(); //Outputs 5.0.3 on my current setup.
?>
```

5.0.3

Naturally, you can also get individual element information about the current PHP settings by using the ini_get() function. You can even set the variables temporarily with the ini_set() function, which can come in handy under certain circumstances. We will discuss the ini_set() function in more detail in Chapter 12, so for now we will cover the ini_get() function. It has a prototype as such:

string **ini_get** (string varname)

Too many arguments exist that can be passed to this function to list here; through this function you can access pretty much any variable that can be set in the php.ini file. You can even view all the configuration values by using the function ini_get_all(). Here is an example of how you can use it:

```php
<?php
  //Check to see the maximum post value size.
  echo ini_get ("post_max_size") . "<br />"; //Outputs 8M on our current server.
  //Output all of the values.
  $myarray = ini_get_all();
  print_r($myarray);
?>
```

8M

Another handy, yet not required, function that PHP can produce for you is the getlastmod() function. This function can return to you a Unix timestamp with the last modified date. This can be helpful to keep track of a given script's past and could potentially be used to track changes to the document. This is not meant to be used as a revision control system, however, as there are other, more powerful methods available for this. Here is a quick example of how to output the last time your script was updated:

```php
<?php
  echo date ("F d Y H:i:s.", getlastmod()) . "<br />"; //June 01 2005 20:07:48.
?>
```

June 01 2005 20:07:48.

A truly powerful way to keep in touch with your script is using the predefined variable $_SERVER. By feeding this variable arguments, you can extract valuable server- and script-related information. It works largely the same as the $_POST or $_GET variable but already has all the arguments it will need. Table 1-3 lists the $_SERVER arguments.

Table 1-3. *PHP* $_SERVER *Arguments*

Argument	Result
PHP_SELF	Returns the filename of the current script with the path relative to the root
SERVER_PROTOCOL	Returns the name and revision of the page-requested protocol
REQUEST_METHOD	Returns the request method used to access the page
REQUEST_TIME	Returns the timestamp from the beginning of the request
DOCUMENT_ROOT	Returns the root directory under which the current script is executing
HTTP_REFERER	Returns the page address that referred to the current page
HTTP_USER_AGENT	Returns the user agent of the header from the current request (handy for browser identification)
REMOTE_ADDR	Returns the IP address of the current user (handy for security)
REMOTE_PORT	Returns the port of the user's machine that is accessing the page
SCRIPT_FILENAME	Returns the absolute filename from the current script
SCRIPT_NAME	Returns the path of the current script

As you can see, you can retrieve a multitude of possible values through the $_SERVER variable. For a complete list, refer to the PHP manual at http://www.php.net/reserved.variables.

The following is an example of a situation in which using the $_SERVER variable would come in handy. Consider that you wanted to create a counter that would track only those website visitors with a unique IP address. By using the $_SERVER variable, you can effectively determine whether the IP address browsing the site is unique to the data collection.

```php
<?php
    //We get the IP address of the current user.
    $curip = $_SERVER['REMOTE_ADDR'];
    //Then we do a database query to see if this IP exists.
    //Let's assume we have already put all of the IP addys in our
    //db into an array called $myarr.
    //We check if the new IP address exists in the array via the in_array() function.
    $myarray = array ();
    if (!in_array ($curip, $myarray)){
      //Then we insert the new IP address into the database.
      echo "We insert the IP addy: " . $curip . " into the database";
    } else {
      echo "The IP addy:" . $curip . " is already in the database.";
    }
?>
```

```
We insert the IP addy: 127.0.0.1 into the database
```

Summary

As you can see, PHP is a powerful and robust language that is growing in popularity and functionality. With the advent of PHP 5, many of the concerns users had regarding certain aspects have been largely resolved, or at least a resolution for them has begun. As you read the rest of this book, you will pick up a large volume of highly useful code (available handily on the Apress website) that can guide you and help you solve the many adversities you may come across in your time as a PHP developer.

Looking Ahead

In the next chapter, Jon Stephens will be taking you through the functionality involved with some of the more important improvements in PHP 5's object-oriented programming. As PHP continues to grow as an object-oriented language, it is continually evolving to respond to the demand for more robust and feature-laden code. Prepare to get structured as you make your way into the next chapter.

CHAPTER 2

■ ■ ■

Overview of Classes, Objects, and Interfaces

If you have worked with PHP in its earlier incarnations, then much of what you will find in PHP 5 is quite familiar, as you no doubt noticed from Lee Babin's survey of the major language features in Chapter 1. Like its predecessor, PHP 5 supports object-oriented programming, but the way in which this is implemented has changed; in fact, it has been expanded significantly from what was formerly available. In this chapter, we will acquaint you with the basics of classes, objects, and interfaces in PHP 5. In doing so, we will address the needs of several groups of readers to make sure that we all (forgive the expression) wind up on the same page.

This book assumes you have prior experience with PHP 4 or some other programming or scripting language. Of course, it is possible to write plenty of useful PHP 4 code (or PHP 5 code, for that matter) without using classes or objects, but we will start with a brief primer on those two concepts so you start to see the advantages of using them. If you are already familiar with the basics of object-oriented programming, then you will still find this chapter to be a useful time-saver; however, it might not be a revelation. If you are not familiar with object-oriented programming, prepare to be taken to the next level as a developer; once you begin to see the advantages of using it, you will likely not want to go back to a purely procedural way of coding.

If you are accustomed to writing object-oriented code in PHP 4, you will find that things have changed quite a bit, and mastering the differences might take some time. By the way, you will likely be happy to learn that the classes and objects you may have written for PHP 4 will usually work in PHP 5, although you may have to do a bit of tweaking here and there. We will point out the differences as we go and highlight any "gotchas" that might make things difficult for you.

If you are new to PHP but you have had some experience programming in a heavily object-oriented language such as Java or C++, you will find that most of the features of PHP 5 classes and objects will look familiar. In fact, the new object-oriented paradigm in PHP 5 is modeled largely on Java and includes interfaces, abstract classes and methods, and exceptions. We will discuss how these are handled in PHP 5 in due course.

Other topics we will cover in this chapter include the following:

- Creating, copying, and destroying objects

- Creating class diagrams

- Finding the methods and properties of an object

- Overriding methods and using polymorphism

- Creating classes and objects dynamically

By the time you have finished reading this chapter, you will have a good grasp of how classes and objects work in PHP 5, how they might prove useful in applications, how to obtain information about them, and the key differences between PHP 4 and PHP 5 in this regard. We will start with a brief look at what classes and objects are and explain some concepts you will need to understand in order to discuss and work with them.

Tip In this chapter, we have barely scratched the surface when it comes to object-oriented design, which is a huge field of its own and largely independent of any particular programming language. For more about object-oriented design principles as applied to PHP 5, refer to Matt Zandstra's excellent *PHP 5 Objects, Patterns, and Practice* (Apress, 2004). If you are serious about digging deep into PHP 5 objects and getting the most from them in your own applications, we strongly recommend you read this book. Since much object-oriented design literature is written with the assumption that the reader is fluent in C++ and/or Java, you will find *PHP 5 Objects, Patterns, and Practice* especially helpful if you do not have a great deal of experience in one of those two languages.

Understanding Basic Concepts

If you have never done any object-oriented programming before, then the terms *class* and *object* may sound mysterious and even a bit scary. (If you have, then you can safely gloss over or even skip the next few paragraphs and proceed to recipe 2-1.) However, classes and objects are really neither mysterious nor scary. After you have used them a few times, you will start to wonder how you managed to get along without them. Once you understand how they work, you should not have any trouble creating your own.

An *object* is basically a type of data that allows you to group data and functions under a single variable. In PHP, the -> operator denotes a member of a specific object, that is, a property (piece of data) or method (function) belonging to an object. You can think of it as meaning "has a," with the arrow pointing from the thing doing the having to the thing being had. In PHP 5, as in previous versions of the language, it is possible to create simple objects by doing nothing more than assigning object properties to an otherwise unused variable. For example:

```php
<?php
  $ball->color = "green";
  $ball->weight = 100;
```

```
  printf("The ball's color is %s, and its weight is %d kilos.",
        $ball->color, $ball->weight);
?>
```

The output of the previous code is as follows:

```
The ball's color is green, and its weight is 100 kilos.
```

If you are familiar with associative arrays, then you will understand what we mean when we say that you can think of an object as being like an associative array with alternative notation. They are quite similar, both being just unordered lists with named elements (rather than indexed elements). Whether you use this

```
$ball['weight'] = 100;
```

or this

```
$ball->weight = 100;
```

each gives you a way of saying "the $ball has something called weight, whose value is 100."

Where objects really become useful is when you have a way to create them on demand from a single pattern. A *class* defines a reusable template from which you can create as many similar objects (*instances* of the class) as you need. For example, if you are writing an inventory system for a pet shop, you are likely to be working with information about lots of birds, and you can write a Bird class to represent a generic bird; each instance of this class then represents an individual bird. You can think of the class as a collection of variables and functions common to all birds. Variables attached to an object in this way are *properties*, and functions manipulating these variables are *methods*. Together, the methods and properties of an object are its *members*.

We have always thought of a programming object as being like a noun, with its properties being adjectives (describing aspects of the objects) and its methods being verbs (representing the object's actions or changes that can be made to its properties). In the case of the Bird class, you would likely want to have properties to account for a bird's name, breed, and price. In this context, you probably are not going to be too concerned about the bird's flight speed or direction of travel, even though most birds are capable of flight—if you are not likely to use some aspect or capability of the thing you are modeling when you define a class, then you should not bother creating a corresponding class member.

Note A class is a template or prototype object. An instance of this class represents a particular case of this class. The word *object* can apply to classes and instances of classes alike.

Of course, programming objects do not have to model concrete objects; you can use them to represent abstractions as well. In subsequent chapters of this book, you will use classes to model abstract concepts such as dates and times (Chapter 5), files and directories (Lee Babin's Chapter 7), and Hypertext Markup Language (HTML) and Extensible Markup Language (XML) tags (Frank M. Kromann's Chapter 14).

2-1. Creating Instances Using Constructors

To create a new instance of a class (also referred to as *instantiating* a class), you can use the new operator in conjunction with the class name called as though it were a function. When used in this way, it acts as what is known as the *class constructor* and serves to initialize the instance. This instance is represented by a variable and is subject to the usual rules governing variables and identifier names in PHP. For example, consider the following:

```
$tweety = new Bird('Tweety', 'canary');
```

This creates a specific instance of Bird and assigns it to the variable named $tweety. In other words, you have defined $tweety as a Bird. So far you have not actually defined any members for the Bird class, and we have not discussed exactly how you define classes in PHP 5, so let's do those tasks now.

The Code

```php
<?php
  class Bird
  {
    function __construct($name, $breed)
    {
      $this->name = $name;
      $this->breed = $breed;
    }
  }
?>
```

How It Works/Variations

This is about as simple a class definition as you can write in PHP 5. As is the case in PHP 4, a PHP 5 class is defined in a block of code that begins with the class keyword and the name of the class. In most cases, a class is not going to be useful unless you can create instances of it (this rule has exceptions, which you will learn about in recipe 2-11). To accomplish this task, you need a class constructor. In PHP 5, you do this by defining a method with the name __construct(); this method is called whenever you create a new instance of the class.

Note It is customary in most programming languages, including PHP, to begin class names with a capital letter and to write names of class instances beginning with a lowercase letter. This is a convention we will observe throughout this book.

Note In PHP 4, a class constructor was written as a method with the same name as the class (for example, using a Bird() method as the constructor for the Bird class). While PHP 5 still supports this way of creating instances of classes for backward compatibility, it is not recommended for new code. You will see why when we talk about extending classes in recipe 2-7.

The $this keyword has a special purpose: it allows you to refer to the instance from within the class definition. It works as a placeholder and means, "the current instance of this class." The Bird class constructor assigns the string 'Tweety' to the name property of the instance you are creating and the string 'canary' to its breed property. You can put this to the test like so:

```php
<?php
  class Bird
  {
    function __construct($name, $breed)
    {
      $this->name = $name;
      $this->breed = $breed;
    }
  }

  $tweety = new Bird('Tweety', 'canary');

  printf("<p>%s is a %s.</p>\n", $tweety->name, $tweety->breed);
?>
```

The resulting output is as follows:

```
Tweety is a canary.
```

To determine the price you want to charge for Tweety, you could set the price property and output it like so:

```php
<?php
  // ...class defined and constructor called as previously shown...

  $tweety->price = 24.95;

  printf("<p>%s is a %s and costs \$%.2f.</p>\n",
          $tweety->name, $tweety->breed, $tweety->price);
?>
```

The output from this is as follows:

```
Tweety is a canary and costs $24.95.
```

Notice that no $price variable is defined within the class itself; you have created one arbitrarily. While this is not a terribly bad thing, it is also not a terribly good one: it means you can easily create Bird objects that are structurally inconsistent with others. If your application depends on all birds having prices, then you will run into trouble the first time you forget to assign a price to a bird. It is much better if you make sure every Bird has a price property by including it in the constructor. We will return to this topic shortly, but first we will finish discussing class instance creation and initialization.

■**Note** It is possible to write a class without a __construct() method and even to instantiate it, but most of the time this is not very useful.

2-2. Using Default Constructors

Suppose also that most—say, 80 percent—of your birds are priced at $15. Wouldn't it be more convenient if all your Bird instances came with prices already set to that amount and you were required to set the prices of only the remaining 20 percent? PHP lets you set default values for function parameters and for class constructors. The following example shows a slightly revised Bird class.

The Code

```php
<?php
  class Bird
  {
    function __construct($name='No-name', $breed='breed unknown', $price = 15)
    {
      $this->name = $name;
      $this->breed = $breed;
      $this->price = $price;
    }
  }

  $aBird = new Bird();
  $tweety = new Bird('Tweety', 'canary');

  printf("<p>%s is a %s and costs \$%.2f.</p>\n",
          $aBird->name, $aBird->breed, $aBird->price);

  $tweety->price = 24.95;

  printf("<p>%s is a %s and costs \$%.2f.</p>\n",
          $tweety->name, $tweety->breed, $tweety->price);
?>
```

Here is the output:

```
No-name is a breed unknown and costs $15.00.

Tweety is a canary and costs $24.95.
```

How It Works

You have created a default constructor for the Bird class. If you forget to set one or more properties when creating a new instance of the class, you will not get caught short later by a division-by-zero error, for example.

2-3. Setting Object Properties

A page or two back, we said it is better to include all properties of an object in its class definition rather than creating them dynamically. This is for two reasons. First, as we mentioned, you want to be sure all instances of a class have the same properties; otherwise, what happens when you forget to set a price for a Bird when some other part of your code expects there to be one? Second, when you assign a value to an object property, PHP does not check to see whether the property already exists. This means that it is all too easy to make a mistake that can be difficult to detect later, such as this one:

```php
<?php
  class Bird
  {
      function __construct($name='No-name', $breed='unknown', $price = 15)
    {
      $this->name = $name;
      $this->breed = $breed;
      $this->price = $price;
    }
  }

  $polly = new Bird('Polynesia', 'parrot');

  $polly->rice = 54.95;  //  ooooops...!

  printf("<p>%s is a %s and costs \$%.2f.</p>\n",
         $polly->name, $polly->breed, $polly->price);
?>
```

The output from this script is as follows:

```
Polynesia is a parrot and costs $15.00.
```

Just in case you have not spotted the error, you can add the following line of debugging code to this script to see all of Polynesia's properties at a glance:

```php
printf("<pre>%s</pre>\n", print_r(get_object_vars($polly), TRUE));
```

The function get_object_vars() makes a handy addition to your object-oriented programming toolkit. It takes any object as a parameter and returns an array whose keys are the names of the object's properties and whose values are the values of the properties. The output in this case is as follows:

```
Array
(
    [name] => Polynesia
    [breed] => parrot
    [price] => 15
    [rice] => 54.95
)
```

The typographical error has resulted in the addition of a new rice property to the $polly object, which is not what you wanted at all. You can avoid this sort of stuff by using methods to get and set properties rather than setting them directly. Let's rewrite the class, except this time we will include a setPrice() method.

The Code

```php
<?php
  class Bird
  {
    function __construct($name='No-name', $breed='unknown', $price = 15)
    {
      $this->name = $name;
      $this->breed = $breed;
      $this->price = $price;
    }

    function setPrice($price)
    {
      $this->price = $price;
    }
  }

  $polly = new Bird('Polynesia', 'parrot');

  printf("<p>%s is a %s and costs \$%.2f.</p>\n",
         $polly->name, $polly->breed, $polly->price);

  $polly->setPrice(54.95);

  printf("<p>%s is a %s and costs \$%.2f.</p>\n",
         $polly->name, $polly->breed, $polly->price);
?>
```

The output from this example is as follows:

```
Polynesia is a parrot and costs $15.00.

Polynesia is a parrot and costs $54.95.
```

Variations

What happens if you change the line containing the call to the setPrice() method to something like the following?

```
$polly->setPice(54.95);
```

Because you are attempting to call a method that has not been defined, the result is an
error message:

```
Fatal error: Call to undefined method Bird::setPice()
in /home/www/php5/bird-5.php on line 22
```

You will probably agree that this makes it much easier to find the source of the problem.
The same situation exists with regard to getting values of object properties: if you ask PHP for
the value of an undeclared variable, the chances are good that you will obtain zero, an empty
string, NULL, or boolean FALSE. If this is the same as the property's default value (or if the property has no default value), then finding the source of the error can be particularly difficult. On
the other hand, defining and using a getPrice() method minimizes the likelihood
of such problems occurring. A construct such as this

```
printf("<p>%s is a %s and costs \$%.2f.</p>\n",
        $polly->getName(), $polly->getBreed(), $polly->getPrice());
```

may require a few extra keystrokes, but you will find that the time saved in tracking down
problems that do not give rise to any error messages is worth the effort.

Note It is customary to name class members beginning with a lowercase letter. (A possible exception
to this is static members, which we will talk about in recipe 2-5.) As for what to do when a name contains
more than one word, two major schools of thought exist. Some programmers prefer to separate the words
using underscores, for example, my_long_method_name(). Others use what is known as intercap notation,
which consists of running the words together and capitalizing the first letter of each word after the first:
myLongMethodName(). We prefer the latter, so that is what we use. If you do not have to work to someone
else's coding conventions, then it is really just a matter of personal taste, as PHP does not care which one
you use. However, you will find it easier in the long run to adopt one style or the other and stick with it.

2-4. Controlling Access to Class Members

We will start the discussion of this topic with a modified version of the previous example. The
following shows the new Bird class, including a complete collection of get and set methods.

The Code<?php

```php
// file bird-get-set.php
class Bird
{
  function __construct($name='No-name', $breed='unknown', $price = 15)
  {
    $this->name = $name;
    $this->breed = $breed;
    $this->price = $price;
  }

  function setName($name)
  {
    $this->name = $name;
  }

  function setBreed($breed)
  {
    $this->breed = $breed;
  }
```

Notice that we have written the setPrice() method in such a way that the price cannot be
set to a negative value; if a negative value is passed to this method, the price will be set to zero.

```php
function setPrice($price)
{
  $this->price = $price < 0 ? 0 : $price;
}

function getName()
{
  return $this->name;
}

function getBreed()
{
  return $this->breed;
}

function getPrice()
{
  return $this->price;
}
```

To save some repetitive typing of the `printf()` statement that you have been using to output all the information you have about a given `Bird` object, you can add a new method named `display()` that takes care of this task:

```
function display()
{
  printf("<p>%s is a %s and costs \$%.2f.</p>\n",
         $this->name, $this->breed, $this->price);
}
}
```

Variations

Now let's create a new instance of `Bird`. Let's say that before you have the chance to write this example, the shop sells Polynesia the parrot; so, you will use a magpie this time. First, call the constructor with some plausible values:

```
$magpie = new Bird('Malaysia', 'magpie', 7.5);

$magpie->display();
?>
```

You can verify that the class is working as expected by viewing the output in a browser:

```
Malaysia is a magpie and costs $7.50.
```

Because the neighborhood cats are begging you to get rid of the magpie—even if it means paying someone to take it off your hands—try using `setPrice()` to set the magpie's asking price to a negative number:

```
$magpie->setPrice(-14.95);

$magpie->display();
```

The `setPrice()` method prevents you from setting the price to a value less than zero:

```
Malaysia is a magpie and costs $0.00.
```

However, it is still possible to circumvent this restriction, whether you do so by accident or the culprit is some particularly crafty, magpie-hating feline hacker:

```
$magpie->price = -14.95;

$magpie->display();
?>
```

As you can see here, this is the output:

```
Malaysia is a magpie and costs $-14.95.
```

How can you stop this sort of thing from happening? The solution lies in a feature that will be familiar to anyone who has studied Java, but it is new in PHP 5: *visibility*. This allows you to control how class members can be accessed through three keywords:

- public: The property or method can be accessed by any other code. This is the default visibility for all class members in PHP 5. (Note: In PHP 4, all class members are public.)

- private: A private class member can be accessed only from within the same class. Attempting to do so from outside the class will raise an error.

- protected: A class member that is declared as protected may be accessed from within the class and from within any class that extends that class. (We will discuss how to extend classes in recipe 2-7.)

Now that you know about visibility, fixing the problem you encountered is simple. Just insert the following into the Bird class before the definition of the constructor:

```
private $name;
private $breed;
private $price;
```

When you reload the example in your browser, you will see something like this:

```
Malaysia is a magpie and costs $7.50.

Malaysia is a magpie and costs $0.00.

Fatal error: Cannot access private property Bird::$price in
 /home/www/php5/bird-7.php on line 60
```

Making the instance variables private forces you (or anyone else using the Bird class) to set its properties via the set methods you have defined, which ensures that any restrictions you have made on the values of those properties are followed.

Tip You can also declare methods as public, private, or protected, which has the same effect as for class variables. You will see some more examples of private methods from recipe 2-5 onward and examples of protected methods in recipe 2-11.

While it is true that the visibility of all class members defaults to `public` and that (unlike the case with Java or C++) you are not required to declare public variables, it is still a good idea to declare the visibility for all your variables. For one thing, it is good from an organizational viewpoint; for example, if you are in the habit of declaring all variables in advance, you will not surprise yourself later by accidentally reusing one of them. For another, the only way you can use private and protected variables is to declare them explicitly.

2-5. Using Static Members and the self Keyword

Sometimes you will want to access a variable or method in the context of a class rather than an object (class instance). You can do this using the `static` keyword, which is new in PHP 5. As an example, let's add a static property and a static method to the `Bird` class as it was in the previous example (in the file `bird-get-set.php`). The ordering does not matter a great deal, but our preference is to list all static members of a class first, so let's insert the new code immediately following the opening bracket in the class declaration.

The Code

```
public static $type = "bird";

public static function fly($direction = 'around')
{
  printf("<p>The bird is flying %s.</p>\n", $direction);
}
```

Note that static members have visibility just like any other class members, and if you do not declare them, they default to `public`. You can place the `static` keyword before or after the `visibility` keyword, but by convention, the visibility is declared first. Static methods are the same as any other method in that they take arguments, can return values, and can have default arguments. However, static methods and static properties are not linked to any partic-ular instance of the class but rather to the class itself. You can reference them in your calling code using the name of the class and the `::` operator. For example:

```
printf("<p>The Bird class represents a %s.</p>\n", Bird::$type);

Bird::fly();
Bird::fly('south');
```

The output from this snippet of code is as follows:

```
The Bird class represents a bird.

The bird is flying around.

The bird is flying south.
```

To access a static member from within an *instance* of the class, you have to do things a bit differently. Let's modify the display() method a bit to illustrate this:

```
public function display()
{
  printf("<p>The %s named '%s' is a %s and costs \$%.2f.</p>\n",
          self::$type, $this->name, $this->breed, $this->price);
}
```

Now you will create a new instance of Bird and see what this change accomplishes. Here is the code:

```
$sam = new Bird('Toucan Sam', 'toucan');
$sam->display();
```

Here is the output of the altered display() method:

The bird named 'Toucan Sam' is a toucan and costs $15.00.

If you look at the new version of the display() method, you will likely notice a new keyword, self. This keyword refers to the class. It is important not to confuse self with this: this means, "the current object" or "the current instance of a class." self means, "the current class" or "the class to which the current object belongs." The differences between them are as follows.

- The self keyword does the following:

  - Represents a class.

  - Is *never* preceded by a dollar sign ($).

  - Is followed by the :: operator.

  - A variable name following the operator always takes a dollar sign ($). (Note that we said this about names of variables, not names of constants. Keep this in mind when you read the next section.) For example: self::$type.

- The this keyword does the following:

  - Represents an object or an instance of a class.

  - Is always preceded by a dollar sign ($).

  - Is followed by the -> operator.

  - A variable name following the operator never takes a dollar sign ($). For example: $this->name.

Tip You will *never* see $this followed by :: in working PHP 5 code.

CLASS DIAGRAMS

For short and simple classes, it is pretty easy to visualize the class and its members as a whole. However, as your classes grow longer and more complex—and particularly as you begin to use and write class libraries—you will probably want to use class diagrams both for designing new classes and for helping you understand classes written by others that you need to use. Fortunately, there's already a way to model classes in a language-neutral fashion. Universal Modeling Language (UML) is a standard for representing classes, their members, and the relationships between classes. UML actually does much more than model classes; it is a fairly lengthy and complex specification, and it would be impossible to cover all of it here. To find out more, visit the UML website at `http://www.uml.org/`, where you can obtain specifications, read tutorials, and get information about UML tools.

We will show you a limited subset of UML here, just enough to let you do some basic diagramming. A class is represented by a box divided into three regions or compartments, with the class name at the top, the class properties (also referred to as *attributes*) listed in the middle, and methods (known as *operations*) at the bottom, as shown in the following illustration. The only required section is the one containing the class name; the other two are optional.

```
[class name]

[properties]

[methods]
```

You list properties like this:

```
<visibility> <property-name> : <data type> [= default-value]
```

You list the property's visibility first and then the name of the property. This is followed by a colon (:) and the property's data type. Optionally, you can include an equals sign followed by the property's default value, if it has one.

You list methods like this:

```
<visibility> <method-name>([<parameter-list>]) : <return-type>
```

As with properties, you list a method's visibility first and then the name of the method. Next comes a set of parentheses containing an optional list of parameters. The parentheses are followed by a colon and a return type. If the method returns no value, you use the keyword `void` to indicate the absence of one. You write input parameters in this form:

```
[in] <parameter-name> : <data type> [= <default-value>]
```

Continued

List each parameter name with a colon and then the parameter's data type. Some languages have both input and output parameters, and for this reason, you can precede parameter names with in, out, or inout. Because PHP has only input parameters, you will sometimes omit the in keyword, although some class diagramming tools may include it regardless. You can optionally follow with an equals sign and the parameter's default value, if it has one.

You indicate visibility with these symbols:

- **public**: + (plus sign)

- **private**: - (minus sign)

- **protected**: # (hash sign)

Static members are underlined or preceded by the modifier <<static>>. Other specifics are also represented by keywords enclosed in doubled angle brackets (also known as *stereotypes*). For instance, class constructors (which appear in recipes 2-8, 2-12, and others) and destructors (which are discussed extensively in recipe 2-10) are often indicated using, respectively, <<create>> and <<destroy>>.

For example, here's a UML representation of the Bird class:

```
                                    Bird
-$name : String = "no-name"
-$breed : String = "unknown"
-$price : Float = 15.00
+$type : String = 'bird'
+fly($direction: String) : void
<<create> + _construct($name: String,$breed: String,$price: float) : Bird
+getName() : String
+getPrice() : Float
+getBreed() : String
+setPrice($price: float) : void
+setName($name: String) : void
+setBreed($breed: String) : void
```

You can use several tools to create UML class diagrams, including Microsoft Visio (Windows platforms only) and Borland Together Designer (Windows, Linux, Mac OS X, Solaris). Many of the more sophisticated tools include code-generation and reverse-engineering capabilities. For most of the diagrams in this book, we used something a bit simpler and less expensive: the open-source Umbrello UML Modeller, which is already included in some Linux distributions as part of the K Desktop Environment (KDE). You can also get the Umbrello source code for Linux from http://uml.sourceforge.net/ and compile it yourself. It is also possible to compile and run Umbrello on Windows platforms using Cygwin, a Unix emulator available from http://www.cygwin.com/. Version 1.4 is included with KDE 3.4. We had no problems compiling or using this release, or the more recent version 1.4.1, with KDE 3.3 and 3.4.

A cross-platform application called ArgoUML is available for free under a Berkeley Software Distribution (BSD) license from `http://argouml.tigris.org/`. Because ArgoUML is written in Java, it should run identically on all common platforms (which is important to us, as we use Linux, Windows, and occasionally FreeBSD and Solaris). It is also easy to install and run:

1. Download the archive for the latest release.

2. Unpack the archive into a convenient directory.

3. Open a shell or DOS prompt.

4. `cd` to the directory in which you unpacked the archive, and run the following command:
   `java -jar argouml.jar` (it should not be difficult to create a shortcut to handle this for you).

The only other requirement for ArgoUML is that you have the Java 2 Virtual Machine installed on your computer. If you run into problems, you can obtain documentation from the project website. While ArgoUML remains under development, the latest version (0.18.1) is sufficiently complete and stable for basic day-to-day use and makes a good learning tool.

In both the open-source modeling applications, the interface is fairly intuitive, and you can generate and save your class diagrams in PNG, JPG, SVG, PostScript, and other formats, as well as store data in the portable XML format. Each will also allow you to generate skeleton class code from your diagrams.

2-6. Using Class Constants

It is also useful sometimes to employ *class constants*. To declare a constant in a class, all you have to do is precede an identifier with the `const` keyword. A class constant is always public and static, and for this reason you cannot use the keywords `public`, `private`, `protected`, or `static` when declaring one. The following is an example of an `Employee` class that uses constants to enumerate classifications of employees. Let's walk through the class listing and some code to test this class. We will explain what is happening along the way.

The Code

```php
<?php
  class Employee
  {
```

Let's say you need to allow for three categories of workers: regular workers, supervisors, and managers. You can define three constants, one per category:

```php
const CATEGORY_WORKER = 0;
const CATEGORY_SUPERVISOR = 1;
const CATEGORY_MANAGER = 2;
```

Each employee classification has an associated job title and rate of pay. With this in mind, it seems reasonable to store those items of information in one or more arrays. Like other constants in PHP, a class constant must be a scalar type such as an integer or a string; you cannot use arrays or objects as constants. Since you might want to access information relating to employee categories independent of any given employee, create a couple of static arrays to hold job titles and rates of pay:

```
public static $jobTitles = array('regular worker', 'supervisor', 'manager');

public static $payRates = array(5, 8.25, 17.5);
```

Next, define a couple of static methods with which you can use the constants defined previously. They are both pretty simple: getCategoryInfo() takes a category number and returns the corresponding job title and rate of pay; calcGrossPay() takes two arguments (a number of hours and a category number) and returns the gross pay due an employee in that category working that many hours. Notice that when referring to static variables from within a method of that class—whether it is a static method or an instance method—you need to prefix the variable name with self::.

■Note It is sometimes customary to use the :: operator when discussing an instance method in relation to a class as a whole. For example, you might use Employee::getFirstName() as shorthand for "the getFirstName() method of the Employee class," even though getFirstName() is an instance method and not a static method. This should usually be clear from the context.

```
public static function getCategoryInfo($cat)
{
  printf("<p>A %s makes \$%.2f per hour.</p>\n",
         self::$jobTitles[$cat],
         self::$payRates[$cat]);
}

public static function calcGrossPay($hours, $cat)
{
  return $hours * self::$payRates[$cat];
}
```

Now let's define some instance variables. Each employee has a first name, a last name, an ID number, and a job category code. These are all private variables; but we will define public methods for manipulating them.

```
private $firstName;
private $lastName;
private $id;
private $category;
```

The Employee constructor is pretty simple. It just assigns its parameters to the corresponding instance variables. For convenience, give $cat (the job category identifier) a default
value, as shown here:

```
public function __construct($fname, $lname, $id, $cat=self::CATEGORY_WORKER)
{
  $this->firstName = $fname;
  $this->lastName = $lname;
  $this->id = $id;
  $this->category = $cat;
}
```

Next, define some (unremarkable) get and set methods:

```
public function getFirstName()
{
  return $this->firstName;
}

public function getLastName()
{
  return $this->lastName;
}

public function getId()
{
  return $this->id;
}

public function getCategory()
{
  return $this->category;
}

public function setFirstName($fname)
{
  $this->firstName = $fname;
}

public function setLastName($lname)
{
  $this->lastName = $lname;
}

public function setId($id)
{
  $this->id = $id;
}
```

Instead of a setCategory() method, you define two methods—promote() and demote()—to update the employee's job category. The first of these increments the category property, but only if it is less than the maximum (Employee::CATEGORY_MANAGER); the second decrements it, but only if it is greater than the minimum (Employee::CATEGORY_WORKER).

Notice that these values are prefixed with self. If you do not do this, you will make PHP think you are trying to use global constants with these names rather than class constants, which is not what you want to do here.

```php
public function promote()
{
  if($this->category < self::CATEGORY_MANAGER)
    $this->category++;
}
```

```php
public function demote()
{
  if($this->category > self::CATEGORY_WORKER)
    $this->category--;
}
```

Finally, define a display() method that outputs the current values of all the properties:

```php
public function display()
{
  printf(
    "<p>%s %s is Employee #%d, and is a %s making \$%.2f per hour.</p>\n",
    $this->getFirstName(),
    $this->getLastName(),
    $this->getId(),
    self::$jobTitles[ $this->getCategory() ],
    self::$payRates[ $this->getCategory() ]
       );
}
} // end class Employee
```

Figure 2-1 shows a UML diagram of the Employee class.

Let's put the Employee class through a few paces. First, test the static getCategoryInfo() method:

```php
Employee::getCategoryInfo(Employee::CATEGORY_SUPERVISOR);
```

Next, create an instance of Employee; Bob Smith is employee number 102 and is a supervisor. You can display() Bob and verify that his attributes are what you would expect them to be:

```php
$bob = new Employee('Bob', 'Smith', 102, Employee::CATEGORY_SUPERVISOR);
$bob->display();
```

Employee
+<<const>> CATEGORY_WORKER : int = 0
+<<const>> CATEGORY_SUPERVISOR : int = 1
+<<const>> CATEGORY_MANAGER : int = 2
-$firstName : string
-$lastName : string
-$id : int
-$category : int
+$payRates : array
+$jobTitles : array
+getCategoryInfo($cat: void) : void
+calcGrossPay($hours: float,$cat: int) : float
<<create>> + _construct($fname: string,$lname: string,$id: int,$cat: int) : Employee
+getFirstName() : string
+getLastName() : string
+getId() : int
+getCategory() : int
+setFirstName($fname: string) : void
+setLastName($lname: string) : void
+setId($id: int) : void
+promote() : void
+demote() : void
+display() : void

Figure 2-1. *UML representation of the* Employee *class*

You can promote Bob and then call the display() method once again to show that the change was made:

```
$bob->promote();
$bob->display();
```

If you try to promote Bob a second time, nothing about him should change; the previous call to the promote() method has already made him a manager, and there's no higher employee category.

```
$bob->promote();
$bob->display();
```

Now you will demote Bob. He should be returned to his original supervisor role:

```
$bob->demote();
$bob->display();
```

Finally, test the static `calcGrossPay()` method:

```
$hours_worked = 35.5;
printf("<p>If %s %s works %.2f hours, he will gross \$%.2f.</p>\n",
        $bob->getFirstName(),
        $bob->getLastName(),
        $hours_worked,
        Employee::calcGrossPay($hours_worked, $bob->getCategory())
      );
?>
```

■**Tip** The `::`, or scope resolution operator, is sometimes referred to as the *paamayim nekudotayim*, which is Hebrew for "double colon." If you see this term as part of a PHP error message (for example, `Parse error: Unexpected T_PAAMAYIM_NEKUDOTAYIM...`), it is often an indicator that you are using the `::` operator where PHP is expecting `->` or the reverse.

You can see this output:

```
A supervisor makes $8.25 per hour.

Bob Smith is Employee #102 and is a supervisor making $8.25 per hour.

Bob Smith is Employee #102 and is a manager making $17.50 per hour.

Bob Smith is Employee #102 and is a manager making $17.50 per hour.

Bob Smith is Employee #102 and is a supervisor making $8.25 per hour.

If Bob Smith works 35.50 hours, he will gross $292.88.
```

In the call to `getCategoryInfo()` (and to `calcGrossPay()`, by inference), you can see the advantage to using named class constants; you do not have to remember that a supervisor has a job category ID of 1. Instead, you just write `Employee::CATEGORY_SUPERVISOR`. In addition, if you add a new job category—say, assistant manager—you do not have to hunt through your code and change a bunch of numbers. You can merely update the appropriate section of the class to read something like this:

```
const CATEGORY_WORKER = 0;
const CATEGORY_SUPERVISOR = 1;
const CATGORY_ASST_MANAGER = 2;
const CATEGORY_MANAGER = 3;

public static $jobTitles
  = array('regular worker', 'supervisor', 'assistant manager', 'manager');

public static $payRates = array(5, 8.25, 12.45, 17.5);
```

   Try making this modification to `Employee`, and you will find that the example code still works (although the output will be slightly different). Obviously, you can make further improvements in this class; for instance, the set methods (including `promote()` and `demote()`) could return boolean values to indicate success or failure. (However, you will look at a feature new in PHP 5 that actually gives you a better strategy when it comes to handling errors in recipe 2-11). We have quite a bit left to cover in this introduction to classes and objects, so we will now show how you can build sets of classes that relate to one another.

2-7. Extending Classes

If you were not already familiar with classes and objects, then by now perhaps you are starting to see just how useful and economical they can be in PHP 5. However, we have not touched on one of their most powerful features, which lies in the ability to reuse an existing class when creating one or more new ones. This technique is known as *extending* a class.

   Extending classes is useful when you have multiple objects that have some but not all properties or methods in common. Rather than write a separate class for each object that duplicates the members that are common to all, you can write a generic class that contains these common elements, extend it with subclasses that inherit the common members, and then add those that are specific to each subclass.

■**Note** Unlike some object-orienting programming languages, PHP 5 does not support multiple inheritance. In other words, a derived class can have only one parent. However, a class *can* have multiple child classes. In addition, a PHP 5 class can implement multiple interfaces (see recipe 2-9 later in this chapter).

   Figure 2-2 shows an example in which we have reworked the `Bird` class from earlier in this chapter and split it up into three classes. The new `Parrot` and `Canary` classes are subclasses of `Bird`. The fact that they each inherit the methods and properties of the `Bird` class is indicated by the arrows, whose heads point to the parent class.

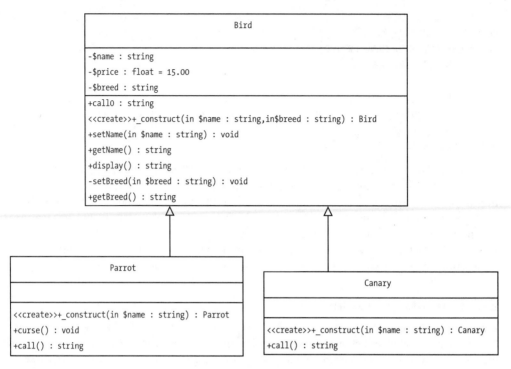

Figure 2-2. *UML diagram showing class inheritance*

The following is some PHP 5 code that implements these three classes. Bird has three properties ($name, $price, and $breed), all of which are private. You can set the first two of these with the public methods setName() and setPrice(), respectively, or in the class constructor. You can set the breed *only* from the Bird class constructor; because the setBreed() method is private, it can be called only from within Bird, not from any other code. Since $breed has no default value, you will receive a warning if you do not set it in the constructor. This seems reasonable—you could rename a bird or change its price easily enough in real life, but you will not often be transforming a pigeon into a bird of paradise unless you are a magician. Notice that you have changed this from the earlier incarnations of this class where you had a default value for this property; here you are saying, "I do not want anyone adding a bird to my inventory unless they say exactly what sort of bird it is." You also force the programmer to name the bird when it is created; however, the price does have a default value.

The Code

```php
<?php
    // file: bird-multi.php
    // example classes for inheritance example
    class Bird
    {
        private $name;
        private $breed;
        private $price;
```

```php
public function __construct($name, $breed, $price=15)
{
  $this->setName($name);
  $this->setBreed($breed);
  $this->setPrice($price);
}

public function setName($name)
{
  $this->name = $name;
}

private function setBreed($breed)
{
  $this->breed = $breed;
}

public function setPrice($price)
{
  $this->price = $price;
}
```

All the get methods of this class are public, which means you can call them at any time from within the Bird class, from within any subclasses of Bird that you might create, and from any instance of Bird or a Bird subclass. The same is true for the display() and birdCall() methods.

```php
public function getName()
{
  return $this->name;
}

public function getBreed()
{
  return $this->breed;
}

public function getPrice()
{
  return $this->price;
}
```

Each bird makes some sort of sound. Unless you override the birdCall() method in a subclass, you assume that the bird chirps. We will discuss overriding class methods in the "Variations" section. (We have named this method birdCall() rather than just call() to avoid writing any confusing bits such as "make a call to call()" in the course of this discussion. Do not let this lead you to think that there's some requirement we are not telling you about to make class names part of the names of their members or anything of that sort.)

```php
public function birdCall()
{
  printf("<p>%s says: *chirp*</p>\n", $this->getName());
}

public function display()
{
  printf("<p>%s is a %s and costs \$%.2f.</p>",
         $this->getName(),
         $this->getBreed(),
         $this->getPrice());
}
} //  end class Bird
```

Variations

Now let's extend `Bird` to create a `Parrot` class. You indicate that `Parrot` extends `Bird` by using the extends keyword as follows. What this means is that `Parrot` inherits all the properties and methods of `Bird`. For example, each instance of `Parrot` has a `birdCall()` method. Because `birdCall()` is a public method, you can redefine it in `Parrot` without it affecting the `birdCall()` method when called by an instance of `Bird` or another subclass. This is what we mean by *overriding* a method of a parent class.

```php
class Parrot extends Bird
{
  public function birdCall()
  {
    printf("<p>%s says: *squawk*</p>\n", $this->getName());
  }
```

You can also override the `Bird` class constructor. In this case, what you do is call the parent's constructor using the parent keyword. This keyword means "the class from which the current class is derived," and when employing it, the double-colon operator is always used to indicate its members.

■**Caution** When extending a class in PHP 5, you should always call the parent constructor in the constructor of the derived class; this is *not* done automatically. If you do not call `parent::__construct()` at some point in the constructor of the subclass, the derived class will not inherit the properties and methods of the parent. Also note that when you do so, you must make sure the parent constructor receives any parameters it is expecting. For this reason, it is often advantageous to write the parent class constructor in a way such that all parameters have default values; however, sometimes you do not want this to happen, and you must judge this for yourself on a case-by-case basis.

The $name is passed to the Parrot constructor; you supply the values parrot and 25 for the $breed and $price parameters. Thus, every Parrot has parrot as its breed and $25 as its price, and while the price can later be updated, the breed cannot be changed once the Parrot has been instantiated.

```
public function __construct($name)
{
  parent::__construct($name, 'parrot', 25);
}
```

Notice that while you cannot call the setBreed() method of Bird directly from within Parrot, you can call the Bird constructor, which does call setBreed(). The difference is that setBreed() gets called *from within Bird*.

■**Note** Is it possible to override a method of a parent class where that method was declared as private? Yes and no. If you try to call the parent class method directly—for example, if you write parent::setBreed() at some point in the Parrot class—you will get a fatal error. If you do some experimenting, you will find that nothing is preventing you from defining a new setBreed() method in Parrot, but you must keep in mind that this method has nothing to do with the method of the same name found in Bird. In any case, you cannot set the $breed property in the Parrot class, because it was defined as private in Bird. The moral of the story is this: if you need to override a parent method in a subclass in any meaningful way, declare the method as either public or protected in the parent class.

Now define a new method that is specific to Parrot, reflecting that parrots are often graced with a vocabulary that is not available to other birds.

```
  public function curse()
  {
    printf("<p>%s curses like a sailor.</p>\n", $this->getName());
  }
} // end class Parrot
```

The curse() method is defined only for Parrot, and attempting to use it with Bird or Canary will give rise to a fatal error.

The Canary class also extends Bird. You override the birdCall() method, but with a bit of a twist: you provide the option to use either the parent's birdCall() method or a different one. To invoke the canary-specific functionality, all that is required is to invoke birdCall() with the value TRUE.

```
class Canary extends Bird
{
  public function birdCall($singing=FALSE)
  {
    if($singing)
      printf("<p>%s says: *twitter*</p>\n", $this->getName());
    else
      parent::birdCall();
  }
```

The Canary constructor overrides the parent's constructor in the same way that the Parrot constructor does, except of course it passes canary as the value for $breed and uses the default value for $price.

```
public function __construct($name)
{
  parent::__construct($name, 'canary');
}
}
?>
```

Let's test these classes:

```
<?php
// file: bird-multi-test.php
// test Bird class and its Parrot and Canary subclasses
// depends on classes defined in the file bird-multi.php
```

Of course, you cannot use the classes defined previously unless they are available to the current script either by including the class code itself or by including the file in which the classes are defined. You use the require_once() function so that the script will fail if the file containing the classes is not found.

```
require_once('./bird-multi.php');
```

The tests themselves are pretty simple. First, create a new Parrot and call those methods that produce output, including the curse() method defined specifically for Parrot. (Because display() is a public method of Bird, you can use it as an instance method of any class deriving from Bird without redefining it.)

```
$polly = new Parrot('Polynesia');
$polly->birdCall();
$polly->curse();
$polly->display();
```

Next, instantiate the Canary class, and call its output methods. In the case of the Bird::birdCall() method, the Parrot object $polly always shows the overridden behavior; $tweety uses the parent's birdCall() method unless you pass boolean TRUE to it, in which case this Canary object's birdCall() method acts in the alternative manner that you defined for it. You can invoke Canary::birdCall() in both ways (with and without TRUE as a parameter) to demonstrate that this is so:

```
$tweety = new Canary('Tweety');
$tweety->birdCall();
$tweety->birdCall(TRUE);
$tweety->display();
```

Now use the setName() method to give the canary a different name, once again invoking its display() method to verify that the name has changed:

```
$tweety->setName('Carla');
$tweety->display();
```

Finally, you can still use the `Bird` constructor directly in order to create a bird of some type other than a parrot or canary. Invoke its `birdCall()` and `display()` methods to illustrate that the object was created and has the attributes and behavior you would expect:

```
$keet = new Bird('Lenny', 'lorakeet', 9.5);
$keet->birdCall();
$keet->display();
?>
```

Here is the output from the test script:

```
Polynesia is a parrot and costs $25.00.

Polynesia says: *squawk*

Polynesia curses like a sailor.

Tweety is a canary and costs $15.00.

Tweety says: *chirp*

Tweety says: *twitter*

Carla is a canary and costs $15.00.

Lenny is a lorakeet and costs $9.50.

Lenny says: *chirp*
```

Tip PHP 5 introduces a feature that makes it easier to include classes in files by allowing you to define an `__autoload()` function, which automatically tries to include a class file for any class that is not found when you attempt to use it. To take advantage of this, you need to save each class in its own file and follow a strict naming convention for these files, such as saving a class named `ClassName` in a file named `ClassName.inc.php`. For example, define the following:

```
function __autoload($classname)
{
    require_once("/includes/classes/$classname.inc.php");
}
```

In this case, if you try to use the class `MyClass` and if it was not already defined in your script, then PHP automatically attempts to load the class named `MyClass` from the file `/includes/classes/MyClass.inc.php`. However, you must be careful to follow the naming convention implied by your `__autoload()` function, because PHP will raise a fatal (unrecoverable!) error if it cannot find the class file. The `__autoload()` function also works with regard to interfaces not already defined in your scripts (see recipe 2-9).

2-8. Using Abstract Classes and Methods

The Bird::birdCall() method you used in the previous example has a fallback in case a derived class does not override it. Now let's suppose you are not interested in providing a default behavior for this method; instead, you want to *force* all Bird subclasses to provide birdCall() methods of their own. You can accomplish this using another feature that is new to PHP in version 5—*abstract* classes and methods.

■**Note** When it is necessary to emphasize that a class or method is *not* abstract (for instance, when a class completely implements an abstract class), it is often referred to as being *concrete*.

An abstract method is one that is declared by name only, with the details of the implementation left up to a derived class. You should remember three important facts when working with class abstraction:

- Any class that contains one or more abstract methods must itself be declared as abstract.

- An abstract class cannot be instantiated; you must extend it in another class and then create instances of the derived class. Put another way, only concrete classes can be instantiated.

- A class that extends the abstract class must implement the abstract methods of the parent class or itself be declared as abstract.

Let's update the Bird class so that its birdCall() method is abstract. We will not repeat the entire class listing here—only two steps are necessary to modify Bird. The first step is to replace the method declaration for Bird::birdCall() with the following:

```
abstract public function birdCall();
```

An abstract method has no method body; it consists solely of the abstract keyword followed by the visibility and name of the function, the function keyword, a pair of parentheses, and a semicolon. What this line of code says in plain English is, "Any class derived from this one must include a birdCall() method, and this method must be declared as public."

The second step is to modify the class declaration by prefacing the name of the class with the abstract keyword, as shown here:

```
abstract class Bird
```

Figure 2-3 shows a UML diagram of the modified three-class package. Abstract classes and methods are usually indicated with their names in italics; alternatively, you can use the stereotype <> for this purpose.

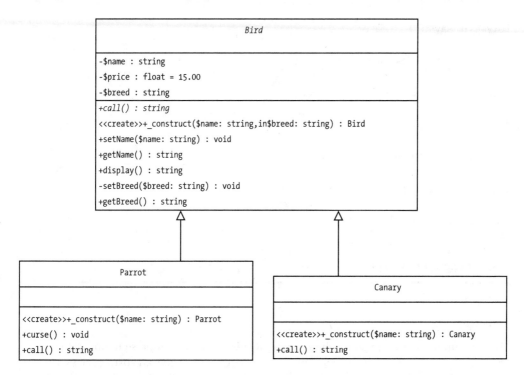

Figure 2-3. *Modified (abstract)* Bird *and derived (concrete) classes*

Now you need to consider how birdCall() is implemented in Parrot and Canary. Parrot::birdCall() is fine the way it is; it is not abstract, and it does not refer to the birdCall() method of the parent class. With Canary's birdCall() method, however, you have a problem: you cannot invoke the parent's version of the method because it is abstract. However, it is not much work to reimplement birdCall() so that this does not happen.

The Code

```
public function birdCall($singing=FALSE)
{
  $sound = $singing ? "twitter" : "chirp";

  printf("<p>%s says: *%s*</p>\n", $this->getName(), $sound);
}
```

Let's see what happens when you rerun the test code in `bird-multi-test.php`:

```
Polynesia is a parrot and costs $25.00.

Polynesia says: *squawk*

Polynesia curses like a sailor.

Tweety is a canary and costs $15.00.

Tweety says: *chirp*

Carla is a canary and costs $15.00.

Carla says: *chirp*

Carla says: *twitter*
```

Fatal error: Cannot instantiate abstract class Bird in
/home/www/php5/bird-multi-test-2.php on line 18

Extension

You run into trouble at the point where you try to create an object representation of Lenny the lorakeet. You cannot create an instance of `Bird` because it is now an abstract class. You can solve this problem in two ways (unless you want to pretend that Lenny is actually a parrot), and they both involve creating another concrete class that extends `Bird`. You can write either a `Lorakeet` class just for use with lorakeets or a generic bird class (which you can call `GenericBird` or whatever you like) that provides a catchall for species of birds for which you do not want to write separate classes. We will leave the choice up to you; as an exercise, spend a bit of time thinking about this sort of problem and the ramifications of both solutions.

Tip If you do not want a method to be overridden in a subclass, you can keep this from happening by declaring it with the `final` keyword, which functions more or less as the opposite to `abstract`. For example, you could have declared `Bird::display()` as `final` without affecting either the `Parrot` class or the `Canary` class as written, since neither subclass tries to override `display()`. You can also declare an entire class as `final`, which means it cannot be subclassed at all. Since this is not difficult to prove, we will leave that task as an exercise for you to do. Note that the `final` keyword comes before `public`, `protected`, or `static`. We should also point out that it makes no sense to use `final` with `private`, since you cannot override a private member of a class in any case, and a class declared as both `final` (no subclassing) and `private` (no direct access) could not be used at all.

2-9. Using Interfaces

As you saw in the previous section, abstract classes and methods allow you to declare some of the methods of a class but defer their implementation to subclasses. So...what happens if you write a class that has *all* abstract methods? We will offer you a somewhat indirect answer to this question: what you end up with is just one step removed from an *interface*. You can think of an interface as a template that tells you what methods a class should expose but leaves the details up to you. Interfaces are useful in that they can help you plan your classes without immediately getting bogged down in the details. You can also use them to distill the essential functionality from existing classes when it comes time to update and extend an application.

To declare an interface, simply use the `interface` keyword, followed by the name of the interface. Within the body of the interface, list declarations (delimited, as with classes, by braces, { }) for any methods to be defined by classes that implement the interface.

Note In PHP 5 you can provide type hints for parameters of functions and methods, but only for types you define. In other words, if you have defined a class named `MyClass` and then define a method `MyMethod` (of `MyClass` or any other class) that takes an instance of `MyClass` as a parameter, you can declare it as (for instance) `public function myMethod(MyClass $myParam)`. This will cause PHP to issue a warning if you try to use a value of some other type with `myMethod`. However, you cannot use type hints for predefined data types such as `int` or `string`; attempting to do so will raise a syntax error.

The Code

Looking at the `Bird` class, you might deduce that you are really representing two different sorts of functional units: a type of animal (which has a name and a breed) and a type of product (which has a price). Let's generalize these into two interfaces, like so:

```
interface Pet
{
  public function getName();
  public function getBreed();
}

interface Product
{
  public function getPrice();
}
```

How It Works

To show that a class implements an interface, you add the `implements` keyword plus the name of the interface to the class declaration. One advantage that interfaces have over abstract classes is that a class can implement more than one interface, so if you wanted to show that `Bird` implements both `Pet` and `Product`, you would simply rewrite the class declaration for `Bird`, as shown here:

```
abstract class Bird implements Pet, Product
```

In fact, if you do this to the existing example that uses the Bird, Parrot, and Canary classes, you will find that the example still runs. This is probably a good place to point out that when you use (for example) implements anInterface in a class declaration, you are basically saying, "I promise to implement in this class any methods listed in anInterface." You cannot defer the implementation of an interface method by declaring it as abstract in the implementing class.

Caution In PHP 5, interfaces may declare only methods. An interface cannot declare any variables.

An interface is represented in UML diagrams by a box with two compartments, the top one containing the stereotype <<Interface>> followed by the name of the interface and the bottom one containing the signatures of the interface's methods. Figure 2-4 shows the updated Bird class diagram with the Pet and Product interfaces and their relationship with the Bird class. Note that the implementation by a class of an interface is indicated by a dashed arrow that points from the class to the interface that it implements.

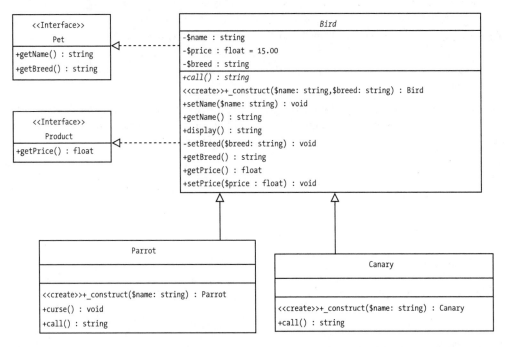

Figure 2-4. *Updated class diagram showing implementation of interfaces by the Bird class*

Using interfaces can help you keep your classes consistent with one another. For example, if you need to write classes to represent additional pets for sale by the pet store, you can, by implementing Pet and Product in those classes, guarantee that they will have the same methods that Bird and its subclasses do.

2-10. Using Class Destructors

In PHP 5, classes can have *destructors* as well as constructors. A destructor is simply a method that is guaranteed to be invoked whenever an instance of the class is removed from memory, either as the result of a script ending or because of a call to the unset() function. For example, suppose that when a user of your e-commerce website—represented by an instance of a SiteUser class—leaves the site, you want to make sure that all the user's preference data is saved to the site's user database. Suppose further that SiteUser already has a savePrefs() method that accomplishes this task; you just need to make sure it is called when the user logs out. In that case, the class listing might include something like the following.

The Code

```
class SiteUser
{
  // class variables...

  public function __construct()
  {
    // constructor method code...
  }

  // other methods...

  public function savePref()
  {
    // code for saving user preferences...
  }

  // Here's the class destructor:

  public function __destruct()
  {
    $this->savePrefs();
  }
}
```

How It Works

As you can see from this listing, all you need to do is to add a __destruct() method to the class containing whatever code you want to be executed when an instance of the class ceases to exist.

"MAGIC" METHODS

Method and function names beginning with a double underscore—such as __construct(),
__destruct(), and __autoload()—are reserved in PHP and are often referred to as *magic.* Several
others, such as those you already looked at in this chapter, are invoked automatically in response to certain
events. (For this reason, you should *never* name your own functions or methods with two leading underscores.)
Here is a listing of most of these magic methods, along with a brief description of each:

- __construct(): Called when a new instance of the class is created.

- __destroy(): Called when an instance of the class passes out of memory; this happens when you
  either unset() the instance or a script finishes running.

- __autoload(): Called when you refer to a class for the first time (for example, call its constructor,
  call one of its static methods, and so on).

- __clone(): Called when you create a copy of an object using the clone keyword.

- __get() and __set(): Called when you attempt to get or set an object property that is not defined
  for that object. __get() takes a single parameter, which represents the name of the property;
  __set() takes two parameters: the name of the property you tried to set and the value you tried to
  assign to it.

- __call(): Called when you try to call an undefined method. It takes two arguments: the method
  name that was used and an array containing any values that were passed to the method.

- __sleep() and __wakeup: __sleep() is called when you try to serialize() an object. This is
  useful when (for example) you need to close a database connection used by an object before saving
  it or when you want to save only some of an object's properties. This method should return an array
  containing the names of the variables you want to be serialized. __wakeup() is called when you
  unserialize() an object; you can use it to re-establish database connections or reinitialize the
  object in whatever other ways you require.

- __toString(): Called when a string representation of the object is required.

Of course, any of these magic methods comes into play only if you have defined it for a given class.
You should also note that they cannot be called directly, only via the event they are supposed to intercept.
For more information on magic methods and their uses, see the PHP manual or *PHP 5 Objects, Patterns, and
Practice* by Matt Zandstra (Apress, 2004).

2-11. Using Exceptions

PHP 5 introduces a much-improved mechanism for handling errors. Like many of PHP 5's new
features, *exceptions* may already be familiar to you if you are a Java programmer. If you are not,
here is your chance to become acquainted with them.

The purpose of exceptions is to help segregate error-handling code from the parts of your
application that are actually doing the work. A typical situation is working with a database.
The following is a bit of code showing how you might do this in PHP 4 or how you might do
this in PHP 5 without using exceptions:

```php
<?php
  $connection = mysql_connect($host, $user, $password)
    or die("Error #". mysql_errno() .": " . mysql_error() . ".");

  mysql_select_db($database, $connection)
    or die("Error: could not select database $database on host $hostname.");

  $query = "SELECT page_id,link_text,parent_id
              FROM menus
              WHERE page_id='$pid'";

  $result = mysql_query($query)
    or die("Query failed: Error #". mysql_errno() .": " . mysql_error() . ".");

  if(mysql_num_rows($result) == 0)
    echo "<h2>Invalid page request -- click <a href=\""
            . $_SERVER["PHP_SELF"] . "?pid=1\">here</a> to continue.</h2>\n";
  else
  {
    $value = mysql_fetch_object($result)
      or die("Fetch operation failed: Error #". mysql_errno()
              . ": " . mysql_error() . ".");
    // ...
  }

  // etc. ...
?>
```

Notice that every time you interact with the database, you include an explicit error check. This is good in that you are practicing defensive programming and not leaving the user with a blank page or half-completed page in the event of an error. However, it is not so good in that the error checking is mixed up with the rest of the code. Using PHP 5 exception handling, the same block might look something like the following example.

The Code

```php
<?php
  function errors_to_exceptions($code, $message)
  {
    throw new Exception($code, $message);
  }

  set_error_handler('errors_to_exceptions');

  try
  {
    $connection = mysql_connect($host, $user, $password);
```

```
    mysql_select_db($database, $connection);

    $query = "SELECT page_id,link_text,parent_id
                FROM menus
                WHERE page_id='$pid'";

    $result = mysql_query($query);

    if(mysql_num_rows($result) == 0)
      echo "<h2>Invalid page request -- click <a href=\""
            . $_SERVER["PHP_SELF"] . "?pid=1\">here</a> to continue.</h2>\n";
    else
    {
      $value = mysql_fetch_object($result);
      // ...
    }

    //  etc. ...
  }
  catch Exception $e
  {
    printf("<p>Caught exception: %s.</p>\n", $e->getMessage());
  }
?>
```

How It Works

The basic structure for exception handling looks like this:

```
try
{
  perform_some_action();
  if($some_action_results_in_error)
    throw new Exception("Houston, we've got a problem...");

  perform_another_action();
  if($other_action_results_in_error)
    throw new Exception("Houston, we've got a different problem...");
}
catch Exception $e
{
  handle_exception($e);
}
```

The try block contains any code that is to be tested for exceptions. When an exception is thrown, either automatically or by using the throw keyword, script execution immediately passes to the next catch block. (If PHP cannot find any catch block following the try block, then it will issue an Uncaught Exception error.)

Having to use throw to signal an exception manually each time an error condition is encountered really is not more efficient or cleaner than using repeated if or or die() constructs. In some programming languages, such as Java, the most common exceptions are thrown automatically, and all you have to worry about is supplying the code that goes inside the try and catch blocks. However, because PHP 5 has to maintain backward compatibility with older code, the traditional error-production mechanism takes precedence. To override this behavior, you can use the set_error_handler() function to call a function to be executed whenever an error is generated, in place of PHP's default behavior. This function takes the name of an error-handling function as its sole argument and causes the function with this name to be executed whenever PHP raises an error. (Note that the name of the function to be executed is passed to set_error_handler() as a string.) In the second version of the database code snippet, you have defined a function named errors_to_exceptions, which simply throws an exception.

You may have noticed that when you throw an exception, you actually use the throw keyword followed by an Exception object. The definition of the Exception class is as follows, and Figure 2-5 shows a UML representation of this class:

```php
<?php
  class Exception
  {
    protected $message = 'Unknown exception';    // Exception message
    protected $code = 0;                          // Exception code (user-defined)
    protected $file;                             // Filename
    protected $line;                             // Line number

    function __construct($message = null, $code = 0);

    final function getMessage();                  // Message
    final function getCode();                     // Code
    final function getFile();                     // Filename
    final function getLine();                     // Line number
    final function getTrace();                    // Backtrace (array)
    final function getTraceAsString();            // Backtrace (string)

    function __toString();                        // Formatted string for display
  }
?>
```

```
                              Exception
 #$message : string = 'Unknown exception'
 #$code : int = 0
 #$file : string
 #$line : int
 +_construct(in $message : string = NULL,in$code : int = 0) : object
 <<final>> + getMessage() : string
 <<final>> + getCode() : int
 <<final>> + getFile() : string
 <<final>> + getTrace() : array
 <<final>> + getTraceAsString() : string
 +_toString() : string
```

Figure 2-5. *The PHP 5* Exception *class (UML representation)*

■**Tip** You can define a __toString() method for any class. It is generally *not* a good idea to declare this method as final. (The only time you might want this to happen is in a class that is itself declared final, in which case there's no need.)

Like any well-designed class, the properties of an Exception are not directly accessible to calling code, and their values must be obtained using the get methods shown. Only the $message and $code can be set by the user, and this must be done via the class constructor. You can extend Exception, which can be a good idea when you are dealing with several classes or different sets of classes with dissimilar functionality. Note that all the get methods are final and thus cannot be overridden in any subclasses. The __toString() method is a "magic" method (as discussed earlier in this chapter) that is called whenever you try to output an instance of Exception directly using echo or print. You can override this method in an Exception subclass.

■**Tip** For some code examples using multiple Exception subclasses, see *MySQL Database Design and Optimization* (Apress, 2004).

Some PHP object-oriented libraries and extensions supply their own exception classes. For example, the Document Object Model (DOM) extension implements a DOMException class and raises an instance of this class whenever an illegal DOM operation is attempted. When using a new PHP 5 class library for the first time, be sure to check whether it includes its own Exception subclasses.

Getting Information About Classes and Objects

What do you do when you need to use one or more classes for which no documentation is available? Since PHP is an interpreted rather than a compiled language, you will usually be able to turn to the source code; however, sometimes this is not possible:

- You may not have access to all the files making up an application.

- Source code can be encrypted using tools such as IonCube.

- You may need to work with an extension that was compiled from C or Java and for which neither complete documentation nor the original sources is available.

- The sources may be available, but you might not be a C or Java programmer or simply not have time to study them in depth.

- You may be writing some highly abstracted code and not know ahead of time whether a given class is available or which of two or more classes might be.

To help you in these situations, PHP 5 provides two mechanisms for obtaining information about classes, class members, and objects. The *class and object functions*, which we will discuss first, are mostly the same as those found in PHP 4, with a few additions and enhancements. These can provide you with basic information about the availability of classes, interfaces, and their public members. For more serious reverse-engineering, PHP 5 has introduced a set of interfaces and classes known collectively as the *Reflection API*. Using this application program- ming interface (API), it is possible to find out just about everything you might want to know about an interface or a class and its members, including private and protected members and the arguments expected by class methods. In fact, using the Reflection API classes, it is possible to reverse-engineer complete extensions.

Using Class and Object Functions

PHP's class and object functions are fairly straightforward and simple to use. You will find most of them in Table 2-1.

Table 2-1. *PHP 5 Class and Object Functions (Partial Listing)*

Function	Arguments/Types	Description/Purpose
class_exists()	string $class, bool $autoload=TRUE	Returns TRUE if the class named $class has been defined. Attempts to call __autoload() if the class is not defined unless $autoload set to FALSE.[1]
is		
class_implements()	object $object	Returns an array containing the names of all interfaces implemented by the class of which $object is an instance.[2]
class_parents()	object $object	Returns an array containing the names of all classes from which $object descends (does not include the name of the class of which $object is an instance).[2]
get_class_methods()	string $class or object $object	Returns an array of class public method names. Can take either the name of a class or an instance of the class as an argument.
get_class_vars()	string $class	Returns an array of default public properties of the class named $class.
get_class()	object $object	Returns the name of the class of an object.
get_declared_classes()	void	Returns an array containing the names of all classes defined in the current script.
get_declared_interfaces()	void	Returns an array of the names of all interfaces defined in the current script.[2]
get_object_vars()	object $object	Returns an associative array whose keys are the names of the properties of $object and whose values are the values of those properties.
get_parent_class()	string $class or object $object	Returns the name of the parent class of the $class or $object.
interface_exists()	string $interface, bool $autoload=TRUE	Returns TRUE if $interface is defined in the current script. Unless $autoload is set to FALSE, this function will attempt to invoke __autoload() (if defined).[2]

Function	Arguments/Types	Description/Purpose
is_a()	object $object, string $class	Returns TRUE if $object is an instance of $class or one of its subclasses.
is_subclass_of()	object $object, string $class	Returns TRUE if $object is a descendant of $class. As of PHP 5.0.3, the first argument may also be the name of a class (as a string).[1]
method_exists()	object $object, string $method	Returns TRUE if $object has a method named $method.

Notes: (1) changed in PHP 5 (2) added in PHP 5

The next few recipes assume you have defined the set of classes (Bird, Parrot, Canary) and interfaces (Pet and Product) shown earlier in Figure 2-4.

2-12. Checking for the Existence of Classes and Interfaces Using class_exists() and interface_exists()

The following defines an additional class Shape that has some static and public variables (the reason for this will become apparent shortly):

```
class Shape
{
  const NUM_SIDES_TRIANGLE = 3;
  const NUM_SIDES_SQUARE = 4;
  const NUM_SIDES_PENTAGON = 5;
  const NUM_SIDES_HEXAGON = 6;

  static $shapeNames = array('triangle', 'quadrilateral', 'pentagon', 'hexagon');

  public $numberOfSides;
  public $perimeter;

  private $name;

  function __construct($numberOfSides = 3, $sideLength = 10)
  {
    if($numberOfSides < 3)
      $this->numberOfSides = 3;
    elseif($numberOfSides > 6)
      $this->numberOfSides = 6;
    else
      $this->numberOfSides = $numberOfSides;

    $this->setName( Shape::$shapeNames[$this->numberOfSides - 3] );
```

```
    $this->perimeter = ($sideLength < 1 ? 1 : $sideLength) * $this->numberOfSides;
  }

  protected function setName($name)
  {
    $this->name = $name;
  }

  public function getName()
  {
    return $this->name;
  }
}
```

Let's also create some class instances to use in the tests:

```
$polly = new Parrot('Polynesia');
$tweety = new Canary('Tweety');
$square = new Shape(Shape::NUM_SIDES_SQUARE);
```

Next you will look at the class_exists() and interface_exists() functions, which do pretty much what their names sound like; they tell you whether a given class or interface is defined. Each takes a string and returns a TRUE or FALSE value.

The Code

```
$classes = array('Parrot', 'Canary', 'Bird', 'Monkey', 'Pet');
$interfaces = array('Pet', 'Product', 'Customer', 'Bird');

print "<p>";
foreach($classes as $class)
  printf("The class '%s' is %sdefined.<br />\n",
         $class,
         class_exists($class, FALSE) ? '' : 'un');

print "</p>\n<p>";

foreach($interfaces as $interface)
  printf("The interface '%s' is %sdefined.<br />\n",
         $interface,
         interface_exists($interface, FALSE) ? '' : 'un');

print "</p>\n";
```

Here is the output:

```
The class 'Parrot' is defined.
The class 'Canary' is defined.
The class 'Bird' is defined.
The class 'Monkey' is undefined.
The class 'Pet' is undefined.

The interface 'Pet' is defined.
The interface 'Product' is defined.
The interface 'Customer' is undefined.
The interface 'Bird' is undefined.
```

2-13. Listing Methods and Interfaces Using get_class_methods()

You can use get_class_methods() to obtain a list of the public methods exposed by either a class or a class instance; you can also use this function with interfaces, as demonstrated in this example:

The Code

```
printf("<p>Parrot class methods: %s</p>\n",
        implode(', ', get_class_methods('Parrot')));
printf("<p>\$polly instance methods: %s</p>\n",
        implode(', ', get_class_methods($polly)));
printf("<p>Shape class methods: %s</p>\n",
        implode(', ', get_class_methods('Shape')));
printf("<p>Pet interface methods: %s</p>\n",
        implode(', ', get_class_methods('Pet')));
```

Here is the output:

```
Parrot class methods: call, __construct, curse, setBreed, setName, ➥
 setPrice, getName, getBreed, getPrice, display

$polly instance methods: call, __construct, curse, setBreed, setName, ➥
 setPrice, getName, getBreed, getPrice, display

Shape class methods: __construct, getName

Pet interface methods: getName, getBreed
```

Notice that the array returned by get_class_methods() contains names of public methods either defined in the class or inherited from a parent class. Private and protected methods are not listed.

2-14. Obtaining Variable Names

PHP has two functions for obtaining the names of public variables; you can use get_class_
variables() with classes (it takes the name of the class as its argument), and you can use
get_object_variables() with objects (it acts on an instance of a class). You might wonder why
two functions exist instead of one function that can act on either a class or a class instance, as
there is for class and object methods. Let's compare the results using these with the class Shape
and the Shape instance $square and see what happens.

The Code

```
printf("<pre>Shape class variables: %s</pre>",
        print_r(get_class_vars('Shape'), TRUE));
printf("<pre>\$square object variables: %s</pre>",
        print_r(get_object_vars($square), TRUE));
```

As you can see here, the output of these two functions can be markedly different, even
when comparing the variables of a class with those of an instance of the same class:

```
Shape class variables: Array
(
    [numberOfSides] =>
    [perimeter] =>
    [shapeNames] => Array
        (
            [0] => triangle
            [1] => quadrilateral
            [2] => pentagon
            [3] => hexagon
        )

)

$square object variables: Array
(
    [numberOfSides] => 4
    [perimeter] => 40
)
```

How It Works

Static variables are shown in the output of get_class_variables() but not in that of
get_object_variables(). In the case of Shape, $numberOfSides and $perimeter have no default
value, so no variable is shown; however, when you call get_object_variables() on an instance
of Shape, the values set by the class constructor for these variables are reported. Variables that
are declared as private or protected are not reported by either of these functions.

> **Tip** When you call get_class_variables() using a class that has no public variables, or get_object_variables() on an instance of that class, the value returned is an empty array. However, it is possible to view an object's private and protected variables using print_r() or var_dump().

2-15. Determining Whether an Object Is an Instance of a Particular Class

You can use the is_a() function to determine whether an object is an instance of a given class. This function takes two parameters, an object ($object) and the name of a class or an interface ('name'), and returns TRUE if any of the following conditions is true:

- $object is an instance of a class named name.

- $object is an instance of a class that descends from a class named name.

- $object is an instance of a class implementing an interface named name.

- $object is an instance of a class that descends from a class implementing an interface named name.

This is one of those things that sounds more complicated than it really is, so perhaps the following code will help make it clearer.

The Code

```
print "<p>";
printf("\$polly is %sa Parrot.<br />\n",
       is_a($polly, 'Parrot') ? '' : 'not ');
printf("\$polly is %sa Canary.<br />\n",
       is_a($polly, 'Canary') ? '' : 'not ');
printf("\$polly is %sa Bird.<br />\n",
       is_a($polly, 'Bird') ? '' : 'not ');
printf("\$polly is %sa Pet.<br />\n",
       is_a($polly, 'Pet') ? '' : 'not ');
print "</p>\n";
```

Here is the output:

```
$polly is a Parrot.
$polly is not a Canary.
$polly is a Bird.
$polly is a Pet.
```

How It Works

Since $polly is an instance of Parrot, the first is_a() test is true. It is not an instance of the Canary class, and it does not descend from Canary, so the second test is false. $polly is an instance of Parrot, which extends the Bird class, so the third test is true. Bird implements the Pet interface, so the fourth test using is_a() also returns TRUE.

Variations

is_a() answers the question, Does object A descend from class B? A closely related question is, What is the parent class of class C? You can answer this with the help of get_parent_class(). This function takes the name of a class and returns the name of its parent, if it has one; otherwise, it returns an empty string. It is not difficult to write a bit of recursive code that takes care of tracing the complete inheritance trail of a class:

```
function write_parents($class)
{
  $parent = get_parent_class($class);

  if($parent != '')
  {
    printf("<p>%s is a child of %s.</p>\n", $class, $parent);
    write_parents($parent);
  }
  else
    printf("<p>%s has no parent class.</p>\n", $class);
}

write_parents('Canary');
```

This yields the following result:

```
Canary is a child of Bird.
Bird has no parent class.
```

However, PHP 5 introduces a simpler way to accomplish this using the class_parents() function. As a bonus, an analogous class_interfaces() function returns a list of all interfaces implemented by a class. Notice that both of these functions take an instance of the class as a parameter:

```
printf("<p>Canary class parents: %s</p>\n",
        implode(', ', class_parents($tweety)));
printf("<p>Canary class implements: %s</p>\n",
        implode(', ', class_implements($tweety)));
```

Here is the output:

```
Canary class parents: Bird

Canary class implements: Product, Pet
```

2-16. Listing Currently Loaded Interfaces and Classes

You can obtain lists of the interfaces and classes currently loaded with the functions get_declared_interfaces() and get_declared_classes(), respectively.

The Code

```
printf("<p>Interfaces currently available: %s</p>",
        implode(', ', get_declared_interfaces()));
printf("<p>Classes currentlyavailable: %s</p>",
        implode(', ', get_declared_classes()));
```

The following is the output generated by this code on one of our test systems running PHP 5.0.4 under Apache 1.3.33 on Windows 2000. Your results are likely to be different, depending on which operating system and web server software you are using, as well as which PHP extensions you have loaded at the time.

```
Interfaces currently available: Traversable, IteratorAggregate,
 Iterator, ArrayAccess, Reflector, RecursiveIterator, SeekableIterator,
 Pet, Product


Classes currently available: stdClass, Exception, ReflectionException,
 Reflection, ReflectionFunction, ReflectionParameter, ReflectionMethod,
 ReflectionClass, ReflectionObject, ReflectionProperty,
ReflectionExtension, COMPersistHelper, com_exception,
 com_safearray_proxy, variant, com, dotnet, RecursiveIteratorIterator,
 FilterIterator, ParentIterator, LimitIterator, CachingIterator,
CachingRecursiveIterator, ArrayObject, ArrayIterator,
DirectoryIterator, RecursiveDirectoryIterator, SQLiteDatabase,
SQLiteResult, SQLiteUnbuffered, SQLiteException, __PHP_Incomplete_Class,
 php_user_filter, Directory, DOMException, DOMStringList, DOMNameList,
 DOMImplementationList, DOMImplementationSource, DOMImplementation,
 DOMNode, DOMNameSpaceNode, DOMDocumentFragment, DOMDocument,
 DOMNodeList, DOMNamedNodeMap, DOMCharacterData, DOMAttr, DOMElement,
 DOMText, DOMComment, DOMTypeinfo, DOMUserDataHandler, DOMDomError,
 DOMErrorHandler, DOMLocator, DOMConfiguration, DOMCdataSection,
 DOMDocumentType, DOMNotation, DOMEntity, DOMEntityReference,
 DOMProcessingInstruction, DOMStringExtend, DOMXPath, SimpleXMLElement,
SimpleXMLIterator, SWFShape, SWFFill, SWFGradient, SWFBitmap, SWFText,
```

SWFTextField, SWFFont, SWFDisplayItem, SWFMovie, SWFButton, SWFAction, SWFMorph, SWFSprite, SWFSound, mysqli, mysqli_result, mysqli_stmt, PDFlibException, PDFlib, tidy, tidyNode, XSLTProcessor, Shape, Bird, Parrot, Canary

---

Variations

The get_declared_classes() function can be handy when writing scripts to run in places where you do not know ahead of time which extensions or programming classes might be available. For example, suppose you need to process an XML file, but you are not sure which XML APIs might be available:

```
$xmlfile = '/xmlfiles/myfile.xml';
$classes = get_declared_classes();

if( in_array('SimpleXMLElement', $classes) )
{
  $xmldoc = simplexml_load_file($xmlfile);
  //  process XML using SimpleXML API...
}
elseif( in_array('DOMDocument', $classes) )
{
  $xmldoc = new DOMDocument();
  $xmldoc->load($xmlfile);
  //  process XML using DOM API...
}
else
{
  //  process XML using Expat or other means...
}
```

You can use these functions with predefined classes as well as those you have written or included yourself. Here is an example showing what you obtain by using class_parents(), class_implements(), get_class_methods(), and get_class_variables() in order to obtain information about the built-in ArrayIterator class:

```
$class = 'ArrayIterator';
eval("@\$object = new \$class();");

printf("<p>%s class parents: %s</p>\n",
        $class,
        print_r(class_parents($object), TRUE));
printf("<p>%s class implements: %s</p>\n",
        $class,
        implode(', ', class_implements($object)));
printf("<p>%s class methods: %s</p>\n",
        $class,
        implode(', ', get_class_methods($class)));
```

```
printf("<p>%s class variables: %s</p>",
        $class,
        print_r(get_class_vars($class), TRUE));
```

We have "cheated" here and used `print_r()` with the arrays that we knew would be empty so you could see that these are in fact empty arrays and not empty strings or NULLs:

```
ArrayIterator class parents: Array()

ArrayIterator class implements: Iterator, Traversable, ArrayAccess, SeekableIterator

ArrayIterator class methods:  __construct, offsetExists, offsetGet,➥
 offsetSet, offsetUnset, append, getArrayCopy, count, rewind, current,➥
 key, next, valid, seek

ArrayIterator class variables: Array()
```

Using the Class Reflection API

PHP 5's class and object functions do not tell you anything about the classes' internals, only about their public members. To make the most of a class, you really need to know about its private and protected members, as well as about the parameters expected by its methods. The Reflection API comes in handy here; it allows you to perform thorough reverse-engineering of any class or interface.

It has been said that he who understands a thing by breaking it apart loses the thing he understands, but in some programming situations you want or need to do exactly that. While the class and object functions you looked at in the previous set of recipes can be useful in this regard, the Reflection API has a number of advantages over those functions:

- It is completely object-oriented.

- You can obtain detailed information about extensions.

- It allows you to access private and protected variables more easily and to obtain default values of properties of classes (without having to instantiate an object using the default constructor).

- It is possible to obtain complete method signatures (except for return types).

- You can examine private and protected methods, which is not possible using the class and object functions.

The Reflection API (as illustrated in Figure 2-6) consists of eight classes, all of which except for the `Reflection` class implement the `Reflector` interface, which is defined as shown here:

```
Interface Reflector
{
  public static function export();
  public function __toString();
}
```

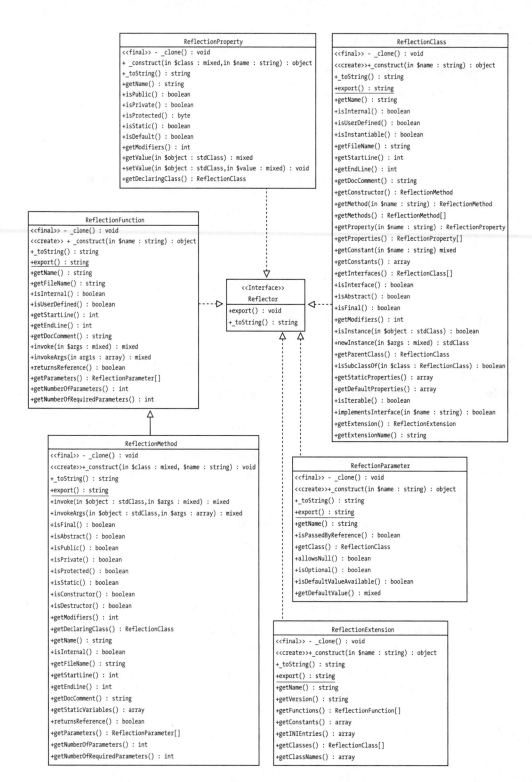

Figure 2-6. *PHP 5 Reflection API classes (UML diagram)*

The Reflection API classes are as follows:

- Reflection: This class implements as a static method the export() method defined by Reflector, although it does not actually implement the Reflector interface. You can use this method to dump all the methods and/or properties of a class, extension, property, method, or parameter.

- ReflectionClass: This class models a PHP 5 class and exposes methods for accessing nearly all aspects of the class, including its properties, methods, any parent classes that it extends or interfaces it implements, whether it is abstract or final, and so on. Note that you can also use the ReflectionClass to represent an interface.

- ReflectionFunction: Represents a function.

- ReflectionMethod: Extends the ReflectionFunction class and is used to model a class method.

- ReflectionParameter: Represents a parameter of a function or method.

- ReflectionProperty: Models a class property.

- ReflectionExtension: Represents a PHP extension.

- ReflectionException: Represents an exception thrown by one of the Reflection API classes. This class actually extends the Exception class.

We will not list all the methods of these classes here; you will get to see some of them used in later recipes, and for the rest you can consult Figure 2-6 or refer to the PHP manual (http://docs.php.net/en/language.oop5.reflection.html).

2-17. Obtaining a Dump of the Reflection API

If you are feeling adventurous, you can use export() to get a dump of the Reflection API. This example shows how to do this, using the Shape class defined earlier, which we have saved to a file named Shape.class.php.

The Code

```php
<?php
 // file: reflection-export-1.php
 // simple Reflection::export() example

 // include class file
 require_once('./Shape.class.php');

 // create new instance of ReflectionClass
 $rc = new ReflectionClass('Shape');

?><pre><?php

 // dump class info
```

```
Reflection::export($rc);

?></pre>
```

How It Works

The ReflectionClass constructor takes the name of the class you want to examine (as a string value). To get a dump of all class members, simply pass the ReflectionClass object you have just created to the static Reflection::export() method. The result contains all properties and methods of the class along with all parameters of those methods, and it even includes line numbers and comments from the source code for the class.

Here is the output:

```
/**
 * An example class for class/object functions
 * and Reflection examples - contains a mix of
 * public/private/protected/static members,
 * constants, etc.
 */
Class [ class Shape ] {
  @@ /home/www/php5/ch2/Shape.class.php 11-66

  - Constants [4] {
    Constant [ integer NUM_SIDES_TRIANGLE ] { }
    Constant [ integer NUM_SIDES_SQUARE ] { }
    Constant [ integer NUM_SIDES_PENTAGON ] { }
    Constant [ integer NUM_SIDES_HEXAGON ] { }
  }

  - Static properties [1] {
    Property [ public static $shapeNames ]
  }

  - Static methods [0] {
  }

  - Properties [3] {
    Property [   public $numberOfSides ]
    Property [   public $perimeter ]
    Property [   private $name ]
  }

  - Methods [3] {
    /**
     * Class constructor
     * input params:
     * int $numberOfSides, int $sideLength
```

```
    */
    Method [   public method __construct ] {
      @@ /home/www/php5/ch2/Shape.class.php 32 - 44

      - Parameters [2] {
        Parameter #0 [   $numberOfSides = 3 ]
        Parameter #1 [   $sideLength = 10 ]
      }
    }

    /**
     * Sets the name value
     * Input param:
     * string $name
     */
    Method [   protected method setName ] {
      @@ /home/www/php5/ch2/Shape.class.php 52 - 55

      - Parameters [1] {
        Parameter #0 [   $name ]
      }
    }

    /**
     * Retrieves the name value
     * returns string
     */
    Method [   public method getName ] {
      @@ /home/www/php5/ch2/Shape.class.php 62 - 65
    }
  }
}
```

Variations

That wasn't so difficult, was it? You can accomplish the same thing for any PHP 5 class by replacing Shape with the class name. This includes built-in classes and those made available by extensions. However, while dumping a pile of data about a class can occasionally be useful during development, this does not use the real power of the Reflection API, which is that it exposes fully object-oriented interfaces for almost any aspect of a class or an object that you might need to use. For example, harking back to the pet shop scenario, suppose you have defined a number of classes implementing the Pet interface. Rather than having a single petCall() method in Pet that you have extended for each class, let's also suppose you have defined a method performing this function but that it is different for each subclass. See Figure 2-7 for an abbreviated UML representation.

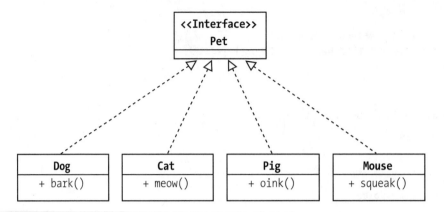

Figure 2-7. *Modified set of* Pets

2-18. Performing Dynamic Class Instantiation

Now imagine that you have to write a module that works with some existing code that uses a Pet class but you have no way of knowing ahead of time which one it might be. Using the Reflection API's ReflectionClass and ReflectionMethod classes, the following code shows one way you could solve this problem.

The Code

```php
<?php
    // Existing code has created an instance of a class
    // implementing the Pet interface as the variable $pet...
    // This array uses the class names as keys and the
    // 'make a noise' method names as values
    $noises = array('Dog' => 'bark', 'Cat' => 'meow',
                    'Pig' => 'oink', 'Mouse' => 'squeak');

    // Now you need for the pet to make a noise...

    // First you need to get the name of the class, and then
    // create a corresponding instance of ReflectionClass
    $pet_name = get_class($pet);
    $pet_rc = new ReflectionClass($pet_name);

    // Get the name of the correct method based on the name of the class
    // (if no match is found, set the method name to NULL):


    // If there was a match on the class name, create
    // an instance of ReflectionMethod using the class name
    // and corresponding method name, and then invoke this method
    // by calling ReflectionMethod's invoke() method
    if( array_key_exists($pet_name, $noises) )
```

```
{
    $pc_method = new ReflectionMethod($pet_rc, $noises[$pet_name]);
    $pc_method->invoke($pet);
}
else  //  Otherwise, indicate that there's no sound for this Pet
    print "This pet does not make a sound";
?>
```

The ReflectionMethod class constructor takes two arguments: the name or an instance of the class and the name of the method. You can use ReflectionMethod::invoke() to simulate a call to the corresponding method; this method requires at least one argument, either NULL (if the referenced object method is static) or an instance of the class. In other words, using the Parrot class defined earlier, you can invoke its birdCall() method dynamically like so:

```
<?php
    require_once('./bird-interface.php');

    $class = 'Parrot';
    $method = 'birdCall';
    $rm = new ReflectionMethod($class, $method);
    $rm->invoke( new $class('Polly') );

    //  Output is: Polly says *squawk*.
?>
```

The output is identical to that produced by the following code:

```
<?php
    require_once('./bird-interface.php');

    $polly = new Parrot('Polly');
    $polly->birdCall();
?>
```

Note that you can also invoke a class constructor dynamically simply by using new $class(), where $class is the name of the class.

2-19. Using the Reflection API to Deconstruct the Shape Class

We will finish this chapter with a more involved example of using the Reflection API to deconstruct the Shape class in an object-oriented fashion by using the ReflectionClass, ReflectionMethod, and ReflectionParameter classes. Let's dive right into the code, and we will explain what is happening along the way.

The Code

```
<?php
    //  file: reflection-example-2.php
    //  more involved Reflection API example
```

```
//  Include the proper class file
$class = 'Shape';

require_once("./$class.class.php");

//  Create a new ReflectionClass instance
$rc = new ReflectionClass($class);

//  Display the name of the class
printf("<p>Name: *%s*<br />\n", $rc->getName());

//  Display the file the class is defined in, and
//   the beginning and ending line numbers
printf("Defined in file '%s', lines %d - %d<br />\n",
        $rc->getFileName(),
        $rc->getStartLine(),
        $rc->getEndLine());
```

It is possible to get documentation comments from the class source; both ReflectionClass and ReflectionMethod provide a getDocComment() method. (Note that these are both instance methods.) ReflectionClass::getDocComment() returns a string containing the multiline comment immediately preceding the class definition; ReflectionMethod::getDocComment() returns a string containing the multiline comment immediately preceding the method declaration in the source. In both cases, the string includes the opening and closing /* and */ comment delimiters. If there is no matching comment, then getDocComment() returns an empty string.

```
printf("<p>Contains the comments:<pre>%s</pre></p>",
        $rc->getDocComment());
```

ReflectionClass has a number of boolean methods that tell you whether the class is public, private, static, abstract, and so on. In addition, because this class can also model an interface, the isInterface() method returns TRUE if you are examining an interface and FALSE if you are introspecting a class.

```
printf("%s is %san interface.<br />\n",
        $rc->getName(),
        $rc->isInterface() ? '' : 'not ');

printf("%s is %sinstantiable.<br />\n",
        $rc->getName(),
        $rc->isInstantiable() ? '' : 'not ');

printf("%s is %sabstract.<br />\n",
        $rc->getName(),
        $rc->isAbstract() ? '' : 'not ');

printf("%s is %sfinal.</p>\n",
        $rc->getName(),
        $rc->isFinal() ? '' : 'not ');
```

The getConstants() method returns an associative array of all class constants. This array's keys are the names of the constants, and their values are those of the corresponding constants.

```
$constants = $rc->getConstants();
$num_constants = count($constants);

printf("%s defines %d constant%s",
        $rc->getName(),
        $num_constants == 0 ? 'no' : $num_constants,
        $num_constants != 1 ? 's' : '');

if($num_constants > 0)
  printf(":<pre>%s</pre>", print_r($constants, TRUE));
```

The instance method ReflectionClass::getProperties() returns an array of class properties (actually an array of ReflectionProperty objects). Here you will just supply each of these in turn as a parameter to the static Reflection::export() method to obtain a dump of the property's attributes, but you can also employ a number of ReflectionProperty methods to determine the property's name, access, whether it is static, and how to get or set the value currently stored by the property represented.

Note Each of the elements in the array returned by getConstants() is an instance of ReflectionParameter.

```
$props = $rc->getProperties();
$num_props = count($props);

printf("%s defines %d propert%s",
        $rc->getName(),
        $num_props == 0 ? 'no' : $num_props,
        $num_props == 1 ? 'y' : 'ies');

if($num_props > 0)
{
  print ':';
  foreach($props as $prop)
  {
    print "<pre>";
    Reflection::export($prop);
    print "</pre>";
  }
}
```

The ReflectionClass method getMethods() returns an array of ReflectionMethod objects, each corresponding to a class method.

```
$methods = $rc->getMethods();
$num_methods = count($methods);

printf("%s defines %d method%s<br />\n",
        $rc->getName(),
        $num_methods == 0 ? 'no' : $num_methods,
        $num_methods != 1 ? 's' : '');

if($num_methods > 0)
{
   print '<p>';

   foreach($methods as $method)
   {
      printf("%s%s%s%s%s%s() ",
             $method->isFinal() ? 'final ' : '',
             $method->isAbstract() ? 'abstract ' : '',
             $method->isPublic() ? 'public ' : '',
             $method->isPrivate() ? 'private ' : '',
             $method->isProtected() ? 'protected ' : '',
             $method->getName());

      $params = $method->getParameters();
      $num_params = count($params);
```

In addition to the methods shown previously for determining access and other method attributes (as well as some others that you can see listed in Figure 2-6 or at http://docs.php.net/en/language.oop5.reflection.html). Each instance of ReflectionMethod has a getParameters() method that returns an array of ReflectionParameter objects. Each of these models a method parameter. In this example script, you list only the names of any parameters using the getName() method; however, this class has several additional methods that are well worth investigating, and we strongly urge you to take a bit of time to do so. You can use this script as a starting point, adding more methods calls and trying it on different classes, and observe the results.

```
      printf("has %s parameter%s%s",
             $num_params == 0 ? 'no' : $num_params,
             $num_params != 1 ? 's' : '',
             $num_params > 0 ? ': ' : '');

      if($num_params > 0)
      {
         $names = array();

         foreach($params as $param)
            $names[] = '$' . $param->getName();
```

```
        print implode(', ', $names);
    }

    print '<br />';
  }
}
?>
```

Here you can see the output from the preceding script:

```
Name: *Shape*
Defined in file '/home/www/php5/ch2/Shape.class.php', lines 11 - 66

Contains the comments:

/**
  * An example class for class/object functions
  * and Reflection examples - contains a mix of
  * public/private/protected/static members,
  * constants, etc.
  */

Shape is not an interface.
Shape is instantiable.
Shape is not abstract.
Shape is not final.

Shape defines 4 constants:

Array
(
    [NUM_SIDES_TRIANGLE] => 3
    [NUM_SIDES_SQUARE] => 4
    [NUM_SIDES_PENTAGON] => 5
    [NUM_SIDES_HEXAGON] => 6
)

Shape defines 4 properties:

Property [ public static $shapeNames ]


Property [   public $numberOfSides ]


Property [   public $perimeter ]
```

```
Property [  private $name ]


Shape defines 3 methods

public __construct() has 2 parameters: $numberOfSides, $sideLength
protected setName() has 1 parameter: $name
public getName() has no parameters
```

Using the Reflection API, it is possible to find out virtually anything you would ever need to know about an extension, interface, class, object, method, or property—whether you need to get information about a library for which you cannot obtain documentation or to be able to work with dynamic classes and objects in your PHP 5 applications. Although we have barely scratched the surface in this chapter, it is well worth your time to read more about this API and experiment with it.

Summary

If we were asked to name the biggest difference between PHP 4 and PHP 5, we would say without hesitation that it is the introduction of the Zend II language engine. The resulting changes in PHP's handling of classes and objects are little short of revolutionary. PHP 4 was a procedural scripting language with some capacity to work with basic objects and classes. PHP 5 is a different animal: it has the capability for being used as a fully fledged object-oriented language with polymorphism, inheritance, and encapsulation. The fact that it has managed to achieve these objectives while maintaining almost complete backward compatibility with PHP 4–style classes and objects is amazing.

In this chapter, we covered the most important and useful of these new capabilities, starting with an overview of basic object-oriented concepts. You looked at what classes and objects are, their major parts (members), and how to create them. One major change in PHP 5 from its predecessors is that true encapsulation is now supported; that is, you can control access to class members by declaring them to be public, private, or protected. In addition, you can now force subclasses to implement methods (using abstract classes and methods) as well as prevent subclasses from modifying class members (by declaring methods or classes as final). PHP 5 also allows for a higher level of abstraction by introducing interfaces; just as a class serves as a template for an object, you can think of an interface as a template for a class— or perhaps it is better to think of a class as implementing one or more interfaces.

Another object-oriented feature making its first appearance in PHP 5 is a new way of handling errors. Exceptions, implemented using an Exception class, make it possible to streamline error handling by reducing the number of checks required. They also make it possible to separate error checking from the functional portions of your code. Because the PHP developers wanted to maintain backward compatibility, it is necessary to do a bit of extra preparation to bypass the default error-handling mechanism if you want to use exceptions. However, as you have now seen, doing so is not terribly difficult to accomplish and makes it possible to write much cleaner code than before.

Object-oriented programming is not really complete without a way to obtain information about classes, class instances, and class members, and PHP 4 provided a number of functions to accomplish this. In this chapter, you looked at how PHP 5 retains these functions and adds a few new ones. PHP 5 also introduces a set of classes whose main purpose is to model classes. These classes, known collectively as the Reflection API, make it possible to examine extensions, interfaces, classes, functions, class methods, and properties and their relationships to one another. In addition to introspecting classes, the Reflection API helps facilitate the dynamic generation and manipulation of classes and objects. Both of these capabilities can prove extremely useful when writing generic routines to handle classes and objects whose identity and composition are not known before runtime.

Looking Ahead

In Chapter 3, Frank M. Kromann shows how to perform math calculations in PHP 5. He will cover a number of useful topics in this area, including a survey of the types of numbers supported in PHP 5, ways to identify them, how they are expressed, and techniques enabling the programmer to format numbers in many different ways for output. PHP 5 has a wealth of mathematical functions and operators, and you will get the opportunity to see how to use some of them to help you solve problems you are likely to encounter in your work with PHP 5; these mathematical functions include all common trigonometric functions and functions for working with exponents and logarithms. Chapter 3 will also cover how to generate random numbers for arbitrary ranges of numbers and intervals within those ranges. Finally, you will examine a couple of "bonus" math libraries: BCMath, used for performing calculations requiring a high degree of precision, and GMP, which allows you to work with large integers. Of course, the chapter will provide heaps of examples and useful bits of code that you can easily adapt and build on for your own PHP 5 projects.

CHAPTER 3

■ ■ ■

Performing Math Operations

Math is one of the fundamental elements of most programming languages. Math allows the programmer to perform anything from simple additions to advanced calculations. Even though PHP was designed to create dynamic Hypertext Markup Language (HTML) documents, it has evolved to a general-purpose programming language that includes a strong and flexible math implementation.

The implementation of math in PHP looks very much like the implementation in C. In fact, many of the functions are implemented as simple wrappers around the math functions found in C libraries.

3-1. Numeric Data Types

Working with numbers or numeric data and math functions in PHP is simple. Basically, you have two data types to work with, floating point and integer. The internal representations for these values are the C data types double and int, and these data types follow the same set of rules as in C.

We've designed most the samples in this chapter to work with the command-line interface (CLI) version of PHP. If you use the samples with a web server and view the results in a browser, you may see different formatting than the results shown in this chapter. This is especially true if a recipe is using a variable-width font to present the data. In most cases, we show the generated output following the code sample. When the output generates HTML output, we will use a figure to display the result.

■**Note** The minimum and maximum values for integer values depend on the system architecture where PHP is running. On a 32-bit operating system, an integer can be between –2,147,483,648 and 2,147,483,647.

PHP is a loosely typed scripting language where variables change the data type as needed by calculations. This allows the engine to perform type conversions on the fly. So, when numbers and strings are included in a calculation, the strings will be converted to a numeric value before the calculation is performed, and numeric values are converted to strings before they are concatenated with other strings. In the following example, a string and an integer value are added, and the result is an integer value.

The Code

```php
<?php
// Example 3-1-1.php
$a="5";
$b= 7 + $a;
echo "7 + $a = $b";
?>
```

How It Works

The variable $a is assigned a string value of 5, and then the variable $b is assigned the value of the calculation of 7 plus the value of $a. The two values are of different types, so the engine will convert one of them so they are both the same type. The operator + indicates the addition of numeric values to the string, which is converted to a numeric value of 5 before the addition. The last line displays the calculation, and the result is as follows:

```
7 + 5 = 12
```

PHP will also convert the data types of one or more values in a calculation in order to perform the calculation correctly. In the following example, the float is converted to an integer before the binary and (&) operation is executed.

The Code

```php
<?php
// Example 3-1-2.php
$a = 3.5;
$b = $a & 2;
echo "$a & 2 = $b";
?>
```

How It Works

The variable $a is assigned a floating-point value of 3.5. Then, the variable $b is assigned the result of the calculation of $a and 2 with the binary and operation. In this case, the floating-point value is converted to an integer (3) before the binary and operation is performed. If you look at the binary values of 3 and 2, you will see these are 011 and 010; if you then perform the operation on each bit, you get the result (0 & 0 = 0, 1 & 0 = 0, and 1 & 1 = 1).

```
3.5 & 2 = 2
```

And as the next example shows, PHP will perform an additional conversion on the resulting data type if the result of a calculation requires that. So, when an integer is divided by an integer, the resulting value might be an integer or a float depending on the result and not on the operation.

The Code

```php
<?php
// Example 3-1-3.php
$a = 5;
$b = $a / 2;
echo "$a / 2 = $b\n";

$a = 6;
$b = $a / 2;
echo "$a / 2 = $b\n";
?>
```

How It Works

This example shows two integer divisions. No data type conversions are needed before the calculations, as both sides of the division operator are numeric, but in the first case where 5 is divided by 2, the result is 2.5, so that value must be stored in a floating-point data type. In the other calculation, where 6 is divided by 2, the result is 6 and can be stored in an integer data type.

```
5 / 2 = 2.5
6 / 2 = 3
```

PHP has a number of functions to test the data type of a variable. Three of these functions test whether the variable contains a numeric value, or, more specifically, whether it is a float or an integer.

The function is_numeric() checks if the value passed as the argument is numeric, and as shown in the next example, it will return a boolean value: true for integers, floats, and string values with a numeric content and false for all other data types. The following example shows how you can use the is_numeric() function.

The Code

```php
<?php
// Example 3-1-4.php
$a = 1;
echo "is_numeric($a) = " . (is_numeric($a) ? "true" : "false") . "\n";

$a = 1.5;
echo "is_numeric($a) = " . (is_numeric($a) ? "true" : "false") . "\n";

$a = true;
echo "is_numeric($a) = " . (is_numeric($a) ? "true" : "false") . "\n";

$a = 'Test';
echo "is_numeric($a) = " . (is_numeric($a) ? "true" : "false") . "\n";
```

```php
$a = '3.5';
echo "is_numeric($a) = " . (is_numeric($a) ? "true" : "false") . "\n";

$a = '3.5E27';
echo "is_numeric($a) = " . (is_numeric($a) ? "true" : "false") . "\n";

$a = 0x19;
echo "is_numeric($a) = " . (is_numeric($a) ? "true" : "false") . "\n";

$a = 0777;
echo "is_numeric($a) = " . (is_numeric($a) ? "true" : "false") . "\n";
?>
```

How It Works

This example shows how you can use the is_numeric() function on variables of different data types. In each of the tests, you use the tertiary operator (?) to print the string value of true or false depending on the result returned by the function.

```
is_numeric(1) = true
is_numeric(1.5) = true
is_numeric(1) = false
is_numeric(Test) = false
is_numeric(3.5) = true
is_numeric(3.5E27) = true
is_numeric(25) = true
is_numeric(511) = true
```

The functions is_int() and is_float() check for specific data types. These functions will return true if an integer or float is passed and false in any other case, even if a string with a valid numeric representation is passed.

The Code

```php
<?php
// Example 3-1-5.php
$a = 123;
echo "is_int($a) = " . (is_int($a) ? "true" : "false") . "\n";

$a = '123';
echo "is_int($a) = " . (is_int($a) ? "true" : "false") . "\n";
?>
```

How It Works

This example shows how the function is_int() will return true if the value passed as the argument is an integer and false if it is anything else, even if the string contains a numeric value.

```
is_int(123) = true
is_int(123) = false
```

To test for other data types, PHP implements is_bool(), is_string(), is_array(), is_object(), is_resource(), and is_null(). All these functions take one argument and return a boolean value.

It is possible to force the engine to change the data type. This is called *typecasting*, and it works by adding (int), (integer), (float), (double), or (real) in front of the variable or value or by using the function intval() or floatval(). This next example shows how you can use the is_int() function with the (int) typecasting to force a string value to be converted to an integer before the type is checked.

The Code

```php
<?php
// Example 3-1-6.php
$a = 123;
echo "is_int($a) = " . (is_int($a) ? "true" : "false") . "\n";

$a = '123';
echo "is_int((int)$a) = " . (is_int((int)$a) ? "true" : "false") . "\n";
?>
```

How It Works

This example works as the previous example does, but because of the implicit typecasting of the string to an integer before calling the is_int() function, both tests will return true.

```
is_int(123) = true
is_int((int)123) = true
```

Using typecasting might force the value to become a zero value. This will happen if the value is an object, an array, or a string that contains a non-numeric value and if this variable is typecast to an integer or floating-point value.

When the intval() function is used on strings, it's possible to pass a second parameter that specifies the base to use for the conversion. The default value is 10, but it's possible to use base 2 (binary), 8 (octal), 16 (hexadecimal), or any other value such as 32 or 36, as shown in the following example.

The Code

```php
<?php
// Example 3-1-7.php
echo intval('123', 10) . "\n";
echo intval('101010', 2) . "\n";
echo intval('123', 8) . "\n";
echo intval('123', 16) . "\n";

echo intval('H123', 32) . "\n";
echo intval('H123', 36) . "\n";
?>
```

How It Works

This example takes numeric values with different bases and converts them to decimal representations (base 10). A decimal value uses the digits 0123456789, a binary value uses the digits 01, an octal value uses the digits 01234567, and a hexadecimal value uses the digits 0123456789abcdef. The digits for base 32 and base 36 are 0123456789 and the first 22 or 26 letters of the alphabet. So, the value H123 does not denote a hexadecimal value.

```
123
42
83
291
558147
794523
```

The intval() function will also work on boolean and float types, returning the integer value. The integer value of a boolean variable is 0 for false and 1 for true. For a float value, this function will truncate the value at the decimal point.

When working with integers, it is sometimes necessary to convert between different base values. The PHP interpreter will accept integers as part of the script, in decimal, octal, and hexadecimal form, and automatically convert these to the internal decimal representation. Using the octal and hexadecimal forms can make the code more readable. You can use the octal form when setting file permissions, as this is the notation used on most Unix and Unix-like systems, and you can use the hexadecimal form when defining constants where you need to have a single bit set in each constant.

```php
<?php
// Example 3-1-8.php
chmod("/mydir", 0755);

define('VALUE_1', 0x001);
define('VALUE_2', 0x002);
define('VALUE_3', 0x004);
define('VALUE_4', 0x008);
define('VALUE_5', 0x010);
define('VALUE_6', 0x020);
?>
```

It is easier to read and define constants based on single bits when using the hexadecimal representation, where each digit represents 4 bits, than when using with decimal representation, where the same values would be 1, 2, 4, 8, 16, and 32.

Sometimes it's also useful to convert integer values to other bases such as binary or base 32 and base 36, as used in the previous example. You can use the function base_convert() to convert any integer value from one base to another. The function takes one numeric and two integer parameters, where the first parameter is the number to be converted. This value can be an integer or a string with a numeric representation. The second parameter is the base to convert from, and the third parameter is the base to convert to. The function will always return a string value, even if the result is an integer in the decimal representation.

The Code

```php
<?php
// Example 3-1-9.php
echo base_convert('123', 10, 10) . "\n";
echo base_convert('42', 10, 2) . "\n";
echo base_convert('83', 10, 8) . "\n";
echo base_convert('291', 10, 16) . "\n";

echo base_convert('558147', 10, 32) . "\n";
echo base_convert('794523', 10, 36) . "\n";

echo base_convert('abcd', 16, 8) . "\n";
echo base_convert('abcd', 16, 2) . "\n";?>
```

How It Works

In this example, you saw the same values as in the previous example, but this example uses the base_convert() function to do the reverse conversion. In addition, this example also shows conversions between bases other than the decimal 10.

```
123
101010
123
123
h123
h123
125715
1010101111001101
```

Remember that the maximum width of an integer value in PHP is 32-bit. If you need to convert integer values with more than 32 bits, you can use the GMP extension (see recipe 3-6).

You can assign a value to a variable in a few ways in PHP (see Chapter 10). The most basic form is the assignment $a = 10;, where $a is given the integer value 10. If the variable exists, the old value will be lost, and if the variable is used for the first time, the internal structure will be allocated. There is no need to declare variables before use, and any variable can be reassigned to another value with another type at any time.

For variables of a numeric type, it is also possible to assign a new value and at the same time use the existing value in the calculation of the new value. You do this with $a += 5;, where the new value of $a will be the old value plus 5. If $a is unassigned at the time the statement is executed, the engine will generate a warning and assume the old value of 0 before calculating the new value.

Tables 3-1, 3-2, and 3-3 show the arithmetic, bitwise, and assignment operators that are available in PHP.

Table 3-1. *Arithmetic Operators*

Example	Operation	Result
-$a	Negation	Negative value of $a
$a + $b	Addition	Sum of $a and $b
$a - $b	Subtraction	Difference of $a and $b
$a * $b	Multiplication	Product of $a and $b
$a / $b	Division	Quotient of $a and $b
$a % $b	Modulus	Remainder of $a divided by $b

Table 3-2. *Bitwise Operators*

Example	Operation	Result
$a & $b	And	Bits that are set in both $a and $b are set.
$a | $b	Or	Bits that are set in either $a or $b are set.
$a ^ $b	Xor	Bits that are set in $$a or $b but not in both are set.
~ $a	Not	Bits that are set in $a are not set, and vice versa.
$a << $b	Shift left	Shift the bits of $a to the left $b steps.
$a >> $b	Shift right	Shift the bits of $a to the right $b steps.

Table 3-3. *Assignment Operators*

Example	Operation	Result
$a += $b	Addition	$a = $a + $b
$a -= $b	Subtraction	$a = $a - $b
$a *= $b	Multiplication	$a = $a * $b
$a /= $b	Division	$a = $a / $b
$a %= $b	Modulus	$a = $a % $b
$a &= $b	Bitwise and	$a = $a & $b
$a |= $b	Bitwise or	$a = $a | $b
$a ^= $b	Bitwise xor	$a = $a ^ $b
$a <<= $b	Left-shift	$a = $a << $b
$a >>= $b	Right-shift	$a = $a >> $b

■Note If you use bitwise operators on strings, the system will apply the operation on the string character by character. For example, 123 & 512 equals 102. First, the values 1 and 5 are "anded" together in binary terms, that is, 001 and 101; only the last bit is common, so the first character becomes 001. The next two values are 2 and 1 (or in binary values, 10 and 01). These two values are "anded" together to make 00, or 0. And finally, 3 and 2 are "anded" together, so that's 11 and 10 with the result of 10, or 2. So, the resulting string is 102.

Integer values can be signed and unsigned in the range from –2,147,483,648 to 2,147,483,647. If a calculation on any integer value causes the result to get outside these boundaries, the type will automatically change to float, as shown in the following example.

The Code

```php
<?php
// Example 3-1-10.php
$i = 0x7FFFFFFF;
echo "$i is " . (is_int($i) ? "an integer" : "a float") . "\n";
$i++;
echo "$i is " . (is_int($i) ? "an integer" : "a float") . "\n";
?>
```

How It Works

The variable $i is assigned a value corresponding to the largest integer number PHP can handle, and then is_int() is called to verify that $i is an integer. Then the value of $i is incremented by 1, and the same check is performed again.

```
2147483647 is an integer
2147483648 is a float
```

In other languages with strict type handling, the increment of $i by 1 would lead to over-flow, and the result would be a negative value of –2,147,483,648.

Comparing integer values is simple and exact because there is a limited number of values and each value is well defined. This is not the case with floating-point values, where the precision is limited. Comparing two integers with = will result in a true value if the two integers are the same and false if they are different. This is not always the case with floating-point values. These are often looked at with a numeric string representation that might change during processing. The following example shows that a simple addition of two floating-point variables compared to a variable with the expected value result can lead to an unexpected result.

The Code

```php
<?php
// Example 3-1-11.php
$a=50.3;
$b=50.4;
$c=100.7;

if ($a + $b == $c) {
  echo "$a + $b == $c\n";
}
else {
  echo "$a + $b != $c\n";
}
?>
```

How It Works

Three variables are each assigned a floating-point value; then, a calculation is performed with the two first values, and the result is compared to the last value. One would expect that the output from this code would indicate that $a + $b == $c.

```
50.3 + 50.4 != 100.7
```

This result indicates that PHP is having trouble with simple floating-point operations, but you will find the same result in other languages. It is possible to compare floating-point values, but you should avoid the == operator and use the <, >, >=, and <= operators instead. In the following example, the loop goes from 0 to 100 in steps of 0.1, and the two checks inside the loop print a line of text when $i reaches the value 50.

The Code

```php
<?php
// Example 3-1-12.php
for ($i = 0; $i < 100; $i += 0.1) {
  if ($i == 50) echo '$i == 50' . "\n";
  if ($i >= 50 && $i < 50.1) echo '$i >= 50 && $i < 50.1' . "\n";
}
?>
```

How It Works

This code creates a loop where the variable $i starts as an integer with the value 0. The code in the loop is executed as long as the value of $i is less than 100. After each run-through, the value of $i is incremented by 0.1. So, after the first time, $i changes to a floating-point value. The code in the loop uses two different methods to compare the value of $i, and, as the result shows, only the second line is printed.

```
$i >= 50 && $i < 50.1
```

Another way to make sure the values are compared correctly is to typecast both sides of the == operator to integers like this: if ((int)$i == 50) echo '$i == 50' . "\n";. This will force the engine to compare two integer values, and the result will be as expected.

3-2. Random Numbers

Random numbers are almost a science by themselves. Many different implementations of random number generators exist, and PHP implements two of them: rand() and mt_rand(). The rand() function is a simple wrapper for the random function that is defined in libc (one of the basic libraries provided by the compiler used to build PHP). mt_rand() is a drop-in replacement with well-defined characteristics (Mersenne Twister), and mt_rand() is even much faster than the version from libc.

Working with random number generation often requires seeding the generator to avoid generating the same random number each time the program is executed. This is also the case for PHP, but since version 4.2.0, this seeding takes place automatically. It is still possible to use the srand() and mt_srand() functions to seed the generators, but it's no longer required.

You can use both random generators with no arguments or with two arguments. If no arguments are passed, the functions will return an integer value between 0 and RAND_MAX, where RAND_MAX is a constant defined by the C compilers used to generate PHP. If two arguments are passed, these will be used as the minimum and maximum values, and the functions will return a random value between these two numbers, both inclusive.

Both random generators provide functions to get the value of MAX_RAND. The next example shows how to use these functions.

The Code

```php
<?php
// Example 3-2-1.php
echo "getrandmax = " . getrandmax() . "\n";
echo "mt_getrandmax = " . mt_getrandmax() . "\n";
?>
```

How It Works

On a Linux or Unix system, this sample code produces this output:

```
Getrandmax() = 2147483647
mt_getrandmax() = 2147483647
```

On a Windows system, the same code produces this output:

```
Getrandmax() = 32767
mt_getrandmax() = 2147483647
```

This difference is caused by the different libc implementations of the random number generators and the MAX_RAND value between different platforms.

You can generate random numbers (integer values) between 0 and MAX_RAND by calling rand() or mt_rand() without any arguments, as shown in the next example.

The Code

```php
<?php
// Example 3-2-2.php
echo "rand() = " . rand() . "\n";
echo "mt_rand() = " . mt_rand() . "\n";
?>
```

How It Works

On Windows and Linux systems, the output from this code would look like the following, though the values will be different each time the script is executed:

```
rand() = 9189
mt_rand() = 1101277682
```

In many cases, it's required to get a random value with other minimum and maximum values than the default. This is where the two optional arguments are used. The first argument specifies the minimum value, and the second specifies the maximum value. The following example shows how to get a random value from 5 to 25.

The Code

```php
<?php
// Example 3-2-3.php
echo "rand(5, 25) = " . rand(5, 25) . "\n";
echo "mt_rand(5, 25) = " . mt_rand(5, 25) . "\n";
?>
```

How It Works

This example prints two random values from 5 to 25.

```
rand(5, 25) = 8
mt_rand(5, 25) = 6
```

Random values are not restricted to positive integers. The following example shows how to get random values from –10 to 10.

The Code

```php
<?php
// Example 3-2-4.php
echo "rand(-10, 10) = " . rand(-10, 10) . "\n";
echo "mt_rand(-10, 10) = " . mt_rand(-10, 10) . "\n";
?>
```

How It Works

This example prints two random values between –10 and 10.

```
rand(-10, 10) = 5
mt_rand( 10, 10) = -6
```

Generating random numbers with these two functions will always result in an integer value. With some simple math it is possible to change this to generate a random floating-point value. So, if you want to generate random floating-point values from 0 to 10 with two decimals, you could write a function called frand(), as shown next.

The Code

```php
<?php
// Example 3-2-5.php
function frand($min, $max, $decimals = 0) {
  $scale = pow(10, $decimals);
  return mt_rand($min * $scale, $max * $scale) / $scale;
}

echo "frand(0, 10, 2) = " . frand(0, 10, 2) . "\n";
?>
```

How It Works

The function takes two mandatory arguments and one optional argument. If the third argument is omitted, the function will work as mt_rand() and return an integer. When the third argument is given, the function calculates a scale value used to calculate new values for the minimum and maximum and to adjust the result from mt_rand() to a floating-point value within the range specified by $min and $max. The output from this sample looks like this:

```
frand(0, 10, 2) = 3.47
```

Working with currency values might require the generation of random numbers with fixed spacing. Generating random values between $0 and $10 and in steps of $0.25 would not be possible with the frand() function without a few modifications. By changing the third parameters from $decimals to $precision and changing the logic a bit, it is possible to generate random numbers that fit both models, as shown in the following example.

The Code

```php
<?php
// Example 3-2-6.php
function frand($min, $max, $precision = 1) {
  $scale = 1/$precision;
  return mt_rand($min * $scale, $max * $scale) / $scale;
}

echo "frand(0, 10, 0.25) = " . frand(0, 10, 0.25) . "\n";
?>
```

Note There are no checks on the $precision value. Setting $precision = 0 will cause a division-by-zero error.

How It Works

The output from the sample looks like this:

```
frand(0, 10, 0.25) = 3.25
```

Changing the precision parameter to 0.01 gives the same result as in the first example, and changing it to 3 causes the function to return random values between 0 and 10 in steps of 3. The possible values are 0, 3, 6, and 9, as shown in the next example.

The Code

```php
<?php
// Example 3-2-7.php
function frand($min, $max, $precision = 1) {
  $scale = 1/$precision;
  return mt_rand($min * $scale, $max * $scale) / $scale;
}

echo "frand(0, 10, 3) = " . frand(0, 10, 3) . "\n";
?>
```

How It Works

The precision parameter has been changed to 3, so the ||$scale value will be 1/3. This reduces the internal minimum and maximum values to 0 and 3, and the result of mt_rand() is divided by $scale, which is the same as multiplying by 3. The internal random value will be 0, 1, 2, or 3, and when that's multiplied by 3, the possible values are 0, 3, 6, or 9.

```
frand(0, 10, 3) = 6
```

> **Note** The arguments to mt_rand() are expected to be integers. If other types are passed, the values are converted to integers before calculating the random value. This might cause the minimum and maximum values to be truncated, If the calculation of $min ⁺ $scale or $max ⁺ $scale results In a floatIng-polnt value.

You can also use the random number generators to generate random strings. This can be useful for generating passwords. The next example defines a function called GeneratePassword() that takes two optional arguments. These arguments specify the minimum and maximum lengths of the generated password.

The Code

```php
<?php
// Example 3-2-8.php
function GeneratePassword($min = 5, $max = 8) {
  $ValidChars = "abcdefghijklmnopqrstuvwxyz123456789";
  $max_char = strlen($ValidChars) - 1;
  $length = mt_rand($min, $max);
  $password = "";
  for ($i = 0; $i < $length; $i++) {
    $password .= $ValidChars[mt_rand(0, $max_char)];
  }
  return $password;
}

echo "New Password = " . GeneratePassword() . "\n";
echo "New Password = " . GeneratePassword(4, 10) . "\n";
?>
```

How It Works

The output from this script could look like this:

```
New Password = bbeyq
New Password = h3igij3bd7
```

The mt_rand() function is first used to get the length of the new password and then used within the for loop to select each character randomly from a predefined string of characters. You could extend this string to include both uppercase and lowercase characters and other characters that might be valid.

The variable $max_char defines the upper limit of the random number generation. This is set to the length of the string of valid characters minus 1 to avoid the mt_rand() function from returning a value that is outside the string's boundaries.

3-3. Logarithms and Exponents

PHP implements the log(), log10(), exp(), and pow() functions, as well as logp1() and expm1() that are marked as experimental, to calculate logarithms and exponents.

The exp() and log() functions are considered to be the inverse of each other, and they use e as the base. This number is called *neperian*, or the natural logarithm base. $e = exp(1); gives the value of e, and it's equal to 2.71828182846. This number is also defined as a constant called M_E, and it's defined as 2.7182818284590452354.

The following example shows the calculation of e and the inverse nature of the two functions.

The Code

```php
<?php
// Example 3-3-1.php
$e = exp(1);
echo "$e\n";
$i = log($e);
echo "$i\n";
?>
```

How It Works

This example calculates the value of e and assigns it to the variable $e, which is printed before it is used as a parameter to the log() function.

```
2.71828182846
1
```

You can calculate logarithms with other base values by dividing the result of the log() function with log(base). If the base is 10, it is faster to use the built-in log10() function, but for all other values of base, you can use this method.

The Code

```php
<?php
// Example 3-3-2.php
$val = 100;
$i = log($val);
echo "log($val) = $i\n";
$i10 = log($val) / log(10);
echo "log($val) / log(10) = $i10\n";
$i10 = log10($val);
echo "log10($val) = $i10\n";
?>
```

How It Works

This example calculates the natural logarithm of 10 and prints it. Then it uses the nature of the logarithmic functions to calculate log10 of the same value, and at last it uses the building log10() function to verify the result. The output from this example looks like this:

```
log(100) = 4.60517018599
log(100) / log(10) = 2
log10(100) = 2
```

The pow() function calculates one number to the power of another number. The function takes two arguments, where the first is the base and the second is the exponent. The return value will be an integer, if possible, or a float value. In the case of an error, the return value will be FALSE. When the base value is e, the pow() function becomes equal to the exp() function.

Note PHP cannot handle negative base values if the exponent is a noninteger.

The following example shows how to use the pow() function with integers, floats, and both negative and positive numbers.

The Code

```php
<?php
// Example 3-3-3.php
echo pow(2, 8) . "\n";
echo pow(-2, 5) . "\n";
echo pow(-2.5, 5) . "\n";
echo pow(0, 0) . "\n";
echo pow(M_E, 1) . "\n";
echo pow(3.2, 4.5) . "\n";
echo pow(2, -2) . "\n";
echo pow(-2, -3) . "\n";
?>
```

How It Works

This example shows how the pow() function can calculate the power of both positive and negative values of both integer and floating-point types.

```
256
-32
-97.65625
1
2.71828182846
187.574977246
0.25
-0.125
```

Another special case of pow() is that when the exponent is 0.5, the function is equal to the sqrt() function.

When presenting data in a graphical form (bar or line charts), it is sometimes practical to use a logarithmic scale to avoid small values being too close to the X axis and to reduce the visual difference between small and large values.

The next example uses a simple HTML-based technology to draw bar charts from an array of data. The script defines two constants used by the ShowChart() function to select a linear or logarithmic scale when drawing the chart. The ShowChart() function takes three arguments, where the first is the array of data used to draw the chart, the second is the optional chart type, and the third is an optional height value used to calculate the scaling of the data. In this case, the data used is hard-coded, but this part of the script could use a database connection or a log file from a web server to fetch the data. The final part of the script is where the HTML document is created and sent to the client.

The Code

```php
<?php
// Example 3-3-4.php
define('BAR_LIN', 1);
define('BAR_LOG', 2);

function ShowChart($arrData, $iType = BAR_LIN, $iHeight = 200) {
  echo '<table border=0><tr>';

  $max = 0;
  foreach($arrData as $y) {
    if ($iType == BAR_LOG) {
      $y = log10($y);
    }
    if ($y > $max) $max = $y;
  }
  $scale = $iHeight / $max;
```

```php
    foreach($arrData as $x=>$y) {
      if ($iType == BAR_LOG) {
        $y = log10($y);
      }
      $y = (int)($y*$scale);
      echo "<td valign=bottom>
              <img src=dot.png width=10 height=$y>
            </td>
            <td width=5> </td>";
    }
  echo '</tr></table>';
}

$arrData = array(
  150,
  5,
  200,
  8,
  170,
  50,
  3
);

echo '<html><body>';

echo 'Show chart with linear scale';
ShowChart($arrData, BAR_LIN);

echo '<br>Show chart with logarithmic scale';
ShowChart($arrData, BAR_LOG);

echo '</body></html>';
?>
```

How It Works

The ShowChart() function uses a small image of 1×1 pixels to generate the bars. Each bar is represented with the image being scaled to a height and width that matches the data in the first array passed to the function. The second parameter selects linear or logarithmic scale, and the third parameter defines the height of the entire chart. Figure 3-1 shows the resulting charts with linear and logarithmic scale.

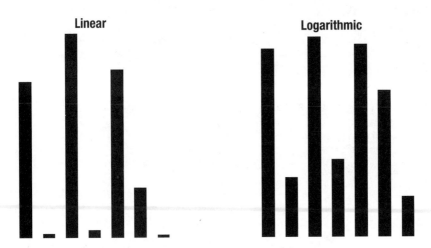

Figure 3-1. *Sample bar charts with linear and logarithmic scale*

Using plain HTML to generate charts is not optimal because of the limitations of the markup language. It's possible to generate more advanced charts with the GD (GIF, PNG, or JPG images) and Ming (Flash movies) extensions. Figure 3-2 shows an example of a bar chart generated with the Ming extension.

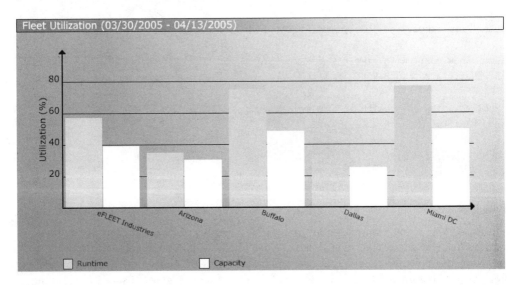

Figure 3-2. *Bar chart generated with the Ming extension*

3-4. Trigonometric Functions

PHP implements a full set of trigonometric and hyperbolic functions as well as a few functions to convert from degrees to radians and back. A number of constants, including M_PI (3.1415926538979323846), and a few derivatives are also defined to make life easier for the developer, as described in Table 3-4 and Table 3-5.

Table 3-4. *Trigonometric Functions*

Name	Description
cos()	Cosine
sin()	Sine
tan()	Tangent
acos()	Arc cosine
asin()	Arc sine
atan()	Arc tangent
atan2()	Arc tangent of two variables
pi()	A function returning pi (the same as M_PI)
deg2rad()	Degree to radians
rad2deg()	Radians to degrees

Table 3-5. *Hyperbolic Functions*

Name	Description
cosh()	Hyperbolic cosine (exp(arg) + exp(-arg))/2
sinh()	Hyperbolic sine (exp(arg) - exp(-arg))/2
tanh()	Hyperbolic tangent sinh(arg)/cosh(arg)
acosh()	Inverse hyperbolic cosine
asinh()	Inverse hyperbolic sine
atanh()	Inverse hyperbolic tangent

Note acosh(), asinh(), and atanh() are not implemented on the Windows platform.

You can use the trigonometric functions to calculate positions of elements in a plane. This can be useful when using GD or Ming extensions to generate dynamic graphical content. If a line that starts in (0, 0) and ends in (100, 0) is to be duplicated starting at (20, 20) and rotated 35 degrees, you can calculate the ending point with the trigonometric functions, as shown in the following example.

The Code

```php
<?php
// Example 3-4-1.php
$start = array(0, 0);
$end = array(100, 0);
$length = sqrt(pow($end[0] - $start[0], 2) + pow($end[1] - $start[1], 2));

$angle = 35;
$r = deg2rad($angle);
$new_start = array(20, 20);
$new_end = array(
   $new_start[0] + cos($r) * $length,
   $new_start[1] + sin($r) * $length
);

var_dump($new_end);
?>
```

How It Works

The first line is defined by two sets of coordinates. These are assigned as arrays to the variables $start and $end and used to calculate the length of the line. Setting the starting point of the new line is as simple as assigning $new_start the coordinates as an array. This is then used together with the angle (35 degrees) to calculate the value of $new_end.

```
array(2) {
  [0]=>
  float(101.915204429)
  [1]=>
  float(77.3576436351)
}
```

The arguments to cos(), sin(), and tan() should always be given in radians, and the values returned by acos(), asin(), and atan() will always be in radians. If you need to operate on angles specified in degrees, you can use the deg2rad() and rad2deg() functions to convert between the two.

Trigonometric functions have a wide range of usages; one of them is to calculate the distance between two locations on the earth. Each location is specified by a set of coordinates. Several different methods with varying accuracy are available, and they can more or less compensate for the fact that the earth is not a perfect sphere. One of the simplest methods is called the Great Circle Distance, and it's based on the assumptions that 1 minute of arc is 1 nautical mile and the radius of the earth is 6,364.963 kilometers (3,955.00465 miles). These assumptions work fine when both locations are far from the poles and equator.

The formula used to calculate the distance takes the longitude and latitude for each location, and it looks like this:

```
D = R * ARCOS (SIN(L1) * SIN(L2) + COS(L1) * COS(L2) * COS(DG))
```

This formula returns the distance in kilometers or miles (depending on the radius value) and assumes all the trigonometric functions to be working in degrees. For most calculators it is possible to choose degrees or radians, but for PHP only radians is available, so you need to convert everything to and from degrees. It would also be nice to have the function return the result in miles or kilometers.

R is the earth's radius in kilometers or miles, L1 and L2 are the latitude of the first and second locations in degrees, and DG is the longitude of the second location minus the longitude of the first location, also in degrees. Latitude values are negative south of the equator. Longitudes are negative to the west with the center being the Greenwich mean time (GMT) line.

Calculating the distance between two locations starts by finding the longitude and latitude of each location and inserting the values in the formula. A Google search is an easy way to find longitude and latitude values for many popular locations. You can use maps and even Global Positioning System (GPS) receivers. As an example, we have chosen Copenhagen and Los Angeles. Copenhagen is located east of the GMT line at 12.56951 and north of the equator at 55.67621, and Los Angeles is located west of the GMT line at –118.37323 and a bit closer to the equator at 34.01241.

To make the calculations a little easier, you can start by creating a function that will return the distance between two locations in either kilometers or miles. The function is called GetDistance(); it takes four mandatory parameters and one optional parameter. The two constants (KM and MILES) select the format of the return value as well as define the earth's radius in both formats.

The Code

```php
<?php
// Example 3-4-2.php
define('KM', 6364.963);
define('MILES', 3955.00465);

function GetDistance($la1, $lo1, $la2, $lo2, $r = KM) {
  $l1 = deg2rad($la1);
  $l2 = deg2rad($la2);
  $dg = deg2rad($lo2 - $lo1);
  $d = $r * acos(sin($l1) * sin($l2) + cos($l1) * cos($l2) * cos($dg));
  return $d;
}

// Copenhagen
$lat1 = 55.67621;
$long1 = 12.56951;
```

```
// Los Angeles
$lat2 =  34.01241;
$long2 = -118.37323;

echo "The distance from Copenhagen to Los Angeles is " .
     round(GetDistance($lat1, $long1, $lat2, $long2)) . " km\n";
echo "The distance from Copenhagen to Los Angeles is " .
     round(GetDistance($lat1, $long1, $lat2, $long2, MILES)) . " miles\n";
?>
```

How It Works

Two constants define the radius of the earth in kilometers and miles. The same two constants are used as parameters to the GetDistance() function, so there is no need for additional constants here. The GetDistance() function takes four mandatory parameters that specify the latitude and longitude of each point for which the distance should be calculated.

The round() function is used on the return value, before printing, to get rid of any decimals, because the calculation is not that accurate anyway. The output from the script is the distance between Copenhagen and Los Angeles in kilometers and in miles:

```
The distance from Copenhagen to Los Angeles is 9003 km
The distance from Copenhagen to Los Angeles is 5594 miles
```

3-5. Formatting of Numeric Data

Except for warnings, errors, and so on, most output from PHP is generated by a few functions, such as echo, print(), and printf(). These functions convert the argument to a string and send it to the client (console or web browser). The PHP-GTK extension uses other methods/functions to generate output. You can use the sprintf() function in the same way as the printf() function, except it returns the formatted string for further processing. The conversion of numbers to string representation takes place in a simple way without any special formatting, except for a few options used with the |printf() function. It is possible to embed integer and floating-point values in strings for easy printing, as shown in the following sample.

The Code

```
<?php
// Example 3-5-1.php
$i = 123;
$f = 12.567;

echo "\$i = $i and \$f = $f\n";
?>
```

How It Works

Two numeric variables are defined and assigned an integer and a floating-point value. The two variables are then embedded in a string. This generates the following output:

```
$i = 123 and $f = 12.567
```

Other functions can format numeric values before the value is output to the client. You can convert an integer into a string representation with a different base using one of these functions: decbin(), decoct(), dechex(), or base_convert(). The base_convert() function can convert an integer to any base, as you saw in recipe 3-1, but the first three functions make the code a bit more readable, and there is no need for additional parameters. Three functions— bindec(), octdec(), and hexdec()—can convert binary, octal, and hexadecimal strings to decimal integer values; again, these conversions can be handled by base_convert(), but the result will be a string value for any conversion, where the three other functions will return an integer or a float depending on the number of bits needed to represent the number.

When decimal numbers (integers or floats) are presented, it's common to use a decimal point, a thousand separator, and a fixed number of decimals after the decimal point. This makes it much easier to read the value when it contains many digits. In PHP the function number_format() converts integers and floating-point values into a readable string representation. The function takes one, two, or four parameters. The first parameter is the numeric value to be formatted. This is expected to be a floating-point value, but the function allows it to be an integer or a string and performs the conversion to a float when needed.

Note If a non-numeric string value is passed as the first parameter, the internal conversion will result in 0. No warnings or errors will be generated.

The second parameter indicates the number of decimals after the decimal point. The default number of decimals is zero. The third and fourth parameters specify the character for the decimal point and thousand separator. The default values are a dot (.) and a comma (,), but you can change to any character. The following example shows how you can format an integer and a floating-point value with the number_format() function.

The Code

```php
<?php
// Example 3-5-2.php
$i = 123456;
$f = 98765.567;

$si = number_format($i, 0, ',', '.');
$sf = number_format($f, 2);

echo "\$si = $si and \$sf = $sf\n";
?>
```

How It Works

Two floating-point values are defined and formatted with the number_format() function. The first value is presented as an integer with zero decimals, the decimal point is represented with a comma (not shown), and the thousand separator is a dot. The second value is formatted with two decimals and uses the system default for the decimal point and thousand separator.

```
$si = 123.456 and $sf = 98,765.57
```

You can use two other functions to format numbers: printf() and sprintf(). Both functions take one or more arguments, where the first argument is a string that describes the format and the remaining arguments replace placeholders defined in the formatting string with values. The main difference between the two functions is the way the output is handled. The printf() function sends the output directly to the client and returns the length of the printed string; sprintf() returns the string to the program. Both functions follow the same formatting rules, where % followed by a letter indicates a placeholder. Table 3-6 lists the allowed placeholders.

Table 3-6. printf() *and* sprintf() *Formatting Types*

Type	Description
%	A literal percent character. No argument is required.
b	The argument is treated as an integer and presented as a binary number.
c	The argument is treated as an integer and presented as the character with that American Standard Code for Information Interchange (ASCII) value.
d	The argument is treated as an integer and presented as a (signed) decimal number.
e	The argument is treated as scientific notation (for example, 1.2e+2).
|u	The argument is treated as an integer and presented as an unsigned decimal number.
f	The argument is treated as a float and presented as a floating-point number (locale aware).
F	The argument is treated as a float and presented as a floating-point number (nonlocale aware). Available since PHP 4.3.10 and PHP 5.0.3.
o	The argument is treated as an integer and presented as an octal number.
s	The argument is treated and presented as a string.
x	The argument is treated as an integer and presented as a hexadecimal number (with lowercase letters).
X	The argument is treated as an integer and presented as a hexadecimal number (with uppercase letters).

The following example shows how you can format an integer and a floating-point value with the printf() function.

The Code

```php
<?php
// Example 3-5-3.php
$i = 123456;
$f = 98765.567;

printf("\$i = %x and \$i = %b\n", $i, $i);
printf("\$i = %d and \$f = %f\n", $i, $f);
printf("\$i = %09d and \$f = %0.2f\n", $i, $f);
?>
```

How It Works

This example shows how the printf() function can format numbers as different data types.

```
$i = 1E240 and $i = 11110001001000000
$i = 123456 and $f = 98765.567000
$i = 000123456 and $f = 98765.57
```

It is also possible to use typecasting to convert numbers to strings; this works as if the variable were embedded in a string, as shown in the next example.

The Code

```php
<?php
// Example 3-5-4.php
$i = 123456;
$f = 98765.567;

echo "\$i = " . (string)$i . "\n";
echo "\$f = " . (string)$f . "\n";
?>
```

How It Works

The two variables are typecast into a string value and used to generate the output.

```
$i = 123456
$f = 98765.567
```

On systems where libc implements the function strfmon(), PHP will also define a function called money_format(). The function takes a formatting string and a floating-point number as arguments. The result of this function depends on the setting of the LC_MONETARY category of the locale settings. You can change this value with the setlocale() function before calling money_format(). This function can convert only one floating-point value at the time, and the formatting string can contain one placeholder along with other characters that will be returned with the formatted number.

The placeholder is defined as a sequence of the following elements:

- The % character indicates the beginning of the placeholder.

- Optional flags.

- Optional width.

- Optional left precision.

- Optional right precision.

- A conversion character.

The following example shows a few ways of formatting currency values and shows how to change the locale setting before showing a money value, as well as a few other formatting options.

The Code

```php
<?php
// Example 3-5-5.php
$number = 1234.56;
setlocale(LC_MONETARY, 'en_US');
echo money_format('%i', $number) . "\n";

setlocale(LC_MONETARY, 'en_DK');
echo money_format('%.2i', $number) . "\n";

$number = -1234.5672;
setlocale(LC_MONETARY, 'en_US');
echo money_format('%(#10n', $number) . "\n";
echo money_format('%(#10i', $number) . "\n";
?>
```

How It Works

A floating-point value is passed to the money_format() function. Before each call to this function, the LC_MONETARY value is changed by a call to the setlocale() function.

```
USD 1,234.56
DKK 1.234,56
($        1,234.57)
(USD        1,234.57)
```

3-6. Math Libraries

PHP comes with two math extensions: BCMath and GMP. BCMath is a binary calculator that supports numbers of any size and precision. This extension is bundled with PHP. (It's compiled by default on Windows systems; on Unix systems it can be enabled with the -enable-bcmath configure option.) There is no need for external libraries. The GMP extension is a wrapper around the GNU MP library, and it allows you to work with arbitrary-length integers. This extension requires the GNU library and can be included by adding -with-gmp when configuring PHP. (For binary Windows distributions this will be included in the php_gmp.dll file). Table 3-7 shows the functions implemented by the BCMath extension.

Table 3-7. *BCMath Functions*

Name	Description
bcadd()	Adds two numbers
bccomp()	Compares two numbers
|bcdiv()	Divides two numbers
bcmod()	Calculates the remainder with the division of two numbers
bcmul()	Multiplies two numbers
bcpow()	Raises one number to the power of another
bcpowmod()	Raises one number to the power of another, raised by the specified modulus
bcscale()	Sets the default scale for all BCMath functions
bcsqrt()	Calculates the square root of a number
bcsub()	Subtracts two numbers

Most of these functions take an optional scale parameter. If the scale parameter is omitted, the functions will use the value defined by a call to bcscale(). The scale parameter defines the number of decimals returned by the function, as shown in the following example.

The Code

```php
<?php
// Example 3-6-1.php
bcscale(3);
$a = 1.123;
$b = 2.345;

$c = bcadd($a, $b);
echo "$c\n";

$c = bcadd($a, $b, 1);
echo "$c\n";
?>
```

How It Works

Two floating-point values are defined and added with the bcadd() function using the default scale (3) set by a call to bcscae(). Then the same two values are added, but this time the default scale is overwritten by the third argument. Note how the result is truncated and not rounded.

```
3.468
3.4
```

The GMP extension implements a long list of functions (see Table 3-8) that can be used to manipulate large integer values (more than 32 bits).

Table 3-8. *GMP Functions*

Name	Description
gmp_abs	Calculates absolute value
gmp_add	Adds numbers
|gmp_and	Logical and
gmp_clrbit	Clears bit
gmp_cmp	Compares numbers
gmp_com	Calculates one's complement
|gmp_div_q	Divides numbers
gmp_div_qr	Divides numbers and gets quotient and remainder
gmp_div_r	Remainder of the division of numbers
gmp_div	Alias of gmp_div_q()
gmp_divexact	Exact division of numbers
gmp_fact	Factorial
gmp_gcd	Calculates GCD
gmp_gcdext	Calculates GCD and multipliers
gmp_hamdist	Hamming distance
gmp_init	Creates GMP number
gmp_intval	Converts GMP number to integer
gmp_invert	Inverse by modulo
gmp_jacobi	Jacobi symbol
gmp_legendre	Legendre symbol
gmp_mod	Modulo operation
gmp_mul	Multiplies numbers
gmp_neg	Negates number
gmp_or	Logical or
gmp_perfect_square	Perfect square check
gmp_popcount	Population count

Name	Description
gmp_pow	Raises number into power
gmp_powm	Raises number into power with modulo
gmp_prob_prime	Checks if number is "probably prime"
gmp_random	Random number
gmp_scan0	Scans for 0
gmp_scan1	Scans for 1
gmp_setbit	Sets bit
gmp_sign	Sign of number
gmp_sqrt	Calculates square root
gmp_sqrtrem	Square root with remainder
gmp_strval	Converts GMP number to string
gmp_sub	Subtracts numbers
gmp_xor	Logical xor

The following is an alternative to base_convert() that works on integers up to 32-bit.

The Code

```php
<?php
// Example 3-6-2.php
if (!extension_loaded("gmp")) {
  dl("php_gmp.dll");
}
/*use gmp library to convert base. gmp will convert numbers > 32bit*/
function gmp_convert($num, $base_a, $base_b)
{
      return gmp_strval(gmp_init($num, $base_a), $base_b);
}

echo "12345678987654321 in hex is: " .
  gmp_convert('12345678987654321', 10, 16) . "\n";
?>
```

How It Works

This example takes a large integer value and converts it into a hexadecimal representation. The output will look like this:

```
12345678987654321 in hex is: 2bdc546291f4b1
```

Note that all the integer values are represented as strings.

■**Note** Loading the GMP extension as a DLL will work only on Windows systems, and using the dl() function will work only for CLI and Common Gateway Interface (CGI) versions of PHP. For the Unix system, the
GMP extension will be built-in or must be loaded as gmp.so.

The large integer values are stored internally as resource types. The function gmp_init()
takes two parameters, where the first is a string representation and the second is an optional
base value if the integer is given in a base value other than 10. The function gmp_strval() can
convert a GMP resource to a readable string value. The rest of the functions manipulate one or
more large integer values.

3-7. A Static Math Class

The math functions in PHP are, for the most part, designed to be used directly as functions
and procedures, but with the new object model introduced in PHP 5 it's possible to create a
static Math() class that will act like math classes in other languages such as Java or JavaScript.

■**Note** It's always faster to call the functions directly than it is to use classes to wrap around the functions.
However, static classes can make function names easier to remember, as they can be defined closer to what
is used in other languages.

The next example shows how you can create and use a simple static Math() class. Using
the static keyword in front of class members and methods makes it possible to use these
without instantiating the class.

The Code

```php
<?php
// Example math.php
define('RAND_MAX', mt_getrandmax());

class Math {
  static $pi = M_PI;
  static $e = M_E;

  static function pi() {
    return M_PI;
  }
  static function intval($val) {
    return intval($val);
  }
```

```php
    static function floor($val) {
      return floor($val);
    }
    static function ceil($val) {
      return ceil($val);
    }
    static function round($val, $decimals = 0) {
      return round($val, $decimals);
    }
    static function abs($val) {
      return abs($val);
    }
    static function floatval($val) {
      return floatval($val);
    }
    static function rand($min = 0, $max = RAND_MAX) {
      return mt_rand($min, $max);
    }
    static function min($var1, $var2) {
      return min($var1, $var2);
    }
    static function max($var1, $var2) {
      return max($var1, $var2);
    }
}

$a = 3.5;

echo "Math::\$pi = " . Math::$pi . "\n";
echo "Math::\$e = " . Math::$e . "\n";
echo "Math::intval($a) = " . Math::intval($a) . "\n";
echo "Math::floor($a) = " . Math::floor($a) . "\n";
echo "Math::ceil($a) = " . Math::ceil($a) . "\n";
echo "Math::round(Math::\$pi, 2) = " . Math::round(Math::$pi, 2) . "\n";
echo "Math::abs(-$a) = " . Math::abs(-$a) . "\n";
echo "Math::floatval($a) = " . Math::floatval($a) . "\n";
echo "Math::rand(5, 25) = " . Math::rand(5, 25) . "\n";
echo "Math::rand() = " . Math::rand() . "\n";
echo "Math::min(2, 28) = " . Math::min(3, 28) . "\n";
echo "Math::max(3, 28) = " . Math::max(3, 28) . "\n";
?>
```

How It Works

The output from this script is simple but shows how the class is used:

```
Math::$pi = 3.14159265359
Math::$e = 2.71828182846
Math::intval(3.5) = 3
Math::floor(3.5) = 3
Math::ceil(3.5) = 4
Math::round(Math::$pi, 2) = 3.14
Math::abs(-3.5) = 3.5
Math::floatval(3.5) = 3.5
Math::rand(5, 25) = 13
Math::rand() = 1651387578
Math::min(2, 28) = 3
Math::max(3, 28) = 28
```

The JavaScript Math() class does not implement the intval(), floatval(), and rand() functions, and the round() function does not take a second argument to specify the number of decimals. The following example shows the same code in JavaScript.

The Code

```
<html>
<!-- Example math.html -->
<body>
<script language=JavaScript>
  a = 3.5;
  document.write('Math.PI = ' + Math.PI + '<br>');
  document.write('Math.E = ' + Math.E + '<br>');
  document.write('floor(' + a + ') = ' + Math.floor(a) + '<br>');
  document.write('ceil(' + a + ') = ' + Math.ceil(a) + '<br>');
  document.write('round(Math.PI) = ' + Math.round(Math.PI) + '<br>');
  document.write('min(3, 28) = ' + Math.min(3, 28) + '<br>');
  document.write('max(3, 28) = ' + Math.max(3, 28) + '<br>');
</script>
</body>
</html>
```

How It Works

Figure 3-3 shows the output in a browser.

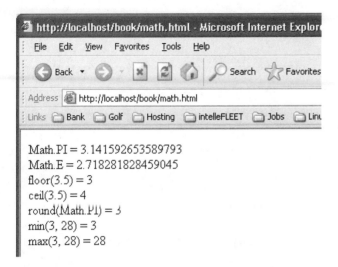

```
Math.PI = 3.141592653589793
Math.E = 2.718281828459045
floor(3.5) = 3
ceil(3.5) = 4
round(Math.PI) = 3
min(3, 28) = 3
max(3, 28) = 28
```

Figure 3-3. *Using the* Math() *class in JavaScript*

Summary

This chapter demonstrated how you can use many of the built-in math functions and operators in conjunction with the advantages of a loosely typed language such as PHP to calculate
simple but advanced computations.

We first covered the basic data types and how PHP handles them when assigning and calculating values. Then we discussed the conversion of integers between different base values.

Next, we talked about random numbers and how to build functions to generate random
values of floating-point or string data types.

The next two topics were logarithmic and trigonometric functions. These functions have
a wide range of usages, but this chapter concentrated on how you can use them to generate
charts and calculate the distance between two points on the earth.

Then, we discussed two extensions for handling math on numbers that do not fit into the
simple numeric data types of PHP. Finally, we showed how you can create a static math class
and use it like you would implement math classes in other languages.

Looking Ahead

In Chapter 4, Jon Stephens will demonstrate how to use arrays as complex data types in PHP.
The chapter will show how you can manipulate arrays, how you can search arrays to find a
specific value, and how you can sort and traverse arrays with different methods.

CHAPTER 4

■ ■ ■

Working with Arrays

If you have worked with PHP 4 or another scripting language, then you have almost certainly worked with arrays—the idea of lists or collections of values is central to programming in general, and PHP is no exception. If you are not already familiar with arrays, you should flip back to Lee Babin's Chapter 1 and get up to speed on just what an array is. Here we will just remind you that the simple definition of the word *array* is "a collection or list of values."

However, when using arrays in PHP, it is important to remember that PHP lumps together two different sorts of constructs under the same name: ordered lists and unordered lists. Ordered lists are often referred to in PHP as *indexed arrays*, in which each value is referenced by a unique number, and unordered lists (collections) are referred to as *associative arrays*, in which each value is identified by a unique name (a string value) and the order usually is not important. It is possible in PHP for a single array to contain both indexed and named values.

Because of this, you will sometimes find that PHP has two ways of performing certain array-related tasks, depending on whether you need to be mindful of keys and key/value relations, such as when you are populating or adding items to arrays or ordering (sorting) arrays. This duplication can sometimes make working with PHP arrays a bit overwhelming. On the other hand, it also means that PHP has many built-in functions for performing common tasks with arrays, and when you do have to "roll your own," you will find that you can handle many of these tasks with just a few lines of code.

In this chapter, we will cover the following topics:

- Creating and populating arrays

- Outputting arrays in various user-friendly formats

- Adding new elements to and removing them from existing arrays, both singly and in sets

- Getting and setting the size or length of an array

- Combining arrays

- Finding array elements and traversing arrays

- Applying functions to arrays

- Sorting arrays according to keys, values, and other criteria

- Comparing arrays and array elements

- Finding combinations and permutations of array elements

Arrays in PHP 5 provide an amazingly huge range of functionality, so we have lots to cover in this chapter. Let's get started by reviewing how to create arrays and how to get data into them once they have been created and then move on from there.

4-1. Creating Arrays

Creating arrays in PHP is quite easy. Both indexed arrays and associative arrays are produced by calling the array() function.

The Code

```
$my_array = array();

$pets = array('Tweety', 'Sylvester', 'Bugs', 'Wile E.');

$person = array('Bill', 'Jones', 24, 'CA');
$customer = array('first' => 'Bill', 'last' => 'Jones',
                  'age' => 24, 'state' => 'CA');
```

How It Works

The simplest way to create an array in PHP is to call array() without any arguments, which creates a new, empty array. You can create an array that is already populated with some elements simply by listing those elements, separated by commas, as arguments to array(). Array elements can be any valid PHP data type, and elements belonging to the same array can be different data types. To create an associative array, list the array's key/value pairs using the => operator to associate each key with its corresponding value, and separate the key/value pairs from each other with commas.

4-2. Accessing Array Elements

To access the elements of an indexed array, just use square brackets ([ ]) and the number of the element in the array starting with 0 (not 1!) and going from left to right.

The Code

```
print "<p>Pet number 1 is named '$pets[0]'.</p>\n";
print "<p>The person's age is $person[2].</p>\n";
print "<p>The customer's age is {$customer['age']}.</p>\n";
```

Assuming you have defined the $pets, $person, and $customer arrays as shown in recipe 4-1, the previous statements will produce the following output:

```
Pet number 1 is named 'Tweety'.

The person's age is 24.
```

■Note The customer's age is 24. In each case, the array element is accessed by using the array's variable name followed by the index of the desired element in square brackets. Note that you must put associative array keys in quotes; in addition, if you want to use variable interpolation when outputting an element from an associative array, you must surround the variable name with braces, as shown in the last print statement of the previous code.

4-3. Creating Multidimensional Arrays

As we said earlier, array elements can be any legal PHP data type, even other arrays. This recipe shows some arrays consisting of other arrays, also referred to as *multidimensional arrays*. To access elements of such arrays, you can use multiple sets of brackets, working your way from the outside in, as shown in the last two statements in the following code.

The Code

```php
$customers
  = array(
          array('first' => 'Bill', 'last' => 'Jones',
                'age' => 24, 'state' => 'CA'),
          array('first' => 'Mary', 'last' => 'Smith',
                'age' => 32, 'state' => 'OH'),
          array('first' => 'Joyce', 'last' => 'Johnson',
                'age' => 21, 'state' => 'TX'),
        );

$pet_breeds
  = array(
          'dogs' => array('Poodle', 'Terrier', 'Dachshund'),
          'birds' => array('Parrot', 'Canary'),
          'fish' => array('Guppy', 'Tetra', 'Catfish', 'Angelfish')
        );
printf("<p>The name of the second customer is %s %s.</p>\n",
        $customers[1]['first'], $customers[1]['last']);

printf("<p>%s and %s</p>", $pet_breeds['dogs'][0], $pet_breeds['birds'][1]);
```

The output of these two statements is as follows:

```
The name of the second customer is Mary Smith.

Poodle and Canary
```

4-4. Using Array Keys

It is possible to use the => operator when creating indexed arrays. This allows you to define an array whose elements do not have contiguous indexes, as shown next. We will show you another means of defining such arrays in the next recipe, coming up shortly.

The Code

```
$primes = array(1 => 'one', 2 => 'two', 3 => 'three', 5 => 'five', 7 => 'seven');
```

Variations

It is entirely possible to use both integer and string keys in the same array. For instance, this is entirely legal:

```
$array = array('name' => 'Bill', 'age' => 32, 1 => '25 Main St.',
               2 => 'Apt. 24', 'city' => 'San Francisco', 'state' => 'CA');
```

If you use the minimal string representation of an integer as an array key, PHP will interpret this as an integer. Note the word *minimal* here—using $array as defined previously, if you assign a value to $array['1'], then the value of $array[1] will be updated; if you assign a value to $array['01'], this will create a new element in $array with that value and with the string key '01'.

4-5. Initializing an Array As a Range or Sequence of Values

It is often useful to be able to create an array and fill it with a sequence or range of values, most often integers. Some examples of these are the arrays (1, 2, 3, 4, 5), (5, 10, 15, 20), and (6, 2, -2, -6, -10). You may already be thinking that we are about to show you some code involving for or foreach loops for constructing such arrays. However, although it is possible to initialize arrays in this way, PHP provides a function that can make things much simpler. In fact, in many cases it can obviate the need to create variables that hold "throwaway" arrays, which are used only once, as you will see shortly. This function has the following prototype:

```
array range(mixed $start, mixed $end[, mixed $step])
```

This function returns an array whose first element is $start and whose last element is $end. If these values are integers (and $step is not used), the result is an array whose elements consist of $start, followed by the integers between $start and $end, followed by $end. For instance, range(0, 4) returns the array (0, 1, 2, 3, 4). If $end is greater than $start, then the array is created in reverse order; in other words, range(4, 0) yields the array (4, 3, 2, 1, 0).

The following are a few examples that ought to give you some ideas regarding the many ways you can use range().

The Code

```
<?php
  function array_list($array)          #  save a bit of typing
  {
    printf("<p>(%s)</p>\n", implode(', ', $array) );
```

```
}
$arr1 = range(5, 11);               # integer start/end
array_list($arr1);

$arr2 = range(0, -5);               # count backward
array_list($arr2);

$arr3 = range(3, 15, 3);            # use $step to skip intervals of 3

array_list($arr3);

array_list( range(20, 0, -5) );     # stepping backward

array_list( range(2.4, 3.1, .1) );  # fractional values

array_list( range('a', 'f') );      # produce a sequence of characters

array_list( range('M', 'A', -2) );  # skip every other letter going backward
?>
```

If you use $start or $end values consisting of more than one character, only the first character is used; any remainder is ignored.

Note If you are not already familiar with implode(), see the following section for more information about this and other ways to display an array's content in an easy-to-read form.

Here is the output:

```
(5, 6, 7, 8, 9, 10, 11)

(0, -1, -2, -3, -4, -5)

(3, 6, 9, 12, 15)

(20, 15, 10, 5, 0)

(2.4, 2.5, 2.6, 2.7, 2.8, 2.9, 3, 3.1)

(a, b, c, d, e, f)

(M, K, I, G, E, C, A)
```

Outputting Arrays

Before performing operations on arrays, it is good to have at least one or two ways to output all the elements of an array so you can check your results. You can do this in numerous ways. Some of these ways are better suited for use with indexed arrays, but most of them can be used equally well with either indexed or associative arrays. Probably the most useful ways to display arrays are as comma-delimited strings and as trees. We will show how you can do both in the next two sections.

4-6. Outputting an Array As a String

Working with ordered (indexed) arrays is generally simpler than with unordered (associative) ones, as shown in the next example.

The Code

```
$languages = array('German', 'French', 'Spanish');

printf("<p>Languages: %s.</p>\n", implode(', ', $languages));
```

Here is the output:

```
Languages: German, French, Spanish.
```

How It Works

The implode() function represents a handy way to output an entire indexed array in one go. It takes two arguments: a "glue" string of zero or more characters used to join the elements of the array into a single string and the array whose elements are to be joined. Here is the formal prototype of this function:

```
string implode(string $glue='', array $pieces)
```

Note The implode() function is also aliased as join(). We prefer implode() (perhaps because it obviously does the reverse of explode()), but you can use either name for this function—it will perform in the same way. Whichever alias you use, we recommend you pick one and stick with it in all your code.

4-7. Outputting Using array_values() and array_keys() for Backward Compatibility

Strictly speaking, you can use the $glue and $pieces arguments in either order, but we recommend you supply these in the order shown. In PHP 5, $glue defaults to an empty string and can be omitted; however, this is not backward compatible and will cause an error in older versions of PHP (prior to PHP 4.3.0). This function does not really work with associative arrays.

To output all the values of an associative array as a string, you can use the array_values() function to get an ordered array consisting of the associative array's values; to do likewise with all of its keys, you can use array_keys().

The Code

```
$countries_languages
    = array('Germany' => 'German', 'France' => 'French', 'Spain' => 'Spanish');

printf("<p>Languages: %s.</p>\n",
        implode(', ', array_values($countries_languages)) );

printf("<p>Countries: %s.</p>\n",
        implode(', ', array_keys($countries_languages)) );
```

Here is the output:

```
Languages: German, French, Spanish.

Countries: Germany, France, Spain.
```

Variations

If you want to add that little extra-special touch, you can wrap these in a couple of functions and surround the joined array elements with parentheses, like so:

```
<?php
  function array_values_string($arr)
  {
    return sprintf("(%s)", implode(', ', array_values($arr)));
  }

  function array_keys_string($arr)
  {
    return sprintf("(%s)", implode(', ', array_key($arr)));
  }

$countries_languages
    = array('Germany' => 'German', 'France' => 'French', 'Spain' => 'Spanish');

  print 'Countries: ';
  print array_keys_string($countries_languages);
  print '<br />Languages: ';
  print array_values_string($countries_languages);
?>
```

The output produced by this is as follows:

```
Countries: (Germany, France, Spain)
Languages: (German, French, Spanish)
```

You might also find these two functions or similar ones useful in dynamically generating code.

4-8. Outputting an Array As a Tree

For debugging purposes, you may also want to use the print_r(), var_export(), and var_dump() functions to output an array as a tree. These are all particularly useful with associative arrays and nested arrays, as they show all keys and values and act recursively. The following example shows how you can do this.

The Code

```php
<?php
  $customers
  = array(
          array('first' => 'Bill', 'last' => 'Jones',
                'age' => 24, 'state' => 'CA'),
          array('first' => 'Mary', 'last' => 'Smith',
                'age' => 32, 'state' => 'OH'),
          array('first' => 'Joyce', 'last' => 'Johnson',
                'age' => 21, 'state' => 'TX'),
          );

  printf("print_r():<pre>%s</pre>", print_r($customers, TRUE));

  printf("var_export():<pre>%s</pre>", var_export($customers, TRUE));

  print 'var_dump():<pre>';
  var_dump($customers);
  print '</pre>';
?>
```

This is the output of the previous code snippet:

```
print_r():
Array
(
    [0] => Array
        (
            [first] => Bill
            [last] => Jones
            [age] => 24
```

```
                [state] => CA
            )

    [1] => Array
        (
                [first] => Mary
                [last] => Smith
                [age] => 32
                [state] => OH
        )

    [2] => Array
        (
                [first] => Joyce
                [last] => Johnson
                [age] => 21
                [state] => TX
        )

)

var_export():
array (
  0 =>
  array (
    'first' => 'Bill',
    'last' => 'Jones',
    'age' => 24,
    'state' => 'CA',
  ),
  1 =>
  array (
    'first' => 'Mary',
    'last' => 'Smith',
    'age' => 32,
    'state' => 'OH',
  ),
  2 =>
  array (
    'first' => 'Joyce',
    'last' => 'Johnson',
    'age' => 21,
    'state' => 'TX',
  ),
)

var_dump():
```

```
array(3) {
  [0]=>
  array(4) {
    ["first"]=>
    string(4) "Bill"
    ["last"]=>
    string(5) "Jones"
    ["age"]=>
    int(24)
    ["state"]=>
    string(2) "CA"
  }
  [1]=>
  array(4) {
    ["first"]=>
    string(4) "Mary"
    ["last"]=>
    string(5) "Smith"
    ["age"]=>
    int(32)
    ["state"]=>
    string(2) "OH"
  }
  [2]=>
  array(4) {
    ["first"]=>
    string(5) "Joyce"
    ["last"]=>
    string(7) "Johnson"
    ["age"]=>
    int(21)
    ["state"]=>
    string(2) "TX"
  }
}
```

How It Works

All three of these functions output a string representation of a variable. In the case of print_r()
and var_export(), you can supply a second optional argument of boolean TRUE in order to have
the function return a string rather than output it directly. var_dump() has no such option; however, you can pass multiple values to this function.

One other item of interest concerning var_export() is that the output of this function is valid PHP code—a fact you can use in your scripts. You might also note that the output from var_dump() contains type and size information about each array element with which it is possible to tell at a glance whether your array elements contain the sort of data you are expecting them to contain.

Tip You can use print_r(), var_export(), and var_dump() with variables and values of *any* type, not just with arrays.

Adding New Elements to Arrays

You can use bracket notation to add new elements to an associative array, like so:

```
$customer['email'] = 'billsmith@mysite.net';
```

This is pretty simple with associative arrays, and it is also possible to set arbitrary elements for indexed arrays this way. However, because you sometimes have to be concerned about both ordering the elements and maintaining the continuity of indexes, you often need to employ some different techniques for adding new elements to an indexed array.

Note From this point on, we will usually refer to indexed (ordered) arrays simply as *arrays*, but we will continue to use *associative array* when speaking of associative or unordered arrays. We will use the term *indexed* or *ordered* only when it seems necessary to avoid confusion.

4-9. Adding an Element to the End of an Array

If you want to add a new element to the end of an array, you can do that using the variable name for the array followed by a set of empty brackets. You can do this regardless of whether the array has any existing elements, as shown in the following example.

The Code

```php
<?php
  $languages = array(); //  create a new, empty array

  $languages[] = 'German';
  $languages[] = 'French';
  $languages[] = 'Spanish';

  printf("<p>Languages: %s.</p>\n", implode(', ', $languages));
?>
```

Here is the output:

```
Languages: German, French, Spanish.
```

Variations

You can also use the array_push() function to accomplish this task, as shown here:

```php
<?php
  $languages = array();

  array_push($languages, 'German', 'French', 'Spanish');

  printf("<p>Languages: %s.</p>\n", implode(', ', $languages));
?>
```

The output of this code snippet is the same as in the previous example. array_push() can be useful when you want to append multiple elements to an array in a single function call. The first argument is the array to which you want to append. You can then use as many values as you want as additional arguments to this function; these will be appended to the array in the order in which they are listed as arguments.

Caution You might be tempted to feed array_push() an array as the second argument rather than list the values separately. Do not do this unless you intend to append to the array an element that is itself an array. If you are looking for a way to add the elements in one array as new elements to another array, see recipe 4-10.

4-10. Appending One Array to Another

If you have two or more sets of elements that you would like to combine sequentially into a single set, you can use the array_merge() function for this purpose. This function takes two or more arrays as arguments and returns a new array whose elements consist of all the elements in the arguments passed to it, in order. That is, it literally appends arrays onto one another. If it helps, you can think of this function as laying out arrays end to end in order to produce a new one.

The Code

```php
<?php
  function array_display($array, $pre=FALSE)
  {
    $tag = $pre ? 'pre' : 'p';
    printf("<%s>%s</%s>\n", $tag, var_export($array, TRUE), $tag);
  }
```

```
$arr1 = array(1, 2, 3);
$arr2 = array(10, 20, 30);
$arr3 = array(5, 10, 15, 20);

$comb1 = array_merge($arr1, $arr2);
$comb2 = array_merge($arr2, $arr1);
$comb3 = array_merge($arr3, $arr2, $arr1);

array_display($comb1);
array_display($comb2);
array_display($comb3);
?>
```

Here is the output:

```
array ( 0 => 1, 1 => 2, 2 => 3, 3 => 10, 4 => 20, 5 => 30, )

array ( 0 => 10, 1 => 20, 2 => 30, 3 => 1, 4 => 2, 5 => 3, )

array ( 0 => 5, 1 => 10, 2 => 15, 3 => 20, 4 => 10, 5 => 20, 6 => 30,
          7 => 1, 8 => 2, 9 => 3, )
```

Variations

You might have noticed that array_merge() reorders the array's indexes. This happens even if you set the indexes explicitly; however, you can get around this behavior by using the + operator instead, as shown here:

```php
<?php
$arr4 = array(10 => 'a', 11 => 'b', 12 => 'c');

array_display(array_merge($arr1, $arr4), TRUE);
array_display($arr1 + $arr4, TRUE);
?>
```

You can compare the results to see the difference:

```
array (
    0 => 1,
    1 => 2,
    2 => 3,
    3 => 'a',
    4 => 'b',
    5 => 'c',
)
```

```
array (
    0 => 1,
    1 => 2,
    2 => 3,
    10 => 'a',
    11 => 'b',
    12 => 'c',
)
```

You also need to be aware of a "gotcha" when using the + operator in this way, which is also known as obtaining the *union* of two arrays. What happens when there are elements with the same index in more than one of the arrays? For example, consider the following:

```php
<?php
    $arr5 = array(1 => 'x', 2 => 'y', 3 => 'z');

    array_display(array_merge($arr1, $arr5), TRUE);
    array_display($arr1 + $arr5, TRUE);
?>
```

Only the first instance of an element with an index matched in the second or subsequent arrays makes it into the result. Any elements having a matching index in a subsequent array are dropped, as shown here:

```
array (
    0 => 1,
    1 => 2,
    2 => 3,
    3 => 'x',
    4 => 'y',
    5 => 'z',
)

array (
    0 => 1,
    1 => 2,
    2 => 3,
    3 => 'z',
)
```

Of course, you can use array_merge() and the + operator with associative arrays as well, as shown here:

```php
<?php
    $dogs1 = array('Lassie' => 'Collie', 'Bud' => 'Sheepdog',
                   'Rin-Tin-Tin' => 'Alsatian');
```

```
$dogs2 = array('Ringo' => 'Dachshund', 'Traveler' => 'Setter');

array_display(array_merge($dogs1, $dogs2), TRUE);
array_display($dogs1 + $dogs2, TRUE);
?>
```

In fact, as long as there are no conflicting keys, you can generally use either method, as shown here:

```
array (
  'Lassie' => 'Collie',
  'Bud' => 'Sheepdog',
  'Rin-Tin-Tin' => 'Alsatian',
  'Ringo' => 'Dachshund',
  'Traveler' => 'Setter',
)

array (
  'Lassie' => 'Collie',
  'Bud' => 'Sheepdog',
  'Rin-Tin-Tin' => 'Alsatian',
  'Ringo' => 'Dachshund',
  'Traveler' => 'Setter',
)
```

These techniques are handy if you want to add new elements onto the end of an array, but what if you want to add an element to the beginning, or even somewhere in the middle? We will show you how to accomplish these tasks in recipes 4-12 and 4-13.

4-11. Comparing Arrays

It is possible to make comparisons between arrays using the ==, ===, >, and < operators.

Two arrays are considered equal if and only if they match with respect to size, keys, and values. The order in which the elements are listed does not affect the output of a comparison for simple equality using the == operator. Two arrays are considered identical if and only if they are identical in every respect, including size, keys, values, and order in which the arrays' elements occur. If all these conditions are not met, then the result of a comparison using the === operator is FALSE.

The following example illustrates equality, identity, and the difference between them with respect to arrays.

The Code

```
<?php
  function array_eq_ident($arr1, $arr2)
  {
    printf("<p>The two arrays are %sequal.</p>\n",
            $arr1 == $arr2 ? '' : 'not ');
```

```
    printf("<p>The two arrays are %sidentical.</p>\n",
            $arr1 === $arr2 ? '' : 'not ');
}

$dogs = array('Lassie' => 'Collie', 'Bud' => 'Sheepdog',
                'Rin-Tin-Tin' => 'Alsatian', 'Snoopy' => 'Beagle');

$pups = array('Lassie' => 'Collie', 'Bud' => 'Sheepdog',
                'Rin-Tin-Tin' => 'Alsatian', 'Snoopy' => 'Beagle');

$mutts = array('Lassie' => 'Collie', 'Rin-Tin-Tin' => 'Alsatian',
                'Bud' => 'Sheepdog','Snoopy' => 'Beagle');

print "<p>\$dogs and \$pups:</p>\n" ;
array_eq_ident($dogs, $pups);

print "<p>\$dogs and \$pups:</p>\n" ;
array_eq_ident($dogs, $mutts);
?>
```

Here is the output:

```
$dogs and $pups:
The two arrays are equal.
The two arrays are identical.

$dogs and $mutts:
The two arrays are equal.
The two arrays are not identical.
```

How It Works

The arrays (2, 4, 6, 8) and (4, 8, 6, 2) are neither equal nor identical. The arrays (2, 4, 6, 8) and (1 => 4, 3 => 8, 2 => 6, 0 => 2) are *equal*, because (2, 4, 6, 8) is the same as (0 => 2, 1 => 4, 2 => 6, 3 => 8), so both arrays have the same indexes pointing to the same values; however, these two arrays are not *identical*, because the elements are not listed in the same order.

You can use the > and < operators to compare the lengths of two arrays. In other words, given the array variables $arr1 and $arr2, the expression $arr1 > $arr2 is a convenient shorthand for count($arr1) > count($arr2) and for sizeof($arr1) > sizeof($arr2). Likewise, $arr1 < $aar2 produces the same result as count($arr1) < count($arr2) and as sizeof($arr1) < sizeof($arr2).

The two array elements $a and $b are considered equal only if (string)$a === (string)$b, that is, only if their string representations are the same.

4-12. Adding an Element to the Beginning of an Array

Prepending an element to an array in PHP is not difficult and requires only that you use the array_unshift() function. This function's prototype is as follows:

```
int array_unshift(array $arr, mixed $val[, mixed $val2[, ...]])
```

The first argument is the array you want to modify; one or more additional arguments are added, in order, to the beginning of the array. The value returned by array_unshift() is the number of elements in the array after it has been modified (however, you are not required to use this if you do not need to do so).

The Code

```php
<?php
  $prices = array(5.95, 10.75, 11.25);
  printf("<p>%s</p>\n", implode(', ', $prices));

  array_unshift($prices, 10.85);
  printf("<p>%s</p>\n", implode(', ', $prices));

  array_unshift($prices, 3.35, 17.95);
  printf("<p>%s</p>\n", implode(', ', $prices));
?>
```

```
5.95, 10.75, 11.25

10.85, 5.95, 10.75, 11.25

3.35, 17.95, 10.85, 5.95, 10.75, 11.25
```

4-13. Inserting New Values at an Arbitrary Point in an Indexed Array

Suppose you are working with this array:

```
$languages = array('German', 'French', 'Spanish');
```

And suppose because of a change in your application requirements, you need to insert Russian as the second element. You might try this:

```
$languages[1] = 'Russian';
```

But when you output the changed array, you discover that what you have done is *overwrite* the second value, and that is not what you want. You want the array to contain the values German, Russian, French, and Spanish. You can do this by using the array_splice() function, whose prototype is as follows:

```
array array_splice(array $original, int $offset, int $length, array $new)
```

The function removes $length elements in $array starting from position $offset and inserts the elements contained in $new to take their place. It returns an array of the elements that were removed from $array. Since you are interested only in inserting new elements into an array (and not in removing any), you will write a new function named array_insert() that is a special case of array_splice(). The following code defines this new function and tests it.

The Code

```php
<?php
  //  file: array-insert.php

  function array_insert(&$array, $offset, $new)
  {
    array_splice($array, $offset, 0, $new);
  }
  $languages = array('German', 'French', 'Spanish');
  printf("<pre>%s</pre>\n", var_export($languages, TRUE));
  array_insert($languages, 1, 'Russian');
  printf("<pre>%s</pre>\n", var_export($languages, TRUE));
  array_insert($languages, 3, array('Swedish', 'Italian'));
  printf("<pre>%s</pre>\n", var_export($languages, TRUE));
?>
```

How It Works

When you call array_splice() with the $length parameter equal to 0, no elements are removed from $array. Because this function works on the array in place, you need to use the indirection operator (&) with this argument so that array_insert() is passed a reference to $array.

After defining the initial elements in the $languages array, you insert Russian into the second position. Since arrays are indexed beginning with 0, you will need to use 1 for the value of the $position argument. Note that when array_splice() is used with a single $new element, it is not required to be an array, so the same is true for the custom function. Then you insert an array containing Swedish and Italian into $languages starting with the fourth position.

```
array (
  0 => 'German',
  1 => 'French',
  2 => 'Spanish',
)

array (
  0 => 'German',
  1 => 'Russian',
  2 => 'French',
  3 => 'Spanish',
)
```

```
array (
  0 => 'German',
  1 => 'Russian',
  2 => 'French',
  3 => 'Swedish',
  4 => 'Italian',
  5 => 'Spanish',
)
```

As you can see, the indexes of the elements in the $languages array are automatically reordered each time new elements are inserted into it using the array_splice() function or the array_insert() function that you have derived from it.

Getting and Setting the Size of an Array

Arrays in PHP are dynamic; their sizes change as elements are added or removed. Because of the way that foreach works with arrays, you often do not need to know an array's size in order to traverse it. Nonetheless, sometimes you do need to know how many elements an array contains.

Unlike the case with some programming languages, you are not obligated to declare the size of a PHP array in advance in order to create it. However, you can cause an array to be padded out to a certain size when it otherwise is not long enough for a given purpose. See recipe 4-15 for one way to handle this sort of problem.

4-14. Counting Array Elements

You might be wondering what happens if you try to insert new elements into an array at a non-existent position. Let's put this to the test, first by assigning an arbitrarily high index to a new element and then by using the array_insert() function defined previously (see recipe 4-13).

```
<?
  // array_insert() defined in previous recipe

  $languages1 = array('German', 'French', 'Spanish');

  array_insert($languages1, 6, 'Russian');
  printf("<pre>%s</pre>\n", var_export($languages1, TRUE));

  $languages2 = array('German', 'French', 'Spanish');

  $languages[6] = 'Russian';
  printf("<pre>%s</pre>\n", var_export($languages2, TRUE));
?>
```

Here is the result:

```
array (
  0 => 'German',
  1 => 'French',
  2 => 'Spanish',
  3 => 'Russian'
)

array (
  0 => 'German',
  1 => 'French',
  2 => 'Spanish',
  6 => 'Russian',
)
```

Which behavior is desirable depends on your circumstances, which you cannot really assess unless you know how to count the elements in an array and how to traverse an array. So, let's take care of those issues without further delay.

You can easily get the size of an array in PHP using the count() function, which works equally well on indexed and associative arrays, as shown next.

The Code

```php
<?php
  $dogs = array('Lassie' => 'Collie', 'Bud' => 'Sheepdog',
                'Rin-Tin-Tin' => 'Alsatian');

  $birds = array('parrot', 'magpie', 'lorikeet', 'cuckoo');

  printf("<p>There are %d dogs and %d birds.</p>", count($dogs), count($birds));

  $birds[] = 'ibis';
  printf("<p>There are now %d birds:</p>", count($birds));
  printf("<pre>%s</pre>\n", var_export($birds, TRUE));

  $birds[10] = 'heron';
  unset($birds[3]);
  printf("<p>There are now %d birds:</p>", count($birds));
  printf("<pre>%s</pre>\n", var_export($birds, TRUE));
?>
```

Here is the output:

```
There are 3 dogs and 4 birds.
There are now 5 birds:
array (
  0 => 'parrot',
  1 => 'magpie',
  2 => 'lorikeet',
  3 => 'cuckoo',
  4 => 'ibis',
)

There are now 5 birds:
array (
  0 => 'parrot',
  1 => 'magpie',
  2 => 'lorikeet',
  4 => 'ibis',
  10 => 'heron',
)
```

How It Works

The count() function always returns the number of elements currently stored in the array. This is true regardless of how the elements are indexed, as you can see from the last portion of the example, where the elements are indexed by the numbers 0, 1, 2, 3, and 10, but count() shows that $birds in fact contains just five elements. You will look at some implications of this when we discuss traversing arrays in the next section. Note that unsetting an array element removes the element but does not reindex the other elements; to see how to do this, refer to the section "Removing Elements from Arrays."

■**Note** You can also use sizeof() in place of count() for obtaining the number of elements in an array. This is nothing more than an alias for count(); the two functions perform identically. We prefer count(), but you can use whichever of the two you prefer. Just do so consistently.

4-15. Setting an Array's Size

If you need to guarantee that an array has a certain number of elements, you might want to look at a PHP function called array_pad(), whose prototype is as follows:

```
array array_pad(array $input, int $size, mixed $value)
```

This function takes as its first argument an array whose length is to be expanded. It does this by copying the array and then adding to the copy a series of new elements whose value is $value until the total length of the array reaches the absolute value of $size. (Why do we say "absolute value" rather than simply "value"? You will see why in a moment.) Then it returns the copy. It does not alter the original array.

The Code

```php
<?php
  $birds = array('parrot', 'magpie', 'lorikeet', 'cuckoo');
  $more_birds = array_pad($birds, 6, 'some bird');

  printf("<p>Birds:</p><pre>%s</pre>\n", var_export($birds, TRUE));
  printf("<p>More birds:</p><pre>%s</pre>\n", var_export($more_birds, TRUE));
?>
```

Here is the output:

```
Birds:
array (
  0 => 'parrot',
  1 => 'magpie',
  2 => 'lorakeet',
  3 => 'cuckoo',
)

More birds:
array (
  0 => 'parrot',
  1 => 'magpie',
  2 => 'lorakeet',
  3 => 'cuckoo',
  4 => 'some bird',
  5 => 'some bird',
)
```

How It Works

The $birds array contains four values, and you have called array_pad() with $size equal to 6 and the padding value 'some bird'. So, the new array $more_birds contains all the values of the original plus two new ones, both equal to some birds, tacked onto the end.

Variations

You can also cause the new values to be added to the beginning of the array by using a negative value for $size:

```php
<?php
  $birds = array('parrot', 'magpie', 'lorikeet', 'cuckoo');

  $more_birds = array_pad($birds, -6, 'some bird');

  printf("<p>More birds:</p><pre>%s</pre>\n", var_export($more_birds, TRUE));
?>
```

```
More birds:
array (
  0 => 'some bird',
  1 => 'some bird',
  2 => 'parrot',
  3 => 'magpie',
  4 => 'lorakeet',
  5 => 'cuckoo',
)
```

Notice that the elements taken from the original array are automatically reindexed and that the padding elements are indexed beginning with 0.

You can also use array_pad() with associative arrays. However, the keys of the additional elements will be numeric, as shown here:

```php
<?php
  $dogs = array('Lassie' => 'Collie', 'Bud' => 'Sheepdog',
                'Rin-Tin-Tin' => 'Alsatian');

  $pups = array_pad($dogs, 5, 'mutt');
  printf("<p>Pups (right padding):</p><pre>%s</pre>\n", var_export($pups, TRUE));

  $pups = array_pad($dogs, -5, 'mutt');
  printf("<p>Pups (left padding):</p><pre>%s</pre>\n", var_export($pups, TRUE));

  printf("<p>Dogs:</p><pre>%s</pre>\n", var_export($dogs, TRUE));
?>
```

```
Pups (right padding):
array (
  'Lassie' => 'Collie',
  'Bud' => 'Sheepdog',
  'Rin-Tin-Tin' => 'Alsatian',
  0 => 'mutt',
  1 => 'mutt',
)
```

```
Pups (left padding):
array (
  0 => 'mutt',
  1 => 'mutt',
  'Lassie' => 'Collie',
  'Bud' => 'Sheepdog',
  'Rin-Tin-Tin' => 'Alsatian',
)

Dogs:
array (
  'Lassie' => 'Collie',
  'Bud' => 'Sheepdog',
  'Rin-Tin-Tin' => 'Alsatian',
)
```

For other techniques you can use for inserting elements into arrays, see recipes 4-11 through 4-14.

Traversing Arrays

Traversing an array means to go through it, element by element. You can also refer to this as *looping through* or *iterating through* an array.

4-16. Looping Through an Associative Array Using foreach

For associative and indexed arrays, the simplest way to do this is to use foreach.

The Code

```php
<?php
  $dogs = array('Lassie' => 'Collie', 'Bud' => 'Sheepdog',
                'Rin-Tin-Tin' => 'German Shepherd', 'Snoopy' => 'Beagle');

  foreach($dogs as $name => $breed)
    print "$name is a $breed.<br />\n";

  $birds = array('parrot', 'magpie', 'lorikeet', 'cuckoo');

  foreach($birds as $bird)
    print "$bird ";

  print "<br />";
```

```php
    $birds[] = 'ibis';
    $birds[10] = 'heron';
    unset($birds[3]);

    foreach($birds as $bird)
        print "$bird ";
?>
```

Here is the output:

```
Lassie is a Collie.
Bud is a Sheepdog.
Rin-Tin-Tin is a German Shepherd.
Snoopy is a Beagle.

parrot magpie lorikeet cuckoo
parrot magpie lorikeet ibis heron
```

As you can see from the output for the changed $birds array, this can be particularly useful with an indexed array when the array is sparse (does not have contiguous indexes).

4-17. Looping Through a Compact Indexed Array Using for and count()

With compact indexed arrays, you can also employ a for loop by using the count() function to obtain the upper limit.

The Code

```php
<?php
    $birds = array('parrot', 'magpie', 'lorikeet', 'cuckoo');

    $limit = count($birds);
    for($i = 0; $i < $limit; $i++)
        printf("<p>(%d) %s.</p>\n", $i, ucfirst($birds[$i]));
?>
```

Here is the output:

```
(1) Parrot.
(2) Magpie.
(3) Lorikeet.
(4) Cuckoo.
```

4-18. Looping Through a Sparse Array

The previous method does not work for sparse arrays, since the value of the greatest index will be greater than the number of elements in the array. Another word of caution is in order regarding a common error in which a programmer attempts to use count() inside the for construct:

```
for($i = 0; $i < count($somearray); i++)
```

The problem with this is that if the code inside the loop adds elements or removes elements from the array, you are likely to obtain inaccurate results, because some elements are skipped or processed twice. Even if the loop does not change the number of elements in the array, using count() directly to set the limiting condition is still inefficient, because the function is called every time execution passes through the for loop. Always set a variable equal to the value returned by count(), and use that variable in the limiting condition.

In mixed arrays (where some elements have integer keys and others have string keys), you can employ foreach to iterate through the entire array; however, using for will retrieve only those elements using integer keys, as shown in this example:

```php
<?php
  error_reporting();
  $array = array('name' => 'Bill', 'age' => 32, 1 => '25 Main St.',
                  2 => 'Apt. 24', 'city' => 'San Francisco', 'state' => 'CA');

  print "<p>Using foreach:</p>\n<ul>";
  foreach($array as $element)
    print("<li>$element</li>\n");
  print "</ul>\n";

  print "<p>Using for:</p>\n<ul>";
  $limit = count($array);
  for($i = 0; $i < $limit; $i++)
    printf("<li>%s</li>\n", $array[$i]);
  print "</ul>\n";
?>
```

Here is what happens when you run the previous code, assuming that error reporting is set to its default level:

```
Using foreach:
. Bill
. 32
. 25 Main St.
. Apt. 24
. San Francisco
. CA

Using for:
```

```
Notice: Undefined offset: 0 in /home/www/php5/for-vs-foreach.php on line 13
.
  25 Main St.
  Apt. 24

Notice: Undefined offset: 3 in /home/www/php5/for-vs-foreach.php on line 13
.

Notice: Undefined offset: 4 in /home/www/php5/for-vs-foreach.php on line 13
.

Notice: Undefined offset: 5 in /home/www/php5/for-vs-foreach.php on line 13
.
```

You can take care of the problem with undefined indexes in such cases by using the isset() function to see whether an array element is defined for a given index.

The Code

```php
<?php
  $array = array('name' => 'Bill', 'age' => 32, 1 => '25 Main St.',
                 2 => 'Apt. 24', 'city' => 'San Francisco', 'state' => 'CA');
  print "<p>Using for:</p>\n<p>";
  $limit = count($array);
  for($i = 0; $i < $limit; $i++)
    if( isset($array[$i]) )
      printf("&middot; %s<br />\n", $array[$i]);
  print "</p>\n";
?>
```

This will produce a more desirable result:

```
Using for:
· 25 Main St.
· Apt. 24
```

Removing Elements from Arrays

You can remove elements from an associative array quite easily by using the unset() function. Here is an example:

```php
<?php
  $dogs = array('Lassie' => 'Collie', 'Bud' => 'Sheepdog',
                'Rin-Tin-Tin' => 'German Shepherd', 'Snoopy' => 'Beagle');
  printf("<pre>%s</pre>\n", var_export($dogs, TRUE));

  unset($dogs['Rin-Tin-Tin']);
  printf("<pre>%s</pre>\n", var_export($dogs, TRUE));
?>
```

You can verify that this works by viewing the output in a web browser:

```
array (
  'Lassie' => 'Collie',
  'Bud' => 'Sheepdog',
  'Rin-Tin-Tin' => 'German Shepherd',
  'Snoopy' => 'Beagle',
)

array (
  'Lassie' => 'Collie',
  'Bud' => 'Sheepdog',
  'Snoopy' => 'Beagle',
)
```

4-19. Removing the First or Last Element from an Array

You can employ the same technique just shown with an indexed array, but this has a potential problem, as noted in recipe 4.15: you wind up with a sparse array. Often what you want is an array whose elements have contiguous indexes. If you want to remove the first or last element while compacting the array's indexes, this is not such a big issue, as PHP has functions for taking care of this easily.

The Code

```php
<?php
  $languages = array('French','German','Russian','Chinese','Hindi', 'Quechua');
  printf("<p>Original array:</p><pre>%s</pre>\n", var_export($languages, TRUE));

  $removed = array_shift($languages);
  printf("<p>Using array_shift():<br />Removed element: %s</p><pre>%s</pre>\n",
          $removed,
          var_export($languages, TRUE));
  $removed = array_pop($languages);
  printf("<p>Using array_pop():<br />Removed element: %s</p><pre>%s</pre>\n",
          $removed,
          var_export($languages, TRUE));
  unset( $languages[count($languages) - 1] );
  printf("<p>Using unset() and count():</p><pre>%s</pre>\n",
          var_export($languages, TRUE));
?>
```

Here is the output:

```
Original array:

array (
  0 => 'French',
  1 => 'German',
  2 => 'Russian',
  3 => 'Chinese',
  4 => 'Hindi',
  5 => 'Quechua',
)

Using array_shift():
Removed element: French

array (
  0 => 'German',
  1 => 'Russian',
  2 => 'Chinese',
  3 => 'Hindi',
  4 => 'Quechua',
)

Using array_pop():
Removed element: Quechua

array (
  0 => 'German',
  1 => 'Russian',
  2 => 'Chinese',
  3 => 'Hindi',
)

Using unset() and count():

array (
  0 => 'German',
  1 => 'Russian',
  2 => 'Chinese',
)
```

How It Works

To remove the first element of an array, just use the array_shift() function. This function returns the element that was removed and reorders the array's indexes. To remove the last element, you can use array_pop(), which also returns the element that was removed. If you do not need to keep track of the element that was removed, you can use unset() along with count() to get the index of the last array element. However, array_pop() acts directly on the array, which is usually more convenient. The same is true for array_shift().

4-20. Removing One or More Arbitrary Array Elements

Now you come to the slightly more challenging case of what to do when you want to remove one or more elements from the middle of an array. You can do this in several ways, but the technique we will show you involves writing an array_remove() function that is really just another special case of your old friend array_splice(). You will use this function to remove the third element of an array named $languages. Since you are removing only one element, you do not need to pass a third argument.

The Code

```php
<?php
  function array_remove(&$array, $offset, $length=1)
  {
    return array_splice($array, $offset, $length);
  }
  $languages = array( 'French', 'German', 'Russian', 'Chinese',
                      'Hindi', 'Quechua', 'Spanish', 'Hausa');
  printf("<p>Original array:</p><pre>%s</pre>\n", var_export($languages, TRUE));

  $removed = array_remove($languages, 2);
  printf("<p>Removed: %s<br />Remaining:</p><pre>%s</pre>\n",
          var_export($removed, TRUE),
          var_export($languages, TRUE));
```

Here is the result of the two array remove() function calls:

```
Original array:
array (
  0 => 'French',
  1 => 'German',
  2 => 'Russian',
  3 => 'Chinese',
  4 => 'Hindi',
  5 => 'Quechua',
  6 => 'Spanish',
  7 => 'Hausa',
)
```

```
Removed: array ( 0 => 'Russian', )
Remaining:
array (
  0 => 'French',
  1 => 'German',
  2 => 'Chinese',
  3 => 'Hindi',
  4 => 'Quechua',
  5 => 'Spanish',
  6 => 'Hausa',
)
```

Notice that even when you remove only a single element, this function still returns an array consisting of the element that was removed.

How It Works

Since `array_splice()` works on an array in place, you have made `array_remove()` do likewise by passing to it as its first argument a reference to the array it is to work on. The second argument (`$offset`) represents the index at which you want to start removing elements. (Do not forget that indexing begins at 0, so you use 2 for this parameter.) The third parameter (`$length`) represents the number of elements to be removed; you make this parameter optional by assigning to it a default value of 1.

You might notice a difference in the way you call `array_splice()` here as opposed to how you used it when writing the `array_insert()` function: you return from `array_remove()` the value returned by `array_splice()`. This is because `array_splice()` returns an array consisting of any elements removed from the array it is called to act upon. Since you did not remove any elements from the array in `array_insert()`, there was no need to do so; however, it could come in handy here, and it does not cost anything extra to do this.

Variations

Let's see how you can use the `array_remove()` function to remove several elements from the beginning and the end of an array:

```php
<?php
  $languages = array( 'French', 'German', 'Russian', 'Chinese',
                      'Hindi', 'Quechua', 'Spanish', 'Hausa');
  printf("<pre>Original array:\n%s</pre>\n", var_export($languages, TRUE));

  $num = 2;
  $removed1 = array_remove($languages, 0, $num);
  $removed2 = array_remove($languages, count($languages) - $num, $num);
  printf("<p>Removed (start): %s<br />Removed (end): %s<br />
          Remaining: %s</p>\n",
        var_export($removed1, TRUE),
        var_export($removed2, TRUE),
        var_export($languages, TRUE));
?>
```

In this example, you have removed the first two and last two elements of the array. Notice that you have used the intermediate variable $num for the number of elements to remove. Here is the output:

```
Original array:
array (
    0 => 'French',
    1 => 'German',
    2 => 'Russian',
    3 => 'Chinese',
    4 => 'Hindi',
    5 => 'Quechua',
    6 => 'Spanish',
    7 => 'Hausa',
)

Removed (start): array ( 0 => 'French', 1 => 'German', )
Removed (end): array ( 0 => 'Quechua', 1 => 'Spanish', )
Remaining: array ( 0 => 'Russian', 1 => 'Chinese', 2 => 'Hindi', 3 => 'Hausa', )
```

Before moving on, you should note that the arrays returned by array_splice(), and thus by array_remove(), are indexed sequentially beginning with 0. The original indexes of the removed elements are not preserved.

4-21. Extracting a Portion of an Array

If you want to extract part of an array while leaving the original array intact, use the array_slice() function, whose full prototype is as follows:

```
array array_slice(array $array, int $offset[, int $length[, bool $preserve]] )
```

This function returns an array whose elements are the $length elements extracted from $array beginning with the element at index $offset. However, unlike the built-in function array_splice() or the custom function array_remove(), this function does not affect the original array. For example, starting with the $languages array as you defined it in the previous example, you can obtain a slice of it consisting of the same elements you ended up with, as shown in the next example.

The Code

```php
<?php
    $languages = array( 'French', 'German', 'Russian', 'Chinese',
                        'Hindi', 'Quechua', 'Spanish', 'Hausa');
    printf("<pre>Original array:\n%s</pre>\n", var_export($languages, TRUE));

    $slice1 = array_slice($languages, 2, count($languages) - 2);
    printf("<pre>Slice 1:\n%s</pre>\n", var_export($slice1, TRUE));
```

Beginning with PHP 5.0.2, you can cause the array returned by this function to preserve the indexes of the original by passing an additional argument of TRUE:

```
$slice2 = array_slice($languages, 2, count($languages) - 2, TRUE);
printf("<pre>Slice 2:\n%s</pre>\n", var_export($slice2, TRUE));
?>
```

How It Works

You can see how this works by examining the output of the previous code and comparing $slice1 and $slice2:

```
Original array:
array (
   0 => 'French',
   1 => 'German',
   2 => 'Russian',
   3 => 'Chinese',
   4 => 'Hindi',
   5 => 'Quechua',
   6 => 'Spanish',
   7 => 'Hausa',
)

Slice 1:
array (
   0 => 'Russian',
   1 => 'Chinese',
   2 => 'Hindi',
   3 => 'Quechua',
   4 => 'Spanish',
   5 => 'Hausa',
)

Slice 2:
array (
   2 => 'Russian',
   3 => 'Chinese',
   4 => 'Hindi',
   5 => 'Quechua',
   6 => 'Spanish',
   7 => 'Hausa',
)
```

You can also use negative values for $offset and/or $length. If $offset is negative, then the slice returned will start abs($offset) elements from the end of the array; if $length is negative, then the slice will end abs($length) elements from the end of the array. For instance, given the following:

```
$slice3 = array_slice($languages, -6, -2, TRUE);
```

then $slice3 will be identical to $slice2 from the previous example.

Finally, you can obtain a slice consisting of all elements of an array beginning with the element at index $offset all the way through to the end of the array simply by omitting the $length argument. Assuming that $languages is the same array as defined in the last two examples, then the following:

```
$last3 = array_slice($languages, -3);
printf("<p>Last 3: %s</p>\n", var_export($last3, TRUE));
```

will produce this output:

```
Last 3: array ( 0 => 'Quechua', 1 => 'Spanish', 2 => 'Hausa', )
```

Note that if you want to preserve the original keys, you must supply $length as well as $preserve_keys, as using 0 (or any value that converts to 0, such as an empty string or NULL) for $length will return an empty array. To get a slice consisting of the last three elements in $languages while preserving the keys, you would need to use something like this:

```
$last3 = array_slice($languages, -3, 3, TRUE);
printf("<p>Last 3: %s</p>\n", var_export($last3, TRUE));
```

This will produce the expected result, as shown here:

```
Last 3: array ( 5 => 'Quechua', 6 => 'Spanish', 7 => 'Hausa', )
```

4-22. Extracting Values from Arrays with extract()

When working with an array, it is sometimes possible to save yourself some time and typing by extracting its elements into simple variables. You do this using the extract() function. This function works by creating a set of variables whose names are taken from the associative array keys and then setting the variables values to the array element values. We find this function particularly handy when handling rows returned from database queries, such as those returned by mysql_fetch_assoc() and mysqli_fetch_assoc(), but you can use this function anytime you are obliged to work with arrays, especially those with many elements.

The Code

```php
<?php
    $customer = array('first' => 'Bill', 'last' => 'Jones', 'age' => 24,
                        'street' => '123 Main St.', 'city' => 'Pacifica',
                        'state' => 'California');
```

```
  extract($customer);
  print "<p>$first $last is $age years old, and lives in $city, $state.</p>";

  extract($customer, EXTR_PREFIX_ALL, 'cust');
  print "<p>$cust_first $cust_last is $cust_age years old,
        and lives in $cust_city, $cust_state.</p>";
?>
```

The print statements each output the following sentence:

Bill Jones is 24 years old, and lives in Pacifica, California.

Variations

extract() offers some additional options that can be helpful when the array keys might not be legal variable identifiers or when you want to avoid overwriting existing variables that might have the same name. (By default, extract() will overwrite such variables.) If you need to see what variables are currently defined, you can call get_defined_vars() to obtain an array of all their names.

EXTR_PREFIX_ALL adds a prefix string to the beginning of each key in the original array. This option and the other extract() options that add a prefix to extracted variable names automatically add an underscore character to the prefix. For example, the following will output each of the values in the $scores array, in turn, on a separate line:

```
<?php
  $scores = array(91, 56, 87, 79);
  extract($scores, EXTR_PREFIX_ALL, "score");

  print "<p>$score_0</p>";
  print "<p>$score_1</p>";
  print "<p>$score_2</p>";
  print "<p>$score_3</p>";
?>
```

Another extremely handy option is EXTR_REFS, which extracts the variables as references to the original associative array elements. The following code shows an example, which also shows how you can combine options passed to extract() by ORing them together using the pipe (|) operator. In this case, you will add the prefix pts to each array key and then make each variable that results into a reference.

```php
<?php
  $points = array('home' => 21, 'away' => 13);

  extract($points, EXTR_REFS|EXTR_PREFIX_ALL, 'pts');

  $pts_home -= 4;
  $pts_away += 6;

  printf("<p>%s</p>", var_export($points, TRUE));
?>
```

Because the extracted variables are references, updating their values updates those of the corresponding elements in the original array:

```
array ( 'home' => 17, 'away' => 19, )
```

You can pass several other options to extract() to exercise more fine-grained control over when variables are or are not overwritten as well as when variable names are or are not prefixed; however, we find that EXTR_PREFIX_ALL and EXTR_REFS satisfy most requirements, so we will let you look up the others in the PHP manual if you are interested.

4-23. Extracting Values from an Array Using list()

The list() operator is technically not a function, even though it looks like one. It is also useful for obtaining values, particularly when dealing with indexed arrays. The easiest way to explain what list() does is to show you first and then explain afterward, so the following simple example gets things started.

The Code

```php
<?php
  $scores = array(88, 75, 91, 84);

  list($maths, $english, $history, $biology) = $scores;

  printf("<p>Maths: %d; English: %d; History: %d; Biology: %d.</p>\n",
          $maths, $english, $history, $biology);
?>
```

As you might expect, the output from this is as follows:

```
Maths: 88; English: 75; History: 91; Biology: 84.
```

How It Works

list() works by assigning values from the array on the right side of the equals sign to the variables passed to it, in order. So, in this example, $maths was set equal to $scores[0], $english to $scores[1], and so on.

Variations

If some values in the array do not interest you, you can skip them by marking their places with an "empty" comma, like so:

```php
<?php
  $scores = array(88, 75, 91, 84);

  list($maths, , $history) = $scores;

  #  using the @ operator to suppress a warning about the undefined variables...
  @printf("<p>Maths: %d; English: %d; History: %d; Biology: %d.</p>\n",
          $maths, $english, $history, $biology);
?>
```

Although only three array positions have been marked, this is completely permissible; list() simply quits trying to make any assignments after it is finished with all the variables you have supplied.

Since %d was used to mark the place of the undefined variable, its value is coerced to integer 0, as shown here:

```
Maths: 88; English: 75; History: 0; Biology: 84.
```

If you try to use more variables with list() than there are elements in the array, you may get a warning about an undefined index. You can suppress this warning with the @ operator (also known as the *error suppression* operator). However, those variables will remain unset, as shown here:

```php
<?php
  $scores = array(88, 75);

  @list($maths, $english, $history) = $scores;

  @printf("<p>Maths: %d; English: %d; History: %d; Biology: %d.</p>\n",
          $maths, $english, $history, $biology);
?>
```

This is the output:

```
Maths: 88; English: 75; History: 0; Biology: 0.
```

Note that list() ignores elements with string keys.

4-24. Combining Arrays

We have already discussed how to insert arrays into one another and have shown how to write a function to help you do so. Now you will tackle something a bit different: combining two indexed arrays to obtain an associative array. For example, suppose you have two arrays defined as shown:

```
$colors = array('red', 'yellow', 'green');
$flavors = array('apple', 'banana', 'lime');
```

And suppose you would like to combine these into a single array that looks like this:

```
$fruit = array('red' => 'apple', 'yellow' => 'banana', 'green' => 'lime');
```

You might think that this requires writing some code that loops through both arrays, assigning one string as a key and the other as its corresponding value, perhaps something like this:

```
$fruit = array();

$limit = count($colors);

for($i = 0; $i < $limit; $i++)
  $fruit[$colors[$i]] = $flavors[$i];
```

Of course, then you are obligated to perform some checks. Are the arrays the same length? Are they both in fact arrays? Fortunately, PHP has a function that handles all these issues for you.

The Code

```php
<?php
  $colors = array('red', 'yellow', 'green');

  $flavors = array('apple', 'banana', 'lime'); # same size as $colors
  $tastes = array('sweet', 'sour');            #  different size
  $prices = array();                           #  empty
  $name = 'lemon';                             #  not an array

  $arrays = array('name' => $name, 'prices' => $prices,
                  'flavors' => $flavors, 'tastes' => $tastes);

  foreach($arrays as $key => $value)
  {
    if($fruits = @array_combine($colors, $value))
      printf("<pre>%s</pre>\n", var_export($fruits, TRUE));
    else
      printf("<p>Couldn't combine \$colors and \$%s.</p>", $key);
  }
?>
```

You are using the @ operator in this example to suppress any warnings or errors triggered by passing invalid parameters to array_combine() so that you can handle those using if ... else. Here is the output from this code:

```
Couldn't combine $colors and $name.

Couldn't combine $colors and $prices.

array (
  'red' => 'apple',
  'yellow' => 'banana',
  'green' => 'lime',
)

Couldn't combine $colors and $tastes.
```

How It Works

array_combine() takes two arrays as arguments, attempts to assign the values from the first arrays as keys to the values found in the second, and returns an associative array if it succeeds. If it fails for any reason (if both arguments are not arrays, if either or both of them are empty, or if they do not contain the same number of values), the function returns FALSE.

4-25. Obtaining Array Keys and Values

What about the converse of the problem you looked at in the previous section? In other words, what if you have an associative array named $fruits that is defined as shown here:

```
$fruits = array('red' => 'apple', 'yellow' => 'banana', 'green' => 'lime');
```

and you like to work with just the colors of the fruits, or just their names? PHP 5 provides a pair of functions intended to make it easy to do this: array_keys() returns an array consisting of only the keys of the array that it acts on, and array_values() returns an array consisting of only the values of the original array. What follows is a simple example in which we have defined an array_display() function to cut down on the repetition of code.

The Code

```php
<?php
  function array_display($array, $pre=FALSE)  # set optional 2nd argument to
  {                                           #  TRUE for preformatted tree display
    $tag = $pre ? 'pre' : 'p';
    printf("<%s>%s</%s>\n", $tag, var_export($array, TRUE), $tag);
  }

  $fruits = array('red' => 'apple', 'yellow' => 'banana', 'green' => 'lime');
```

```
    $colors = array_keys($fruits);
    $flavors = array_values($fruits);

    array_display($fruits);
    array_display($colors);
    array_display($flavors);
?>
```

How It Works

This is pretty straightforward stuff. You start with the associative array $fruits as defined previously. You then use array_keys() to get the keys from $fruit and assign its return value to the variable $colors. Next you use array_values() to get its values, assigning that function's return value to $flavors. Finally, you output all three variables using array_display(), which is really nothing more than a wrapper for the var_export() function you looked at earlier in the chapter (in recipe 4-8). The result is easy enough to predict, but we will show it to you anyway for the sake of completeness:

```
array ( 'red' => 'apple', 'yellow' => 'banana', 'green' => 'lime', )

array ( 0 => 'red', 1 => 'yellow', 2 => 'green', )

array ( 0 => 'apple', 1 => 'banana', 2 => 'lime', )
```

Tip If you use array_values() on an indexed array, you will just obtain an array whose structure is identical to the first one, with one important exception: its indexes will be reordered. This can be a handy way to "compact" sparse arrays.

4-26. Working with Unique Values

Often you will find yourself dealing with sets of data (arrays) containing duplicate values. Although nothing is wrong with this in and of itself, many times you will be interested only in *unique* values. For example, suppose you are involved with internationalizing a website, and you are working with some logging data concerning countries from which your site has had visitors and the languages spoken in those countries. Let's assume you have already parsed the log files and have ended up with an array defined as follows:

```
$countries = array( 'USA' => 'English', 'Spain' => 'Spanish',
                    'Brazil' => 'Portuguese', 'UK' => 'English',
                    'Mexico' => 'Spanish', 'Germany' => 'German',
                    'Colombia' => 'Spanish', 'Canada' => 'English',
                    'Russia' => 'Russian', 'Austria' => 'German',
                    'France' => 'French', 'Argentina' => 'Spanish');
```

To get the unique values in this array, all that is necessary is to use the built-in array_unique() function, as shown next.

The Code

```
$languages = array_unique($countries);
printf("<pre>%s</pre>\n", var_export($languages, TRUE));
```

The output looks like this:

```
array (
  'USA' => 'English',
  'Spain' => 'Spanish',
  'Brazil' => 'Portuguese',
  'Germany' => 'German',
  'Russia' => 'Russian',
  'France' => 'French',
)
```

How It Works

The array_unique() function returns an array from which all duplicate values have been removed. In cases of duplicate values, only the first element having that value is included each time. (This can occasionally prove useful.) The key associated with each of these values is preserved, as you can see in the previous output. This is true whether the array in question is associative or indexed. If you want only the values, without the keys, you will need to use the array_values() function (discussed in the previous section) on the result.

4-27. Getting and Displaying Counts of Array Values

Another frequent task is getting the number of elements that have unique values. The following example shows one way you can do this, as applied to the $countries array defined in the previous recipe.

The Code

```
<?php
  $language_counts = array_count_values($countries);
?>
  <table border="1" cellpadding="3" cellspacing="0">
    <tbody>
      <tr><th>Language</th><th>Number<br />of<br />Countries</th></tr>
<?php
  foreach($language_counts as $language => $number)
    print "        <tr><td>$language</td><td>$number</td></tr>\n";
?>
    </tbody>
  </table>
```

How It Works

This works by using the function `array_count_values()`, which creates a new array whose keys are the values of the array passed to it as a parameter and whose values are the number of times each of those values occurs in the original array.

We have dressed up the output just a bit this time by using a HTML table. To obtain this, just loop through the `$language_count` array, writing a new two-column row for each element and inserting the key into one table cell and the value into another cell. Figure 4-1 shows the result as viewed in a typical web browser.

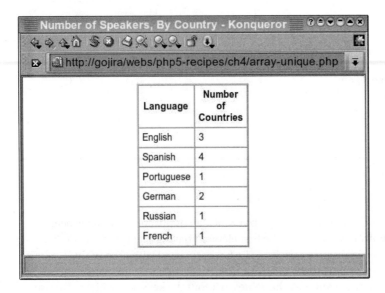

Figure 4-1. *Output of the countries and languages example (counts of unique values)*

Notice that the keys of this array are the unique values from the original array. In other words, `array_keys($language_count)` is identical to `array_values(array_unique($countries))`.

Finding and Working with Array Values

If you know the key for a given array element, whether the key is a string or an integer, finding the matching value is trivial. Doing the opposite is not that difficult, but it does require a bit more effort. In this section, we will show you how to answer questions such as these:

- Does an element with a given value exist in an array?

- Does an array contain an element with a given key?

- At what position can you find an element with a desired value in an array? That is, what key or keys correspond to the value being sought?

- How can you find the elements in an array whose values meet a set of criteria or pass a certain test?

- What is the best way to find the maximum or minimum value in an array?

- How do you apply a function to all the elements in an array?

PHP has functions that can help you with all these issues. In addition, we will show you a programming algorithm or two that might be beneficial in solving some of these problems and maybe slip in one or two other bits of useful array-related functionality.

4-28. Determining Whether an Element Is in an Array

Often you will need to find out whether a set of values contains one value in particular. Recall the internationalization example (see recipe 4-26); you have data reflecting the countries from which website visitors originated, and the languages spoken in those countries, represented by the following array:

```
$countries = array( 'USA' => 'English', 'Spain' => 'Spanish',
                    'Brazil' => 'Portuguese', 'UK' => 'English',
                    'Mexico' => 'Spanish', 'Germany' => 'German',
                    'Colombia' => 'Spanish', 'Canada' => 'English',
                    'Russia' => 'Russian', 'Austria' => 'German',
                    'France' => 'French', 'Argentina' => 'Spanish');
```

A natural question might be, do any of the site's visitors speak Spanish? To obtain an answer, you might be tempted to use brute force by traversing the $countries array and testing each element's value in turn until you either find a match for the desired value or exhaust all of the array's elements. Fortunately, PHP has a function that does this for you.

The following example tests in_array() by using the $countries array defined previously as a "haystack" in which to search for a couple of likely values.

The Code

```php
<?php
  #  $countries array previously defined in text

  $language = 'Spanish';
  printf("<p>%s of our visitors speak %s.</p>\n",
         in_array($language, $countries) ? 'Some' : 'None',
         $language);

  $language = 'Swahili';
  printf("<p>%s of our visitors speak %s.</p>\n",
         in_array($language, $countries) ? 'Some' : 'None',
         $language);
?>
```

The output from this bit of code is as follows:

```
Some of our visitors speak Spanish.
```

```
None of our visitors speak Swahili.
```

How It Works

in_array() takes two arguments, a value to be matched and the array to be searched for the value. It returns TRUE if the value is found and FALSE if it is not. Here is the function's prototype:

```
bool in_array(mixed $value, array $array[, bool $strict])
```

The matching of strings is case-sensitive; in other words, spanish is not considered a match for Spanish. The optional $strict parameter, if TRUE, forces this function to use strict equality (as with ===) in making any comparisons rather than allowing type conversions to occur (as if the function were using ==). In other words, if you use strict mode, then the number 12 will not match the string "12".

This function works just as well with indexed arrays as it does with associative arrays; we used an associative array in the previous example to emphasize that in_array() matches values and not keys. We will show how to do that in the next recipe.

4-29. Testing for the Existence of a Key in an Array

Sometimes you need to answer a question such as, is there an item number 5 in this set? Or you might ask, does the information for this customer include a postcode? If the datasets in question are arrays, then PHP makes it simple to find the answer. To determine whether an array contains an element with a given key or index, all you need to do is use the array_key_exists() function.

Once again, using the $countries array defined in the previous section (and assuming that this array includes language data for all countries from which the site has had hits), this example asks and answers the question, has our site had any visitors from Country X?

The Code

```php
<?php
  #  $countries array from previous recipe

  $country = 'Kazakhstan';
  printf("<p>%s of our visitors are from %s.</p>\n",
         array_key_exists($country, $countries) ? 'Some' : 'None',
         $country);

  $country = 'Argentina';
  printf("<p>%s of our visitors are from %s.</p>\n",
         array_key_exists($country, $countries) ? 'Some' : 'None',
         $country);
?>
```

None of our visitors are from Kazakhstan.

Some of our visitors are from Argentina.

How It Works

The prototype for array_key_exists() is as follows:

bool array_key_exists(mixed $key, array $array)

If an element with a key matching $key is found in $array, the function returns TRUE; otherwise, it returns FALSE. The comparisons made by this function are case-sensitive but not strict. In other words, a search for a "usa" key will not match a "USA" key, but a search for a "2" key (string value) will return TRUE if the array contains an element with the index 2 (integer).

4-30. Obtaining Array Keys with a Given Value

Another common task involves obtaining one or more keys of array elements with a known value. In other words (harking back once again to the $countries array you have been using in the past few sections), you want to know the answer to the question, in which of the countries where you have users is Spanish spoken? No built-in function gives you this sort of information, but you can write one of your own easily enough.

The Code

```php
<?php
  # Note: $countries array as previously defined

  # prototype: mixed array_get_keys(mixed $search, array $array)

  function array_get_keys($search, $array)
  {
    $keys = array();                      #  array to contain keys for output

    foreach($array as $key => $value)     #  traversing the array...
       if($value == $search)              #  if the current value matches $search
          $keys[] = $key;                 #  append the current key to the output array

    if(count($keys) == 0)                 #  if no keys were appended to $keys
       $keys = FALSE;                     #  set its value to boolean FALSE

    return $keys;
  }

  $language = 'Spanish';

  $spoken = array_get_keys($language, $countries);
```

```
printf("<p>Countries where %s is spoken: %s.</p>\n",
       $language,
       $spoken ? implode(', ', $spoken) : 'None');

$language = 'Tagalog';

$spoken = array_get_keys($language, $countries);
printf("<p>Countries where %s is spoken: %s.</p>\n",
       $language,
       $spoken ? implode(', ', $spoken) : 'None');
?>
```

How It Works

You have defined array_get_keys() in such a way that it returns FALSE if no matching keys are found on the premise that most code calling this function would need to test this in any case. Of course, if you prefer, you could always rewrite the printf() statement (and get rid of the intermediate variable $spoken) using something like this:

```
printf("<p>Countries where %s is spoken: %s</p>",
       $language,
       array_key_exists($language)
           ? implode(', ', array_get_keys($language, $country))
           : 'None');
```

In any case, the output from the example code is as follows:

```
Countries where Spanish is spoken: Spain, Mexico, Colombia, Argentina.

Countries where Tagalog is spoken: None.
```

4-31. Finding the Greatest and Least Values in an Array

One common task in computing is to find the minimum and maximum among a set of values. In PHP, the min() and max() functions work not only on sets of values (for example, $max = max(2, 8, 6, -3, 17)) but also on arrays.

The Code

```
<?php
  $prices = array(12.95, 24.5, 10.5, 5.95, 7.95);
  printf("<p>Highest price: \$%.2f; lowest price: \$%.2f.</p>\n",
         max($prices), min($prices));
?>
```

Here is the output:

```
Highest price: $24.50; lowest price: $5.95.
```

Variations

These functions also work with associative arrays:

```php
<?php
$clothes = array( 'hats' => 75, 'coats' => 32, 'shoes' => 102,
                  'gloves' => 15, 'shirts' => 51, 'trousers' => 44);

uasort($clothes, 'evenfirst');

var_export($clothes);

printf("<p>Most items: %d; least items: %d.</p>\n",
       max($clothes), min($clothes));
?>
```

This is the output:

```
Most items: 102; least items: 15.
```

Because they do not provide access to array keys, these functions are mostly useful with one-dimensional, indexed arrays. In many cases, you are better off using one of the sorting techniques later in this chapter. For example:

```php
<?php
$clothes = array( 'hats' => 75, 'coats' => 32, 'shoes' => 102,
                  'gloves' => 15, 'shirts' => 51, 'trousers' => 44);
$names = array_keys($clothes);
$items = array_values($clothes);
array_multisort($items, $names);
$num = count($clothes) - 1;

printf("<p>Most items: %s (%d); least items: %s (%d).</p>\n",
       $names[$num], $items[$num], $names[0], $items[0]);
?>
```

This is the output:

```
Most items: shoes (102); least items: gloves (15).
```

Another problem with trying to get by on min() and max() is that they assume all values passed to them are numeric, which means strings are coerced to zero. For more about sorting arrays, see the "Sorting Arrays" section of this chapter.

4-32. Finding the Sum and Average of the Values in an Array

Obtaining the sum of a set of numbers in PHP is trivially easy, thanks to the array_sum() function, which adds all of the array's values and returns the total. For example, this code returns the value 12:

```
array_sum( array(2, 2, 8) )
```

This function attempts to convert any non-numeric values to numbers. This may or may not be desirable behavior, depending upon your circumstances, so keep this in mind whenever you use this function.

■**Note** In older versions of PHP (through PHP 4.2.1), a bug in array_sum() caused this function to perform a type conversion of numbers of all the elements in the array it was used on, with the result that string values could be converted to zero. In PHP 5 this is not an issue, and you may safely use array_sum() on an array without having to worry about creating a copy for fear of modifying the original.

Calculating the average value is also fairly simple, since all you need are the sum of the array values and how many of them there are. Then you just perform a straightforward division. The following array_average() function does this. It also checks for the argument type and makes sure the array has at least one element so you do not get tripped up by a possible division-by-zero error.

The Code

```php
<?php
    #  obtain the average value of an array's elements
    #  prototype (returns a number or FALSE if an average cannot be calculated):
    #  mixed array_average(array $array)
    function array_average($array)
    {
      $retval = FALSE;

      if(is_array($array) && count($array))        #  if the argument is an array
                                                   #  with at least one element...
        $retval = array_sum($array) / count($array); #  divide the sum of the element
                                                   #  values by the number of values

      return $retval;
    }
```

```
#  test the function
$scores = array('Bill' => 87.5, 'Jan' => 94.8, 'Terry' => 80.0,
                'Andy' => 91.5, 'Lisa' => 95.5);

printf("<p>There are %d scores, totaling %.2f and averaging %.2f.</p>",
        count($scores), array_sum($scores), array_average($scores));

?>
```

The result of this test is as follows:

```
There are 5 scores, totaling 449.30 and averaging 89.86.
```

Applying Functions to Arrays

If you need to make a uniform alteration in all the elements of an array (that is, apply a function to each element in the array), you could traverse the array using a for, foreach, or while loop. Similarly, if you need to select elements from an array that meet a given condition, you could traverse the array, applying a test to each element in turn and then copying that element into a new array if it meets the test or (if you want to alter the original array) unsetting the element if it fails to meet a converse test. PHP provides alternatives for both of these tasks, which you will investigate in the following two recipes.

PHP 5 has two ways you can apply a function to each of the elements in an array; such a function is a *callback function* (or simply a *callback*). Your choice depends on whether you want to act upon the array's elements already in place or create a new array consisting of the elements from the original after they have been modified. In the former case, you will want to use the array_walk() function (see recipe 4-34); in the latter, the proper function to use is array_map() (see recipe 4-35).

Both array_walk() and array_map() can be powerful and useful, so we encourage you to spend some time experimenting with them—you will be amazed at what you can accomplish with them. Here is a quick summary of the differences between them:

array_walk() works on a single array in place; you can think of it as walking through an array, changing it as it goes. It returns a value of only TRUE or FALSE to indicate success or failure. It modifies element values and can access array keys as well as a value supplied by the programmer, although it cannot modify the keys themselves. The callback function used with array_walk() does not need to return a value and must include a reference to the value of an array element in its signature. If the callback includes a user-supplied value in its signature, the signature must also include a parameter corresponding to an element's key, even if the key is not used within the callback function.

array_map() works on one or more arrays; think of it as mapping from one array (or set of arrays) to another array. It does not modify the original array(s) and can access only the values of the array(s), not the keys. In addition, you can't pass a user value to it. The callback function used with array_map() must return a value, and array_map() itself returns an array. If more than one array is used, the arrays do not need to be the same size; if they are not, array_map() will pad any "missing" values with nulls.

Another way in which functions can be applied to arrays is by filtering them. When we speak of filtering arrays, we mean the process of inspecting each element in an array to see whether it meets a certain test or set of conditions and retaining the element for subsequent use or tossing it into the trash bin, so to speak, as result of that test. In the array_filter() function, which is used for filtering arrays, you have another example of a PHP language construct that can save you a great deal of time and energy that would otherwise be spent writing and debugging loops.

In the recipes that follow, we will demonstrate how to use array_walk(), array_map(), and array_filter().

4-33. Applying Functions to Array Elements Using array_walk()

The following example shows the simplest case for using array_walk() to apply a function to each element of an array; you will apply a function named modify() to each element of an array named $array. The outcome you are trying to achieve in this case is to multiply each number in $array by a constant without writing a loop. Let's look at the code first, and then we will provide some explanation and elaborate on this theme.

The Code

```php
<?php
  function array_display($array, $pre=FALSE)
  {
    $tag = $pre ? 'pre' : 'p';
    printf("<%s>%s</%s>\n", $tag, var_export($array, TRUE), $tag);
  }
```

In this case, you are not using the array key for anything, and you are not passing in any values to the callback, so its signature requires only a single parameter (a reference to the current array element's value).

```php
  function modify(&$value)
  {
    $value *= 1.5;
  }
```

```php
  $array = array(10, -3.5, 2, 7);  #  array containing some numbers
  array_display($array, TRUE);     #  display it as defined

  array_walk($array, 'modify');    #  apply modify() to all the elements in $array
  array_display($array, TRUE);     #  display the modified array
?>
```

Here is the output of this script, showing that the values stored in $array have indeed been updated by the callback function:

```
array (
  0 => 10,
  1 => -3.5,
  2 => 2,
  3 => 7,
)

array (
  0 => 15,
  1 => -5.25,
  2 => 3,
  3 => 10.5,
)
```

How It Works

The prototype for array_walk() is as follows:

```
bool array_walk(array &$array, string $funcname[, mixed $data])
```

This function returns TRUE if successful and FALSE in the event of failure. When called, the function named funcname acts on the elements of an array. The prototype for the callback function is generally of the following form:

```
void funcname(mixed &$value[, $mixed $key[, mixed $data]])
```

The callback does not return a value; instead, it acts on each array value in place (indicated by the & operator), which it expects to receive as the first argument. The second argument is the element's key. An optional third argument representing data to be used in the function may also be present. Note that if the callback uses a data parameter, then a key parameter must be present in the callback's signature whether or not it is actually used in the callback function.

Tip If for some reason you need to pass more than one user value to the callback function, you will need to pass it via some structure such as an array, as there can be only one data variable.

Variations

Here is a slightly more complex example that uses both the array key and a passed-in value to modify each element value:

```php
<?php
  function change(&$element, $key, $mark)
  {
    $element = "$mark$key$mark, the $element";
  }

  $dogs = array('Lassie' => 'Collie', 'Bud' => 'Sheepdog',
                'Rin-Tin-Tin' => 'Alsatian', 'Snoopy' => 'Beagle');
  array_display($dogs, TRUE);

  array_walk($dogs, 'change', '*');
  array_display($dogs, TRUE);
?>
```

The output, which displays the $dogs array before and after modification, is as follows:

```
array (
  'Lassie' => 'Collie',
  'Bud' => 'Sheepdog',
  'Rin-Tin-Tin' => 'Alsatian',
  'Snoopy' => 'Beagle',
)

array (
  'Lassie' => '*Lassie*, the Collie',
  'Bud' => '*Bud*, the Sheepdog',
  'Rin-Tin-Tin' => '*Rin-Tin-Tin*, the Alsatian',
  'Snoopy' => '*Snoopy*, the Beagle',
)
```

Of course, the actual names you assign to the callback function's parameters are not important as long as you know which one is which and use them appropriately.

Caution A callback function used by array_walk() may not modify the array, only the values of the array's elements. In other words, the callback may not insert or delete elements, and it may not modify any keys.

4-34. Applying Functions to Array Elements Using array_map()

Now let's look at applying a function to array elements using `array_map()`. This time we will also apply a slightly more complex callback function to create a *negative-safe* square root function, which tests the input value to see whether it is a negative number and takes appropriate action if it does.

The Code

```php
<?php
  function array_display($array, $pre=FALSE)
  {
    $tag = $pre ? 'pre' : 'p';
    printf("<%s>%s</%s>\n", $tag, var_export($array, TRUE), $tag);
  }


  function safe_sqrt($num)
  {
    return sqrt( abs($num) ) . ($num < 0 ? 'i' : '');
  }

  $values = array(3, 8, -3, 0, 14, -4);

  $roots = array_map('safe_sqrt', $values);

  print '<p>Values:</p>';
  array_display($values, TRUE);

  print '<p>Square roots:</p>';
  array_display($roots, TRUE);
?>
```

Here is the output generated by this example:

```
Values:
array (
  0 => 3,
  1 => 8,
  2 => -3,
  3 => 0,
  4 => 14,
  5 => -4,
)
```

```
Square roots:
array (
    0 => '1.7320508075689',
    1 => '2.8284271247462',
    2 => '1.73205080756891',
    3 => '0',
    4 => '3.7416573867739',
    5 => '21',
)
```

How It Works

The callback function safe_sqrt() is applied to each number from the $values array in turn. As you might recall from mathematics classes, the square root of a negative number can be represented using i or j (a so-called imaginary number equal to the square root of -1). Using this notation, you can represent the square root of -4 as $2i$, so that 2i * 2i = (2 * 2) * (i * i) = 4 * -1 = -4.

As already mentioned, the array_map() function returns a new array whose elements are the modified values of the array it acts upon. Its prototype is as follows:

```
array array_map(string $funcname, array $arr1[, array $arr2...])
```

The arguments to this function are the name of the callback function followed by one or more array variables. This callback function works somewhat differently than the one that is used by array_walk(). Its prototype is as follows:

```
mixed funcname(array $arr1[, array $arr2[, array $arr3[, ...]]])
```

In other words, the callback takes one or more array variables as parameters, and these parameters must be the same number of array variables as passed to array_map(). When you pass an array variable to array_map(), the callback function actually "sees" a single element of this array at a time.

Also, do not forget that the first argument to array_map() is a string and must be quoted. This means that since the name of the callback function in the example is safe_sqrt, you need to refer to it as "safe_sqrt" (including the quotation marks) when calling it from array_map().

Tip You are not limited to user-defined functions with array_map(); you can also employ native PHP functions. For example, if you need to check the sort order for some special characters, you can generate a string containing all the printable characters available in the Extended ASCII character set, in order, with this bit of code that uses the chr() function: $chars = implode('', array_map('chr', range(32, 255)));.

You can also use the array_map() function without any callback function to generate nested arrays. See recipe 4-24 for an example.

4-35. Filtering Arrays Using array_filter()

In the previous two sections, you had a chance to see how you can use a function to modify all the elements of an array. Now you will look at a slightly different way to apply a function to an array's elements: you will subject each element to a test and derive a new array containing only those elements that have passed the test.

If you recall the website internationalization scenario from a few sections back, you will remember that you were working with a list of countries and the languages spoken in those countries, defined like so:

```
$countries = array( 'USA' => 'English', 'Spain' => 'Spanish',
                    'Brazil' => 'Portuguese', 'UK' => 'English',
                    'Mexico' => 'Spanish', 'Germany' => 'German',
                    'Colombia' => 'Spanish', 'Canada' => 'English',
                    'Russia' => 'Russian', 'Austria' => 'German',
                    'France' => 'French', 'Argentina' => 'Spanish');
```

Let's say you want a list of only those countries in which romance languages are spoken. You can also represent these as an array: ('French', 'Spanish', 'Portuguese', 'Italian'). What you want to do is check each country (element in $countries) in turn and see whether its value is one of the values in this array of romance language names. You might recall that to determine whether a given value is found in an array, you can use the in_array() function somehow. Rather than write a loop that uses that function, there is a better way to use in_array().

The Code

```
function is_rom($lang)
{
  return in_array($lang, array('French', 'Spanish', 'Portuguese', 'Italian')));
}
```

Now let's put this altogether:

```php
<?php
  function array_display($array, $pre=FALSE)
  {
    $tag = $pre ? 'pre' : 'p';
    printf("<%s>%s</%s>\n", $tag, var_export($array, TRUE), $tag);
  }

  function is_romance($lang)
  {
    return in_array($lang, array('French', 'Spanish', 'Portuguese', 'Italian'));
  }

  $countries = array( 'USA' => 'English', 'Spain' => 'Spanish',
                      'Brazil' => 'Portuguese', 'UK' => 'English',
                      'Mexico' => 'Spanish', 'Germany' => 'German',
                      'Colombia' => 'Spanish', 'Canada' => 'English',
```

```
                                'Russia' => 'Russian', 'Austria' => 'German',
                                'France' => 'French', 'Argentina' => 'Spanish');

   $rom_countries = array_filter($countries, 'is_romance');

   array_display($rom_countries, TRUE);
?>
```

Here is the output:

```
array (
  'Spain' => 'Spanish',
  'Brazil' => 'Portuguese',
  'Mexico' => 'Spanish',
  'Colombia' => 'Spanish',
  'France' => 'French',
  'Argentina' => 'Spanish',
)
```

How It Works

The function prototype for array_filter looks like this:

```
array array_filter(array $array, string $funcname)
```

This function filters an array represented by the variable $array using a callback function whose name is funcname. The callback acts on an element of this array and returns a boolean value. In this case, when array_filter() is invoked, it calls is_rom() for each value in $countries one after another. If is_rom() returns TRUE, then that element is appended to the output of array_filter(). As you can see by examining the output of this example, the original array keys are preserved.

The callback function can be virtually anything you like, as long as it takes a single input parameter (corresponding to an array element's value) and returns a boolean. The only other restriction is that the original array may not be altered by the callback function.

Variations

A quick way to rid an array of "empty" array elements is to call array_filter() with no callback function. This has the effect of providing a copy of the original array except for those elements whose values evaluate to FALSE, as shown here:

```
<?php
  #  array_display() function as was defined previously

  $arr = array(2, 'two', 0, 'NULL', NULL, 'FALSE', FALSE, 'empty', '');
  $copy = array_filter($arr);
  $reindexed = array_values($copy);
```

```
    print '<p>Original:</p>';
    array_display($arr, TRUE);
    print '<p>Filtered:</p>';
    array_display($copy, TRUE);
    print '<p>Filtered and reindexed:</p>';
    array_display($reindexed, TRUE);
?>
```

Notice that when you want to use array_filter() in this way, you simply omit the call-back parameter. Once again, you can see that the original keys are preserved. If you want the elements to be reindexed, you can always use array_values(), as discussed earlier in this chapter (see recipe 4-25).

```
Original:
array (
  0 => 2,
  1 => 'two',
  2 => 0,
  3 => 'NULL',
  4 => NULL,
  5 => 'FALSE',
  6 => false,
  7 => 'empty',
  8 => '',
)

Filtered:
array (
  0 => 2,
  1 => 'two',
  3 => 'NULL',
  5 => 'FALSE',
  7 => 'empty',
)

Filtered and reindexed:
array (
  0 => 2,
  1 => 'two',
  2 => 'NULL',
  3 => 'FALSE',
  4 => 'empty',
)
```

Sorting Arrays

PHP 5 has a rich collection of sorting functions that allow you to sort by values and keys and even use your own comparison algorithms. Variants on most of these functions facilitate sorting in forward or reverse order and provide you with the option of preserving or resetting the associations between array keys and values. In this section of the chapter, we will show you how to sort arrays in all these ways and perhaps one or two more.

Note All of PHP's array sorting functions work on arrays in place and return TRUE to indicate success or FALSE in the event of failure.

4-36. Sorting an Array by Its Values

To order an array's elements using their values, use the sort() function. This function takes as its arguments the array to be sorted and an optional sort flag, and, like PHP's other sorting functions, this one sorts the array in place.

The Code

```php
<?php
  $nums = array(15, 2.2, -4, 2.3, 0);

  sort($nums);

  printf("<pre>%s</pre>\n", var_export($nums, TRUE));

  $words = array('bird', 'fish', 'George', 'Aden');

  sort($words);

  printf("<pre>%s</pre>\n", var_export($words, TRUE));

  $dogs = array('Lassie' => 'Collie', 'Bud' => 'Sheepdog',
                'Rin-Tin-Tin' => 'Alsatian', 'Snoopy' => 'Beagle');

  sort($dogs);
  printf("<pre>%s</pre>\n", var_export($dogs, TRUE));
?>
```

Let's look at the output produced by this code:

```
array (
  0 => -4,
  1 => 0,
  2 => 2.2,
  3 => 2.3,
```

```
    4 => 15,
)

array (
  0 => 'Aden',
  1 => 'George',
  2 => 'bird',
  3 => 'fish',
)

array (
  0 => 'Alsatian',
  1 => 'Beagle',
  2 => 'Collie',
  3 => 'Sheepdog',
)
```

How It Works

The array $nums, whose values are numbers, is sorted in numerical order. The second array, $words, consists of string values. These are sorted in the order of the characters' ASCII codes, so capital letters come before lowercase ones. (If you do not have a list of characters in their ASCII ordering handy, use the ord() function to obtain the ASCII codes for the characters in question.) The values from $dogs, being strings, are also sorted in the order of their ASCII codes.

Variations

What has become of the keys from the associative array $dogs? You appear to have a bit of a problem. Because sort() resets all the indexes, you have lost the original keys. To get around this issue, you can use the asort() function instead. This works in the same way as sort() except in one respect: it preserves the array's original key/value associations.

```php
<?php
  $dogs = array('Lassie' => 'Collie', 'Bud' => 'Sheepdog',
                'Rin-Tin-Tin' => 'Alsatian', 'Snoopy' => 'Beagle');

  asort($dogs);
  printf("<pre>%s</pre>\n", var_export($dogs, TRUE));
?>
```

```
array (
  'Rin-Tin-Tin' => 'Alsatian',
  'Snoopy' => 'Beagle',
  'Lassie' => 'Collie',
  'Bud' => 'Sheepdog',
)
```

In general, as you can see, when you need to sort arrays by value, you are most likely to want to use sort() with indexed arrays and asort() with associative arrays.

For sorting an array by value in reverse order, see recipe 4-39 later in this chapter.

4-37. Sorting an Array by Its Keys

Particularly with regard to associative arrays, it is just as important to be able to sort arrays by their keys as it is by their values. The ksort() function accomplishes this while maintaining the relationship between keys and values. The next example should suffice to demonstrate how to use this function.

The Code

```php
<?php
  $dogs = array('Lassie' => 'Collie', 'Bud' => 'Sheepdog',
                'Rin-Tin-Tin' => 'Alsatian', 'Snoopy' => 'Beagle');

  ksort($dogs);
  printf("<pre>%s</pre>\n", var_export($dogs, TRUE));
?>
```

Here is the output:

```
array (
  'Bud' => 'Sheepdog',
  'Lassie' => 'Collie',
  'Rin-Tin-Tin' => 'Alsatian',
  'Snoopy' => 'Beagle',
)
```

Extension

Of course, you can also sort an indexed array by index using this function; one situation in which you might need this is after using asort() to return the array's elements to their original order:

```php
<?php
  $nums = array(15, 2.2, -4, 2.3, 0);
  asort($nums);
  printf("<pre>%s</pre>\n", var_export($nums, TRUE));
  ksort($nums);
  printf("<pre>%s</pre>\n", var_export($nums, TRUE));
?>
```

```
array (
   2 => -4,
   4 => 0,
   1 => 2.2,
   3 => 2.3,
   0 => 15,
)

array (
   0 => 15,
   1 => 2.2,
   2 => -4,
   3 => 2.3,
   4 => 0,
)
```

It is also possible to sort an array by key in reverse order using krsort(); see recipe 4-38 for particulars.

4-38. Reversing an Array Using arsort()

To sort an associative array by value in reverse order, use arsort(). Like asort(), this function preserves the array's keys, as you can see in the following code.

The Code

```php
<?php
  $dogs = array('Lassie' => 'Collie', 'Bud' => 'Sheepdog',
                'Rin-Tin-Tin' => 'Alsatian', 'Snoopy' => 'Beagle');
  arsort($dogs);
  printf("<pre>%s</pre>\n", var_export($dogs, TRUE));
?>
```

Here is the output:

```
array (
  'Bud' => 'Sheepdog',
  'Lassie' => 'Collie',
  'Snoopy' => 'Beagle',
  'Rin-Tin-Tin' => 'Alsatian',
)
```

4-39. Reversing an Array Using krsort()

The krsort() function sorts an array by key in reverse order.

The Code

```php
<?php
  $dogs = array('Lassie' => 'Collie', 'Bud' => 'Sheepdog',
                'Rin-Tin-Tin' => 'Alsatian', 'Snoopy' => 'Beagle');
  krsort($dogs);
  printf("<pre>%s</pre>\n", var_export($dogs, TRUE));
?>
```

```
array (
  'Snoopy' => 'Beagle',
  'Rin-Tin-Tin' => 'Alsatian',
  'Lassie' => 'Collie',
  'Bud' => 'Sheepdog',
)
```

As you can see, krsort() preserves the relationship between keys and values.

4-40. Reversing an Array Using array_reverse()

The array_reverse() function does just what you would expect; it reverses the order in which the elements of an array are listed.

The Code

```php
<?php
  $dogs = array('Lassie' => 'Collie', 'Bud' => 'Sheepdog',
                'Rin-Tin-Tin' => 'Alsatian', 'Snoopy' => 'Beagle');

  array_reverse($dogs);
  printf("<pre>%s</pre>\n", var_export($dogs, TRUE));

  $nums = array(15, 2.2, -4, 2.3, 0);
  array_reverse($nums);
  printf("<pre>%s</pre>\n", var_export($nums, TRUE));
?>
```

Like the array sorting functions, array_reverse() works on an array in place. It leaves all key/value associations intact.

```
array (
  'Lassie' => 'Collie',
  'Bud' => 'Sheepdog',
  'Rin-Tin-Tin' => 'Alsatian',
```

```
  'Snoopy' => 'Beagle',
)

array (
  0 => 15,
  1 => 2.2,
  2 => -4,
  3 => 2.3,
  4 => 0,
)
```

4-41. Randomizing an Array Using shuffle(), kshuffle(), and array_rand()

To reorder an array's elements so they are in random order, PHP provides the shuffle() function. Like the sort functions, shuffle() acts on the array in place and can be called repeatedly without obtaining the same result over and over, as shown in the next example.

The Code

```php
<?php
  $nums = array(15, 2.2, -4, 2.3, 0);

  shuffle($nums);
  printf("<pre>%s</pre>\n", var_export($nums, TRUE));

  shuffle($nums);
  printf("<pre>%s</pre>\n", var_export($nums, TRUE));

  shuffle($nums);
  printf("<pre>%s</pre>\n", var_export($nums, TRUE));
?>
```

Some example output follows. You should keep in mind that if you run the same code on your own PHP installation, the results will be similar, but almost certainly not identical to this:

```
array (
  0 => 2.3,
  1 => -4,
  2 => 0,
  3 => 2.2,
  4 => 15,
)

array (
  0 => 0,
  1 => -4,
```

```
  2 => 2.3,
  3 => 2.2,
  4 => 15,
)

array (
  0 => 15,
  1 => 2.3,
  2 => -4,
  3 => 2.2,
  4 => 0,
)
```

4-42. Sorting an Array Using Comparison Functions

It is also possible to set your own criteria for sorting by using a comparison function that you have written yourself. PHP has three functions—usort(), uasort(), and uksort()—that make this a much less painful exercise than it might be otherwise. (If you have ever taken a C or C++ programming class in which you were required to write routines from scratch for sorting strings according to custom rules, you will know what we are talking about here.)

Suppose you want to sort some numbers so that even numbers will be sorted first, followed by odd numbers, with the numbers sorted from highest to lowest within each of the two groups. You will write a function evenfirst() to do this and then apply evenfirst() when sorting an array that represents inventory in a clothing shop. The reason you want to perform the custom sort is because the shop is having a two-for-one sale, and you want to know at a glance which categories of items will have leftovers, as well as which categories have the most items. (Admittedly this is a bit silly, but forgive us for the sake of the example.) You will call the array representing the shop's current inventory $clothes. Let's look first at the code used to perform the sort and then discuss how it does its job.

The Code

```php
<?php
  function evenfirst($i, $j)
  {
    $value = 0;            #  default return value (do nothing)
    if($i % 2) $value++;
    if($j % 2) $value--;
    if($value == 0) $value = $j > $i;
    return $value;
  }
  $clothes = array( 'hats' => 75, 'coats' => 32, 'shoes' => 102,
                    'gloves' => 15, 'shirts' => 51, 'trousers' => 44);
  usort($clothes, 'evenfirst');
  var_export($clothes);
?>
```

How It Works

The usort() function takes two arguments, an array to be sorted in place and the name of a comparison function. The comparison function takes two parameters—two array elements to be compared—and returns an integer whose value is interpreted according to the following rules:

- If the result is negative, then the first argument is considered to be less than the second, and the first argument is sorted first.

- If the result is positive, then the first argument is considered to be greater than the second, and the second argument is sorted first.

- If the result is zero, then the order of the arguments is left unchanged in the array.

The function firsteven() might look a bit odd (if you will excuse the pun), but what it does is this: it takes two values, $i and $j, to be compared; these represent adjacent values from the array to be sorted. In this case, if $i is even and $j is odd, then $value will be positive 1, and $i will be sorted first; if $j is even and $i is odd, then $value will be negative 1, and $j will be sorted first. If both $i and $j are odd, or if both are even, then $value is 0, and nothing is changed (yet). If both $i and $j are odd, or if both are even, then you want to see whether $j is greater than $i; if it is, then you want $j to be sorted first. You do this by setting $value equal to $j > $i, which will evaluate as 1 if the condition is true and 0 if it is not. Finally, you return $value to the sort function, which takes the appropriate action based on its value.

```
array ( 0 => 102, 1 => 44, 2 => 32, 3 => 75, 4 => 51, 5 => 15, )
```

Variations

usort() performed the sort but did not preserve the keys, which would be much more helpful. To do this, use uasort() instead:

```
uasort($clothes, 'evenfirst');
var_export($clothes);
```

Here is the output:

```
array ( 'shoes' => 102, 'trousers' => 44, 'coats' => 32, 'hats' => 75,
        'shirts' => 51, 'gloves' => 15, )
```

This is a bit more useful, since it still tells you which amounts go with which items of clothing.

To perform a custom sort on the keys of an array, you can use the uksort() function in the same way as we have shown you with usort() and uasort(), the only difference being that your comparison function will be comparing keys rather than values.

4-43. Sorting Multidimensional Arrays

Not all arrays are one-dimensional, and PHP recognizes this with a function that can be used to sort multiple-dimensional arrays. array_multisort() takes a number of arrays as arguments, each followed optionally by one or more sort flags. This can be useful in cases such as sorting through database result sets.

Let's return to the website internationalization scenario and expand upon it a bit. First, let's suppose you have retrieved the visitor/country/language data from a database using a query along the lines of this:

```
SELECT country, language, visitors FROM visits v;
```

A result set row from such a query might look something like this:

```
array('country'=>'Spain', 'language'=>'Spanish', 'visitors'=>1289)
```

You might assemble a multidimensional array called $data using a construct such as this:

```
$data = array();

while($row = $result->fetch_assoc())
    $data[] = $row;
```

For this example, suppose that $data is populated as shown in the following code. The objective here is to sort that array in the order of language, then country, and then number of visitors.

The Code

```php
<?php
  $data
    = array(
        array('country'=>'Spain', 'language'=>'Spanish', 'visitors'=>1289),
        array('country'=>'France', 'language'=>'French', 'visitors'=>984),
        array('country'=>'Argentina', 'language'=>'Spanish', 'visitors'=>812),
        array('country'=>'UK', 'language'=>'English', 'visitors'=>3111),
        array('country'=>'Germany', 'language'=>'German', 'visitors'=>2786),
        array('country'=>'Canada', 'language'=>'English', 'visitors'=>2331),
        array('country'=>'Austria', 'language'=>'German', 'visitors'=>1102),
        array('country'=>'Mexico', 'language'=>'Spanish', 'visitors'=>1071)
    );

  # printf("<pre>%s</pre>\n", var_export($data, TRUE));

  $cols = array();

  foreach($data as $row)
  {
    foreach($row as $key => $value)
    {
```

```
        if( !isset($cols[$key]) )
          $cols[$key] = array();
        $cols[$key][] = $value;
    }
  }

  $data = $cols;

  array_multisort($data['language'], $data['country'], $data['visitors']);

  printf("<pre>%s</pre>\n", var_export($data, TRUE));
?>
```

Here is the output:

```
array (
  'country' =>
  array (
    0 => 'Canada',
    1 => 'UK',
    2 => 'France',
    3 => 'Austria',
    4 => 'Germany',
    5 => 'Argentina',
    6 => 'Mexico',
    7 => 'Spain',
  ),
  'language' =>
  array (
    0 => 'English',
    1 => 'English',
    2 => 'French',
    3 => 'German',
    4 => 'German',
    5 => 'Spanish',
    6 => 'Spanish',
    7 => 'Spanish',
  ),
  'visitors' =>
  array (
    0 => 2331,
    1 => 3111,
    2 => 984,
    3 => 1102,
    4 => 2786,
    5 => 812,
    6 => 1071,
```

```
    7 => 1289,
  ),
)
```

How It Works

To be effective, array_multisort() requires that multidimensional arrays be arranged in a columnar fashion. You can convert $data from an array of rows to an array of columns, as shown here:

```
$cols = array();
```

```
foreach($data as $row)
{
  foreach($row as $key => $value)
  {
    if( !isset($cols[$key]) )
      $cols[$key] = array();
    $cols[$key][] = $value;
  }
}
```

```
$data = $cols;
```

$data now looks like this:

```
array(
        'country' => array('Spain', 'France', 'Argentina', 'UK',
                           'Germany', 'Canada', 'Austria', 'Mexico'),

        'language' => array('Spanish', 'French', 'Spanish', 'English',
                            'German', 'English', 'German', 'Spanish'),

        'visitors' => array(1289, 984, 812, 3111, 2786, 2331, 1102, 1071)
)
```

Now comes the easy part. To sort this array by language and then country, you merely call array_multisort(), like so:

```
array_multisort($data['language'], $data['country'], $data['visitors']);
```

Then you output the sorted array using var_export(). Note that the values in all three columns have been sorted into their correct positions relative to one another. The data has been sorted first by language, then by country, and then by number of visitors.

You can change the order simply by changing the order of the columns in the call to array_multisort(). You can also sort by a column in reverse order by following that column with a comma and SORT_DESC. For example, to perform the same sort except with the languages in reverse order, you could use this:

```
array_multisort($data['language'], SORT_DESC,
    $data['country'], $data['visitors']);
```

Try this on your own, and experiment with it a bit. You will be surprised at how many ways you can use it.

■**Caution** When using `array_multisort()`, you must specify all columns you want to sort. Any omitted columns will be left in their original order (this means omitted columns will not participate in the sort and cannot be used reliably). If you do not intend to use values from that column, then this is not a problem, but we usually include all columns, just in case we later change our minds.

4-44. Sorting Multiple Arrays

You can also use `array_multisort()` with multiple arrays. Consider a set of arrays that serves as a sort of mini-dictionary that contains four words in each of four languages. Each language's words are contained in an array, and the corresponding digits are stored in a fifth array. The objective is to sort the arrays so that the words from one language appear in alphabetical order and the corresponding words in the other three languages match up with them.

The Code

```php
<?php
    $eng = array('one', 'two', 'three', 'four');  # 1-4 in English
    $esp = array('uno', 'dos', 'tres', 'cuatro'); # 1-4 in Spanish
    $deu = array('eins', 'zwei', 'drei', 'vier'); # 1-4 in German
    $rus = array('odin', 'dva', 'tri', 'chetire'); # 1-4 in Russian
    $digits = range(1,4);
    array_multisort($rus, $esp, $deu, $eng, $digits);

    foreach(range(0, 3) as $j)
        printf("<p>Russian: %s (%d); Spanish: %s; German: %s; English: %s.</p>",
               $rus[$j], $digits[$j], $esp[$j], $deu[$j], $eng[$j]);
?>
```

Here is the output:

Russian: chetire (4); Spanish: cuatro; German: vier; English: four.

Russian: dva (2); Spanish: dos; German: zwei; English: two.

Russian: odin (1); Spanish: uno; German: eins; English: one.

Russian: tri (3); Spanish: tres; German: drei; English: three.

How It Works

All that is required is to list all the arrays as arguments to `array_multisort()`. The first array is sorted in normal order, and the corresponding elements of the other arrays are sorted to match. The only restriction is that all the arrays must have the same number of elements.

Finding Permutations and Combinations

In order to understand recursion, one first must understand recursion.

—Anonymous

Both combinations and permutations of a set of values involve different arrangements of those values. In this section, we will define what these terms mean and show you how to do the following:

- Calculate numbers of possible permutations and combinations of an array's elements

- Generate permutations and combinations

4-45. Finding All Permutations of an Array's Elements

An array's permutations are defined as the set of all possible combinations of the elements in that array. For example, suppose you have defined an array like this:

`$letters = array('a', 'b', 'c');`

This array has six permutations: abc, bca, cab, cba, bac, and acb.

Assuming that all an array's elements can be uniquely identified, the number of permutations is equal to the factorial of the number of elements in the array. In this case, since there are three elements, the number of permutations is three factorial, written as so:

`3! = 3 * 2 * 1 = 6`

More generally, the factorial of a positive integer N is defined as follows:

`N! = N * (N-1) * (N-2) * ... * 3 * 2 * 1`

where $N!$ is read as "N factorial." The factorial of 0 is defined to be 1, and the factorial of a negative number is undefined.

This is a natural consequence of a mathematical principle known as the Law of Counting, which can be stated as follows:

If something can be chosen, or can happen, or be done, in m different ways, and, after that has happened, something else can be chosen in n different ways, then the number of ways of choosing both of them is m* n.

For example, say you have five cards, and each one is printed with one of the letters *a*, *b*, *c*, *d*, and *e*. If you pick one card, there are exactly five different possible outcomes—one outcome per letter. If you select one of the remaining four cards, there are four possible outcomes of that event, regardless of which card was selected in the first draw. Thus, there are twenty outcomes when two cards are drawn from five. At this point, there are three cards remaining and hence three choices, or sixty possible outcomes. This may also be expressed as $N!/(N-k)!$, where N is the total number of objects and k the number of objects chosen from amongst them. For five cards, taken two at a time, there are $5! / (5-2)! = 120 / 6 = 20$ possible outcomes, and for five cards taken three at a time, there are $5! / (5-3)! = 120 / 2 = 60$ possible outcomes.

■**Caution** Factorials increase in size extremely quickly as the base increases. 5! equals 120. 10! equals 3628800. 20! equals approximately 2.43E+18, which is rather larger than the maximum acceptable size of an integer on most systems.

We can sum up this discussion in two rules:

- The total number of permutations of N objects is $N!$.

- The number of permutations of N objects taken k objects at a time is $N! / (N-k)!$.

Now that you know what permutations are and how many a given set of elements has, the following example shows how you can generate them.

The Code

```php
<?php
  function array_permutations($input, $num)
  {
    $perms = $indexed = $output = array();
    $base = count($input);
    $i = 0;

    foreach($input as $in)
      $indexed[$i++] = $in;

    foreach(range(0, pow($base, $num) - 1) as $i)
      $perms[] = sprintf("%'0{$num}d", base_convert($i, 10, $base));

    foreach(array_filter($perms, 'catch_duplicate_chars') as $perm)
    {
      $temp = array();

      foreach(str_split($perm) as $digit)
        $temp[] = $indexed[$digit];
```

```
      $output[] = $temp;
    }

    return $output;
}

function catch_duplicate_chars($val)
{
    $arr = str_split($val);
    return $arr == array_unique($arr);
}

$test = array_permutations(array('a', 'b', 'c'), 2);

$display = '';
foreach($test as $row)
    $display .= implode('', $row) . "\n";

print "<pre>$display</pre>";
?>
```

Here is the output:

```
ab
ac
ba
bc
ca
cb
```

How It Works

You can reduce the rule for permutations to make it more efficient. Both the numerator and denominator will contain the terms $(N - k) * (N - (k - 1)) * (N - (k - 2)) * ... * (N - 1)$, which means that the result consists of the series $N * (N - 1) * (N - 2) * ... * (N - (k + 1))$. For example, if you are taking five objects, three at a time, then the number of permutations is 5 * 4. The permutations() function acts recursively to find the number of permutations for $total objects taken $num at a time. It multiplies the current value of $total by $total minus 1 and then calls itself using $total minus 1 until $total is no longer greater than $limit, which is set equal to the difference of the original value of $total and $num.

```
function permutations($total, $num)
{
    $limit = func_num_args() == 2 ? $total - $num : func_get_arg(2);

    return $total > $limit ? $total * permutations($total - 1, $num, $limit) : 1;
}
```

That takes care of the number of permutations. To generate the permutations themselves, you take a slightly different tack. array_permutations() takes two arguments: an array $input and the number $num of elements from that array you want to take at a time. First, you get the number of elements in the array and use that as a base for generating a sequence of numbers with $num digits, which you then store in an array $perms. For example, for five objects taken three at a time, you generate all the three-digit numbers to the base 5. You filter $perms to remove all elements with duplicate digits using catch_duplicate_chars(), which splits up each number into separate digits and then compares the resulting array with the same array after array_unique() is applied to it; if the two arrays are not the same, you know that the number contains one or more repeated digits, so it is dropped from $perms. Once the numbers with duplicate digits are removed from $perms, you can iterate through $perms and, for each number in this array, assemble a string from the elements corresponding to each digit. This string is then appended to the array that is returned by array_permutations().

Caution Exercise prudence when using these scripts (or similar ones) to generate listings of all possible permutations or combinations for large values of N; it is not difficult to bog down your server quickly. This should not be too surprising when you consider, for example, that there are 311,875,200 permutations of 52 playing cards drawn 5 at a time and 2,598,960 unique combinations. Either one of these figures represents quite a lot of records to display or to save to a file.

4-46. Finding All Combinations of an Array's Elements

The difference between permutations and combinations is that combinations represent unique subsets regardless of order. For example, the groupings abc and acb are two different permutations, but because they contain the same elements, they are not considered to be separate combinations.

The Code

```php
<?php
 #  depends array_permutations() function
 #  defined in previous section

 function array_combinations($input, $num)
 {
   $combos = array();
   foreach(array_permutations($input, $num) as $row)
   {
     $copy = $row;
     sort($copy);
     $combos[implode('', $row)] = implode('', $copy);
   }

   return array_keys( array_unique($combos) );
 }
```

```
$array_combinations = array_combinations(array('a', 'b', 'c', 'd'), 3);

$display = '';
foreach($array_combinations as $row)
  $display .= "$row\n";

print "<pre>$display</pre>"
?>
```

Here is the output:

```
abc
abd
acd
bcd
```

How It Works

You simply leverage the permutation generation function from the previous section for generating combinations, since all you need to do is throw out any duplicates. You do this using the array_unique() function provided by PHP 5.

Summary

Different programming languages call arrays by different names and have different methods for manipulating them, but any programming language worth using provides some means of working with sets of data. PHP is no different in this regard. In fact, as you had the chance to see in this chapter, PHP excels in its array-handling capabilities. What PHP refers to simply as an *array* really encompasses two related but different structures—ordered and unordered lists.

In this chapter, we covered PHP arrays and array functions, starting with creating and populating them and then looking at different techniques for adding elements to existing arrays and removing elements from them either singly or in groups. We also discussed how to determine whether a given element exists in an array, how to access that element once you have made that determination, and how to traverse an array in a systematic fashion.

You also saw some techniques for outputting arrays in formats that are easy to read, as well as for obtaining information about the array as a whole, such as its size and the sum and average of its values.

From there you learned about ways to manipulate arrays using functions acting on all or selected array elements, as well as ways to filter arrays to retrieve or remove elements that do or do not meet your criteria. By now, you should also have a fair idea of how you can combine arrays in several ways; you can append them to one another in a linear fashion or use one array as the keys and another as the values of a new array.

In the last few sections of this chapter, you had the opportunity to see some sophisticated uses of arrays, such as PHP's ability to sort arrays according to different criteria or according to completely arbitrary rules that you can implement by using callback functions. This includes an extremely powerful technique for sorting multiple arrays and multidimensional arrays with the aid of the `array_multisort()` function. Finally, we showed you some techniques for determining how many permutations and combinations of elements are possible for a given dataset and how to generate them.

Looking Ahead

In Chapter 5, we will discuss PHP 5's handling of times and dates. We will give you a guided tour of the most important functions available for this purpose and show you some ways you can use these functions to perform tasks such as outputting formatted times and dates; calculating differences between different times and dates; accounting for time zones, locales, and Universal Time, Coordinated (UTC); and finding out what day of the week a given date is. We will also share with you a `Date` class, based on the ECMA standard, that we have developed in our work and that we have upgraded to PHP 5 for this book.

CHAPTER 5

■ ■ ■

Working with Dates and Times

Dates and times are quite unlike most other sorts of data you are likely to encounter when programming with PHP 5. Arrays, whether they are indexed arrays or associative arrays, are nicely structured. So are strings. Numbers are—well, they are numbers, and despite a few bumps here and there because of issues such as rounding, you are still obliged to work with a fairly limited set of mathematical operations and formatting functions. However, dates are rather messy with respect to both calculation and representation, and one is about as bad as the other.

Quick question: what were the date and time exactly 101 hours, 44 minutes, and 15 seconds prior to 7:35 p.m. on September 17, 1989? And what day of the week was that? If you can answer that in 30 seconds or less unaided, then you are a rare individual indeed. The problems with calculating that date and time the rest of us experience arise because humans have so far resisted adopting something like the metric system for dates and times. Instead, we have conventions such as 60 seconds per minute, 60 minutes per hour, 24 hours per day, and 7 days per week. And if that is not bad enough, when we get to that point, we throw all semblance of regularity out the window. Months have differing numbers of days, and weeks do not match up precisely with either months or years. People cannot even agree on which day of the week comes first. And it does not end there: sooner or later, we have to deal with time zones and daylight-saving time.

Then there are the issues of representation and localization. Consider the following dates and times:

- 2:50:30 p.m., 17 March 2005

- 2005-03-17 14:50:30

- 2:50:30 p.m. 17/03/2005

- March 17, 2005, 2:50:30 p.m.

- 1111035030000

- Nine-and-a-half minutes before 3 o'clock on Thursday afternoon

Each of these is a common and valid way of representing the same time and date. All of them are equally precise, except for the last one, which depends upon the context in which it is being used for accuracy. (If it is used sometime between March 11 and March 16, 2005, then it will be taken to mean the same as the others.)

It is not that difficult for humans to sort these things out (although most people would balk at 1111035030000). For instance, 17/03/2005 is pretty obviously March 17, 2005—even if you are accustomed to writing the month first—since there is no 17th month in the year. Computers, being fairly literal, do not have it quite so easy. They prefer it if dates and times are more consistent.

Fortunately, PHP has a number of functions to help you keep dates and times simple for computers. In the first part of this chapter, we will show you how to use some of these functions to perform tasks such as the following:

- Obtaining the current date and time

- Accounting for time zones

- Converting between different date and time formats

- Performing calculations involving dates and times (the earlier "quick question" being one example)

- Determining whether a given date and time representation is a valid one

Some or all of these functions might be familiar to you from PHP4. While PHP's built-in date and time functions are easy enough for computers to work with, they are somewhat cumbersome for humans, for reasons we will discuss in due course. So, we will devote the latter portion of this chapter to leveraging some of PHP 5's new object-oriented capabilities; specifically, we will show how to create and use a couple of classes that will vastly simplify reading, writing, and performing calculations with dates. Because we will be dealing with Date objects having clearly defined properties and methods that dispense with some of the crypticness of PHP's built-in functions, you should find these classes much easier to use and remember than the functions PHP provides for this purpose.

Overview of PHP 5's Date and Time Functions

The PHP 5 date and time function library makes up a core part of the language. The library is included by default, and no special compilation or configuration directives are required to use these functions: they are available in any working PHP installation. No external dependencies such as shared libraries need to be installed on the server in addition to PHP. Also, this library does not define any special constants or resource types.

> **Note** GMT stands for Greenwich mean time, which is standard time at the Greenwich meridian at zero degrees of longitude (so-called because it passes through the old Royal Observatory at Greenwich, England). Zero degrees of longitude is also sometimes referred to as the *prime meridian*. UTC, which stands for Universal Time, Coordinated, means basically the same thing. (Actually, a GMT second is defined as 1/86,400 of the time required for the earth to complete one rotation, while a UTC second is based on a more accurate unit as determined by an atomic clock. However, for these purposes this makes no appreciable difference.) Many institutions that must deal with multiple time zones, such as weather bureaus and military establishments, use GMT/UTC, and many if not most computers running Unix operating systems base their dates and times on GMT/UTC.

Table 5-1 lists the functions included in the date and time library.

Table 5-1. *PHP 5 Date/Time Functions*

Function	Description
checkdate()	Validates set of Gregorian year, month, and day values (for example, 2005, 3, 17).
date_sunrise()	Returns time of sunrise for a given day and location (new in PHP 5).
date_sunset()	Returns time of sunset for a given day and location (new in PHP 5).
date()	Formats a local date/time, given a Unix timestamp (for example, 1111035030000 from the introduction to this chapter) and a formatting string.
getdate()	Given a Unix timestamp, returns an associative array containing date and time information (defaults to current time).
gettimeofday()	Returns an associative array containing information about the current system time. In PHP 5.1, it is possible for this function to return a float as well.
gmdate()	Formats a GMT/UTC date/time. Uses the same formatting characters as the date() function.
gmmktime()	Converts a set of GMT date/time values into a Unix timestamp (analogous to mktime()).
gmstrftime()	Formats a GMT/UTC date/time according to locale settings (similar to strftime() except the time used is GMT/UTC).
idate()	Formats a local time/date value as an integer. Uses many of the same formatting characters as the date() function (those that produce numeric output). However, idate() accepts just *one* formatting character (new in PHP 5).
localtime()	Given a Unix timestamp, returns an array of date/time values. In PHP 5, this array can be returned as an associative array as well as an indexed array.
microtime()	Returns a string representation of the current Unix timestamp with microseconds. In PHP 5, this function can also return a float.
mktime()	Converts a set of local date/time values into a Unix timestamp.
strftime()	Given a timestamp and a formatting string, returns a representation of a local date/time according to locale settings.
strptime()	Given a date/time string generated with strftime() and the formatting string used to generate it, returns a Unix timestamp (new in PHP 5.1).
strtotime()	Converts an English textual date/time description into a Unix timestamp.
time()	Returns the current system date and time as a Unix timestamp.

Most of these functions depend on the concept of a Unix timestamp. Simply, a Unix timestamp reflects the time elapsed since the beginning of what is known as the *Unix epoch*, that is, midnight on January 1, 1970, GMT. Usually this is expressed in seconds, although sometimes milliseconds or microseconds are used.

■**Note** When we refer to *local* time, we really mean the *web server's* time. Since PHP is a server technology, it has no way to obtain a web client's local time (at least, not directly). If you want a website visitor's local time, you will need to use a client-side technology such as JavaScript to accomplish this task.

In the next few sections, you will learn how to use some of these functions to accomplish typical date-related tasks.

Displaying Dates and Times

The three functions that you most need to be familiar with for displaying human-readable dates in English are time(), mktime(), and date(). time() and mktime() provide ways to represent date/time values that are locale independent and easy for computers to use.

- **Locale independent**: You do not have to worry about whether 06-04-2005 means April 6 (as most Britons and Australians would interpret it) or June 4 (as most Americans would understand it to mean).

- **Easy for computers to use**: Both of these functions return integer values, and it does not get much easier than that for a computer.

Each of these functions returns a time expressed as seconds since the Unix epoch. The difference between time() and mktime() is that time() does not take any arguments and always returns a value corresponding to the current system time, whereas mktime() retrieves a Unix timestamp for an arbitrary date and time. This latter function takes from zero to seven arguments; when you call it without any arguments, it acts just like time() and uses the current system date and time. The arguments, along with their usual ranges of values, are as follows (in the order you must specify them):

- hour (0–23).

- minute (0–59).

- second (0–59).

- month (1–12).

- day (1–28|29|30|31).

- Year (four-digit year recommended). It is important to note that on Windows operating systems the range of possible years for a PHP date extends from only 1970 to 2038 UTC. This is because, unlike Unix systems where PHP can accommodate years between 1901 and 2038, Windows does not support negative values for timestamps.

- is_daylight (boolean). This is TRUE or 1 for daylight-saving time and FALSE or 0 for standard time.

It is possible to omit arguments, but the arguments that are used must start with the hour argument and continue in the order shown previously, without skipping any in between. In other words, if you specify the day, you must specify the hour, minute, second, and month as well. It is also possible to use out-of-range values (except for years, on Windows); we will show what happens in these cases in a moment.

Note If you use floating-point numbers where PHP's date and time functions expect integers, any digits to the right of the decimal point are ignored. For example (in our current time zone), `date('r', mktime(2.5, 0, 0, 3, 15, 2005))` yields `Tue, 15 Mar 2005 02:00:00 +1000`.

5-1. Displaying Human-Readable Dates and Times

To obtain a timestamp for the current system date and time, it is necessary only to call the `time()` function, as shown here:

```php
<?php
  echo time();
?>
```

In a web browser, this produces output such as the following:

1110638611

This is not helpful for users, who are likely to be expecting something more along the lines of `May 23, 2005, 12:25 p.m.` For obtaining a human-readable date and time, PHP provides the `date()` function. When called with a single argument (a formatting string), this function returns a string representation of the current date and/or time. The optional second argument is a timestamp. The following example shows a few ways you can use various formatting strings with `date()`.

The Code

```php
<?php
  $time = time();
  $formats = array(
                    'U',
                    'r',
                    'c',
                    'l, F jS, Y, g:i A',
                    'H:i:s D d M y',
                    'm/j/y g:i:s O (T)'
                  );

  foreach($formats as $format)
    echo "<p><b>$format</b>: " . date($format, $time) . "</p>\n";
?>
```

How It Works

Here is the output of this script as it might be viewed in a browser:

U: 1110643578

r: Sun, 13 Mar 2005 02:06:18 +1000

c: 2005-03-13T02:06:18+10:00

l, F jS, Y, g:i A: Sunday, March 13th, 2005, 2:06 AM

H:i:s D d M y: 02:06:18 Sun 13 Mar 05

m/j/y g:i:s a O (T): 03/13/05 2:06:18 am +1000 (E. Australia Standard Time)

As you may have guessed from comparing the formatting strings to the corresponding lines in the output, the letters stand for various portions of a date or time; punctuation characters including period (.), comma (,), hyphen (-), colon (:), parentheses (()), and slash (/) are inserted directly into the output. The function is defined in such a way that any characters not recognized as formatting characters are passed through as is, but best practice in this regard is that any letters intended to be displayed verbatim in the output of date() should be escaped using a backslash, whether or not they are listed as formatting characters. Table 5-2 lists the most useful formatting characters, grouped according to the units involved.

Table 5-2. *Formatting Characters for the* date() *Function*

Character	Description
Month	
F	Full name of the month (January, February, and so on).
M	Three-letter abbreviation for the month (Jan, Feb, and so on).
m	Numeric representation for the month, with leading zero (two digits).
n	Numeric representation for the month (no leading zero).
Day	
d	Day of the month, with leading zeros (two digits).
j	Day of the month (no leading zeros).
S	Ordinal suffix for the day of the month, two characters (st, nd, th); most commonly used in combination with j.
l (lowercase *L*)	Full name of the day of the week (Monday, Tuesday, and so on).
D	A textual representation of a day, three letters (Mon, Tue, and so on).
w	Numeric representation of the day of the week (0 = Sunday, 6 = Saturday).

Character	Description
Year	
y	Two-digit year.
Y	Four-digit year.
Hour	
h	Hour in 12-hour format, with leading zero (two digits).
g	Hour in 12-hour format (no leading zero).
H	Hour in 24-hour format, with leading zero (two digits).
G	Hour in 24-hour format (no leading zero).
a	am/pm (lowercase).
A	AM/PM (uppercase).
O (uppercase o)	String representation of the difference in hours between local time and GMT/UTC (for example, +1000, –0500).
Minute	
i	Minute, with leading zero (two digits).
j	Minute (no leading zero).
Second	
s	Second, with leading zero (two digits).
Z	Integer representation of the difference in seconds between local time and GMT/UTC (for example, 36000 for GMT+1000 and –18000 for GMT–0500).
Complete Date and Time	
c	ISO-8601 format (*YYYY-MM-DDTHH:MM:SS±HHMM*, for example, 2005-03-14T19:38:08+10:00).
r	RFC-2822 format *WWW, DD MMM YYYY HH:MM:SS ±HHMM*, for example, Mon, 14 Mar 2005 19:38:08 +1000).
U	Seconds since the Unix epoch. Calling date('U') with no timestamp argument produces the same output as the time() function.

We will discuss some additional date() formatting characters in recipes 5-5, 5-9, and 5-12.

The difference between local time and GMT/UTC is always positive for points east of Greenwich and always negative for locations to its west. For example, Eastern Australia Standard Time is GMT+1000 and U.S. Eastern Standard Time is GMT–0500, as shown in Figure 5-1.

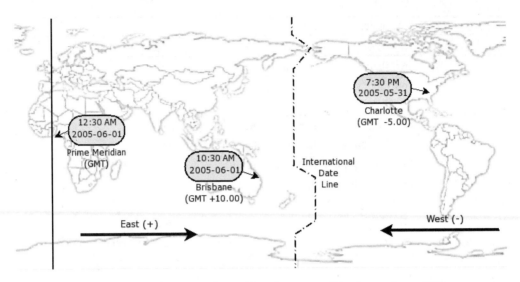

Figure 5-1. *Points east of Greenwich add to GMT; points west of it subtract from GMT.*

5-2. Displaying Arbitrary Dates and Times

Displaying arbitrary dates and times requires passing the Unix timestamp for the desired date and time to the date() function as its second parameter. As already mentioned, you can obtain this with mktime(), which is pretty straightforward to use. In this example, you can get the Unix timestamp for 6:30 p.m. on August 10, 1997, and test the result by passing it to the date() function.

The Code

```php
<?php
  $timestamp = mktime(18, 30, 0, 8, 10, 1997);
  echo date('r (T)', $timestamp);
?>
```

How It Works

The output from this on our server is as follows:

```
Sun, 10 Aug 1997 18:30:00 +1000 (E. Australia Standard Time)
```

Of course, if the locale for your machine is different, you will see something different in place of +1000 (E. Australia Standard Time). Note that the string supplied for T probably will vary according to your operating system and other environmental factors.

■**Tip** The rules for daylight-saving time vary from country to country and are not necessarily uniform even within countries. (For example, Arizona in the United States and Queensland in Australia do not observe day-light-saving time.) In the Southern hemisphere, the height of the summer comes in late December (when it is mid-winter in the United States and Europe), and daylight-saving time in those countries is generally observed from October through March. Helsinki and Johannesburg are both in the GMT +0200 time zone, but in July, Helsinki is an hour ahead of Johannesburg because of Summer Time (daylight-saving time) in Europe; in January, it is the other way around. A good starting place for more information about daylight-saving time and when it is in effect for different countries and regions is `http://webexhibits.org/daylightsaving/g.html`.

5-3. Converting Human-Readable Dates Into Unix Timestamps Using strtotime()

Of course, you are not limited to employing `mktime()` to obtain a timestamp for use with the `date()` function. You can also convert dates in the form of English-language strings into Unix timestamps using the `strtotime()` function. This function is surprisingly flexible and can accept nearly any sensible string as an argument:

- You can use two-digit years (00–69 = 2000s, 70–99 = 1900s) and four-digit years. An unformatted four-digit number in isolation will be treated as a time; that is, 2004 used by itself will be interpreted as 20:04 (8:04 p.m.).

- Numeric days and months are accepted in either one- or two-digit formats. Note that numbers cannot be spelled out.

- You can use names of months in full or the standard three- and four-letter abbreviations for months. For instance, both 24 Sep 1990 and 24 September 1990 will be interpreted correctly.

- Days of the week are allowed, either spelled out in full or as three-letter abbreviations.

- Numeric dates in the formats [[yy]y]y-[m]m-[d]d or [m]m/[d]d/[yy]yy are permitted. That is, 05-01-25, 05-1-5, and 2005-1-05 are all interpreted as January 5, 2005, and so are 01/05/05 and 1/5/2005. Unformatted five- or six-digit numbers will be interpreted as a date in (y)y-mm-dd format; 020430 and 20430 will both be resolved to the time-stamp equivalent of April 30, 2002. (A single digit in the year position will be taken to mean the year ending in that digit from the current decade.)

- If you need a timestamp for the beginning of a month, *do not* use a zero for the day of the month; this will be parsed as the last day of the previous month. Use 1 or 01 as the first day of the month.

- You can use 24-hour times and 12-hour times with the *am/pm* or *AM/PM* indicator. Leading zeroes are optional for hours, minutes, and seconds, which must be separated with a colon (:).

- You can use units such as *hour, day, week, fortnight, month, year,* and so on, and the symbols + and - (the + is optional) along with numerals to indicate future and past. Note that any numbers you use in this fashion cannot be spelled out.

- You can use many (English-speaking!) ordinary words relating to dates and times, such as *now, last, today, yesterday, ago,* and so on.

The following example shows how this works.

The Code

```
<table>
<?php
  $mydatestrings = array(
                    "now", "today", "tomorrow", "yesterday",
                    "Thursday", "this Thursday", "last Thursday",
                    "+2 hours", "-1 month", "+10 minutes",
                    "30 seconds", "+2 years -1 month", "next week",
                    "last month", "last year", "2 weeks ago"
                  );

  // remember: strtotime() returns a timestamp
  foreach($mydates as $mydate)
    echo "<tr><td>$mydate:</td><td>" . date('r', strtotime($mydate)) .
         "</td></tr>\n";
?>
</table>
```

How It Works

The output of this loop in a browser is as follows (for the time, date, and time zone shown in the first line):

```
now:                 Tue, 15 Mar 2005 15:23:52 +1000
today:               Tue, 15 Mar 2005 15:23:52 +1000
tomorrow:            Wed, 16 Mar 2005 15:23:52 +1000
yesterday:           Mon, 14 Mar 2005 15:23:52 +1000
Thursday:            Thu, 17 Mar 2005 00:00:00 +1000
this Thursday:       Thu, 17 Mar 2005 00:00:00 +1000
last Thursday:       Thu, 10 Mar 2005 00:00:00 +1000
+2 hours:            Tue, 15 Mar 2005 17:23:52 +1000
-1 month:            Tue, 15 Feb 2005 15:23:52 +1000
+10 minutes:         Tue, 15 Mar 2005 15:33:52 +1000
-3 weeks:            Tue, 22 Feb 2005 15:23:52 +1000
+2 years -1 month: Thu, 15 Feb 2007 15:51:46 +1000
last month:          Tue, 15 Feb 2005 15:23:52 +1000
last year:           Mon, 15 Mar 2004 15:23:52 +1000
2 weeks ago:         Tue, 1 Mar 2005 16:05:24 +1000
```

As you can see, it is even possible to combine some of these. For example, `-1 year -1 month` will produce the same results as `-13 months`. Also note that the *s* suffix for the plural forms is optional, so `-13 month` will produce the same result as `-13 months`.

Caution You can use the word *next* with `strtotime()`, but this can be interpreted a bit oddly, in that it will sometime skip a unit. For example, given the current date March 15, 2005 (a Tuesday), then `next Friday` will yield Friday, March 25, 2005, which is probably what you would expect, given that most people would refer to Friday, March 18 as *this* Friday, but `next year` will return a date in 2007 rather than 2006. This behavior is known to occur in PHP versions 4.3.0 through 5.0.3.

Note Generally speaking, relative words relating to time were misinterpreted in PHP versions through and including 5.0.2, and timestamps derived by using them were calculated in terms of midnight on the current date. This has been corrected in PHP 5.0.3, which was the current version when this book was written.

5-4. Finding the Date for a Weekday

By combining `date()` and `strtotime()`, it is possible get the day for any desired weekday in a given month. For example, suppose that your firm's sales employees are supposed to turn in their monthly sales reports on the first Tuesday of each month. The following example shows how you can determine the date of the first Tuesday in the month following the current one.

The Code

```php
<?php
  $nextmonth = date('Y-' . (date('n') + 1) . '-01');
  $nextmonth_ts = strtotime($nextmonth);
  $firsttue_ts = strtotime("Tuesday", $nextmonth_ts);
  echo 'Today is ' . date('d M Y') . '.<br />\n';
  echo 'The first Tuesday of next month is ' . date('d M Y', $firsttue_ts) . '.';
?>
```

How It Works

Here is some sample output in a browser:

```
Today is 15 Mar 2005.
The first Tuesday of next month is 05 Apr 2005.
```

Let's step through the script line by line to see what is happening:

`$nextmonth = date('Y-' . (date('n') + 1) . '-01');`: The inner call to date() returns an integer corresponding to the current month, to which you add 1. You then use this as part of the argument to another date() call, which returns the string 2005-4-01.

`$nextmonth_ts = strtotime($nextmonth);`: This stores the timestamp equivalent to 2005-4-01 in $nextmonth_ts.

`$firsttue_ts = strtotime("Tuesday", $nextmonth_ts);`: Using the timestamp just obtained as the second argument to strtotime(), you get a new timestamp, $firsttue_ts. Since the first argument to strttime() is simply the string Tuesday, the function looks for the first date following the date corresponding to $nextmonth_ts that falls on a Tuesday. (As you will see in the next example, the range of dates searched includes the original date.) The timestamp corresponding to this date is stored as $firsttue_ts.

`echo 'Today is ' . date('d M Y') . '.<br />\n';`: To provide a basis for comparison, you output the current date in *dd-MM-yyyy* format.

`echo 'The first Tuesday of next month is ' . date('d M Y', $firsttue_ts) . '.';`: Finally, you feed the $firsttue_ts timestamp to date() and output the result in *dd-MM-yyyy* format.

Variations

"All this is nice," you might be saying, "but what happens when the current month is December?" As it turns out, that's not a problem: PHP's time and date functions are fairly forgiving when it comes to arguments that are out of range. Let's put this assertion to the test by creating a list of the first Tuesdays in each of the next 12 months:

```php
<?php
  echo 'Today is ' . date('d M Y') . '.';

  for($i = 1; $i <= 12; $i++)
  {
    $nextmonth = date('Y-' . (date('n') + $i) . '-01');
    $nextmonth_ts = strtotime($nextmonth);
    $firsttue_ts = strtotime("Tuesday", $nextmonth_ts);

    echo '\n<br />The first Tuesday in ' . date('F', $firsttue_ts)
        . ' is ' . date('d M Y', $firsttue_ts) . '.';
  }
?>
```

This is similar to the previous example, except that you add a successively larger integer to the result of the call to date('n') each time through the loop. Here is the output of this script when it was run on March 15, 2005:

```
Today is 15 Mar 2005.
The first Tuesday of April is 05 Apr 2005.
The first Tuesday of May is 03 May 2005.
The first Tuesday of June is 07 Jun 2005.
The first Tuesday of July is 05 Jul 2005.
The first Tuesday of August is 02 Aug 2005.
The first Tuesday of September is 06 Sep 2005.
The first Tuesday of October is 04 Oct 2005.
The first Tuesday of November is 01 Nov 2005.
The first Tuesday of December is 06 Dec 2005.
The first Tuesday of January is 03 Jan 2006.
The first Tuesday of February is 07 Feb 2006.
The first Tuesday of March is 07 Mar 2006.
```

When the number corresponding to the month is set to 13, the month and year roll over to January 2006. PHP handles this internally, so you do not have to worry about it.

Let's conclude this section by writing a generic function to find the Xth weekday of a given month:

```php
<?php
  function find_weekday($month, $year, $weekday, $offset=1)
  {
    $month_ts = strtotime("$year-$month-01");

    if(--$offset > 0)
      $month_ts = strtotime("+$offset week", $month_ts);

    $month_ts = strtotime($weekday, $month_ts);

    return $month_ts;
  }
?>
```

This function takes four arguments: $month and $year are both integers, and $month is the number for the desired month. The string $day is the name or three-letter abbreviation for the day of the week. The optional fourth argument, $offset, determines whether to look for the first such weekday in the month, the second, and so on, and defaults to a value of 1. The return value is a timestamp representing the desired date.

Let's test this function by finding the first, second, third, and fourth Fridays in May 2000:

```php
<?php
    // (find_weekday() function as defined previously goes here...)
    // omit optional $offset; should be 1st Friday
    echo date('d M Y', find_weekday(5, 2000, "Friday")) . "<br />";
    // specify the 1st Friday explicitly
    echo date('d M Y', find_weekday(5, 2000, "Friday", 1)) . "<br />";
    // 2nd Friday, using the 3-letter abbreviation
    echo date('d M Y', find_weekday(5, 2000, "Fri", 2)) . "<br />";
    // 3rd and 4th Fridays
    echo date('d M Y', find_weekday(5, 2000, "Friday", 3)) . "<br />";
    echo date('d M Y', find_weekday(5, 2000, "Friday", 4));
?>
```

When this is run, the result is as follows:

```
05 May 2000
05 May 2000
12 May 2000
19 May 2000
26 May 2000
```

Validating this output is as easy as checking any desktop calendar program, as shown in Figure 5-2.

Figure 5-2. *Fridays in the month of May 2000*

With a small bit of work, you can adapt this function to accept names of months and two-digit years instead of the argument types specified here or (by testing the argument types and branching appropriately) even in addition to those.

Finding the day of the week for a given date is even easier. If you want the result as a string, you can use date('D', $ts) or date('l', $ts), where $ts is a timestamp corresponding to the desired date. For example, to find the day of the week on which July 4 will fall in 2007, you can use something such as this:

```php
$ts = strtotime('04 Jul 2007');
```

or this:

```
$ts = mktime(0, 0, 0, 7, 4, 2007);
```

followed by either this:

```
$day = date('D', $ts);  //  $day = 'Wed'
```

or this:

```
$day = date('l', $ts);  //  $day = 'Wednesday';
```

If you need the name of this day in a language other than English, you can call setlocale() with the appropriate language/locale string and then use strftime('%a', $ts) (abbreviated) or strftime('%A', $ts) (full weekday name). We will discuss some localization issues in recipes 5-12 and 5-13.

To obtain a number corresponding to the day of the week, use getdate() instead:

```
<?php
  $ts = strtotime('04 Jul 2007');  // or: $ts = mktime(0, 0, 0, 7, 4, 2007);
  $gd = getdate($ts);
  $day = $gd["wday"];  //  $day = 3;
```

Do not forget that getdate() reports the weekday number as 0–6, corresponding to Sunday–Saturday.

■Tip For a complete description of date and time formats accepted by strtotime(), see Chapter 7 of the GNU Tar Manual at http://www.gnu.org/software/tar/manual/html_chapter/tar_7.html.

5-5. Getting the Day and Week of the Year

Obtaining the day of the year is fairly simple; you need use only a lowercase z in the first argument to the date() function.

The Code

```
<?php
  $mydates = array('2005-01-01', '2005-06-30', '2005-12-31');

  foreach($mydates as $mydate)
  {
    $ts = strtotime($mydate);
    echo 'Day ' . date('d M Y: z', $ts) . "<br />\n";
  }
?>
```

How It Works

This shows the output, which illustrates a little "gotcha":

```
01 Jan 2005: Day 0
30 Jun 2005: Day 180
31 Dec 2005: Day 364
```

The numbering of the days of the year as derived using date('z') begins with 0, which means you will likely need to add 1 to the result before displaying it.

Getting the number of the week in the year is also quite simple: all that is required is to pass an uppercase *W* as a formatting character to date(). This brief example illustrates its use and what to expect from it in the way of output:

```php
<?php
    $mydates = array('2005-01-01', '2005-01-03', '2005-05-22', '2005-05-23',
                        '2005-12-31');

    foreach($mydates as $mydate)
        echo date("D d M Y: \w\e\e\k W", strtotime($mydate)) . "<br />\n";
?>
```

Notice how the characters making up the word week have been escaped using backslashes in order to prevent them from being parsed as formatting characters. Since w is the only formatting character in the word week, this could have been written as \week, but we prefer to escape *all* letter characters that are not to be parsed, for two reasons:

- Doing so helps make your scripts forward-compatible. In the event that new formatting characters are added in future releases—as c was in PHP 5—you do not have to worry about your date() calls producing output you never intended at a later, well, date.

- Unless you know all the formatting characters by heart (and we freely admit that we do not remember them all), it saves you the time of checking the list in the PHP manual to make sure that you do not use one accidentally.

This shows what happens when you run the script:

```
Sat 01 Jan 2005: week 53
Mon 03 Jan 2005: week 1
Sun 22 May 2005: week 20
Mon 23 May 2005: week 21
Sat 31 Dec 2005: week 52
```

If the first line of the output looks a bit strange, it is because week numbers are calculated according to the ISO-8601 standard, which means Monday is considered the first day of the week, and week 1 of the year is the first *full* week of the year, that is, the first week containing a Monday. For a year beginning on a day other than Monday, any days prior to the first Monday in January are considered to be part of week 53 from the previous year.

■**Tip** For a good overview of the ISO-8601 standard for dates and times, see Marcus Kuhn's summary at http://www.cl.cam.ac.uk/~mgk25/iso-time.html.

5-6. Determining Whether a Given Year Is a Leap Year

The date() function employs another one-letter argument; it uses *L* to determine if a given year is a leap year. When this is used, date() returns 1 if the year in question is a leap year and 0 if it is not. Rather than make repeated calls to date() and strtotime(), you can wrap this in a simple function that takes the year to be tested as an argument, as shown in the following example.

The Code

```php
<?php
  //  takes a 2- or 4-digit year,
  //  returns 1 or 0
  function is_leap_year($year)
  {
    $ts = strtotime("$year-01-01");
    return date('L', $ts);
  }

  //  test the function for a set of 11 consecutive years
  for($i = 2000; $i <= 2010; $i++)
  {
    $output = "$i is ";
    if( !is_leap_year($i) )
      $output .= "not ";
    $output .= "a leap year.<br />\n";

    echo $output;
  }
?>
```

How It Works

The result of the test loop is as follows:

```
2000 is a leap year.
2001 is not a leap year.
2002 is not a leap year.
2003 is not a leap year.
2004 is a leap year.
2005 is not a leap year.
2006 is not a leap year.
```

2007 is not a leap year.
2008 is a leap year.
2009 is not a leap year.
2010 is not a leap year.

A final note regarding leap years: you should remember that years ending in 00 are leap years *only* if the first two digits of the year taken as a two-digit number are evenly divisible by 4. This means that although 2000 was a leap year (20 % 4 = 0), 1900 and 2100 are not (19 % 4 = 3; 21 % 4 = 1).

5-7. Getting Times and Dates of Files

PHP supplies the function getlastmod() that returns the time and date the current file was last modified in the form of a Unix timestamp that can be used with date(), as shown in the following example.

The Code

```
<?php
  echo 'This file was last updated on '
        . date('l d F Y, \a\t H:i:s T', getlastmod())
        . '.';
?>
```

How It Works

The sample output is as follows:

```
This file was last updated on Wednesday 16 March 2005, at 15:07:33
E. Australia Standard Time.
```

Variations and Fixes

However, getlastmod() can have problems on some servers, which arise when PHP and Apache are compiled with different values for the –DFILE_OFFSET_BITS variable. (Do not worry about what this actually means, but if the values you are getting for the last modified date seem to be off, this is probably why. Ask your server administrator to be sure.) In this case, you can use the following workaround:

```
<?php
  $lastmod = filemtime($_SERVER['SCRIPT_FILENAME']);
  echo 'This file was last updated on '
        . date('l d F Y, \a\t H:i:s T', $lastmod)
        . '.';
?>
```

`filemtime()` returns a Unix timestamp, so this will produce the same sort of output as the version using `getlastmod()` did. You can also use this technique to obtain the last modified date and time for a file other than the current one:

```php
<?php
  $file = "testfile.html";
  echo "The file <b>$file</b> was last updated on "
        . date('l d F Y, \a\t H:i:s T', filemtime("./$file"))
        . '.';
?>
```

The `stat()` function also returns Unix timestamps for the date and time data that it provides relating to files:

```php
<?php
  $file = 'testfile.html';
  $data = stat($file);

  $accessed = $data['atime'];
  $modified = $data['mtime'];
  $created = $data['ctime'];

  echo "The file <b>$file</b> was...<br />\n"
        . 'last accessed ' . date('l d F Y, \a\t H:i:s', $accessed) . ',<br />\n'
        . 'last modified ' . date('l d F Y, \a\t H:i:s', $modified) . ',<br />\n'
        . 'and created ' . date('l d F Y, \a\t H:i:s', $created)
        . '.';
?>
```

The output of this script might look something like this:

```
The file testfile.html was...
last accessed Wednesday 16 March 2005, at 17:34:57,
last modified Wednesday 16 March 2005, at 17:34:57,
and created Wednesday 16 March 2005, at 17:08:02.
```

In sum, you can use the values provided by `getlastmod()`, `filemtime()`, and `stat()` with `date()` in the same way you can use the values obtained from `time()` and `mktime()`. You should be able to turn the previous code snippet into a reusable function that takes the filename and path as its argument and outputs the information it provides in a format of your choosing. You might even want to consider making it a method of a `File` class; see Chapter 7 for more ideas and examples of this sort.

5-8. Setting Time Zones and GMT/UTC

The time(), mktime(), and strtotime() functions return timestamps based on the server's local time. This is fine if your PHP application lives on an intranet or the majority of your users are in the same time zone as your server. However, consider the situation we found ourselves in when building an e-commerce site hosted on a server located in the United States for an Australian client (who was in a different time zone in Australia from us). The client did not want his customers (all in eastern Australia) to have to contend with times that were 15 or 16 hours different from their own. This presented a type of problem you may encounter.

You might think of solving this by adding or subtracting the difference between the server time and that of your users whenever you need to display times and dates to them. However, this is likely to become cumbersome and error-prone, even if you write your own wrapper functions to handle the differences. Fortunately, you can handle this in a much easier way. You can change the effective time zone for a PHP script using a single function call, as shown here:

```
putenv('TZ=Australia/Melbourne');
```

Let's look at this in action in a slightly more complete example.

The Code

```php
<?php
  $ts = time();

  echo date('r', $ts) . "<br />\n";

  putenv('TZ=Australia/Melbourne');
  echo date('r', $ts) . "<br />\n";
?>
```

How It Works

When we ran this script on a Linux server observing U.S. Eastern Standard Time, this was the result:

```
Wed, 16 Mar 2005 06:49:31 -0500
Wed, 16 Mar 2005 22:49:31 +1100
```

That was pretty easy, was it not? In general, you can use the name of the country and the nearest large city in the same time zone, separated by a slash, for the TZ value. These values are not standardized (they can vary slightly even between different Linux distributions), so you may have to experiment. If all else fails, consult the documentation for your operating system or a C programming manual for developers who write software for the platform on which your server runs.

■Caution A significant difference exists in the behavior between Unix and Windows platforms when using putenv() to adjust the time zone setting. On Unix, the change remains in effect for the duration of the current script only, and you must make a new call to putenv() at the beginning of each PHP page. On Windows, once the time zone setting is changed using putenv(), the server ignores any subsequent attempts to change the time zone in this way, and the new setting remains in effect until the web server is restarted. This is true whether you are running Apache or IIS.

Variations and Fixes

You should be aware of one potential stumbling block. It is possible for PHP to be configured so that scripts cannot change this setting. If the safe_mode_protected_env_vars configuration variable includes the TZ variable and safe mode is enabled, then you cannot change the time zone using putenv().

When your site has visitors from many different time zones, and especially if your audience is likely to be somewhat more technically savvy than the norm, you might want to display dates and times using GMT/UTC. To get a GMT timestamp for the current GMT time and date, just use the gmmktime() function, which acts identically to and takes the same arguments as mktime(), with two exceptions:

- The optional is_dst argument has no effect on the return value.

- The return value is a Unix timestamp representing the equivalent to the GMT time values passed to gmmktime().

The second item may be a bit confusing, so let's illustrate it with this example:

```php
<?php
  echo 'Output of <code>mktime()</code>: ' . mktime() . ".<br>\n";
  echo 'Output of <code>gmmktime()</code>: ' . gmmktime() . ".<br>\n";
  echo 'Local time zone: ' . date('O') . ".<br>\n";
?>
```

The output from this bit of code is as follows:

```
Output of mktime(): 1111041977.
Output of gmmktime(): 1111077977.
Local time zone: +1000.
```

This is what is happening: in the absence of any other arguments, both mktime() and gmmktime() base their output on the current local (system) time. Notice that the server's time zone is GMT plus ten hours, so PHP adds this amount of time to what is produced by mktime() in order to arrive at a value to return for gmmktime(). Here is the same code run on a server keeping U.S. Eastern Standard Time:

```
Output of mktime(): 1111043160.
Output of gmmktime(): 1111025160.
Local timezone: -0500.
```

In this case, the local time is GMT minus five hours, so PHP subtracts 5 * 3600 = 18,000 seconds from the local timestamp to derive the output of gmmktime(). In other words, PHP uses the local date and time value for *both* functions but with different time zone settings: the timestamp corresponding to 5:02 p.m. on March 17, 2005, Eastern Australian Time (GMT+1000) is 1111043160 (the value returned by mktime()), and the timestamp corresponding to 5:02 p.m. on March 17, 2005, GMT is 1111025160 (the value returned by gmmktime()).

The reason we are taking a somewhat circuitous route in explaining this is in order to clear up a common misconception. Those who are new to working with dates and times in PHP often seem to think that gmmktime() returns a GMT timestamp for a set of local date and time values. In other words, they think, "gmmktime() will give me the timestamp for the GMT corresponding to the current time on my server." In fact, what gmmktime() does is to give the timestamp for the current local clock time as if that were the current GMT time.

■**Tip** mktime() actually produces a GMT timestamp. Keep that thought in mind—we will cover it in a moment, in this recipe, and use it in the next few recipes as well.

We will now talk about another PHP function, gmdate(), which is a GMT-specific function analogous to date(). Like date(), it takes a format string and an optional timestamp as arguments. It returns a GMT time and date string. Some potential for confusion exists when it comes to using date(), gmdate(), mktime(), and gmmktime() in combination. To make this clearer, the following expands the previous example:

```php
<?php
    echo 'Output of <code>mktime()</code>: ' . mktime() . ".<br>\n";
    echo 'Output of <code>gmmktime()</code>: ' . gmmktime() . ".<br>\n";
    echo 'Local timezone: ' . date('O') . ".<br>\n";
    echo 'date/mktime: ' . date('r', mktime()) . ".<br>\n";
    echo 'date/gmmktime: ' . date('r', gmmktime()) . ".<br>\n";
    echo 'gmdate/mktime: ' . gmdate('r', mktime()) . ".<br>\n";
    echo 'gmdate/gmmktime' . gmdate('r', gmmktime()) . ".<br>\n";
?>
```

When you run this on two servers set to different time zones, you will see something like Figure 5-3.

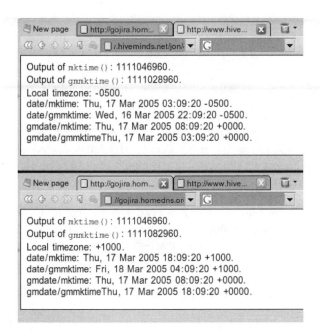

Figure 5-3. *The* date()/gmdate()/mktime()/gmktime() *matrix*

In both cases, the correct local time is displayed using the timestamp produced by mktime() with the date() function *or* the timestamp produced by gmmktime() with gmdate(). The current GMT date and time is displayed when you use the timestamp produced by mktime() as the second argument to gmdate(). As you can see, it is the same on both servers.

Caution We have worked on a couple of Red Hat Linux servers running various 4.*x* versions of PHP where the time() function did not produce the same timestamp values as mktime() and strtotime() but was an hour ahead of them. We have not observed this behavior on any installation of PHP 5, but it cannot hurt to play it safe and check for this when starting development work on a given PHP installation for the first time. Other than this case, all three functions produce a timestamp based on local time, which can be used with gmdate() or gmstrftime() to output a current GMT/UTC time and date string.

5-9. Displaying Times and Dates in Other Languages

So far, all the date and time output has been in English. From the point of view of someone for whom English is the primary language, this is not necessarily a bad thing. However, quite a lot of people in the world use other languages and prefer to use websites in those languages. You do not want to display something like "Guten Morgen! Heute is Monday, der 15th March" to users of a German-language news portal any more than English-speaking users would want to see something like "Good Morning! It's Montag, the 15. of März" on an English-language site!

You might consider writing your own functions to deal with this type of situation, but this is not very appealing, not only because it is extra work for a German-language site but because the same task would then have to be repeated for each language. Fortunately, a much better way to accomplish this task exists. You can use the setlocale() function to change PHP's language and related settings in a number of ways. Here you are concerned primarily with how dates and times are represented, but if internationalization is of any concern to you in your work with PHP, you should investigate this function more thoroughly.

setlocale() takes two arguments: a *category* (a predefined constant) and a *language code* (a string). To localize time and date settings, you can use either LC_ALL or LC_TIME for the category.

You can determine whether the locale was set successfully by testing the return value of setlocale(), which is either the language string on success or FALSE on failure. The languages or locales actually supported will vary from system to system; if you cannot find a value for a desired language or locale, check with your system administrator or consult the operating system documentation. On Unix systems, you can often find out what is supported by examining the contents of the /usr/share/locale directory. On Windows, use Regional Settings in the Control Panel.

If you do not know ahead of time what is supported, you can pass multiple language/locale strings to setlocale(), and PHP will test each one in succession until (you hope) one is used successfully. For example:

```php
<?php
  if($lc = setlocale(LC_ALL, "de_DE", "de_DE@euro", "deu", "deu_deu", "german"))
    echo "<p>Locale setting is \"$lc\".</p>";
  else
    echo "<p>Couldn't change to a German locale.</p>";
?>
```

Once you have set the locale, you are ready to output dates and times in the target language without resorting to brute-force translation (and possible transliteration). However, you cannot use date() for this. Instead, you must use a separate function, strftime(). This function is similar to date() in that it takes a format string and an optional timestamp as arguments. Unfortunately, the similarity ends there, because the formatting characters are quite unlike those used by date(). Table 5-3 lists the characters you are most likely to need, arranged by the part of the date or time they represent. Note that not all of these are available on all platforms, and Windows has some of its own. See http://msdn.microsoft.com/library/en-us/vclib/html/_crt_strftime.2c_.wcsftime.asp for a complete listing.

Table 5-3. *Format Characters Used by the* strftime() *Function*

Character	Description
Day	
%A	Full weekday name.
%a	Abbreviated weekday name.
%u	Weekday number (1 = Monday, 7 = Saturday).
%d	Day of the month, with leading zero.

Character	Description
%e	Day of the month, with leading space.
%j	Day of the year (001–366). Note that numbering begins with 1 and not 0.
Week	
%U	Number of the week of the year, with Sunday as the first day of the week.
%V	ISO-8601 number of the week of the year, with Monday as the first day of the week (01–53).
%W	Number of the week of the year, with Monday as the first day of the week (decimal number).
Month	
%B	Full name of the month.
%b or %h	Abbreviated name of the month.
%m	Number of the month, with leading zero.
Year	
%g	Two-digit year for ISO-8601 week of the year.
%G	Four-digit year for ISO-8601 week of the year.
%y	Two-digit year.
%Y	Four-digit year.
Hour	
%H	Hour (00–23).
%I	Hour (01–12)
Minute	
%M	Minute.
Second	
%S	Second.
Full Date and/or Time	
%c	Preferred date and time representation for the current locale.
%D	Current date; equivalent to %m/%d/%y.
%p	a.m./p.m. indicator.
%R	Time in 24-hour notation.
%r	Time in 12-hour (am/pm) notation.
%T	Current time; equivalent to %H:%M:%S.
%x	Preferred date representation.
%X	Preferred time representation.
%z or %Z	Time zone.
Formatting Characters	
%n	New line.
%t	Tab.
%%	The percent character.

Now you are ready to put this together in a simple working example. Actually, since browsers have problems displaying more than one character set in a single page, we will use three examples.

The Code

```php
<?php
  if($loc_de = setlocale(LC_ALL, 'de_DE@euro', 'de_DE', 'deu_deu'))
  {
    echo "<p>Preferred locale for German on this system is \"$loc_de\".<br />";
    echo 'Guten Morgen! Heute ist ' . strftime('%A %d %B %Y', mktime()) . ".</p>\n";
  }
  else
    echo "<p>Sorry! This system doesn't speak German.</p>\n";
?>
```

```php
<?php
  if($loc_ru = setlocale(LC_ALL, 'ru_RU.utf8', 'rus_RUS.1251', 'rus', 'russian'))
  {
    echo "<p>Preferred locale for Russian on this system is \"$loc_ru\".<br />\n";
    echo '&#x0414&#x043E&#x0431&#x0440&#x043E&#x0435 '
      . '&#x0423&#x0442&#x0440&#x043E! '
      . '&#x0421&#x0435&#x0433&#x043E&#x0434&#x043D&#x044F '
      . strftime('%A %d %B %Y', mktime()) . ".</p>\n";
  }
  else
    echo "<p>Couldn't set a Russian locale.</p>\n";
?>
```

```php
<?php
  if($loc_zh = setlocale(LC_ALL, 'zh_ZH.big5', 'zh_ZH', 'chn', 'chinese'))
  {
    echo "<p>Preferred locale for Chinese on this system is \"$loc_zh\".<br />\n";
    echo '???! ???... ' . strftime('%A %d %B %Y', mktime()) . ".</p>\n";
  }
  else
  {
    echo "<p>Sorry! No Chinese locale available on this system.</p>\n";
    $lc_en = setlocale(LC_TIME, 'en_US', 'english');
    echo "<p>Reverting locale to $lc_en.</p>\n";
  }
?>
```

How It Works

Figure 5-4 shows the output in a web browser from each of these scripts when run on a
Windows system that supports German and Russian locales but no Chinese locale.

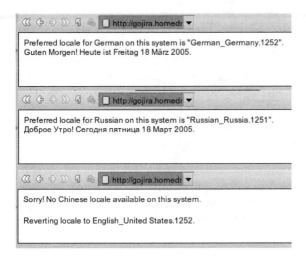

Figure 5-4. *Output from the three* `setlocale()`/`strftime()` *examples*

■**Note** `LC_TIME` changes only the way in which dates and times are reported but does not change other
locale-dependent items such as character sets. If you use an English-language locale and need to display
dates in a language (German or Spanish, for example) that uses the Latin-1 character set or a close relative
such as ISO-8559-1, ISO-8859-15, or Windows-1252, you may be able to use `LC_TIME`. However, in the
case of a language that uses non-Latin characters (such as Russian, Chinese, and some Eastern European
languages with special characters not represented in Western European character sets), you will most likely
have to use `LC_ALL`. Be aware that using `setlocale()` with `LC_ALL` will change *all* locale settings, not just
those related to dates and times. If you will be working with currency, numbers, or sorting of strings, be sure
to check the PHP manual for `setlocale()` and understand what all the implications might be before doing so.

The format of the language string differs between Unix and Windows systems. On Unix
systems, this varies somewhat but generally takes the form `lc_CC.charset`, where `lc` represents the two-letter language code, `CC` represents the two-letter country code, and `charset`
is the designation of the character set to be used. (The `charset` designation—including the
period—is often optional.) For example, `pt_BR.ISO-18859-1` might be used to represent Brazil-
ian Portuguese. On Windows, you can use either Microsoft's three-letter language codes or the
names of the languages, for example, `deu` or `german` for German-language dates and times.

5-10. Generating Localized GMT/UTC Time and Date Strings

It is important to remember that using `setlocale()` to set `LC_ALL` or `LC_TIME` does *not* handle time zone differences for you, as this example illustrates:

```php
<?php
  $ts = mktime();
  echo '<p>' . date('r (T)', $ts) . "</p>\n";

  if($loc_de = setlocale(LC_ALL, 'de_DE@euro', 'de_DE', 'deu_deu'))
    echo 'Guten Abend! Heute ist ' . strftime('%A %d %B %Y, %H.%M Uhr', $ts)
    . ".</p>\n";
  else
    echo "<p>Sorry! This system doesn't speak German.</p>\n";
?>
```

The following shows the output for the date and time in standard format, along with the name of the time zone, and then it shows a greeting, date, and time in German. As you can see here, the time may be *in* German, but it is not German time that is being reported:

```
Fri, 18 Mar 2005 17:14:30 +1000 (E. Australia Standard Time)

Guten Abend! Heute ist Freitag 18 März 2005, 17.14 Uhr.
```

To report local time for any Germans who might be viewing this page, you have to calculate the time zone offset yourself:

```php
<?php
  $ts_au = mktime();  //  local time in Brisbane (GMT +1000)
  $ts_de = $ts_au - (9 * 3600);  //  Berlin time is GMT +0100; difference is 9 hours

  echo 'Good evening from Brisbane, where it\'s ' . date('H:m \o\n l d m Y', $ts_au)
       . ".<br />";

  setlocale(LC_ALL, 'de_DE', 'german');

  echo 'Guten Morgen aus Berlin. Hier ist es '
       . strftime('%H.%M Uhr, am %A dem %d %B %Y', $ts_de) . '.';
?>
```

The output from the previous code snippet should look something this:

```
Good evening from Brisbane, where it's 18:03 on Friday 18 03 2005.
Guten Morgen aus Berlin. Hier ist es 09.30 Uhr, am Freitag dem 18 März 2005.
```

To generate a localized GMT/UTC time and date string, you can use the `gmstrftime()` function. It works in the same way as `strftime()`, except it produces a date and time string in accordance with GMT/UTC rather than local time.

Tip For more information about language and other codes that can be used with the `setlocale()` function, see the following URLs:

- C-1766, "Tags for the Identification of Languages": `http://www.faqs.org/rfcs/rfc1766`

- ISO-639, "3-Letter Language Codes": `http://www.w3.org/WAI/ER/IG/ert/iso639.htm`

- You can find identifiers available on Windows systems for languages, countries, and regions here:

  - MSDN, "Language Strings (Visual C++ Libraries)":
    `http://msdn.microsoft.com/library/en-us/vclib/html/_crt_language_strings.asp`

  - MSDN, "Run-Time Library Reference: Country/Region Strings":
    `http://msdn.microsoft.com/library/en-us/vclib/html/_crt_country_strings.asp`

One final note before moving on: most if not all Hypertext Transfer Protocol (HTTP) headers use GMT/UTC dates and times that are expressed in English. Generally speaking, these must conform to the RFC-1123 format *ddd, dd mmm yyyy HH:mm:ss GMT*, such as `Mon, 28 Mar 2005 12:05:30 GMT`. Here is an example showing how to generate a `Content-Expires` header that tells user agents that a page should be considered "stale" exactly ten days after it has been served by your site:

```
header('Expires: ' . gmdate('D, d M Y H:i:s', strtotime("+10 days")) . ' GMT');
```

The same is true for `If-Modified-Since`, `If-Unmodified-Since`, `Last-Modified`, and other time- and date-sensitive HTTP headers. To generate these programmatically, you should always use `gmdate()` and *not* `strftime()` and *not* `gmstrftime()`, as the latter two may contain locale-specific information or be in a language other than English.

Note For definitions of HTTP 1.1 headers, see `http://www.w3.org/Protocols/rfc2616/rfc2616-sec14.html`.

5-11. Obtaining the Difference Between Two Dates

As you have already had the chance to see, altering a date by a given interval is not difficult. Getting the difference between two dates is a bit more complicated.

The Code

```php
<?php
    $date1 = '14 Jun 2002';
    $date2 = '05 Feb 2006';

    $ts1 = strtotime($date1);
    $ts2 = strtotime($date2);

    printf("<p>The difference between %s and %s is %d seconds.<p>\n",
            $date1, $date2, $ts2 - $ts1);
?>
```

How It Works

The output looks like so:

```
The difference between 14 Jun 2002 and 05 Feb 2006 is 115084800 seconds.
```

This *is* an answer, and you can verify that it is a *correct* one (a bit more than three years), but it is not really a *good* answer—unless you know for certain that your users will not object to performing a bit of long division.

Variations and Fixes

Let's create a function that you can use to obtain the difference between two dates and times and to present the results in a manner humans can easily understand. This function, which we will call date_diff(), normally takes one or two arguments, each of which is either an integer representing a timestamp or a time/date string in a format understood by strtotime(). (Actually, it can be called without *any* arguments, but the results will not be terribly interesting or useful; also, you can set an optional third argument to enable debugging output.) This function returns an array consisting of three elements—two arrays and an integer, which will be described for you in a moment.

We are breaking up the code listing here in order to provide some commentary as you read through it, but you can get it in the single file date_diff.php in the chapter5 directory of the code download package that accompanies this book and that you can download for free from the Downloads section of the Apress website at http://www.apress.com/.

```php
<?php
    function date_diff($date1=0, $date2=0, $debug=FALSE)
    {
```

The first task is to check the argument types passed to this function. (Note that they both default to zero.) For each of the values, you check its type using is_numeric(). If it is a number, you treat it as an integer and thus a timestamp; otherwise, you treat it as a string to be passed to strtotime(). In production, you may want to perform some additional checks (for instance, on a Windows system, you need to make sure that neither of the first two arguments represents a date prior to the Unix epoch), but this is sufficient for the current purposes.

Once you have decided how to handle the input parameters and have converted any strings to timestamps, you assign the timestamps to the variables $val1 and $val2 and then subtract one from the other. To avoid problems with negative values, you can actually obtain the absolute value of the difference. This value is then assigned to the variable $sec.

```php
$val1 = is_numeric($date1) ? $date1 : strtotime($date1);
$val2 = is_numeric($date2) ? $date2 : strtotime($date2);

$sec = abs($val2 - $val1);

//  **DEBUG **
if($debug)
  printf("<p>Date 1: %s ... Date2: %s</p>\n",
          date('r', $val1), date('r', $val2));
```

The reason for getting the absolute value is so that you can pass it to getdate(), assigning the value that is returned by this function to the variable $units. You also create an array named $output, which you will use for storing the data to be returned from this function.

```php
$units = getdate($sec);

//  **DEBUG**
if($debug)
  printf("<pre>%s</pre>\n", print_r($units, TRUE));

$output = array();
```

Before continuing, let's see what sort of data $units contains at this point by calling the function with the $debug argument set to TRUE:

```php
<?php
  date_diff('12 Sep 1984 13:30:00', '10 Sep 1984 09:15:45', TRUE');
?>
```

This is the output:

```
Date 1: Wed, 12 Sep 1984 13:30:00 +1000 ... Date2: Mon, 10 Sep 1984 09:15:45 +1000

Array
(
    [seconds] => 15
    [minutes] => 14
    [hours] => 14
    [mday] => 3
    [wday] => 6
    [mon] => 1
    [year] => 1970
    [yday] => 2
    [weekday] => Saturday
    [month] => January
    [0] => 188055
)
```

We also need to talk about the output from this function. As we have said already, the return value is an array consisting of three elements:

components: This is an array whose elements are the difference between the dates when expressed as a single quantity broken down into years, months, days, hours, minutes, and seconds. Given the two dates shown previously, you would expect this to be 0 years, 0 months, 2 days, 4 hours, 14 minutes, and 15 seconds. But some obvious discrepancies exist between those values shown; we will return to this issue and discuss these shortly.

elapsed: This element is also an array, whose elements are named for years, months, weeks, days, hours, minutes, and seconds. However, each of these is a stand-alone value; in other words, the elements of this array will—in the case of the dates used previously— make it possible to express the difference as (approximately) .0060 years, *or* 0.073 months, *or* 0.31 weeks, *or* 2.2 days, *or* 52.24 hours, *or* 3,134.25 minutes, *or* 188,055 seconds.

order: This is simply an integer value: -1 if the second date is earlier than the first and 1 if otherwise.

You will look at the complete output of date_diff() a bit later in this recipe. Right now, we will discuss how to reconcile the output you just saw with what you know ought to go into the array $output["components"]. Keep in mind that what you are doing is treating a value representing elapsed time as though it were a timestamp and using getdate() to get an approximation of the number of years, months, days, and so on, that it breaks down into.

Let's start with the hours, because they are a bit tricky. getdate() handles a timestamp with the same attitude (so to speak) as mktime(), in that the values it returns are calculated in terms of system time. What this means is that the difference in hours between system time and GMT is added to $units["hours"], and you need to subtract the same amount in order to correct for this. You can get the difference in seconds by obtaining date('Z'); then you just divide this amount by 3600 to get the difference in hours and subtract the result from $units["hours"] to find the value for $hours.

```
$hours = $units["hours"] - (date('Z') / 3600);
```

You also have to consider that half the time zones on the planet are negative with respect to GMT, and thus what will actually happen is that some number of hours will be added to $units["hours"]. This means you could end up with a value greater than 24. To handle this possibility, you need to test whether the number of hours is greater than 24; if it is, then you will have to increment the number of days and subtract 24 from $hours:

```
$days = $units["mday"];

while($hours > 23)
{
  $days++;
  $hours -= 24;
}
```

Now you are ready to actually assign values to keys in the $outputs["components"] array. To get an accurate number of years, you need to subtract 1970 (the base year for timestamps) from $units["years"].

■**Note** If your system uses a time zone west of Greenwich (chiefly, the Americas), you will need to take into account that the Unix epoch will be represented as something such as 31 December 1969 19:00:00 for U.S. Eastern Standard Time (GMT–0500). In this case, the value of the years element would be 1969.

Now consider the situation when the time difference between the two dates that were passed to date_diff() is less than one month; getdate() will return a value of 1 for the months, where you actually want a value of 0 (no months elapsed). The same is true of days. Putting this together, you can now assign values to all the elements of $output["components"]:

```
$epoch = getdate(0);   //  the Unix epoch in the server's local time zone
$output["components"] = array(
                        "years"   => $units["year"] - $epoch["year"],
                        "months"  => --$units["mon"],
                        "days"    => --$days,
                        "hours"   => $hours,
                        "minutes" => $units["minutes"],
                        "seconds" => $units["seconds"]
                        );
```

Let's look at the second element in $output, the $output["elapsed"] array. This is actually fairly straightforward, since all that is required is to divide the total number of seconds elapsed by the number of seconds in a year, in a month, in a week, and so on, and assign these values appropriately:

```
$output["elapsed"] = array(
                        "years"   => $sec / (365 * 24 * 60 * 60),
                        "months"  => $sec / (30 * 24 * 60 * 60),
                        "weeks"   => $sec / (7 * 24 * 60 * 60),
                        "days"    => $sec / (24 * 60 * 60),
                        "hours"   => $sec / (60 * 60),
                        "minutes" => $sec / 60,
                        "seconds" => $sec
                        );
```

Finally, you set $output["order"] equal to -1 if the second date is earlier than the first and to 1 if it is not, and then you return the $output array to the calling code:

```
    $output["order"] = $val2 < $val1 ? -1 : 1;

    return $output;
  }
?>
```

Let's test this function with a couple of sample values. Note that you can omit the $debug argument—in fact, you might want to take the debugging portions from the function when using it in production, but we will leave that decision up to you. First we will use print_r() to output a sample array and then write a message that tells the reader exactly how long our last stay in New Zealand was. We have saved the following test file as ch5/date-diff-test.php in this book's code download:

```php
<?php
  require('./date-diff.php');

  $arrived = mktime(11, 30, 0, 6, 9, 2002);
  $departed = mktime(17, 20, 0, 6, 22, 2002);

  $holiday = date_diff($arrived, $departed);

  //  display the entire $holiday array
  printf("<pre>%s</pre>\n", print_r($holiday, TRUE));

  $components = $holiday["components"];

  $output = array();

  //
  foreach($components as $period => $length)
    if($length > 0)
      $output[] = "$length $period";

  printf("<p>My holiday in Auckland began on %s, and lasted %s.</p>\n",
         date('l, jS F Y', $arrived), implode($output, ', '));
?>
```

The following is the output:

```
Array
(
    [components] => Array
        (
            [years] => 0
            [months] => 0
            [days] => 13
            [hours] => 5
            [minutes] => 50
            [seconds] => 0
        )

    [elapsed] => Array
        (
            [years] => 0.036282343987823
            [months] => 0.44143518518519
            [weeks] => 1.8918650793651
            [days] => 13.243055555556
            [hours] => 317.83333333333
```

```
        [minutes] => 19070
        [seconds] => 1144200
    )

    [order] => 1
)
```

My holiday in Auckland began on Sunday, 9th June 2002, and lasted 13 days,
 5 hours, 50 minutes.

Tip If you need to work with dates including years outside the range 1901–2038 on Unix platforms or
1970–2038 on Windows, or if you need to work with negative timestamp values, you might want to try the
ADOdb Date library. This library provides replacements for the regular PHP date and time functions that work
much like their counterparts, except that the function names are all prefixed with adodb_, and a few of the
formatting characters used with date(), gmdate(), strftime(), and gmstrftime() are not supported by
their ADOdb analogs. However, the library adds some extended functionality for setting and tracking daylight-saving time, so it seems a fair trade. You can download this library and read its documentation at
http://phplens.com/phpeverywhere/adodb_date_library.

5-12. Project: Constructing and Using a Date Class

PHP's date functions are quite flexible but can be somewhat frustrating to use. In a recent conversation with a friend who is the author of a popular book on PHP and MySQL, we mentioned
to him that we wanted to include a date-related class or two in this chapter. His response was,
"Great! I hope you'll come up with something that's easier to remember than all those formatting characters—I can't believe how often I still have to look them up."

Lots of formatting characters is not the only issue. date() and gmdate() use a *different* set
of formatting characters than strftime() and gmstrftime(), and there is not a one-to-one cor-
respondence between the two sets. Moving further afield, you will find that the getdate() and
gettimeofday() functions (as well as localtime(), which we did not really cover in this chapter) have made a couple of attempts to offer a more structured representation of a date using
arrays. The problem with these is that the arrays have different structures. Basically, PHP's
date and time functions do not present a unified picture of dates and times, other than them
all relating to Unix timestamps.

In the following sections, we will offer a solution to some of these problems by creating a
couple of date- and time-related classes that expose a well-defined and consistent interface,
as well as methods that are easy to use and to remember.

A Model: The ECMA Date Class

Different programming languages can be better at doing certain things than others. For example, Python provides some extremely powerful functionality for handling arrays (or *lists* and
tuples, as they are known in that language), Perl is handy for string processing, C is good for
building data structures, and so on. We have always found the Date class provided in

JavaScript (or, more properly, EMCAScript) to offer a simple, unambiguous, no-frills way to work with dates. This class, which bears some resemblance to Java 1.0's java.util.Date, is defined in the ECMAScript Standard, third edition, also known as EMCA-262, which can be found at http://www.ecma-international.org/publications/standards/ECMA-262.htm. The class has three properties—all private—and about three dozen public methods that are used to get and set these properties according to different criteria. This may sound like a lot of methods, but they are really quite straightforward. You can see a complete listing of these, as we have adapted them for use in PHP 5, in Figure 5-5.

Date				
Properties				
protected	$time	: int		= 0
protected	$offset	: int		= 0
protected	$UTCDate	: int		= 0
Methods				
public	static parse	($date : string = '' $now : int = mktime()) : int		
public	static UTC	($year : int $month : int $day : int $hours : int = 0 $minutes : int = 0 $seconds : int = 0) : int		
public	__construct	([variable arguments]) : void		
public	__toString	(void) : string		
public	getDate	(void) : int		
public	getDay	(void) : int		
public	getFullYear	(void) : int		
public	getHours	(void) : int		
public	getMinutes	(void) : int		
public	getMonth	(void) : int		
public	getSeconds	(void) : int		
public	getTime	(void) : int		
public	getTimeZoneOffset	(void) : int		
public	getUTCDate	(void) : int		
public	getUTCDay	(void) : int		
public	getUTCFullYear	(void) : int		
public	getUTCHours	(void) : int		
public	getUTCMonth	(void) : int		
public	getUTCSeconds	(void) : int		
public	setDate	($date : int) : int		
public	setFullYear	($year : int) : int		
public	setHours	($hours : int) : int		
public	setMinutes	($minutes : int) : int		
public	setMonth	($month : int) : int		
public	setSeconds	($seconds : int) : int		
public	setTime	($time : int) : int		
public	setTimeZoneOffset	($offset : int) : int		
public	setUTCDate	($date : int) : int		
public	setUTCFullYear	($year : int) : int		
public	setUTCHours	($hours : int) : int		
public	setUTCMinutes	($minutes : int) : int		
public	setUTCMonth	($month : int) : int		
public	setUTCSeconds	($seconds : int) : int		
public	toGMTString	(void) : string		
public	toLocaleString	(void) : string		
public	toUTCString	(void) : string		
public	valueOf	(void) : int		

Figure 5-5. *Base* Date *class members, showing input parameters and return types*

The Date class provides two static methods that we will discuss shortly. All the remaining methods exposed by Date are instance methods and can be grouped according to two different criteria:

- **Get vs. set methods**: Each instance method either gets or sets the value of a different component of a date and time object represented by an instance of Date, such as hours, minutes, years, months, and so on.

- **Local vs. UTC**: Each instance method references a Date object expressed as either a local (system) or as a UTC (GMT) time.

For example, you can obtain the hours portion of a local date and time by calling the corresponding Date object's getHours() method and the same time in terms of UTC by calling its getUTCHours() method. To set the hours portion of a local date and time, call its setHours() method. To set the hours portion of a Date instance in UTC, use the setUTCHours() method.

All Date instance methods, without exception, return integers. No methods are provided for the purpose of adding leading zeroes for single-digit values. And no methods return names of months or days of the week. Times are expressed in 24-hour format only. We will show you how to take care of these last two issues later in this recipe by extending the Date class. Other than in the case of the toLocaleString() method, ECMA-262 dates do not support localization. Because localization in PHP depends on so many factors external to the language itself, we have chosen not to attempt to make provisions for it here; however, we will offer some suggestions on how you might extend Date in different circumstances to accommodate at least some of your localization needs.

One other point needs to be addressed before continuing. If you are familiar with ECMAScript in one or more of its incarnations—browser JavaScript, Flash ActionScript, Microsoft JScript, and so on—then you are probably aware that ECMA-262 dates are stored internally as millisecond timestamps. That is, an ECMAScript date that complies with the specification is supposed to be stored as a number of thousandths of a second elapsed since the Unix epoch. Because PHP does not provide a ready means to obtain milliseconds for any date and time other than the current one, we have chosen to define Date using whole seconds only.

Now let's look at the class; the source code is included in this book's code download package in the file ch5/Date.class.inc.php.

The Code

```php
<?php
//  file: Date.class.inc.php
//  purpose: implements an ECMA-style Date class for PHP 5

class Date
{
```

This defines two class variables, both of which are protected so that they cannot be accessed directly by the user of the class but are accessible by subclasses. (You will see why you want to control access in this fashion later in this chapter in recipe 5-13, when we look at extending the Date class.)

Note If you are not familiar with protected class members, see Chapter 2 for an explanation.

The $time variable stores the local date's internal representation in seconds (a Unix time-stamp). $offset stores the number of minutes by which $time differs from UTC. Note that this value is negative for time zones west of Greenwich.

```
protected $time;
protected $offset;
```

Next, let's look at the two static methods mentioned previously. Date::parse() takes an RFC-1123 date as its argument and returns a timestamp (in seconds). We have used strtotime() to implement this method, so you could in theory use any string accepted by that function, but we advise against doing so.

```
//  STATIC METHODS
public static function parse($date)
{
  return strtotime($date);
}
```

The other static method, Date::UTC(), returns the UTC timestamp in seconds for a local date and time passed to it as a set of three to six arguments. These arguments are as follows, in order:

- $year: A four-digit year.

- $month: The number of the month (January = 0; December = 11). Note that all Date methods number the months of the year beginning with 0.

- $day: The day of the month (1–31).

- $hours: Hours (0–23).

- $minutes: Minutes (0–59).

- $seconds: Seconds (0–59).

The $year, $month, and $day parameters are required. Each of the remaining three arguments is optional, but those that are used must be present in the order listed. Note that this method does not work on Windows for dates/times previous to January 1, 1970, 12 a.m. UTC.

```
public static function UTC($year, $month, $day)
{
  $hours = $minutes = $seconds = 0;
  $num_args = func_num_args();
  if($num_args > 3)
    $hours = func_get_arg(3);
  if($num_args > 4)
    $minutes = func_get_arg(4) + ((int)date('Z') * 60);
  if($num_args > 5)
```

```
    $seconds = func_get_arg(5);
  return mktime($hours, $minutes, $seconds, ($month + 1), $day, $year);
}
```

The Date constructor is a bit tricky to implement in PHP, because (as indicated in Figure 5-4) it can take varying types and numbers of arguments. It has four options in this regard:

- **No arguments**: In this case, the Date instance corresponds to the current local date and time.

- **One argument, of type int**: The argument is interpreted as a local timestamp in seconds.

- **One argument, of type string**: The argument is interpreted as a local date and time in RFC-1123 format (for example, Wed, 8 May 1996 17:46:40 -0500). (See http://www.ietf.org/rfc/rfc1123.txt for details of the specification.)

- **Two to six arguments, all of type int**: Similar to the way in which Date::parse handles its arguments, these are interpreted in the following order:

  - Four-digit year

  - Month (0 = January, 11 = December)

  - Day (0–31)

  - Hours (0–23)

  - Minutes (0–59)

  - Seconds (0–59)

In addition, because you might want to extend this class later, and because you do not know ahead of time what the number and type(s) of argument(s) might be, it is also necessary to allow for the possibility that the arguments might be passed in the form of an array.

The following is the code for the class constructor. No input parameters are specified in the declaration; instead, you will use func_num_args() to find the number of arguments passed to the constructor and the array returned by func_get_args() to access the arguments. (For more about these functions, see Lee Babin's Chapter 11.)

```
// CONSTRUCTOR

  public function __construct()
  {
```

You can determine how many arguments were passed to the constructor with this:

```
$num_args = func_num_args();
```

If the constructor has been called with at least one argument, then you assign the arguments array to a variable named $args:

```
if($num_args > 0)
{
  $args = func_get_args();
```

Here is where you have to perform a bit of sleight of hand. If the Date constructor has been called by a child class of Date, then the Date constructor will have been invoked with a single argument, an array whose elements are the arguments that were passed to the child class constructor. Fortunately, it is not difficult to find out if this is the case: just use the is_array() function to test whether this is so.

Tip When you need to determine a value's type in production code, you should always use the is_*() functions, such as is_array(), is_int(), is_string(), and so on, in preference to gettype(). The reason for this is that the strings returned by gettype() are not guaranteed always to have the same values as PHP evolves. In other words, if you performed a test such as if(gettype($somevar) == 'integer')..., it might work today on your server, but a few versions down the road, or on a different platform, gettype() might return int rather than integer , so the test would fail even if $somevar really does hold an integer value. Writing the test as if(is_int())... avoids this problem.

Here is where the sleight of hand comes in. If the first element of $args is itself an array, then you assign this array to the variable $args and update $num_args to hold the number of arguments in this array.

```
if( is_array($args[0]) )
{
    $args = $args[0];
    $num_args = count($args);
}
```

If $num_args is greater than 1, then you know that multiple arguments representing the different portions of a date (seconds, minutes, hours, day, and so on) were passed to the constructor, and you create and initialize variables to hold these values.

```
if($num_args > 1)
    $seconds = $minutes = $hours = $day = $month = $year = 0;
}
```

Now you can continue, using a switch .... case to set the values of the variables that were passed in, in order. For instance, if six arguments are passed in, then you know the sixth argument corresponds to seconds and assign its value to $seconds; if there are at least five arguments, then you assign the value of the fifth to $minutes, and so on. If there are two arguments, you know they correspond to the month and year, respectively. You might notice that there are no break statements for any of the cases until you reach the case where the number of arguments is equal to 2. At this point, you have set all the temporary variables, so now you can use them in making a call to mktime() and setting the class $time variable to the result.

If a single argument is passed to the constructor, you check to see if it is an integer or a string. If it is an integer, you assume that it is a timestamp and set $time to that value. Otherwise, if it is a string, you assume that it represents an RFC-formatted date, pass this to strtotime(), and set $time equal to the value that is returned by that function. It is important to remember that if the value is neither an integer nor a string, then $time will never get set.

This is something we might fix in a future version of this class—or that you can change your-self if you want—but for now we have left it as it is.

If no arguments are passed to the constructor, then $time is set to the default value returned by mktime() when called without any input parameters. In other words, the resulting Date instance will in this case represent the current system date and time.

```
switch($num_args)
{
  case 6:
    $seconds = $args[5];
  case 5:
    $minutes = $args[4];
  case 4:
    $hours = $args[3];
  case 3:
    $day = $args[2];
  case 2:
    $month = $args[1];
    $year = $args[0];
    $this->time = mktime($hours, $minutes, $seconds, ($month + 1), $day , $year);
    break;
  case 1:
    if( is_int($args[0]) )
    {
      $this->time = $args[0];
    }
    elseif( is_string($args[0]) )
    {
      $this->time = strtotime($args[0]);
    }
    break;
  case 0:
    $this->time = mktime();
    break;
}
```

Now you have two tasks remaining for the constructor: you need to get the time zone off-set, which you can obtain using PHP's built-in gettimeofday() function; as we noted earlier, this function returns an array, so you need to set the class variable $offset to the value of this array's "minuteswest" element. That completes what is required of the constructor.

```
    $temp = gettimeofday();
    $this->offset = (int)$temp["minuteswest"];
  }
```

You may have noticed that it ought to be possible to change the time zone setting for a date and time directly, and it is—the ECMA specification includes appropriate methods for doing this, and as you will see shortly, we have implemented them in this class. But let's not get ahead of ourselves.

Before proceeding to the Date class's get*() and set*() methods, you need to take care of one more ECMA requirement, which is also just a good idea for any class representing a complex data structure. The toString() method should return an implementation-dependent string representation of the local date and time that is human-readable but that *does not* use locale-specific formatting. We have chosen to use a MySQL-style DATETIME for this purpose, which you can derive from the output of date('c') quite easily, as you can see here:

```
public function toString()
{
    return str_replace('T', ' ', date('c', $this->time));
}
```

Now you are ready for some getter methods. The first seven of these are quite straightforward; except in the case of getTime() and getTimeZoneOffset(), all that is necessary is to map each to the appropriate date() call. (You could also use the idate() function for this purpose.) getTime() and getTimeZoneOffset() merely return the values stored as the instance variables $time and $offset, respectively. Note that the ECMA getMilliseconds() method is not implemented (for reasons we have already given). For particulars, see the code comments preceding each method definition.

```
//  returns day of month (1-31)
public function getDate()
{
    return (int)date("j", $this->time);
}


//  returns day of week (0=Sunday, 6=Saturday)
public function getDay()
{
    return (int)date("w", $this->time);
}


//  returns 4-digit year
//  JS 1.0 defined a getYear() method as well, but it has been deprecated
//  in favor of this one because it was not defined or implemented very well
public function getFullYear()
{
    return (int)date("Y", $this->time);
}


//  returns hours field (0-23)
public function getHours()
{
    return (int)date("H", $this->time);
}


//  returns minutes field (0-59)
public function getMinutes()
{
```

```
    return (int)date("i", $this->time);
  }


  // returns month (0=January, 11=December)
  public function getMonth()
  {
    $temp = (int)date("n", $this->time);
    return --$temp;
  }


  // returns seconds field (0-59)
  public function getSeconds()
  {
    return (int)date("s", $this->time);
  }


  // returns a complete Date as elapsed seconds
  // since the Unix epoch (midnight on January 1, 1970, UTC)
  // note that this is not actually ECMA-compliant since
  // it returns seconds and not milliseconds
  public function getTime()
  {
    return $this->time;
  }


  // returns difference between local time and UTC
  // as measured in minutes
  // (east of Greenwich = positive, west of Greenwich = negative)
  public function getTimezoneOffset()
  {
    return $this->offset;
  }
```

The UTC-specific get*() methods are defined in much the same way except you use gmdate() rather than date(). Once again, just see the comment preceding each method definition for any required explanations.

```
  // returns day of month (1-31) (UTC)
  public function getUTCDate()
  {
    return (int)gmdate("j", $this->time);
  }


  // returns day of week (0=Sunday, 6=Saturday) (UTC)
  public function getUTCDay()
  {
    return (int)gmdate("w", $this->time);
  }
```

```php
//  returns the 4-digit year (UTC)
public function getUTCFullYear()
{
   return (int)gmdate("Y", $this->time);
}


//  returns the hours field (0-59) (UTC)
public function getUTCHours()
{
   return (int)gmdate("H", $this->time);
}


//  returns minutes field (0-59) (UTC)
public function getUTCMinutes()
{
   return (int)gmdate("i", $this->time);
}


//  returns month (0=January, 11=December) (UTC)
public function getUTCMonth()
{
   $temp = (int)gmdate("n", $this->time);
   return ($temp - 1);
}


//  returns seconds field (0-59) (UTC)
public function getUTCSeconds()
{
   return (int)gmdate("s", $this->time);
}

/*
//  deprecated in JS 1.2 in favor of Date.getUTCFullYear()
//  because it was so badly implemented in JS 1.0/1.1
//  We have chosen not to do so here
function getUTCYear()
{
}
*/
```

The get*() methods let you read the components of a Date object in both local and UTC time. However, Date will be much more useful if you are able to set these component values (year, month, day, and so on) as well. Let's look at the setDate() method as an example, as the remaining set*() methods will follow the same pattern.

This method sets the day of the month for a given Date object. It takes a single integer argument that should be the number of the desired day of the month. As mandated by ECMA-262 for all the Date class set*() methods, it returns the updated value for this Date instance's $time variable. setDate() works by calling the built-in mktime() function and using

the Date's get*() methods to derive current values for all components of the date and time
except for the day of the month, for which it uses the value supplied as $date. It then sets the
$time value for the Date to the resulting timestamp value from the mktime() call.

```
//  set day of month (1-31)
public function setDate($date)
{
    $this->time = mktime(
                        $this->getHours(),
                        $this->getMinutes(),
                        $this->getSeconds(),
                        $this->getMonth() + 1,
                        $date,
                        $this->getFullYear()
                    );
    return $this->time;
}


//  set 4-digit year
public function setFullYear($year)
{
    $this->time = mktime(
                        $this->getHours(),
                        $this->getMinutes(),
                        $this->getSeconds(),
                        $this->getMonth() + 1,
                        $this->getDate(),
                        $year
                    );

    return $this->time;
}


//  set hours (0-23)
public function setHours($hours)
{
    $this->time = mktime(
                        $hours,
                        $this->getMinutes(),
                        $this->getSeconds(),
                        ($this->getMonth() + 1),
                        $this->getDate(),
                        $this->getFullYear()
                    );
    return $this->time;
}


//  set minutes (0-59)
```

```php
public function setMinutes($minutes)
{
    $this->time = mktime(
                        $this->getHours(),
                        $minutes,
                        $this->getSeconds(),
                        ($this->getMonth() + 1),
                        $this->getDate(),
                        $this->getFullYear()
                        );

    return $this->time;
}

//  set month (0-11)
public function setMonth($month)
{
    $this->time = mktime(
                        $this->getHours(),
                        $this->getMinutes(),
                        $this->getSeconds(),
                        $this->getMonth() + 1,
                        $this->getDate(),
                        $this->getFullYear()
                        );

    return $this->time;
}

//  set seconds (0-59)
public function setSeconds($seconds)
{
    $this->time = mktime(
                        $this->getHours(),
                        $this->getMinutes(),
                        $seconds,
                        $this->getMonth() + 1,
                        $this->getDate(),
                        $this->getFullYear()
                        );

    return $this->time;
}
```

The setTime() and setTimeZoneOffset() methods set the $time and $offset variables, respectively. Do not forget that $offset is measured in minutes to accommodate time zones that are not defined in whole hours. India, for example, uses GMT+0530, and some parts of Australia use GMT+0930 for local times. Also note that $offset is negative for points west of Greenwich. This means that the offset is added to local time to find the equivalent UTC date and time and subtracted from UTC to get the local date and time.

```
//  set time in seconds since the Unix epoch
//  note that in ECMA-262 this should actually
//  be a value in milliseconds, not seconds
public function setTime($time)
{
  $this->time = $time;

  return $this->time;
}


//  set time zone offset in minutes
//  (negative values for points west of Greenwich,
//  positive values are east of it)
public function setTimeZoneOffset($offset)
{
  $this->offset = $offset;

  return $this->time;
}
```

The next methods of this class set dates and times in terms of their UTC equivalents. These are quite similar to the set*() methods you have already seen for Date, except that you subtract the time zone offset from the value returned by getUTCMinutes() and pass this adjusted value to mktime().

```
//  set day of month (1-31) (UTC)
public function setUTCDate($date)
{
  $this->time = mktime(
                    $this->getUTCHours(),
                    $this->getUTCMinutes() - $this->offset,
                    $this->getUTCSeconds(),
                    $this->getUTCMonth() + 1,
                    $date,
                    $this->getUTCFullYear()
                );


  return $this->time;
}


//  set 4-digit year (UTC)
public function setUTCFullYear($year)
{
```

```
    $this->time = mktime(
                        $this->getUTCHours(),
                        $this->getUTCMinutes() - $this->offset,
                        $this->getUTCSeconds(),
                        $this->getUTCMonth() + 1,
                        $this->getUTCDate(),
                        $year
                    );

    return $this->time;
}

//  set hours (0-23) (UTC)
public function setUTCHours($hours)
{
    $this->time = mktime(
                        $hours,
                        $this->getUTCMinutes() - $this->offset,
                        $this->getUTCSeconds(),
                        $this->getUTCMonth() + 1,
                        $this->getUTCDate(),
                        $this->getUTCFullYear()
                    );

    return $this->time;
}
```

In the case of setUTCMinutes(), the time zone adjustment is made to the value that has been passed to this method for the $minutes argument:

```
//  set minutes (0-59) (UTC)
public function setUTCMinutes($minutes)
{
    $this->time = mktime(
                        $this->getUTCHours(),
                        $minutes - $this->offset,
                        $this->getUTCSeconds(),
                        $this->getUTCMonth() + 1,
                        $this->getUTCDate(),
                        $this->getUTCFullYear()
                    );

    return $this->time;
}
```

```php
//  set month (0-11) (UTC)
public function setUTCMonth()
{
    $this->time = mktime(
                    $this->getUTCHours(),
                    $this->getUTCMinutes() - $this->offset,
                    $this->getUTCSeconds(),
                    $month + 1,
                    $this->getUTCDate(),
                    $this->getUTCFullYear()
                );
    return $this->time;
}


//  set seconds (0-59) (UTC)
public function setUTCSeconds($seconds)
{
    $this->time = mktime(
                    $this->getUTCHours(),
                    $this->getUTCMinutes() - $this->offset,
                    $seconds,
                    $this->getUTCMonth() + 1,
                    $this->getUTCDate(),
                    $this->getUTCFullYear()
                );

    return $this->time;
}
```

■Note The ECMA specification originally defined the methods getYear() and setYear() that were used
to get and set the year portion of a date. setYear() could accept either a two-digit or a four-digit year.
However, because of ambiguities in the definitions of these methods, and because of differing implementations of them, they were eventually deprecated in favor of getFullYear() and setFullYear(), which
always act with regard to four-digit years. Because of this, and because we think it is a more sensible practice always to work with four-digit years whenever possible, we have chosen not to implement the older
methods. If you really want, you can always implement a getShortYear() method to return a two-digit
year in a child class, such as the DateExtended class you will look at in recipe 5-13. We recommend not
implementing a method to set two-digit years.

The next three methods return a date in two different formats. Both toGMTString() and toUTCString() return the current local date and time expressed in UTC and in RFC-1123 format. In fact, they are synonymous; an earlier version of the ECMA specification named this method toGMTString(), but this was later deprecated in favor of toUTCString(). The toLocaleString() method returns a date and time formatted according to local conventions. We have chosen to express this as the string returned by date('r').

```php
public function toGMTString()
{
  return $this->toUTCString();
}


// returns the date formatted according to local
// conventions and using local time
public function toLocaleString()
{
  return date('r', $this->time);
}


// returns RFC-formatted date (see toGMTString())
public function toUTCString()
{
  return date("D d M Y H:i:s", ($this->time + ($this->offset * 60))) . " UTC";
}
```

Finally, the ECMA specification defines a valueOf() method that returns a numeric representation of the local date and time. (Although ECMA uses milliseconds, we have used seconds.) This is a good programming practice, even though in this case this method is really just an alias for getTime().

```php
// this is an alias for getTime()
// once again ECMA specifies milliseconds rather than seconds
// as it's implemented here
public function valueOf()
{
  return $this->time;
}
}
  // end class Date
?>
```

Trying It Out

Here is some code that demonstrates how to use this class. It should be fairly self-explanatory.

```php
<?php
  // file: ch5/date-class-test.php
  require("./Date.class.inc.php");

  $today = new Date();
```

```php
printf("<p>Current date and time: %s</p>\n", $today->toLocaleString());

echo "<p>'Get' methods:</p>";

printf("<p>Month: %d.</p>\n", $today->getMonth());
printf("<p>Day of month: %d.</p>\n", $today->getDate());
printf("<p>Day of Week: %d.</p>\n", $today->getDay());
printf("<p>Year: %d.</p>\n", $today->getFullYear());
printf("<p>Hours: %d.</p>\n", $today->getHours());
printf("<p>Minutes: %d.</p>\n", $today->getMinutes());
printf("<p>Seconds: %d.</p>\n", $today->getSeconds());

echo "<p>UTC 'get' methods used on the same <code>Date()</code> instance...</p>";

printf("<p>UTC Month: %d.</p>\n", $today->getUTCMonth());
printf("<p>UTC Day of month: %d.</p>\n", $today->getUTCDate());
printf("<p>UTC Day of Week: %d.</p>\n", $today->getUTCDay());
printf("<p>UTC Year: %d.</p>\n", $today->getUTCFullYear());
printf("<p>UTC Hours: %d.</p>\n", $today->getUTCHours());
printf("<p>UTC Minutes: %d.</p>\n", $today->getUTCMinutes());
printf("<p>UTC Seconds: %d.</p>\n", $today->getUTCSeconds());

$timezone = $today->getTimeZoneOffset();
printf("Value returned by <code>getTimeZoneOffset()</code>: %d",
        $timezone);

$date = "Sat, 5 April 2003 15:15:25 +1000";
$timestamp = Date::parse($date);
printf("<p>Test date: %s; <code>Date::parse()</code> yields: %d.</p>\n",
        $date, Date::parse($date));

printf("<p><code>Date::UTC()</code> method: %d</p>\n", ➡
          Date::UTC(2002, 3, 4, 23, 30));

printf("<p>Using <code>toUTCString()</code>: %s</p>", $today->toUTCString());

echo "<p>Now for some 'set' methods...</p>";

echo "<p>Let's try advancing the date by one day... :";
$today->setDate($today->getDate() + 1);
echo $today->toLocaleString() . "</p>";

echo "<p>Now let's try advancing that date by one year... :";
$today->setFullYear($today->getFullYear() + 1);
echo $today->toLocaleString() . "</p>";

echo "<p>Now we're going to set the month for that date to 0 (January):";
```

```php
$today->setMonth(0);
echo $today->toLocaleString() . ".</p>\n";

echo "<p>Now we're going to set the month for that date to 13
      (should be February of the following year):";
$today->setMonth(13);
echo $today->toLocaleString() . ".</p>\n";

echo "<p>Now for <code>setMinutes()</code> and <code>setSeconds()</code>:</p>\n";
echo "<p>Test code: <code>\$today->setMinutes(30);
      \$today->setSeconds(45);</code>.</p>\n";

$today->setMinutes(30);
$today->setSeconds(45);

printf("<p>Date is now: %s.</p>\n", $today->toLocaleString());

echo "<p>Using the <code>toString()</code> method
      on the same date yields: " . $today->toString() . ".</p>\n";

echo "Finally, let's try some other ways to call the constructor...</p>";

echo "First, the RFC-formatted date <code>24 Sept 2005</code>: ";
$myBirthday = new Date("24 Sept 2005");
echo $myBirthday->toString() . "</p>.\n";

echo "<p>And now we'll try it with<br />
      <code>\$xmas2k = new Date(2000, 11, 25);</code>
      followed by<br />
      <code>echo \$xmas2k->toLocaleString();</code><br />
      and then<br />
      <code>echo \$xmas2k->toUTCString();</code>...</p>";
$xmas2k = new Date(2000, 11, 25);
echo "<p>" . $xmas2k->toLocaleString() . "</p>";
echo "<p>" . $xmas2k->toUTCString() . "</p>";

echo "<p>Now for some UTC methods, using <code>\$xmas2k</code>...</p>\n";

echo "Calling <code>\$xmas2k->setUTCDate(30);</code></p>\n";
$xmas2k->setUTCDate(30);
printf("<p>UTC date: %s; local date: %s</p>\n",
       $xmas2k->toUTCString(),
       $xmas2k->toLocaleString());

echo "Calling <code>\$xmas2k->setUTCHours(48);</code></p>\n";
$xmas2k->setUTCHours(48);
printf("<p>UTC date: %s; local date: %s</p>\n",
```

```
          $xmas2k->toUTCString(),
          $xmas2k->toLocaleString());

    echo "Calling <code>\$xmas2k->setUTCFullYear(2008);</code></p>\n";
    $xmas2k->setUTCFullYear(2008);
    printf("<p>UTC date: %s; local date: %s</p>\n",
          $xmas2k->toUTCString(),
          $xmas2k->toLocaleString());
?>
```

The output from this file is as follows:

```
Current date and time: Fri, 25 Mar 2005 21:49:37 +1000
'Get' methods:
Month: 2.
Day of month: 25.
Day of Week: 5.
Year: 2005.
Hours: 21.
Minutes: 49.
Seconds: 37.
UTC 'get' methods used on the same Date() instance...
UTC Month: 2.
UTC Day of month: 25.
UTC Day of Week: 5.
UTC Year: 2005.
UTC Hours: 11.
UTC Minutes: 49.
UTC Seconds: 37.
Value returned by getTimeZoneOffset(): -600

Test date: Sat, 5 April 2003 15:15:25 +1000; Date::parse() yields: 1049519725.

Date::UTC() method: 1147527000
Using toUTCString(): Fri 25 Mar 2005 11:49:37 UTC

Now for some 'set' methods...
Let's try advancing the date by one day: Sat, 26 Mar 2005 21:49:37 +1000
Now let's try advancing that date by one year: Sun, 26 Mar 2006 21:49:37 +1000
Setting the month for that date to 0 (January): Thu, 26 Jan 2006 21:49:37 +1000
Setting the month for that date to 13 (should be February of the following year):
Mon, 26 Feb 2007 21:49:37 +1000.

Now for setMinutes() and setSeconds()...
Test code: $today->setMinutes(30);
$today->setSeconds(45);.
```

```
Date is now: Mon, 26 Feb 2007 21:30:45 +1000.
Using the toString() method on the same date yields: 2007-02-26 21:30:45+10:00.
Finally, let's try some other ways to call the constructor...
First, the RFC-formatted date 24 Sept 2005: 2005-09-24 00:00:00+10:00.

And now we'll try it with
$xmas2k = new Date(2000, 11, 25); followed by
echo $xmas2k->toLocaleString();
echo $xmas2k->toUTCString();

Mon, 25 Dec 2000 00:00:00 +1000
Sun 24 Dec 2000 14:00:00 UTC

Now for some UTC methods, using $xmas2k...
Calling $xmas2k->setUTCDate(30);

UTC date: Sat 30 Dec 2000 14:00:00 UTC; local date: Sun, 31 Dec 2000 00:00:00 +1000

Calling $xmas2k->setUTCHours(48);
UTC date: Mon 01 Jan 2001 00:00:00 UTC; local date: Mon, 1 Jan 2001 10:00:00 +1000

Calling $xmas2k->setUTCFullYear(2008);
UTC date: Tue 01 Jan 2008 00:00:00 UTC; local date: Tue, 1 Jan 2008 10:00:00 +1000
```

This may seem like a lot of work just to get and set dates, but the payoff comes from having a clear and well-defined interface for dealing with a complex structure. However, so far, you are able to use this class to work with dates only as numbers or sets of numbers. What about being able to output dates in a more conventional format, such as March 15, 2005, 8:25 p.m.? Do you have to sacrifice PHP's capabilities in this regard in order to have a "nice" programming construct? The answer to this question is, "No, you do not." As you saw in Chapter 2, it is possible to extend classes to provide additional functionality. This is exactly what you are going to do in the next example.

5-13. Extending the Date Class

PHP's native date and time functions provide lots of output options, which the Date class you developed in the previous section does not really let you take advantage of. You could go back and add new methods to that class to take care of this shortcoming, but you do not really want to do this for a couple of reasons:

The Date class, having more than two dozen methods, is already fairly long and complex. Any advantage you might gain from adding methods to it is likely to be offset by increased difficulty in maintaining it.

As it is now, the class comes close to being a complete implementation of a class that is a recognized and open standard. (It is actually a subset of the standard, since there are four methods, all relating to milliseconds, which the Date class does not include.) By leaving its class members as they are, you help guarantee its interoperability. Someone else can implement an ECMA-compliant Date class with different internals, and code written against our Date class should still work.

However, you can leverage the capabilities of the existing class in a new class that extends Date. You will call this new class DateExtended, and in it you will provide methods for displaying names and abbreviations for the months and for the days of the week, a method for displaying times in formats that humans are accustomed to reading, a method for obtaining the interval between two dates/times, and a couple of other methods based on information that you can obtain readily from calling PHP's native date() function with different arguments. This class also implements one static method and adds no new class variables to the two defined by the parent class (which are available to DateExtended because they were declared as protected in Date). Figure 5-6 shows a description of the methods exposed by this class, all of which are public methods.

DateExtended		
<< extends Date >>		
Properties		
[inherited from Date]		
Methods		
public static isLeapYear	($year : int	) : bool
public __construct	[calls parent::__construct()]	
public getClockTime	($twelveHour : bool = TRUE $upperCaseAMPM : bool = TRUE $includeSeconds : bool = TRUE $separator : string = ':'	) : string
public getDayFullName	(void	) : string
public getDayShortName	(void	) : string
public getDaysInMonth	(void	) : int
public getDifference	($date : Date	) : array
public getISOWeek	(void	) : int
public getMonthFullName	(void	) : string
public getMonthShortName	(void	) : string
public getOrdinalDate	(void	) : string
public getTimeZoneName	(void	) : string
public isWeekDay	(void	) : bool
public toISOString	(void	) : string
public getUTCClockTime	($twelveHour : bool = TRUE $upperCaseAMPM : bool = TRUE $includeSeconds : bool = TRUE $separator : string = ':'	) : string
public getUTCDayFullName	(void	) : string
public getUTCDayShortName	(void	) : string
public getUTCDaysInMonth	(void	) : int
public getUTCISOWeek	(void	) : int
public getUTCMonthFullName	(void	) : string
public getUTCMonthShortName	(void	) : string
public getUTCOrdinalDate	(void	) : string
public isUTCWeekDay	(void	) : bool
public toUTCISOString	(void	) : string

Figure 5-6. DateExtended *class members, with input parameters and return types*

Without further ado, let's look at the code for this new class, which you can find in the code download for this book as ch5/Date-Extended.class.inc.php.

The Code

```php
<?php
// file: Date-Extended.class.inc.php
// purpose: provide additional output methods for
// the ECMA-compliant Date class (Date.class.inc.php)
```

Since this class extends the existing Date class, you need to include the file containing the Date class definition and use extends Date in the declaration line of the DateExtended class:

```php
require_once('./Date.class.inc.php');
```

```php
class DateExtended extends Date
{
```

Sometimes it is necessary to determine whether a given year is a leap year. Since PHP's date() function provides an easy way to do that, you will wrap it in a static method of DateExtended. Why use a static method instead of an instance method? It is a matter of convenience and economy. Since you are concerned with a year value only, no other date or time values affect the outcome. It does not matter if you are talking about 8:32 p.m. on July 24, 2001, or 12:05 a.m. on April 15, 2001; either 2001 is a leap year or it is not. It therefore seems easier to write a function or method that requires you to supply the year only than to create a Date or DateExtended instance with dummy arguments. (In fact, passing some meaningless arguments is exactly what is needed in order to invoke date('L') for an arbitrary year.) By implementing isLeapYear() as a static method, you do not have to worry about performing either of these tasks. If you do need to test the year component of an existing Date, you can use something like this:

```php
if( DateExtended::isLeapYear( $someDate->getFullYear() ) ){...}
```

Of course, if you find yourself using isLeapYear() in this fashion more often than not, you can always reimplement it as an instance method. In any case, this method does its job by invoking mktime() to create a timestamp for the first day of the year passed to isLeapYear() as $year and using this timestamp as the second argument for a call to date(). date('L'), as you will recall from earlier in the chapter, returns 1 if the year is a leap year and 0 if it is not, and you use a tertiary operator on this result to force the return of a boolean TRUE or FALSE to the calling code.

```php
// takes a 4-digit year and returns TRUE or FALSE
// depending on whether the year is a leap year
public static function isLeapYear($year)
{
    return date('L', mktime(0, 0, 0, 1, 1, $year)) == 1 ? TRUE : FALSE;
}
```

You might notice here that we have implemented this method using mktime() rather than strtotime() as we did in the stand-alone is_leap_year() function. Is there any particular reason for that? Well, yes and no: we did it differently to show that when you call this method, it does not really make any difference, as long as it accepts the expected parameters and returns correct values. (So, if you prefer, you can reimplement the method using strtotime(). It makes no difference to anyone using it, *as long as what goes in and what comes out remain the same.*)

Unlike the constructor for its parent class, the constructor for DateExtended is simple. In fact, all it does is invoke the Date class constructor and pass on any arguments it receives as an array by means of the func_get_args() function. This is necessary because you do not know ahead of time how many arguments the DateExtended constructor will be called with. This also helps explain the sleight of hand you performed in the Date constructor in order to accommodate the possibility that it might be invoked on an array of arguments.

```
//  class constructor: passes whatever arguments it
//  receives back to the parent class constructor
public function __construct()
{
  parent::__construct( func_get_args() );
}
```

The first instance method of DateExtended provides the option to override the parent's toLocaleString() method and output a formatted date in a more verbose form, such as Wednesday, 24th February 2010, 8:25 a.m. To specify this behavior, pass TRUE to the method. Passing FALSE or no argument at all will produce the same output as the parent's toLocaleString() method, for example, Wed, 24 Feb 2005 08:25:20 +1000.

```
public function toLocaleString($long=FALSE)
{
  $output = "";

  if($long)
  {
    $day = $this->getDayFullName();
    $date = $this->getOrdinalDate();
    $month = $this->getMonthFullName();
    $year = $this->getFullYear();
    $time = $this->getClockTime(TRUE, TRUE, FALSE);

    $output = "$day, $date $month $year, $time";
  }
  else
    $output = date('r', $this->getTime());

  return $output;
}
```

We wrote the getClockTime() method to simplify the task of displaying a time in human-readable format. It takes four optional parameters:

- $twelve: If this is TRUE, display the time using 12-hour format with an a.m./p.m. indicator; if FALSE, display the time using 24-hour format. The default value is TRUE.

- $uppercaseAMPM: If this parameter is TRUE, display the a.m./p.m. indicator in uppercase or in lowercase if FALSE. The default value is TRUE. Note that setting this parameter has no effect on the output if the value of $twelve is FALSE.

- $includeSeconds: If this is TRUE, then seconds are included in the output. The default is TRUE.

- $separator: The character to use as the hours/minutes/seconds separator. The default value is ':' (a colon).

Here is the code:

```
public function getClockTime($twelve = TRUE, $uppercaseAMPM = TRUE,
                             $includeSeconds = TRUE, $separator = ':')
{
  $am_pm = "";

  $hours = $this->getHours();
  if($twelve)
  {
    $am_pm = " " . ($hours >= 12 ? "pm" : "am");
    if($uppercaseAMPM)
      $am_pm = strtoupper($am_pm);

    if($hours > 12)
      $hours -= 12;
  }
  else
  {
    if($hours < 10)
      $hours = "0$hours";
  }

  $minutes = $this->getMinutes();
  if($minutes < 10)
    $minutes = "0$minutes";

  $minutes = "$separator$minutes";

  $seconds = "";

  if($includeSeconds)
  {
    $seconds = $this->getSeconds();
    if($seconds < 10)
      $seconds = "0$seconds";

    $seconds = "$separator$seconds";
  }

  return "$hours$minutes$seconds$am_pm";
}
```

The next three methods are basically wrappers for the date() function (merely calling it with different formatting characters) and should be explained adequately by the comments preceding each one.

```
//  returns full English name of day of week
//  (e.g. Sunday, Monday, etc.)
public function getDayFullName()
{
   return date('l', $this->time);
}


//  returns 3-letter abbreviation for day of week
//  (Sun, Mon, etc.)
public function getDayShortName()
{
   return date('D', $this->time);
}


//  returns number of days in current month
    public function getDaysInMonth()
{
   return date('t', $this->time);
}
```

The getDifference() method is a reimplementation of the stand-alone date_difference() function, which calculates the difference between dates in years, months, and days. Since this version is now a method of DateExtended, it requires only a single argument—a Date object to compare with the current one. Of course, nothing is stopping you from passing another instance of DateExtended to this method instead of a Date, since it inherits all the requisite Date class methods.

```
public function getDifference(Date $date)
  {
    $val1 = $this->getTime();
    $val2 = $date->getTime();
    $sec = abs($val2 - $val1);
    $units = getdate($sec);

    $hours = abs($units["hours"] - (date('Z') / 3600));
    $days = $units["mday"];

    if($hours > 23)
    {
      $days++;
      $hours %= 24;
    }

    $output = array();
```

```
$output["components"] = array(
                            "years"   => $units["year"] - 1970,
                            "months"  => --$units["mon"],
                            "days"    => --$days,
                            "hours"   => $hours,
                            "minutes" => $units["minutes"],
                            "seconds" => $units["seconds"]
                        );

    $output["elapsed"] = array(
                            "years"   => $sec / (365 * 24 * 60 * 60),
                            "months"  => $sec / (30 * 24 * 60 * 60),
                            "weeks"   => $sec / (7 * 24 * 60 * 60),
                            "days"    => $sec / (24 * 60 * 60),
                            "hours"   => $sec / (60 * 60),
                            "minutes" => $sec / 60,
                            "seconds" => $sec
                        );

  $output["order"] = $val2 < $val1 ? -1 : 1;

  return $output;
}
```

The getMonthFullName() and getMonthShortName() methods are wrappers for date('F') and date('M'), respectively.

```
//  returns full English name of month
//  (January, February, etc.)
public function getMonthFullName()
{
  return date('F', $this->time);
}
```

```
//  returns 3-letter abbreviation for month
//  (Jan, Feb, etc.)
public function getMonthShortName()
{
  return date('M', $this->time);
}
```

The next method, getOrdinalDate(), returns the day of the month with an ordinal suffix, for example, 1st, 2nd, 3rd, and so on. It is a wrapper for date('jS'); note that it does *not* include leading zeroes for days of the month before the tenth.

```
public function getOrdinalDate()
{
return date('jS', $this->time);
}
```

The methods in the group that follows should be adequately explained by the comments preceding the methods.

```php
//  returns name or abbreviation of current time zone
public function getTimeZoneName()
{
  return date('T', $this->time);
}


//  returns ISO week number
public function getISOWeek()
{
  return (int)date('W', $this->time);
}


//  returns TRUE if current date/time is daylight-saving time, FALSE if not
public function isDST()
{
  return date('I', $this->time) == 1 ? TRUE : FALSE;
}


//  returns TRUE if day is a weekday (Mon-Fri), FALSE if not
public function isWeekDay()
{
  $w = $this->getDay();
  return ($w > 0 && $w < 6) ? true : FALSE;
}


//  returns ISO representation of date and time
//  e.g., 2005-03-26T18:59:07+10:00
public function toISOString()
{
  return date('c', $this->time);
}
```

We have also included UTC versions of the methods described previously. They differ from their local counterparts only in that they either use the Date class's getUTC*() methods instead of the get*() methods or invoke gmdate() in place of the date() function.

```php
//  returns "friendly" representation of UTC time
//  see getClockTime() for parameters
public function getUTCClockTime($twelve = TRUE, $uppercaseAMPM = TRUE,
                                $includeSeconds = TRUE, $separator = ':')
{
  $am_pm = "";

  $hours = $this->getUTCHours();
  if($twelve)
```

```
    {
      $am_pm = " " . ($hours >= 12 ? "pm" : "am");
      if($uppercaseAMPM)
        $am_pm = strtoupper($am_pm);

      if($hours > 12)
        $hours -= 12;
    }
    else
    {
      if($hours < 10)
        $hours = "0$hours";
    }

    $minutes = $this->getUTCMinutes();
    if($minutes < 10)
      $minutes = "0$minutes";

    $minutes = "$separator$minutes";

    $seconds = "";

    if($includeSeconds)
    {
      $seconds = $this->getUTCSeconds();
      if($seconds < 10)
        $seconds = "0$seconds";

      $seconds = "$separator$seconds";
    }

    return "$hours$minutes$seconds$am_pm";
  }

  // returns full English name for day of the week (UTC)
  public function getUTCDayFullName()
  {
    return gmdate('l', $this->time);
  }

  // returns 3-letter abbreviation for day of the week (UTC)
  public function getUTCDayShortName()
  {
    return gmdate('D', $this->time);
  }

  // returns number of days in month (UTC)
  public function getUTCDaysInMonth()
```

```
    {
      return gmdate('t', $this->time);
    }


    //  returns full English name of month (UTC)
    public function getUTCMonthFullName()
    {
      return gmdate('F', $this->time);
    }


    //  returns 3-letter abbreviation for month (UTC)
    public function getUTCMonthShortName()
    {
      return gmdate('M', $this->time);
    }


    //  returns ordinal form for day of the month (UTC)
    public function getUTCOrdinalDate()
    {
      return gmdate('jS', $this->time);
    }


    //  returns time zone name or abbreviation (UTC)
    public function getUTCTimeZoneName()
    {
      return 'UTC';
    }


    //  returns ISO week number (UTC)
    public function getUTCWeek()
    {
      return gmdate('W', $this->time);
    }


    //  returns TRUE/FALSE depending on whether day is a weekday (UTC)
    public function isUTCWeekDay()
    {
      $w = $this->getUTCDay();
      return ($w > 0 && $w < 6);
    }


    //  returns ISO representation of date (UTC)
    public function toUTCISOString()
    {
      return gmdate('c', $this->time);
    }
  } //  end class DateExtended
?>
```

Trying It Out

Let's take this class for a spin. Remember that since it extends the Date class, an instance of DateExtended can access any of the methods exposed by the parent class. Here is the source of the test file, ch5/date_ext_test.php, which is included in the code download that accompanies this book:

```php
<?php
    //  file: date_ext_test.php
    //  demonstrating the DateExtended class

    //  include the class file
    require_once("Date-Extended.class.inc.php");

    //  create a new instance, using the current date and time
    $today = new DateExtended();

    printf("<p>Current date and time (long toLocaleString()): %s.</p>\n",
            $today->toLocaleString(TRUE));
    printf("<p>Current date and time (parent toLocaleString()): %s.</p>\n",
            $today->toLocaleString());
    printf("<p>Current date and time (ISO format): %s.</p>\n",
            $today->toISOString());
    printf("<p>Current UTC date and time: %s %s %s %s %s</p>\n",
            $today->getUTCDayShortName(),
            $today->getUTCDate(),
            $today->getUTCMonthShortName(),
            $today->getUTCFullYear(),
            $today->getUTCClockTime());

    printf("<p>Today is %s (%s).</p>\n",
            $today->getDayFullName(),
            $today->getDayShortName());

    printf("<p>Today is %s %s, %d.</p>\n",
            $today->getOrdinalDate(),
            $today->getMonthFullName(),
            $today->getFullYear());

    printf("<p>12-hour time: %s.</p>\n", $today->getClockTime(TRUE, TRUE, FALSE));

    printf("<p>24-hour time: %s (%s).</p>\n",
            $today->getClockTime(FALSE, TRUE, TRUE, '.'),
            $today->getTimeZoneName());

    echo "<p>";
    for($year = 2000; $year <= 2010; $year++)
    {
```

```
    printf("%s is %sa leap year.<br />\n",
            $year,
            DateExtended::isLeapYear($year) ? '' : 'not ');
}
echo "</p>";

$past = new DateExtended(1997, 6, 4, 15, 30, 45);
printf("<p>Past date is %s.</p>\n", $past->toLocaleString());

$diff = $today->getDifference($past);

$components = $diff["components"];

$output = array();

foreach($components as $period => $length)
  if($length > 0)
    $output[] = "$length $period";

printf("<p>Difference in dates is: %s.</p>", implode($output, ', '));
printf("<p>Difference in dates is: %s years.</p>", $diff["elapsed"]["years"]);
?>
```

Here is the output from this script:

```
Current date and time (long toLocaleString()): Sunday, 27th March 2005, 1:44 AM.
Current date and time (parent toLocaleString()): Sun, 27 Mar 2005 01:44:39 +1000.
Current date and time (ISO format): 2005-03-27T01:44:39+10:00.

Current UTC date and time: Sat 26 Mar 2005 3:44:39 PM

Today is Sunday (Sun).
Today is 27th March, 2005.

12-hour time: 1:44 AM.
24-hour time: 01.44.39 (E. Australia Standard Time).
2000 is a leap year.
2001 is not a leap year.
2002 is not a leap year.
2003 is not a leap year.
2004 is a leap year.
2005 is not a leap year.
2006 is not a leap year.
2007 is not a leap year.
2008 is a leap year.
2009 is not a leap year.
2010 is not a leap year.
```

Past date is Friday, 4th July 1997, 3:30 PM.

Difference in dates is: 7 years, 8 months, 22 days, 10 hours,
                                13 minutes, 54 seconds.
Difference in dates is: 7.732674847793 years.

So, why exactly did we go to the trouble of writing these classes? In part it is because it is somewhat easier to remember something like echo $mydate->getOrdinalDate(); than it is something like echo date('jS', $mydate);. You might argue that being able to write a single statement such as echo date('M jS, Y', strtotime('+2 weeks')); makes for more compact code than the alternatives offered by the Date and DateExtended classes. We will not claim that terseness is not a virtue, but like any good thing, it can be counterproductive when carried to extremes.

You do not have to stop with what we have given you here. In general, if you find yourself reusing the same block of code repeatedly in an application, it is a good idea to turn it into a function. If invoked using methods of the Date or DateExtended classes, there is no reason why you cannot extend DateExtended further. For example, if it is often the case that you are adding or subtracting complex intervals to or from different times, maybe it is time to write a method that does that, with a signature such as that shown here:

```
void public function addInterval(int $hours=0, int $minutes=0, int $seconds=0){}
```

(Or you might decide that you need a $days parameter and maybe one for weeks as well. It is really up to you and depends on what you require.) It is usually not a good idea to modify the interface provided by a base class such as Date, but you could make this a method of DateExtended. Or you might decide to create a CustomDate class that extends DateExtended. Again, this depends on your circumstances: if this is the only method you would like to add for your application, and it will not adversely affect any existing code, then you might be able to get away with modifying DateExtended. If you are planning on adding a lot of new functionality, and especially if you need to override existing methods, then you are better off extending an existing class.

This latter approach is probably a good one when it comes to localization issues. Because localization in PHP depends on what is available in the server environment, and this can vary widely from one server to the next, we will just provide part of such a class here and let you "fill in the blanks" as is appropriate to your requirements and what is available to you.

```
class DateLocalised extends Date
{
  static protected $locale;

  public function __construct()
  {
    parent::__construct( func_get_args() );
  }

  public function getLocaleFullDay
  {
    return strftime('%A', $this->time);
  }
```

```
  public function getLocaleShortDay()
  {
    return strftime('%a', $this->time);
  }

  // ...

  public function getLocale()
  {
    return $self::locale;
  }

  public function setLocale($lc_strings)
  {
    $self::locale = setlocale(LC_ALL, $lc_strings);
  }
}
```

This might represent an acceptable implementation on a Linux or other Unix server where it is possible to control the locale on a script-by-script basis. When on a Windows-based server, when in safe mode or other circumstances prevent you from changing the locale, or when a desired locale is not available, you might have to set up constants or static variables containing the names of days and months in various languages.

You can accommodate daylight-saving time in a similar fashion, say, by adding a $dst variable and the setDST() and isDST() methods to DateExtended or to your own extension of this class or of the Date class.

Summary

Dates are probably the most complex data types that programmers commonly have to deal with, and you will seldom if ever find any quick miracles for working with them or performing date arithmetic. PHP, like most if not all modern programming languages, reduces this complexity to timestamps internally, but even though PHP takes care of much of the overhead for you, turning these into human-readable formats can still be a tricky proposition.

In the first part of this chapter, you looked at the most important and useful functions that PHP provides for displaying dates and times, including the date(), time(), and mktime() functions. Also, certain functions exist for working with dates and times in UTC as opposed to local or server time (gmdate() and gmmktime()), and you saw how to use these to convert between local and UTC/GMT dates and times. In addition, PHP provides some ways to localize formatted dates and times (using the strftime() function).

You also did some date arithmetic, taking advantage of some of the relative, ordinary-language arguments (such as +1 week or -3 days) that can be used with the strtotime() function. This technique can be handy; it can take care of rollover issues so you do not have to worry about what happens when, for instance, you add 12 hours to 8 p.m. and the resulting time is on the following day.

However, PHP's date and time functions have some drawbacks, in particular with regard to those used to output formatted dates. In the first place, the arguments used for these are somewhat cryptic and can be difficult to remember. In addition, the formatting characters used with local dates and times (used with date()) and those for locale-specific dates and times (those used as arguments to strftime()) are not at all consistent with one another; in fact, the two sets of formatting characters do not even come close to mapping to one another.

The second half of this chapter was devoted to taking care of the first of these problems by developing a couple of classes to provide a clear and consistent means of working with dates that does not involve having to look up formatting characters, many of which are not especially memorable but *are* easily confused with one another. The Date class implements a well-known interface that is defined in a recognized international standard (ECMA-262), providing the means to define Date instances and to set and to retrieve aspects of them (such as months and hours) that are easily recognizable to human beings. Since this class in and of itself does not provide much flexibility in formatting dates for output, you extended it in a DateExtended class that does a better job at making this functionality available to the programmer. These classes also simplify the tasks of converting between local time and UTC as well as other time zones.

In wrapping things up, we also gave you some suggestions for taking the PHP 5 classes in this chapter and building on them to handle issues such as extended date arithmetic. We also sketched the outline of a class you might want to write that would extend Date and DateExtended for localization purposes. In any case, we have been using these classes and their predecessors for a couple of years now in our own projects. They have let us handle many of the date and time tasks we have needed to accomplish much more quickly and easily than by using the native PHP functions alone, and we hope you will also find them to be beneficial in your own work and that they will serve as a basis you can build upon to meet your needs.

Looking Ahead

In Chapter 6, Lee Babin will show you some tips and tricks for solving common problems that PHP programmers encounter when working with strings, including putting strings together and splitting them up. He will also cover accessing specific portions of strings (substrings), removing them, replacing them, and inserting them into other strings. He will also discuss some issues that often come up in displaying web pages and text, such as trimming and wrapping text. Finally, he will show you how to wrap many of these techniques into your own String class, which you can use as is or modify for your work with strings in PHP.

CHAPTER 6

■■■

Working with Strings

Considered pretty much a staple of any programming language, the ability to work with, maneuver, and ultimately control strings is an important part of a daily programming routine. PHP, unlike other languages, has no trouble using data typing to handle strings. Thanks to the way PHP is set up—that is to say, that when a value is assigned to a variable, the variable automatically typecasts itself—working with strings has never been easier. PHP 5 has not done much to improve upon, or modify, the way strings are handled in PHP itself, but it has provided you with new and improved class functionality so you can more readily create tools to help support PHP's somewhat clunky string function naming conventions.

This chapter's focus will be threefold. First, we will offer a bit of a refresher course on how PHP's versatile string functions can be quite an asset to the aspiring developer. Second, we will display some real-world examples not just on how using strings is both important and practical while deploying applications but also on how to use them to your best advantage. Last, we will use what we have learned and apply it towards a fully functional, working example of a possible string dilemma (see Table 6-1).

Table 6-1. *PHP 5 String Functions*

Function	Description
substr_count()	Counts the number of substring occurrences
strstr()	Finds the first occurrence of a string
strchr()	Can be used as an alias of strstr()
strrchr()	Finds the last occurrence of a character in a string
stristr()	Performs the same functionality as strstr() but is case-insensitive
substr_replace()	Replaces text within a portion of a string
strpos()	Finds the position of the first occurrence of a string
substr()	Returns a piece of a string
strlen()	Returns the length of a string
strtok()	Splits a string into smaller tokens
explode()	Returns an array of substrings of a target string, delimited by a specific character
implode()	Takes an array of items and puts the items together, delimited by a specific character

Continued

Table 6-1. *Continued*

Function	Description
join()	Acts as an alias to implode()
str_split()	Converts a string to an array
strtoupper()	Converts an entire string to uppercase characters
strtolower()	Converts an entire string to lowercase characters
ucfirst()	Changes a given string's first character into uppercase
ucwords()	Changes a given string's first character of each word into uppercase
trim()	Strips whitespace from the beginning and end of a string
chop()	Acts as an alias for rtrim()
rtrim()	Strips whitespace from the end of a string only
ltrim()	Strips whitespace from the beginning of a string only
strcmp()	Performs a string comparison

Manipulating Substrings

One of the common occurrences developers will come across is the problem of deducing what is needed, where certain aspects are, or even what order is necessary from a string. *Substrings* make up part of a full string. Since manipulating different portions of a string is a common task while building applications, PHP has granted you the use of some rather powerful functions. None of the string functions need to be included, and the basic string functions are prepackaged with the PHP 5 release, thus removing the problem of including them as extensions or packaging them with libraries. Table 6-2 lists the functions that prove useful (and sometimes quite invaluable) when working with substrings.

Table 6-2. *PHP 5 Substring Functions*

Function	Description
substr_count()	Counts the number of substring occurrences
strstr()	Finds the first occurrence of a string
strchr()	Can be used as an alias of strstr()
strrchr()	Finds the last occurrence of a character in a string
stristr()	Performs the same functionality as strstr() but is case-insensitive
substr_replace()	Replaces text within a portion of a string
strops()	Finds the position of the first occurrence of a string
substr()	Returns a piece of a string

6-1. Testing for Substrings

The first thing you might do when working with substrings is test a string for occurrences of a specific substring. You can put this sort of functionality to use in almost any kind of application. The most obvious usage of this sort of algorithm would be when building a search engine. Depending on what exactly it is you are building the search engine to do, testing for substrings manually with PHP may not always be the most efficient plan. For instance, if you were searching something in a database, more than likely it would be beneficial to do a query comparison using the built-in SQL engine to find whether a substring exists, but certainly sometimes you will not have the luxury of letting another system's workhorse do the brunt of the task for you.

Obviously, if you were going to do a search within a given block of text using PHP, it might be a smart move to check whether any instances of the search query appear within the text; there is no point in proceeding with your search algorithm if you find no instance of the search term. Thankfully, PHP has a nicely built function, substr_count(), that is perfect for the task. The standard definition for the substr_count() function is as follows:

```
int substr_count ( string haystack, string needle )
```

That is to say, you provide the block of text you want to search as the first parameter for the function (string haystack), and then you provide the substring you want to obtain as the second parameter (string needle). The function will then provide you with a return value of the number of occurrences of the needle parameter from the haystack search block.

The following block of code is basically a mundane search engine.

The Code

```php
<?php
  function searchtext ($haystack, $needle){
    //First, let's deduce whether there is any point in going on with our little
    //string hunting charade.
    if (substr_count ($haystack, $needle) == 0){
      echo "No instances were found of this search query";
    } else {
      //Now, we will go through the haystack, find out the
      //different positions that the string occurs at, and then output them.

      //We will start searching at the beginning.
      $startpos = 0;
      //And we will set a flag to stop searching once there are no more matches.
      $lookagain = true;

      //Now, we search while there are still matches.
      while ($lookagain){
        if ($pos = strpos ($haystack, $needle, $startpos)){
          echo "The search term \"$needle\" was found at position:  ➥
$pos<br /><br />";
          //We increment the position we are searching in order to continue.
          $startpos = $pos + 1;
        } else {
```

```
            //If there are no more matches, then we want to break out of the loop.
            $lookagain = false;
        }
    }

    echo "Your search for \"$needle\" within \"$haystack\" ➥
returned a total of \"" . substr_count ($haystack, $needle) . "\" matches.";
    }
}

searchtext ("Hello World!","o");
?>
```

```
The search term "o" was found at position: 4
The search term "o" was found at position: 7
Your search for "o" within "Hello World!" returned a total of "2" matches.
```

How It Works

The previous function is a bare-bones search engine that is primed to take a block of text and then output not only whether there are any matches within the block of text but exactly where those matches occur. For ease of use and cleanliness, the total number of matches found is displayed at the bottom. Take a moment to review the function, and we will discuss how exactly it does what it does by using the built-in PHP string functions.

By using substr_count() to make sure there are no instances of the substring, you let the user know that there were no matches if, indeed, you find no matches.

The next matter that this function attends to is the meat and potatoes of this function; it actually loops through the search string and outputs the position of all instances of the substring.

```
//Now, we search while there are still matches.
while ($lookagain){
    if ($pos = strpos ($haystack, $needle, $startpos)){
        echo "The search term \"$needle\" was found at position:  $pos<br /><br />";
        //We increment the position we are searching in order to continue.
        $startpos = $pos + 1;
    } else {
        //If there are no more matches, then we want to break out of the loop.
        $lookagain = false;
    }
}
```

By using the strpos() function, which outputs the position within the string of the given substring, you can go through the entire block of search text, outputting where exactly the search term falls.

Now, this is a scaled-down idea for a search engine, but by using these basic concepts you can see the power you get by taking advantage of built-in string functions.

6-2. Counting the Occurrences of a Substring

As discussed in the previous recipe, counting the number of occurrences of a substring within a search string is a simple process. PHP has included the function substr_count() that does the work for you. Naturally, there are more manual ways of doing this (consider adding a counter to the previous script as it loops), but since this is a stable function that has been around for some time, there is no need to reinvent the wheel. Thus, when it comes time in the previous function to output a total search tally, you simply call the substr_count() function, as in the following example.

The Code

```php
<?php
    //Let's find the number of o's in our string.
    $counter = substr_count ("Hello World!","o");
    echo "There are " . $counter . " instance (s) of \"o\" in Hello World!.";
?>
```

```
There are 2 instances of "o" in Hello World!.
```

How It Works

As you can see, by providing the substr_count() function with a needle substring and a haystack string to search through, you can determine quickly and easily how many instances of a given substring exist within the supplied string.

6-3. Accessing Substrings

A fairly common day-to-day activity you might be required to perform while programming would be to access, and then do something with, a certain substring. PHP has a rather versatile and powerful function that will allow you to do just that. Aptly named substr(), this function will allow you to access any part of a string using the concise method detailed here:

string **substr** (string string, int start [, int length])

Basically, the function substr() takes as arguments the string you want to divide, the position you want to begin dividing from, and (optionally) the end point at which you want to stop dividing. The function then returns a nicely packaged (in the form of a string) substring ready for your use and (potentially) abuse.

As you can imagine, the substr() function is a handy tool. You can use it in many real-world applications, and it is a great help with everything from validation to properly formatted output. Imagine, for instance, that you have been tasked with building a content management system (CMS) that takes in information from a client and then outputs it onto the home page of a website. Sound easy? Now imagine that the design for the website has been built so the height of the block where the text is supposed to be output is big enough to handle only 300 characters of text. If the amount of text outputted exceeds that, the site could potentially "break," causing the entire design to look flawed; this is not good considering this is an important client.

In addition, consider that the client is not sure at all how many characters to use and even if you had informed them to use only 300, there is still a real chance they would try their luck anyway. How then can you guarantee that the design will not break? Well, this sounds like a lovely test for our good friend Mr. substr() and his buddy Ms. strlen().

The Code

```php
<?php

    $theclientstext = "Hello, how are you today? I am fine!";

    if (strlen ($theclientstext) >= 30){
      echo substr ($theclientstext,0,29);
    } else {
      echo $theclientstext;
    }

?>
```

```
Hello, how are you today? I a
```

How It Works

The first thing this block of code does is check to make sure the text provided by the client is within the length you need it to be:

```php
if (strlen ($theclientstext) >= 30){
```

If it happens to fall outside the range of acceptable length, you then use the lovely substr() function to echo only the portion of the text that is deemed acceptable. If the client has entered a proper block of text, then the system merely outputs the text that was entered, and no one is the wiser.

By using the function substr(), you have averted a potential disaster. People browsing the site will see nothing but a slightly concatenated set of verbiage, so the site's integrity remains sound. This sort of rock-solid validation and programming can save business relationships, as clients are seldom fond of having their site appear "broken" to potential customers or intrigued individuals.

6-4. Using Substring Alternatives

You can consider the substr() function as something of a jack of all trades. It can get you whatever you are looking for in a string with the greatest of ease. Sometimes, however, it may not be necessary to go to the trouble of using such a versatile function. Sometimes it is just easier to use a more specialized function to accomplish a task; fortunately, PHP has a fairly decent selection of such methods.

For instance, if you are interested in using only the first instance of a substring, you can use the function strstr() (or strchr(), which is merely an alias of the former), which takes a block of text and a search value as arguments (the proverbial haystack and needle). If you are not concerned with the case of the subjects, the function stristr() will take care of any problems you may have. Alternatively, you may be interested in obtaining the last instance of a substring within a block of text. You can accomplish this particular maneuver with the strrchr() function, also available from PHP. The prototypes for strstr() and stristr() are as follows:

```
string strstr ( string haystack, string needle )
string stristr ( string haystack, string needle )
```

The Code

```php
<?php
  $url = "www.apress.com";
  $domain = strstr ($url, ".");
  echo $domain;
?>
```

```
.apress.com
```

How It Works

In this example in which you are attempting to find the domain name of the current string, the strstr() function finds the first instance of the dot (.) character and then outputs everything starting with the first instance of the dot. In this case, the output would be ".apress.com".

6-5. Replacing Substrings

How often do you find yourself using the search-and-replace function within your word processor or text editor? The search-and-replace functionality found within such applications is a testament to how much easier it is to do things using a computer rather than manually. (How helpful would it be to have such a function while, say, skimming the local newspaper for classified ads?) Thankfully, PHP has heard the cries of the people and has provided a function called substr_replace() that can quickly turn the tedious task of scanning and editing a large block of text into a lofty walk through the park where you let PHP do your task for you while you grab yourself another coffee (preferably a white-chocolate mocha...). The substr_replace() function is defined as follows:

```
string substr_replace ( string str, string replacmnt, int start [, int len] )
```

The function substr_replace() is a powerful and versatile piece of code. While you can access the core functionality of it easily and painlessly, the depth and customization you can accomplish through the function is rather daunting. Let's start with the basics. If you want to simply make a replacement to the substring, and you want to start from the beginning and replace the entire instance (say, by changing the ever-so-clichéd "Hello World!" into the more "l33t" phrase "H3110 W0r1d!" and hence proving your "l33t" status), you could simply invoke the substr_replace() function as shown in the following example.

The Code

```php
<?php
  //By supplying no start or length arguments,
  //the string will be added to the beginning.
  $mystring = substr_replace("Hello World", "H3110 W0r1d!", 0, 0);
  echo $mystring . "<br />"; //Echoes H3110 W0r1d!Hello World

  //Where if we did this:
  $mystring = substr_replace("Hello World", "0 w0", 4, 4);
  echo $mystring; //Echoes Hell0 w0rld.

?>
```

```
H3110 W0r1d!Hello World
Hell0 w0rld
```

How It Works

This is not all that useful, is it? Happily, the substr_replace() function can do much more than that. By changing the third argument (the start position) and the last argument (which is optional and represents a length of characters that you want to replace), you can perform some pretty powerful and dynamic operations. Let's say you simply want to add the catchy "H3110 W0r1d!" phrase to the front of a string. You could perform this operation by simply using the substr_replace() function as follows:

```php
<?php
  substr_replace("Hello World", "H3110 W0r1d!", 0, 0);
?>
```

You can also do some pretty fancy operations by changing the start and length arguments of the function from positive to negative values. By changing the start value to a negative number, you can start the function counting from the end of the string rather than from the beginning. By changing the length value to a negative number, the function will use this number to represent the number of characters from the end of the given string argument at which to stop replacing the text.

Processing Strings

Now that we have gone into how to manipulate and use the more intricate substrings contained within a string value, it is only natural to get right into using strings for more powerful applications. In any given piece of software, it is likely that some sort of string processing will be involved. Be it a block of text that is being collected from an interested Internet user (for example, an e-mail address for a newsletter) or a complete block of text for use in a CMS, text is here to stay, so it is important to be able to put it to good use.

Of particular note in this day and age is security. No matter what form of content is being submitted, and no matter the form it takes (query strings, post variables, or database submittal), it is important to be able to validate both when collecting the necessary information and when outputting it. By knowing what is available to you in the form of string processing, you can quickly turn a security catastrophe into a well-managed, exception-handled occurrence. In the next recipes, we will show what you can do with the current string functions available through PHP and what you can do to help preserve the integrity of a data collection.

6-6. Joining and Disassembling Strings

The most basic functionality of strings is joining them. In PHP joining strings is easy. The simplest way to join a string is to use the dot (.) operator. For example:

```php
<?php
  $string1 = "Hello";
  $string2 = " World!";
  $string3 = $string1 . $string2;
?>
```

The end result of this code is a string that reads "Hello World!" Naturally, this is the easiest way to do things; in the real world, applications will likely call for a more specific approach. Thankfully, PHP has a myriad of solutions available to take care of the issue.

A common, and rather inconvenient, dilemma that rears its ugly head is dealing with dates. With the help of Jon Stephen's date class (see Chapter 5), you will not have to deal with this issue; rather, you may have to deal with date variables coming from the database. Generally, at least in MySQL, dates can either be stored as type date or be stored as type datetime. Commonly this means they will be stored with a hyphen (-) delimiting the month from the day from the year. So, this can be annoying when you need just the day or just the month from a given string. PHP has the functions explode(), implode(), and join() that help you deal with such situations. The prototypes for the functions implode() and explode() are as follows:

```
string implode ( string glue, array pieces )
array explode ( string separator, string string [, int limit] )
```

Consider the following block of code:

```php
<?php
  //Break the string into an array.
  $expdate = explode ("-","1979-06-23");
  echo $expdate[0] . "<br />"; //echoes 1979.
  //Then pull it back together into a string.
  $fulldate = implode ("-", $expdate);
  echo $fulldate; //Echoes 1979-06-23.
?>
```

```
1979
1979-06-23
```

This block of code will create an array called $expdate that will contain three values: 1979, 06, and 23. Basically, explode() splits a string at every occurrence of the character specified and packs the individual contents into an array variable for ease of use. Now, if you want to simply display the year an individual was born (a famous author perhaps?), you can easily manage to do so, like this:

```php
<?php
  echo $expdate[0];
?>
```

```
1979
```

Similarly, if you then want to repackage the contents of an array into a delimited string, you can use the function implode() by doing something like this:

```php
<?php
  $fulldate = implode ("-", $expdate);
  echo $fulldate;
?>
```

```
1979-06-23
```

The result of this line of code will repackage the array of date fragments back into a fully functioning string delimited by whatever character you choose as an argument, in this case the original hyphen. The join() function acts as an alias to implode() and can be used in the same way; however, for the sake of coherence, the explode()/implode() duet is probably the better way to do things if for nothing more than clarity's sake.

By using explode() and implode() to their fullest, you can get away with some classy and custom maneuvers. For example, if you want to group like fields into just one hidden field, perhaps to pass along in a form, you can implode them into one string value and then pass the string value in the hidden field for easy explosion when the data hits your processing statement.

The strtok() function performs a similar task to explode(). Basically, by entering strings into the strtok() function, you allow it to "tokenize" the string into parts based on a dividing character of your choosing. The tokens are then placed into an array much like the explode() function. Consider the following prototype for strtok():

```
string strtok ( string str, string token )
```

The Code

```php
<?php
  $anemail = "lee@babinplanet.ca";
  $thetoken = strtok ($anemail, "@");
  while ($thetoken){
    echo $thetoken . "<br />";
    $thetoken = strtok ("@");
  }
?>
```

Lee
babinplanet.ca

How It Works

As you can see, the strtok() function skillfully breaks the string down into highly useable tokens that can then be applied to their desired task.

In this example, say you want to tokenize the string based upon the at (@) symbol. By using strtok() to break the string down at the symbol, you can cycle through the string outputting the individual tokens one at a time. The strtok() function differs from the explode() function in that you can continue to cycle through the string, taking off or outputting different elements (as per the dividing character), where the explode() function simply loads the individual substrings into an array from the start.

Further, sometimes you will probably prefer to split a string up without using a dividing character. Let's face it, strings don't always (and in fact rarely do) follow a set pattern. More often than not, the string will be a client- or customer-submitted block of text that reads coherently across, left to right and up to down (just like the book you currently hold in your hands). Fortunately, PHP has its answer to this as well; you can use a function called str_split(). The definition of str_split() is as follows:

```
array str_split ( string string [, int split_length] )
```

Basically, str_split() returns an array filled with a character (or blocks of characters) that is concurrent to the string that was placed as an argument. The optional length argument allows you to break down a string into chunks of characters. For example, take note of the following block of code:

```php
<?php
  $anemail = "lee@babinplanet.ca";
  $newarray = str_split($anemail);
?>
```

This instance would cause an array that looks like this:

```
Array {
  [0] => l
  [1] => e
  [2] => e
  [3] => @
  [4] => b
  [5] => a
  [6] => b
  [7] => i
  [8] => n
  [9] => p
  [10] => l
  [11] => a
  [12] => n
  [13] => e
  [14] => t
  [15] => .
  [16] => c
  [17] => a
}
```

You can also group the output into blocks of characters by providing the optional length argument to the function call. For instance:

```php
$newarray = str_split ("lee@babinplanet.ca",3);
```

In this case, the output array would look like this:

```
Array {
  [0] => lee
  [1] => @ba
  [2] => bin
  [3] => pla
  [4] => net
  [5] => .ca
}
```

6-7. Reversing Strings

While we are on the subject of working with strings, we should note that you can also reverse strings. PHP provides a bare-bones, yet highly functional, way to take a string and completely reverse it into a mirror image of itself. The prototype of the function strrev(), which performs the necessary deed, is as follows:

```
string strrev ( string string )
```

Therefore, you can take a basic string, such as the fan favorite "Hello World," and completely reverse it by feeding it into the strrev() function as an argument.

The Code

```php
<?php
  $astring = "Hello World";
  echo strrev ($astring);
?>
```

```
dlroW olleH
```

How It Works

The output for such code would change the value of "Hello World" into the rather more convoluted "dlroW olleH" string. Quite apart from those who prefer to read using a mirror, the strrev() function can come in handy in a myriad of ways ranging from using encryption to developing Internet-based games.

6-8. Controlling Case

From time to time, it can be important to control the case of text strings, particularly from user-submitted data. For instance, if you have created a form that allows a customer to create an account with your site and allows them to enter their preferred username and password, it is probably a good idea to force a case-sensitive submittal. Confusion can occur if a client creates a password that contains one wrongly created capital letter, especially when using a password field (with all characters turned into asterisks). If the client meant to enter "mypass" but instead entered "myPass" accidentally, an exact string match would not occur.

PHP has several ways to control the case of a string and hence remove the potential for such a disaster. The ones most relevant to the previous problem are the functions strtoupper() and strtolower(). The prototypes for these two functions are as follows:

```
string strtoupper ( string string )
string strtolower ( string str )
```

These functions do what you would expect them to do. The function strtoupper() turns an entire block of text into uppercase, and strtolower() changes an entire string into lowercase. By using either of these functions, you can quickly turn troubles with case sensitivity into things of the past.

The Code

```php
<?php
  //The value passed to use by a customer who is signing up.
  $submittedpass = "myPass";
  //Before we insert into the database, we simply lowercase the submittal.
  $newpass = strtolower ($submittedpass);

  echo $newpass; //Echoes mypass
?>
```

```
mypass
```

How It Works

This code will work fine if there was a user mistake when entering a field or if you want all the values in your database to be a certain case, but what about checking logins? Well, the code can certainly apply there as well; the following block of code will check for a valid username and password match:

```php
<?php
  if (strcmp (strtolower ($password), strtolower ($correctpassword) == 0){
    //Then we have a valid match.
  }
?>
```

This function also uses the strcmp() function, which is described in more detail later in this chapter (see recipe 6-12).

By turning both the correct password and the user-submitted password into lowercase, you alleviate the problem of case sensitivity. By comparing the two of them using the strcmp() function (which returns a zero if identical and returns a number greater than zero if the first string is greater than the second, and vice versa), you can find out whether you have an exact match and thusly log them in properly.

Besides turning an entire block of text into a specific case, PHP can also do some interesting things regarding word-based strings. The functions ucfirst() and ucwords() have the following prototypes:

```
string ucfirst ( string str )
string ucwords ( string str )
```

Both functions operate on the same principle but have slightly differing scopes. The ucfirst() function, for instance, changes the first letter in a string into uppercase. The ucwords() does something slightly handier; it converts the first letter in each word to uppercase. How does it determine what a word is? Why, it checks blank spaces, of course. For example:

```php
<?php
  $astring = "hello world";
  echo ucfirst ($astring);
?>
```

```
Hello world
```

This would result in the function outputting the "Hello world" phrase. However, if you changed the function slightly, like so:

```php
<?php
  $astring = "hello world";
  echo ucwords ($astring);
?>
```

you would get the (far more satisfying) result of a "Hello World" phrase:

```
Hello World
```

As you can see, controlling the case of strings can be both gratifying and powerful; you can use this feature to control security in your applications and increase readability for your website visitors.

6-9. Trimming Blank Spaces

A potentially disastrous (and often overlooked) situation revolves around blank spaces. A frequent occurrence is for website visitors (or CMS users) to enter content that contains a myriad of blank spaces into forms. Of particular frequency is the copy-and-paste flaw. Some people may compose text in a word processor or perhaps copy text from another web browser. The problem occurs when they then try to paste the submission into a form field. Although the field may look properly filled out, a blank space can get caught either at the beginning or at the end of the submittal, potentially spelling disaster for your data integrity goal. PHP has a few ways to deal with this.

The more common way of removing blank space is by using PHP's trim(), ltrim(), and rtrim() functions, which go a little something like this:

```
string trim ( string str [, string charlist] )
string ltrim ( string str [, string charlist] )
string rtrim ( string str [, string charlist] )
```

The trim() function removes all whitespace from the front and back of a given string; ltrim() and rtrim() remove it exclusively from the front or back of a string, respectively. By providing a list of characters to remove to the optional charlist argument, you can even specify what you want to see stripped. Without any argument supplied, the function basically strips away certain characters that should not be there; you can use this without too much concern if you are confident about what has to be removed and what does not.

The Code

```php
<?php
  $blankspaceallaround = " somepassword ";
  //This would result in all blank spaces being removed.
  echo trim ($blankspaceallaround) . "<br />";
  //This would result in only the blank space at the beginning being trimmed.
  echo ltrim ($blankspaceallaround) . "<br />";
  //And, as you can imagine, only the blank space at the end would be trimmed here.
  echo rtrim ($blankspaceallaround) . "<br />";
?>
```

How It Works

For security purposes and all-around ease of use, it makes sense to use trim() on pretty much any field you encounter. Blank spaces cannot be seen and more often than not will cause trouble for the individual who entered them. Particularly disastrous are login fields that can be next to impossible to decipher should some unruly blank spaces make their appearance. It is highly recommended that you take care of any information that is integral to the system (validation, please!), and using the trim functions provides the means to an end in that regard.

As a side note, data storing is not the only place this sort of validation can come in handy. Pretty much any form consisting of user submittal can benefit from a little extra cleanliness. Search queries with blank spaces accidentally entered at the beginning or end of a search term can provide a frustrating experience for visitors to your website, for instance.

6-10. Wrapping Text

Sometimes it is not always a matter of ensuring a proper submittal of data that makes string manipulation so important; it is frequently important to ensure that strings are displaying properly to the end user. There is no point in having a beautiful set of information that displays in a choppy, chunky manner. Once again, PHP comes to your rescue by providing a couple of clever text formatting functions.

We will first talk about the function nl2br(), whose prototype is as follows:

```
string nl2br ( string string )
```

Basically, nl2br() changes any new line characters found in the data string into
 Hypertext Markup Language (HTML) code. This can be extremely handy when building CMS type systems with end users who are unfamiliar with HTML code. Which would you consider easier out of the following two choices? First, is it easier teaching clients who have absolutely no technical expertise whatsoever (and no time for any) how to use the cryptic <br /> every time they want a new line, or, second, is it easier just telling them to hit the Enter key whenever they want a new line? If you chose the second option, go grab yourself a cookie (we recommend the white-chocolate, macadamia-nut variety).

Basically, the nl2br() function can be a lifesaver because it allows your client (or whoever is entering information) to enter text into a text area in a way that looks normal to them. Then, rather than displaying one big chunk of run-on text on the website, you can allow the already formatted text to "automagically" display using this function.

The Code

```php
<?php
  $astring = "Hello\nWorld\n\nHow are you?";
  echo nl2br ($astring);
?>
```

This block of code would result in something that looks like this:

```
Hello
World

How are you?
```

How It Works

The nl2br() function is nice if the person submitting the data is aware of carriage returns and whatnot, but what if they just feel like copying and pasting a huge block of text into your painstakingly prepared web layout? Well, there is a simple way of dealing with this sort of occurrence as well, using the highly useful wordwrap() function that has the following prototype:

```
string wordwrap ( string str [, int width [, string break [, bool cut]]] )
```

By using this function, you can set a block of text to wrap to a width of your choosing and then even choose the character you want to break it with. Consider the following block of code as an example:

```php
<?php
  $textblock = "See spot run, run spot run.  See spot roll, roll spot roll!";
  echo wordwrap ($textblock, 20, "<br />");
?>
```

This would create a paragraph whereby the text block would go only to a width of 20 and then break into a new line. Not only does this help lay out the page in a more readable format, it can also be a lifesaver in certain circumstances. The output would look something like this:

```
See spot run, run
spot run. See spot
roll, roll spot roll!
```

Unfortunately, while HTML layout elements such as tables or divs can contain text and wrap the text automatically, they do have one interesting flaw. Basically, HTML will wrap text only if there is a blank space contained (that is, a new word). Sadly, this does not encompass the end result of someone entering a word that is really long and does not contain a blank space. For example:

```php
<?php
  $alongstring = "Helllllllllllllllllllllllllllllllllloooooooooooooo World";
?>
```

Now, if the very long "Hello" happened to be contained by a certain design HTML wrapper and it exceeded the length of the wrapper, the design could potentially break. But if you put the wordwrap() function to good use, you should be safe even in such an eventuality.

6-11. Checking String Length

A common occurrence that is quite easily handled in PHP is attempting to find out how long a string is. This can come in handy in multitudes of places, including validation of form elements, output of user-submitted data, and even database insertion preparation. PHP's strlen() function will instantly retrieve for you the length of any given string. The prototype for strlen() is as follows:

```
int strlen ( string string )
```

Since validation and security are such vital issues, it is important to know a few common string types that should always be checked for proper length. First up is data that will soon be inserted into a database and that has been submitted from a form by a user. Without going too in depth into MySQL (Chapter 15 goes into more detail in that regard), we will just begin by saying that certain data fields in a database can handle only a certain size field. If a string field, for instance, goes into a database field that cannot take the length of the string, an error will definitely be generated; and that is no fun for anyone. What is the simple way around this problem? You can simply validate the string's length using strlen(), as shown in the following example.

The Code

```php
<?php
  //Define a maximum length for the data field.
  define ("MAXLENGTH", 10);
  if (strlen ("Hello World!") > MAXLENGTH){
    echo "The field you have entered can be only " ➥
  . MAXLENGTH . " characters in   length.";
  } else {
    //Insert the field into the database.
  }
?>
```

```
The field you have entered can be only 10 characters in length.
```

How It Works

As you can see, by checking to make sure the length of the string is less than the maximum length that your database field will allow, you prevent a potential tragedy. You can use this in many occasions such as making sure a password submitted by a user is at least a certain number of characters in length and when outputting user-submitted text that could potentially break a design to which a CMS has been applied.

6-12. Comparing Strings

No matter what language you are programming in, comparing values becomes a common dilemma. Unlike in most programming languages, however, PHP makes comparing easy, at least on the surface. The easiest way to compare two strings is with the == operator. The == operator, in PHP, basically determines an exact equal match when using a conditional statement. The following block of code shows how to use it.

The Code

```php
<?php
  $stringone = "something";
  $stringtwo = "something";
  if ($stringone -- $stringtwo){
    echo "These two strings are the same!";
  }
?>
```

```
These two strings are the same!
```

How It Works

However, sometimes a simple string comparison as shown previously just will not cut it. Sometimes a more precise comparison is in order; once again PHP has given you an answer in the form of strcmp().

int **strcmp** (string str1, string str2)

The function strcmp() does slightly more than your average == operator as well. Not only does it check for an exact binary match between strings, but it can also return a result that lets you know if a string is greater than or less than the other. More specifically, if the value returned is less than zero, then string 1 is less than string 2; and, as you might expect, if the returned value is greater than zero, then string 1 is greater than string 2.

A real-world way in which you may want to use a full-on binary comparison function such as strcmp() is when dealing with usernames and passwords. Quite realistically, it is not good enough for a string to be "almost" the same as the other one. What we mean by that is if blank spaces get in the way or some such circumstance, occasionally the == operator will return a match even when the two strings are not completely identical. By using the strcmp() function, you can be assured that if the two values are not a complete and absolute match, the function will not return you a zero.

PHP also has a few other cousin functions to the mighty strcmp() that are a little more advanced and provide slightly different functionality. The more similar function available is the strncmp() function, which does almost the same thing as strcmp() but adds the benefit of being able to choose the length of the characters you want to compare. The strncmp() function has a prototype that looks like this:

int **strncmp** (string str1, string str2, int len)

Similarly, should you not be interested in case sensitivity when comparing strings, you can use the functions strcasecmp() and strncasecmp(), which look like this:

```
int strcasecmp ( string str1, string str2 )
int strncasecmp ( string str1, string str2, int len )
```

Basically, these two functions do exactly what their case-sensitive counterparts do, only they completely ignore case sensitivity. The slightly confusing part of the strncmp() and strncasecmp() functions is the len argument. What this means is that it will compare len amount of characters from the first string with the second string. For example:

```php
<?php
  if (strncmp ("something","some",4) == 0){
    echo "A correct match!";
  }
?>
```

```
A correct match!
```

6-13. Comparing Sound

A common use for comparing strings has always been a search engine. By entering appropriate terms as arguments, you can then compare them against similar fields using string comparison. In quite a few modern-day applications, direct string comparisons may not be enough to satisfy the ever-growing need for a powerful search application.

To help make search engines a touch friendlier, a concept was created that will allow you to return accurate search results even if the search term is pronounced in a similar tone. PHP 5 has a function that can determine matching strings based on something called a *soundex key*. The function soundex() has the goal of identifying a match based on pronunciation. The prototype for the function is as follows:

```
string soundex ( string str )
```

The Code

```php
<?php

  echo soundex ("Apress") . "<br />";
  echo soundex ("ahhperess") . "<br />";

  echo soundex ("Lee") . "<br />";
  echo soundex ("lhee") . "<br />";

  echo soundex ("babin") . "<br />";
  echo soundex ("bahbeen") . "<br />";
```

```
//Now, say I wanted to buy a xylophone online but had no idea how to spell it.
echo soundex ("xylophone") . "<br />";

//Here is a common misspelling no doubt.
echo soundex ("zilaphone");
//Note, how the end 3 numbers are the same? That could be used to perform a match!

?>
```

```
A162
A162
L000
L000
B150
B150
X415
Z415
```

How It Works

As you can see, similar-sounding pronunciations can result in similar (if not exact) results. The first character returned is the first letter used in the query, and the next set of three numerical values is the soundex key that is based on how the word sounds. By integrating this sort of functionality into your search engines, you can return a set of potential results with much greater accuracy than if you were using exact matches.

Project: Creating and Using a String Class

It is certainly one thing to show how string functions could be used but quite another to apply them to a real-world example. String manipulation is a common solution to many programming dilemmas, and sometimes the ability to put string functionality to use on the fly can mean the difference between a botched project and a fully functional web solution. In the next example, we have created an actual real-world project that draws on string functionality to process a wide range of applications.

6-14. Using a Page Reader Class

One of the more amusing algorithms that you can use is a web page reader, more commonly referred to as a *spider*. Basically, the point of the pagereader class is to read a web page that is located somewhere on the Internet and then parse it for appropriate or interesting information.

The next class's intent is to read a page and uncover a listing of all links, e-mails, and words contained within a given web page. The same sort of functionality is applied to many modern-day, large-scale operations including web search engines and, sadly, spam e-mail collectors. The following class will show you the basics of using a wide variety of string functions to process an effective application.

The Code

```php
<?php

    //Class to read in a page and then output various attributes from said page.
    class pagereader {

        protected $thepage;

        //The constructor function.
        public function __construct (){

            $num_args = func_num_args();

            if($num_args > 0){
                $args = func_get_args();
                $this->thepage = $args[0];
            }
        }

        //Function to determine the validity of a file and then open it.
        function getfile () {
            try {
                if ($lines = file ($this->thepage)){
                    return $lines;
                } else {
                    throw new exception ("Sorry, the page could not be found.");
                }
            } catch (exception $e) {
                echo $e->getmessage();
            }
        }

        //Function to return an array of words found on a website.
        public function getwords (){
            $wordarray = array ();
            $lines = $this->getfile ();
            //An array of characters we count as an end to a word.
            $endword = array ("\"","<",">"," ",";","(",")","}","{");
            //Go through each line.
            for ($i = 0; $i < count ($lines); $i++){
                $curline = $lines[$i];
                $curline = str_split ($curline);
                for ($j = 0; $j < count ($curline); $j++){
                    //Then start counting.
                    $afterstop = false;
                    $afterstring = "";
                    $counter = 0;
```

```
    for ($k = $j; $k < count ($curline); $k++){
      $counter++;
      if (!$afterstop){
        if (!in_array ($curline[$k],$endword)){
          $afterstring = $afterstring . $curline[$k];
        } else {
          $afterstop = true;
          //Set j to the next word.
          $j = $j + ($counter - 1);
        }
      }
    }
    if (trim ($afterstring) != ""){
      $wordarray[] = $afterstring;
    }
  }
}
  return $wordarray;
}

//Function to deliver an array of links from a website
public function getlinks (){
  //Read the file.
  $lines = $this->getfile ();
  $impline = implode ("", $lines);
  //Remove new line characters.
  $impline = str_replace ("\n","",$impline);
  //Put a new line at the end of every link.
  $impline = str_replace("</a>","</a>\n",$impline);
  //Then split the impline into an array.
  $nlines = split("\n",$impline);

  //We now have an array that ends in an anchor tag at each line.
  for($i = 0; $i < count($nlines); $i++){
    //Remove everything in front of the anchor tag.
    $nlines[$i] = eregi_replace(".*<a ","<a ",$nlines[$i]);
    //Grab the info in the href attribute.
    eregi("href=[\"']{0,1}([^\"'> ]*)",$nlines[$i],$regs);
    //And put it into the array.
    $nlines[$i] = $regs[1];
  }

  //Then we pass back the array.
  return $nlines;
}

//Function to deliver an array of e-mails from a site.
```

```php
public function getemails (){
    $emailarray = array ();
    //Read the file.
    $lines = $this->getfile ();
    //Go through each line.
    for ($i = 0; $i < count ($lines); $i++){
        //Then, on each line, look for a string that fits our description.
        if (substr_count ($lines[$i],"@") > 0){
            //Then go through the line.
            $curline = $lines[$i];
            //Turn curline into an array.
            $curline = str_split ($curline);
            for ($j = 0; $j < count ($curline); $j++){
                if ($curline[$j] == "@"){
                    //Then grab all characters before and after the "@" symbol.
                    $beforestring = "";
                    $beforestop = false;
                    $afterstring = "";
                    $afterstop = false;
                    //Grab all instances after the @ until a blank or tag.
                    for ($k = ($j + 1); $k < count ($curline); $k++){
                        if (!$afterstop){
                            if ($curline[$k] != " " && $curline[$k] != "\"" ➡
&& $curline[$k] != "<"){
                                $afterstring = $afterstring . $curline[$k];
                            } else {
                                $afterstop = true;
                            }
                        }
                    }
                    //Grab all instances before the @ until a blank or tag.
                    for ($k = ($j - 1); $k > 0; $k--){

                        if (!$beforestop){
                            if ($curline[$k] != " " && $curline[$k] != ">" ➡
&& $curline[$k] != ":"){
                                $beforestring = $beforestring . $curline[$k];
                            } else {
                                $beforestop = true;
                            }
                        }
                    }
                    //Reverse the string since we were reading it in backwards.
                    $beforestring = strrev ($beforestring);
                    $teststring = trim ($beforestring) . "@" . trim ($afterstring);
                    if (preg_match("/^([a-zA-Z0-9])+([.a-zA-Z0-9_-])*@([a-zA-Z0-9_-])➡
+(.[a-zA-Z0-9_-]+)+[a-zA-Z0-9_-]$/",$teststring)){
```

```
                //Only include the e-mail if it is not in the array.
                if (!in_array ($teststring,$emailarray)){
                    $emailarray[] = $teststring;
                }
            }
        }
      }
    }


    }
    //Then we pass back the array.
    return $emailarray;
  }

}

$myreader = new pagereader ("http://www.apress.com");

//None found ;).
?><p style="font-weight: bold;">Emails:</p><?php
print_r ($myreader->getemails ());
//Whoa, a few links.
?><p style="font-weight: bold;">Links:</p><?php
print_r ($myreader->getlinks ());
//Hold on to your hats, this will take a while...
?><p style="font-weight: bold;">Words:</p><?php
print_r ($myreader->getwords ());

?>
```

How It Works

The pagereader class's core functionality is based around reading a web page on the Internet and then performing operations on the read. Therefore, it comes with the validated method getfile(), whose sole purpose is to attempt to read in a web page using the file() function. If the function receives a valid read, then you can begin work on the received information.

The class has three main functions, and they all perform somewhat differently to accomplish their goals. The getwords() method is perhaps the simplest of the three merely because of its somewhat global goal. The purpose of the getwords() method is to collect an array filled with all words contained on a website. The problem is, what constitutes a word? The answer to such a question will probably vary from user to user, so an array filled with characters that will be omitted when determining the end of a word has been instantiated. By changing the values contained within this array, you can determine what constitutes a word and thus change the way the script reads in a word list.

The way it works after that is quite simple. The script takes in each line of the received file individually and then splits it into an array. It then parses through the array and waits until it finds a character that is not in the current array of end characters. After it finds such a character, it loops through the string of characters found after the start character and waits until it finds another character in the array, adding to a final string as it goes. Once it reaches a final character, it stores the "word" into an array to be returned when the script has finished processing.

The getemails() method works similarly to the getwords() method, except it bases everything upon the @ symbol. So, although it also goes through each line received from the file and breaks it down, it instead breaks it down according to the @ symbol. When a valid symbol has been found, it cycles through all characters before and after the symbol and quits cycling once an end character has been found. Once an end character has been found before and after the @ symbol, a full string is concocted and compared against a valid e-mail string using the preg_match() function. (For more information, see Nathan A. Good's Chapter 9.) If a valid match is received, the e-mail is returned in an array filled with e-mail addresses.

The last method in this class also differs the most. It combines string functionality with regular expressions to create a link targeting script. Basically what this method does is break the received lines down into a single line and kill off all new line characters. Then, it searches for any instances of an anchor tag and places a new line character after the closing anchor tag. Then, with an array of anchor tags delimited by a new line character in place, it strips out everything from in front of the leading anchor tag and grabs all information from within the href argument. At this point, the data contained within is stored into an array for returning.

As you can see, you can perform a wide range of functionality using the received file information; what is shown here is only a small glimpse. With the wide range of functionality available in the form of string functions, anything is possible.

Summary

So, as you can see, strings will always be a rather important subject when dealing with a programming language such as PHP. Thankfully, because of PHP 5's new class functionality, it is becoming easier to take matters into your own hands and concoct some truly powerful classes to help make your life just a little easier. It is important to experiment and use the tools available to you. As you can see from the real-world example in this chapter of a pagereader class, the ability to use string functionality on the fly is a learned and highly appreciated skill.

Looking Ahead

In the next chapter, we will go through the ins and outs of working with your current file system. This is a handy set of functionality that will likely serve you well in your quest for the perfect web application. While operating systems and server configurations may differ, the ability to react to such changes, with a bit of help from this book, will define you as the master programmer that you are.

CHAPTER 7

■■■

Working with Files and Directories

Although a web page may appear as a nicely collected and displayed grouping of images and text, the actual underlying structure comprises a wide collection of files that are sorted amongst (we hope) well-structured directories. Website file structures generally consist of specifically formatted files that run on a server-enabled computer.

Just as you would explore your current computer using some form of command (perhaps Windows Explorer for Windows-based operating systems or something such as the `ls` command in Linux), so too can you use PHP to navigate the internal structure of the computer from which it is currently processing.

PHP 5 is truly effective not just at navigating and browsing the file structure of a given server but also at manipulating it. Capable of creating, navigating, deleting, and modifying, PHP is a powerful tool for maintaining a web directory from a dynamic level.

Further, PHP can work with and manipulate the underlying file structure of a server, and it can provide functionality to independent files. No matter what it is you are attempting to do with your script, you generally need a way to pass along values from one script to another. Multiple ways exist for doing this, including storing and retrieving data to and from a database or even in the virtual memory of the server (sessions), but one popular way, certainly before the advent of secure database functionality, is using text files (referred to as *flat files*).

Working with Files

PHP 5 is more than adept at opening, closing, reading, writing, and manipulating text files, including Hypertext Markup Language (HTML), JavaScript, and Extensible Markup Language (XML) files. The list of reasons you would want to use PHP to manipulate text files is rather vast, but in this chapter we will go with a basic one and assume you want to create a visitor counter for your website.

7-1. Opening Files

The first task you must accomplish when working with a file (be it a `.txt` file, an `.xml` file, or another file) is to open the file. Naturally, since you are a sound-minded developer and realize that exceptions may occur, you must validate such an occurrence against mishaps. Keep in mind that a file that is to be opened must have proper permissions set to allow it to be read or written to, so those working on a Linux server should CHMOD the file to read (and potentially write, as in this case) values. Those on a Windows server should check the read/write permission setting. As a general rule, if you are not concerned too heavily about the security behind a particular file, you cannot go wrong by setting it to 777. If you are concerned about the security of a given writable file, however, you should consider a more advanced method of protecting your files (such as htaccess).

The following example uses two pertinent file-related functions: file_exists() checks (relatively) for a file's existence, and fopen() attempts to open a file. The prototypes for the functions are as follows:

```
bool file_exists ( string filename )
resource fopen (string fname, string mode [, bool useincpth [, resource zcontext]])
```

The Code

```php
<?php
  //sample7_1.php

  //First, declare the file you want to open.
  $file = "samplefile1.txt";
  //Now, you use the file_exists() function to confirm its existence.
  if (file_exists ($file)){
    //Then you attempt to open the file, in this case for reading.
    try {
      if ($readfile = fopen ($file, "r")){
        //Then you can work with the file.
        echo "File opened successfully.";
      } else {
        //If it fails, you throw an exception.
        throw new exception ("Sorry, the file could not be opened.");
      }
    } catch (exception $e) {
      echo $e->getmessage();
    }
  } else {
    echo "File does not exist.";
  }
?>
```

```
File opened successfully.
```

How It Works

As you can see, you first confirm that the file does in fact exist and then try to open the file for reading. By using PHP 5's new exception handling, you take care of the eventuality that the file might not have the proper permissions to read. Table 7-1 shows many other ways of opening a file. Should you neglect to supply an argument to the fopen() function designating how to open it, PHP will supply a warning, and the file will not open correctly.

Table 7-1. *PHP 5 Arguments for Opening a File*

Argument	Description
r	Opens a file for reading
r+	Opens a file for both reading and writing
w	Opens a file for writing only
w+	Opens a file for reading and writing
a	Opens a file for appending (write-only)
a+	Opens a file for appending (read/write)
X	Creates a file and opens it for writing only
x+	Creates a file and opens it for reading and writing

7-2. Reading from Files

PHP 5 has a nice way of reading from files. Not only can you open a file for reading, but you can also have PHP attempt to create the file for you and then open it. Created files are owned by the server by default (on Linux servers) and should thus be given proper permissions by the script to ensure that you (and your script) can access the file later. Similarly, when reading files, you can go about doing this in a few ways. Which way you choose to use depends on what the goal of your script is. You need to ask yourself exactly what it is you want to accomplish by reading in data from the text file.

The most common means of acquiring information from a text file is by using the functions fgetc(), fgets(), and fread(). Each of these functions is similar in use but has its own separate strengths and weaknesses; the idea is to pick the right one for the job. The methods are as follows:

- `string` **fgetc** (resource handle)

- `string` **fgets** (resource handle [, int length])

- `string` **fread** (resource handle, int length)

The function fgetc() returns a character from a line in a file, fgets() returns a single line from a file, and fread() returns a requested amount of bytes worth of data from a file. Typically, if you are on the lookout for only one character at a time, use the fgetc() method. If you need access to the entire line of a file, use the fgets() function; should you need a specific set of information for a line in a file, use the fread() method.

In the case of the sample script, since we have no idea how large the counter could get, the example will use the fread() function combined with the filesize() function (which returns the size of the file in question) to read the entirety of the current counter so as to handle any eventuality.

The Code

```php
<?php

//sample7_2.php

//First, declare the file you want to open.
$file = "samplefile1.txt";
//Now, you use the file_exists() function to confirm its existence.
if (file_exists ($file)){
  //Then you attempt to open the file, in this case for reading.
  try {
    if ($readfile = fopen ($file, "r")){
      //Then you can work with the file.
      //Get the current value of the counter by using fread().
      $curvalue = fread ($readfile,filesize($file));
      //Then you can output the results.
      echo $curvalue;
    } else {
      //If it fails, throw an exception.
      throw new exception ("Sorry, the file could not be opened.");
    }
  } catch (exception $e) {
    echo $e->getmessage();
  }
} else {
  echo "File does not exist.";
}
?>
```

The result would be a numerical value such as the following:

9

How It Works

Notice the following line:

```php
$curvalue = fread ($readfile,filesize($file));
```

In this line, you simply read in the current value of the counter using the fread() function. The variable $curvalue will now be assigned the value at which the counter is currently sitting.

7-3. Writing to Files

When working with files, you will also need to know how to make changes to them, that is, how to write to files. Similar with reading from files, you can write to files in a multitude of ways. The most common way of accomplishing this task is by using the function fwrite(), but several methods exist:

- int **fwrite** (resource handle, string string [, int length])

- int **file_put_contents** (string filename, mixed data [, int flags [, resource context]])

- fputs (alias of fwrite())

Generally, the fwrite() function acts as a simple way to write something to a file and should be used if you are opening and closing a file using the fopen() and fclose() functions. The (new-to-PHP 5) function file_put_contents() allows you to open, write to, and then close a file—all at the same time. Lastly, the function fputs() merely acts as an alias to fwrite() and can be used in the same manner.

Since writing to files is a little more sensitive than reading from them (because you wouldn't want any script to overwrite sensitive information), you have to perform a few more checks to ensure that you can actually write to the file in question. Thankfully, PHP 5 supports the function is_writable(), which will return a boolean value that lets you know whether you can write to a file. As a careful and methodic programmer, it is your duty to perform this sort of validation. Consider the following addition to the counter script, which will update the counter by 1 and then write the new value to the file.

The Code

```php
<?php

//sample7_3.php

//First, declare the file you want to open.
$file = "samplefile1.txt";
//Now, you use the file_exists() function to confirm its existence.
if (file_exists ($file)){
  //Then you attempt to open the file, in this case for reading.
  try {
    if ($readfile = fopen ($file, "r")){
      //Then you can work with the file.
      //Get the current value of the counter by using fread().
      $curvalue = fread ($readfile,filesize($file));
      //Increment our counter by 1.
      $curvalue++;
      //Then attempt to open the file for writing, again validating.
      if (is_writable ($file)){
        try {
          if ($writefile = fopen ($file, "w")){
            //Then write the new value to the file.
```

```
                    fwrite ($writefile, $curvalue);
                    echo "Wrote $curvalue to file.";
                  } else {
                      throw new exception ("Sorry, the file could not be opened");
                  }
                } catch (exception $e){
                  echo $e->getmessage();
                }
              } else {
                echo "File could not be opened for writing";
              }
            } else {
              //If it fails, you throw an exception.
              throw new exception ("Sorry, the file could not be opened.");
            }
        } catch (exception $e) {
          echo $e->getmessage();
        }
    } else {
      echo "File does not exist.";
    }
?>
```

```
Wrote 11 to file.
```

How It Works

Note how you now increment the counter and then write to the file the new value of the counter. This means when the next person to visit your site loads the counter script, they will find the new value written to the file and subsequently increment that by 1, increasing the counter. Also note the error handling involved once again.

7-4. Closing Files

The last thing you must do, once you have finished working with your file, is to clean up the mess. By this we mean that you must close the current file pointer. Those of you paying careful attention to the previous scripts will note the distinct lack of any cleanup operations, which is just a poor way of handling code.

Closing a file in PHP is just as simple as opening one; you simply need to invoke the fclose() method, which will close the file pointer link. This is the prototype for fclose():

```
bool fclose ( resource handle )
```

The following example finalizes the counter code by outputting the value of the counter to the website (hence making it a functional script) and cleaning up your work with the fclose() function.

The Code

```php
<?php

  //sample7_4.php

  //First, declare the file you want to open.
  $file = "samplefile1.txt";
  //Now, you use the file_exists() function to confirm its existence.
  if (file_exists ($file)){
    //Then you attempt to open the file, in this case for reading.
    try {
      if ($readfile = fopen ($file, "r")){
        //Then you can work with the file.
        //Get the current value of our counter by using fread().
        $curvalue = fread ($readfile,filesize($file));
        //Close the file since you have no more need to read.
        fclose ($readfile);
        //Increment the counter by 1.
        $curvalue++;
        //Then attempt to open the file for writing, and again, validating.
        if (is_writable ($file)){
          try {
            if ($writefile = fopen ($file, "w")){
              //Then write the new value to the file.
              fwrite ($writefile, $curvalue);
              //Close the file, as you have no more to write.
              fclose ($writefile);
              //Then lastly, output the counter.
              echo $curvalue;
            } else {
              throw new exception ("Sorry, the file could not be opened");
            }
          } catch (exception $e){
            echo $e->getmessage();
          }
        } else {
          echo "File could not be opened for writing";
        }
      } else {
        //If it fails, throw an exception.
        throw new exception ("Sorry, the file could not be opened.");
      }
    } catch (exception $e) {
      echo $e->getmessage();
    }
  } else {
    echo "File does not exist.";
  }
?>
```

How It Works

Notice these lines:

```
fclose ($readfile);
fclose ($writefile);
```

Both of these lines finalize the reading and writing business by closing the file pointer links. With that out of the way, you can simply output the current count, and there you have it—a fully functional, PHP 5–driven, heavily validated counter script.

7-5. Reading and Writing Comma-Separated Data

A frequent operation you will need to perform, particularly in this day and age of standardizing data, is the process of removing data from a source to convert it into another format. With XML arising as a common form of storing data, and database interactivity becoming easier and cheaper every year, it is rather commonplace to have to take data from an antiquated source (such as a point-of-sale system) and convert it into a more usable, modern-day form of data storage.

One way that many point-of-sale systems export data (and most database applications as well) is in the form of comma-delimited files. In other words, each row of every table (or whatever it is that is being used to store the data) can be exported and then delimited by a comma, typically in the form of a text file. This is a universal way to export data, and most database systems have features that allow them to read such a file.

Luckily, reading and writing comma-separated data with PHP 5 is simple, quick, and efficient. By using some of the functions from the previous example, plus the explode() string function, you can quickly and efficiently parse or create a set of comma-delimited data.

For this example, we have created a text file that will represent a dump of a book repository database. Each row in the theoretical table contains a unique ID number, the name of the book, and the author who wrote the book. For clarity's sake, we have written only three lines to the text file, but in real life, it could very well be 30,000 lines; this script will take care of it either way.

The text file looks like this:

```
1,Book 1,An Author
2,Book 2,Another Author
3,Book 3,Yet Another Author
```

The Code

```php
<?php

  //sample7_5.php

  //First, find the comma-separated file.
  $commafile = "samplefile2.txt";
  //Now, you use the file_exists() function to confirm its existence.
  if (file_exists ($commafile)){
```

```php
    //In this case, you will use the file() function to read an entire file
    //into an array.
    $rows = file ($commafile);
    for ($i = 0; $i < count ($rows); $i++){
        //You use the explode function to break the current row into the sum
        //of its comma-delimited parts.
        $exprow = explode (",", $rows[$i]);
        //Normally at this point you would insert the data into a database
        //or convert it into XML.  In this case, for brevity, you will simply
        //output it.
        echo "ID: " . $exprow[0] . "<br />";
        echo "Name: " . $exprow[1] . "<br />";
        echo "Author: " . $exprow[2] . "<br />";
        echo "<hr />";
    }
} else {
    echo "File does not exist.";
}
//Reading the data back into a comma-delimited file is just as easy.
//Generally you would do this from a database, but in this case, you
//will create a set of arrays to output.
$idarray = array ("1","2","3");
$namearray = array ("Book 1","Book 2","Book 3");
$authorarray = array ("An Author","Another Author","Yet Another Author");

$newfile = "samplefile2.txt";
//You will open it in such a way that it creates a new file if one
//does not exist.
try {
    if ($readfile = fopen ($newfile, "w")){
        //You then go through the array and write a line at a time.
        for ($i = 0; $i < count ($idarray); $i++){
            $writestring = $idarray[$i] . "," . $namearray[$i] . ","➥
. $authorarray[$i] . "\n";
            fwrite ($readfile, $writestring);
        }
    fclose ($readfile);
    } else {
        //If it fails, you throw an exception.
        throw new exception ("Sorry, the file could not be opened.");
    }
} catch (exception $e) {
    echo $e->getmessage();
}
?>
```

```
ID: 1
Name: Book 1
Author: An Author

ID: 2
Name: Book 2
Author: Another Author

ID: 3
Name: Book 3
Author: Yet Another Author
```

How It Works

In this case, you use a function called `file()` that reads the contents of a file into an array effectively, one line at a time. The `file()` function's prototype is as follows:

```
array file ( string filename [, int use_include_path [, resource context]] )
```

7-6. Reading Fixed-Width Delimited Data

Sometimes you will have to build an algorithm that allows you to read exact coordinates in a text file. For example, variables could have been set within a text file and flat files could have been created to hold information in lieu of a proper database. In this sort of occurrence, you must take a few more precautions when reading and writing the data in the file, because it must be done rather precisely. Figure 7-1 shows an inventory listing where the fields are kept within two exact coordinates in a text file.

```
Soap                    8
Towels                  11
Body Lotion             3
```

Figure 7-1. *A fixed-width, delimited data text file*

In this example, the name of the inventory item is being kept within the first 20 characters of each line in a text file, and the next 20 characters contain the amount of inventory remaining in the system. By using a handy string function (discussed in more detail in Chapter 6) called `substr()`, you can cycle through the text file, use the method to break the required parts of the file into appropriate variables, and proceed to perform the needed algorithm.

The Code

```php
<?php

  //sample7_6.php

  $flatfile = "samplefile3.txt";
  //Now, you use the file_exists() function to confirm its existence.
  if (file_exists ($flatfile)){
    //In this case, you will use the file() function to read an entire file
    //into an array.
    $rows = file ($flatfile);
    for ($i = 0; $i < count ($rows); $i++){
      //Now, you use the substr() function to parse out the appropriate parts.
      $item = substr ($rows[$i],0,20);
      $amount = substr ($rows[$i],20,40);
      //Note that you trim the end spaces just in case.
      echo "Item: " . rtrim ($item) . " has " . rtrim ($amount)➥
. " unit (s) left.<br />";
    }
  } else {
    echo "File does not exist.";
  }
?>
```

How It Works

Using this particular flat file, you will end up with a result that looks something like this:

```
Item: Soap has 8 unit (s) left.
Item: Towels has 11 unit (s) left.
Item: Body Lotion has 3 unit (s) left.
```

The method for handling this functionality is quite efficient when using the substr() function. By pulling in each line of the text file and then parsing out the appropriate sections of the file using the substr() function, you are left with only the data in which you are interested. With this data in hand, it is simply a matter of what to do with it; in this case, you merely output the results.

7-7. Reading and Writing Binary Data in a File

Reading and writing binary data in a file is quite similar to performing the same functionality demonstrated previously but is slightly more portable across different platforms. Binary files can be read on pretty much any platform and can be a composition of any type of file format (rather than just text files). You can typically see what a binary file might look like by opening an image or music file in a text editor such as Notepad. You will notice that most of the characters are nonalphabetic and look rather like gibberish to the untrained eye (or computer).

The functions fopen(), fread(), fwrite(), and fclose() will still work just fine with binary files. The function fgets(), however, will not work exactly as planned because of its reliance on string types. The fread() function is generally the function of choice for reading from binary files.

Basically, the major change when working with binary files is to add a *b* to the end of the argument you assign when opening the file. The following example showcases how to read and write to a forced binary file.

The Code

```php
<?php

  //sample7_7.php

  //First, dictate a file.
  $binfile = "samplefile4.txt";
  //Now, you use the file_exists() function to confirm its existence.
  if (file_exists ($binfile)){
    //Then open the file for binary read and writing.
    try {
      if ($readfile = fopen ($binfile, "rb+")){
        //Now, you can read an write in binary.
        $curtext = fread ($readfile,filesize($binfile));
        echo $curtext; //Hello World!

        //Then you can write to it.
        fwrite ($readfile, "Hi World!");

        //Then you close the file.
        fclose ($readfile);
      }
    } catch (exception $e) {
      echo $e->getmessage();
    }
  } else {
    echo "Sorry, file does not exist.";
  }
?>
```

```
Hello World!Hi World!
```

How It Works

As you can see, reading and writing with binary files is quite similar to reading or writing normal text-based files. The big difference comes into play within the fopen() function, as you must tell the system to read in the file as a binary file. With the binary option in place (in this case rb+, or reading a binary file and creating it if it does not exist), the system is now free to read in whatever binary file has been specified.

7-8. Getting the Number of Lines in a File

Finding the number of lines in a file is also quite handy. Luckily, with PHP it is also rather easy to accomplish. Because the file() function creates an array filled with each line in a separate index, you can simply read a file into an array and use count() to retrieve what is essentially the number of lines in a file.

The Code

```php
<?php

  //sample7_8.php

  //First, dictate a file.
  $afile = "samplefile5.txt";
  //Now, you use the file_exists() function to confirm its existence.
  if (file_exists ($afile)){
    //Read it using the file() function.
    $rows = file ($afile);
    //You can then use the count() function to tell you the number of lines.
    echo count ($rows) . " lines in this file"; //Outputs 4 in this case
  } else {
    echo "Sorry, file does not exist.";
  }
?>
```

```
4 lines in this file
```

How It Works

The highly useful nature of the file() function really shows itself with this example. Because the file() function reads each line of a file into an array, all you need to do to find the number of lines in the file is to call the count() function to determine an array size. Since each index in the array would be filled with one line from the file, the count() function will retrieve the line number with no issue whatsoever.

7-9. Getting the Number of Characters, Words, or Paragraphs in a File

Working with PHP and files allows for some rather powerful functionality. Consider, for example, that you want to find the number of characters, the number of words, or even the number of paragraphs within a certain text file. Naturally, performing this in any conventional way could potentially take forever. Fortunately, while harnessing the power of PHP 5, you can loop your way through the text file, stopping only when you get to the end of a file using the function feof(), whose prototype is as follows:

```
bool feof ( resource handle )
```

The following example counts all three of the previous queries (characters, words, and paragraphs) as it runs through the file. Assume a paragraph is separated by an end line character, and a word is separated by a blank character. Naturally, you will accept any character for the character count.

The Code

```php
<?php

//sample7_9.php

//First, dictate a file.
$afile = "samplefile6.txt";
//Now, you use the file_exists() function to confirm its existence.
if (file_exists ($afile)){
  try {
$charcounter = 0;
$wordcounter = 0;
//You default the paragraph counter to 1, as there is bound to be at least 1 line.
$paragraphcounter = 1;
$haveanewline = false;
  if ($readfile = fopen ($afile, "r")){
    while (!feof ($readfile)){
      $curchar = fgetc ($readfile);
      $charcounter++;
      //If you have a blank character, that's a word.
      if ($curchar == " "){
        $wordcounter++;
      }
      //If you have a new line, then you increment the counter.
      if ($curchar == "\n"){
        $paragraphcounter++;
      }
    }
  }
//Now, you close the file.
  fclose ($readfile);
```

```
   //And output the results.
    echo "Number of characters: " . $charcounter . "<br />";
    echo "Number of words: " . $wordcounter . "<br />";
    echo "Number of paragraphs: " . $paragraphcounter;
      } else {
         throw new exception ("Sorry, the file could not be opened");
      }
    } catch (exception $e){
      echo $e->getmessage();
    }
  } else {
    echo "Sorry, file does not exist.";
  }
?>
```

```
Number of characters: 1343
Number of words: 204
Number of paragraphs: 3
```

How It Works

As you can see, the output created is a handy listing of the number of characters, words, and paragraphs found within the file. Naturally, you could customize this script for some specific features such as instances of each letter within a file, special characters, and many other intricate uses.

The actual work involved with gathering statistics from a text file is strictly a matter of taste. For all the figures, you merely loop through the entire file and compile a list of what the script finds. Of course, any character it finds will be added to a character counter because the example considered something a new word instance only if the previous character was a space. Finding the number of paragraphs is a little trickier. We prefer to think of a new line as a new paragraph, but some, no doubt, prefer to include a paragraph only after two new line characters; the choice is up to you. In any case, the script continues to read the file until it reaches the end and then outputs the results as shown previously.

7-10. Project: Creating and Using a File Class

When dealing with files, you will spend a lot of time checking to make sure a file is open, is closed, exists, and so on. Because validation is key when dealing with text files, and because a hefty amount of validation is needed at all times, it makes sense to create a more usable class that does all the legwork for you. The following cfile class takes most of the guesswork and validation out of working with files. You simply create a new instance of the class by pointing it to a specified file path, and the system takes care of the rest. You can easily read, write, or append, and the class and PHP 5's handy new exception handling system handles all the validation.

The Code

```php
<?php

//sample7_10.php

//  Copyright 2005, Lee Babin (lee@thecodeshoppe.com)
//  This code may be used and redistributed without charge
//  under the terms of the GNU General Public
//  License version 2.0 or later -- www.gnu.org
//  Subject to the retention of this copyright
//  and GPL Notice in all copies or derived works

class cfile {

    //The path to the file you want to work with.
    protected $thepath;

    //Error messages in the form of constants for ease of use.
    const FOUNDERROR = "Sorry, the file in question does not exist.";
    const PERMERROR = "Sorry, you do not have the proper permissions on this file";
    const OPENERROR = "Sorry, the file in question could not be opened.";
    const CLOSEERROR = "Sorry, the file could not be closed.";

    //The constructor function.
    public function __construct (){

        $num_args = func_num_args();

        if($num_args > 0){
            $args = func_get_args();
            $this->thepath = $args[0];
        }
    }

    //A function to open the file.
    private function openfile ($readorwrite){
        //First, ensure the file exists.
        try {
            if (file_exists ($this->thepath)){
                //Now, you need to see if you are reading or writing or both.
                $proceed = false;
                if ($readorwrite == "r"){
                    if (is_readable($this->thepath)){
                        $proceed = true;
                    }
                } elseif ($readorwrite == "w"){
                    if (is_writable($this->thepath)){
                        $proceed = true;
                    }
```

```php
      } else {
        if (is_readable($this->thepath) && is_writable($this->thepath)){
          $proceed = true;
        }
      }
      try {
        if ($proceed){
          //You can now attempt to open the file.
          try {
            if ($filepointer = fopen ($this->thepath, $readorwrite)){
              return $filepointer;
            } else {
              throw new exception (self::OPENERROR);
              return false;
            }
          } catch (exception $e) {
            echo $e->getmessage();
          }
        } else {
          throw new exception (self::PERMERROR);
        }
      } catch (exception $e) {
        echo $e->getmessage();
      }
    } else {
      throw new exception (self::FOUNDERROR);
    }
  } catch (exception $e) {
    echo $e->getmessage();
  }
}

//A function to close a file.
function closefile () {
  try {
    if (!fclose ($this->thepath)){
      throw new exception (self::CLOSEERROR);
    }
  } catch (exception $e) {
    echo $e->getmessage();
  }
}

//A function to read a file, then return the results of the read in a string.
public function read () {
  //First, attempt to open the file.
  $filepointer = $this->openfile ("r");

  //Now, return a string with the read data.
```

```
    if ($filepointer != false){
      //Then you can read the file.
      return fread ($filepointer,filesize ($this->thepath));
    }

    //Lastly, close the file.
    $this->closefile ();
  }

  //A function to write to a file.
  public function write ($towrite) {
    //First, attempt to open the file.
    $filepointer = $this->openfile ("w");

    //Now, return a string with the read data.
    if ($filepointer != false){
      //Then you can read the file.
      return fwrite ($filepointer, $towrite);
    }

    //Lastly, close the file.
    $this->closefile ();
  }

  //A function to append to a file.
  public function append ($toappend) {
    //First, attempt to open the file.
    $filepointer = $this->openfile ("a");

    //Now, return a string with the read data.
    if ($filepointer != false){
      //Then you can read the file.
      return fwrite ($filepointer, $toappend);
    }

    //Lastly, close the file.
    $this->closefile ();
  }

  //A function to set the path to a new file.
  public function setpath ($newpath) {
    $this->thepath = $newpath;
  }

}

?>
```

The code and the comments speak for themselves. The only truly complicated part of this class has already been discussed in the earlier examples. The way that the class can work for you is the rather exciting part. Consider the following example, for instance:

```php
<?php
  //Include the class.
  require_once ("file.class.inc.php");
  //Then create a new instance of the class.
  $myfile = new cfile ("sample7_9.txt");

  //Now, let's try reading it.
  echo $myfile->read();

  //Then let's try writing to the file.
  $myfile->write ("Hello World!");

  //Then, let's try appending.
  $myfile->append ("Hello Again!");

?>
```

```
Hello World!Hello Again!
```

How It Works

As you can see, reading and writing has been completely simplified. You simply instantiate a cfile object, and from there you can read and write by simply passing the appropriate arguments. The read() function returns a complete string from the text file, the write() method automatically writes the specified verbiage into the file, and the append() method adds the text you specify to the end of the file. All in all, writing $myfile->read() is much easier and more efficient than validating the opening and closing of the file every time.

Working with Directories

Just like with files, PHP 5 also does an effective job of parsing and reading directories. In fact, the amount of flexibility is rather daunting when you consider you could effectively search and output an entire directory structure by using recursive functionality. This sort of algorithm can be a valuable use of your time as a developer. The following are several examples of just how powerful PHP can be when working with a file server's directory listing.

PHP 5 consists of some handy directory parsing functions. opendir() opens a directory for reading, is_dir() verifies the existence of a directory, readdir() parses through a directory, closedir() closes an opened directory, and scandir() allows you to scan through a directory to retrieve an array of files within the directory. The prototypes for these useful functions are as follows:

```
resource opendir ( string path )
bool is_dir ( string path )
string readdir ( resource dir_handle )
void closedir ( resource dir_handle )
array scandir ( string directory [, int sorting_order [, resource context]] )
```

7-11. Listing All Files in the Current Directory

A handy script you may find yourself in need of is a script with the ability to list all the files within a directory. This sort of dynamic script can be helpful when dealing with mass client-submitted uploads or multiple XML files. PHP is set up to handle such occurrences, and the result is an effective way of handling the directory and file structure that you have within your server. The following example creates a function that will read through a directory of choice and output all the files within the directory.

The Code

```php
<?php

//sample7_11.php

function numfilesindir ($thedir){
  //First, you ensure that the directory exists.
  if (is_dir ($thedir)){
    //Now, you scan the files in this directory using scandir.
    $scanarray = scandir ($thedir);
    //Then you begin parsing the array.
    //Since scandir() counts the "." and ".." file navigation listings
    //as files, you should not list them.
    for ($i = 0; $i < count ($scanarray); $i++){
      if ($scanarray[$i] != "." && $scanarray[$i] != ".."){
        //Now, you check to make sure this is a file, not a directory.
        if (is_file ($thedir . "/" . $scanarray[$i])){
          echo $scanarray[$i] . "<br />";
        }
      }
    }
  } else {
    echo "Sorry, this directory does not exist.";
  }
}
//You then call the function pointed to the directory you want to look through.
echo numfilesindir ("sample1");
?>
```

1.txt
2.txt

How It Works

This example is a combination of exception handling and the scandir() function. It is always important when dealing with files or directories to validate and ensure that a file or directory is present before you begin working with it. In this case you ensure a valid directory and then move through it using the scandir() function. As the script moves through the directory, it checks to ensure a valid file and then outputs the filename if it exists.

7-12. Listing All Files of a Certain Type

While you are working on displaying directory and file structure, you might find that display-ing all the files of a certain type is useful. For instance, let's assume you have been hired to create a content management system (CMS) in which the client is allowed to log in and then browse a list of editable files within the current directory. By harnessing the power of PHP, you can output the files for selection from the client, and you can even prechoose which file types you will allow them to see.

You can use a similar block of code to what you saw in recipe 7-11, but this time you will create an array of allowable file types. The system will then check the file type of the current file that is being scanned and determine whether it is a file you want to display to the client. By doing this, you allow common file types to be worked on while maintaining a sense of directory integrity.

The Code

```php
<?php

  //sample7_12.php

  function outputfiles ($allowedtypes, $thedir){

    //First, you ensure that the directory exists.
    if (is_dir ($thedir)){

      //Now, you scan the files in this directory using scandir.
      $scanarray = scandir ($thedir);

      //Then you begin parsing the array.
      //Since scandir() counts the "." and ".." file navigation listings
      //as files, you should not list them.
      for ($i = 0; $i < count ($scanarray); $i++){
        if ($scanarray[$i] != "." && $scanarray[$i] != ".."){

          //Now, you check to make sure this is a file, not a directory.
          if (is_file ($thedir . "/" . $scanarray[$i])){

            //Now, since you are going to allow the client to edit this file,
            //you must check if it is read and writable.
            if (is_writable ($thedir. "/" . $scanarray[$i]) &&➥
```

```
          is_readable($thedir . "/" . $scanarray[$i])){

                    //Now, you check to see if the file type exists➥
          within the allowed type array.
                    $thepath = pathinfo ($thedir . "/" . $scanarray[$i]);
                    if (in_array ($thepath['extension'], $allowedtypes)){

                        //If the file follows your stipulations,➥
          then you can proceed to output it.
                        echo $scanarray[$i] . "<br />";
                    }
                }
            }
          }
        }
      } else {
        echo "Sorry, this directory does not exist.";
      }
    }
    //You then call the function pointed to the directory you want to look through.
    //In this case you pass it an array with allowed file extensions.
    //You want them to edit only .txt files.
    $allowedtypes = array ("txt","html");
    echo outputfiles ($allowedtypes, "sample2");
?>
```

```
test.html
test1.txt
test2.txt
```

How It Works

You will notice we have thrown a couple of new functions into the fray. The functions
is_readable() and is_writable() tell you whether the file in question will allow you to read
or write to it, respectively, and the function pathinfo() provides you with an array containing
the prominent features of the file path. These three functions have prototypes as follows:

```
bool is_readable ( string filename )
bool is_writable ( string filename )
array pathinfo ( string path [, int options] )
```

   As you can see, you can edit the $allowedtypes array to completely customize the allowed
types that will appear in the list. This can be handy, as some clients will no doubt be provided
different privileges than others.

7-13. Sorting Files by Date

Just as you can sort a directory using your operating system in a number of ways, so too may it be important to be able to sort a directory of files using certain parameters. PHP is rather powerful in its ability to access files; you can acquire a wide range of information about a file using some of the prebuilt PHP functionality. Obviously, several ways exist to sort a directory of files (size, modified date, type, and so on), but in this recipe we will show you a quick and easy way to sort all the files in a directory by date.

We have already gone over how to list files in a directory, so now you just need to implement an algorithm that will take the listing and return it in a date-sorted fashion. This solution simply requires a little bit of ingenuity; rather than actually outputting the list directly, you will do this in the form of a function that returns a sorted array of filenames (by date, of course).

The Code

```php
<?php

//sample7_13.php

function sortfilesbydate ($thedir){
  //First, you ensure that the directory exists.
  if (is_dir ($thedir)){
    //Now, you scan the files in this directory using scandir.
    $scanarray = scandir ($thedir);
    $finalarray = array();
    //Then you begin parsing the array.
    //Since scandir() counts the "." and ".." file navigation listings
    //as files, you should not list them.
    for ($i = 0; $i < count ($scanarray); $i++){
      if ($scanarray[$i] != "." && $scanarray[$i] != ".."){
        //Now, you check to make sure this is a file, not a directory.
        if (is_file ($thedir . "/" . $scanarray[$i])){
          //Now what you need to do is cycle the data into an associative array.
          $finalarray[$thedir . "/" . $scanarray[$i]] =➡
filemtime ($thedir . "/" . $scanarray[$i]);
        }
      }
    }
    //Finally, when you have gone through the entire array,➡
you simply asort() it.
    asort ($finalarray);
    return ($finalarray);
  } else {
    echo "Sorry, this directory does not exist.";
  }
}
//You then call the function pointed to the directory➡
you want to look through.
```

```
   $sortedarray = sortfilesbydate ("sample3");
   //You could then output it as such:
   while ($element = each ($sortedarray)){
      echo "File: " . $element['key'] . " last modified: " . ➥
date ("F j, Y h:i:s", $element['value']) .      "<br />";
   }
?>
```

```
File: sample3/test1.txt was last modified: April 12, 2005 06:04:18
File: sample3/test2.txt was last modified: April 12, 2005 06:04:26
File: sample3/test.html was last modified: April 12, 2005 06:05:10
File: sample3/test.php was last modified: April 12, 2005 06:05:18
```

How It Works

In this particular function, you use a couple of new concepts. For starters, you use an associative array that is discussed in more detail in Jon Stephen's Chapter 4. By using an associative array, you can assign the filename to the key value and associate it with the file modification date stored in the value portion. To actually retrieve the last modified time, you use the filemtime() function, which returns a Unix timestamp of the last time the file was modified. You could have also used the filectime() function, which returns pretty much the same thing; however, filemtime() seems to work better on a multitude of platforms, while filectime() does not seem to work properly on all Windows servers.

   Notice the use of the asort() function that sorts the array. Should you want to sort the array in reverse order, the arsort() function can take care of that predicament for you. The prototypes for all these new functions are as follows:

```
int filemtime ( string filename )
int filectime ( string filename )
bool asort ( array &array [, int sort_flags] )
bool arsort ( array &array [, int sort_flags] )
```

7-14. Generating a Recursive Directory Listing

Naturally, a powerful application that can be extremely useful for outputting a complete directory listing is the infamous recursive directory listing. Basically what this example shows is how to take a function that outputs all files in a directory and use it recursively by allowing it to call itself if it hits another directory. It is something of an age-old script that has been written a million times; however, we show how to do it the PHP 5 way and bring things up-to-date. The following example recursively outlines an entire directory with all the files and directories beneath it.

The Code

```php
<?php

  //sample7_14.php

  function recurdir ($thedir) {
    //First attempt to open the directory.
    try {
      if ($adir = opendir ($thedir)){
        //Scan through the directory.
        while (false !== ($anitem = readdir ($adir))){
          //Do not count the . or .. in a directory.
          if ($anitem != "." && $anitem != ".."){
            //Now, if it is another directory, then you indent a bit
            //and go recursive.
            if (is_dir ($thedir . "/" . $anitem)){
              ?><span style="font-weight: bold;"><?php echo $anitem; ?></span><?php
              ?><div style="margin-left: 10px;"><?php
              recurdir ($thedir . "/" . $anitem );
              ?></div><?php
            } elseif (is_file ($thedir . "/" . $anitem)){
              //Then echo the file.
              echo $anitem . "<br />";
            }
          }
        }
      } else {
        throw new exception ("Sorry, directory could not be opened.");
      }
    } catch (exception $e) {
      echo $e->getmessage();
    }
  }

  //Run the function.
  recurdir ("sample4");
?>
```

How It Works

As you can see, the function uses exception handling to run the validation and then outputs all files unless it hits a directory, in which case it then calls itself to do the same thing with a new path. The result is a recursive function that will output an entire directory listing. The following shows how the output might look:

```
test1
    test1_1
      2levelsdown.txt
      2levelsdownagain.txt
    2levelsdown.txt
test2
    test2.txt
test0.txt
test01.txt
```

7-15. Using the SPL DirectoryIterator Object

The Standard PHP Library (SPL) set of classes and interfaces is a truly promising step toward enforcing a bit of conformity among PHP developers. By bringing together some truly functional and helpful methods contained within some easy-to-use classes, PHP developers from all around the globe can begin to write reusable applications that conform to the same standard. The SPL set of classes is an overlooked piece of functionality in the PHP 5 build, in which it is now included by default.

Although the SPL is constantly expanding, it already contains a good amount of functionality ready for use. Of particular note in regard to this chapter are the DirectoryIterator and RecursiveDirectoryIterator objects. You can clean up much of the redundant code you have been writing by using a set of methods designed specifically for the purpose at hand. Although the following small example cannot cover the entirety of the functionality contained within these objects, Table 7-2 lists all the methods available (currently). You can obtain more research at http://www.php.net/spl.

Table 7-2. *PHP 5 SPL DirectoryIterator and RecursiveDirectoryIterator Methods*

Method	Description
DirectoryIterator::__construct	Constructs a new directory iterator from a path
DirectoryIterator::current	Returns this (needed for the Iterator interface)
DirectoryIterator::getATime	Gets last access time of file
DirectoryIterator::getCTime	Gets inode modification time of file
DirectoryIterator::getChildren	Returns an iterator for the current entry if it is a directory
DirectoryIterator::getFilename	Returns filename of current directory entry
DirectoryIterator::getGroup	Gets file group

Method	Description
DirectoryIterator::getInode	Gets file inode
DirectoryIterator::getMTime	Gets last modification time of file
DirectoryIterator::getOwner	Gets file owner
DirectoryIterator::getPath	Returns directory path
DirectoryIterator::getPathname	Returns path and filename of current directory entry
DirectoryIterator::getPerms	Gets file permissions
DirectoryIterator::getSize	Gets file size
DirectoryIterator::getType	Gets file type
DirectoryIterator::isDir	Returns true if file is directory
DirectoryIterator::isDot	Returns true if current entry is . or ..
DirectoryIterator::isExecutable	Returns true if file is executable
DirectoryIterator::isFile	Returns true if file is a regular file
DirectoryIterator::isLink	Returns true if file is symbolic link
DirectoryIterator::isReadable	Returns true if file can be read
DirectoryIterator::isWritable	Returns true if file can be written
DirectoryIterator::key	Returns current directory entry
DirectoryIterator::next	Moves to next entry
DirectoryIterator::rewind	Rewinds directory back to the start
DirectoryIterator::valid	Checks whether directory contains more entries
RecursiveDirectoryIterator::getChildren	Returns an iterator for the current entry if it is a directory
RecursiveDirectoryIterator::hasChildren	Returns whether current entry is a directory and not . or ..
RecursiveDirectoryIterator::key	Returns path and filename of current directory entry
RecursiveDirectoryIterator::next	Moves to next entry
RecursiveDirectoryIterator::rewind	Rewinds directory back to the start
RecursiveIteratorIterator::current	Accesses the current element value
RecursiveIteratorIterator::getDepth	Gets the current depth of the recursive iteration
RecursiveIteratorIterator::getSubIterator	Gets the current active sub iterator
RecursiveIteratorIterator::key	Accesses the current key
RecursiveIteratorIterator::next	Moves forward to the next element
RecursiveIteratorIterator::rewind	Rewinds the iterator to the first element of the top-level inner iterator
RecursiveIteratorIterator::valid	Checks whether the current position is valid

The following example takes the previous one and shows how it might look if you used the RecursiveDirectoryIterator instead of the regular means.

The Code

```php
<?php

  //sample7_15.php

  //Create a new instance of a recursivedirectoryiterator.
  $di = new RecursiveDirectoryIterator ("sample4");

  function dirrecurse ($di){

    //Cycle through the directory.
    for ( ; $di->valid(); $di->next()){
      //Ensure that you have a directory and exclude the dots.
      if ($di->isDir() && !$di->isDot()){
        //Output the directories in bold.
        ?><span style="font-weight: bold;"><?php echo $di->current(); ?></span><?php
        ?><div style="margin-left: 10px;"><?php
        //Check if the current directory has any children.
        if ($di->hasChildren()){
          //And if so, run the function again.
          dirrecurse ($di->getChildren());
        }
        ?></div><?php
        //Else, if you have a file.
      } elseif ($di->isFile()){
        //Then echo the file.
        echo $di->current() . "<br />";
      }
    }

  }

  //Run the recursion.
  dirrecurse ($di);
?>
```

How It Works

If this code runs correctly, you should see the same result as you did in recipe 7-14. This code, however, is much smoother and abides much better by object-oriented guidelines. Our favorite part of this code is how the object can check in advance for any children. If a child entity exists (and keep in mind, it checks against the dots as well), then it can perform its duty. All in all, we prefer the iterator means of handling directories and look forward to what the PHP developers will come up with next.

Summary

As it is, PHP 5 has no trouble in the slightest when it comes to dealing with files and directories. As the software continues to improve and more features are added, it may be time to begin porting your code to the much more flexible, object-oriented SPL. As you saw, the SPL can quickly and efficiently take care of any directory issues you may have.

In the meantime, however, you can put the regular PHP means of dealing with files and directories to good use by writing your own classes and then extending them. The functionality involved is quite robust and should enable a solution no matter what the problem entails.

It is important to remember to exception handle any potential trouble spots. When dealing with files, especially on a Linux-based server, it is quite important to keep permissions in mind, both when reading and writing. With a proper contingency plan in place, your code will deal with potential issues in a much more competent manner.

Looking Ahead

In the next chapter, Chapter 8, you will learn the ins and outs of one of our favorite, and lesser known, sets of PHP functionality: creating and maintaining images on the fly. PHP 5 provides a nice base for working with images, and now that the GD libraries and font systems are in place by default, it has never been easier to harness their power. See you in the next chapter.

Working with Dynamic Imaging

Working with dynamic images in PHP 5 is easier than it has ever been. PHP 5 includes the GD extension right in the `php.ini` file. Simply remove the comment from the GD extension, and you are set to go. The GD library included with PHP 5 happens to be the upgraded GD2 library, which contains some useful JPG functionality that allows for true-color imaging.

Dynamic imaging becomes especially handy when dealing with servers that do not support PHP or when working with online applications that allow only Hypertext Markup Language (HTML). Because PHP allows you to embed links into a PHP document within an image's SRC tag, you can pull dynamic images from a PHP-enabled server by simply putting the uniform resource locator (URL) of the PHP document into the SRC tag. Using techniques such as these, you can implement some imaginative solutions, including online polls and visitor counters.

Working with Image Types

The first thing you need to know about dynamic imaging is that, like embedding an image with a SRC tag, PHP needs to know what type of image you are going to be working with, and it has pre-built functions that differ slightly depending on the image type. Although many variations of image types exist, for the vast majority of your web career you will be concerned mainly with GIFs, JPGs, and PNGs.

Each file type has its own strengths and weaknesses; and when working with images, you will want to select the right tool for the job. For instance, GIF files are good for small, cartoon- or icon-style graphics. JPGs are excellent for photorealism but are generally larger in file size. PNGs, on the other hand, are quite a bit more powerful (being 16-bit rather than 8-bit) and have a few features (such as lossless compression) that make them an excellent choice for pretty much any task. It is important, however, to remember that PNGs are not fully supported yet on the Internet and should be deployed with relative caution (although newer versions of popular browsers have no problem with PNGs).

8-1. Working with JPGs

Quite often, as a developer, you will find yourself working with JPGs. For crystal-clear imagery, JPG (along with PNG) is the file type of choice. Because JPGs lend themselves well to photo galleries and dynamic thumbnail generation tasks, you will commonly find JPGs to be the right file type for the job.

The Code

```php
<?php

//sample8_1.php

//The first thing to do is check for GD compatibility.
try {
  //First you create a blank canvas.
  if ($animage = imagecreate (200, 200)){
    //Then you can create a new background color for this image.
    $red = imagecolorallocate ($animage, 255, 0, 0);
    //Then you can draw a rectangle on the canvas.
    imagerectangle ($animage, 0, 0, 200, 200, $red);
    //Then you output the new jpg.
    imagejpeg ($animage);
    //And then header the image.
    header ("Content-type: image/jpeg");
    //Finally you destroy the image.
    imagedestroy ($animage);
  } else {
    throw new exception ("Sorry, the GD library may not be set up.");
  }
} catch (exception $e) {
  echo $e->getmessage();
}
?>
```

How It Works

The first aspects of this code that you need to pay attention to are a few image-related functions. In this code you are using a function called imagecreate() to create a blank image (using the size specifications you give it). Note that you use PHP 5's exception handling to take care of any issues that may arise. Also, keep in mind that if the GD library is turned off, the code will throw an exception.

The next thing to understand about images is that in order to deal with colors, you must allocate a specific color to the image in every script in which you want to use color. Colors are based on the red-green-blue (RGB) spectrum with a maximum value being 255 and a minimum value being 0. In this case, you are trying to create a bright red, so you allocate the full 255 to the red attribute of the function imagecolorallocate(), which you can then use for a wide variety of tasks such as creating a red rectangle against the canvas using the imagerectangle() function.

Next, to actually display the image, you must designate what type of image you are using. Since you are attempting to do some JPG work here, you use the imagejpeg() function to designate a JPG image and then use the header() function to output the image. Keep in mind that headers must be outputted before any HTML or output is displayed, so here is where calling a script from the SRC attribute of an IMG tag is highly efficient.

Being the good developer you are, you now must clean up the mess. To take care of the temporary image that is created, you merely call the function imagedestroy(), which, as per its name, sends the temporary image to "sleep with the fishes."

The following are the prototypes for the image functions you can use:

```
resource imagecreate ( int x_size, int y_size )
int imagecolorallocate ( resource image, int red, int green, int blue )
int imagerectangle ( resource image, int x1, int y1, int x2, int y2, int col )
bool imagejpeg ( resource image [, string filename [, int quality]] )
void header ( string string [, bool replace [, int http_response_code]] )
bool imagedestroy ( resource image )
```

Figure 8-1 shows the output for recipe 8-1.

Figure 8-1. *Output of recipe 8-1*

8-2. Working with GIFs

Working with GIF images is largely the same as working with JPG images but with fewer options. For instance, you can sharpen the quality of a JPG image, but GIFs were not intended to be displayed in a photorealistic way and hence look slightly duller.

GIF has its share of history in the online community. Of particular note is when CompuServe (the creator of GIF) attempted to heavily enforce the use of the file format and requested a tax of sorts. Lawsuits and the like went on for years but seem to have cooled down in recent times.

In any case, the GIF is ideal for cartoon- or icon-type images, and it works similarly to JPGs.

The Code

```php
<?php

  //sample8_2.php

  //The first thing you do is check for GD compatibility.
  try {
    //First you create a blank canvas.
    if ($animage = imagecreate (200, 200)){
      //Then you can create a new background color for this image.
      $red = imagecolorallocate ($animage, 255, 0, 0);
      //Then you can draw a rectangle on the canvas.
      imagerectangle ($animage, 0, 0, 200, 200, $red);
      //To make things more interesting, you can add text this time.
      //Let's create a "white" color.
      $white = imagecolorallocate ($animage, 255, 255, 255);
      //Then write on the image.
     imagestring($animage, 5, 45, 50, "Hello World!", $white);
      //Then you output the new gif.
      imagegif ($animage);
      //And then header the image.
      header ("Content-type: image/gif");
      //Finally you destroy the image.
      imagedestroy ($animage);
    } else {
      throw new exception ("Sorry, the GD library may not be setup.");
    }
  } catch (exception $e) {
    echo $e->getmessage();
  }
?>
```

How It Works

As you can see, there really isn't much difference between creating and outputting a JPG image and doing the same for a GIF image; you merely replace the imagejpeg() function with the imagegif() function and then alter the header() function slightly. The important factor to note here is the end file size of both of these images. The JPG image comes in at 1.34KB in size. While this is hardly huge, consider that the same image, outputted in GIF format and with more features (saying "hello" to the world is a feature), is only a third of the size at .45KB. This may not be a substantial difference between these two images, but when the size and quality go up in both, the correlation in size becomes much more evident.

You will notice a few more features in this particular image. First, note that you have created a new color for use, white. You then take the newly assigned white color and use it to write on the image with the imagestring() function. The result is the rather gaudy red GIF image that displays a friendly greeting to the world.

The prototypes for the imagegif() and imagestring() functions are as follows:

```
bool imagegif ( resource image [, string filename] )
int imagestring ( resource image, int font, int x, int y, string s, int col )
```

Figure 8-2 shows the output for recipe 8-2.

Figure 8-2. *Output of recipe 8-2*

8-3. Working with PNGs

Superior to GIF in almost every conceivable way, PNG is the file format of the future. You can look at PNGs as something like higher-quality GIFs. Everything about them looks sharper than GIFs, and they can be even smaller in size. The reaction to PNGs has been quite enthusiastic, but sadly it is taking its time catching on, as the GIF format is so widely used amongst your average computer user. The following example adds to the common theme of creating dynamic images.

The Code

```php
<?php

  //sample8_3.php

  //The first thing you do is check for GD compatibility.
  try {
    //First you create a blank canvas.
    if ($animage = imagecreate (200, 200)){
      //Then you can create a new background color for this image.
      $red = imagecolorallocate ($animage, 255, 0, 0);
      //Then you can draw a rectangle on the canvas.
      imagerectangle ($animage, 0, 0, 200, 200, $red);
      //Now, let's create a circle in the middle of the red rectangle.
      //Let's make it black.
      $black = imagecolorallocate ($animage, 0, 0, 0);
      imagefilledellipse($animage, 100, 100, 150, 150, $black);
      //To make things more interesting, you can add text this time.
      //Let's create a "white" color.
      $white = imagecolorallocate ($animage, 255, 255, 255);
      //Then write on the image.
      imagestring($animage, 5, 48, 95, "Hello World!", $white);
      //Then you output the new png.
      imagepng ($animage);
      //And then header the image.
      header ("Content-type: image/png");
      //Finally you destroy the image.
      imagedestroy ($animage);
    } else {
      throw new exception ("Sorry, the GD library may not be setup.");
    }
  } catch (exception $e) {
    echo $e->getmessage();
  }
?>
```

How It Works

As you can see, the major differences in outputting a PNG image are the calls to the header() function and the imagepng() function. The important thing to note is the file size. Weighing in at a mere .57KB in size, even with the addition of a circle, means that the PNG file is a smaller file size even than the GIF file. Further, when you put the same circle into the GIF image, the GIF's size increases to .83KB. As you can see, the PNG file format is quite preferable for use, whether you need photorealism or not. The prototype for imagepng() is as follows:

```
bool imagepng ( resource image [, string filename] )
```

Figure 8-3 shows some output of recipe 8-3.

Figure 8-3. *Output of recipe 8-3*

Working with Image Libraries

The most widely used and supported set of library functions for PHP 5 belongs to the GD library. Currently, the GD2 library comes prepackaged in the ext folder with a fresh install of PHP 5 and requires you only to remove the comment from the extension in the php.ini file to make the functions available. Highly robust and well-tested (and hence relatively bug free), the GD library can take care of pretty much any concern you may have with creating an image from scratch.

To find out more information about what is enabled or disabled in your current configuration, you can call the function gd_info(), which will return a listing of all pertinent information to the library. For more information on the GD library, you should refer to the PHP manual at http://www.php.net/gd. Far too many functions exist to mention in the scope of this book, and the features list is quite extensive.

Creating an Image from Scratch

A common use for dynamic imaging is to take data and create a graph with it. Because there is no need for an external image, you can create a blank canvas and then, based on information collected from some source (a database perhaps), create a detailed bar chart or pie graph.

8-4. Creating a Blank Canvas

Creating a blank canvas is rather easy in PHP; the tricky part is creating a size that will contain the amount of data you want to display. Since you are dealing with pixels here, you have to ensure that the canvas you create is meant to hold enough information. Over the next few examples we will show you step by step how to create a bar graph image in PNG format.

The Code

```php
<?php

//sample8_4.php

//The first thing you do is check for GD compatibility.
try {
  //First you create a blank canvas.
  if ($animage = imagecreate (500, 500)){
    //Now, let's allocate the background color and line color.
    $white = imagecolorallocate ($animage, 255, 255, 255);
    $black = imagecolorallocate ($animage, 0, 0, 0);
    //Now, let's draw the rectangle over the background, and surround
    //it with a black line.
    imagefilledrectangle ($animage, 0, 0, 500, 500, $black);
    imagefilledrectangle ($animage, 1, 1, 498, 498, $white);

    //Designate the image.
    imagepng ($animage);
    //Then output it.
    header ("Content-type: image/png");
    //Lastly, clean up.
    imagedestroy ($animage);

  } else {
    throw new exception ("Sorry, the GD library may not be setup.");
  }
} catch (exception $e) {
    echo $e->getmessage();
}
?>
```

How It Works

This particular example is a matter of aesthetics. By using the imagefilledrectangle() function, you create what is essentially a white image with a 1-pixel line around the edge. This will
serve as the basic template for outputting the bar graph, which we will explain in more detail
in the next example. The prototype for imagefilledrectangle() is as follows:

```
int imagefilledrectangle (resource img, int x1, int y1, int x2, int y2, int color)
```

Figure 8-4 shows some output of recipe 8-4.

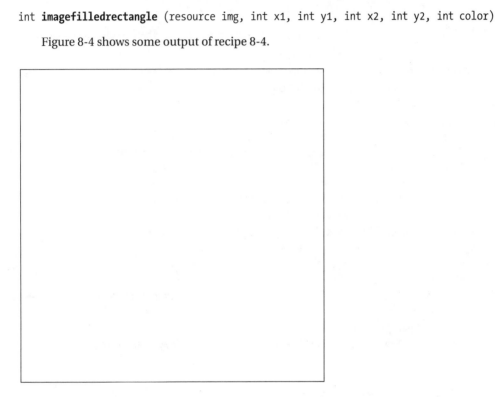

Figure 8-4. *Output of recipe 8-4*

8-5. Creating and Using Colors

Because we are dealing with a graphical topic, the concept of what color to display it in is
a rather important one. As mentioned, colors for dynamic imaging are handled in an RGB
method. To apply colors to a particular element of a dynamic image, you must first allocate
the color to a variable resource that can then be used on other image elements. You use the
imagecolorallocate() function to facilitate this necessity. The following example shows how
to start using the new colors to create a title for the graph.

The Code

```php
<?php

  //sample8_5.php

  //The first thing you do is check for GD compatibility.
  try {
    //First you create a blank canvas.
    if ($animage = imagecreate (500, 500)){
      //Now, let's allocate the background color and line color.
      //Here is the way to do it with RGB.
      $white = imagecolorallocate ($animage, 255, 255, 255);
      //And here is an example with hex.
      $black = imagecolorallocate ($animage, 0x00, 0x00, 0x00);
      //Now, let's draw the rectangle over the background, and surround
      //it with a black line.
      imagefilledrectangle ($animage, 0, 0, 500, 500, $black);
      imagefilledrectangle ($animage, 1, 1, 498, 498, $white);
      //Now, let's create some more colors for the title.
      $blue = imagecolorallocate ($animage, 0, 0, 255);
      $green = imagecolorallocate ($animage, 0, 255, 0);
      //Now, let's center the text at the top of the image.
      $title = "A Sample Poll";
      imagestring ($animage, 4, ((500 - (strlen($title) * imagefontwidth(4))) / 2)➥
, 5, $title, $blue);
      $copy = "Copyright Lee Babin";
      imagestring ($animage, 4, ((500 - (strlen($copy) * imagefontwidth(4))) / 2)➥
, 25, $copy, $green);

      //Designate the image.
      imagepng ($animage);
      //Then output it.
      header ("Content-type: image/png");
      //Lastly, clean up.
      imagedestroy ($animage);
    } else {
      throw new exception ("Sorry, the GD library may not be setup.");
    }
  } catch (exception $e) {
    echo $e->getmessage();
  }
?>
```

How It Works

As you can see in this example, you are beginning to turn the little graphing system into a more cohesive image. By using some green and blue color allocations, the image is starting to obtain some style. Keep in mind that you can use hex values or numerical values when setting up color allocations, so use what is most efficient for your project. Also note how easy it is to center text. By using the function imagefontwidth(), you can determine how long each character will be using the current font. By using a little math, you can easily determine where the X coordinate should begin in order to allow the text to sit squarely in the middle, regardless of what that text may be. Figure 8-5 shows some output of recipe 8-5.

Figure 8-5. *Sample output of recipe 8-5*

8-6. Creating and Applying Different Shapes and Patterns

Using shapes and patterns is where the current application will begin to shine. By calculating values from the current data, you can create bar graphs or pie graphs that will show off the data in a usable format. PHP 5 supports a wide range of shapes and patterns including rectangles, ellipses, lines, and polygons. Choose the best fit for the job and a couple of nice colors, and away you go.

The Code

```php
<?php

  //sample8_6.php

  //The first thing you do is check for GD compatibility.
  try {
    //First you create a blank canvas.
    if ($animage = imagecreate (500, 500)){
      //Now, let's allocate the background color and line color.
      $white = imagecolorallocate ($animage, 255, 255, 255);
      $black = imagecolorallocate ($animage, 0, 0, 0);
      //Now, let's draw the rectangle over our background, and surround
      //it with a black line.
      imagefilledrectangle ($animage, 0, 0, 500, 500, $black);
      imagefilledrectangle ($animage, 1, 1, 498, 498, $white);
      //Now, let's create some more colors for the title.
      $blue = imagecolorallocate ($animage, 0, 0, 255);
      $green = imagecolorallocate ($animage, 0, 255, 0);
      //Now, let's center the text at the top of the image.
      $title = "A Sample Poll";
      imagestring ($animage, 4, ((500 - (strlen($title) * imagefontwidth(4))) / 2)➡
, 5, $title, $blue);
      $copy = "Copyright Lee Babin";
      imagestring ($animage, 4, ((500 - (strlen($copy) * imagefontwidth(4))) / 2)➡
, 25, $copy, $green);
      //Now, usually this data would come from a database, ➡
but since that is not within
      //the scope of this chapter, you will assume you ➡
retrieved this array of data from
      //someplace meaningful.
      $myvalues = array ("4","7","1","9","5","8");
      //Now, you need to do some calculations.
      //Since you have 6 values here, you need to determine ➡
the ideal width each bar
      //should be while leaving room on the sides for clarity.
      $barwidth = (int) (500 / ((count ($myvalues) * 2)+ 1));
      //You now have the width, so you need a height to represent the values.
      //You take 30 pixels off the top to account for the title.
      $barheightpernum = (int) (500 / 10);
      //Now, you run through the values.
      for ($i = 0; $i < count ($myvalues); $i++){
```

```
        //And for every value you output the bar and a line around for aesthetics.
        imagefilledrectangle ($animage, ((($barwidth * $i) * 2) + $barwidth)➥
 - 1, 500 - (($barheightpernum *     (int) $myvalues[$i]) - 35)➥
 - 1,(((($barwidth * $i) * 2) + $barwidth) + $barwidth) + 1,498, $black);
        imagefilledrectangle ($animage, ((($barwidth * $i) * 2) + $barwidth)➥
, 500 - (($barheightpernum * (int) $myvalues[$i]) - 35),(((($barwidth * $i) * 2)➥
 + $barwidth) + $barwidth),498, $green);
    }

    //Designate the image.
    imagepng ($animage);
    //Then output it.
    header ("Content-type: image/png");
    //Lastly, clean up.
    imagedestroy ($animage);
  } else {
    throw new exception ("Sorry, the GD library may not be setup.");
  }
 } catch (exception $e) {
   echo $e->getmessage();
 }
?>
```

How It Works

Here is where things get a tad tricky. Since you are dealing with a fixed-width table, you need to create an algorithm that can deduce a maximum-sized bar to be displayed depending on the number of values you need to display. After that, the script must be able to also figure out a scale of sorts. Since in this case you are using a scale of one to ten, you can easily figure out how many units of pixel height each increment in the number should indicate by taking the maximum height and dividing it by ten. If you needed to create a scale on the fly, you could simply create an algorithm that would check for the highest and lowest values in the data set and then create a range from that.

Once you have figured out how wide and how tall each unit on the graph should be, it is a simple matter to run through the array and create the appropriately sized bar. For aesthetics, you can also apply a black outline to the bars to make them look nice. The black bar was easy to apply after figuring out the original green bars, as it is simply a matter of setting the same bar, just one pixel bigger. Figure 8-6 shows some output of recipe 8-6.

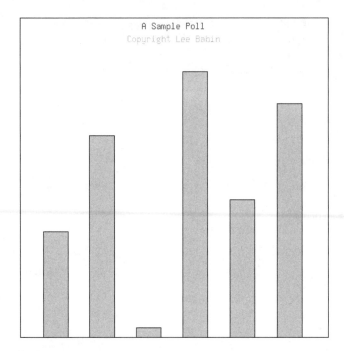

Figure 8-6. *Output of recipe 8-6*

8-7. Outputting an Image

One of the more powerful features to note about PHP 5's dynamic imaging is that you can call a PHP script that outputs a dynamic image from within an IMG tag's SRC attribute, even from a server that is not currently set up to handle PHP. Time and again this sort of functionality has allowed companies to produce web-ready applications that can be distributed even on websites that support only HTML. You can even pass arguments in as $_GET values, which means you can use the script on the receiving end to retrieve a value through the SRC attribute and then display the image based on that argument.

For instance, you could have a polling system in place that will dynamically display the results of a poll based on the ID number passed to the script. By doing this, you can recycle code and have it ready for use by anyone who passes the script a correct argument. Naturally, some validation will be in order, but you can begin to see just how powerful this can be. The following example shows how to call the bar graph building function, but instead of getting the values from an array, you will pass them into the script from the SRC attribute using a $_GET method.

The Code

```php
<?php

//sample8_7_script.php

//The first thing you do is check for GD compatibility.
try {
  //First you create a blank canvas.
  if ($animage = imagecreate (500, 500)){
    //Now, let's allocate the background color and line color.
    $white = imagecolorallocate ($animage, 255, 255, 255);
    $black = imagecolorallocate ($animage, 0, 0, 0);
    //Now, let's draw the rectangle over the background, and surround
    //it with a black line.
    imagefilledrectangle ($animage, 0, 0, 500, 500, $black);
    imagefilledrectangle ($animage, 1, 1, 498, 498, $white);
    //Now, let's create some more colors for the title.
    $blue = imagecolorallocate ($animage, 0, 0, 255);
    $green = imagecolorallocate ($animage, 0, 255, 0);
    //Now, let's center the text at the top of the image.
    $title = "A Sample Poll";
    imagestring ($animage, 4, ((500 - (strlen($title) * imagefontwidth(4))) / 2)➡
, 5, $title, $blue);
    $copy = "Copyright Lee Babin";
    imagestring ($animage, 4, ((500 - (strlen($copy) * imagefontwidth(4))) / 2)➡
, 25, $copy, $green);
    //Now retrieve an array of values from the GET superglobal.
    $myvalues = array ($_GET['v1'],$_GET['v2'],$_GET['v3'],$_GET['v4'],➡
$_GET['v5'],$_GET['v6']);
    //Now, you need to do some calculations.
    //Since you have 6 values here, you need to determine the ideal width each bar
    //should be while leaving room on the sides for clarity.
    $barwidth = (int) (500 / ((count ($myvalues) * 2)+ 1));
    //You now have the width, so you need a height to represent the values.
    //You take 30 pixels off the top to account for the title.
    $barheightpernum = (int) (500 / 10);
    //Now, you run through the values.
    for ($i = 0; $i < count ($myvalues); $i++){
      //And for every value you output the bar and a line around for aesthetics.
      imagefilledrectangle ($animage, ((($barwidth * $i) * 2) + $barwidth)➡
- 1, 500 - (($barheightpernum *     (int) $myvalues[$i]) - 35) - 1,➡
(((($barwidth * $i) * 2) + $barwidth) + $barwidth) + 1,498, $black);
      imagefilledrectangle ($animage, ((($barwidth * $i) * 2) + $barwidth)➡
, 500 - (($barheightpernum * (int) $myvalues[$i]) - 35),(((($barwidth * $i) * 2)➡
+ $barwidth) + $barwidth),498, $green);
    }
```

```
        //Designate the image.
        imagepng ($animage);
        //Then output it.
        header ("Content-type: image/png");
        //Lastly, clean up.
        imagedestroy ($animage);
      } else {
        throw new exception ("Sorry, the GD library may not be setup.");
      }
    } catch (exception $e) {
      echo $e->getmessage();
    }
?>
<!DOCTYPE html PUBLIC "-//W3C//DTD XHTML 1.0 Transitional//EN"➥
  "http://www.w3.org/TR/xhtml1/DTD/xhtml1-transitional.dtd">
<html xmlns="http://www.w3.org/1999/xhtml">
<title>Sample 8-7</title>
<meta http-equiv="Content-Type" content="text/html; charset=iso-8859-1" />
</head>
<body>
  <div align="center">
    <img src="sample8_7_script.php?v1=2&v2=7&v3=3&v4=9&v5=1&v6=6" alt="" title="" />
  </div>
</body>
</html>
```

How It Works

The code for actually creating the image in this example has changed very little. The only real change is where you actually obtain your values. If you look at the line of code where you assign your value to the $myvalues array, you will notice that you are now loading the values in dynamically from the $_GET superglobal. When you look at the second block of code, you will notice that it references the script via the SRC attribute of the IMG tag. On top of all that, you even pass the values to change the bar graph within the SRC tag.

By using this method, you can create all kinds of ingenious applications including web counters, polling systems, and more. Try experimenting with this, and see how far your ingenuity and PHP 5's dynamic imaging can take you.

Creating an Image from an Existing Image

One of the more powerful aspects of the GD library is the ability to take a premade image and then add to or modify aspects of it on the fly using PHP 5's dynamic imaging. The end result can be some fancy functionality that you probably have already had the opportunity to witness. Have you ever seen one of those forms on the Internet that allows you to enter a block of text and then the text shows up on a sign within an image? Did you ever wonder how it was done? Well, let us fill you in on a little secret—it is really not all that difficult.

8-8. Loading an Existing Image

In the following example, you will see piece by piece how to construct an image that will allow you to write to a dialog box contained within the picture shown in Figure 8-7. Keep in mind that the poor photo victim, Tiger, was neither actually drunk nor is quite as cool as he appears to be. That being said, with the power of PHP 5, you can at least create something unique for him to include in his conversation. To play with the code for the upcoming examples, please feel free to download the image within the code download at the Apress website.

Loading the actual image is not much different from creating a blank image. The only major difference is in the function call to create the image. Rather than using the generic function, imagecreate(), you use the imagecreatefrom… function depending on the file type of the image. In the following example, you will use a JPG flavor because of its photorealism.

The Code

```php
<?php

  //sample8_8_script.php

  //The first thing you do is check for GD compatibility.
  try {
    //First you create a blank canvas.
    if ($animage = imagecreatefromjpeg ("images/tiger.jpg")){

      //Designate the image.
      imagejpeg ($animage);
      //Then output it.
       header ("Content-type: image/jpeg");
      //Lastly, clean up.
      imagedestroy ($animage);
    } else {
      throw new exception ("Sorry, the GD library may not be setup.");
    }
  } catch (exception $e) {
    echo $e->getmessage();
  }
?>
<!DOCTYPE html PUBLIC "-//W3C//DTD XHTML 1.0 Transitional//EN"➥
 "http://www.w3.org/TR/xhtml1/DTD/xhtml1-transitional.dtd">
<html xmlns="http://www.w3.org/1999/xhtml">
<title>Sample 8-8</title>
<meta http-equiv="Content-Type" content="text/html; charset=iso-8859-1" />
</head>
<body>
  <div align="center">
    <img src="sample8_8_script.php?whattosay=Hello World!" alt="" title="" />
  </div>
</body>
</html>
```

How It Works

The only real new function to learn (and, in fact, the function that makes this whole script work) is imagecreatefromjpeg(). Creating a new image from an existing one is almost too easy. You simply pass in the location of the file you want to work with, and there you have it—instant image. The prototype for the function imagecreatefromjpeg() is as follows:

```
resource imagecreatefromjpeg ( string filename )
```

Figure 8-7 shows some output from recipe 8-8.

Figure 8-7. *Output of recipe 8-8*

8-9. Applying Modifications to an Existing Image

Now that you know how to load an existing image, it is time to start doing something with the image. Since the loaded image now acts as something of a canvas, all the tricks you have been using up until now are still quite applicable. You can draw shapes, draw lines, and even write words on your new canvas. The following example demonstrates how to write onto the new canvas.

The Code

```php
<?php

  //sample8_9_script.php

  //The first thing you do is check for GD compatibility.
  try {
    //First you create a blank canvas.
    if ($animage = imagecreatefromjpeg ("images/tiger.jpg")){
      //For now, the font will be in black.
      $black = imagecolorallocate ($animage, 0, 0, 0);
      //Now, write to the speech balloon.
```

```php
        //First, you need to designate the rectangular area you want to write to.
        $topleftx = 479;
        $toplefty = 35;
        $bottomrightx = 741;
        $bottomrighty = 90;
        //Then get the length of the string.
        $strlen = (strlen ($_GET['whattosay']) * imagefontwidth (5));
        //Find the X coordinate to center it.
        $xcoord = (((($bottomrightx - $topleftx) - $strlen) / 2) + $topleftx);
        imagestring($animage, 5, $xcoord, 50, $_GET['whattosay'], $black);
        //Designate the image.
        imagejpeg ($animage);
       //Then output it.
        header ("Content-type: image/jpeg");
        //Lastly, clean up.
        imagedestroy ($animage);

    } else {
      throw new exception ("Sorry, the GD library may not be setup.");
    }
  } catch (exception $e) {
    echo $e->getmessage();
  }
?>
<!DOCTYPE html PUBLIC "-//W3C//DTD XHTML 1.0 Transitional//EN"➥
 "http://www.w3.org/TR/xhtml1/DTD/xhtml1-transitional.dtd">
<html xmlns="http://www.w3.org/1999/xhtml">
<title>Sample 8-9</title>
<meta http-equiv="Content-Type" content="text/html; charset=iso-8859-1" />
</head>
<body>
  <div align="center">
    <img src="sample8_9_script.php?whattosay=Hello World!" alt="" title="" />
  </div>
</body>
</html>
```

How It Works

In this case, the desired canvas area happens to be within the speech balloon. To get centered text within that balloon, open the image in an image-editing program such as MS Paint and deduce the exact coordinates of where you want the text to be. As you can see from the variables $topleftx, $toplefty, $bottomrightx, and $bottomrighty, we have decided to keep the text within those constraints.

By doing a little mathematical work, we have managed to make the text appear centered within the constraints given. Naturally, in a real-world application, you would definitely manage the length of the string allowed, combined with the height of the string, but in this case, which has been simplified a bit, it was not really necessary.

Figure 8-8 shows some output from recipe 8-9.

Figure 8-8. *Sample output of recipe 8-9*

8-10. Saving and Outputting the Modified Image

As part of this type of functionality, you may want to save the images you are dynamically creating (particularly those generated as a result of user participation) to a folder. Once the images have been saved, you can then access them at any time as a record of what was generated. Luckily, using PHP 5, you can copy the created image to a folder for later reference.

The Code

```php
<?php

//sample8_10_script.php

//The first thing you do is check for GD compatibility.
try {
  //First you create a blank canvas.
  if ($animage = imagecreatefromjpeg ("images/tiger.jpg")){
    //For now, the font will be in black.
    $black = imagecolorallocate ($animage, 0, 0, 0);
    //Now, write to the speech balloon.
    //First, you need to designate the rectangular area you want to write to.
    $topleftx = 479;
    $toplefty = 35;
    $bottomrightx = 741;
    $bottomrighty = 90;
    //Then get the length of the string.
    $strlen = (strlen ($_GET['whattosay']) * imagefontwidth (5));
    //Find the X coordinate to center it.
    $xcoord = (((($bottomrightx - $topleftx) - $strlen) / 2) + $topleftx);
```

```
      imagestring($animage, 5, $xcoord, 50, $_GET['whattosay'], $black);
      //Designate the image.
      imagejpeg ($animage);
      //Then output it.
      header ("Content-type: image/jpeg");
      //Now, you want to save it.
      //Let's name the image after the current timestamp.
      imagejpeg ($animage,"savedimages/" . time() . ".jpg");

      //Lastly, clean up.
      imagedestroy ($animage);
    } else {
      throw new exception ("Sorry, the GD library may not be setup.");
    }
  } catch (exception $e) {
    echo $e->getmessage();
  }
?>
<!DOCTYPE html PUBLIC "-//W3C//DTD XHTML 1.0 Transitional//EN"➥
 "http://www.w3.org/TR/xhtml1/DTD/xhtml1-transitional.dtd">
<html xmlns="http://www.w3.org/1999/xhtml">
<title>Sample 8-10</title>
<meta http-equiv="Content-Type" content="text/html; charset=iso-8859-1" />
</head>
<body>
<div align="center">
<img src="sample8_10_script.php?whattosay=Hello World!" alt="" title="" />
</div>
</body>
</html>
```

How It Works

As you can see, this script is not doing all that much more than the previous one. Fortuitously, you can also pass the imagejpeg() function an argument to dictate where the image should be output. By using it in this case to direct it to the save directory and name it as the current timestamp, you ensure a unique image creation every time. Using this script you can quickly and efficiently save a copy of the works of art that your user base will likely be creating for you.

Using TrueType Fonts

Although generating dynamic images can be fun and generally appealing to the eye, the font selection and display can be somewhat less than aesthetically pleasing. But because of the FreeType library, you can now integrate real fonts in your dynamic imaging. This is the final touch for making your images looks as pristine as possible. Developed through the open-source community, the FreeType library can either be downloaded from the website or, if you are using PHP 5, be installed as part of the default GD library. If you must download it, the website is at http://www.freetype.org/.

8-11. Loading Fonts

To use TrueType fonts in PHP, you must first load the font you want to use. Loading a font is a combination of a few different complexities. First, you must find where in your system the font is located. In a typical Windows XP install, you can find them in the C:\WINDOWS\Fonts folder. In the next example, you will begin the font loading process by locating the verdana.ttf file that is stored in (on our particular operating system) the C:\WINDOWS\Fonts folder.

The Code

```php
<?php

  //sample8_11_script.php

  //The first thing you do is check for GD compatibility.
  try {
    //First you create a blank canvas.
    if ($animage = imagecreatefromjpeg ("images/tiger.jpg")){
      //For now, the font will be in black.
      $black = imagecolorallocate ($animage, 0, 0, 0);
      //Now, write to the speech balloon.
      //First, you need to designate the rectangular area you want to write to.
      $topleftx = 479;
      $toplefty = 35;
      $bottomrightx = 741;
      $bottomrighty = 90;

      //Give the location of the font you want to use.
      $verdana = "C:\WINDOWS\Fonts\verdana.ttf";

      //Designate the image.
      imagejpeg ($animage);
      //Then output it.
      header ("Content-type: image/jpeg");

      //Lastly, clean up.
      imagedestroy ($animage);
    } else {
      throw new exception ("Sorry, the GD library may not be setup.");
    }
  } catch (exception $e) {
    echo $e->getmessage();
  }
?>
<!DOCTYPE html PUBLIC "-//W3C//DTD XHTML 1.0 Transitional//EN"➥
 "http://www.w3.org/TR/xhtml1/DTD/xhtml1-transitional.dtd">
<html xmlns="http://www.w3.org/1999/xhtml">
<title>Sample 8-11</title>
```

```
<meta http-equiv="Content-Type" content="text/html; charset=iso-8859-1" />
</head>
<body>
  <div align="center">
    <img src="sample8_11_script.php?whattosay=Hello World!" alt="" title="" />
  </div>
</body>
</html>
```

How It Works

As you can see, loading fonts is as easy as showing the script where the font is located. On a Windows machine, such as the one we are currently using, you can find them within the C:\WINDOWS\Fonts\ folder generally. The nice thing about this is that you can even copy the font and upload it relative to the script. By doing this you can place the fonts you enjoy using in a fonts folder on your web server. This also gets around the problem of different machines storing fonts in different places and makes your code a lot more portable.

8-12. Applying TrueType Fonts to an Image

Now that you know how to get fonts into your code, let's begin the fun stuff, which is actually outputting the font onto the dynamically created image. Doing so involves manipulating the script slightly to center the text, as the imagefontwidth() function no longer works in this case. A function called imagettfbbox() can do roughly the same thing but with even more options.

The Code

```php
<?php

  //sample8_12_script.php

  //The first thing you do is check for GD compatibility.
  try {
    //First you create a blank canvas.
    if ($animage = imagecreatefromjpeg ("images/tiger.jpg")){
      //For now, the font will be in black.
      $black = imagecolorallocate ($animage, 0, 0, 0);
      //Now, write to the speech balloon.
      //First, you need to designate the rectangular area you want to write to.
      $topleftx = 479;
      $toplefty = 35;
      $bottomrightx = 741;
      $bottomrighty = 90;

      //Give the location of the font you want to use.
      $verdana = "C:\WINDOWS\Fonts\verdana.ttf";
```

```
    //Then get the length of the string.
    //First you need to the width of the font.
    $dimensions = imagettfbbox (14,0,$verdana, $_GET['whattosay']);
    $strlen = ($dimensions[2] - $dimensions[0]);
    //Find the X coordinate to center it.
    $xcoord = (((($bottomrightx - $topleftx) - $strlen) / 2) + $topleftx);

    imagettftext($animage, 14, 0, $xcoord, 60, $black, $verdana➥
, $_GET['whattosay']);

    //Designate the image.
    imagejpeg ($animage);
    //Then output it.
    header ("Content-type: image/jpeg");

    //Lastly, clean up.
    imagedestroy ($animage);
  } else {
    throw new exception ("Sorry, the GD library may not be setup.");
  }
} catch (exception $e) {
  echo $e->getmessage();
}
?>
<!DOCTYPE html PUBLIC "-//W3C//DTD XHTML 1.0 Transitional//EN"➥
 "http://www.w3.org/TR/xhtml1/DTD/xhtml1-transitional.dtd">
<html xmlns="http://www.w3.org/1999/xhtml">
<title>Sample 8-12</title>
<meta http-equiv="Content-Type" content="text/html; charset=iso-8859-1" />
</head>
<body>
  <div align="center">
    <img src="sample8_12_script.php?whattosay=Hello World!" alt="" title="" />
  </div>
</body>
</html>
```

How It Works

In this case, by using the imagettftext() function, you can perform roughly the same action as the previous text display examples, only with TrueType font compatibility. The result speaks for itself (see Figure 8-9), but by using some nice fonts you can truly make your dynamic image look that much more professional. The prototypes for both TrueType functions are as follows:

```
array imagettfbbox ( float size, float angle, string fontfile, string text )
array imagettftext (resource img,float size,float angl, int x, int y,➥
 int color, string fontfile, string text)
```

Figure 8-9. *Output of recipe 8-12*

8-13. Project: Creating and Using a Dynamic Thumbnail Class

One of the more common uses of dynamic imaging is creating a dynamic thumbnail on the
fly. To create a photo gallery that allows the user to upload images, this task is almost certainly
a must. The reason this is so important is due in part to download speeds but mostly to user
error. We cannot count the number of times we have built a system that allows users to upload
images, and they upload their pictures straight from their digital cameras. Those of you who
own digital cameras know that the default setting on them is to output the images with huge
dimensions. Needless to say, even one of those large images would be enough to slow the site
down to a crawl, let alone a gallery of them.

Creating dynamic thumbnails and then displaying them is actually simpler than it sounds.
By creating a function that will deduce the new scaled-down size for you and then one that will
do the sizing for you, you can easily create thumbnails on the fly.

Note that it is important to remember that both the image that is to be resampled and the
folder that the resampled image will be saved to must have the proper writable (and readable)
permissions. For the sake of clarity, simply CHMOD them both to 777 for this example to work
properly.

The Code

```php
<?php

  //sample8_13.php

  //This function takes in the current width and height of an image
  //and also the max width and height desired.
  //It then returns an array with the desired dimensions.
  function setWidthHeight($width, $height, $maxwidth, $maxheight){
    if ($width > $height){
      if ($width > $maxwidth){
        //Then you have to resize it.
```

```
      //Then you have to resize the height to correspond to the change in width.
      $difinwidth = $width / $maxwidth;

      $height = intval($height / $difinwidth);

      //Then default the width to the maxwidth;
      $width = $maxwidth;

      //Now, you check if the height is still too big in case it was to begin with.
      if ($height > $maxheight){
        //Rescale it.
        $difinheight = $height / $maxheight;

        $width = intval($width / $difinheight);

        //Then default the height to the maxheight;
        $height = $maxheight;

      }
    } else {
      if ($height > $maxheight){
        //Rescale it.
        $difinheight = $height / $maxheight;

        $width = intval($width / $difinheight);

        //Then default the height to the maxheight;
        $height = $maxheight;

      }
    }
  } else {
    if ($height > $maxheight){
      //Then you have to resize it.

      //You have to resize the width to correspond to the change in width.
      $difinheight = $height / $maxheight;

      $width = intval($width / $difinheight);

      //Then default the height to the maxheight;
      $height = $maxheight;

      //Now, you check if the width is still too big in case it was to begin with.
      if ($width > $maxwidth){
        //Rescale it.
        $difinwidth = $width / $maxwidth;
```

```php
      $height = intval($height / $difinwidth);

      //Then default the width to the maxwidth;
      $width = $maxwidth;


    }
  } else {
    if ($width > $maxwidth){
      //Rescale it.
      $difinwidth = $width / $maxwidth;

      $height = intval($height / $difinwidth);

      //Then default the width to the maxwidth;
      $width = $maxwidth;
    }
  }
}
$widthheightarr = array ("$width","$height");
return $widthheightarr;
}

//This function creates a thumbnail and then saves it.
function createthumb ($img, $constrainw, $constrainh){

  //Find out the old measurements.
  $oldsize = getimagesize ($img);
  //Find an appropriate size.
  $newsize = setWidthHeight ($oldsize[0], $oldsize[1], $constrainw, $constrainh);

  //Create a duped thumbnail.
  $exp = explode (".", $img);

  //Check if you need a gif or jpeg.
  if ($exp[1] == "gif"){
    $src = imagecreatefromgif ($img);
  } else {
    $src = imagecreatefromjpeg ($img);
  }
  //Make a true type dupe.
  $dst = imagecreatetruecolor ($newsize[0],$newsize[1]);
  //Resample it.
  imagecopyresampled ($dst,$src,0,0,0,0,$newsize[0],$newsize[1],➥
$oldsize[0],$oldsize[1]);
  //Create a thumbnail.
  $thumbname = $exp[0] . "_th." . $exp[1];
```

```php
    if ($exp[1] == "gif"){
      imagejpeg ($dst,$thumbname);
    } else {
      imagejpeg ($dst,$thumbname);
    }

    //And then clean up.
    imagedestroy ($dst);
    imagedestroy ($src);

    return $thumbname;


  }

  $theimg = "images/tiger.jpg";
  $thumb = createthumb ($theimg, 300, 300);
  ?><img src="<?php echo $thumb; ?>" style="border: none;" alt="" title="" /><?php
  ?>
```

How It Works

Basically, the setWidthHeight() function takes the current width and height and the desired maximum width and height as arguments and then resizes the image proportionally. Those who have changed an image size in Adobe Photoshop will have some idea of what we are talking about. To keep the image from skewing, the height and width are downsized in proportional amounts so the image still looks fairly decent, no matter what the size ends up being. The function then returns an array with two values, which are the width and the height that the new image should be.

The next function in the script, createthumb(), accepts a maximum width and height and the location of the image you want resized. It calls the setWidthHeight() function to find the dimensions to resize the image to, and then it creates a duplicate of the image using the new dimension measurements. The new image then gets saved to the same folder as the current image but has a _th tacked on at the end to indicate a thumbnail.

Lastly, you simply call the function and feed it in the arguments of your choosing. The end result is a nicely resized image that is generated on the fly. Rather than deal with enormous file sizes, this method makes the web page a lot more manageable, particularly for those with a dial-up Internet connection. Figure 8-10 shows some output for recipe 8-13.

Figure 8-10. *Output of recipe 8-13*

Summary

In this chapter, we provided you with a quick overview of dynamic imaging. We find that dynamic imaging is at its most efficient when being used for creative purposes. Working with images can be rewarding if given the chance.

The most important aspect of this topic to keep in mind is what file format to do your work in. If you ever find yourself at a loss, consider both the audience that will be using your application and the type of effect you want. A general rule is to use the JPG file type if you want something to be photorealistic, the GIF file format if you need a small image, and the PNG file type if you need a clean or potentially transparent nonphotorealistic image.

Working with images requires some patience. A vast majority of your time can easily be consumed by simply trying different pixel combinations to determine what size is the best and where to position elements. With a little practice, however, you can quickly develop methods to get the job done with a minimal amount of work. You now have a good starting point for working on your own exciting dynamic, image-driven applications.

Looking Ahead

In the next chapter, Nathan A. Good will explain one of the more difficult concepts in PHP, regular expressions.

CHAPTER 9
■ ■ ■
Using Regular Expressions

Sometimes when you are processing strings, you will run into a problem that is difficult to solve with `strcomp` or other functions. For instance, you might have to validate an e-mail address, which requires you to look at many difficult-to-check rules.

This is where regular expressions come in handy. Regular expressions are powerful, concise groups of characters that can contain quite a bit of logic, especially considering how short they are.

Think of regular expressions as mathematical expressions that work on strings. Like mathematical expressions, regular expressions have certain characters that mean something special. Like + says "plus" in a mathematical expression, a character such as ^ says "the beginning of the line."

If you are not familiar with regular expressions, it may become tempting to put them everywhere once you learn how to use them. But follow this general rule when deciding between using `strcomp` and using regular expressions: if you are searching for something specific, with no fancy rules, use `strcomp` and other string functions like it. If you are searching for something and are using special rules, consider using regular expressions.

Overview of Regular Expression Syntax

An expression either can be a single atom or can be more than one atom joined together. An *atom* is a single character or a metacharacter. A *metacharacter* is a single character that has a special meaning other than its literal meaning. The letter *a* is an example of an atom; the symbol ^ is an example of both an atom and a metacharacter (a metacharacter that I will explain in a minute). You can put these atoms together to build an expression, like so: ^a.

You can put atoms into groups using parentheses, as shown in this expression: (^a). Putting atoms in a group builds an expression that can be captured for back referencing, modified with a qualifier, or included in another group of expressions.

(starts a group of atoms.

)   ends a group of atoms.

Qualifiers

Qualifiers restrict the number of times the preceding expression may appear in a match. The common single-character qualifiers are ?, +, and *.

?   means "zero or one," which matches the preceding expression found zero or one time.

+   means "one or more." An expression using the + qualifier will match the previous expression one or more times, making it required but matching it as many times as possible.

*   means "zero or more." You should use this qualifier carefully; since it matches zero occurrences or the preceding expression, some unexpected results can occur.

The + and * qualifiers do greedy matching, which is covered in more detail in recipe 9-3.

Ranges

Ranges, like qualifiers, specify the number of times a preceding expression can occur in the string. Ranges begin with { and end with }. Inside the brackets, either a single number or a pair of numbers can appear. A comma separates the pair of numbers.

When a single number appears in a range, it specifies how many times the preceding expression can appear. If commas separate two numbers, the first number specifies the least number of occurrences, and the second number specifies the most number of occurrences.

{   specifies the beginning of a range.

}   specifies the end of a range.

{n}   specifies the preceding expression is found exactly n times.

{n,}   specifies the preceding expression is found at least n times.

{n,m}   specifies the preceding expression is found at least n but no more than m times.

Line Anchors

The ^ and $ metacharacters are *line anchors*. They match the beginning of the line and the end of the line, respectively, but they do not consume any real characters. When a match *consumes* a character, it means the character will be replaced by whatever is in the replacement expression. The fact that the line anchors do not match any real characters is important when making replacements, because the replacement expression does not have to be written to put the ^ or $ metacharacter back into the string.

^   specifies the beginning of the line.

$ specifies the end of the line.

An Escape

You can use the *escape* character \ to precede atoms that would otherwise be metacharacters but that need to be taken literally. The expression \+, for instance, will match + and does not mean \ is found one or many times.

\   indicates the escape character.

Saying OR

You use the | metacharacter as an *OR operator* in regular expressions. You use it between expressions, which can consist of a single atom or an entire group.

| indicates OR.

Character Classes

Character classes are defined by square brackets ([and]) and match a single character, no matter how many atoms are inside the character class. A sample character class is [ab], which will match a or b.

You can use the - character inside a character class to define a range of characters. For instance, [a-c] will match *a*, *b*, or *c*. It is possible to put more than one range inside brackets. The character class [a-c0-2] will not only match *a*, *b*, or *c* but will also match 0, 1, or 2.

[indicates the beginning of a character class.

-    indicates a range inside a character class (unless it is first in the class).

^   indicates a negated character class (if found first).

]   indicates the end of a character class.

To use the - character literally inside a character class, put it first. It is impossible for it to define a range if it is the first character in a range so that it is taken literally. This is also true for most of the other metacharacters.

The ^ metacharacter, which normally is a line anchor that matches the beginning of a line, is a negation character when it is used as the first character inside a character class. If it is not the first character inside the character class, it will be treated as a literal ^.

The character classes \s, \t, and \n are examples of character classes supported by PCRE expressions, which are explained next.

POSIX vs. PCRE

PHP supports two implementations of regular expressions—Portable Operating System Implementation (POSIX) and Perl-Compatible Regular Expressions (PCREs). These implementations offer different features, which are outlined in the next sections.

POSIX

POSIX regular expressions comply to standards that make them usable with many regular expression implementations. For instance, if you write a POSIX regular expression, you will be able to use it in PHP, use it with the grep command, and use it with many editors that support regular expressions.

Table 9-1 lists the POSIX regular expressions.

Table 9-1. *POSIX Regular Expressions Character Classes*

Expression	Meaning
[[:alpha:]]	A letter, such as A–Z or a–z
[[:digi:]]	A number 0–9
[[:space:]]	Whitespace, such as a tab or space character
4.60\< or \>	Word boundaries

ereg and eregi

The ereg method accepts the regular expression and the string to search as arguments.

```
ereg("SEARCH", $inmystring)
```

It evaluates to true if the match is found, so you can use it inside if statements and while loops to control flow.

```
if (ereg("FIND", $needleinahaystack))
{
    print "Success!";
}
```

The eregi method is a case-insensitive alternative.

ereg_replace

The ereg_replace method also uses POSIX regular expressions. It takes the expression, replacement expression, and string as arguments.

```
$mynewstring = ereg_replace("SEARCH", "REPLACE", $inmystring )
```

In this example, "SEARCH" is the string to search for, and "REPLACE" is the string that will be put in the place of "SEARCH" if it is found. The variable $inmystring is the string that contains the value that is to be replaced. To change *Hello* to *Goodbye* in a Hello World! example, use this:

```
$inmystring = "Hello World!";
$mynewstring = ereg_replace("Hello", "Goodbye", $inmystring);
```

PCRE

On the other hand, PCREs are based on the regular expression syntax supported in Perl. PCREs have more character classes that give you shortcuts, so PCREs are generally more powerful to use.

Table 9-2 lists the PCRE regular expression character classes.

Table 9-2. *PCRE Regular Expressions Character Classes*

Expression	Meaning
\d	A number 0–9
\b	A word boundary
\w	A word character, which matches anything A–Z, a–z, 0–9, and _
\s	Whitespace, like a tab or a space
\t	A tab

Another big advantage of using PCREs is that they support *look-arounds*. You can use a *look-around* to match what is before or after an expression without capturing what is in the look-around. For instance, you might want to replace a word but only if it is not preceded or followed by something else.

(?=   starts a group that is a positive look-ahead.

(?!   starts a group that is a negative look-ahead.

(?<=   starts a group that is a positive look-behind.

(?<!   starts a group that is a negative look-behind.

)   ends any of the previous groups.

A *positive look-ahead* will cause the expression to find a match only when what is inside the parentheses can be found to the right of the expression. The expression \.(?=   ), for instance, will match a dot (.) only if it is followed immediately by two spaces. The reason for using a look-around is because any replacement will leave what is found inside the parentheses alone.

A *negative look-ahead* operates just like a positive one, except it will force an expression to find a match when what is inside the parentheses *is not* found to the right of the expression. The expression \.(?!   ), for instance, will match a dot (.) that *does not* have two spaces after it.

Positive and *negative look-behinds* operate just like positive and negative look-aheads, respectively, except they look for matches to the left of the expression instead of the right. Look-behinds have one ugly catch: many regular expression implementations do not allow the use of variable-length look-behinds. This means you cannot use qualifiers inside look-behinds.

preg_match

The `preg_match` method takes two to three parameters: the regular expression, the string to search, and optionally a variable that holds the array of matches found.

```
preg_match("/FIND/", $mystr)
```

Alternatively, you could use the following:

```
preg_match("/FIND/", $mystr, $matchArray)
```

Notice that the regular expressions in the first parameter must start and end with a delimiter, which in this chapter will be /.

preg_replace

The `preg_replace` method accepts the regular expression for searching, the expression for the replacement, and the variable containing the string to replace. The `preg_replace` method returns the new string with the replacements made. The following is an example of using `preg_replace`:

```
$newstring = preg_replace("/OLD/", "NEW", $original)
```

The PCREs in `preg_replace` support back references in the replacement by using \1 to access the first group, \2 to access the second group, and so on.

When considering which implementation to use, keep in mind the skills of those who will be maintaining the code after you write it, if that is not you. Also, think about whether you will ever use the same expression elsewhere.

You can learn more about PCREs at `http://www.pcre.org/pcre.txt`.

Putting Regular Expressions to Work

The rest of this chapter contains recipes for using regular expressions, both POSIX and PCRE. These recipes demonstrate practical examples of using regular expressions in PHP to find and parse text.

9-1. Using String Matching vs. Pattern Matching

Usually, you should try to use the standard string-matching functions to keep things simple if you are trying to match a known, simple value with no real logic behind the searching. A good example is an internal value, such as an ID of some kind or a username or password. These matches do not require anything special such as the ability to search for more than one word or the ability to see what is before or after the string you are trying to match.

If you have rules that accompany your search, such as finding more than one of several words in a search or making sure something is in a certain format, use regular expressions— they allow you to define these rules. The following code shows how to look for a complete word using `strrpos` vs. regular expressions.

The Code

```php
<?php

    $value = "my username";

    // This won't match because the value contains more than just
    // user.
    if (strcmp($value, "user") == 0) {
        echo "Found match in '" . $value . "' using strcmp.\n";
    } else {
        echo "Didn't find match in '" . $value . "' using strcmp.\n";
    }

    // Use strrpos to find out if user is somewhere in
    // the string. Fair enough--this will return true because user
    // will be found in username.
    if (!(strrpos($value,"user") === false)) {
        echo "Found match in '" . $value . "' using strrpos.\n";
    } else {
        echo "Didn't find match in '" . $value . "' using strrpos.\n";
    }

    // But what if you want to make sure user is a
    // word all by itself, not part of username?
    if (ereg("\<user\>", $value)) {
        echo "Found match in '" . $value . "' using ereg.\n";
    } else {
        echo "Didn't find match in '" . $value . "' using ereg.\n";
    }

?>
```

This is the output:

```
Didn't find match in 'my username' using strcmp.
Found match in 'my username' using strrpos.
Didn't find match in 'my username' using ereg.
```

How It Works

This example demonstrates how you can use regular expressions to introduce some logic into your string comparisons—albeit simple logic in this case. In this example, you are looking for the word *user*. The string in which you are searching for the word *user* is *my username*, so although you will find *user* in *username*, you will not find *user* as a word by itself.

This is where regular expressions come in handy, because they support functionality such as word boundaries (\< and \> in the expression here). Since the word *user* is wrapped in these word boundaries, a match would be found if the value was *a user* but not *my username*.

Perhaps you are thinking, "Well, that is easy! I will just add a space in front of *user* in the strrpos function, and that will find it." That is true, in this case. But what if *user* is by itself or in quotes? The regular expression will still work in these cases, because it is smart about word boundaries. Any punctuation, or the beginning or end of a line, is considered a word boundary.

9-2. Finding the *n*th Occurrence of a Match

One of the powerful capabilities the PCRE functions give you is the ability to get an array of captures (a *capture* is the part that the pattern matched). This can be useful if you are trying to do something such as extract the second occurrence of something.

The Code

```php
<?php
    // This function will put all of the matches found into
    // the $matches array
    preg_match("/\d/", "1 and 2 and 3 and 4", $matches);
    // The 0 element of the $matches array holds another
    // array of the matches.
    echo "Value: " . $matches[0][2] . "\n";
?>
```

This is the output:

```
Value: 3
```

How It Works

When you call the preg_match function as shown here, the 0 element in the $matches array will contain elements that are matched by the whole pattern, which in this case is just \d. If groups exist in the pattern, then the matches that are captured by the groups get put into the other elements of the array. Anything captured by the first group from left to right in the pattern gets put into the 1 element of the array, and so on.

9-3. Matching with Greedy vs. Nongreedy Expressions

By default, regular expression engines perform *greedy* matching. This means as they are looking through the string and searching for a match to the pattern, they will gobble up as much of your string as they can while making the match.

This presents an interesting problem if you want to stop at the first occurrence of something in your string. The following block of code demonstrates the difference between greedy and nongreedy matching. If you use nongreedy matching, you have to use PCREs.

The Code

```php
<?php
    // The test string has two words in quotes.  The
    // greedy matching will replace everything from
    // the first to the last quotes.
    $teststring = '"Hello" and "Goodbye."';
    // This result will contain
    // "***"
    // because everything from the first to the last " is replaced.
    $greedyresult = preg_replace('/".*"/', '"***"', $teststring);
    // This  result will be:
    // "***" and "***"
    // because the match stops at the first " found.
    $nongreedyresult = preg_replace('/".*?"/', '"***"', $teststring);
    echo "Original: $teststring\n";
    echo "Greedy Replace: $greedyresult\n";
    echo "Nongreedy Replace: $nongreedyresult\n";
?>
```

This is the output:

```
Original: "Hello" and "Goodbye."
Greedy Replace: "***"
Nongreedy Replace: "***" and "***"
```

How It Works

Notice that the first preg_replace function uses the * qualifier to modify the . wildcard. The .* combination matches anything and everything, so ".*" will match anything between two double quotes (including other double quotes).

By contrast, the second expression uses the *? combination, which is the nongreedy version of the * qualifier. So, ".*?" will match anything between two double quotes, but it will stop making the match at the first sign of a double quote.

Table 9-3 lists the greedy qualifiers, and Table 9-4 lists the nongreedy qualifiers.

Table 9-3. *Greedy Qualifiers*

Qualifier	What It Matches
*	The preceding expression can be found any number of times, including one.
+	The preceding expression can be found one or more times.
?	The preceding expression can be found at most once.

Table 9-4. *Nongreedy Qualifiers*

Qualifier	What It Matches
*?	The preceding expression can be found any number of times, but the matching will stop as soon as it can.
+*	The preceding expression can be found one or more times, but the matching will stop as soon as it can.

9-4. Matching a Valid IP Address

Form validation, an area where you can use regular expressions to great effect, sometimes requires more than matching just normal text characters. Sometimes it is necessary to do something a little extra, such as finding ranges of numbers.

The following code shows how to verify Internet Protocol (IP) addresses with a regular expression. IP addresses are in the form of four numbers separated by periods. Each number can be at most 255, so an address such as 270.300.10.0 is a bad IP address.

The Code

```php
<?php

    $good_ip = "192.168.0.1";
    $bad_ip = "1.334.10.10";
    $regex = "^(([1-9]?[0-9]|1[0-9]{2}|2[0-4][0-9]|25[0-5]).){3}➥
([1-9]?[0-9]|1[0-9]{2}|2[0-4][0-9]|25[0-5])$"

    if (ereg($regex, $good_ip)) {
        echo "'" . $good_ip . "' is a valid ip address.\n";
    } else {
        echo "'" . $good_ip . "' is an INVALID ip address.\n";
    }

    if (ereg($regex, $bad_ip)) {
        echo "'" . $bad_ip . "' is a valid ip address.\n";
    } else {
        echo "'" . $bad_ip . "' is a INVALID ip address.\n";
    }

?>
```

This is the output:

```
'192.168.0.1' is a valid ip address.
'1.334.10.10' is a INVALID ip address.
```

How It Works

This example demonstrates a regular expression technique that can match numbers. You can use the same technique to make sure a month is represented with a number less than 12 when matching dates or that there are fewer than 31 days.

The regular expression ([1-9]?[0-9]|1[0-9]{2}|2[0-4][0-9]|25[0-5]) matches the numbers 0–255. The range 0–255 breaks down into other ranges: 0–99, 100–199, 200–249, and 250–255. The expression to match this is ([1-9]?[0-9]|1[0-9]{2}|2[0-4][0-9]|25[0-5]) and can be broken down into [1-9]?[0-9], which will match 0–99; 1[0-9]{2}, which will match 100–199; 2[0-4][0-9], which will match 200–249; and 25[0-5], which will match 250–255.

After taking out the IP address validation expression, the rest of it breaks down like this:

^	the beginning of the line…
(	the beginning of a group that contains…
(…)	the IP address expression explained previously…
\.	a literal dot…
)	the end of the group…
{3}	occurring exactly three times…
(…)	another occurrence of the IP address…
$	the end of the line.

This example uses the ereg function because the regular expression used here is POSIX compliant. But with a little effort, you can change this expression to use the PCRE function preg_match instead.

9-5. Validating Pascal Case Names

Using PHP, you might design web front ends or scripts that allow you to build classes or database tables. If you are accepting input from users, you might want to verify that the input follows certain naming conventions.

The following script shows how to inspect text to make sure it follows pascal case naming convention rules, sometimes called *upper camel case*.

The Code

```php
<?php
// This example will iterate through the array
// and check the values to see which one is a
// valid pascal case name.

    $values = array(
        "PascalCase", // Valid
        "notPascalCase",  // Invalid
        "not_valid",  // Valid
        "Valid",  // Valid
        "ValidPascalName",  // Valid
```

```
            "_notvalid",  // Not Valid
            );

    foreach ($values as $value) {
        if(preg_match("/^([A-Z][a-z]+)+$/", $value)) {
            printf("'%s' is a valid name.\n", $value);
        } else {
            printf("'%s' is NOT a valid name.\n", $value);
        }
    }

?>
```

This is the output:

```
'PascalCase' is a valid name.
'notPascalCase' is NOT a valid name.
'not_valid' is NOT a valid name.
'Valid' is a valid name.
'ValidPascalName' is a valid name.
'_notvalid' is NOT a valid name.
```

How It Works

This example demonstrates a couple techniques. The first is finding a string that starts with a certain range of characters. In this case, the first character is an uppercase letter, A–Z. Other regular expressions, however, can match variable names, domain names, or Extensible Markup Language (XML) tag names (which all have rules that say they must begin with certain characters).

The other technique is using the uppercase letter as a delimiter that separates names. It is the first character in a group that is modified by a qualifier, which in this case is +. You will see a similar structure in recipe 9-5, where the , character is found first as a delimiter in groups of numbers and - is used as a delimiter in the globally unique identifiers (GUIDs). This is the regular expression broken down into parts:

^	the beginning of the line, followed by...
(	a group that contains...
[A-Z]	the letters *A* through *Z*, followed by...
[a-z]	the letters *a* through *z* (lowercase)...
+	found one or more times...
)	the end of the group...
+	where the group is found one or more times...
$	the end of the line.

9-6. Validating U.S. Currency

While doing validation on web forms, one relatively common task is to validate a number that a user can enter based on a couple of rules. As an example to demonstrate this, we have chosen to validate U.S. currency and have added a couple of rules. One is that the dollar sign ($) is optional. The second is that there must be two decimal places in the number. The last rule is that the comma used as a thousands separator is optional; however, if it is used, it must be used correctly, which means 10,00.00 is an invalid number.

The Code

```php
<?php
// This example will build an array of values and then
// iterate through that array to check each value against
// the regular expression. Each value below is marked
// Valid if it is expected to be valid and Invalid if it
// is an invalid value.

    // Set up the regular expression as a variable.
    $regex = "/^\\$?(\d{1,3}(,\d{3})*|\d+)\.\d\d$/";

    $values = array(
        "1,000.00", // Valid
        "$100.00",  // Valid
        "$1.0",  // Invalid
        "1,0000.0",  // Invalid
        "$1,000,000.00",  // Valid
        "4",  // Invalid
        "1000.00"  // Valid
        );
    // Now go through the array, and use preg_match to
    // try to find a match in each value
    foreach ($values as $value) {
        if (preg_match($regex, $value)) {
            echo "'" . $value . "' is a valid number.\n";
        } else {
            echo "'" . $value . "' is NOT a valid number.\n";
        }
    }

?>
```

This is the output:

```
'1,000.00' is a valid number.
'$100.00' is a valid number.
'$1.0' is NOT a valid number.
'1,0000.0' is NOT a valid number.
'$1,000,000.00' is a valid number.
'4' is NOT a valid number.
'1000.00' is a valid number.
```

How It Works

In this example, to easily demonstrate the values that would be matched with the regular expression, you have built an array of strings that hold various values. The valid values in the array are 1,000.00, $100.00, $1,000,000.00, and 1000.00 because these values match the various rules you set for a valid U.S. currency format. The other values in the array—$1.0, 1,0000.0, and 4—are invalid.

The expression uses the | operator to match values with or without commas, as shown in (\d{1,3}(,\d{3})*|\d+). The first condition, \d{1,3}(,\d{3})*, is explained here:

\d	a number, zero through nine...
{1,3}	found between one and three times...
(	the beginning of a group that contains...
,	a comma, followed by...
\d	a number...
{3}	found three times...
)	the end of the group...
*	where the group may be found any number of times...
\.	a literal dot (.)...
\d	a number...
\d	another number...
$	the end of the line.

The group (,\d{3})* matches groups of three numbers preceded by a comma, such as ,999 and ,000. The * qualifier also means the group doesn't have to appear at all. The expression before the group, \d{1,3}, captures between one and three digits, so numbers such as 1,999 and 22,000 are valid. Since the group of three numbers preceded by a comma is completely optional, numbers such as 1 and 12 are also valid. This expression requires at least one leading number before the decimal point, which is still fine if the number is less than $1, such as $0.34.

The part of the expression after |, which is \d+, matches one or more digits without commas. Before the group you have \\$?, which finds a literal dollar sign that is optional because it is followed by the ? qualifier. After the group is \.\d\d$, which matches a period or decimal followed by two digits (\d\d) and the end of the line ($).

9-7. Formatting a Phone Number

If you are building user interfaces with PHP, no doubt you will run across the situation when you might have stored values that you want to format nicely before displaying them to a user.

An example is a phone number, which might be stored as 8005551234 in the data, but you want to display the value to the user as (800) 555-1234. The following code will not only reformat that number but will also reformat other "ugly" combinations such as 800.555.1234, 800-555-1234, and 800 555.1234.

The Code

```php
<?php
// This example will build an array of values and then
// iterate through that array to replace each value with
// a formatted version of the number. The new formatted
// number is echoed out to the screen

    // The regular expression is set to a variable.
    $regex = "/^(\(?\d{3}\)?)?[- .]?(\d{3})[- .]?(\d{4})$/";


    $values = array(
        "8005551234", // (800) 555-1234
        "800.555.1234",  // (800) 555-1234
        "800-555-1234",  // (800) 555-1234
        "800.555.1234",  // (800) 555-1234
        "800 5551234",  // (800) 555-1234
        "5551234",  // () 555-1234
        );

    // Go through each one, and use preg_replace to
    // reformat the number
    foreach ($values as $value) {
        $formattedValue = preg_replace($regex, "(\\1) \\2-\\3",
            $value);

        echo $formattedValue . "\n";
    }

?>
```

This is the output:

```
(800) 555-1234
(800) 555-1234
(800) 555-1234
(800) 555-1234
(800) 555-1234
()  555-1234
```

How It Works

Back references are the key to the replacement string in this example. \\1, \\2, and \\3 put what was found in the various groups back into the replacement, allowing you to introduce formatting such as parentheses, spaces, and hyphens into a string without having to use substring functions.

The group that captures the values for the \\1 back reference is (\(?\d{3}\)?)?. Because the value is optional, a value such as the last line in the previous output may be printed, with nothing in the parentheses. The group broken down is as follows:

(the parenthesis that captures the group for the back reference…

\(?   a literal parenthesis that is optional…

\d{3}   a number, zero to nine, found three times…

\)?   an optional parenthesis…

)   the close of the capturing group…

?   where the group itself may be optional.

In the examples in the array, this expression will capture 800, no matter what it is surrounded by.

Similar to the first group in the expression, the second group is (\d{3}). It is separated from the first group by an optional character class [- .] that will match a hyphen, space, period, or (since it is optional) nothing at all. This second group captures exactly three numbers.

The third group captures the last four numbers, (\d{4}), which is followed by the end of the line, matched by the line anchor $. Like the second group, the third group is separated by the one before it with a [- .] character class that has been marked as optional by the ? qualifier.

9-8. Finding Repeated Words

You can use back references, as shown in the previous example, not only in replacements but also in the searches themselves. When used in searches, they say, "Whatever you found there, look for it here, too." This provides an easy way to look for things such as repeated words and Hypertext Markup Language (HTML) and XML tags.

The following code looks for repeated words, regardless of case. It will find a match in strings such as *The the* and *that that*.

The Code

```php
<?php

// This example will look for repeated words next to each
// other, regardless of case. The case insensitivity is
// provided by the i option, which is used to modify the
// expression given to preg_match.

// Here, a function is used to contain common code that
// will be run on each string down below.

function showMatchResults($str) {
    if (preg_match("/\b(\w+)\s+\\1\b/i", $str)) {
        echo "Match successful: '" . $str . "'\n";
    } else {
        echo "Match failed: '" . $str . "'\n";
    }
}

showMatchResults("Hello World!");
showMatchResults("The the is repeated.");
showMatchResults("No match here");
showMatchResults("That that is that.");
showMatchResults("Goodbye World!");


?>
```

This is the output:

```
Match failed: 'Hello World!'
Match successful: 'The the is repeated.'
Match failed: 'No match here'
Match successful: 'That that is that.'
Match failed: 'Goodbye World!'
```

How It Works

The most important aspect of this regular expression is the back reference, which is \1. The \ must be escaped in PHP, so in the example it appears as \\1. The back reference is just a way of saying, "Whatever you found in the first group, look for it here." The parentheses in the expression define the group. Here is a breakdown of the expression:

\b   is a word boundary, followed by...

(...)   a group, then...

\s   a space...

+   one or more times, then...

\1   whatever was found in the group, and lastly...

\b   a word boundary.

The group is simply (\w+), which is as follows:

\w   a word character...

+   found one or more times.

This will match a word. The expression begins and ends with a word boundary anchor. This is to prevent the expression from matching a string such as password wordsmith. If the word boundary anchors are removed, the expression will start matching subsections of words.

9-9. Finding Words Not Followed by Other Words

PCREs provide look-arounds, which are one of the many features not provided by POSIX expressions. The following code shows a negative look-ahead, which will make a match if what is inside the look-ahead does not appear in the string.

The Code

```php
<?php
// This example uses a negative look-ahead,
// to make sure that the word "world" is not
// found after "hello".

    $regex = "/\bhello\b(?!\sworld\b)/";

    $valid = "hello";
    $invalid = "hello world!";

    if (preg_match($regex, $valid)) {
        echo "Found match:  '" . $valid . "'\n";
    } else {
        echo "No match:  '" . $valid . "'\n";
    }
```

```php
    if (preg_match($regex, $invalid)) {
        echo "Found match:  '" . $invalid . "'\n";
    } else {
        echo "No match:  '" . $invalid . "'\n";
    }

?>
```

This is the output:

```
Found match:  'hello'
No match:  'hello world!'
```

How It Works

PCREs support negative look-aheads, which allow you to build a regular expression that finds matches when the group is *not* found ahead of the expression. In this case, the match will be made as long as the word *world* is not found after *hello*.

9-10. Matching a Valid E-mail Address

If you are using PHP in web development, you will probably have to do a lot of validation on web forms. This is where regular expressions really work well, because there are a lot of rules in validation, even with something simple such as an e-mail address where the exact input is not known. You can find the specific rules that govern how a valid e-mail address is put together in RFC-2882.

For instance, in an e-mail address, two parts of the address are separated by an @ sign. The first part is the username, and the second part is the domain name. The first part can contain almost any number of American Standard Code for Information Interchange (ASCII) characters except control characters, spaces, and a few other special characters. (See RFC-2882 for a complete list.)

The domain name consists of one or more labels separated by periods. These labels must start with either an ASCII letter or a number, must end with either an ASCII letter or a number, and can contain letters, numbers, and hyphens in between. The following code shows how to validate e-mail addresses.

The Code

```php
<?php
// This example will build an array of values and then
// iterate through that array to replace each value with
// a formatted version of the number. The new formatted
// number is echoed out to the screen.

    // The regular expression is set to a variable.
    $regex = "/^[\w\d!#$%&'*+-\/=?^`{|}~]+(\.[\w\d!#$%&'*+-\/=?^`{|}~]+)*➥
@([a-z\d][-a-z\d]*[a-z\d]\.)+[a-z][-a-z\d]*[a-z]$/";
```

```
$values = array(
    "user@example.com",              // Valid
    "first.last@mail.example.com",   // Valid
    "user",                          // Invalid
    "user@example",                  // Invalid
    "user_name@my_example_com",      // Invalid
    "user0203@example.com",          // Valid
    );

// Go through each one, and use preg_replace to
// reformat the number
foreach ($values as $value) {
    if (preg_match($regex, $value)) {
        printf("Found valid address:   %s\n", $value);
    } else {
        printf("INVALID address:   %s\n", $value);
    }
}

?>
```

This is the output:

```
Found valid address:    user@example.com
Found valid address:    first.last@mail.example.com
INVALID address:    user
INVALID address:    user@example
INVALID address:    user_name@my_example_com
Found valid address:    user0203@example.com
```

How It Works

In this example, the value entered into the input box is compared against a regular expression
to validate the e-mail address. The part of the expression that validates the username is
[\w\d!#$%&'*+-\/=?^`{|}~]+(\.[\w\d!#$%&'*+-\/=?^`{|}~]+)*, which although really long
basically matches only the characters that are allowed by RFC-2882 for an e-mail address. Part
of the expression, [\w\d!#$%&'*+-\/=?^`{|}~], is repeated twice after the beginning of the line
(^). It matches A–Z, a–z, 0–9, and _ (which are all matched by \w) and the rest of the characters
found inside the brackets: !, #, $, %, &, ', *, +, -, / (escaped), =, ?, ^, `, {, |, }, and ~. These are
all the ASCII characters that are not control characters, spaces, or other special characters.

This group is repeated a second time, but after a literal \. that allows groups of letters to
be separated by a dot.

The domain name follows the same technique. An ASCII letter or a number is matched
by using [a-z\d], which appears at the beginning and the end of a domain label. Between the
first and last characters in the domain label, a letter, a number, or a hyphen can appear. This
is represented by the character class [-a-z\d]. Notice that when the hyphen should be taken
literally inside a character class, it needs to be first.

Finally, the top-level domain (.com, .org, and so on, in the address) complies with slightly different rules than labels in the domain name. The top-level domain can start with a letter and end in a letter (no numbers allowed) and in between can have a hyphen, a letter, or a number. The top-level domain is matched by the expression [a-z][-a-z\d]*[a-z]$.

9-11. Finding All Matching Lines in a File

Because you can open files and go through them line by line in PHP, you can combine regular expressions with your searching to give you more flexibility than you would have with basic string comparison functions.

The Code

```php
<?php
    // Open the file with the fopen command. The $file variable
    // holds a handle to the file that will be used when
    // getting the line from the file.
    $file = fopen("testfile.txt", "r") or die("Cannot open file!\n");

    // this will be false if you can no longer get a line from
    // the file.
    while ($line = fgets($file, 1024)) {
        if (preg_match("/Hello( World!)?/", $line)) {
            echo "Found match:  " . $line;
        } else {
            echo "No match: " . $line;
        }
    }
    // Make sure to close the file when you are done!
    fclose($file);

?>
```

This is the output for the file contents:

```
Hello
Goodbye World
Hello World
Goodbye
```

This is the command output:

```
Found match:  Hello
No match: Goodbye World
Found match:  Hello World
No match: Goodbye
```

How It Works

This example demonstrates how to open a file, loop through the file line by line, and, while you are looping through it, compare each line to a regular expression to see whether you can find a match.

The fopen command opens the file specified by string, which in this case is testfile.txt. The contents of the file are as follows:

```
Hello
Goodbye World
Hello World
Goodbye
```

Once the file is open, use the 20.370 fgets function to get the next line from the file and assign it to a variable ($line). The loop will stop when there are no more lines in the file to get. When you are done processing the file, make sure to close the file with the fclose command.

9-12. Finding Lines with an Odd Number of Quotes

Odd numbers of quotes on a line in source code or in text files can sometimes be difficult to track down. Particularly if you're using an editor that does not offer syntax highlighting, you can spend a long time trying to track down lines with unmatched quotes in large files.

This script will isolate lines in a file that have unmatched quotes. It uses a regular expression to make sure that quotes are found in even numbers, if at all, in each line of a file and will print lines that have unmatched quotes.

The Code

```php
<?php
// Open a file in which to search for lines that may contain
// odd numbers of quotes.
    $file = fopen("oddquotes.txt", "r") or die("Cannot open file!\n");

    // lineNbr is used to keep track of the current line number
    // so the user can get an informational message.
    $lineNbr = 0;

    // This will be false if you can no longer get a line from
    // the file.
    while ($line = fgets($file, 1024)) {
        $lineNbr++;
        if (preg_match("/^[^\"]*\"([^\"]*|([^\"]*\"[^\"]*\"[^\"]*)*)$/",
            $line)) {
            echo "Found match at line " . $lineNbr . ":  " . $line;
        }
    }
    // Make sure to close the file when you are done!
    fclose($file);

?>
```

This is the output for the file contents:

```
"Valid"
"Invalid
"\"Invalid\"
"\"Valid\""
Valid
"Invalid "Closed" Invalid "Closed"
```

This is the command output:

```
Found match at line 2:  "Invalid
Found match at line 3:  "\"Invalid\"
Found match at line 6:  "Invalid "Closed" Invalid "Closed"
```

How It Works

This expression begins at the start of a line and searches the rest of the line to make sure any quote that is found is followed by either no more quotes (remember, you are searching for lines with odd numbers of quotes here) or, if there are more quotes, an even number of them found between the odd quote and the end of the line. The expression without the escaped double quotes is ^[^"]*"([^"]*|([^"]*"[^"]*"[^"]*)*)$, and it is important to remember that the escape characters in front of the double quotes are not used by the regular expression interpreter.

The first few characters in the expression, ^[^"]*", match anything from the beginning of the line up to the first double quote in the line. ([^"] matches any character that is not a quote.) After that, the group ([^"]*|([^"]*"[^"]*"[^"]*)*) looks for either no quote between the one found and the end of the line ([^"]*) or an even number of quotes (([^"]*"[^"]*"[^"]*)*). The even number is grouped so that there can be closed quoted strings found in the line along with an odd number somewhere.

9-13. Capturing Text Inside HTML or XML Tags

Like the preg_match function shown in recipe 9-2, the ereg function can put what it finds into an array if one is passed as a parameter. The array is optional, so if you do not supply it, the ereg will not put the matches it finds anywhere. The function returns the number of matches found and will return 0 if no matches were found.

The following code demonstrates how to capture text and display it. The text that is going to be captured by ereg is whatever is inside two HTML tags. You can easily modify the expression to get the text from any tag, including XML.

The Code

```php
<?php
    // Assign some sample text to a variable.  The regular expression
    // should pull out anything in between the two p tags.
    $text = "<p>This is some text here \"</p>\".</p>";
    // This expression is so long because it is doing this match without
    // using lazy qualifiers.  Plus, there are other things to think
    // about, such as ignoring the </p> in double quotes above.
    ereg("<p>(([^<\"]|[^<]*<[^\/][^<])*(\"[^\"]*\"([^<\"]|➡
[^<]*<[^\/][^<])*)*)?<\/p>", $text, $matches);
    echo "Found text: " . $matches[1] . "\n";
?>
```

This is the output:

```
Found text: This is some text here "</p>".
```

How It Works

This example showcases a scenario where the rules for capturing text are a little more complicated than when they first appear. For instance, in this case you want to ignore strings that look like tags but really are not, such as tags within quotes. The tag shown in this example is the <p> tag.

Inside the <p> tags, this regular expression looks for three conditions. The first is that a less-than sign or a double quote is not found between the end of the opening tag and the beginning of the closing tag. This part is relatively straightforward, as shown here:

[^<"]   any character that is not a less-than sign or a double quote...

*   found any number of times.

The next condition that the regular expression searches for is whether a less-than sign exists. This can happen in script, where a less-than sign is in a comparison, such as i < 0. Fortunately, there is no operator called </, so if a less-than sign is found, it cannot be followed by a slash. This is what the second condition checks for:

(a group that contains...

[^<]   a character class that matches anything but a less-than sign...

*   found any number of times...

<   a less-than sign, followed by...

[^/]   any character except a slash...

[^<]   any character except a less-than sign...

*   found any number of times...

)   the end of the group...

*   where the group may appear any number of times.

The third condition checks to make sure that if any quotes are found in the string, they are closed before the ending script tag:

...   the first group, followed by...

(a group that contains...

"   a double quote, followed by...

[^"]   a character class that matches anything that is not a double quote...

*   found any number of times...

"   a double quote...

...   the group repeated again...

)   the end of the group...

*   where the group may be found any number of times.

This will allow several quoted strings within the script tags but will make sure the quotes are closed before the ending tag.

For the sake of simplicity, this regular expression does not do a couple of things—the point is to demonstrate the technique to get you started without being overwhelmed. After you feel comfortable with the regular expression, you can modify it. For instance, aside from double quotes, you could change the regular expression to also check for single quotes. Also, you could modify the regular expression to look for HTML comments.

9-14. Escaping Special Characters

Sometimes you need to do some complicated replacements that involve looking at what you are replacing to make sure you actually want to replace it. In this example, the string getting replaced is > in HTML. It is getting replaced by <.

One thing to note is that certain functions are available to do a transformation that is similar to this one—look at htmlspecialchars, for instance, This function will work most of the time, but in this case you want to replace some of the > characters and leave others alone. The htmlspecialchars function does not allow you to make this distinction. If htmlspecialchars meets your needs, use it. You should always use a standard function that has been tested and has been in use for a while rather than writing your own.

The Code

```php
<?php
    // This example shows how to escape a > character in HTML.
    $html = "<p> replace > and >> and >>> </p>";
    print "<b>Original text was: '" . $html . "'\n";
    // This is the part that gets a little difficult.  Not even PCRE
    // supports variable-length look-behinds, which would be
    // necessary to make sure that the > is not part of an HTML tag.
    // So, the technique here is to reverse the string and then make
    // the substitution because variable-width look-aheads are
```

```
    // okay.
    $html = strrev( $html );
    // Replace the >, but only if it is not inside or part of an
    // HTML tag.  With (?![^><]+?\/?<), you are looking for a tag
    // that has been closed.
    $newhtml = preg_replace( "/>(?![^><]+?\/?<)/", ";tl&", $html );
    $newhtml = strrev( $newhtml );
    print "<b>New text is: '" . $newhtml . "'\n";
?>
```

This is the output:

```
<b>Original text was: '<p> replace > and >> and >>> </p>'
<b>New text is: '<p> replace &lt; and &lt;&lt; and &lt;&lt;&lt; </p>'
```

How It Works

In this example, look-arounds escape the > character with the HTML escape <. Using look-arounds has a problem, though: the +? nongreedy qualifier, which is necessary because you do not know how many characters are between the beginning of the HTML tag and the special character, makes the regular expression variable length. Look-behinds do not support variable-length expressions, so you have to instead use a look-ahead, but that does not work well because the reason you are using the look-around is to make sure the > you are replacing is not actually part of an HTML tag.

The solution is to first reverse the string and then use a look-ahead to make sure the > is not part of an unclosed HTML tag. Here the expression is broken down into parts:

>	a > sign...
(?!	a negative look-ahead that contains...
[^	a character class that *does not* include...
>	a greater-than sign...
<	or less-than sign...
+?	found one or more times, but matching as little as possible...
\/	a forward slash (escaped for the PCRE)...
?	found zero or one time...
<	a less-than sign...
)	the end of the look-ahead.

The look-ahead does not capture any text, so when the replacement is made, whatever has been matched by the look-ahead will remain unaffected. The >, however, will be replaced by < (well, ;tl& because it is still backward), as long as it is not followed by what looks like an open HTML tag that has not been closed.

The expression [^<>]+?/?< matches an open HTML tag because it is looking for a < that does not have a < or > after it.

9-15. Replacing URLs with Links

With PHP 5, you can build powerful web interfaces for almost any application. One cool feature to make available to users of applications such as forums is to automatically replace Uniform Resource Locators (URLs) with hyperlinks to those URLs.

The Code

```php
<?php

    $hostRegex = "([a-z\d][-a-z\d]*[a-z\d]\.)*[a-z][-a-z\d]*[a-z]";
    $portRegex = "(:\d{1,})?";
    $pathRegex = "(\/[^?<>#\"\s]+)?";
    $queryRegex = "(\?[^<>#\"\s]+)?";

    $urlRegex = "/(?:(?<=^)|(?<=\s))((ht|f)tps?:\/\/" . $hostRegex . ➥
$portRegex . $pathRegex . $queryRegex . ")/";

    $str = "This is my home page:  http://home.example.com.";
    $str2 = "This is my home page:  http://home.example.com:8181/index.php";

    echo $urlRegex . "\n";

    $sample1 = preg_replace($urlRegex, "<a href=\"\\1\">\\1</a>", $str);
    $sample2 = preg_replace($urlRegex, "<a href=\"\\1\">\\1</a>", $str2);

    // Result will be:
    //
    // This is my home page:  <a ➥
href="http://home.example.com">home.example.com</a>.

    echo $sample1 . "\n";

    // Result will be:
    //
    // This is my home page:  <a href="http://home.example.com:8181/index.php">➥
home.example.com:8181/index.php</a>

    echo $sample2 . "\n";

?>
```

This is the output:

```
This is my home page:   <a href="http://home.example.com">➡
http://home.example.com</a>.
This is my home page:   <a href="http://home.example.com:8181/index.php">➡
http://home.example.com:8181/index.php</a>
```

How It Works

The full regular expression is /(?:(?<=^)|(?<=\s))((ht|f)tps?:\/\/([a-z\d][-a-z\d]*
[a-z\d]\.)*[a-z][-a-z\d]*[a-z](:\d{1,})?(\/[^\s?]+)?(\?[^<>#"\s]+)?)/, but it has been
broken down in this example to make it a little easier to digest. Parts of the expression match
various parts of the URL, such as the hostname, port number, and path. We will break down
each part of the expression and explain why it works, starting with the expression assigned
to $hostRegex, which matches the hostname part of the URL.

RFC-1035, under the "Preferred Name Syntax" section, describes that domain labels
should begin with a letter, end with a letter or a digit, and contain a letter, a digit, or a hyphen.
In RFC-1123, the requirement for the first character in a domain label is relaxed to also
include a digit. In URLs, the domain label is delimited from the scheme by : and //.

Here's the expression broken down:

(	a group that contains...
[a-z\d]	a character class that matches a letter or digit...
[-a-z\d]*	another character class that matches a hyphen, letter, or digit...
[a-z\d]	a character class that matches a letter or digit...
\.	a dot (or period)...
)	the end of the first group...
+	found one or more times.

The domain label is followed by the top-level domain, which has similar rules; according
to RFC-2396, it should start with a letter; contain a letter, a hyphen, or a digit; and end with a
letter or a digit. Here is that part of the expression broken down:

[a-z]	a character class that matches a letter from *a* to *z*, followed by...
[-a-z\d]	a character class that matches a hyphen, letter, or digit...
*	found any number of times...
[a-z\d]	a letter or digit.

After the hostname, a URL can optionally include a port if the site is found on a nonstandard port such as 8181 in the example. According to RFC-2396, a port can contain only a number and is delimited from the domain label by a colon. This makes the recipe relatively short, as shown here:

:	a colon, followed by...
(	a group that contains...
\d	a digit...
{1,}	found one or more times...
)	the end of the group.

The next part of the expression matches any valid URL characters, up to the ?, which is the delimiter that separates the querystring from the rest of the URL, or a space (\s), which is not allowed in URLs. (Delimiters are those characters mentioned earlier: <, >, #, and ".) This is how that part breaks down:

(	a group that contains...
[^?<>#\"\s]	a character class that does not match a ?, , <, >, +, ", or whitespace...
+	found one or more times...
)	the end of the group.

The last part of the URL is the querystring. The expression is basically the same one used to match a path, with the exception of ?, which is not included in the negated character class, as shown here:

\?	a question mark, escaped so it represents a literal question mark...
(	a group that contains...
[^<>#"]	a character class that does not match the delimiters <, >, #, and "...
+	found one or more times...
)	the end of the group.

When the parts of the expression are all put together, the entire expression will match complete URLs including everything from the schema (http:// and https://) to the querystring. You can use the expression to locate URLs and replace them with other text. In this expression, the other text is simply the anchor tag <a> with the href set to the URL that was captured by the expression. In PHP, the way to specify a back reference is \1, but you need to use a second \ to escape the backward slash in the string. The replacement string is <a href=\"\\1\">\\1</a>, which will place the URL between the quotes in the href attribute and inside the <a> tag.

9-16. Replacing Smart Quotes with Straight Quotes

Some programs such as word processors can make automatic replacements that help you with formatting. Smart quotes are quotes that have special formatting depending on whether they are at the beginning or end of the quoted phrase. This means strings such as *"Hello World"* will be replaced with *"Hello World"*.

You can use the character \x that is used to find smart quotes in this example to replace values such as trademark symbols, copyright symbols, and other special characters.

The Code

```php
<?php
// If the form is being posted to itself, it will take
// the value inside the text box and print it back out
// to the HTML with the smart quotes replaced with straight
// quotes.
$orig = '"Hello world!"'
$mynewstr = preg_replace('/\x93|\x94/', '"', $orig);
print "$mynewstr\n";
?>
```

This is the output:

```
"Hello world!"
```

How It Works

The expression shown in the example uses the \x character class, which in the regular expressions in PHP specifies characters by their hex values.

Other common replacements that you might make are the copyright symbol and the trademark symbol, which are \x97 and \x99, respectively.

9-17. Testing the Complexity of Passwords

You can also use a regular expression to test the complexity of a password—for instance, to make sure that the password is a certain length or has a combination of uppercase and lowercase letters and numbers.

The Code

```php
<?php
// This array holds different passwords, some good and
// some bad. The script will iterate through the
// array and use a regular expression to find the good
// passwords.

    $values = array(
        "password",    // Bad
```

```
    "P4ssw0rd",    // Good
    "XRokzX0z12k", // Good`
    "I5NB5YzW",    // Good
    "secret",      // Bad
    "12345",       // Bad
    );


    // Go through the array of values, and look at each password
    // to see if it is a good one.
    foreach ($values as $value) {
        if (! preg_match( '/^(?=.*[A-Z])(?=.*[a-z])(?=.*[0-9]).{8,16}/', $value)) {
            printf("Bad password.  '%s'\n", $value);
        } else {
            printf("Good password:  '%s'!\n", $value);
        }
    }
?>
```

This is the output:

```
Bad password:   'password'
Good password:  'P4ssw0rd'!
Good password:  'XRokzX0z12k'!
Good password:  'I5NB5YzW'!
Bad password:   'secret'
Bad password:   '12345'
```

How It Works

This expression uses a feature available in PCREs called a *look-ahead*. Look-aheads are anything inside (?=...). In this expression, each look-ahead will match any number of characters (.*) followed by uppercase characters ([A-Z]), lowercase characters ([a-z]), or numbers ([0-9]). At the end of the expression, there is a wildcard (.) that matches any character qualified by {8,16} to make sure there are between eight and sixteen occurrences of any character.

9-18. Matching GUIDs/UUIDs

GUIDs/UUIDs are pseudorandom numbers that are "guaranteed" to be unique. They are not really 100 percent guaranteed to be unique, but since the numbers are so large, the chance of getting two of the same numbers is so distant that the risk is acceptable in most applications. You can use GUIDs/UUIDs to uniquely identify objects in code.

The following code shows how to isolate GUIDs/UUIDs that are not valid. You can find the rules used to know what a valid GUID/UUID looks like at http://en.wikipedia.org/wiki/GUID.

The Code

```php
<?php

// This example will match valid GUIDs/UUIDs in
// the format specified at http://en.wikipedia.org/wiki/GUID

$uuid = "B15BC71E-D94C-11D9-9D71-000A95B70106";
$bad = "E34B13ED-D94C-11D9-9628-Z00A95B70106";

function printResults($str) {
    // Alternatively, you could also add [0-9a-f]{32} with |
    // to look for either format--with or without dashes.
    if (eregi("^[0-9a-f]{8}(-[0-9a-f]{4}){3}-[0-9a-f]{12}$", $str)) {
        printf("'%s' is a valid GUID/UUID.\n", $str);
    } else {
        printf("'%s' is NOT a valid GUID/UUID.\n", $str);
    }
}

printResults($uuid);
printResults($bad);

?>
```

This is the output:

```
'B15BC71E-D94C-11D9-9D71-000A95B70106' is a valid GUID/UUID.
'E34B13ED-D94C-11D9-9628-Z00A95B70106' is NOT a valid GUID/UUID.
```

How It Works

Since GUIDs/UUIDs are in hexadecimal, each character will be either a number or a letter between A and F. This is matched pretty easily with a character class: [0-9e-f]. If the GUID has hyphens in it, it has eight characters, then three groups of four characters, and finally twelve characters all separated by dashes.

9-19. Reading Records with a Delimiter

Reading records with a delimiter can be useful when providing rich features in an application in PHP. By being able to parse records with delimiters, you can build applications that work with comma-separated value (CSV) files, tab-delimited files, and even pipe-delimited files.

The techniques for working with these various files are the same; once you learn them, it is easy to add more formats to your application. The following code shows how to work with CSV files.

Before getting into the example, first be aware of what a properly formatted CSV file looks like. The CSV format has many implementations, so for this example we will focus specifically on the format that you will find if you export a CSV file in Microsoft Excel. This will probably be the most common CSV file format you will see. Also, you will learn why a simple replacement of a comma or a split on a comma into an array to get the fields does not cut it.

When a comma is included in a field in a CSV file, the field is wrapped with double quotes. Since double quotes have special meaning as text qualifiers, they are escaped in a CSV file by doubling them. You can find more about the makeup of a properly formed CSV file at http://en.wikipedia.org/wiki/Comma-separated_values.

The Code

```php
<?php
    // Open the file with in read-only mode.  This is the same
    // code you will find in recipe 9-5.
    $file = fopen("testfile.csv", "r") or die("Cannot open file!\n");

    // this will be false if you can no longer get a line from
    // the file.
    while ($line = fgets($file, 1024)) {
        preg_match_all("/[^,\"]+|\"([^\"]|\"\")*\"/", $line, $fields);
        // Print out the second first and second fields, just to
        // get an idea that it is working okay.
        echo "First field is:  " . $fields[0][0] . "\n";
        echo "Second field is: " . $fields[0][1] . "\n";
    }
    // Make sure to close the file when you are done!
    fclose($file);

?>
```

This is the output for the file contents:

```
"Doe, John",Anytown,MN,55555
"""Jon""",Anycity,NE,11111
"Doe, Jon ""Jon Boy""",Anytropolis,IA,77777
```

This is the command output:

```
First field is:  "Doe, John"
Second field is: Anytown
First field is:  """Jon"""
Second field is: Anycity
First field is:  "Doe, Jon ""Jon Boy"""
Second field is: Anytropolis
```

How It Works

To see how iterating through the file works, you can look at recipe 9-5 and recipe 9-2 for more information about how `preg_match_all` works. In this example, we will focus specifically on how the regular expression works.

When you are processing records in a file, you must define what a field is so that `preg_match_all` can extract the fields. This is part of the technique that is the same for all delimited records. In any delimited record, a field simply consists of characters that are not the delimiter. If the delimiter is allowed to appear in the field, it must probably be escaped somehow, or any application that processes the record will not be able to tell delimiters apart from values inside fields. This is the case with CSV records—remember that fields separated by a comma can actually include a comma as long as the field is wrapped in quotes to tell the processor to ignore the comma inside the field.

In CSV files, you also have to be wary of double quotes, since they can also be in a field where they are to be taken literally. To process this file, you use the expression `[^,"]+|"([^"]|"")*"`. Note that in the previous PHP example, the double quotes are escaped with a backward slash, but it is important to make the distinction that escaping double quotes is not a requirement of the regular expression interpreter; therefore, we will go through the expression as if they were not there.

The first part of the expression is `[^,"]+`, which is a negated character class that matches one or more characters that is not a comma or a double quote. In the example file, this matches fields with values such as `Anytown` and `11111`.

An OR operator, `|`, separates the first part from the second part of the expression, which is `"([^"]|"")*"`. This expression matches fields wrapped in quotes and is better explained like this:

`"`	a double quote, followed by...
`(`	a group that contains...
`[^"]`	any character that is not a double quote...
`|`	or...
`""`	an escaped double quote, followed by...
`)`	the end of the group...
`*`	where the group is found any number of times, ending in...
`"`	a double quote.

So, the expression `"([^"]|"")*"` will match any field in double quotes because it starts and ends with a double quote and cannot contain another double quote inside of it unless the double quote is escaped with another one. As long as the field is correctly wrapped in double quotes, you do not have to care whether there is a comma inside of it. The first part of the expression (`[^,"]+`) will make sure there is not one outside double quotes.

You can use this same technique to process tab-delimited files and other files that have records with fields separated by a delimiter. Depending on the specification of the file, you might have to tweak the expression just a little bit. The expression for dealing with tab-delimited files as exported by Microsoft Excel is this: `[^\t]+`.

9-20. Creating Your Own RegExp Class

If you have worked with other languages that support a Regex or RegExp class of some kind, you might miss the convenience of working with the class over calling various methods such as ereg and preg_match. Fortunately, PHP 5 has many improved features that allow you to build a similar class that supports finding matches and making replacements.

The following code demonstrates how to build a class called RegExp that will make working with regular expressions easier. This class allows you to define a pattern and find matches in strings or make replacements. It even has a function for getting an array of matches from a string.

The Code

```php
<?php

class RegExp {

    public $pattern;

    // Constructor
    // Creates a new instance of the RegExp object
    // with the pattern given.
    function __construct($pattern) {
        $this->pattern = $pattern;
    }

    // prints the string representation of the RegExp object,
    // which in this case is the pattern
    function __toString() {
        return $this->pattern;
    }

    // isMatch($str)
    // Returns the number of matches found, so is 0 if
    // no match is present.
    function isMatch($str) {
        $result = preg_match($this->pattern, $str);
        return $result;
    }

    // getMatches($str)
    // Returns an array of matches found in the string $str
    function getMatches($str) {
        preg_match_all($this->pattern, $str, $matches);
        return $matches;
    }

    // replace($replaceStr, $str)
    // Makes a replacement in a string
    //      -$replaceStr:  The string to use as a replacement
    //          for the pattern.
```

```
        //     -$str:  The string in which to make the replacement
        function replace($replaceStr, $str) {
            $result = preg_replace($this->pattern, $replaceStr, $str);
            return $result;
        }

}


$re = new RegExp('/Hello/');

// echo $re . "\n";
echo $re->pattern . "\n";

if ($re->isMatch('Goodbye world!')) {
    echo "Found match!\n";
} else {
    echo "Didn't find match!\n";
}

if ($re->isMatch('Hello world!')) {
    echo "Found match!\n";
} else {
    echo "Didn't find match!\n";
}

$res = $re->replace('Goodbye', 'Goodbye world!');
echo $res . "\n";

?>
```

How It Works

In this example, many new PHP 5 features are being used to build a powerful RegExp class that you can use in your code. At the end of the example, code demonstrates how to use the new class.

The __construct constructor is used with the regular expression as an argument to the constructor. When a new RegExp object is created, the pattern is kept inside the object to use in its future matches and replacements. The class declaration and constructor are as follows:

```
class RegExp {

    public $pattern;

    // Constructor
    // Creates a new instance of the RegExp object
    // with the pattern given.
    function __construct($pattern) {
        $this->pattern = $pattern;
    }
}
```

To create an instance of the RegExp class, just create it using new as shown here and in the test code at the bottom of the example:

```
$re = new RegExp('/Hello/');
```

In the previous example, '/Hello/' will be stored in the $pattern variable in the class. The __toString method is declared in this class to print the regular expression in the pattern variable, so using echo to print the object will print the pattern only:

```
echo $re;
```

This is the result:

```
/Hello/
```

Now that the object has been created and is storing a regular expression internally, the isMatch function, shown next, will make it easy to see if there is a match found inside a string:

```
function isMatch($str) {
    $result = preg_match($this->pattern, $str);
    return $result;
}
```

As you can see, this class uses the PCRE function preg_match to look at the string to see if there is a match, with $this->pattern used as the regular expression. This is why the example regular expression /Hello/ includes the / delimiters. Likewise, the preg_match_all function is used in getMatches to return an array of matches. The getMatches function is as follows:

```
function getMatches($str) {
    preg_match_all($this->pattern, $str, $matches);
    return $matches;
}
```

To complete the class's functionality, a replace function is included that allows you to make replacements using the RegExp class's $pattern to search for a string to replace. The replace function is as follows:

```
function replace($replaceStr, $str) {
    $result = preg_replace($this->pattern, $replaceStr, $str);
    return $result;
}
```

So far, this class uses PCRE to make its matches and replacements. But what if you want a class that can use either PCRE or POSIX expressions? With additions in PHP 5 such as constants, implementing this in a class is much cleaner than it would have been in prior versions of PHP.

Modify the class to include a $mode variable in the constructor. If $mode is not defined, set it to the value of the PCRE constant so PCRE methods are the default method of searching and replacing. Inside the class, if $mode is set to PCRE, the class uses preg_match and preg_replace to find matches and make replacements, and if $mode is set to POSIX, the class uses ereg and ereg_replace.

The modified class is as follows, with the additions in bold:

```php
<?php

class RegExp {

    const POSIX = 'POSIX';
    const PCRE = 'PCRE';

    public $pattern;
    public $mode;

    // Constructor
    // Creates a new instance of the RegExp object
    // with the pattern given.
    function __construct($pattern, $mode) {
        $this->pattern = $pattern;
        if (! $mode) {
            // Defaults to PCRE if there is no mode defined
            $this->mode = self::PCRE;
        } else {
            // In a real implementation, this $mode should be validated—check
            // it against the PRCE and POSIX constants
            $this->mode = $mode;
        }
    }

    // prints the string representation of the RegExp object,
    // which in this case is the pattern
    function __toString() {
        return $this->pattern;
    }

    // isMatch($str)
    // Returns the number of matches found, so is 0 if
    // no match is present.
    function isMatch($str) {
        if (strcmp($this->mode, self::PCRE)==0) {
            $result = preg_match($this->pattern, $str);
        } else {
            $result = ereg($this->pattern, $str);
        }
        return $result;
    }

    // getMatches($str)
    // Returns an array of matches found in the string $str
    function getMatches($str) {
```

```
        if (strcmp($this->mode, self::PCRE)==0) {
            preg_match_all($this->pattern, $str, $matches);
        } else {
            ereg($this->pattern, $str, $matches);
        }
        return $matches;
    }

    // replace($replaceStr, $str)
    // Makes a replacement in a string
    //      -$replaceStr:  The string to use as a replacement
    //           for the pattern.
    //      -$str:  The string in which to make the replacement
    function replace($replaceStr, $str) {
        if (strcmp($this->mode, self::PCRE)==0) {
            $result = preg_replace($this->pattern, $replaceStr, $str);
        } else {
            $result = ereg_replace($this->pattern, $replaceStr, $str);
        }
        return $result;
    }

}

?>
```

The strcmp function compares the mode against the PCRE constants because it is a value that needs exact matching, and strcmp is a more efficient method of doing this particular comparison.

The following code uses this new and improved class that supports both PCRE and POSIX regular expressions:

```
$re = new RegExp('/Hello/', RegExp::PCRE);
$re2 = new RegExp('Hello', RegExp::POSIX);

print "Using PCRE: \n\n";

print "Pattern:  " . $re->pattern . "\n";

if ($re->isMatch('Goodbye world!')) {
    echo "Found match!\n";
} else {
    echo "Didn't find match!\n";
}

if ($re->isMatch('Hello world!')) {
    echo "Found match!\n";
} else {
```

```
        echo "Didn't find match!\n";
}

$res = $re->replace('Goodbye', 'Hello world!');
echo $res . "\n";

print "\n\nUsing POSIX: \n\n";

print "Pattern:   " . $re2->pattern . "\n";

if ($re2->isMatch('Goodbye world!')) {
    echo "Found match!\n";
} else {
    echo "Didn't find match!\n";
}

if ($re2->isMatch('Hello world!')) {
    echo "Found match!\n";
} else {
    echo "Didn't find match!\n";
}

$re2s = $re2->replace('Goodbye', 'Hello world!');
echo $re2s . "\n";
```

When the code here is executed, the output will look like this:

```
Using PCRE:

Pattern:  /Hello/
Didn't find match!
Found match!
Goodbye world!


Using POSIX:

Pattern:  Hello
Didn't find match!
Found match!
Goodbye world!
```

Notice that the patterns are a little different between the two objects. This is because the PCRE version of the regular expression requires delimiters at the beginning and the end of the expression—in this case, the / character.

Summary

PHP supports two implementations of regular expressions—POSIX and PCRE. PCREs support more character classes and special features such as nongreedy matching and look-arounds.

Regular expressions allow you to do much more than simple searching and replacing within strings. Using regular expressions in PHP, you can find strings according to specific rules, validate user input, process files such as CSV and tab-delimited files, and make complicated replacements in text. Combined with the other capabilities in PHP, the possibilities are nearly endless.

For more about using regular expressions, see *Regular Expression Recipes: A Problem-Solution Approach* (Apress, 2005) and *Regular Expression Recipes for Windows Developers: A Problem-Solution Approach* (Apress, 2005).

Looking Ahead

In the next chapter, Frank M. Kromann explores the world of variables in PHP, showing some advanced variable functions that you will find invaluable in your everyday programming.

CHAPTER 10

■ ■ ■

Working with Variables

Variables are an important part of any programming language, and that goes for PHP too. Variables are blocks of memory associated with a name and a data type, and variables contain data to be used in calculations, program flow, presentation, and so on.

PHP is a loosely typed language where variables can be used without declarations and where they can change type from line to line, in some cases without losing the content. This makes programming much easier than in more strictly typed languages, but it can also make it more difficult to debug the code.

All variable names in PHP start with a dollar ($) sign. This makes it easy for the scripting engine, as well as the reader, to identify variables anywhere in the code, including when they are embedded in strings. Also, using the $ sign allows the developer to use variable names that would otherwise be reserved by the engine for function names and language constructs. This means writing code where function names are used as variable names, such as `$strlen = strlen("This is a test");`, is allowed.

The first character after the $ sign in a variable name must be a letter or an underscore (_). The remaining characters can be letters, numbers, and underscores, and there is no limit on the length of a variable name (but it makes sense to keep them short and meaningful to ensure the readability of the code). Using short variable names means less typing when writing the code, and using longer names means more descriptive names. Valid letters are any of the characters a–z, the characters A–Z, and any ASCII character from 127 to 255. This makes it possible to use international characters when naming variables. $LøbeNummer is a valid variable name but most likely readable only to Danish developers. We prefer to keep variable and function names as well as all comments in English like all the language constructs and built-in functions.

It is also important to note that although function names are case-insensitive in PHP, this is not the case for variables. $MyVar and $myvar are two different variables in PHP, and this is often the cause of scripting warnings. If PHP is configured to hide errors and warnings, it will be difficult to catch programming errors caused by the misspelling of variables as well as other mistakes. It is recommended to configure PHP (on the development system) to display all errors and warnings; you can do this by defining these two values in `php.ini`:

```
error_reporting  =  E_ALL
display_errors = On
```

■**Note** On a production site it is good practice to hide most or all errors and warnings from the user, but during development it makes sense to display as much information as possible so you can correct errors.

10-1. Using Variable Types

PHP implements a number of variable types. Any variable can be assigned a value of any of these types or the special NULL value. The special NULL value is not case-sensitive, so NULL and null are the same value. When a variable is assigned the NULL value, it does not have a type, and it is considered to be empty. Table 10-1 lists all types that can be used in PHP.

Table 10-1. *PHP Data Types*

Type	Description
Boolean	Possible values are True and False.
Float	Floating-point values.
Integer	Integer values.
String	Any series of ASCII characters 0–255. PHP strings are binary safe.
Array	An indexed list of other values. All data types are allowed as values.
Object	A class instance.
Resource	A handle to an internal data structure. This can be a database connection or a result set.

Variables of the types boolean, float, and integer use a fixed amount of memory, and the remaining types use memory as needed; if additional memory is needed, the engine automatically allocates it.

The internal representation of a string value has two parts—the string data and the length. This causes the function strlen() to be very efficient, as it will return the stored length value without having to count the number of characters in the string. It also allows a string to contain any of the 256 available ASCII values, so you can use a string to store the content of any file or other form of binary data.

PHP's array implementation is an indexed list of values. The index is often called the *key*, and it can be either an integer or a string value. If boolean or float values are used as keys, they are converted to integers before the value is added or updated in the array. Using boolean or floats as keys might lead to unexpected results. The value corresponding to each key can be of any type, so it is possible to create arrays of arrays, and it is also possible to mix the types for both keys and values (see the next section for some examples). More strictly typed languages require that arrays are defined as lists of the same data type and that the memory must be allocated before the arrays are used.

Objects are usually created as an instance of a class or are generated by the engine, and they will contain methods and/or properties. Properties and methods are accessed with the -> indirection symbol, for example, $obj->property or $obj->method($a, $b).

Resources are a special type that can be created only by the engine (built-in or extension functions). The data structure and memory usage is known only to a few functions used to create, modify, and destroy the resource. It is not possible to convert any other type to a resource type.

Operating in a loosely typed language can make it difficult to know the type of a variable. PHP has a number of functions that can determine the current type of a variable (see Table 10-2).

Table 10-2. *Functions to Check Data Type*

Name	Description
is_null()	Returns true if the value is null (no type)
is_string()	Returns true if the value is a string
is_int()	Returns true if the value is an integer
is_float()	Returns true if the value is a floating-point value
is_array()	Returns true if the value is an array
is_object()	Returns true if the value is an object
is_a()	Deprecated; checks if an object is a specified class
instanceof()	Checks if an object is an instance of a class

In addition to these functions, two more functions are important when variables are checked. The isset() function checks if a variable has been defined, and the empty() function checks if the value of a variable is empty. Using one of the is_*() functions will give a compiler notice if the variable is undefined. This is not the case for isset() and empty(). They will return false and true if the variable is undefined. The next example shows what the empty() function will return when passed different values.

The Code

```php
<?php
// Example 10-1-1.php
$text = array(
  "0", "1", "\"\"", "\"0\"", "\"1\"",
  "true", "false", "array()", "array(\"1\")"
);
$values = array(0, 1, "", "0", "1", true, false, array(), array("1"));
foreach($values as $i=>$val) {
  echo "empty(" . $text[$i] . ") is " . (empty($val) ? "True" : "False") . "\n";
}
?>
```

How It Works

This example defines two arrays with the same number of elements. The $text array prints the values that are checked, and the second array, $values, is used in the loop to check the result of a call to the empty() function. The output looks like this:

```
empty(0) is True
empty(1) is False
empty("") is True
empty("0") is True
empty("1") is False
empty(true) is False
empty(false) is True
empty(array()) is True
empty(array("1")) is False
```

Note that the values 0, "", "0", and array() all are considered empty.

10-2. Assigning and Comparing

Assigning a value to a variable takes place with one of the assignment operators: =, +=, -=, *=, /=, %=, .=, &=, |=, ^=, <<=, or >>=. The simple form (=) creates a new variable of any type or assigns a new value. The left side is the variable, and the right side is the value or an expression. The remaining assignment types are more complex; they all assume that the variable on the left side is defined before the statement is reached. The result will be the current value of the variable on the left side and the value on the right side after performing the operation identified by the operator. $a += $b; is the same as $a = $a + $b;.

If the variable is in use when a value is assigned (with simple assignment using the = operator), the old value will be discarded before the new variable is created. All the other assignment operators will reuse the existing value to create a new value. If needed, the existing value will be converted to the proper type before the calculation and assignment. For instance, if $a is an integer and it is used with the string concatenation operator, then $a .= "string value";.

PHP uses a reference-counting system on all variables, so you do not need to free variables when they are no longer used. All allocated memory will be released at the end of the request, but for scripts that use a lot of memory or long-running processes, such as command-line interface (CLI) scripts or PHP-GTK scripts, it might be necessary to free unused variables to allow other variables to use the memory. You can free any variable from memory by assigning it to NULL ($a = NULL;) or by using the unset() function.

Note If more than one variable name references the same variable, all of them must be unset before the memory is released. Creating multiple references to the same data in memory is discussed in this recipe.

You can add values to arrays in two ways. If the left side is a variable, the right side can be an array definition like this: $a = array(9, 7, "orange", "apple");. This will create an array with four elements, and the index or key values will be assigned automatically in numeric order starting with 0. New values can be added, or existing values can be replaced with an expression where the left side points to one of the values in the array. So, setting $a[2] = "pear"; will replace the third element, orange, with pear because the key value of 2 was in use already. A new element will be added to the array if the key does not exist already. Setting $a[5] = "orange"; will add orange with the key 5, and the array will now have five elements. Note that this will not have an element with the key 4. If you try to access or use $a[4], you will get an undefined variable notice. You can use a special notation to let PHP assign the key values automatically. You do this by simply omitting the key in the assignment, such as $a[] = "apricot". This will create the key 6 and assign it the value apricot. This notation will always use numeric indexes, and the next value will be one higher than the highest numeric index value in the array.

You can also assign the key values to force a specific relation between keys and values, as shown the following example, where both keys and values are mixed between numeric and string values.

The Code

```php
<?php
// Example 10-2-1.php
$a = array(
   0=>1,
   1=>2,
   2=>"orange",
   3=>"apple",
   "id"=>7,
   "name"=>"John Smith"
);
print_r($a);
?>
```

How It Works

In this example you create an array with six values where the keys are assigned with the => operator. The first four values are assigned numeric keys, and the last two are assigned string keys. The output from this code looks like this:

```
Array
(
    [0] => 1
    [1] => 2
    [2] => orange
    [3] => apple
    [id] => 7
    [name] => John Smith
)
```

You can get rid of a single value in an array with the unset() function. This will remove the value from the array but not rearrange any of the key values. The code unset($a[3]); will remove apple from the array in the previous example. PHP implements many functions that manipulate arrays. One of these requires special attention. It is the list() function, or language construct. Like array(), it is not really a function but a way to tell the engine how to handle special data. It is used on the left side of the assignment operator, when the right side is an array or an expression that results in an array, and it can assign values to multiple variables at the same time.

Note list() works only on numerical arrays and assumes numerical indexes start at 0.

The next example shows how to use the list() function.

The Code

```php
<?php
// Example 10-2-2.php
$net_address = array("192.168.1.101", "255.255.255.0", "192.168.1.1");
list($ip_addr, $net_mask, $gateway) = $net_address;
echo "ip addr  = $ip_addr\n";
echo "net mask = $net_mask\n";
echo "gateway  = $gateway\n";
?>
```

How It Works

First, you define an array with three elements. This could be the return value from a function call. Second, these values are extracted from the array and stored in individual variables with a call to the list() function. Finally, the three new variables are printed to form this output:

```
ip addr  = 192.168.1.101
net mask = 255.255.255.0
gateway  = 192.168.1.1
```

When a variable is assigned a value, it will actually get a copy of that value. Using the special & operator makes it possible to create a new variable that references the same value in memory as another variable. This is best demonstrated with a small example, where two values are defined. In the first part of the code, $b is assigned a copy of $a, and in the second part, $b is assigned a reference to $a.

The Code

```php
<?php
// Example 10-2-3.php
$a = 5;
$b = $a;
$a = 7;
echo "\$a = $a and \$b = $b\n";

$a = 5;
$b = &$a;
$a = 7;
echo "\$a = $a and \$b = $b\n";
?>
```

How It Works

In the first part, $a and $b will have independent values, so changing one variable will not affect the other. In the second part, the two variables share the same memory, so changing one variable will affect the value of the other.

```
$a = 7 and $b = 5
$a = 7 and $b = 7
```

When two or more variables share the same memory, it is possible to use the unset() function on one of the variables without affecting the other variables. The unset() function will simply remove the reference and not the value.

PHP has two kinds of comparison operators. The loose comparison operators will compare values even if the two values are of different data types. The strict comparison operators will compare both the values and the data types. So, if two variables are of different types, they will always be different when compared to the strict operators, even if the values are identical otherwise. Tables 10-3 and 10-4 explain the comparison operators.

Table 10-3. *Loose Comparison Operators*

Example	Name	Description
$a == $b	Equal to	True if $a is equal to $b
$a != $b	Not equal to	True if $a is not equal to $b
$a < $b	Less than	True if $a is less than $b
$a > $b	Greater than	True if $a is greater than $b
$a <= $b	Less than or equal to	True if $a is less than or equal to $b
$a >= $b	Greater than or equal to	True if $a is greater than or equal to $b

Table 10-4. *Strict Comparison Operators*

Example	Name	Description
$a === $b	Equal to	True if $a is equal to $b and they are of the same type
$a !== $b	Not equal to	True if $a is not equal to $b or they are not of the same type

   When the loose operators are used and the data types are different, PHP will convert one of the variables to the same type as the other before making the comparison.
   To show how these different operators work, the next example creates a script that loops through an array of different data types and compares all the values to each other.

The Code

```php
<?php
// Example 10-2-4.php
$Values = array(
  NULL,
  True,
  False,
  1,
  0,
  1.0,
  0.0,
  "1",
  "0",
  array(1),
  (object)array(1)
);

function dump_value($var) {
  switch (gettype($var)) {
    case 'NULL':
      return "NULL";
      break;
    case 'boolean':
      return $var ? "True" : "False";
      break;
    default :
    case 'integer':
      return $var;
      break;
    case 'double':
      return sprintf("%0.1f", $var);
      break;
    case 'string':
      return "'$var'";
      break;
```

```
    case 'object':
    case 'array':
      return gettype($var);
      break;
  }
}

function CreateTable($Values, $type = "==") {
  echo "<table border=1>";
  echo "<tr><td>$type</td>";
    foreach ($Values as $x_val) {
      echo "<td bgcolor=lightgrey>" . dump_value($x_val) . "</td>";
    }
  echo "</tr>";
  foreach ($Values as $y_val) {
    echo "<tr><td bgcolor=lightgrey>" . dump_value($y_val) . "</td>";
    foreach ($Values as $x_val) {
      if ($type == "==") {
        $result = dump_value($y_val == $x_val);
      }
      else {
        $result = dump_value($y_val === $x_val);
      }
      echo "<td>$result</td>";
    }
    echo "</tr>";
  }
  echo "</table>";
}

echo "<html><body>";
CreateTable($Values, "==");
CreateTable($Values, "===");
echo "</body></html>";
?>
```

How It Works

The script defines the array with values of different types, a function to format the output, and a function to create a Hypertext Markup Language (HTML) table with the result. The formatting function dump_value() is needed to print readable values for booleans and floats. The CreateTable() function is called once for each comparison type. The output from this script, viewed in a browser, looks like Figure 10-1 and Figure 10-2.

==	NULL	True	False	1	0	1.0	0.0	'1'	'0'	array	object
NULL	True	False	True	False	True	False	True	False	False	False	False
True	False	True	False	True	False	True	False	True	False	True	True
False	True	False	True	False	True	False	True	False	True	False	False
1	False	True	False	True	False	True	False	True	False	False	False
0	True	False	True	False	True	False	True	False	True	False	False
1.0	False	True	False	True	False	True	False	True	False	False	False
0.0	True	False	True	False	True	False	True	False	True	False	False
'1'	False	True	False	True	False	True	False	True	False	False	False
'0'	False	False	True	False	True	False	True	False	True	False	False
array	False	True	False	False	False	False	False	False	False	True	False
object	False	True	False	False	False	False	False	False	False	False	True

Figure 10-1. *Comparing variables of different types with loose operators*

===	NULL	True	False	1	0	1.0	0.0	'1'	'0'	array	object
NULL	True	False	False	False	False	False	False	False	False	False	False
True	False	True	False	False	False	False	False	False	False	False	False
False	False	False	True	False	False	False	False	False	False	False	False
1	False	False	False	True	False	False	False	False	False	False	False
0	False	False	False	False	True	False	False	False	False	False	False
1.0	False	False	False	False	False	True	False	False	False	False	False
0.0	False	False	False	False	False	False	True	False	False	False	False
'1'	False	False	False	False	False	False	False	True	False	False	False
'0'	False	False	False	False	False	False	False	False	True	False	False
array	False	False	False	False	False	False	False	False	False	True	False
object	False	False	False	False	False	False	False	False	False	False	True

Figure 10-2. *Comparing variables of different types with strict operators*

10-3. Typecasting

Typecasting is a method used to force the conversion of a variable from one type to another. During typecasting, the value is preserved and converted if possible, or the result is assigned a default value with the specified type. Converting a string with abc to an integer will give the value 0. The next example shows how a string with a numeric value can be typecast to an integer and how an array, which has at least one element, is typecast to an integer that will result in a value of 1.

The Code

```php
<?php
// Example 10-3-1.php
$a = "10";
$b = (int)$a;
echo 'gettype($a) = ' . gettype($a) . "\n";
echo 'gettype($b) = ' . gettype($b) . ", \$b = $b\n";
$a = array(5,4,5);
$b = (int)$a;
echo 'gettype($a) = ' . gettype($a) . "\n";
echo 'gettype($b) = ' . gettype($b) . ", \$b = $b\n";
?>
```

How It Works

You define $a as a string and then $b as the integer value of $a. Then you use the gettype() function to get a string representation of the variable type. The output from this script looks like this:

```
gettype($a) = string
gettype($b) = integer, $b = 10
gettype($a) = array
gettype($b) = integer, $b = 1
```

Note Converting from arrays and objects to integers is undefined by the engine, but it currently works as if the variable was converted to a boolean and then to an integer. You should not rely on this, and you should avoid typecasting arrays and objects to any other types.

When arrays are used with an if clause, they are implicitly converted to booleans. This is useful when checking if an array has any elements. If $a is an array, then the code if ($a) echo "$a has elements"; will print a statement only if $a is a nonempty array.

Jon Stephen's Chapter 4 discussed numeric values and showed how an integer value could change its type to floating point if the result of a calculation was outside the boundaries of an integer.

In this chapter you have seen how you can convert string values with numeric content into integers. You can apply the same conversion to floating-point values but not to boolean values. For example, (bool)"true"; and (bool)"false"; will both return a true value. An empty string will convert to false, and any nonempty string will convert to true when typecast to a boolean.

It is also possible to convert variables from arrays to objects and back again. You can do this to change how elements/properties are accessed, as shown in the following example.

The Code

```php
<?php
// Example 10-3-2.php
$a = array(
  "Name" => "John Smith",
  "Address" => "22 Main Street",
  "City" => "Irvine",
  "State" => "CA",
  "Zip" => "92618"
);
echo "Name = " . $a["Name"] . "\n";

$o = (object)$a;
echo "Address = $o->Address\n";?>
```

How It Works

First, you define an array with five elements. Each element is defined as a key and a value, and all the keys are string values. Second, you use traditional array accessors to print the Name value from the array. Finally, a new variable is created by typecasting the array to an object. When elements/properties are accessed on an object, you use the -> symbol between the object name and the property.

```
Name = John Smith
Address = 22 Main Street
```

Converting an object to an array will convert properties to elements of the resulting array only (see recipe 10-5 for a discussion of the public, private, and protected properties).

The Code

```php
<?php
// Example 10-3-3.php
class myclass {
  public $name;
  public $address;
  private $age;
  function SetAge($age) {
    $this->age = $age;
  }
}

$obj = new myclass;
$obj->name = "John Smith";
$obj->address = "22 Main Street";
$obj->SetAge(47);

$arr = (array)$obj;
print_r($arr);
?>
```

How It Works

The class myclass() has a couple of public properties, a private property, and a method used to set the private property. When an object is created as an instance of myclass, you can use -> to assign values to the public properties and use the SetAge() method to assign a value to the private property. The object is then converted to an array and dumped with the print_r() function.

```
Array
(
    [name] => John Smith
    [address] => 22 Main Street
    [ myclass age] => 47
)
```

Formatting output requires different types to be converted into strings before they are sent to the client. You can do this by concatenating different values using the . operator. The engine will automatically convert nonstring values to strings, if possible. Integer and floating-point values are converted into a decimal representation, and booleans are converted into an empty value or 1.

■**Note** If an expression is concatenated with other values or strings, you must enclose the expression in ( ). For instance, $a = "test " . 5 + 7; is not the same as $a = "test " . (5 + 7);. The first will calculate to the value 7, as the concatenation will take place before the addition, so the string "test 5" is created and added to the value 7. The second expression will calculate to "test 12".

Arrays, objects, and resources contain values too complex to be converted to strings in a unified and automated way, so these are converted into strings showing the data type.

It is also possible to embed variables directly into strings, when the string is created with double quotes. A string with single quotes will not expand the value of any variable included in the string. The next example shows how embedded variables are handled when the string is created with single or double quotes.

The Code

```php
<?php
// Example 10-3-4.php
$a = 10;
$b = 15.7;
echo "The value of \$a is $a and the value of \$b is $b\n";
echo 'The value of .\$a is $a and the value of \$b is $b\n';
?>
```

How It Works

This example will output two lines, where the first line will expand the values of $a and $b and where the variable names are printed in the second line. The \ escapes the $ signs to prevent the engine from converting the first $a into the value, and it just prints the variable name. Note how the string with single quotes prints all the escape characters.

```
The value of $a is 10 and the value of $b is 15.7
The value of \$a is $a and the value of \$b is $b\n
```

The same example with the concatenation operator looks like the following.

The Code

```php
<?php
// Example 10-3-5.php
$a = 10;
$b = 15.7;
echo "The value of \$a is " . $a . " and the value of \$b is " . $b . "\n";
echo 'The value of $a is ' . $a . ' and the value of $b is ' . $b . "\n";
?>
```

How It Works

Note how the last line combines strings created with single and double quotes. This allows you to use $a without escaping the $ sign and the new line at the end of the line.

Embedding numbers and strings into other strings is simple, but what if the value is stored in an array or object? It is still possible to embed these more complex types in strings, but you need to follow a few rules:

- You can use only one dimension.

- You should not include key values in quotes, even if strings are used as keys.

- You can embed more complex values with the syntax ${}.

The next example shows how arrays embedded in strings will be converted.

The Code

```php
<?php
// Example 10-3-6.php
$arr = array(
    1 => "abc",
    "abc" => 123.5,
    array(1,2,3)
);
$key = "abc";
```

```
echo "First value = $arr[1]\n";
echo "Second value = $arr[abc]\n";
echo "Third value = $arr[2]\n";
echo "Third value = $arr[2][2]\n";

echo "Second value = ${arr['abc']}\n";
echo "Second value = ${arr["abc"]}\n";
echo "Second value = ${arr[$key]}\n";
?>
```

How It Works

After defining an array with three elements and a string value with the index of one of tho olo ments, you use the different embedding methods to see how the values are resolved. The three first lines in the output, shown next, shows how the simple embedding works. The first two of these actually print the value of the element, but the third line prints Array. The same goes for the fourth line where you tried to print a single value from a two-dimensional array. The last three lines used the ${} syntax that allows embedding of more complex types, but this is limited to one-dimensional arrays. Use string concatenation if you want to combine values from multidimensional arrays in a string.

```
First value = abc
Second value = 123.5
Third value = Array
Third value = Array[2]
Second value = 123.5
Second value = 123.5
Second value = 123.5
```

The following example is the same but with objects.

The Code

```
<?php
// Example 10-3-7.php
$arr = array(
    "abc" => "abc",
    "def" => 123.5,
    "ghi" => array(1,2,3)
);
$key = "abc";
$obj = (object) $arr;

echo "First value = $obj->abc\n";
echo "Second value = $obj->def\n";
echo "Third value = $obj->ghi\n";
?>
```

```
First value = abc
Second value = 123.5
Third value = Array
```

> **Note** It is important that the index values of the array are strings. Values that use an integer as an index cannot be converted to a valid property name. Variable and property names must start with a letter or an underscore.

10-4. Using Constants

You can use variables to define values that have one value for the duration of the script. The nature of a variable allows the content to be changed, and this might lead to unexpected behavior of the program. This is where constants become handy. Constants are identifiers for simple values. The value can be defined once, while the script is running, and never changed. The function define() assigns a simple constant value (bool, int, float, or string) to a constant name. By default the constant names are case-sensitive like variables, but a third optional argument to the define() function makes it possible to create case-insensitive constant names. Constant names are often defined as uppercase only to make it easier to identify them in the code. The define() function will return true if the constant could be defined or false if it was defined already.

Unlike variables that start with a $ sign, constants are defined by name; this makes it impossible for the engine to identify constants with the same name as language constructs or functions. If a constant is defined with a name that is reserved for language constructs or function names, it can be retrieved only with the constant() function. This function takes a string as the argument and returns the value of the constant. The constant() function is also helpful when different constants are retrieved by storing the constant name in a variable or returning it from a function.

The Code

```php
<?php
// Example 10-4-1.php
define('ALIGN_LEFT', 'left');
define('ALIGN_RIGHT', 'right');
define('ALIGN_CENTER', 'center');

$const = 'ALIGN_CENTER';
echo constant($const);
?>
```

How It Works

This example defines three constants and assigns the name of one of the constants to a string that is used as the parameter to the constant() function. The result is the value of the constant.

```
center
```

You can use the function `defined()` to check if a constant is defined, before trying to define it again or before using it to avoid undefined constants (which will generate a warning).

Using constants makes it easy to change the values used to control program flow without having to break code. If you use hard-coded values and want to change one or more values, you must make sure all the places you compare to each value are updated to match the new values. If, on the other hand, you use constants, then you can get by with changing the value in the constant definition, and all the places you use that constant will automatically have the new value.

Consider an example where you have three values controlling the program flow and you want to change the values for some reason. Your code could look like the following example.

The Code

```php
<?php
// Example 10-4-2.php
switch($justify) {
  case 1 :  // left
    break;
  case 2 :  // center
    break;
  case 3 :  // right
    break;
}
?>
```

How It Works

Each constant is used only once in the example, but you could have several functions that use a justification value to print the content in different ways, and using numbers is less readable than the constant names.

The Code

```php
<?php
// Example 10-4-3.php
define('ALIGN_LEFT', 1);
define('ALIGN_CENTER', 2);
define('ALIGN_RIGHT', 3);

switch($value) {
  case ALIGN_LEFT :
    break;
  case ALIGN_CENTER :
    break;
  case ALIGN_RIGHT :
    break;
}
?>
```

How It Works

So, to change the values of these constants, you need to change only the definitions, and you get the benefit of writing more readable code without having to add a lot of comments.

PHP has a large number of predefined constants (M_PI, M_E, and so on, from the math functions), and many extensions define and use constants (MYSQL_NUM, MYSQL_ASSOC, and MYSQL_BOTH, to mention a few) that allow you to write more readable code.

It is not possible to define a constant as an array or object, but as discussed in recipe 10-4, you can convert these data types into strings with the serialize() function. You can use the result of this function, or any other function that returns a simple value, to define constant values. These constants can then be accessed globally (as discussed in recipe 10-5). The only downside is the need to unserialize the value before it can be used. The next example shows how to use this technique to store an array in a constant and use that from within a function. This makes it possible to access a global constant in the form of an array, without having to use global $arr; or $GLOBALS['arr'];.

The Code

```php
<?php
// Example 10-4-4.php
$arr = array("apple", "orange", "pear");
define('MYARRAY', serialize($arr));

function MyTest() {
  print_r(unserialize(MYARRAY));
}

MyTest();
?>
```

How It Works

The variable $arr is assigned an array with three values, serialized (converted to string form), and stored in a constant called MYARRAY. The constant is then used inside the function MyTest(), where it is converted back to an array and the content is printed. The output looks like this:

```
Array
(
    [0] => apple
    [1] => orange
    [2] => pear
)
```

10-5. Defining Variable Scope

Variables are visible and usable in the scope where they are defined, so if a variable is defined in the global scope, it is visible there and not in any functions or class methods. If the variable $a is defined globally, another variable with the same name might be defined in a function. The two variables are not the same even though they share the same name.

The Code

```php
<?php
// Example 10-5-1.php
$a = 7;
function test() {
   $a = 20;
}
test();
echo "\$a = $a\n";
?>
```

How It Works

The variable $a is defined in the global scope and assigned the value 7. Inside the function test() you define another variable with the same name but the value 20. When the code is executed, you call the function test and then print the value of $a. The two versions of $a do not share the same memory, so the output will be the original value of $a from the global scope.

```
$a = 7
```

You have two ways to access global variables from within a function or method of a class. You can use the global keyword to associate a variable inside a function with a global variable. The variable does not need to be defined globally before the association is made, so if the line $a = 7; in the following example is omitted, the result will still be 20.

The Code

```php
<?php
// Example 10-5-2.php
$a = 7;
function test() {
  global $a;
  $a = 20;
}
test();
echo "\$a = $a\n";
?>
```

How It Works

The only change from the previous example is the line global a$; inside the function. This line makes the two variables reference the same memory, so when you change the value inside the function, you also change the value of the variable in the global scope.

```
$a = 20
```

The other way of accessing global variables is by using the true global or superglobal variable called $GLOBALS. This is an associative array that is available in any scope, and it has references to all variables defined in the global scope.

The Code

```php
<?php
// Example 10-5-3.php
$a = 7;
function test() {
  $GLOBALS['a'] = 20;
}
test();
echo "\$a = $a\n";
?>
```

How It Works

By using the superglobal $GLOBAL, it is possible to access or change any variable from the global space, without defining it as global as you did in the previous example.

```
$a = 20
```

As in the previous example, it is possible to define variables in the global scope from within a function or class method. Using $GLOBALS['newvar'] = 'test'; will create a variable called $newvar in the global scope and assign it the string value 'test'.

You can use a few other PHP variables like this. These are in general called *superglobals*, and they do not belong to any special scope (see Table 10-5).

Table 10-5. *PHP Superglobals*

Name	Description
$GLOBALS	An associated array with references to every variable defined in the global scope
$_SERVER	Variables set by the server
$_ENV	Environment variables
$_GET	Variables provided to the script via the Uniform Resource Locator (URL)
$_POST	Variables provided to the script via HTTP POST
$_COOKIE	Variables provided to the script via HTTP cookies
$_FILE	Variables uploaded via HTTP POST file uploads
$_REQUEST	A combination of variables provided by GET, POST, and COOKIE methods
$_SESSION	Variables currently registered in the session

Constants are another form of true global data. If a script has a need for defining values that should be accessed from any scope, constants might be a good way of defining these. This, of course, requires that the values should remain constant for the duration of the script. You can define constants in the global scope or in a function, but they will always belong to the global scope, as shown in the next example.

The Code

```php
<?php
// Example 10-5-4.php
define('CONST1', 1);

function MyTest() {
  define('CONST2', 2);
}

MyTest();
echo "CONST1 = " . CONST1 . " and CONST2 = " . CONST2 . "\n";
?>
```

How It Works

In this example, you define a constant from the global scope and one from inside a function. As the output shows, both constants are available in the global scope.

```
CONST1 = 1 and CONST2 = 2
```

Working with classes and objects introduces another form of variable called a *property*, or a *member*. This is basically a normal PHP variable, but access to it can be restricted with one of the keywords public, private, protected, or static. You can use the same keywords when declaring functions or methods. Older versions of PHP (before version 5.x) used var to declare members, and they were all considered to be public. When updating scripts from PHP 4 to PHP 5, you should convert all var declarations to one of the new modifiers. Table 10-6 lists the class member and method definitions.

Table 10-6. *Class Member and Method Definitions*

Name	Description
Const	Defines a constant member.
Public	Accessible from any object of the class.
Protected	Accessible from the class where it is defined and from inherited classes.
Private	Accessible from the class where it is defined.
Static	Modifier. When used alone, public is assumed.

The Code

```php
<?php
// Example 10-5-5.php
class myclass {
   public $a;

   function set_value($val) {
      $this->a = $val;
   }
}

$obj = new myclass;
$obj->set_value(123);
echo "Member a = $obj->a\n";
$obj->a = 7;
echo "Member a = $obj->a\n";
?>
```

How It Works

This example declares a class called myclass(). It has the public member $a and a method called set_value(). An object is defined as an instance of myclass(), and then you use the set_value() method to assign a value to the member. This value is later changed by accessing the member directly.

```
Member a = 123
Member a = 7
```

Changing the member $a to protected or private will give the following result.

The Code

```php
<?php
// Example 10-5-6.php
class myclass {
  private $a;

  function set_value($val) {
    $this->a = $val;
  }
}

$obj = new myclass;
$obj->set_value(123);
echo "Member a = $obj->a\n";
$obj->a = 7;
echo "Member a = $obj->a\n";
?>
```

How It Works

This small change will cause the script to fail.

```
Fatal error: Cannot access private property myclass::$a
in /Samples/11-5-5.php on line 12
```

This feature is useful when you develop classes that are used by other developers. It will protect the class from being misused by accessing the members directly for both reading and writing. The class should expose functions to set and get values that are supposed to be available (the class API) to other developers. So, you should modify this class as shown in the following example.

The Code

```php
<?php
// Example 10-5-7.php
class myclass {
  private $a;

  function set_value($val) {
    $this->a = $val;
  }

  function get_value() {
    return $this->a;
  }
}
```

```
$obj = new myclass;
$obj->set_value(123);
echo "Member a = " . $obj->get_value() . "\n";
?>
```

How It Works

You can access the member $a only through one of the methods.

```
Member a = 123
```

This will allow read and write access to the member but will not allow direct access to modify the member without calling a method. The method should check the value and return a value indicating if the property could be set. If a member is private, it can be accessed only by members of the class where it is created; if a member is protected, it can be modified only by the class or any inherited classes.

You can use the static modifier to change a member or method so it is accessible without instantiating the class. A static member will be defined only once regardless of the number of instantiated objects of the class.

The Code

```php
<?php
// Example 10-5-8.php
class myclass {
   const MYCONST = 123;
   static $value = 567;
}

echo 'myclass::MYCONST = ' . myclass::MYCONST . "\n";
echo 'myclass::$value = ' . myclass::$value . "\n";
?>
```

How It Works

In this example, a simple class defines two members. One is defined as a const, and the other is defined as a static. Both members can be accessed with the name of the class and two colons and the name of the member. As for normal PHP constants, the const members of a class are read-only.

```
myclass::MYCONST = 123
myclass::$value = 567
```

Note how the constant definition automatically is considered a static member of the class (only one copy will be stored in memory for all instances of the class) and how the static modifier is used without a public, private, or protected keyword. This makes the variable public. If the variable was defined as private static, it would not be possible to access it directly, as shown in the next example.

The Code

```php
<?php
// Example 10-5-9.php
class myclass {
  const MYCONST = 123;
  private static $value = 567;
}

echo 'myclass::MYCONST = ' . myclass::MYCONST . "\n";
echo 'myclass::$value = ' . myclass::$value . "\n";
?>
```

How It Works

The first part of the code works as in the previous example, but when you try to access the private member, the script will stop with a fatal error.

```
myclass::MYCONST = 123
Fatal error: Cannot access private property myclass::$value
in /Samples/10-5-9.php on line 9
```

10-6. Parsing Values to Functions

The function name and the number of parameters it takes define a function. Each parameter can be defined as *pass by value* or *pass by reference* or can be assigned a default value. Using default values makes it possible to call the function with fewer arguments, and parameters with default values should always be placed at the end of the parameter list.

When a variable is passed by value, it means that the function will operate on a copy of the variable. The function can change the content and type of the variable without affecting the code that called the function (that is, that passed the argument). If a variable is passed by reference, it means that the variable will share the same memory, and any changes to the content or type will affect the code that called the function. The next example shows two functions that both take one variable as a parameter.

The Code

```php
<?php
// Example 10-6-1.php
function by_value($a) {
  $a *= 2;
}
function by_reference(&$a) {
  $a *= 2;
}
$b = 5;
by_value($b);
```

```php
echo "\$b is now $b\n";
by_reference($b);
echo "\$b is now $b\n";
by_value(&$b);
echo "\$b is now $b\n";
?>
```

How It Works

The two functions are almost identical. They both take the value passed as the argument and multiply by 2. The difference is how the variable is passed. In the first function, the variable is passed by value, so $a is considered a copy of the variable. The second function forces the variable to be passed by reference. This makes the two variables share the same memory; therefore, when the variable is changed inside the function, it affects the variable that was passed. You can force parsing by reference at call time. You do this by adding the & sign in front of the variable name. The output from this example looks like this:

```
$b is now 5
$b is now 10
$b is now 20
```

Passing values by reference is a useful way to have a function return more than one value. A function that performs a database query to get a result set could also return information about the columns selected, and the actual return value could be used to indicate success or failure. To illustrate this, create an example with two functions. GetData() simulates a database query, and ListData() creates an HTML table with the rows returned from GetData(). You can also extend this example to include another function to present data, when only a single row is returned from the GetData() function.

The Code

```php
<?php
// Example 10-6-2.php
define('COLUMN_NAME', 0);
define('COLUMN_TYPE', 1);

define('COLUMN_STRING', 1);
define('COLUMN_INTEGER', 2);

function GetData(&$data, &$meta) {
  $meta = array(
    array(
      COLUMN_NAME => "First Name",
      COLUMN_TYPE => COLUMN_STRING
    ),
```

```php
    array(
      COLUMN_NAME => "Last Name",
      COLUMN_TYPE => COLUMN_STRING
    ),
    array(
      COLUMN_NAME => "Age",
      COLUMN_TYPE => COLUMN_INTEGER
    )
  );
  $data = array(
    array("John", "Smith", 55),
    array("Mike", "Johnson", 33),
    array("Susan", "Donovan", 29),
    array("King", "Tut", 3346)
  );
  return sizeof($data);
}

function ListData($data, $meta) {
  echo "<table border=1>";
  foreach($data as $row) {
    echo "<tr>";
    foreach($row as $col=>$cell) {
      switch ($meta[$col][COLUMN_TYPE]) {
        case COLUMN_STRING :
          echo "<td align=left>$cell</td>";
          break;
        case COLUMN_INTEGER :
          echo "<td align=right>" . number_format($cell) . "</td>";
          break;
      }
    }
    echo "</tr>";
  }
  echo "</table>";
}

$d = array();
$m = array();
if (GetData($d, $m)) {
  ListData($d, $m);
}
?>
```

How It Works

You define the two variables $d and $m. Both are assigned the value of empty arrays. The call to GetData() defines the content of the two variables passed by reference. The two variables are then passed to the ListData() function, which generates an HTML table showing the values, as shown in Figure 10-3.

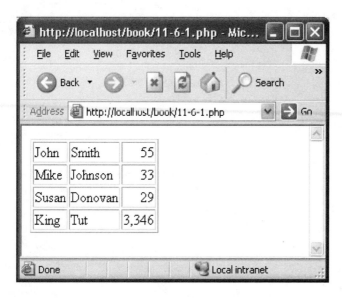

Figure 10-3. *Getting and listing data*

A special case of pass by value is used for arrays. Arrays can be very large, and in order to improve speed these values are always passed by reference. If the definition is called for pass by value, the array will be copied when the function first attempts to modify the content or data type. This is called *copy on write*, so if an array is passed by value and the function never changes the content of the array, you have no need to perform the copy.

You can define whether a variable is passed by value or reference either in the function definition or when the function is called, as shown in the following example.

The Code

```php
<?php
// Example 10-6-3.php
function f1($a) {
    $a += 4;
}
function f2(&$a) {
    $a += 10;
}
$b = 5;
f1(&$b);
```

```
f2($b);
echo "\$b = $b\n";
?>
```

How It Works

This example defines two functions. The first function, f1(), takes an argument passed by value, and the second function, f2(), takes one argument passed by reference. When the first function is called, the value that is passed is a reference to $b, forcing the function to operate on the same value in memory. When the second function is called, the value passed is the actual value, but the function automatically converts that to a reference to the value.

```
$b = 19
```

10-7. Using Dynamic Variable and Function Names

You can use variable variables or variable function names to reduce the number of if, else, or switch statements and make the code more readable. It is all about being able to calculate the name of the variable to store (or get data from) or the name of the function to execute.

Calculating the index or key value for an array is useful if the data is stored in an array. You can specify the key value with a hard-coded value or with a value stored in a variable or returned from a function.

The Code

```php
<?php
// Example 10-7-1.php
$fruits = array(
   'apple', 'orange', 'pear', 'apricot',
   'apple', 'apricot', 'orange', 'orange'
);
$fruit_count = array();
foreach ($fruits as $i=>$fruit) {
  if (isset($fruit_count[$fruit])) {
    $fruit_count[$fruit]++;
  }
  else {
    $fruit_count[$fruit] = 1;
  }
}
asort($fruit_count);
foreach ($fruit_count as $fruit=>$count) {
  echo "$fruit = $count\n";
}
?>
```

How It Works

The script produces this output:

```
pear = 1
apple = 2
apricot = 2
orange = 3
```

This example loops through an indexed array of fruit names and creates a new array with the count of each fruit name. The $fruit_count array is filled with key and value pairs as you loop through the $fruits array. For each fruit you test to see if it is a new name or if it already exists in the array. This code can be written a little more compactly by using the @ modifier. This will suppress any warnings from using the increment operator (++) on an undefined variable. If a variable is undefined when the increment operator is used, a new variable will be declared with a 0 value, and a warning will be issued. This warning can be suppressed by adding @ in front of the statement. You can also use the @ modifier to suppress warnings from function calls, but this will not suppress errors.

```php
<?php
// Example 10-7-1a.php
$fruits = array(
  'apple', 'orange', 'pear', 'apricot',
  'apple', 'apricot', 'orange', 'orange'
);
$fruit_count = array();
foreach ($fruits as $i=>$fruit) {
  @$fruit_count[$fruit]++;
}
asort($fruit_count);
foreach ($fruit_count as $fruit=>$count) {
  echo "$fruit = $count\n";
}
?>
```

Caution Using the @ modifier in front of variables or functions could hide warnings that may indicate a programming error. You should use it with caution.

It is also possible to calculate the variable name for simpler variables and use that name to access the value of that variable. You do this with the double $ sign. Adding another $ sign in front of a variable will take the value of that variable and access the value of another variable with that name. If $a = 'test';, then $$a will access a variable called $test. The following example shows how a series of variables is accessed to print a string composed from the values of these variables.

The Code

```php
<?php
// Example 10-7-2.php
$a0 = 'This';
$a1 = 'is';
$a2 = 'a';
$a3 = 'test';

for ($i = 0; $i < 4; $i++) {
  $var = "a$i";
  echo "${$var} ";
}
?>
```

How It Works

The script defines four variables that all start with $a and end with an integer. You then create a loop from 0 to 3, and for each execution of the loop you output the value of the variable with the name calculated from the contents of the string $var.

```
This is a test
```

The calculation of each variable is simple, but you could easily extend the same method to include more advanced calculations or database lookups.

Note When a variable is embedded in a string, it is necessary to use a different notation to avoid errors. $$var becomes ${$var} when it is embedded in a string.

You can also use constants in the calculation of variable variables. You need to use a different modifier, because a $ sign in front of a constant would look like a variable. By putting {} around the constant name and then applying the $ sign in front of it, you will create a reference to a variable with the name of the constant's value.

The Code

```php
<?php
// Example 10-7-3.php
define('CONST_A', 'test');

${CONST_A} = 27;
echo "\$test = $test\n";
?>
```

How It Works

First you define a variable with the value test, and then you use that constant to calculate a new variable name and assign that variable the value of 27. To avoid creating a new variable called $CONST_A, you use the extended notation ${CONST_A} to tell the engine to use the constant.

```
$test = 27
```

It is also possible to use the value of a variable to point to a function name and thereby change the program flow without needing flow control. This might not always make the code readable, but it makes it possible to create code where the flow control can be moved to a database in the form of parameters.

The Code

```php
<?php
// Example 10-7-4.php
function ShowSimple($val) {
   echo "$val\n";
}
function ShowComplex($val) {
   echo "The value is " . number_format($val) . "\n";
}

$v = 1234567;

$a = "ShowSimple";
$b = "ShowComplex";

$a($v);
$b($v);
?>
```

How It Works

You define two functions and assign the names of each function to a variable. When the new variables are written as $a($v);, the system will convert $a to a function name and call that function.

```
1234567
The value is 1,234,567
```

You can use this method to return the function name from a function call or calculation. It might make the code less readable, and you can obtain the same effect by adding an extra parameter to one function so it will be able to handle both simple and complex printing.

10-8. Encapsulating Complex Data Types

You can format numbers and strings and use them as output or store them in files or databases without modifications. The more complex data types—arrays and objects—can also be stored, but that generally requires some advanced formatting or multiple records in the database (one for each element in the array). This was demonstrated in recipe 10-6, where one function generated multiple arrays and another function presented the generated data in an HTML table structure.

However, using user-defined functions to convert arrays and objects into data that can be stored in a database or file is not the fastest or simplest solution. This is where the built-in functions serialize() and unsearialize() become handy. These functions can convert an array or an object into a string representation that can be stored in a single column in a database (or a file) and later retrieved and converted to the original data type.

The serialize() function takes a PHP variable and converts it into a string representation, and the unserialize() function takes a string (most often created with serialize()) and converts it to its original type.

■**Note** Variables of the resource type cannot be serialized. They contain data created and maintained by the engine. Any other type can be serialized.

The Code

```php
<?php
// Example 10-8-1.php
$fruits = array(
    'apple', 'orange', 'pear', 'apricot',
    'apple', 'apricot', 'orange', 'orange'
);

$str = serialize($fruits);
echo "$str\n";

$new_fruits = unserialize($str);
$new_fruits[] = 'apple';
print_r($new_fruits);
?>
```

How It Works

This example uses the serialize() function to convert the contents of an array to a string. The string is printed and then converted to a new array, where you add a new element.

```
a:8:{i:0;s:5:"apple";i:1;s:6:"orange";i:2;s:4:"pear";i:3;s:7:"apricot";i:4;
s:5:"apple";i:5;s:7:"apricot";i:6;s:6:"orange";i:7;s:6:"orange";}
Array
(
    [0] => apple
    [1] => orange
    [2] => pear
    [3] => apricot
    [4] => apple
    [5] => apricot
    [6] => orange
    [7] => orange
    [8] => apple
)
```

Database-driven websites are often designed in a way so the content stored in a database can be retrieved and presented without much formatting. When a web page is created from numeric data and processing, it can be useful to cache the results for easy access and presentation for the next user who requests the same page. You can do this by serializing the results, storing them in the database or in a file, and then checking if a cached version exists before a new page is generated.

The next example demonstrates how to build a class that can cache an array of values between requests. The class will work on files, but you can easily change it to store the values in a database. The caching class is stored in an include file (cache.inc) so it can be used in many different applications.

Table 10-7 lists the methods.

Table 10-7. *Caching Class Methods*

Name	Description
__construct()	Class constructor. Initiates properties.
Check()	Checks if the cache file exists and if it is still valid.
Save()	Writes the cached value to the file.
SetValue()	Adds or updates a value in the cache.
GetValue()	Retrieves a value in the cache.

The Code

```php
<?php
// Example cache.inc
class Cache {
  private $name = null;
  private $value = array();
  private $ttl;

  function __construct($name, $ttl = 3600) {
    $this->name = $name;
    $this->ttl = $ttl;
  }

  function Check() {
    $cached = false;
    $file_name = $this->name . ".cache";
    if (file_exists($file_name)) {
      $modified = filemtime($file_name);
      if (time() - $this->ttl < $modified) {
        $fp = fopen($file_name, "rt");
        if ($fp) {
          $temp_value = fread($fp, filesize($file_name));
          fclose($fp);
          $this->value = unserialize($temp_value);
          $cached = true;
        }
      }
    }
    return $cached;
  }

  function Save() {
    $file_name = $this->name . ".cache";
    $fp = fopen($file_name, "wt");
    if ($fp) {
      fwrite($fp, serialize($this->value));
      fclose($fp);
    }
  }

  function SetValue($key, $value) {
    $this->value[$key] = $value;
  }
```

```php
   function GetValue($key) {
     if (isset($this->value[$key])) {
       return $this->value[$key];
     }
     else {
       return NULL;
     }
   }
  }
}
?>
```

How It Works

This caching class is used in the next example, where a cache object is created from the caching class and checked to see if the file exists. If not, the values are calculated and stored in the cache. If cached data exists and it is valid, the data will be retrieved and displayed.

The Code

```php
<?php
// Example 10-8-2.php
include 'cache.inc';

$cache = new Cache('data');
if ($cache->Check()) {
  echo "Retrieving values from cache\n";
  $arr = $cache->GetValue('arr');
  $fruits = $cache->GetValue('fruits');
  print_r($arr);
}
else {
  $arr = array("apple", "orange", "apricot");
  $fruits = sizeof($arr);
  $cache->SetValue('arr', $arr);
  $cache->SetValue('fruits', $fruits);
  $cache->Save();
  echo "Values are stored in cache\n";
}
?>
```

How It Works

The first time the script is executed, the output will look like this:

```
Values are stored in cache
```

The second time, when the values are retrieved from the cache, it will look like this:

```
Array
(
    [0] => apple
    [1] => orange
    [2] => apricot
)
```

10-9. Sharing Variables Between Processes

When a user is navigating through a web application, it is useful to store user- or session-specific data on the web server so it is easy to access each time a page is requested. This can be information about the user, user preferences, or data related to the application, such as data in a shopping chart. Each time the user requests a page that contains a call to the session_start() function, the server will start a new process (or reuse an idle), and the PHP engine will look for a session ID in the query string or cookie data. This will fetch the saved session data and build the $_SESSION array.

As mentioned in recipe 10-5, $_SESSION is a superglobal and can be accessed directly from any code segment. When a session is active, it is possible to retrieve, add, update, and delete values from the $_SESSION array. You do this like any other variable. The engine will automatically store the values of the array when the script ends, unless it was stopped with an error. The session data file will be locked to keep multiple processes from accessing (writing to) the same data at the same time. If you have scripts that take a long time to execute or you are loading multiple frames from the same server, it might optimize the application to use session_write_close() or session_commit() to close the session data file. After either of these commands are used, it is not possible to add new values to the $_SESSION array.

Shared memory is another way of sharing data between processes. This is used when the two processes are running at the same time and might be started by different clients. Shared memory will in most cases be faster than a shared file or a table in a database. To use shared memory in PHP, it must be compiled with the –enable–shmop parameter.

■**Note** Using shared memory requires that the processes are persistent such as Apache modules, IIS ISAPI, or PHP-GTK applications.

The shmop extension implements six simple functions, as shown in Table 10-8.

Table 10-8. *shmop Functions*

Name	Description
shmop_open()	Opens or creates a memory block for sharing
shmop_close()	Closes a shared memory block
shmop_delete()	Deletes a shared memory block
shmop_read()	Reads data from a shared memory block
shmop_write()	Writes data to a shared memory block
shmop_size()	Gets the size of a shared memory block

You must create a shared memory block before you can use it. You can use the shmop_open() function to do this; this function takes four arguments. The first is a unique ID (an integer) used to identify the memory block. The second parameter is a flag that specifies how the block is accessed (a = read-only, c = create or read/write, w = write and read, and n = create new or fail). The third argument specifies the access to the memory block and should be passed as an octal such as file system rights (for example, 0644). The fourth and last argument sets the size of the block. The third and fourth arguments should be set to 0 if you are opening an existing block.

■**Note** The size of a shared memory block is fixed on creation and cannot be changed.

The following example shows how to create and write to a memory block. The block is deleted and closed at the end of the script, so in order to demonstrate how it works, the script will wait 60 seconds before it terminates. This should be enough time to run the next example and see the shared memory in action.

The Code

```php
<?php
// Example 10-9-1.php
if (!extension_loaded("shmop")) {
  dl("php_shmop.dll");
}

$shm_id = shmop_open(0x123, 'c', 0644, 250);
shmop_write($shm_id, "Data in shared memory", 0);
$value = shmop_read($shm_id, 8, 6);
echo "$value";
shmop_delete($shm_id);
shmop_close($shm_id);
sleep(60);
?>
```

If the memory block should be used by another process, it should not be deleted, and another process could access the data, like this:

```php
<?php
// Example 10-9-2.php
if (!extension_loaded("shmop")) {
  dl("php_shmop.dll");
}

$shm_id = shmop_open(0x123, 'a', 0, 0);
if ($shm_id) {
  $value = shmop_read($shm_id, 0, 100);
  echo "$value";
  shmop_close($shm_id);
}
?>
```

How It Works

Sharing memory between two scripts requires that both scripts run at the same time. The first script defines a shared memory block with a string and reads six bytes from the block. The second script connects to the same block through the same handle (0×123). The entire string is read and sent to the client.

10-10. Debugging

Printing and storing information during development and testing will help eliminate errors caused by variables having other values than expected or by using the wrong variable names. PHP implements several functions that make debugging a lot easier (see Table 10-9).

Table 10-9. *Functions Used for Debugging*

Name	Description
echo()	Prints a simple variable or value
print()	Prints a simple variable or value
printf()	Prints a formatted string
var_dump()	Prints the type and content of a variable
print_r()	Recursively prints the content of an array or object
debug_backtrace()	Returns an array with the call stack and other values

The functions echo(), print(), and printf() generate normal output, so using these to produce debug output might be a bit confusing, but this is the way to generate any output.

Having a function called debug_print() will make it easy to use debugging information and to turn it on and off when needed. This function could be defined in an include file along with a constant DEBUG set to true or false.

The Code

```php
<?php
// Example debug.inc
define('DEBUG', true); // set to false for disabling

function debug_print($var) {
  if (DEBUG) {
    switch (strtolower(substr(php_sapi_name(), 0, 3))) {
      case 'cli' :
      var_dump($var);
        break;
      default :
        print("<pre>");
      var_dump($var);
        print("</pre>");
        break;
    }
  }
}
?>
```

How It Works

When the DEBUG constant is set to true, the function will generate output; when it is set to
false, the function will be silent. This is an easy way to turn debug information on and off.
The debug_print() function calls the php_sapi_name() function to determine how the PHP
script is executed. Depending on the process type, it will generate different output.

Defining the debug_print() function in the file debug.inc makes it possible to reuse the
same function in many scripts with a simple include statement and one or more calls to
the function.

The Code

```php
<?php
// Example 10-10-1.php
include 'debug.inc';

$a = array('orange', 'apple');
debug_print($a);
?>
```

How It Works

The include file with the debug information is included in the top of the script and used to
print the content of an array.

```
array(2) {
  [0]=>
  string(6) "orange"
  [1]=>
  string(5) "apple"
}
```

PHP implements a few so-called magic constants. These are not really constants, because they change value depending on where they are used (see Table 10-10).

Table 10-10. *Magic Constants*

Name	Description
__FILE__	Name of current file
__LINE__	Current line number
__FUNCTION__	Name of current function
__CLASS__	Name of current class
__METHOD__	Name of current method

You can modify the debug_print() function from the previous example to use __FILE__ and __LINE__ to print where the debug information originated.

The Code

```php
<?php
// Example debug1.inc
define('DEBUG', true); // set to false for disabling

function debug_print($var, $file = __FILE__, $line = __LINE__) {
  if (DEBUG) {
  $where = "File = $file ($line)";
    switch (strtolower(substr(php_sapi_name(), 0, 3))) {
      case 'cli' :
        echo "$where\n";
        var_dump($var);
        break;
      default :
        echo "$where<br>";
        print("<pre>");
        var_dump($var);
        print("</pre>");
        break;
    }
  }
}
```

```php
?>
<?php
// Example 10-10-2.php
include 'debug1.inc';

$a = array('orange', 'apple');
debug_print($a, __FILE__, __LINE__);
?>
```

How It Works

In this example, you add two parameters to the debug_print() function. As shown in the following output, the debug_print() function can produce two forms of output. The first call to the function uses the default values for $file and $line. This causes the system to insert the name of the include file and the line where the function is defined. In the second call, you use __FILE__ and __LINE__ as parameters to the function call, and these will be replaced with the filename and line number where the function was called.

```
File = /Samples/debug1.inc (5)
array(2) {
  [0]=>
  string(6) "orange"
  [1]=>
  string(5) "apple"
}
File = /Samples/10-10-2.php (7)
array(2) {
  [0]=>
  string(6) "orange"
  [1]=>
  string(5) "apple"
}
```

Note how the two magic constants are used as default values for $file and $line in the definition of the function. If one or both of these two arguments are omitted from the call, they will be replaced by values that indicate the include file and the line where the function is defined.

Summary

This chapter demonstrated the strengths of PHP when it comes to variables and data types. The loosely typed behavior of PHP makes it easy to work with, and there is little reason to spend time on memory cleanups, as the engine handles these when the scripts terminate.

We discussed how variables are handled from creation, and we discussed how to manipulate data, how to test for values and types, and how to use the more advanced features of variable variables and functions.

We also showed examples of using the serialize() and unserialize() functions to format data so the data can be shared between calls or stored in a database. Finally, we showed some examples of how data can be shared between processes that run simultaneously.

Looking Ahead

The next chapter will discuss how functions are created and used in PHP.

■ ■ ■

CHAPTER 11

Using Functions

Redundant code is rarely a good thing. Rewriting code over and over again is not time efficient and looks rather shoddy from a layout point of view. Like any good programming language, PHP alleviates the problem of redundant code in a number of ways; the most commonly used and simple-to-implement way is by using functions.

A *function* is basically a block of code that performs a given action from the script that has access to it, via includes, code insertions, or other methods. Rather than repeatedly rewrite the same block of code to, say, check if the current user is logged into your site, you can put the code into what is essentially a code wrapper and then call it at your convenience with a simple function call.

To be truly versatile, functions can receive values passed into them, perform some sort of functionality, and then return a value (or set of values using an array or object). Taking an entire block of code that was redundantly placed all over your scripts and replacing it with a one-line function call does wonders for the cleanliness of your code and is the first step to becoming an efficient programmer.

11-1. Accessing Function Parameters

The first thing any good programmer should realize about a function is that in order to do something meaningful with an exterior set of data, you must pass the function the values that are to be worked with. Parameters in PHP 5 are passed when the function itself is called and then worked on within the block of code. Because of PHP's ease of use with data types, passing a value to a function as a parameter is quite simple. The following example passes a username and password to the function to confirm that a valid match exists.

The Code

```php
<?php

  //sample11_1.php

  //A function to validate a username and password.
  function validatelogin ($username, $password){
    //Typically the username and password would be validated against information
    //in the database. For the sake of simplicity in this example, the username
    //and password are hard-coded into variables.
    $actualuser = "myusername";
```

```
    $actualpass = "mypassword";

    //Now, you do a quick comparison to see if the user ➥
has entered the correct login.
    if (strcmp ($username, $actualuser) == 0 &&➥
 strcmp ($password, $actualpass) == 0){
        return true;
    } else {
        return false;
    }
}

    //You then call the function and pass in the values you want checked.
    if (validatelogin ("myusername","mypassword")){
        echo "You are logged in correctly";
    } else {
        echo "You have an incorrect username and/or password";
    }
?>
```

```
You are logged in correctly
```

How It Works

This is a basic example of how easy it is to pass to, and then access, a set of parameters. In this case, the function receives two values from the function (denoting a username and password) and then checks to see that they match with the existing username and password (preferably in a database). If you receive a valid match, then the function returns a `true` boolean type; if not, then the function returns a `false` boolean type. Note how much easier it is to call the function `validatelogin()` rather than type out that entire block of code. Not only is it much cleaner and more efficient, but it also alleviates the problem of redundancy when you undoubtedly call the function again.

As for accessing the actual values within the script, you simply access them according to whatever you named them in the function's argument list. In this case, you named them `$username` and `$password`, allowing you to reference them using their variable names within the function.

11-2. Setting Default Values for Function Parameters

When you are passing arguments to a function, you may want the parameters to default to a certain value. Doing so within a PHP function is simple. In most programming languages, any values you are concerned might not be passed to the function properly (or at all) can be defaulted to a certain value. You might prefer to default the parameters being passed to a function for two reasons. First, you do not have to worry so much about exception handling and can rest assured that any argument that does get passed in properly will override the default. Second, when using functions that generally receive the same values but sometimes

require different values to be passed in, having the defaults in place prevents you from constantly having to pass in the same set of values. The following example returns the sum of
three values.

The Code

```php
<?php

//sample11_2.php

//A function to return the sum of three values.
function addvalues ($value1 = 0, $value2 = 0, $value3 = 0){
  //Now the function takes the three values and adds them
  $total = $value1 + $value2 + $value3;
  return $total;
}

//Now, if you forget a value or two, it will still work.
echo addvalues (1) . "<br />"; //Echoes a 1.
//If you pass all the arguments, you will still get a valid result.
echo addvalues (1,2,3); //Echoes a 6.
?>
```

1

6

How It Works

Now, if you had not defaulted the values in the argument list to zeros, the function call you
just made would have returned a warning telling you that you were missing arguments to your
function call. Rather than face the possibility of an incorrectly called function, you can cover
all your bases by defaulting the values to zeros. Therefore, if someone were to call the function
(as you did in the previous example) with an incorrect number of arguments, the function
would still perform its given action using the default values assigned to its arguments.

11-3. Passing Values by Reference

The default when passing a parameter to a function in PHP 5 is to pass the argument by value.
In other words, when the function receives the value, it will then work on it as if that variable
was an entirely separate entity to the one that was passed to it originally. If you pass by reference, however, the variable that was passed in will be manipulated within the function as if
the value were still within the script it was passed in from. Think of passing arguments by
value as creating a temporary copy to work with; alternatively, passing by reference uses, and
can make changes to, the original copy. The following example allows you to concatenate text
to an existing block of text.

The Code

```php
<?php

 //sample11_3.php

 //A function to concatenate text.
 function attachtext (&$newtext = ""){
   //Now the function attaches the received text.
   $newtext = $newtext . " World!";
 }

 //Here is the current block of text.
 $mystring = "Hello";
 //Then you call the function to attach new text.
 attachtext ($mystring);
 //And when you echo the variable now...
 echo $mystring; //Outputs Hello World!
?>
```

```
Hello World!
```

How It Works

As you can see, the major difference in the argument list is that you place an ampersand (&) character in front of the passed-in variable. This tells PHP to treat the variable as a referenced object. This means any change to the passed-in value will affect the original passed-in variable. Therefore, when you output $mystring after the function call has been made, the new value has been concatenated onto the old value. Had you passed in the argument by value, the script would have merely output "Hello" because it would have treated the value as a copy of the original, not as an alias to the original.

11-4. Creating Functions That Take a Variable Number of Arguments

Sometimes you will need to create a function that could receive a multitude of values but the number of values to be received will not be set in stone. Take, for instance, a function that will add any number of values passed to it provided that they are integer values. In this case, you want the function to be versatile enough to add any number of values that are passed to it—kind of like a math crunching machine.

The Code

```php
<?php

  //sample11_4.php

  //A function to add up any number of values.
  function addanything (){
    //Default the return value.
    $total = 0;
    //Get the full list of arguments passed in.
    $args = func_get_args ();
    //Loop through the arguments.
    for ($i = 0; $i < count ($args); $i++){
      //Make sure the value is an integer.
      if (is_int ($args[$i])){
        //And add to it if necessary.
        $total += $args[$i];
      }
    }
    //Then return the total.
    return $total;
  }

  //Now, you can pass the function any numbers.
  echo addanything (1,5,7,8,11) . "<br />"; //Outputs 32.
  echo addanything (1,1) . "<br />"; //Outputs 2.
  //It will ignore noninteger values.
  echo addanything (1,1,"Hello World"); //Still outputs 2.
?>
```

32
2
2

How It Works

The benefactor in this case happens to be the lovely func_get_args() function, which grabs an array of all the passed-in values. The great thing about this is that you can then cycle, or loop through, the list of arguments and do what you want with them. This sort of functionality serves you well in this case, because you loop through, adding to the total as you go. For the sake of validation, the script adds only integer values in order to keep a valid result in mind. The end result is a highly flexible function that will take care of all your integer adding needs. The prototype for func_get_args() and the prototype for func_get_arg(), which will grab an argument at a certain reference, are as follows:

```
array func_get_args ( void )
mixed func_get_arg ( int arg_num )
```

11-5. Returning More Than One Value

Naturally, it is handy to have a single value returned from a function, and it is even more help-ful in some instances to have a function return multiple values. Since the return statement is really set up to return only a single value, you can get a little tricky and pass an array of items for use.

If you want to get even more involved, you can return entire objects from a function, thus allowing you to pass back whatever values were associated with the object. Through some careful manipulation, you can use functions to return whatever it is you need returned from them.

The following example is a function that allows you to return an array of values, thus getting around the problem of being able to return only a single value.

The Code

```php
<?php

 //sample11_5.php

 //Function that will take in a set of values, calculate them,➡
 then return the values.
  function addandsubtract ($firstvalue, $secondvalue){
    //The first thing we need to do is add the values.
    $firstreturnvalue = ($firstvalue + $secondvalue);
    $secondreturnvalue = ($firstvalue - $secondvalue);

    //Now, you declare an array.
    $myarray = array ();

    //Then put the two return values into the first two indexes of the array.
    $myarray[0] = $firstreturnvalue;
    $myarray[1] = $secondreturnvalue;

    //Then you can return the entire array.
    return $myarray;
  }

 //Now, when you call the function, it will return the two values in array format.
 $myarray = array ();
 $myarray = addandsubtract (10, 3);

 echo $myarray[0] . "<br />"; //Will echo 13.
 echo $myarray[1]; //Will echo 7.
?>
```

13
7

How It Works

As you can see, the method for returning an array from a function is rather simple. All that is required is to have an array declared (and probably filled with a value or two) and then return it to the function call using the `return` method. Then, when you receive the value from the function, you can assign the result of the function to an array and use it as you would any other array.

11-6. Returning Values by Reference

Sometimes passing back an argument by value may not be all that efficient. Fortunately, PHP 5 allows returning values by reference, but you should keep in mind a few new syntaxes both when declaring the function and when calling the function.

Returning values by reference can be rather obscure, but when used properly, this technique can be quite handy in specific circumstances. The following example allows you to search through an array of objects and then return the exact object for which you are looking.

The Code

```php
<?php

//sample11_6.php

//Create a class that stores values.
class myclass {

    //A defining value.
    private $thevalue;
    //A word to prove you have found the right object.
    private $theword;

    public function __construct (){
        $num_args = func_num_args();

        if($num_args > 0){
            $args = func_get_args();
            $this->theword = $args[0];
        }
    }

    public function setvalue ($newvalue){
        $this->thevalue = $newvalue;
    }
    public function getvalue () {
        return $this->thevalue;
    }
    public function getword () {
        return $this->theword;
```

```
    }
}

//Now, create four different instances of this class.
$myclass1 = new myclass ("Abra");
$myclass1->setvalue (1);

$myclass2 = new myclass ("Kadabra");
$myclass2->setvalue (2);

$myclass3 = new myclass ("Hocus");
$myclass3->setvalue (3);

$myclass4 = new myclass ("Pocus");
$myclass4->setvalue (4);

//Create a global array of
$classarr = array ($myclass1,$myclass2,$myclass3,$myclass4);

//Now, you can create a function that searches for a correct instance of a class.
function &findclass ($whichclass,$classarr){
    for ($i = 0; $i < count ($classarr); $i++){
        if ($classarr[$i]->getvalue() == $whichclass){
            return $classarr[$i];
        }
    }
}

//Search for the id number 3, and return the word if it is found.
$myobject = new myclass ("");
$myobject =& findclass (3,$classarr);
echo $myobject->getword();

?>
```

Hocus

How It Works

In this example, you create four objects of a certain class and fill them with four sets of values. Next, you create an array of the objects and a function that will sift through the array until it finds the object in question. If the object is found, the function can return the actual object through the magic of returning values by reference.

Although this may seem like overkill with four objects, consider if you had a hundred—or a thousand. The ability to sift through a mountain of objects and return the exact one you are looking for is incredibly valuable and can give you instant use of the object in question.

11-7. Returning Failure

A simplistic yet rather important aspect of functions is returning a failure value should something go wrong with the function. Functions can make wonderful systems for performing validation on different parts of your code, and they can be used as true/false values by simply returning a boolean result on success or failure. This sort of functionality can clean up your code and, with the right naming conventions, create code that is much easier to read. The following example returns a true or false value based on whether the e-mail value passed to it is a valid format.

The Code

```php
<?php

  //sample11_7.php

  //A function to return a true/false value based on e-mail format.
  function validemail ($email = ""){
    return preg_match("/^([a-zA-Z0-9])+([.a-zA-Z0-9_-])*@([a-zA-Z0-9_-])➥
+(.[a-zA-Z0-9_-]+)+[a-zA-Z0-9_-]$/",$email);
  }
  $anemail = "lee@babinplanet.ca";
  //Use the function to confirm a valid e-mail.
  if (validemail ($anemail)){
    echo $anemail . " is in valid e-mail format.<br />";
  } else {
    echo $anemail . " is not valid.<br />";
  }

  //And of course, an invalid e-mail.
  $bademail = "abademail";
  if (validemail ($bademail)){
    echo $bademail . " is in valid e-mail format.<br />";
  } else {
    echo $bademail . " is not valid.<br />";
  }
?>
```

```
lee@babinplanet.ca is in valid e-mail format.
abademail is not valid.
```

How It Works

As you can see, the code to check the validity of an e-mail string's format is quite clear and easy to read. The function returns a true value if the format is valid and a false value if the format is incorrect. By using this in the code, you can easily see what the script is attempting to accomplish, so now you have a handy function to validate against user-submitted e-mail addresses that can be called at any time.

11-8. Calling Variable Functions

The concept of calling variable functions is an interesting one. Basically, by adding parentheses to the end of a variable you can force PHP to attempt to call a function of whatever name the value of the variable equates to. This can make for some nice conditional handling, as you can essentially determine which function is to be called on the fly by using a specific variable. Say, for instance, that you have three functions: one function adds two values, one subtracts two values, and the last multiplies two values. Based on what the user enters into a form, the script determines which function to use and then assigns a value to the variable that will be used to call the function.

The Code

```php
<?php

//sample11_8.php

//A function to add two values.
function addvalues ($firstvalue = 0, $secondvalue = 0){
  return $firstvalue + $secondvalue;
}

//A function to subtract two values.
function subtractvalues ($firstvalue = 0, $secondvalue = 0){
  return $firstvalue - $secondvalue;
}

//A function to multiply two values.
function multiplyvalues ($firstvalue = 0, $secondvalue = 0){
  return $firstvalue * $secondvalue;
}
//And let's assume these are the values you want to work with.
$firstvalue = 10;
$secondvalue = 3;

//Let's say this value represents a user-submitted value.
$whattodo = "addvalues";

//You can then call the function as a variable.
echo $whattodo($firstvalue, $secondvalue) . "<br />";
```

```
//Let's say this value represents a user-submitted value.
$whattodo = "subtractvalues";

//You can then call the function as a variable.
echo $whattodo($firstvalue, $secondvalue) . "<br />";

//Let's say this value represents a user-submitted value.
$whattodo = "multiplyvalues";

//You can then call the function as a variable.
echo $whattodo($firstvalue, $secondvalue) . "<br />";

?>
```

```
13
7
30
```

How It Works

The key aspect to note about this code is where you actually perform the function call. Does it look a little strange to you? Thanks to the power of variable function calls, you can assign a value dynamically to a variable and then have the script look for a function that is named the same as the variable's value. Naturally, if PHP cannot find a function by that name, you will get the regular errors you would get for attempting to call a function that does not exist. The powerful aspect of this code is that you can use conditional statements to determine which function gets called.

11-9. Accessing a Global Variable from Within a Function

While generally considered a quick-fix approach and not really a valid way to code because of programmers preferring more rigidly structured code (globals can easily get lost/changed), sometimes having global variables around is useful. Quite possibly the most useful aspect to global variables is using them within functions without having to pass them in as arguments. Because the variables are global, any script within the scope of the variable (basically, any script that has access to the originally declared global variable) will be able to use it without having to pass it around.

The current standard in PHP 5 is to use superglobals to access the global variables, and the following script shows you how to do it properly. PHP has the predefined superglobal variable $GLOBALS that can be used to create, access, and maintain global variables. The following function uses a global value that is set to tell you what the current username and password for the site are.

The Code

```php
<?php

//sample11_9.php

$GLOBALS['user'] = "myusername";
$GLOBALS['pass'] = "mypassword";

//A function to check the validity of a login.
function validatelogin ($username, $password){
  //Now, you do a quick comparison to see if the user➥
has entered the correct login.
    if (strcmp ($username, $GLOBALS['user']) == 0 &&➥
strcmp ($password, $GLOBALS['pass']) == 0){
      return true;
    } else {
      return false;
    }
}

//You then call the function and pass in the values you want checked.
if (validatelogin ("myusername","mypassword")){
  echo "You are logged in correctly";
} else {
  echo "You have an incorrect username and/or password";
}
?>
```

```
You are logged in correctly
```

How It Works

You will notice that this example looks like recipe 11-1. You will, however, notice one key difference. Rather than assigning the current correct username and password values within the function, you can set the values anywhere within the scope of the script using the superglobal $GLOBALS. This means that rather than having to search the database within the function for the current proper login, you can search it within a hidden include file and then reference the values. It looks a little cleaner and helps hide what is potentially hazardous information from the wrong viewer.

11-10. Creating Dynamic Functions

One of the advantages of using PHP functions is that you can create conditional occurrences that allow you to write functions only if strictly necessary. By placing function declarations within conditional statements, you can force PHP to create a function only if a condition has been met. By using this sort of functionality, you can actually create functions dynamically by allowing functions to be born based on a certain condition.

Let's say you want to take in a value from the user, and based on that value you create a function that performs a certain task. For instance, based on what the user enters, you need a function either to add two values, to subtract two values, or to multiply two values. Rather than clutter your code with functions you may not use, you can create the valid function on the fly and call it by just one name.

The following example is useful in a site where a user can log in and log out based upon their current status.

The Code

```php
<?php

//sample11_10.php

if ($_GET['go'] == "yes"){

  //Now, if you are logged in, you want the function to log you out.
  if ($_GET['loggedin'] == "true"){

    //Create a logout function.
    function dosomething (){
      $_GET['loggedin'] = false;
      echo "You have been successfully logged out.<br />";
    }

  }

  //Now, if you were not logged in, you want to be able to log in.
  if ($_GET['loggedin'] == "false"){

    //Create a login function.
    function dosomething (){
      $_GET['loggedin'] = true;
      echo "You have been successfully logged in.<br />";
    }
  }

  dosomething();

}
```

```
  if ($_GET['loggedin']){
    ?><a href="sample11_10.php?go=yes&amp;loggedin=true">➡
click here to log out</a><?php
  } elseif (!$_GET['loggedin']){
    ?><a href="sample11_10.php?go=yes&amp;loggedin=false">➡
click here to log in</a><?php
  }
?>
```

If you click to log in, you should get this message and hence be logged in:

```
You have been successfully logged in.
click here to log out
```

If, however, you click to log out, you should get the following result:

```
You have been successfully logged out.
click here to log in
```

How It Works

This particular instance is based on a login principle. If a person is logged in, you want the function to allow them to log out. If, however, the person is logged out, you want to provide them with a means to log in. Through the power of dynamic function creation, you can make the same function call but actually have it perform two (or more) different actions.

Summary

As you can see, PHP 5 not only supports a myriad of ways to clean up and modularize your code, but it also allows you to manipulate your functions in a wide variety of ways. By using functions to ensure that you are never using redundant code in your applications, you cut back on the time you will spend coding and make your code more applicable both for others to use and for you to clean up should the need arise.

PHP 5 supports passing and receiving values by reference as well as by value, and you should always use the defaults if you think the validity of the code calling the function could ever come into question. The ideal way to do things is to evaluate the task at hand and then select the most efficient method for the job. Passing and returning by reference can be an ideal solution for keeping integrity within a variable or group of variables, and passing and returning by value is ideal for working with a given data set.

PHP also supports many ways to base your code upon dynamic dealings. By using dynamic functions or variable function calls, you can reduce the processing and preloading time of your script by deciding on the fly what calls are necessary and which function declarations are important. This allows for a wide range of ingenuity and good, clean coding.

All in all, you can make a powerful set of PHP code that much more efficient by proper, smart function use, and the amount of time it will save you in the end is well worth the initial investment.

Looking Ahead

In the next chapter, we will introduce a topic that is quite far from basic, web basics. We will cover a wide variety of important web aspects to show you how to turn a bland, static website into a dynamic, living, breathing entity. No good web application is complete without the upcoming knowledge contained within Chapter 12.

CHAPTER 12

■ ■ ■

Understanding Web Basics

In the world of online applications, a wide variety of functionality needs to be on hand for the programmer. Thankfully, PHP 5 has done its best to ensure that anything that makes a system work is readily available to a crafty programmer. Algorithms that track a unique individual on a website or functions that work with headers and querystrings are common pieces of functionality that make up the backbone of most well-written online software applications.

This chapter shows how to set up and maintain a wide variety of functionality that will come in handy with your everyday applications. Considered kind of a "bells and whistles" chapter, this chapter covers some of the functionality that will no doubt serve you well in applications to come. Sit back, relax, and enjoy the ride through some of PHP 5's fun and rewarding functionality.

Using Cookies

Before the advent of sessions, there were *cookies*. Cookies are files that get written to a temporary file on a user's computer by a web application. Cookies store information that can be read by the online application, thus authenticating a user as unique. By allowing a web application to identify whether a user is unique, the application can then perform login scripts and other functionality.

The problem with cookies is that because they are stored on a user's computer, they have developed a bad rap as being highly insecure. And because of possible insecurities with cookies, users have begun to turn them off in their browser security settings; in fact, users often do not accept cookies.

Cookies themselves are not bad or insecure if used correctly by a developer. However, since users have the ability to turn them off (and since the actual cookie must be stored on the user's computer), most good developers have migrated their code to sessions (which are explained in the "Using Sessions" section). For now, though, cookies are certainly functional enough to get the job done, so the following recipes show how they work.

12-1. Setting Cookies

To be able to use cookies and store values in them, you must first set a cookie on a user's computer. You can use plenty of parameters to take full advantage of a cookie, including the expiration time, path of use, name, value, and so on. By using the different parameters, you can customize the way the cookie works for you. The way to set a cookie is by using the function setcookie(), which has the following prototype:

```
bool setcookie ( string name [, string value [, int expire➥
 [, string path [, string domain [, bool secure]]]]] )
```

Table 12-1 lists the parameters available to you when creating a cookie using setcookie().

Table 12-1. *PHP 5* setcookie() *Parameters*

Parameter	Description
name	The name to set the cookie variable to and hence the name to access it with
value	The value of the current cookie
expire	When a cookie will expire (in the form of a Unix timestamp)
path	The directory where the cookie will be available for use
domain	The domain at which the cookie will be available
secure	Whether a cookie can be read on a non-SSL enable script

The Code

```php
<?php

 //sample12_1.php

 //Let's say that the correct login is based on these global user and pass values.
 //In the real world, this would be taken from the database most likely.
 $GLOBALS['username'] = "test";
 $GLOBALS['password'] = "test";

 //Here is an example to set a cookie based on a correct login.
 function validatelogin ($username, $password){
   //Check for a valid match.
   if (strcmp ($username, $GLOBALS['username']) == 0➥
 && strcmp ($password, $GLOBALS['password']) == 0){
     //If you have a valid match, then you set the cookies.
     //This will set two cookies, one named cookie_user set to $cookieuser,
     //and another set to cookie_pass, which contains the value of $password.
     //When storing passwords, it is a good idea to use something like md5() to
     //encrypt the stored cookie.
     setcookie ("cookie_user", $username, time()+60*60*24*30);
     setcookie ("cookie_pass", md5 ($password), time()+60*60*24*30);
     return true;
   } else {
```

```
      return false;
    }
  }

  //You call the validatelogin() script.
  if (validatelogin ("test","test")){
    echo "Successfully logged in.";
  } else {
    echo "Sorry, invalid login.";
  }
?>
```

How It Works

As you can see from this example, login validation is a common use for cookies. In this example, you compare a username and password that you have passed into the function and then set cookies based on a proper login. In a real-world scenario, the username and password would have likely come from a login form, and the comparable variables would likely have been stored in a database, but the functionality is largely the same.

Of note as well is the actual structure of the cookies themselves. These particular cookies are set to be usable anywhere, with no changes depending on SSL or otherwise. You set two of them, one named cookie_user and one named cookie_pass. It is important to keep these names in mind, as this is how you will reference the cookies. You will also note that this script uses the md5() function to encrypt the cookies. Because cookies are stored on a user's machine, it is important to use some manner of encryption to keep others from going to the cookie file and determining a login. The prototype for md5() is as follows:

```
string md5 ( string str [, bool raw_output] )
```

12-2. Reading Cookies

Naturally, there would be little use for cookies if you could not read from them, hence allowing you to use them in your applications. Cookies can indeed be read—and quite easily. By using the $_COOKIE superglobal, you can have full access to your cookie for reading and writing to it from your script. The following script allows you to determine if you are properly logged in using a function that returns a true value upon proper validation of login.

The Code

```php
<?php

  //sample12_2.php

  //Let's say the correct login is based on these global user and pass values.
  //In the real world, this would be taken from the database most likely.
  $GLOBALS['username'] = "test";
  $GLOBALS['password'] = "test";
```

```
//Let's assume you already have a valid set of cookies in place.
setcookie ("cookie_user", "test", time()+60*60*24*30);
setcookie ("cookie_pass", md5 ("test"), time()+60*60*24*30);

//Here is an example to set a cookie based on a correct login.
function validatelogin (){
  //Check for a valid match.
  if (strcmp ($_COOKIE['cookie_user'], $GLOBALS['username']) == 0➥
&& strcmp ($_COOKIE['cookie_pass'], md5 ($GLOBALS['password'])) == 0){
    return true;
  } else {
    return false;
  }
}

//You call the validatelogin() script.
if (validatelogin ()){
  echo "Successfully logged in.";
} else {
  echo "Sorry, invalid login.";
}
?>
```

How It Works

As you can see, using a set of cookies is rather simple; you can simply access them via the $_COOKIE superglobal. In this case, you compare the (currently) global username and password against the cookies that have been set. If a match is acquired, the unique user is logged in, and the script will remember him until the cookie is expired or until the user physically removes the cookies from their collection. Note also the ease of use with encrypted cookies. If you know how and if a cookie has been encrypted, it is a simple matter of comparing the cookie against an md5()-enabled variable.

12-3. Deleting Cookies

Removing cookies is also a simple task. You should note that cookies will disappear by themselves if you have set them up to do so. Cookies that have not been assigned a time to die will simply be removed when the browser window closes. Sometimes, however, a user will want to be able to clear the cookies on a site. Such functionality typically goes by the name of "logout" and is a staple of a well-programmed user interface. The following code allows a user to log out.

The Code

```php
<?php

//sample12_3.php

//Let's assume you already have a valid set of cookies in place.
setcookie ("cookie_user", "test", time()+60*60*24*30);
setcookie ("cookie_pass", md5 ("test"), time()+60*60*24*30);

//Here is a function that will kill the cookies and hence "log out."
function logout (){
  //To remove a cookie, you simply set the value of the cookie to blank.
  setcookie ("cookie_user", "", time()+60*60*24*30);
  setcookie ("cookie_pass", "", time()+60*60*24*30);
}

//You call the logout script.
logout();

//You can no longer access the cookies.
echo $_COOKIE['cookie_user'] . "<br />";

echo "You have successfully logged out.";
?>
```

How It Works

As you can see, removing cookies is as easy as setting them and leaving the value blank.
It is important to remember that when removing the cookies, the parameters passed to the
setcookie() function must be identical to the parameters that were passed to it initially. If
the parameter list varies from the original, PHP will assume you are trying to remove a different cookie, and the removal will not take place. Once a cookie has been removed, your scripts
will no longer have access to it, and the physical cookie itself will have been deleted from your
collection.

12-4. Writing and Using a Cookie Class

Cookies should be as easy to use as sessions are. To cut down on some of the more underused
functionality that cookies are capable of and make them nice and easy to manage, you can use
the following class, which can manage a cookie with the greatest of ease by making instances
of a cookieclass.

The Code

```php
<?php

//sample12_4.php

//A class to manage a very simple cookie set.
class cookieclass {

    private $cookiename;
    private $cookievalue;
    private $cookieexpiry;

    //A function to construct the class.
    public function __construct (){
      $num_args = func_num_args();

      if($num_args > 0){
        $args = func_get_args();
        $this->cookiename = $args[0];
        $this->cookievalue = $args[1];
        $this->cookieexpiry = $args[2];

        $this->cookieset();
      }
    }

    //The function to actually set a cookie.
    public function cookieset (){
        try {
          if ($this->cookiename != "" && $this->cookievalue != "" ➥
&& $this->cookieexpiry != ""){
              setcookie ($this->cookiename,➥
 $this->cookievalue, time() + $this->cookieexpiry);
          } else {
              throw new exception ("Sorry, you must assign a ➥
name and expiry date for the cookie.");
          }
        } catch (exception $e){
          echo $e->getmessage();
        }
    }

    //A function to change the value of the cookie.
    public function change ($newvalue){
      $_COOKIE[$this->cookiename] = $newvalue;
    }
```

```
  //A function to retrieve the current value of the cookie.
  public function getvalue (){
    return $_COOKIE[$this->cookiename];
  }

  //A function to remove the cookie.
  public function remove (){
    $this->change ("");
  }
}

//Create a cookie.
$mycookie = new cookieclass ("cookieid","1","60");

echo $mycookie->getvalue() . "<br />"; //Echoes 1.
$mycookie->change ("Hello World!");
echo $mycookie->getvalue() . "<br />"; //Echoes Hello World!

//Now, you kill off the cookie.
$mycookie->remove();

echo $mycookie->getvalue(); //Outputs nothing as the cookie is dead.
?>
```

How It Works

As you can see, this class makes it easy to create, maintain, and output a cookie. Having the functionality available to you from an easy-to-manage object can be an organizational benefit. Consider that you could keep an array of cookie objects and manage them as such. Of course, you could also build this class to include path and domain settings, but for the scope of this project, it works rather well.

Using HTTP Headers

HTTP headers are slightly finicky but rather powerful sets of functionality. The most important aspect to remember about headers is that they can be called only before any output has been written to the web page. If you attempt to call a header after output has been sent to the page, you will generate an error; hence, your script will fail on you.

That being said, the functionality of headers is rather powerful. You can use them to control everything, including setting the current page location, finding out what file format is being displayed, and managing all aspects of the browser cache. In the following examples, you will learn how to use the header() function in a variety of ways. The header() function's prototype is as follows:

```
void header ( string string [, bool replace [, int http_response_code]] )
```

12-5. Redirecting to a Different Location

One of the more common uses for HTTP headers is redirecting a script. By using headers inside processing scripts, you can force the browser to return to any page you want. We prefer to use headers to control exception handling within process scripts. The following script makes sure that all input coming from a form is not blank.

The Code

```
<!DOCTYPE html PUBLIC "-//W3C//DTD XHTML 1.0 Transitional//EN" ➥
"http://www.w3.org/TR/xhtml1/DTD/xhtml1-transitional.dtd">
<html xmlns="http://www.w3.org/1999/xhtml">
<title>Sample 12.5</title>
<meta http-equiv="Content-Type" content="text/html; charset=iso-8859-1" />
</head>
<body>
  <form action="sample12_5.php" method="post">
    Name: <input type="text" name="yourname" maxlength="150" /><br />
    <input type="submit" value="Submit" style="margin-top: 10px;" />
  </form>
</body>
</html>
```

The form in the previous block of code will then call the processing statement as follows:

```
<?php

  //sample12_5.php

  //You will assume that this scripts main focus is to validate➥
  against a blank entry.
  if (trim ($_POST['yourname']) == ""){
    header ("Location: sample12_5.html");
    exit;
  }
  //If you have a value, then it would do something with said value➥
  . Like, say, output it.
  echo $_POST['yourname'];

?>
```

How It Works

The header() function is rather nice in that it will redirect you automatically to the appropriate file (providing it exists) without a single hiccup in the processing. You will simply find yourself at the appropriate page. You can even use the header() function with the Location parameter to send you to a page not currently on the server on which the script is located. As such, this functionality can be rather effective even as a simple page redirection script.

12-6. Sending Content Types Other Than HTML

Naturally, sometimes you will want to use the header() function to output a type of file format that may not be an actual web page. Thankfully, the header function is more than versatile enough to take care of this issue. To make the most out of this function, you can effectively output other file types by simply declaring the content type you want to output.

This functionality can be handy in circumstances where you want to deploy a document to a user or perhaps even output a dynamic image. You can use the following script to output a JPG image to the user.

The Code

```
<!DOCTYPE html PUBLIC "-//W3C//DTD XHTML 1.0 Transitional//EN"
 "http://www.w3.org/TR/xhtml1/DTD/xhtml1-transitional.dtd">
<html xmlns="http://www.w3.org/1999/xhtml">
<title>Sample 12.6</title>
<meta http-equiv="Content-Type" content="text/html; charset=iso-8859-1" />
</head>
<body>
  <div align="center">
    <img src="sample12_6.php" alt="" title="" style="border: none;" />
  </div>
</body>
</html>
<?php

  //sample12_6.php

  //The location of the image.
  $path = "images/winter.jpg";
  try {
    if (is_file ($path)){
      if ($file = fopen($path, 'rb')) {
        while(!feof($file) and (connection_status()==0)) {
          $f .= fread($file, 1024*8);
        }
        fclose($file);
      }
      //Use the header function to output an image of .jpg.
      header ("Content-type: image/jpeg");
      print $f;
    } else {
      throw new exception ("Sorry, file path is not valid.");
    }
  } catch (exception $e){
    //Create a dynamic error message.
    $animage = imagecreate (500, 500);
```

```
    $red = imagecolorallocate ($animage, 255, 0, 0);
    $white = imagecolorallocate ($animage, 255, 255, 255);
    imagefilledrectangle ($animage, 0, 0, 500, 500, $white);
    imagestring ($animage, 4, ((500 - (strlen($e->getmessage()) ➥
 * imagefontwidth(4))) / 2), 5, $e->getmessage(), $red);
    imagejpeg ($animage);
    header ("Content-type: image/jpeg");
    imagedestroy ($animage);
  }

?>
```

How It Works

Although the error handling for this particular function may be a tad beyond the scope of this particular chapter, those who have studied Chapter 8 should have no trouble with it. Exception handling aside, what you are doing here is basically reading a file as a binary object. Then, by utilizing the header() function, you can output it as a JPG by merely printing it. You can use this same sort of procedure to read pretty much any file as a binary object and then output it in much the same way, provided you use the proper content type (more widely known as a MIME type). Table 12-2 lists a few of the popular MIME types you may be interested in using as output.

Table 12-2. *Common File Format Content Types*

Content Type	Application
application/pdf	Adobe Portable Document Format (PDF) types
application/msword	Microsoft Word documents
application/excel	Microsoft Excel documents
image/gif	GIF images
image/png	PNG images
application/octet-stream	Zip files
text/plain	Plain text (text files)

12-7. Forcing File "Save As" Downloads

Because web browsers can output many different file types directly onto the screen, the default when you use headers to output a wide variety of file types is to make them automatically appear on the screen. What if you would rather have the file appear as a download, though? You can use the header() function to force a Save As dialog box to appear for the user to accept a download. The following example uses largely the same code as the previous example but instead forces the user to download the file.

The Code

```php
<?php

//sample12_7.php

//The location of the image.
$path = "images/winter.jpg";
try {
  if (is_file ($path)){
    if ($file = fopen($path, 'rb')) {
      while(!feof($file) and (connection_status()==0)) {
        $f .= fread($file, 1024*8);
      }
      fclose($file);
    }
    //Use the header function to output an image of .jpg.
    $outputname = "myimage";
    header ("Content-type: image/jpeg");
    //This will force a download.
    header("Content-disposition: attachment; filename=".$outputname.".jpg");
    print $f;
  } else {
    throw new exception ("Sorry, file path is not valid.");
  }
} catch (exception $e){
  echo $e->getmessage();
}

?>
```

How It Works

The key point in this code is showing content-disposition in the header. By making content-disposition an attachment value, the browser will force a download rather than display the file inline. By using this, you can force the download to appear with any particular filename you prefer and also with pretty much any file extension. By using content-type, you force the browser to output a file of the requested type.

Using Sessions

Because cookies are getting less and less trusted, a means had to be created to allow user authentication without having to store physical files on a remote computer. As a solution, *sessions* came onto the scene. Considered the best solution for user authentication that allows for script control, sessions store their files on the actual server.

12-8. Implementing Sessions

Sessions are handled much like cookies but with a major difference. While cookies are pretty much declared as global members of the site, a session state must be enabled to use them effectively. While in the session state, sessions can be accessed just like cookies, in a global sense, and can be manipulated, added to, or removed with relative ease.

Setting sessions requires less overhead than creating cookies. Instead of having to completely define how and where a cookie will be in use, with sessions you control most of that through the PHP configuration file.

You use sessions in PHP 5 using the $_SESSION superglobal. You can assign and access a session using the superglobal, provided the script that is doing the work is within the session state. The following example creates a session state, sets a session, and then outputs the session value.

The Code

```php
<?php

    //sample12_8.php

    //First, create a session states.
    session_start();

    $GLOBALS['user'] = "test";
    $GLOBALS['pass'] = "test";

    //Now, here is a function that will log you in.
    function login ($username, $password){
       if (strcmp ($username, $GLOBALS['user']) == 0 ➥
&& strcmp ($password,      $GLOBALS['pass']) == 0){
          $_SESSION['user'] = $username;
          $_SESSION['pass'] = md5 ($password);
          return true;
       } else {
          return false;
       }
    }

    //Function to logout.
    function logout (){
       unset ($_SESSION['user']);
       unset ($_SESSION['pass']);
       session_destroy();
    }

    //Now, you can login.
```

```php
if (login("test","test")){
    //And output our sessions with the greatest of ease.
    echo "Successfully logged in with user: " . $_SESSION['user']➥
. " and pass: " . $_SESSION['pass'];
} else {
    echo "Could not login.";
}

//Now, you logout.
logout();

//And hence cannot use our sessions anymore.
if (isset ($_SESSION['user'])){
    echo $_SESSION['user']; //Outputs nothing.
}

?>
```

How It Works

The code works quite simply. You create a session state using the session_start() function and then use and access these session values using the $_SESSION superglobal. Using the superglobal, you can then add to, remove, or modify the session values. You can use the sessions anywhere the session state is enabled, which means the session_start() function needs to be called at the beginning of every page where you want session access. When you have finished with the sessions, you can simply use the unset() function on the session values and finish off the session state using the session_destroy() function. The prototypes for these session-related functions are as follows:

```php
bool session_start ( void )
bool session_destroy ( void )
```

12-9. Storing Simple Data Types in Sessions

Up until PHP 5, short of using a bit of serialization (which is somewhat inconvenient at best), sessions have really been useful only for passing simple data types around. Sessions handle simple data types, and they handle them well. Like any PHP variable, however, the data type of a current session is based upon what was last assigned to it and can be changed quite easily. The following example passes three values by session: an integer, a string, and a floating-point value.

The Code

```php
<?php

//sample12_9.php

//First, create a session states.
session_start();
```

```php
(int) $_SESSION['integer_value'] = "115";
(string) $_SESSION['string_value'] = "Hello World";
(float) $_SESSION['float_value'] = "1.07";

//This function exists for the sole purpose of showing how sessions can be called
//from anywhere within the scope of the session state.
function outputsessions (){
  echo $_SESSION['integer_value'] . "<br />"; //Outputs 115.
  echo $_SESSION['string_value'] . "<br />"; //Outputs Hello World.
  echo $_SESSION['float_value'] . "<br />"; //Outputs 1.07.
}

//Then you can call the function from here:
  outputsessions();
?>
```

How It Works

As you can see, sessions that have been set can be called and accessed from anywhere within the scope of the session state. In this case, you have an integer, a string, and a float value (which have been typecast) that can be accessed from anywhere. The script was called without passing in any values, yet it can access and output the session values.

12-10. Storing Complex Data Types in Sessions

One of the major improvements to PHP 5 is the ability to store complex data types within a session. In the past, code that tracked information such as shopping carts had to be stored within temporary database tables and such, which was incredibly clunky and not space efficient. Fortunately, PHP now allows you to store objects within sessions. Using this technique, you can easily store large quantities of data within a single object (such as a shopping cart object), use the functionality within the session for these purposes, and then pass the data along to other pages. The following example shows how to pass an object and then access the object from a session.

The Code

```php
<?php

  //sample12_10.php

  //First, create a session states.
  session_start();

  //A class that does not do too much.
  class myclass {
    protected $myvalue;

    public function setmyvalue ($newvalue){
```

```
      $this->myvalue = $newvalue;
   }

   public function getmyvalue (){
      return $this->myvalue;
   }
}

$_SESSION['myclass_value'] = new myclass ();

//This function exists for the sole purpose of showing how sessions can be called
//from anywhere within the scope of the session state.
function outputsessions (){
   $_SESSION['myclass_value']->setmyvalue ("Hello World");
   echo $_SESSION['myclass_value']->getmyvalue ();
}

//Then you can call the function from here:
outputsessions();
?>
```

How It Works

As you can see, the ability to use and set an object through a session variable is now just as simple as doing so with regular data types. This ability will prove to be quite effective in future applications, as web developers can now use the system memory to perform certain functionality rather than wasting space within a database or text/Extensible Markup Language (XML) file.

12-11. Detecting Browsers

To determine the browser version of the user who is currently viewing your site in PHP, several algorithms are at your disposal. The most useful and easiest to implement is the $_SERVER superglobal. By grabbing the contents of $_SERVER['HTTP_USER_AGENT'], you can retrieve a fairly conclusive string offering of the system that is currently accessing your website. Once you have the string in hand, it is a simple matter of using regular expressions to break down the different parts of the string into something usable.

The other way to detect a browser in PHP is through the get_browser() function. Sadly, using this method is not nearly as reliable and involves quite a bit more server configuration. For starters, you are going to need a browscap.ini file. Now, the problem with this file is that it needs to be constantly up-to-date. You can find browscap.ini files for download on the Internet, but finding a recent one that will work properly with your current version of PHP and whatever server you are running can be tricky.

Once you have located a browscap.ini file that works with your current setup, it is a simple matter of changing this line inside your php.ini file:

```
;browscap =
```

to this:

```
browscap = my/path/to/browscap.ini
```

From there you merely call the get_browser() function, and it will return an associative array filled with all the pertinent details. Since using the get_browser() function can be tricky to set up and the installation is rather platform dependent, the following example uses $_SERVER, which should work on just about any PHP 5 platform.

The Code

```php
<?php

  //sample12_11.php

  //A class to determine a browser and platform type.
  class browser {
      //Our private variables.
      private $browseragent;
      private $browserversion;
      private $browserplatform;

      //A function to set the browser agent.
      private function setagent($newagent) {
         $this->browseragent = $newagent;
      }
      //A function to set the browser version.
      private function setversion($newversion) {
         $this->browserversion = $newversion;
      }
      //A function to set the browser platform.
      private function setplatform($newplatform) {
         $this->browserplatform = $newplatform;
      }
      //A function to determine what browser and version you are using.
      private function determinebrowser () {
       if (ereg('MSIE ([0-9].[0-9]{1,2})',$_SERVER['HTTP_USER_AGENT'],$version)) {
           $this->setversion($version[1]);
           $this->setagent("IE");
       } else if (ereg( 'Opera ([0-9].[0-9]{1,2})',➥
$_SERVER['HTTP_USER_AGENT'],$version)) {
           $this->setversion($version[1]);
           $this->setagent("OPERA");
       } else if (ereg( 'Mozilla/([0-9].[0-9]{1,2})',➥
$_SERVER['HTTP_USER_AGENT'],$version)) {
           $this->setversion($version[1]);
           $this->setagent("MOZILLA");
       } else {
           $this->setversion("0");
           $this->setagent("OTHER");
       }
      }
```

```
    //A function to determine the platform you are on.
    private function determineplatform () {
        if (strstr ($_SERVER['HTTP_USER_AGENT'],"Win")) {
            $this->setplatform("Win");
        } else if (strstr ($_SERVER['HTTP_USER_AGENT'],"Mac")) {
            $this->setplatform("Mac");
        } else if (strstr ($_SERVER['HTTP_USER_AGENT'],"Linux")) {
            $this->setplatform("Linux");
        } else if (strstr ($_SERVER['HTTP_USER_AGENT'],"Unix")) {
            $this->setplatform("Unix");
        } else {
            $this->setplatform("Other");
        }
    }
    //A function to return the current browser.
    public function getbrowser (){
        $this->determinebrowser ();
        return $this->browseragent . " " . $this->browserversion;
    }
    //A function to return the current platform.
    public function getplatform (){
        $this->determineplatform ();
        return $this->browserplatform;
    }
}
//Now, you simply create a new instance of the browser class.
$mybrowser = new browser ();
//And then you can determine out current browser and platform status.
echo "Browser: " . $mybrowser->getbrowser() . "<br />";
echo "Platform: " . $mybrowser->getplatform() . "<br />";
//The bare bones output looks as such:
echo $_SERVER['HTTP_USER_AGENT'];
?>
```

How It Works

As you can see, by creating a class, you can easily parse the $_SERVER superglobal for the nec-
essary information. The raw output from $_SERVER['HTTP_USER_AGENT'] on our current system
returns this result, which is not so great looking:

```
Mozilla/5.0 (Windows; U; Windows NT 5.1; en-US; rv:1.7.7)➡
 Gecko/20050414 Firefox/1.0.3
```

By using the class set up previously, you can quickly and easily determine the platform
and browser in use. It would be quite simple as well to throw in a function or two to return
boolean types depending on whether you want to test for a certain browser or platform. Keep
in mind that this script is set up to handle only a few of the popular browsers—you could easily expand it to encompass a few more. All in all, by using regular expressions, this is not too
difficult of a script.

Using Querystrings

You will frequently want to pass values to a page through a means other than a form. You can pass values through the address bar of your browser in PHP by using *querystrings*. Basically, by using special characters and values in the address bar of your browser, you can pass values into a script and then have the script pass more values.

This provides a convenient method to pass values from page to page and also provides a valuable method for reusing the same page to perform multiple forms of functionality. Sadly, although passing values this way is convenient, it is also insecure. Users can insert whatever they would like into the address bar of their browser and hence force your script to do unpredicted things if you do not take the time to validate against such an occurrence.

Querystrings are often the target of SQL injection attacks whereby a value passed through a querystring to your script creates a dynamic SQL statement. Utilizing the right code injection, hackers can potentially cause a lot of damage to the integrity of your site using querystrings. It is with this in mind that the following examples use optimal security.

12-12. Using Querystrings

Using querystrings has always been a relatively easy task, but let's look at it from a PHP 5 point of view. The current way to handle querystrings is to use the $_GET superglobal (are you starting to see where PHP is going yet?). By using the $_GET superglobal to handle your querystring, you can at least determine where the value is coming from and deal with it accordingly.

Passing querystrings is usually handled with the HREF attribute of an <A> tag. The first value of a querystring must always be denoted by the question mark (?), followed by the name of the variable and then the value of the character. Any following variables must be denoted by the ampersand (&) character, then the variable name, and lastly the value.

Keep in mind that using current Extensible HTML (XHTML) standards, you should use & to substitute for & when you encode the link. Also note that blank spaces do not carry over well using querystrings; therefore, it is a good idea to use the urlencode() function to prepare a string value for passing along to a querystring and the urldecode() function to extract it. The prototypes for these functions are as follows:

```
string urlencode ( string str )
string urldecode ( string str )
```

The following example shows the HTML necessary to pass several values to the current page.

The Code

```
<!DOCTYPE html PUBLIC "-//W3C//DTD XHTML 1.0 Transitional//EN"➡
 "http://www.w3.org/TR/xhtml1/DTD/xhtml1-transitional.dtd">
<html xmlns="http://www.w3.org/1999/xhtml">
<title>Sample 12.12</title>
<meta http-equiv="Content-Type" content="text/html; charset=iso-8859-1" />
</head>
<body>
  <div align="center">
    <a href="sample12_12.html?firstvalue=1&amp;secondvalue=2➡
```

```
&amp;thirdvalue=3">Click Me!</a>
  </div>
</body>
</html>
```

How It Works

With this simple example, you can see how to pass values to the current page. Notice the address bar of your browser when you click the link. The following examples show ways to deal with the information that will be passed and read.

12-13. Passing Numeric Values in a Querystring

Passing numeric values in the address bar as a querystring can be one of the handiest ways to use them but also one of the most vulnerable to attack. Website attacks quite frequently occur when you pass an integer value (quite often indicative of the ID value in a database for a particular record), which then shows you a record in the database. This is a prime target for SQL injection attacks and should definitely be dealt with using the proper validation.

The following example shows you how to pass an integer value, read it in by the page, perform a specified action with it, and keep it in the form of an integer the entire time for validation purposes.

The Code

```
<!DOCTYPE html PUBLIC "-//W3C//DTD XHTML 1.0 Transitional//EN"➥
 "http://www.w3.org/TR/xhtml1/DTD/xhtml1-transitional.dtd">
<html xmlns="http://www.w3.org/1999/xhtml">
<title>Sample 12.13</title>
<meta http-equiv="Content-Type" content="text/html; charset=iso-8859-1" />
</head>
<body>
<div align="center">
  <p>Click a link to change the text color of the verbiage below:</p>
  <a href="sample12_13.html?color=1">Green</a><br />
  <a href="sample12_13.html?color=2">Red</a><br />
  <a href="sample12_13.html?color=3">Blue</a><br />
  <a href="sample12_13.html">Reset</a>
  <?php
    //The first thing you must do is read in the value.
    //Note the use of the intval() function.
    //By forcing an integer value, you kill off SQL injection problems.
    if (isset ($_GET['color'])){
      $color = intval ($_GET['color']);
    } else {
      $color = "";
    }

    //Now, you can perform an action based on the result.
```

```
    if ($color == 1){
      $fontcolor = "00FF00";
    } elseif ($color == 2){
      $fontcolor = "FF0000";
    } elseif ($color == 3){
      $fontcolor = "0000FF";
    } else {
      $fontcolor = "000000";
    }
  ?><p style="color: #<?php echo $fontcolor; ?>; font-weight: bold;">➟
Hello World!</p><?php
?>
</div>
</body>
</html>
```

How It Works

Passing integer values is really rather simple. As you can see in the previous example, you code the proper value into each link that you deem necessary for the functionality. Based on the value received, the verbiage changes color. You will note, for validation purposes, that not only do you ensure an integer value (using the intval() function), but you also provide a default in all cases to ensure that if you do not get a desired value, the system still dies gracefully.

12-14. Passing String Values in a Querystring

Passing string values in a querystring is slightly more complicated than passing integer values. Because you know pretty well what format an integer will be in when you receive it, it makes matters slightly easier than receiving a string value that could potentially take on a variety of forms. You must be careful when sending as well as when receiving to prevent against SQL injection attacks and other such nonsense that could potentially break your script. You can use the following example to maintain a system whereby you create a design shell and then pass in the content for the site dynamically through querystring page locations.

The Code

```
<!DOCTYPE html PUBLIC "-//W3C//DTD XHTML 1.0 Transitional//EN"➟
 "http://www.w3.org/TR/xhtml1/DTD/xhtml1-transitional.dtd">
<html xmlns="http://www.w3.org/1999/xhtml">
<title>Sample 12.14</title>
<meta http-equiv="Content-Type" content="text/html; charset=iso-8859-1" />
</head>
<body>
  <div align="center">
  <p>Click a link to move to a new page:</p>
  <a href="sample12_14.html?page=content1.html">Content 1</a><br />
  <a href="sample12_14.html?page=content2.html">Content 2</a><br />
  <a href="sample12_14.html?page=content3.html">Content 3</a><br />
```

```php
<?php
    //The first thing you do is decode, remove slashes, ➡
and trim the incoming value.
    $page = trim (urldecode (stripslashes ($_GET['page'])));
    //First, you see if there is a page.
    if (isset ($page) && $page != ""){
      //Now, you determine if this is a valid page.
      if (is_file ($page)){
        require_once ($page);
      } else {
        echo "<p>Sorry, the page you have requested does not exist.</p>";
      }
    }
?>
</div>
</body>
</html>
```

How It Works

This page works by requiring a filename that is dynamically passed in by the querystring. The first operation you perform is ensuring that the values being received are properly formatted types. Next, you confirm that the page that is to be loaded is indeed a relative file. If the file to be loaded is valid, then you include the file in the page. This sort of functionality can be powerful because it takes away the problem of copying and pasting design code across pages. Using this method you can create a design "wrapper" and simply insert content pages dynamically.

12-15. Passing Complex Values in a Querystring

Passing complex values in a querystring takes a little more effort than passing regular data-typed values. To pass a value such as an array or an object, you must first serialize the value into a format that can be passed easily and effectively. PHP contains two handy functions that must be utilized in order for such functionality to become feasible. The serialize() function will transform a variable into a format that is capable of being passed in a querystring, and the unserialize() function is required to retrieve the value and turn it back into a usable variable. The prototypes for the functions are as follows:

```
string serialize ( mixed value )
mixed unserialize ( string str )
```

The Code

```
<!DOCTYPE html PUBLIC "-//W3C//DTD XHTML 1.0 Transitional//EN"➡
 "http://www.w3.org/TR/xhtml1/DTD/xhtml1-transitional.dtd">
<html xmlns="http://www.w3.org/1999/xhtml">
<title>Sample 12.15</title>
<meta http-equiv="Content-Type" content="text/html; charset=iso-8859-1" />
<?php
```

```php
  class someclass {
  protected $someval;

    public function setsomeval ($newval){
      $this->someval = $newval;
    }

   public function getsomeval (){
      return $this->someval;
    }
  }

  $myclass = new someclass ();
  $myclass->setsomeval ("Hello World!");

  $myarray = array();
  $myarray[0] = "Hello";
  $myarray[1] = "World!";

  $myarray = serialize ($myarray);
  $myarray = urlencode ($myarray);

  $myclass = serialize ($myclass);
  $myclass = urlencode ($myclass);
?>
</head>
<body>
<div align="center">
<a href="sample12_15.html?passedarray=<?php echo $myarray; ?>➡
&amp;passedclass=<?php echo $myclass; ?>">Output Current Value</a><br />
<?php
  if (isset ($_GET['passedclass']) && isset ($_GET['passedarray'])){

    $newclass = new someclass;
    $newclass = $_GET['passedclass'];
    $newclass = stripslashes ($newclass);
    $newclass = unserialize ($newclass);
    echo "Object: " . $newclass->getsomeval() . "<br />";

    $newarray = array ();
    $newarray = $_GET['passedarray'];
    $newarray = stripslashes ($newarray);
    $newarray = unserialize ($newarray);
    print_r ($newarray);
}
?>
</div>
</body>
</html>
```

How It Works

As you can see, to make this code work, the object variable and the array variable must both be serialized into a format that can be passed from page to page and then unserialized when received. If you were to try to pass the variables along without serializing them, they would lose all stored information and could not be read properly when received. Serialization can be helpful in circumstances such as this, but a better way to maneuver may be to create session objects and pass them that way instead.

Authenticating Your Users

No matter what type of online application you are building, if you need to keep sections of it private, you will at some point need to create a way of authenticating your users so that you know you have a valid user accessing the site. You can handle authentication in a variety of ways, but the two most common methods for securing a file or set of files is through HTTP-based authentication and through cookie authentication. Neither is technically superior to the other, and they both have their own uses. Both can be set up dynamically, and both will stop users in their tracks should they not meet the authenticated demands.

12-16. Setting Up HTTP-Based Authentication

HTTP-based authentication can be a true challenge from a scripting point of view. The interesting part about it is that most server interfaces (such as Cpanel or Ensim) can create HTTP-based authentication on the fly. In this case, we have written a class to do this for you.

We are not the biggest fans of HTTP-based authentication because the login mechanism is largely the same. You can set a few variables to customize it slightly, but in the end, it is the same pop-up window asking for your username and password. That being said, this class lets you handle the authentication on the fly.

For this code to work properly, you must first set up a file called .htaccess and ensure that you set the proper path to it when calling the class. You must also have a proper password file prepared (and once again specify the proper path to it). Keep in mind that the .htaccess file must also be read and write enabled (a simple CHMOD of 777 can accomplish this).

The Code

```php
<?php

//sample12_16.php

//Class to create and maintain http authorization.
class httpauth {

  protected $filepath;
  protected $passpath;

  //A function to construct the class.
  public function __construct (){
    $num_args = func_num_args();
```

```php
if($num_args > 0){
  $args = func_get_args();
  $this->filepath = $args[0];
  //Check the validity of the file path.
  try {
    if (is_file ($this->filepath)){
      //Validate that the file is named .htaccess.
      try {
        $expfilename = explode ("/", $this->filepath);
        if ($expfilename[count($expfilename) - 1] != ".htaccess"){
          throw new exception ("Sorry, file must be named .htaccess.");
        } else {
          try {
            //Make sure the file is writable.
            if (!is_writable ($this->filepath)){
              throw new exception ("File must be writable.");
            }
          } catch (exception $e){
            echo $e->getmessage();
          }
        }
      } catch (exception $e){
        echo $e->getmessage();
      }
    } else {
      throw new exception ("Sorry, file does not exist.");
    }
  } catch (exception $e){
    echo $e->getmessage();
  }
  //Now, check the validity of the password file.
  $this->passpath = $args[1];
  try {
    if (is_file ($this->passpath)){
      //Make sure the file is writable.
      try {
        if (!is_writable ($this->passpath)){
          throw new exception ("Password file must be writable.");
        }
      } catch (exception $e){
        echo $e->getmessage();
      }
    } else {
      throw new exception ("Sorry, password file does not exist.");
    }
  } catch (exception $e){
    echo $e->getmessage();
```

```
        }
      }
    }
    //Function to add a user to the password file.
    public function adduser ($user, $pass) {
      //Make sure a given user does not already exist.
      try {
        if ($file = fopen ($this->passpath,"r")){
          $proceed = true;
          //Run through the file.
          while ($input = fgets ($file, 200)){
            $exp = explode (":", $input);
            //If this user already exists, then you stop right here.
            if ($user == $exp[0]){
              $proceed = false;
            }
          }
          fclose ($file);
        } else {
          throw new exception ("Sorry, could not open the➡
password file for reading.");
        }
      } catch (exception $e) {
        echo $e->getmessage();
      }
      try {
        //If you are good to go, then write to the file.
        if ($proceed){
          try {
            //Open the password file for appending.
            if ($file = fopen ($this->passpath,"a")){

              //And then append a new username and password.
              fputs($file,$user . ":" . crypt ($pass) . "\n");
              fclose($file);
            } else {
              throw new exception ("Error opening the password file for appending");
            }
          } catch (exception $e) {
            echo $e->getmessage();
          }
        } else {
          throw new exception ("Sorry, this username already exists.");
        }
      } catch (exception $e){
        echo $e->getmessage();
      }
```

```
    }
    //Function to add http authorization.
    public function addauth ($areaname = "Protected Zone") {
      //Now, protect the directory.
      try {
        if ($file = fopen ($this->filepath, "w+")){
          fputs($file, "Order allow,deny\n");
          fputs($file, "Allow from all\n");
          fputs($file, "AuthType        Basic\n");
          fputs($file, "AuthUserFile    " . $this->passpath . "\n\n");
          fputs($file, "AuthName        \"" . $areaname . "\"\n");
          fputs($file, "require valid-user\n");
          fclose($file);
        } else {
          throw new exception ("Sorry, could not open htaccess file for writing.");
        }
      } catch (exception $e) {
        echo $e->getmessage();
      }
    }
    //Function to remove a user from the password listing.
    public function removeuser ($user) {
      //Run through the current file and get all of the usernames and passwords.
      $userarray = array ();
      $passarray = array ();
      $arrcounter = 0;
      try {
        if ($file = fopen ($this->passpath,"r")){
          //Run through the file.
          while ($input = fgets ($file, 200)){
            $exp = explode (":", $input);
            //If this user already exists, then you stop right here.
            if ($user != $exp[0]){
              //Then add to the list.
              $userarray[$arrcounter] = $exp[0];
              $passarray[$arrcounter] = $exp[1];
              $arrcounter++;
            }
          }
          fclose ($file);
        } else {
          throw new exception ("Sorry, could not open the➡
password file for reading.");
        }
      } catch (exception $e) {
        echo $e->getmessage();
      }
```

```php
    //Then go through the file again and write back all the logins in the array.
    try {
      if ($file = fopen ($this->passpath,"w")){
        //Run through the file.
        for ($i = 0; $i < count ($userarray); $i++){
          if ($userarray[$i] != "" && $passarray[$i] != ""){
            fputs ($file, $userarray[$i] . ":" . $passarray[$i] . "\n");
          }
        }
        fclose ($file);
      } else {
        throw new exception ("Sorry, could not open the➡
password file for writing.");
      }
    } catch (exception $e) {
      echo $e->getmessage();
    }
  }
  //Function to change the password of a user.
  public function changepass ($user,$newpass){
    try {
      if ($newpass == ""){
        throw new exception ("Sorry, you must supply a new password");
      } else {
        $userarray = array ();
        $passarray = array ();
        $arrcounter = 0;
        try {
          if ($file = fopen ($this->passpath,"r")){
            //Run through the file.
            while ($input = fgets ($file, 200)){
              $exp = explode (":", $input);
              //If you don't have a match you to the array.
              if ($user != $exp[0]){
                //Then add to the list.
                $userarray[$arrcounter] = $exp[0];
                $passarray[$arrcounter] = $exp[1];
                $arrcounter++;
              } else {
                //Else you change the pass.
                $userarray[$arrcounter] = $exp[0];
                $passarray[$arrcounter] = crypt ($newpass);
                $arrcounter++;
              }
            }
            fclose ($file);
          } else {
```

```
                    throw new exception ("Sorry, could not open the➥
        password file for reading.");
                }
            } catch (exception $e) {
              echo $e->getmessage();
            }
            //Then go through the file again and write back all the➥
        logins in the array.
            try {
                if ($file = fopen ($this->passpath,"w")){
                    //Run through the file.
                    for ($i = 0; $i < count ($userarray); $i++){
                      if ($userarray[$i] != "" && $passarray[$i] != ""){
                        fputs ($file, $userarray[$i] . ":" . $passarray[$i] . "\n");
                      }
                    }
                    fclose ($file);
                } else {
                    throw new exception ("Sorry, could not open the➥
        password file for writing.");
                }
            } catch (exception $e) {
              echo $e->getmessage();
            }
          }
        } catch (exception $e){
          echo $e->getmessage();
        }
      }

      //Function to kill the authorization.
      public function removeauth () {
        unlink ($this->filepath);
      }
    }
    //Set this path to your password file.
    $passpath = "/home/ensbabin/public_html/php5recipes/chapter12/code/htpasswd";
    //Set this path to the folder you want to protect.
    $toprotect = "/home/ensbabin/public_html/php5recipes/➥
chapter12/code/foldertoprotect/.htaccess";
    //Create a new instance of an httpauth.
    $myhttp = new httpauth ($toprotect, $passpath);
    //Add user.
    $myhttp->adduser ("test","test");
    //Protect a directory.
    $myhttp->addauth ("My Protected Zone");
    //Add another user.
```

```php
  $myhttp->adduser ("phpauth","sample");
  //Change a user's password.
  $myhttp->changepass ("phpauth","testing");
  //Remove a user.
  $myhttp->removeuser ("phpauth");
  //Remove the protection entirely.
  $myhttp->removeauth ();
?>
```

How It Works

Basically, to set up authentication, you must first set up a username and password that can access the authentication. You can perform this action in this particular script by using the adduser() method. Once you have set up a user, you can then set up authentication on a particular directory using the addauth() method. Any users you have added to the password file can have access to the protected directory.

This class also comes with a few bells and whistles such as the ability to change the password for a user, remove a user entirely, or remove the authentication, but the functionality for the methods speaks for itself.

At its core, creating and maintaining users and HTTP authorization is simply a matter of maintaining a few text files—the .htpasswd and .htaccess files. Because these are basically text-based, all the class needs to do is read and write to the files in question (hence the hefty file-opening validation).

12-17. Setting Up Cookie Authentication

Managing user authentication through cookies or sessions is a little harder than using HTTP-based authentication, but it can ultimately be more flexible and rewarding. Some of the nice features of cookie-based authentication are being able to set your own error messages, being able to control what happens upon login, and being allowed to make your login form blend seamlessly into your application (rather than being forced to use the pop-up boxes of the HTTP-based variety).

Two schools of thought exist on the whole cookie vs. sessions issue; the advantages of sessions being kept on the server side and working on any platform outweigh the cookie method's advantage of being slightly more flexible. By using sessions you will know that your script should work on pretty much any platform and will be a reliable, secure way of handling authentication. You can use the following example as a login system.

The Code

```php
<?php
  session_start();
?>
<!DOCTYPE html PUBLIC "-//W3C//DTD XHTML 1.0 Transitional//EN"➥
 "http://www.w3.org/TR/xhtml1/DTD/xhtml1-transitional.dtd">
<html xmlns="http://www.w3.org/1999/xhtml">
<title>Sample 12.17</title>
<meta http-equiv="Content-Type" content="text/html; charset=iso-8859-1" />
```

```php
<?php

   //Normally your username and pass would be stored in a database.
   //For this example you will assume that you have already retrieved them.
   $GLOBALS['user'] = "test";
   $GLOBALS['pass'] = "test";

   //Now, check if you have a valid submission.
   if (isset ($_POST['user']) && isset ($_POST['pass'])){
     //Then check to see if you have a match.
     if (strcmp ($_POST['user'], $GLOBALS['user']) == 0↩
&& strcmp ($_POST['pass'], $GLOBALS['pass']) == 0){
       //If you have a valid match, then set the sessions.
        $_SESSION['user'] = $_POST['user'];
        $_SESSION['pass'] = $_POST['pass'];
     } else {
        ?><div align="center"><p style="color: #FF0000;">↩
Sorry, you have entered an incorrect login.</p></div><?php
     }
   }

   //Check if you need to logout.
   if ($_POST['logout'] == "yes"){
     unset ($_SESSION['user']);
     unset ($_SESSION['pass']);
     session_destroy();
   }

   //You then use this function on every page to check for a valid login at all
times.
   function checkcookies () {
     if (strcmp ($_SESSION['user'], $GLOBALS['user']) == 0↩
&& strcmp ($_SESSION['pass'], $GLOBALS['pass']) == 0){
        return true;
     } else {
        return false;
     }
   }

?>
</head>
<body>
  <div align="center">
    <?php
      //Check if you have a valid login.
      if (checkcookies()){
        ?>
```

```
        <p>Congratulations, you are logged in!</p>
        <form action="sample12_17.html" method="post" style="margin: 0px;">
          <input type="hidden" name="logout" value="yes" />
          <input type="submit" value="Logout" />
        </form>
        <?php
        //Or else present a login form.
      } else {
        ?>
        <form action="sample12_17.html" method="post" style="margin: 0px;">
          <div style="width: 500px; margin-bottom: 10px;">
            <div style="width: 35%; float: left; text-align: left;">
              Username:
            </div>
            <div style="width: 64%; float: right; text-align: left;">
              <input type="text" name="user" maxlength="25" />
            </div>
            <br style="clear: both;" />
          </div>
          <div style="width: 500px; margin-bottom: 10px;">
          <div style="width: 35%; float: left; text-align: left;">
            Password:
          </div>
          <div style="width: 64%; float: right; text-align: left;">
            <input type="password" name="pass" maxlength="25" />
          </div>
          <br style="clear: both;" />
        </div>
        <div style="width: 500px; text-align: left;">➥
<input type="submit" value="Login" /></div>
      </form>
      <?php
    }
    ?>
  </div>
</body>
</html>
```

How It Works

Basically, you are running the entire login algorithm from this one script. If the script detects that you have submitted a username and password, it will then check for a valid match and set proper sessions upon the match. If the system detects that the sessions are already in place and are proper (as handled by the checkcookies() function), it does not display the login form and instead displays a means to log out. The logout algorithm is handled in mostly the same way. If the script detects a logout field is in place, it then goes through the algorithm to kill off the session variables.

Using Environment and Configuration Variables

PHP provides a means to use and verify the configuration settings and environment variables relative to the server space the script is occupying. Having access to this feature set can come in handy on many occasions. By having access to environment variables, you can customize your scripts to work optimally on the platform that is available. By having access to the configuration variables of PHP, you can customize the PHP environment your script is working in for special occurrences.

A common use of the environment variables in PHP is for dynamic imaging. While Windows systems commonly store their fonts in one folder, Linux-based systems keep theirs in another. By using PHP's environment variables to determine the current operating system, you can make your code slightly more portable.

Using configuration variables can also come in quite handy, particularly with file upload scripts. The base PHP installation leaves only enough processing time to upload files that are generally 2MB or smaller in size. By manipulating the PHP configuration files temporarily, you can increase the limit enough to allow a script to process much larger files.

12-18. Reading Environment and Configuration Variables

PHP 5 makes reading environment and configuration variables easy. The $_ENV superglobal is PHP's method for reading a system's environment variables and has an argument set that is based upon the current environment that is available to it. Because of its relative flexibility, there is no real set argument list, as it is generated based on the current server environment. You can use the phpinfo() function to determine the current environment variables, and you can retrieve them using the getenv() function, which needs to be supplied a valid environment variable name.

Reading configuration variables, on the other hand, takes place through two functions, ini_get() and ini_get_all(). The function ini_get() will retrieve the value of a specified configuration variable, and the function ini_get_all() will retrieve an array filled with the entire selection of configuration variables that are available.

The following example shows how to retrieve both environment and configuration variables.

The Code

```php
<?php

  //sample12_18.php

  //Here is an example of retrieving an environmental variable or two.
  echo $_ENV['ProgramFiles'] . "<br />"; //Outputs C:\Program Files.
  echo $_ENV['COMPUTERNAME'] . "<br />"; //Outputs BABINZ-CODEZ.
  echo getenv("COMPUTERNAME") . "<br />"; //Also Outputs BABINZ-CODEZ.

  //Now, let's look at reading configuration variables.
  echo ini_get ("post_max_size") . "<br />"; //Outputs 8MB.

  //And you can output the entire listing with this function.
  print_r (ini_get_all());
?>
```

How It Works

As you can see, there is really no problem when reading environment and configuration variables. You can get the job done in a bunch of ways, and predefined functions exist in all aspects of PHP to take care of any issue you may encounter.

12-19. Setting Environment and Configuration Variables

Setting environment and configuration variables is just as easy as it is to get them. While working with environment variables, you merely need to assign a new value to the $_ENV superglobal to process a temporary change. The change will be in effect for the script's duration. The same applies for configuration variables but with a different approach. To set a configuration variable, you have to use the PHP function ini_set(), which will allow you to set a configuration variable for the script's duration. Once the script finishes executing, the configuration variable will return to its original state. The prototype for ini_set() is as follows:

string **ini_set** (string varname, string newvalue)

The Code

```php
<?php

//sample12_19.php

//Setting an environment variable in php is as easy as assigning it.
echo $_ENV['COMPUTERNAME'] . "<br />"; // Echoes BABINZ-CODEZ.
$_ENV['COMPUTERNAME'] = "Hello World!";
echo $_ENV['COMPUTERNAME'] . "<br />"; //Echoes the new COMPUTERNAME.
//Of course the change is relevant only for the current script.

//Setting a configuration variable is the same in that it is in effect only for
//the duration of the script.
echo ini_get ('post_max_size'); //Echoes 8MB.

//Then you set it to 200M for the duration of the script.
ini_set('post_max_size','200M');

//Any files that are to be uploaded in this script will be OK up to 200M.
?>
```

How It Works

As you can see, setting environment and configuration variables is a rather simple task. It can be a handy task, and it can help you modify the current environment to work for you. Many times in your coding career you will have to code around a certain server's configuration. By combining a means to analyze your environment and a means to subsequently work with it, PHP ensures that your scripts will be able to operate to their fullest.

Summary

You could say that the chapter title of "Understanding Web Basics" is somewhat misleading. This chapter has operated more as a guide to some of the optional functionality offered by PHP that can come in handy when building your web applications. We have not covered some of the really basic stuff you perhaps expected; instead, we have gone further than that and given you some solutions that you might have found challenging to work out by yourself.

Whether it is building a system for authenticating users or passing values from page to page, PHP 5 has a solution for you. It is key to use the right technology for the job, however, so having knowledge of a wide variety of methods can be the difference between a well-conceived web application and a complete flop.

Keep these technologies in mind when building your applications; although they may not come in handy for every task, they are there for your use should you need them.

Looking Ahead

In the next chapter, you will look into all aspects of the web form. Web forms are a way to accommodate software creation on the Internet and can be an in-depth topic. You will learn about security, validation, file types, and much more.

■ ■ ■

Creating and Using Forms

To create a fully functional web application, you need to be able to interact with your users. The common way to receive information from web users is through a form. Forms have evolved to be quite all-encompassing. Over time, savvy web developers have taken the elements available to them through the form interface and figured out ways to accomplish pretty much any goal.

On the surface, web forms are merely Hypertext Markup Language (HTML) elements. The way that the elements are processed, however, relies on the processing script that will take care of the elements. PHP 5 is built so that it seamlessly integrates with form elements. Over the past few versions of PHP, its methodology for dealing with form information has gradually evolved and is now quite robust.

This chapter will discuss how best to use PHP 5's form handling functionality with respect to precision, ease of use, features, and security.

On the surface, you have several options when dealing with forms. More specifically, you have control over what elements you want to provide to your user, how you handle the information passed to you, and in what format you choose to receive the data. Obviously, when dealing with information that is passed from a user, it is imperative that you spend some time validating the data passed to your script.

Issues such as user error and malicious scripts affect dealing with forms, so it is important you maintain the integrity of whatever device you are using to store information garnered from users. Over time malicious individuals have come up with ways to extract information they should not be privy to and with ways to potentially cripple your scripts. These individuals generally prey upon forms that have not been properly secured against intrusion, so it is important to maintain a proper amount of validation. Recipes in this chapter that discuss validating form input and globals vs. superglobals will give you a few good ideas of how to maintain the integrity of your web forms.

Understanding Common Form Issues

When dealing with forms, the most important aspect to remember is that you are limited to a certain variety of fields that can be applied to a form. The fields that have been created are non-negotiable and work in only the way they were created to work. It is important, therefore, to fully understand what is available and how best to use the form features to your advantage. Table 13-1 lists the form elements that are available to you.

Table 13-1. *HTML Form Elements*

Element	Description
TEXT INPUT	A simple text box
PASSWORD INPUT	A text box that hides the characters inputted
HIDDEN INPUT	A field that does not show on the form but can contain data
SELECT	A drop-down box with options
LIST	A select box that can have multiple options selected
CHECKBOX	A box that can be checked
RADIO	A radio button that can act as a choice
TEXTAREA	A larger box that can contain paragraph-style entries
FILE	An element that allows you to browse your computer for a file
SUBMIT	A button that will submit the form
RESET	A button that will reset the form to its original state

13-1. GET vs. POST

When dealing with forms, you must specify the way that the information entered into the form is transmitted to its destination (method=""). The two ways available to a web developer are GET and POST. When sending data using the GET method, all fields are appended to the Uniform Resource Locator (URL) of the browser and sent along with the address as data. With the POST method, values are sent as standard input. Sending data using the GET method means that fields are generally capped at 150 characters, which is certainly not the most effective means of passing information. It is also not a secure means of passing data, because many people know how to send information to a script using an address bar.

Sending data using the POST method is quite a bit more secure (because the method cannot be altered by appending information to the address bar) and can contain as much information as you choose to send. Therefore, whenever possible, use the POST method for sending information and then adjust your script to handle it.

PHP 5's current methods for dealing with GET and POST variables are the $_GET and $_POST superglobals, respectively. By using these two superglobals, you can designate exactly where the information should be coming from and subsequently handle the data in the way you want. The following example shows the difference between using the GET and POST methods.

The Code

```
<!DOCTYPE html PUBLIC "-//W3C//DTD XHTML 1.0 Transitional//EN"➥
  "http://www.w3.org/TR/xhtml1/DTD/xhtml1-transitional.dtd">
<html xmlns="http://www.w3.org/1999/xhtml">
<title>Sample 13.1</title>
<meta http-equiv="Content-Type" content="text/html; charset=iso-8859-1" />
</head>
<body>
```

```php
<div style="width: 500px; text-align: left;">
<?php
  //Handle incoming data.
  //This will trigger if you submit using GET
  if ($_GET['submitted'] == "yes"){
    if (trim ($_GET['yourname']) != ""){
      echo "Your Name (with GET): " . $_GET['yourname'];
    } else {
      echo "You must submit a value.";
    }
    ?><br /><a href="sample13_1.php">Try Again</a><?php
  }
  if ($_POST['submitted'] == "yes"){
    if (trim ($_POST['yourname']) != ""){
      echo "Your Name (with POST): " . $_POST['yourname'];
    } else {
      echo "You must submit a value.";
    }
    ?><br /><a href="sample13_1.php">Try Again</a><?php
  }
?>
<?php
  //Show the forms only if you don't already have a submittal.
  if ($_GET['submitted'] != "yes" && $_POST['submitted'] != "yes"){
    ?>
    <form action="sample13_1.php" method="get">
      <p>GET Example:</p>
      <input type="hidden" name="submitted" value="yes" />
      Your Name: <input type="text" name="yourname" maxlength="150" /><br />
      <input type="submit" value="Submit with GET" style="margin-top: 10px;" />
    </form>
    <form action="sample13_1.php" method="post">
      <p>POST Example:</p>
      <input type="hidden" name="submitted" value="yes" />
      Your Name: <input type="text" name="yourname" maxlength="150" /><br />
      <input type="submit" value="Submit with POST" style="margin-top: 10px;" />
    </form>
    <?php
  }
?>
</div>
</body>
</html>
```

How It Works

This block of code demonstrates the difference between the GET and POST methods using the two different forms. You should remember a few things when using such code. Specifically, try hitting the Refresh button after submitting data using the POST form. You will note that the browser will ask you if you want to resubmit the data that was passed to it previously. If you want to resend the data, you must select Yes to this option. On the other hand, when using the GET method, you will not be presented with this issue. (The browser will automatically send the data again.)

Other than a mild bit of validation, this script is pretty simple. It receives either a POST method or a GET method submission of a text field and then displays it if it is not an empty field. Note that because you are using the $_POST and $_GET superglobals, you can determine from where the information is coming. Although each form has a field called submitted, the script knows which value to display based upon the way the information was passed to it.

13-2. Superglobals vs. Globals

Before the advent of superglobals, data was passed along from script to script with loose security. In the php.ini file, you can change a value called register_globals to either on or off. If you leave it on, then whenever you pass a value using the GET or POST method, you can access the variable simply by putting an ampersand (&) character in front of the name of the element you are passing. The problem with this method is that malicious users can insert values into your code to bypass the form entirely.

Therefore, if you want your code to be as secure as possible (and who doesn't?), you should definitely code your applications with register_globals turned off and ensure that you receive your values from where you expect them to come. Using superglobals allows you to do this. The following example shows how you can submit values using globals or superglobals. Note that for this example to work properly, you must temporarily switch your register_globals value to on (don't forget to turn it off afterward!).

The Code

```
<!DOCTYPE html PUBLIC "-//W3C//DTD XHTML 1.0 Transitional//EN"➥
 "http://www.w3.org/TR/xhtml1/DTD/xhtml1-transitional.dtd">
<html xmlns="http://www.w3.org/1999/xhtml">
<title>Sample 13.2</title>
<meta http-equiv="Content-Type" content="text/html; charset=iso-8859-1" />
</head>
<body>
  <div style="width: 500px; text-align: left;">
  <?php
    //Handle the incoming data.
    //Here is how you could handle it with register_globals turned on.
    if ($submitted == "yes"){
      if (trim ($yourname) != ""){
        echo "Your Name: $yourname.";
      } else {
        echo "You must submit a value.";
      }
```

```
        ?><br /><a href="sample13_2.php">Try Again</a><br /><?php
      }
      //Now, here is how it SHOULD be handled with register_globals turned off.
      if ($_POST['submitted'] == "yes"){
        if (trim ($_POST['yourname']) != ""){
          echo "Your Name: " . $_POST['yourname'] . ".";
        } else {
          echo "You must submit a value.";
        }
        ?><br /><a href="sample13_2.php">Try Again</a><br /><?php
      }
    ?>
    <?php
      //Show the forms only if you don't already have a submittal.
      if ($_POST['submitted'] != "yes"){
        ?>
        <form action="sample13_2.php" method="post">
          <p>Example:</p>
          <input type="hidden" name="submitted" value="yes" />
          Your Name: <input type="text" name="yourname" maxlength="150" /><br />
          <input type="submit" value="Submit" style="margin-top: 10px;" />
        </form>
        <?php
      }
    ?>
  </div>
</body>
</html>
```

How It Works

Note how the code that does not use the $_POST superglobal looks pretty much identical, minus the $_POST preceding the field name. The interesting thing to note is that if you run this code with register_globals turned on, both scripts will fire. If, however, you run this code with register_globals turned off, only the second script will fire. Now, consider how easily someone could inject some code into the first script and potentially change the received value. Since the script would not recognize where the value is coming from, it could be easily intercepted. Using the second script, the value passed has to be the one coming from the $_POST superglobal. It should become common practice to code only with register_globals turned off to create as secure an application as possible.

13-3. Validating Form Input

In this day and age of constant attacks on websites, one of the biggest issues is attacking forms directly. To ensure a suitable submission of form data, validation is key. You have many ways to validate a form and many form elements to consider. Generally, you need to determine what qualities you want a piece of data to adhere to and then ensure that the submitted data comes in the correct form. If the data comes in a format that is not to your liking, you must be ready to take care of this. The following example shows a few examples of form validation using PHP.

The Code

```
<!DOCTYPE html PUBLIC "-//W3C//DTD XHTML 1.0 Transitional//EN"➥
 "http://www.w3.org/TR/xhtml1/DTD/xhtml1-transitional.dtd">
<html xmlns="http://www.w3.org/1999/xhtml">
<title>Sample 13.3</title>
<meta http-equiv="Content-Type" content="text/html; charset=iso-8859-1" />
</head>
<body>
  <div style="width: 500px; text-align: left;">
    <?php
      //Function to determine a valid e-mail address.
      function validemail($email){
        return preg_match("/^([a-zA-Z0-9])+([.a-zA-Z0-9_-])*@([a-zA-Z0-9_-])➥
+(.[a-zA-Z0-9_-]+)+[a-zA-Z0-9_-]$/",$email);
      }
      //Handle the incoming data.
      if ($_POST['submitted'] == "yes"){
        //Let's declare a submission value that tells you if you are fine.
        $goodtogo = true;
        //Validate the name.
        try {
          if (trim ($_POST['yourname']) == ""){
            $goodtogo = false;
            throw new exception ("Sorry, you must enter your name.<br />");
          }
        } catch (exception $e) {
          echo $e->getmessage();
        }
        //Validate the select box.
        try {
          if ($_POST['myselection'] == "nogo"){
            $goodtogo = false;
            throw new exception ("Please make a selection.<br />");
          }
        } catch (exception $e) {
          echo $e->getmessage();
        }
        //And lastly, validate for a proper e-mail addy.
        try {
          if (!validemail (trim ($_POST['youremail']))){
            $goodtogo = false;
            throw new exception ("Please enter a valid email address.<br />");
          }
        } catch (exception $e) {
          echo $e->getmessage();
        }
        //Now, if there were no errors, you can output the results.
```

```php
        if ($goodtogo){
            echo "Your Name: " . $_POST['yourname'] . "<br />";
            echo "Your Selection: " . $_POST['myselection'] . "<br />";
            echo "Your Email Address: " . $_POST['youremail'] . "<br />";
        }
        ?><br /><a href="sample13_3.php">Try Again</a><br /><?php
    }
  ?>
  <?php
    //Show the forms only if you don't already have a submittal.
    if ($_POST['submitted'] != "yes"){
      ?>
      <form action="sample13_3.php" method="post">
        <p>Example:</p>
        <input type="hidden" name="submitted" value="yes" />
        Your Name: <input type="text" name="yourname"➥
maxlength="150" /><br /><br />
        Selection:
        <select name="myselection">
          <option value="nogo">make a selection...</option>
          <option value="1">Choice 1</option>
          <option value="2">Choice 2</option>
          <option value="3">Choice 3</option>
        </select><br /><br />
        Your Email: <input type="text" name="youremail" maxlength="150" /><br />
        <input type="submit" value="Submit" style="margin-top: 10px;" />
      </form>
      <?php
    }
  ?>
  </div>
</body>
</html>
```

How It Works

Since, for this example, you have chosen three types of fields, it is important to take care of them in individual ways. For this example, you want to receive a name value that will not be blank, a selected value that must not be the default, and an e-mail address that must be in the proper format. To make sure you do not have a blank field, you can validate the name value by ensuring that it does not equal a blank string. In the case of the selection, if the user has not chosen a different value than the default, the value will be a nogo, against which you can then validate. For the last value, the e-mail address, you use a regular expression to ensure that the e-mail address is properly formatted. By using this type of validation, you ensure that all the submitted values are in the format you need. (See Nathan A. Good's Chapter 9 for more about regular expressions.)

13-4. Working with Multipage Forms

Sometimes you will need to collect values from more than one page. Most developers do this for the sake of clarity. By providing forms on more than one page, you can separate blocks of information and thus create an ergonomic experience for the user. The problem, therefore, is how to get values from each page onto the next page and finally to the processing script. Being the great developer that you are, you can solve this problem and use the hidden input form type. When each page loads, you merely load the values from the previous pages into hidden form elements and submit them.

The Code

```
<!DOCTYPE html PUBLIC "-//W3C//DTD XHTML 1.0 Transitional//EN"➥
 "http://www.w3.org/TR/xhtml1/DTD/xhtml1-transitional.dtd">
<html xmlns="http://www.w3.org/1999/xhtml">
<title>Sample 13.4 Page 1</title>
<meta http-equiv="Content-Type" content="text/html; charset=iso-8859-1" />
</head>
<body>
  <div style="width: 500px; text-align: left;">
    <form action="sample13_4_page2.php" method="post">
      <p>Page 1 Data Collection:</p>
      <input type="hidden" name="submitted" value="yes" />
      Your Name: <input type="text" name="yourname" maxlength="150" /><br /><br />
      <input type="submit" value="Submit" style="margin-top: 10px;" />
    </form>
  </div>
</body>
</html>
<!DOCTYPE html PUBLIC "-//W3C//DTD XHTML 1.0 Transitional//EN"➥
 "http://www.w3.org/TR/xhtml1/DTD/xhtml1-transitional.dtd">
<html xmlns="http://www.w3.org/1999/xhtml">
<title>Sample 13.4 Page 2</title>
<meta http-equiv="Content-Type" content="text/html; charset=iso-8859-1" />
</head>
<body>
  <div style="width: 500px; text-align: left;">
    <form action="sample13_4_page3.php" method="post">
      <p>Page 2 Data Collection:</p>
      Selection:
      <select name="yourselection">
        <option value="nogo">make a selection...</option>
        <option value="1">Choice 1</option>
        <option value="2">Choice 2</option>
        <option value="3">Choice 3</option>
      </select><br /><br />
      <input type="hidden" name="yourname" ➥
```

```
value="<?php echo $_POST['yourname']; ?>" />
      <input type="submit" value="Submit" style="margin-top: 10px;" />
    </form>
  </div>
</body>
</html>
<!DOCTYPE html PUBLIC "-//W3C//DTD XHTML 1.0 Transitional//EN"➥
 "http://www.w3.org/TR/xhtml1/DTD/xhtml1-transitional.dtd">
<html xmlns="http://www.w3.org/1999/xhtml">
<title>Sample 13.4 Page 3</title>
<meta http-equiv="Content-Type" content="text/html; charset=iso-8859-1" />
</head>
<body>
  <div style="width: 500px; text-align: left;">
    <form action="sample13_4_page4.php" method="post">
      <p>Page 3 Data Collection:</p>
      Your Email: <input type="text" name="youremail" maxlength="150" /><br />
      <input type="hidden" name="yourname"➥
 value="<?php echo $_POST['yourname']; ?>" />
      <input type="hidden" name="yourselection"➥
 value="<?php echo _POST['yourselection']; ?>" />
      <input type="submit" value="Submit" style="margin-top: 10px;" />
    </form>
  </div>
</body>
</html>
<!DOCTYPE html PUBLIC "-//W3C//DTD XHTML 1.0 Transitional//EN"➥
 "http://www.w3.org/TR/xhtml1/DTD/xhtml1-transitional.dtd">
<html xmlns="http://www.w3.org/1999/xhtml">
<title>Sample 13.4 Page 4</title>
<meta http-equiv="Content-Type" content="text/html; charset=iso-8859-1" />
</head>
<body>
  <div style="width: 500px; text-align: left;">
    <?php
      //Display the results.
      echo "Your Name: " . $_POST['yourname'] . "<br />";
      echo "Your Selection: " . $_POST['yourselection'] . "<br />";
      echo "Your Email: " . $_POST['youremail'] . "<br />";
    ?>
    <a href="sample13_4_page1.php">Try Again</a>
  </div>
</body>
</html>
```

How It Works

As you can see, by passing the values in the hidden form fields, you can continue to collect information. In a real-world example, you most certainly want to perform validation to make sure you have all the information you need at every point in the script. For this particular example, for the sake of brevity, no validation is used, but you should definitely consider including some of the lessons you learned in recipe 13-3. In any case, if you follow the flow of the script, you will see that on each subsequent page the values from the previous pages are included and hence displayed once the final display page is reached.

13-5. Redisplaying Forms with Preserved Information and Error Messages

When receiving information submitted from a user, the information may not be submitted in the format you need. To ensure that users do not get frustrated, it is important to inform them of what they did wrong and clearly tell them how to fix the problem. It is also bad practice to force users to completely rewrite all the proper information they may have already submitted on the form. If users are forced to do redundant work, they may become irritated and potentially disregard your service altogether. Therefore, to keep users happy, it is important to validate properly and clearly while keeping matters as simple for them as possible.

The Code

```
<!DOCTYPE html PUBLIC "-//W3C//DTD XHTML 1.0 Transitional//EN"➥
 "http://www.w3.org/TR/xhtml1/DTD/xhtml1-transitional.dtd">
<html xmlns="http://www.w3.org/1999/xhtml">
<title>Sample 13.5</title>
<meta http-equiv="Content-Type" content="text/html; charset=iso-8859-1" />
<style>
  .error {
    font-weight: bold;
    color: #FF0000;
  }
</style>
</head>
<body>
  <div style="width: 500px; text-align: left;">
    <?php
      //Function to determine a valid e-mail address.
      function validemail($email){
        return preg_match("/^([a-zA-Z0-9])+([.a-zA-Z0-9_-])*@([a-zA-Z0-9_-])➥
+(.[a-zA-Z0-9_-]+)+[a-zA-Z0-9_-]$/",$email);
      }
      //Default to showing the form.
      $goodtogo = false;

      //Handle the incoming data.
      if ($_POST['submitted'] == "yes"){
```

```php
        //Let's declare a submission value that tells you if you are fine.
        $goodtogo = true;
        //Validate the name.
        try {
          if (trim ($_POST['yourname']) == ""){
            $goodtogo = false;
            throw new exception ("Sorry, you must enter your name.<br />");
          }
        } catch (exception $e) {
          ?><span class="error"><?php echo $e->getmessage(); ?></span><?php
        }
        //Validate the select box.
        try {
          if ($_POST['myselection'] == "nogo"){
            $goodtogo = false;
            throw new exception ("Please make a selection.<br />");
          }
        } catch (exception $e) {
          ?><span class="error"><?php echo $e->getmessage(); ?></span><?php
        }
        //And lastly, validate for a proper e-mail addy.
        try {
          if (!validemail (trim ($_POST['youremail']))){
            $goodtogo = false;
            throw new exception ("Please enter a valid e-mail address.<br />");
          }
        } catch (exception $e) {
          ?><span class="error"><?php echo $e->getmessage(); ?></span><?php
        }
        //Now, if there were no errors, you can output the results.
        if ($goodtogo){
          echo "Your Name: " . $_POST['yourname'] . "<br />";
          echo "Your Selection: " . $_POST['myselection'] . "<br />";
          echo "Your E-mail Address: " . $_POST['youremail'] . "<br />";
          ?><br /><a href="sample13_5.php">Try Again</a><br /><?php
        }

    }

    //Show the forms only if you do not have all the valid information.
    if (!$goodtogo){
      ?>
      <form action="sample13_5.php" method="post">
        <p>Example:</p>
        <input type="hidden" name="submitted" value="yes" />
        Your Name: <input type="text" name="yourname" maxlength="150"➥
value="<?php echo $_POST['yourname']; ?>" /><br /><br />
```

```
          Selection:
          <select name="myselection">
              <option value="nogo">make a selection...</option>
              <option value="1"<?php if ($_POST['myselection'] == 1){?>➡
selected="selected"<?php } ?>>Choice 1</option>
              <option value="2"<?php if ($_POST['myselection'] == 2){?>➡
selected="selected"<?php } ?>>Choice 2</option>
              <option value="3"<?php if ($_POST['myselection'] == 3){?>➡
selected="selected"<?php } ?>>Choice 3</option>
          </select><br /><br />
          Your Email: <input type="text" name="youremail" maxlength="150"➡
value="<?php echo $_POST['youremail']; ?>" /><br />
          <input type="submit" value="Submit" style="margin-top: 10px;" />
      </form>
      <?php
    }
  ?>
  </div>
</body>
</html>
```

Figure 13-1 shows the potential output if you input a valid name field but leave the selection and e-mail address empty.

Please make a selection.
Please enter a valid e-mail address.

Example:

Your Name: Lee Babin

Selection: make a selection...

Your E-mail:

Submit

Figure 13-1. *Telling users to properly enter information*

How It Works

In this example, you have seen how you may want to handle your validation. Keep in mind that your objective is to ensure that users know what they did wrong and keep their properly submitted information for ease of use. To ensure that the user of this form sees the error messages, the Cascading Style Sheet (CSS) class called `error` will be used every time an error message is displayed. The error message will display in bold and red, thus directing the users to realize what they did wrong.

By providing the value fields, and in the case of the select box a selected argument if you have valid data, the form fields will retain any current, proper information. If there is no current, proper data to use, nothing will display. This form has now become decidedly easy to use, is quite secure, and ensures a happy, well-directed user.

Preventing Multiple Submissions of a Form

One possible occurrence that happens often is that users become impatient when waiting for your script to do what it is doing, and hence they click the submit button on a form repeatedly. This can wreak havoc on your script because, while the user may not see anything happening, your script is probably going ahead with whatever it has been programmed to do.

Of particular danger are credit card number submittals. If a user continually hits the submit button on a credit card submittal form, their card may be charged multiple times if the developer has not taken the time to validate against such an eventuality.

13-6. Preventing Multiple Submissions on the Server Side

You can deal with multiple submittal validation in essentially two ways. The first occurs on the server. *Server side* refers to a script located on the server that is receiving the data; *client side* is more browser related (and explained in the next example). Because the server has no actual access to the browser, validating multiple submissions can be a bit trickier. While you can accomplish this goal in a number of ways from a server-side perspective, we prefer to use a session-based method. Basically, once the submit button has been clicked, the server logs the request from the individual user. If the user attempts to resubmit a request, the script notes a request is already in motion from this user and denies the subsequent request. Once the script has finished processing, the session is unset, and you have no more worries.

For the following example, you will need a test.txt text file that you can create and place relative to the script. (Or you can ensure that you have write privileges on the working directory, and the script will attempt to create it for you.) Keep in mind that the file must have the proper privileges set for writing (CHMOD to 777 to keep things simple).

The Code

```
<!DOCTYPE html PUBLIC "-//W3C//DTD XHTML 1.0 Transitional//EN"
 "http://www.w3.org/TR/xhtml1/DTD/xhtml1-transitional.dtd">
<html xmlns="http://www.w3.org/1999/xhtml">
<title>Sample 13.6</title>
<meta http-equiv="Content-Type" content="text/html; charset=iso-8859-1" />
</head>
<body>
  <div style="width: 500px; text-align: left;">
    <form action="sample13_6_process.php" method="post">
      <p>Example:</p>
      <input type="hidden" name="submitted" value="yes" />
      Your Name: <input type="text" name="yourname" maxlength="150" /><br />
      <input type="submit" value="Submit" style="margin-top: 10px;" />
    </form>
  </div>
</body>
</html>
<?php
  //Start the session state.
  session_start ();
```

```php
//Set a session started value for this user.
if (!isset ($_SESSION['processing'])){
  $_SESSION['processing'] = false;
}

//Now you ensure you haven't already started processing the request.
if ($_SESSION['processing'] == false){
  //Now, you let the script know that you are processing.
  $_SESSION['processing'] = true;

  //Create a loop that shows the effect of some heavy processing.
  for ($i = 0; $i < 2000000; $i++){
    //Thinking...
  }

  //Every time you do this, write to a text file so you can test that
  //the script isn't getting hit with multiple submissions.
  if ($file = fopen ("test.txt","w+")){
    fwrite ($file, "Processing");
  } else {
    echo "Error opening file.";
  }

  //Then you start doing the calculations.
  echo $_POST['yourname'];

  //Then, once you have finished calculating, you can kill the session.
  unset ($_SESSION['processing']);
  }
}
?>
```

How It Works

Now, enter your name and continue to jam on the submit button. Rather than allow the script to continually run time and time again, the script verifies your existence via a session and determines if it is already processing your server call. If the script sees you are already processing, then it will not allow you to try again no matter how many times you click the same button. Once the script has finished performing its action, it merely unsets the session variable, and you could theoretically start again. By checking the session, the script ensures that it is the same user attempting to access the script and can therefore block multiple attempts from the same user.

13-7. Preventing Multiple Submissions on the Client Side

Handling multiple submittals from a client-side perspective is actually much simpler than doing it on the server side. With well-placed JavaScript, you can ensure that the browser will not let the submittal go through more than once. The problem with this method, of course, is that JavaScript is not always foolproof because of the user's ability to turn it off. That being said, however, most users will have JavaScript enabled, so this script will likely work for

90 percent of web users. The following example uses JavaScript to cut off multiple submittals from a client-side (browser) level.

Don't forget to ensure that you have a valid test.txt file (CHMOD to 777), as specified in the previous recipe.

The Code

```
<!DOCTYPE html PUBLIC "-//W3C//DTD XHTML 1.0 Transitional//EN"➥
 "http://www.w3.org/TR/xhtml1/DTD/xhtml1-transitional.dtd">
<html xmlns="http://www.w3.org/1999/xhtml">
<title>Sample 13.7</title>
<meta http-equiv="Content-Type" content="text/html; charset=iso-8859-1" />
<script language="javascript" type="text/javascript">
  <!--
    function checkandsubmit() {
        //Disable the submit button.
        document.test.submitbut.disabled = true;
        //Then submit the form.
        document.test.submit();
    }
  //-->
</script>
</head>
<body>
  <div style="width: 500px; text-align: left;">
    <form action="sample13_6_process.php" method="post" name="test"➥
 onsubmit="return checkandsubmit ()">
      <p>Example:</p>
      <input type="hidden" name="submitted" value="yes" />
      Your Name: <input type="text" name="yourname" maxlength="150" /><br />
      <input type="submit" value="Submit" style="margin-top: 10px;"➥
 id="submitbut" name"submitbut" />
    </form>
  </div>
</body>
</html>
<?php

  //Create a loop that shows the effect of some heavy processing.
  for ($i = 0; $i < 2000000; $i++){
    //Thinking...
  }

  //Every time you do this, let's write to a text file so you can test that
  //out script isn't getting hit with multiple submissions.
  if ($file = fopen ("test.txt","w+")){
    fwrite ($file, "Processing");
  } else {
```

```
    echo "Error opening file.";
  }

  //Then you start doing the calculations.
  echo $_POST['yourname'];

?>
```

How It Works

We realize that this particular piece of functionality is based on JavaScript and this is a book about PHP, but PHP is a server-side language. Therefore, to do a little client-side validation, you must use a language that can interact with the browser, such as JavaScript. In any case, the way this script works is by actually disabling the submit button once the form has been submitted. The button is clicked, which forces the browser to redirect first to the JavaScript function checkandsubmit(), which immediately disables the submit button and then submits the form for you. At this point, it does not matter how long the script takes to finish executing; the submit button is disabled and hence cannot be clicked again until the page is revisited.

13-8. Performing File Uploads

Handling file uploads in PHP is not exactly difficult from a syntax point of view, but it is important (extremely important in fact) to ensure that the file being uploaded is within the upload constraints you lay out for it. In other words, an individual user could easily upload a virus or some other form of malicious software if you are not careful about allowing them to upload only what you want from them. A similar consideration is file size. You could easily find your server under some heavy loads if you are not careful about what size of files are being uploaded. The following example allows you to upload an image (of the file type JPG only) that is smaller than 500KB in size.

Keep in mind that in order for this script to work, you must have a directory created (relative to the script) that is called uploads and is writable (again, using a CHMOD of 777 is the simplest way of accomplishing this).

The Code

```
<!DOCTYPE html PUBLIC "-//W3C//DTD XHTML 1.0 Transitional//EN"➥
 "http://www.w3.org/TR/xhtml1/DTD/xhtml1-transitional.dtd">
<html xmlns="http://www.w3.org/1999/xhtml">
<title>Sample 13.8</title>
<meta http-equiv="Content-Type" content="text/html; charset=iso-8859-1" />
</head>
<body>
  <div style="width: 500px; text-align: left;">
  <?php
    //If you have received a submission.
    if ($_POST['submitted'] == "yes"){
      $goodtogo = true;
      //Check for a blank submission.
```

```php
      try {
        if ($_FILES['image']['size'] == 0){
          $goodtogo = false;
          throw new exception ("Sorry, you must upload an image.");
        }
      } catch (exception $e) {
        echo $e->getmessage();
      }
      //Check for the file size.
      try {
        if ($_FILES['image']['size'] > 500000){
          $goodtogo = false;
          //Echo an error message.
          throw new exception ("Sorry, the file is too big at approx: "➥
. intval ($_FILES['image']['size'] / 1000) . "KB");
        }
      } catch (exception $e) {
        echo $e->getmessage();
      }
      //Ensure that you have a valid mime type.
      $allowedmimes = array ("image/jpeg","image/pjpeg");
      try {
        if (!in_array ($_FILES['image']['type'],$allowedmimes)){
          $goodtogo = false;
          throw new exception ("Sorry, the file must be of type .jpg.➥
  Yours is: " . $_FILES['image']['type'] . "");
        }
      } catch (exception $e) {
        echo $e->getmessage ();
      }
      //If you have a valid submission, move it, then show it.
      if ($goodtogo){
        try {
          if (!move_uploaded_file ($_FILES['image']['tmp_name'],"uploads/".➥
$_FILES['image']['name'].".jpg")){
            $goodtogo = false;
            throw new exception ("There was an error moving the file.");
          }
        } catch (exception $e) {
          echo $e->getmessage ();
        }
      }
      if ($goodtogo){
        //Display the new image.
        ?><img src="uploads/<?php echo $_FILES['image']['name'] . ".jpg"; ?>"➥
  alt="" title="" /><?php
      }
```

```
        ?><br /><a href="sample13_8.php">Try Again</a><?php
        }
        //Only show the form if there is no submission.
        if ($_POST['submitted'] != "yes"){
        ?>
        <form action="sample13_8.php" method="post" enctype="multipart/form-data">
            <p>Example:</p>
            <input type="hidden" name="submitted" value="yes" />
            Image Upload (.jpg only, 500KB Max):<br />➥
    <input type="file" name="image" /><br />
            <input type="submit" value="Submit" style="margin-top: 10px />
        </form>
        <?php
        }
        ?>
    </div>
</body>
</html>
```

A sample execution of this script could lead to a certain someone appearing on your monitor (see Figure 13-2).

Try Again

Figure 13-2. *Beware of Darth Vader.*

How It Works

The first aspect of this script you need to know about is that PHP 5 handles file uploads through the superglobal $_FILES. By accessing certain elements of this superglobal, you can find out certain information about the file upload. Table 13-2 lists data you can retrieve from the $_FILES superglobal. The next important aspect to uploading files takes place in the form element itself. If you plan to pass along a file, you must include the code enctype="multipart/form-data", or else the script will appear to function successfully without ever actually passing along a file.

Table 13-2. $\_$FILES *Arguments*

Argument	Description
name	The original filename that was uploaded
type	The MIME type of the uploaded file
size	The size of the uploaded file (in bytes)
tmp_name	The temporary name of the file that has been uploaded
error	The error code that may be generated by the file upload

From this point on, the rest is merely a matter of validation. By comparing the file type against an array of allowed MIME types, you can completely shut out malicious file uploads (because the MIME type will return the absolute type of the file). Size validation is handled in bytes, so if you plan on limiting it according to megabytes or kilobytes, you must do a few calculations (such as bytes multiplied by 1,000 in this case to return a kilobyte result).

As for moving the actual file and saving it, you can use two methods for performing this action. The two functions in PHP that will allow you to save a file are the copy() and move_uploaded_file() functions. We prefer to use the move_uploaded_file() function, as it will work even when PHP's safe mode is enabled. If PHP has its safe mode enabled, the copy() function will fail. They both work largely the same, so there is no real downside to using the move_uploaded_file() function over the copy() function.

13-9. Handling Special Characters

An added security feature, particularly when dealing with database submittal, is validating against special characters being inserted into your script. Be it a database insertion script, a contact form, or even a mailer system, you always want to ensure that no malicious users are attempting to sabotage your script with bad (or special) characters. PHP allots a number of functions to use in this regard. In the following example, you will look at the functions trim(), htmlspecialchars(), strip_tags(), and addslashes(). Their prototypes are as follows:

```
string trim ( string str [, string charlist] )
string htmlspecialchars ( string string [, int quote_style [, string charset]] )
string strip_tags ( string str [, string allowable_tags] )
string addslashes ( string str )
```

The Code

```
<!DOCTYPE html PUBLIC "-//W3C//DTD XHTML 1.0 Transitional//EN"➥
 "http://www.w3.org/TR/xhtml1/DTD/xhtml1-transitional.dtd">
<html xmlns="http://www.w3.org/1999/xhtml">
<title>Sample 13.9</title>
<meta http-equiv="Content-Type" content="text/html; charset=iso-8859-1" />
</head>
<body>
  <div style="width: 500px; text-align: left;">
    <?php
      //If you have received a submission.
```

```
        if ($_POST['submitted'] == "yes"){
            $yourname = $_POST['yourname'];
            //You can trim off blank spaces with trim.
            $yourname = trim ($yourname);
            //You can cut off code insertion with strip_tags.
            $yourname = strip_tags ($yourname);
            //You can turn any special characters into safe➥
    representations with htmlspecialchars.
            $yourname = htmlspecialchars ($yourname);
            //And you can prepare data for db insertion with addslashes.
            $yourname = addslashes ($yourname);

            //And echo the result.
            echo $yourname . "<br />";
            ?><a href="sample13_9.php">Try Again</a><?php
        }
        //Show the form only if there is no submission.
        if ($_POST['submitted'] != "yes"){
            ?>
            <form action="sample13_9.php" method="post">
              <p>Example:</p>
              <input type="hidden" name="submitted" value="yes" />
              Your Name: <input type="text" name="yourname" maxlength="150" /><br />
              <input type="submit" value="Submit" style="margin-top: 10px;" />
            </form>
            <?php
        }
    ?>
  </div>
</body>
</html>
```

How It Works

The four functions you have put into play perform different actions on a submitted variable. The `trim()` function removes any blank space found at the beginning or end of the submitted string. The `htmlspecialchars()` function turns attempted HTML into its special character equivalent. For instance, if you enter an ampersand (&) symbol, the system will change that symbol into a harmless &. The `strip_tags()` function completely removes any characters it sees as being a tag. You can delimit to the function which tags you want stripped as well. The last function, `addslashes()`, places a slash in front of any characters that could be harmful to the database such as apostrophes. The end result is a string that is quite squeaky clean, and you can feel safe performing functionality on it.

13-10. Creating Form Elements with Multiple Options

From time to time, it will occur to you as a developer that you may need to retrieve several values from the same select box. Luckily, HTML and PHP 5 have made an allowance for such a feature. Commonly referred to as a *list box*, the functionality involved allows you to select a multitude of items (by holding down the Control key) and then submit them as one. The following example allows you to select a number of items and then display only the selected items in the script.

The Code

```
<!DOCTYPE html PUBLIC "-//W3C//DTD XHTML 1.0 Transitional//EN"➥
 "http://www.w3.org/TR/xhtml1/DTD/xhtml1-transitional.dtd">
<html xmlns="http://www.w3.org/1999/xhtml">
<title>Sample 13.10</title>
<meta http-equiv="Content-Type" content="text/html; charset=iso-8859-1" />
</head>
<body>
  <div style="width: 500px; text-align: left;">
    <?php
      //If you have received a submission.
      if ($_POST['submitted'] == "yes"){
        //Check if any have been selected.
        if (count ($_POST['fruit']) != 0){
          echo "Your Selections:<br />";
        } else {
          echo "You have not made any selections.<br /><br />";
        }
        //You can actually treat the submittal as an array.
        for ($i = 0; $i < count ($_POST['fruit']); $i++){
          echo $_POST['fruit'][$i] . "<br />";
        }
        ?><a href="sample13_10.php">Try Again</a><?php
      }
      //Show the form only if there is no submission.
      if ($_POST['submitted'] != "yes"){
        ?>
        <form action="sample13_10.php" method="post">
          <p>Example:</p>
          <input type="hidden" name="submitted" value="yes" />
          Your Choice (s): <br />
          <select name="fruit[]" multiple="multiple" style="width: 400px;➥
 height: 100px;">
            <option value="Bananas">Bananas</option>
            <option value="Apples">Apples</option>
            <option value="Oranges">Oranges</option>
            <option value="Pears">Pears</option>
            <option value="Grapes">Grapes</option>
            <option value="Kiwi">Kiwi</option>
          </select><br />
          <input type="submit" value="Submit" style="margin-top: 10px;" />
        </form>
```

```
        <?php
    }
  ?>
  </div>
</body>
</html>
```

How It Works

You should note a few key features when examining this code. In the form element itself, you
will witness a few new attributes to the select tag. You can designate the element as a list box
by adding the attribute multiple="multiple", and you designate the field as something that
can be read as an array by adding the [] to the end of the element name. Once PHP gets a hold
of the posted value, it treats the value as an array. By walking through the array one element at
a time using a for loop, you can output the selections by merely outputting the value of the
array. If a particular option was not selected, it simply will not show up in the array.

13-11. Creating Form Elements Based on the Current Time and/or Date

Occasionally, it makes sense to create a form-based element that will react according to the
current date and/or time on the server. Doing so speeds up form entry for the user and can
make things slightly more ergonomic. To create this sort of functionality, you merely embed
some PHP into the HTML to create a dynamic element set. Those of you who have studied
Jon Stephens's Chapter 5 will find this section of code to be no trouble at all. The following
example allows you to select a value with the form elements being preset to the current
date and time.

The Code

```
<!DOCTYPE html PUBLIC "-//W3C//DTD XHTML 1.0 Transitional//EN"➥
 "http://www.w3.org/TR/xhtml1/DTD/xhtml1-transitional.dtd">
<html xmlns="http://www.w3.org/1999/xhtml">
<title>Sample 13.11</title>
<meta http-equiv="Content-Type" content="text/html; charset=iso-8859-1" />
</head>
<body>
  <div style="width: 500px; text-align: left;">
    <?php
      //If you have received a submission.
      if ($_POST['submitted'] == "yes"){
        echo $_POST['month'] . "/" . $_POST['day'] . "/" . $_POST['year']➥
. " - " . $_POST['hour'] . ":" . $_POST['minute']➥
. ":" . $_POST['second'];
        ?><br /><a href="sample13_11.php">Try Again</a><?php
      }
      //Only show the form if there is no submission.
      if ($_POST['submitted'] != "yes"){
```

```
      ?>
      <form action="sample13_11.php" method="post">
        <p>Example:</p>
        <input type="hidden" name="submitted" value="yes" />
        Select a Date and Time: <br />
        <select name="month">
        <?php
        for ($i = 1; $i <= 12; $i++){
          ?><option value="<?php echo $i; ?>"<?php if ($i == date ("n")){?>➥
selected="selected"<?php } ?>><?php echo $i; ?></option><?php
        }
        ?>
      </select> /
      <select name="day">
        <?php
        for ($i = 1; $i <= 31; $i++){
          ?><option value="<?php echo $i; ?>"<?php if ($i == date ("j")){?>➥
selected="selected"<?php } ?>><?php echo $i; ?></option><?php
        }
        ?>
      </select> /
      <select name="year">
        <?php
        for ($i = 1950; $i <= date ("Y"); $i++){
          ?><option value="<?php echo $i; ?>"<?php if ($i == date ("Y")){?>➥
selected="selected"<?php } ?>><?php echo $i; ?></option><?php
        }
        ?>
      </select> -
      <select name="hour">
        <?php
        for ($i = 1; $i <= 24; $i++){
          ?><option value="<?php echo $i; ?>"<?php if ($i == date ("G")){?>➥
selected="selected"<?php } ?>><?php echo $i; ?></option><?php
        }
        ?>
      </select> :
      <select name="minute">
        <?php
        for ($i = 1; $i <= 60; $i++){
          //Deal with leading zeros.
          if ($i < 10){
            $comparem = "0" . $i;
          } else {
            $comparem = $i;
          }
          ?><option value="<?php echo $i; ?>"➥
```

```
        <?php if ($comparem == date ("i")){?> selected="selected"<?php } ?>>➡
        <?php echo $i; ?></option><?php
                }
                ?>
            </select> :
            <select name="second">
                <?php
                for ($i = 1; $i <= 60; $i++){
                    //Deal with leading zeros.
                    if ($i < 10){
                        $compares = "0" . $i;
                    } else {
                        $compares = $i;
                    }
                    ?><option value="<?php echo $i; ?>"➡
        <?php if ($compares == date ("s")){?> selected="selected"<?php } ?>>➡
        <?php echo $i; ?></option><?php
                }
                ?>
            </select>
            <br /><input type="submit" value="Submit" style="margin-top: 10px;" />
        </form>
        <?php
    }
    ?>
    </div>
</body>
</html>
```

How It Works

The way this script works is by providing the selected="selected" value in the case where the current date element equals its counterpart in the select box. By being marked as selected when the proper element approaches, the form provides the ability to select the current date and time with the greatest of ease. Of course, should users want to select a different date and/or time, that is entirely up to them. This is merely meant to act as a time-saver to improve the ergonomics of the web application.

Summary

Like it or not, dealing with forms will become a common occurrence with pretty much any script you happen to be building. The opportunity to collect information from a user is limited almost entirely to form collection and is the standard for such functionality.

With this in mind, it is important to create forms based on a number of elements. While any developer can create a form to collect information, the way to single yourself out as a competent developer is to consider factors such as security, ergonomics, validation, and ease of use.

A form should collect the information required and do it in such a way that the user feels as though the form flows quite easily and effectively. You should perform error handling at all times, and errors should die gracefully with helpful error messages and an intuitive return to the form with the information that was originally submitted.

Choosing the correct form element for the job is a task you should not take lightly, and each form should be designed from the ground up with ease of use in mind. Ask yourself the question, what would be the most effective? Also, what would be the easiest means of collecting a certain amount of information?

With a properly thought-out plan of attack, you can create forms that will do more than just serve their purpose; they will function almost as a wizard does, with the user constantly able to understand what is happening and not being allowed to perform any functionality they should not have access to do.

Looking Ahead

In the next chapter, Frank M. Kromann will guide you through the fairly modern concepts of markup and Extensible Markup Language (XML). The industry is leaning more and more toward XML as a portable and extremely valuable form of both data collection and data porting, and Chapter 14 will showcase some of PHP 5's robust handling of XML.

CHAPTER 14

■ ■ ■

Working with Markup

PHP was originally designed as a way to use a special Hypertext Markup Language (HTML) tag to access custom-made business logic written in C. This system has since evolved to a full programming language that allows an HTML developer to add and parse code or a programmer to create advanced scripts that generate HTML documents, images, or other forms of documents. The processing of the special PHP tag takes place on the server side, before the final document is transferred to the browser or client. This is why the language used to be called PHP Hypertext Preprocessor.

When you request that a web server serve a document, the document is usually read from a disk or other storage device and transferred directly to the client. You can instruct the web server to preprocess the document before sending it to the client. This is how PHP documents or scripts are handled. It is not the document but the output from the preprocessor that is sent to the client when a browser requests a PHP script. The script can define the document type—or, as it is called in the web world, the *content type*—before any content is sent to the client. This makes it possible for a PHP script to return a simple text file, an HTML document, or even binary images files generated on the fly.

14-1. Understanding Markup Concepts

You can pass any text document to the PHP engine for parsing, and the engine will scan the document and divide it into sections. The content that falls between the special PHP tags `<?php` and `?>` will be treated as script code and executed by the engine. Everything else will be transferred directly to the client without any parsing or changes. A PHP document can be one big script starting and ending with the PHP tags, or it can be an HTML document with one or more embedded PHP tags. In fact, it could be any document type with embedded PHP tags, but the engine sets the document type to text/html by default in the Hypertext Transfer Protocol (HTTP) header. You can change this by using the `default_mimetype` parameter in `php.ini` or by setting a new content type with the `header()` function before sending any other output. The following code shows how to use PHP to generate a standard text file where part of the file is untouched by the engine and other parts of the document are parsed by the engine.

The Code

```php
<?php
// Example 14-1-1.php
header("Content-Type: text/plain");
?>
Hello and welcome to the random number generator!

Your random number is: <?php echo mt_rand(0,100); ?>

This is all for today
```

How It Works

When the document (in this case 14-1-1.php) is requested from a browser, the web server will pass it through PHP. The engine will see two PHP tags. The first one contains a comment and a call to the header function. This sets a new content type for the output. The second PHP tag contains script code to generate a random number from 0 to 100 and to print that value as part of the document. All the text outside the two tags will be returned to the browser without any changes. The result looks like this:

```
Hello and welcome to the random number generator!

Your random number is: 67
This is all for today
```

Plain text is just one of many content types that can tell the client how to handle the content. The client is most often a web browser that was designed to read and render HTML content, so the default setting of text/html is a good choice. But web servers are used more and more to serve other types of content as well. A good example of this is news feeds in the form of an RDF Site Summary/Rich Site Summary (RSS) file or an Extensible Markup Language (XML) file. An RSS file is an XML file with a specific set of tags. This RSS file can be a static file stored on a hard drive, or it can be a PHP document where the content is generated from database lookups when the document is requested. Some browsers support the rendering of RSS files, but dedicated feed readers are also available; you can configure these readers to scan a list of RSS feeds from different servers and display a headline and short abstract for each news article. The PHP website provides a number of RSS feeds; one of them is http://www.php.net/news.rss. In recipe 14-7, you will take a closer look at RSS feeds and see how they work.

14-2. Manually Generating Markup

You can manually generate output from PHP with print or echo statements in the code. PHP also provides several functions that offer helpful output for more complex data types, but echo or print are the most common output functions when it comes to manually generating content. You can generate almost any content type, but this opens the possibility for generating documents with errors. A missing closing tag will cause an error in an XML document but might not do that in HTML.

The next example shows how a result set from a database query can generate a simple XML document. The example uses a FrontBase database, but you can easily change this to Microsoft SQL Server, MySQL, or any other PHP-supported database.

The Code

```php
<?php
// Example 14-1-2.php
header("Content-Type: text/xml");

echo "<?xml version=\"1.0\" encoding=\"iso-8859-1\" ?>\n";
echo "<inventory>\n";
$con = fbsql_connect("localhost", "user", "password");
if ($con) {
  fbsql_select_db("database", $con);
  $rs = fbsql_query("select * from products;", $con);
  if ($rs) {
    while($row = fbsql_fetch_assoc($rs)) {
      echo "<product id=\"$row[id]\">\n" .
          "<name>$row[name]</name>\n" .
          "</product>\n";
    }
    fbsql_free_result($rs);
  }
  fbsql_close($con);
}
echo "</inventory>";
?>
```

How It Works

This script starts by setting the content type to text/xml, and then it outputs the XML definition tag, where the XML version and encoding is specified. Then it prints the first half of the outermost tag of the XML document. The other half, or the closing tag, is printed as the last statement of the script. The code included in the inventory tags is where the work takes place. A connection is created to the database, and a query that selects all columns and all rows from the product table is executed. For each of the returned rows, it prints a product tag that has one attribute and includes one child element with the product name.

Note how attributes are enclosed in double quotes. Unlike HTML or JavaScript documents that allow a mix of single and double quotes, XML documents are stricter and require double quotes. XML is in fact bound by much stricter rules in many areas than you may be used to when working with HTML documents. Depending on the browser, it is possible to forget a </tr> tag before the next <tr> tag without any visible effect on the result. The browser's rendering function will render the document anyway. With XML, it is required that tags come in pairs, so <inventory> must have a corresponding </inventory> tag for the document to be valid. The only exception to this is for a tag that is empty and does not contain any children. You can write such a tag as <tag id="test" />. The slash before the end of the tag indicates that this is a stand-alone tag. You can get the same effect by using <tag id="test"></tag>, but obviously the first version is shorter.

When it comes to special characters such as & and national characters such as æøå, you might usually use these directly in an HTML document, but that will not work in XML documents. You must represent these special characters with HTML entities (&, æ, ø, and å). As you will see in the next recipe, certain sophisticated tools will handle this for you when generating XML documents.

14-3. Using DOM to Generate Markup

Manually generating markup will in most cases require that the document be generated from the top down. And it is up to the developer to make sure all tags are complete with matching opening and closing tags. You can optimize this with the help of a few PHP functions or classes, but PHP comes with a set of built-in objects and functions. The Document Object Model (DOM) provides a treelike structure that makes it easy to create and handle markup. PHP has two implementations of DOM: DOM and DOMXML.

The DOMXML extension was moved to the PHP Extension and Application Repository (PECL) repository and will no longer be bundled with PHP as of PHP 5.0.0.

The DOM extension is bundled and enabled by default (no need for recompilations to use it) on both Unix and Windows platforms from PHP 5.0.0. It is a replacement for the DOMXML extension from PHP 4, and it follows the DOM Level 2 standard.

You can handle DOM documents by creating an instance of the DomDocument() class. This class provides methods to create and add elements to the object tree. The DomDocument() constructor takes two parameters; the first is a string indicating the DOM version to be used, and the second is an optional encoding parameter. These values create the content of the <?xml ?> tag located as the first tag in an XML document.

The DOM extension makes it possible to create both HTML and XML documents from the same object tree by calling saveHTML() or saveXML() on the DomDocument()object. The next example shows how to create a simple HTML document with the DOM extension.

The Code

```php
<?php
// Example 14-3-1.php
$root = new DomDocument('1.0', 'iso-8859-1');
$html = $root->createElement("html");

$body = $root->createElement("body");
$table = $root->createElement("table");
$row = $root->createElement("tr");

$cell = $root->createElement("td", "value1");
$row->appendChild($cell);
$cell = $root->createElement("td", "value2");
$row->appendChild($cell);
```

```
$table->appendChild($row);
$body->appendChild($table);
$html->appendChild($body);

$root->appendChild($html);

echo $root->saveHTML();
?>
```

How It Works

The first step is to create an instance of DomDocument(). This then creates instances of the DomElement() class for each tag you want in the file.

This example uses two methods to create and add elements to the object tree. The createElement() method can be called with one or two string parameters. The first parameter specifies the node or element name, and the second parameter specifies an optional value. If a value is passed, it will be added between the opening and closing tags for that element. In the previous example, you created the html, body, table, and tr elements without any values. These elements will only contain other elements. The two td elements were created with a value, and the value will end up as the data in the table cells in the resulting HTML document.

The other method, appendChild(), places the elements in the object tree, and as shown in the example, you can use this method both on the root element and on any of the child elements in the tree.

The output from this code will be sent to the client in the form of a valid HTML document. The default content type for output generated with PHP is text/html, so you do not have to send an explicit header.

```
<html><body><table><tr>
<td>value1</td>
<td>value2</td>
</tr></table></body></html>
```

The object tree is maintained in memory, so it is possible to add elements to a node even after it has been added to the tree. So, if you want to add another row to the table in the previous example, you can do so at any time before the output is generated, as shown next.

The Code

```php
<?php
// Example 14-3-2.php
$root = new DomDocument('1.0', 'iso-8859-1');
$html = $root->createElement("html");

$body = $root->createElement("body");
$table = $root->createElement("table");
$row = $root->createElement("tr");
```

```
$cell = $root->createElement("td", "value1");
$row->appendChild($cell);
$cell = $root->createElement("td", "value2");
$row->appendChild($cell);

$table->appendChild($row);
$body->appendChild($table);
$html->appendChild($body);

$root->appendChild($html);

$row = $root->createElement("tr");
$cell = $root->createElement("td", "value3");
$row->appendChild($cell);
$cell = $root->createElement("td", "value4");
$row->appendChild($cell);
$table->appendChild($row);

echo $root->saveHTML();
?>
```

How It Works

This is basically the same code as used in the previous example, but it shows how you can add elements to other elements deep in the tree, even after these have been added to the tree. This will generate the following output:

```
<html><body><table>
<tr>
<td>value1</td>
<td>value2</td>
</tr>
<tr>
<td>value3</td>
<td>value4</td>
</tr>
</table></body></html>
```

When an element has been created with or without the optional value, it is possible to add text or character data to the element. You can do this with createTextNode() or createCDATASection(). Both methods are available on the DomDocument() object, and they both return an object that must be appended to the object tree with the appendChild() method. The next example shows how you can use the createTextNode() method to add multiple text strings to a body element in an HTML document.

The Code

```php
<?php
// Example 14-3-3.php
$root = new DomDocument('1.0', 'iso-8859-1');
$html = $root->createElement("html");
$body = $root->createElement("body");

$txt = $root->createTextNode(
  utf8_encode("This is a text with Danish characters æøå\n")
);
$body->appendChild($txt);
$txt = $root->createTextNode(
  utf8_encode("& we could continue to add text to this document")
);
$body->appendChild($txt);

$html->appendChild($body);
$root->appendChild($html);

echo $root->saveHTML();
?>
```

How It Works

This example will create a document with two elements (html and body). Inside the inner body tag, you will add two text nodes. Using the utf8_encode() function will ensure that all special characters are converted correctly.

```
<html><body>This is a text with Danish characters &aelig;&oslash;&aring;
&amp; we could continue to add text to this document</body></html>
```

Using CDATA sections, or *character data* sections, is important when handling XML documents. The CDATA sections allow the document to contain sections with special characters and linefeeds. You can use the CDATA sections to include JavaScript code in an XML document, as shown in the next example.

The Code

```php
<?php
// Example 14-3-4.php
$root = new DomDocument('1.0', 'iso-8859-1');
$html = $root->createElement("html");
$body = $root->createElement("body");
$script = $root->createElement("script");
```

```
$txt = $root->createCDATASection(
"function SubmitForm() {
  if (document.myform.name.value == '') {
    alert('Name cannot be empty');
    document.myform.name.focus();
  }
}"
);
$script->appendChild($txt);

$body->appendChild($script);
$html->appendChild($body);
$root->appendChild($html);

header("Content-Type: text/xml");
echo $root->saveXML();
?>
```

How It Works

You can use the `createCDATASection()` method like the other create methods to create the node that is later appended to the object tree with the `appendChild()` method. This example also uses the `header()` function to overwrite the default content type, and it uses the `saveXML()` method to create an XML document.

```
<?xml version="1.0" encoding="iso-8859-1"?>
<html><body><script><![CDATA[function SubmitForm() {
  if (document.myform.name.value == '') {
    alert('Name cannot be empty');
    document.myform.name.focus();
  }
}]]></script></body></html>
```

14-4. Creating and Setting Attributes

So far you have seen documents where all the elements are as simple as a tag name. In many cases, documents require that the elements or tags have attributes that specify additional information for each tag. An example is the `table` element in the HTML documents you have created. The `table` element can include attributes such as `width`, `height`, and `border` as well as several others. The `createElement()` method does not provide a way to add these attributes or attribute values, but the `DomDocument()` object has a method that handles this. The `createAttribute()` method creates the attribute by giving it a name. Each attribute can then be appended to the element with the `appendChild()` method. When attributes are appended to the element, they do not have a value assigned to them. The values are assigned with the `setAttribute()` method. This method must be applied to the element where the attribute is defined, and it takes two string parameters. The first parameter is the name of the attribute, and the second parameter is the value. If the attribute name does not exist on the element where setAttribute is called, the attribute will be created.

You can now extend the HTML example from earlier (example 14-3-1.php) to include the creation of attributes on the table element.

The Code

```php
<?php
// Example 14-4-1.php
$root = new DomDocument('1.0', 'iso-8859-1');
$html = $root->createElement("html");

$body = $root->createElement("body");
$table = $root->createElement("table");

$w = $root->createAttribute("width");
$table->appendChild($w);
$h = $root->createAttribute("height");
$table->appendChild($h);
$b = $root->createAttribute("border");
$table->appendChild($b);
$table->setAttribute("width", "100%");
$table->setAttribute("height", "50%");
$table->setAttribute("border", "1");

$row = $root->createElement("tr");

$cell = $root->createElement("td", "value1");
$row->appendChild($cell);
$cell = $root->createElement("td", "value2");
$row->appendChild($cell);

$table->appendChild($row);
$body->appendChild($table);
$html->appendChild($body);

$root->appendChild($html);

echo $root->saveHTML();
?>
```

How It Works

In this example, you create and append the tree attributes to the `table` element and assign them some values. The output will then look like this:

```
<html><body><table width="100%" height="50%" border="1"><tr>
<td>value1</td>
<td>value2</td>
</tr></table></body></html>
```

Because attributes are automatically created, you can reduce this example a bit without impacting the result. The next example shows how to remove the creation and appending of attributes and simply assign the needed attributes to the elements where you need them.

The Code

```php
<?php
// Example 14-4-2.php
$root = new DomDocument('1.0', 'iso-8859-1');
$html = $root->createElement("html");

$body = $root->createElement("body");
$table = $root->createElement("table");

$table->setAttribute("width", "100%");
$table->setAttribute("height", "50%");
$table->setAttribute("border", "1");

$row = $root->createElement("tr");

$cell = $root->createElement("td", "value1");
$row->appendChild($cell);
$cell = $root->createElement("td", "value2");
$row->appendChild($cell);

$table->appendChild($row);
$body->appendChild($table);
$html->appendChild($body);

$root->appendChild($html);

echo $root->saveHTML();
?>
```

The `DomElement` object also includes methods to check for the existence of an attribute, remove an attribute, and get the value of an attribute. The methods are called `hasAttribute()`, `removeAttribute()`, and `getAttribute()`. These functions all take the attribute name as the only parameter.

14-5. Parsing XML

So far we have been discussing generating HTML and XML documents, but you can also use the DOM extension to load and parse both HTML and XML documents. Unlike XML documents, HTML documents do not have to be well formatted (browsers can render HTML documents with missing end tags), so it is likely to see errors or warnings when these documents are loaded. The DomDocument() class includes methods to parse string values as HTML or XML and methods to load the content directly from a file or as a stream. The next example does not make much sense, but it demonstrates how to read the HTML content directly from a Uniform Resource Locator (URL). The resulting HTML document is then echoed directly to the client. The loadHTMLFile() method is called statically, and this will create the DomDocument() object automatically. You can also create the DomDocument() object first and then have the loadHTMLFile() applied to it, with the same result.

The Code

```php
<?php
// Example 14-5-1.php
$doc = DOMDocument::loadHTMLFile("http://php.net");
echo $doc->saveHTML();
?>
```

How It Works

This example will load the content of the default HTML document from http://php.net into a DomDocument() object, and it will create the object tree for all elements and child elements for the entire document. The entire document is the echoed back to the browser without any changes. The result from this script is too long to show here, but it might include lines like these:

```
Warning: DOMDocument::loadHTMLFile(): htmlParseEntityRef: no name in
http://php.net, line: 119 in Samples/14.10.php on line 2
```

This indicates that the content includes & or other undefined entities. To be well formatted, & should be replaced with &.

Parsing documents with the DOM extension is more useful if the document is an XML document; as an example, you can use http://slashdot.org/slashdot.xml. This is a document that provides a list of the current stories on Slashdot. The file is structured with a root element called backslash and a number of story elements, each containing title, url, time, author, and other elements. The basic structure of this file is as follows with a single story entry. The complete file contains multiple story sections.

```xml
<?xml version="1.0"?><backslash
xmlns:backslash="http://slashdot.org/backslash.dtd">

  <story>
    <title>Dell Axim X50 Running Linux</title>
    <url>http://slashdot.org/article.pl?sid=05/06/15/022211</url>
    <time>2005-06-15 04:10:00</time>
```

```
    <author>timothy</author>
    <department>tempty-tempty</department>
    <topic>100</topic>
    <comments>0</comments>
    <section>hardware</section>
    <image>topichandhelds.gif</image>
  </story>
...
</backslash>
```

The following code shows a simple script that loads the content of this file into a DOM object tree.

The Code

```php
<?php
// Example 14-5-2.php
$slashdot = DOMDocument::load("http://slashdot.org/slashdot.xml");
```

■Caution Many sites that provide XML feeds require that you fetch an updated version only at certain intervals. Please respect this, and store a local copy of the file on your own system until it is time to request a new file from the server. For Slashdot, the minimum time between requests is 30 minutes. If the previous code is excecuted too often, it will return errors, as the document read from the server will no longer be a valid XML document.

The next example handles the local caching of the document and uses that as long as the local version is valid.

The Code

```php
<?php
// Example 14-5-3.php
$local_file = "slashdot.xml";
$ttl = 30 * 60;      // Cache in 30 min.
if (file_exists($local_file) && filemtime($local_file) > time() - $ttl) {
  echo "Loading from cache\n";
  $slashdot = DOMDocument::load($local_file);
}
else {
  echo "Loading from server\n";
  $slashdot = DOMDocument::load("http://slashdot.org/slashdot.xml");
  $fp = fopen($local_file, "wt");
  if ($fp) {
    fwrite($fp, $slashdot->saveXML());
    fclose($fp);
```

```
    }
  }
?>
```

How It Works

First you define variables for the local document name and the time to live in the cache. Then you check whether the local document exists and whether it is valid. If that is the case, you load the document from the local file. If the document is invalid, you load a new copy from the original website and store that copy on the disk.

```
Loading from server
```

Any other execution of the code will produce output like this:

```
Loading from cache
```

When the document is loaded into the object tree, you can get the different elements by using either getElementsByTagName() or getElementsById(). The first function looks for all the elements in the document where the tag name is equal to the parameter. The second function uses the special attribute called id to build a list of elements.

So, if you want to use this document to create a new HTML document that contains a list of all the titles with links to the full stories, you could get the individual stories by starting from the top. You can extract all the story elements with a single call to the getElementsByTagName() method. This will return a list of nodes that can be examined one at the time in a foreach() loop, as shown next.

The Code

```php
<?php
// Example 14-5-4.php
$slashdot = DOMDocument::load("http://slashdot.org/slashdot.xml");
$stories = $slashdot->getElementsByTagName("story");
foreach($stories as $story) {
  $titles = $story->getElementsByTagName("title");
  foreach($titles as $title) {
    echo $title->nodeValue . " - ";
  }
  $urls = $story->getElementsByTagName("url");
  foreach($urls as $url) {
    echo $url->nodeValue . "\n";
  }
}
?>
```

How It Works

This example uses the special property on the DomElement object, called nodeValue, to extract the actual value for the title and url elements. The getElementsByTagName() method exists on the DomDocument() object as well as the DomElement object. This allows you to scan for the title and URL for a selected element only.

The output from this example will look like this:

```
FDA OKs Brain Pacemaker for Depression -
            http://slashdot.org/article.pl?sid=05/07/21/1657242
Do Not Call List Under Attack - http://slashdot.org/article.pl?sid=05/07/21/1439206
Firefox 1.1 Scrapped - http://slashdot.org/article.pl?sid=05/07/21/142215
World of Warcraft For The Win - http://slashdot.org/article.pl?sid=05/07/21/1341215
Space Shuttle Discovery to Launch July 26
            http://slashdot.org/article.pl?sid=05/07/21/1220218
Microsoft Continues Anti-OSS Strategy -
            http://slashdot.org/article.pl?sid=05/07/21/1218247
Security Hackers Interviewed - http://slashdot.org/article.pl?sid=05/07/21/1215217
Pay-Per-Click Speculation Market Soaring -
            http://slashdot.org/article.pl?sid=05/07/21/124230
Websurfing Damaging U.S. Productivity? -
            http://slashdot.org/article.pl?sid=05/07/21/0132206
VoIP Providers Worry as FCC Clams Up -
            http://slashdot.org/article.pl?sid=05/07/21/0135213
```

PHP 5.0 includes a new extension for parsing XML documents called SimpleXML. The SimpleXML extension makes the parsing of files such as slashdot.xml much easier. You can handle the previous example with the following small piece of code.

The Code

```php
<?php
// Example 14-5-5.php
$stories = simpleXML_load_file("http://slashdot.org/slashdot.xml");
foreach($stories as $story) {
  echo $story->title . " - ";
  echo $story->url . "\n";
}
?>
```

How It Works

This code produces the same output as the previous example. The content is loaded directly from the URL, but the resulting SimpleXML object is a list of all the story elements. The backslash element is ignored, because XML files can contain exactly one root-level element. You do not need to call functions or methods to get values or attributes on a SimpleXML object.

These are made available directly on the object structure (such as PHP objects), as shown in the next two examples where the attributes are extracted from the same XML file using first the DOM method and then the SimpleXML method. In the first example, you create a file that contains the XML content; in this case, use a short list of books. Each book has an ID defined as an attribute on the book element and a title defined as a child element to the book element.

```xml
<?xml version="1.0" ?>
<!-- example books.xml -->
<books>
  <book book_id="1">
    <title>PHP 5 Recipes</title>
  </book>
  <book book_id="2">
    <title>PHP Pocket Reference</title>
  </book>
</books>
```

Note You can use comment elements in XML documents in the same way you use them in HTML.

In the next example, you create the script that uses the DOM extension to create a list of title and book_id attributes.

The Code

```php
<?php
// Example 14-5-6.php
$doc = DOMDocument::load("books.xml");
$books = $doc->getElementsByTagName("book");
foreach($books as $book) {
  $titles = $book->getElementsByTagName("title");
  foreach($titles as $title) {
    echo $title->nodeValue . " - ";
  }
  $id = $book->getAttribute("book_id");
  echo "book_id = $id\n";
}
?>
```

Now create the same example with the SimpleXML extension.

The Code

```php
<?php
// Example 14-5-7.php
$books = simpleXML_load_file("books.xml");
```

```
foreach($books as $book) {
  echo $book->title . " - ";
  echo "book_id = $book[book_id]\n";
}
?>
```

How It Works

Both examples use the same XML file to create a DOM object tree or a Simple XML tree, and both examples create the same output with the title and book_id attributes for each book:

```
PHP 5 Recipes - book_id = 1
PHP Pocket Reference - book_id - 2
```

This example uses a small and simple XML file. If the file were more complex, the advantages of using SimpleXML to parse the content would be obvious. The SimpleXML extension does not include any features to manipulate the XML document in memory, but both extensions have functions that allow for the exchange of documents between the two standards. It's possible to use the DOM extension to build a document with values from a database or other source and then convert it to SimpleXML before the document is passed to another process for further processing. The advantage of the DOM extension is the ability to add, remove, and change elements and attributes in the object tree.

14-6. Transforming XML with XSL

Transforming XML documents to other XML documents or even to HTML documents is an important part of handling XML documents. Before PHP 5.0, you could do this with the XSLT extension. (XSLT stands for XSL Transformations, and XSL stands for Extensible Stylesheet Language.) The XSLT extension was built as a processor-independent application programming interface (API) with support for the Sabletron library. Since PHP 5.0, a new extension called XSL is available for transformations, and the XSLT extension has been moved to the PECL repository. The XSL extension builds on libxslt and is available on both Unix and Windows platforms. Unlike the DOM and SimpleXML, this extension is not enabled/loaded by default; you must load it from php.ini or with the dl() function. You can also compile it as a static module with no need for loading. You do this by including the -with-xsl option when running the configure script on a Unix platform.

If you return to the Slashdot example, where an XML file is loaded into a DomDocument() object, you can use the same file to see how XSL can transform this document to an HTML document that can be included on other web pages. Working with XSL is in many ways similar to how DOM works, though the methods and functions are different. The following document shows how to create an instance of xsltProcessor(), import a stylesheet, and transform the slashdot.xml document.

The Code

```php
<?php
// Example 14-6-1.php
if (!extension_loaded("xsl")) {
  dl("php_xsl.dll");
}

$xslt = new xsltProcessor;
$xslt->importStyleSheet(DomDocument::load('slashdot.xsl'));
$slashdot = new DomDocument("1.0", "iso-8889-1");
$slashdot->preserveWhiteSpace = false;
$local_file = "slashdot.xml";
$ttl = 30 * 60;  // Cache in 30 min.
if (file_exists($local_file) && filemtime($local_file) > time() - $ttl) {
  $slashdot->load($local_file);
}
else {
  $slashdot->load('http://slashdot.org/slashdot.xml');
  $fp = fopen($local_file, "wt");
  if ($fp) {
    fwrite($fp, $slashdot->saveXML());
    fclose($fp);
  }
}
echo $xslt->transformToXML($slashdot);
?>
```

■**Note** The code assumes the XSL extension is compiled in on Unix Unix platforms and available as a DLL on Windows platforms.

How It Works

The biggest differences are that you need to load the XSL extension and that you are working with two documents. The slashdot.xml file is loaded from the local cache or from the remote server (so it will always be up-to-date without violating the rules of usage for the service), and the stylesheet is loaded from the local hard drive. You could use the static method to load the XML file as well, but in this case you want to get rid of whitespace in the XML file, so create a DomDocument() object manually and set the property preserverWhiteSPace to false before you load the document.

The stylesheet, called slashdot.xsl, is itself an XML file that includes definitions for how different elements in the slashdot.xml file should be converted.

The Stylesheet

```
<xsl:stylesheet version="1.0" xmlns:xsl="http://www.w3.org/1999/XSL/Transform">
<!-- Example slashdot.xsl -->
 <xsl:param name="site" select="'slashdot.org'"/>
 <xsl:output method="html" encoding="iso-8859-1" indent="no"/>
 <xsl:template match="/">
  <html><body><center>
  <h1>Welcome to latest extract from <xsl:value-of select="$site"/></h1>
  <table border="1" width="75%">
  <xsl:apply-templates/>
  </table>
  </center></body></html> </xsl:template>
 <xsl:template match="story">
  <tr>
   <td>
    <a>
     <xsl:attribute name="href">
      <xsl:value-of select="url"/>
     </xsl:attribute>
     <xsl:value-of select="title"/>
    </a>
   </td>
   <td><xsl:value-of select="author"/></td>
  </tr>
 </xsl:template>
</xsl:stylesheet>
```

■**Note** The root element is named / in the first template. This could also be named backslash in this case, as that is the name of the root element.

The template file has two templates. The first one is for the backslash element (the root element in the XML file), and the second template is for the story element. It does not matter which order the two templates are defined in the XSL file. The <xsl:apply-templates/> element used in the first template defines where the second template is inserted.

Figure 14-1 shows the output from converting slashdot.xml to an HTML document.

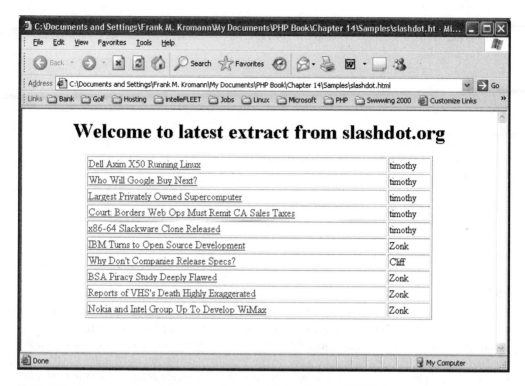

Figure 14-1. *Browser output from converting* `slashdot.xml` *to an HTML document*

14-7. Using RSS Feeds

RSS is an XML standard for syndicating web content. It was originally developed by Netscape but is widely used by many websites. An RSS feed has two parts. The first part is the XML document that contains one Resource Description Framework (RDF) `<rdf:RDF>` element and a list of the elements for the actual content. The second part is one or more files described in the `rdf` tag. These files contain additional descriptive information about the feed's structure.

An easy way to work with RSS feeds is to use the `PEAR::XML_RSS` class. You can use this class to read the RSS file from the remote server and parse the file so the contents will be stored in a number of PHP arrays. The RSS file has a number of sections that will be converted into a PHP array with the `PEAR` class (see Table 14-1).

Table 14-1. *RSS Sections*

Name	Description
Channel	Information about the channel, the publisher, and so on
Items	A short list of items with a direct link to the full story
Item	A detailed description of each item, often with a short abstract of the story
Images	A list of images provided by the file (can be empty)
TextInputs	A list of text input fields provided by the file (can be empty)

The next example shows how to read the news feed from the PHP website with the XML_RSS class. You must have PEAR and the classes PEAR::XML and PEAR::XML_RSS installed to run this example.

The Code

```php
<?php
// Example 14-7-1.php
require "XML/RSS.php";
$rss = new XML_RSS("http://php.net/news.rss");
$rss->parse();

foreach($rss->getItems() as $item) {
  print_r($item);
}
?>
```

How It Works

The XML_RSS class is a subclass of the XML class, so this example requires both PEAR::XML and PEAR::XML_RSS to be installed on the system. First the XML_RSS class is included, and then you create an rss object as a new instance of the CML_RSS class. The parameter to the constructor is the URL to the file. This could also be a file on the local hard drive. You must parse the file before you can get any information from it. At the end of this example, you print the content of each item included in the file, and the output will look like this (only the first element is shown here):

```
Array
(
    [title] => PHP 5.1 Beta 2 Available
    [link] => http://www.php.net/downloads.php#v5.1
    [description] => PHP 5.1 Beta 2 is now available! A lot of work has been put
into this upcoming release and we believe it is ready for public testing. Some of
the key improvements of PHP 5.1 include: PDO (PHP Data Objects) - A new
native database abstraction layer providing performance, ease-of-use, and
flexibility. Significantly improved language performance mainly due to the new
Zend Engine II execution architecture. The PCRE extension has been updated
to PCRE 5.0. Many more improvements including lots of new functionality & many
bug fixes, especially in regard to SOAP, streams, and SPL. See the bundled NEWS
file for a more complete list of changes. Everyone is encouraged to start playing
with this beta, although it is not yet recommended for mission-critical production
use.
    [dc:date] => 2005-06-23
)
```

   RSS feeds are available from a broad range of servers and organizations, and you can use the simple script in the previous example to create a script that will replicate the content of multiple RSS feeds into a local database. Many of these feeds require local caching to avoid overloading the service; as shown in the next example, you can do this with a simple database structure. We have used a FrontBase database, but you can easily convert the code and SQL statements into other databases supported by PHP. The example is split into three files. The first file (rss_db.inc) is where the database class is defined. This class connects to the database server and retrieves or updates entries. The two other files fetch the content of the feeds and present a list of data in a browser.
   Before you view the code, you need to create a database structure:

```
--
-- Example rss.sql
   Database structure needed for local caching
--
create table tRSSFeed (
      Xid             int                 default unique,
      Title           varchar(500)        ,
      Link            varchar(200)        ,
      Url             varchar(200)        not null,
      Frequency       int                 not null,
      LastUpdate      int                 ,
      Description     varchar(32768),
      primary key (xid)
);

create table tRSSItem (
      Xid             int                 default unique,
      RSSXid          int                 not null,
      Title           varchar(500)        ,
      Link            varchar(200)        ,
      ItemDate        int                 ,
      Description     varchar(32768)      ,
      primary key (xid)
);
insert into tRSSfeed (Url, Frequency)
  values ('http://php.net/news.rss', 7200);
insert into tRSSfeed (Url, Frequency)
  values ('http://slashdot.org/slashdot.rss', 3600);
```

   This example uses two tables. The first table describes the feeds, and the second table contains all the items from each feed. To initiate the system, you insert two feeds with the URL to the RSS file and a frequency (in seconds) between each update. The update script will look at the data in the first table and retrieve the file for each feed. The script will update the channel information and add new items for each feed.

The Code

```php
<?php
// Example 14-6-2.php
require "XML/RSS.php";
require "./rss_db.inc";

$RSS = new RSSdb('localhost', 'rss', 'secret', 'rssdb');
$feeds = $RSS->GetFeeds();
foreach($feeds as $feed) {
  $rss_feed = new XML_RSS($feed['url']);
  $rss_feed->parse();
  $channel = $rss_feed->getchannelInfo();
  $RSS->UpdateChannel(
    $feed['xid'],
    $channel['title'],
    $channel['link'],
    $channel['description']
);
  foreach($rss_feed->getItems() as $item) {
    $RSS->AddItem(
      $feed['xid'],
      $item['title'],
      $item['link'],
      $item['description'],
      $item['dc:date']
    );
  }
}
?>
```

How It Works

The script includes the XML_RSS class from PEAR and a special RSS database class, described in the next example. The script has two loops. The outer loop traverses through all the feeds defined in the tRSSFeed table, and the inner loop traverses the data returned by the RSS feed and inserts new items. This script should be executed through the cron daemon or through Windows-scheduled tasks that are executed as often as updates are needed.

Table 14-2 lists the methods of the RSSdb() class.

Table 14-2. RSSdb *Methods*

Name	Description
__construct()	Class constructor that will create a connection to the database.
__dtor()	Class destructor. It will disconnect from the database.
GetFeeds()	Returns a list of feeds from the database.
UpdateChannel()	Writes the latest channel information to the database.
AddItem()	Checks for the existence of an item and inserts it if it does not exist.
GetItems()	Returns a list of items for a given feed.

The Code

```php
<?php
// Example rss_db.inc
if (!extension_loaded("fbsql")) {
  dl("php_fbsql.dll");
}

class RSSdb {
  private $con;
  function __construct($host, $user, $passwd, $database) {
    $this->con = fbsql_connect($host, $user, $passwd);
    if ($this->con) {
      fbsql_select_db($database, $this->con);
    }
  }

  function __dtor() {
    if ($this->$con) {
      fbsql_close($this->com);
    }
  }

  function GetFeeds($for_update = true) {
    $res = array();
    $ts = time();
    $SQL = "select xid, url, link, title, description from tRSSFeed";
    if ($for_update) {
      $SQL .= " where LastUpdate is null or LastUpdate + Frequency < $ts";
    }
    $rs = fbsql_query("$SQL order by title;", $this->con);
    if ($rs) {
      while ($row = fbsql_fetch_assoc($rs)) {
        if (is_array($row)) {
          $row = array_change_key_case($row, CASE_LOWER);
        }
        $res[] = $row;
      }
      fbsql_free_result($rs);
    }
    return $res;
  }

  function UpdateChannel($xid, $title, $link, $description) {
    $title = str_replace("'", "''", $title);
    $description = str_replace("'", "''", $description);
    $ts = time();
    fbsql_query("update tRSSFeed " .
      "set LastUpdate=$ts, title='$title', " .
      "link='$link', description='$description' " .
      "where xid=$xid;", $this->con);
  }
```

```
function AddItem($rssxid, $title, $link, $description, $date) {
    $title = str_replace("'", "''", $title);
    $description = str_replace("'", "''", $description);
    $arrDate = split("[ T:+-]", $date);
    while(sizeof($arrDate) < 6) $arrDate[] = 0;
    $ts = gmmktime((int)$arrDate[3], (int)$arrDate[4], (int)$arrDate[5],
        (int)$arrDate[1],(int)$arrDate[2], (int)$arrDate[0]);
    $rs = fbsql_query("select xid from tRSSItem " .
        "where ItemDate=$ts and title='$title' and rssxid=$rssxid;", $this->con);
    if ($rs) {
        $row = fbsql_fetch_assoc($rs);
        fbsql_free_result($rs);
    }
    if (empty($row)) {
        fbsql_query(
            "insert into tRSSItem (RSSXid, title, link, description, itemdate) " .
            "values ($rssxid, '$title', '$link', '$description', $ts);", $this->con
        );
    }
}

function GetItems($rssxid, $count = 10) {
    $res = array();
    $rs = fbsql_query("select top $count xid, url, link, " .
        " title, description, itemdate from tRSSItem " .
        "where rssxid = $rssxid order by itemdate desc;", $this->con);
    if ($rs) {
        while ($row = fbsql_fetch_assoc($rs)) {
            if (is_array($row)) {
                $row = array_change_key_case($row, CASE_LOWER);
            }
            $res[] = $row;
        }
        fbsql_free_result($rs);
    }
    return $res;
}
}
?>
```

How It Works

This code does not produce any output. It is a class definition used by the next example. The method GetFeeds() takes an optional argument. When this argument is true, the method will return the feeds that need to be updated. When it is false, it will return all feeds in the database. This makes it possible to use the same method for the automated update and the presentation script. The UpdateChannel() and AddItem() methods take a number of parameters used to update the database. Both functions replace a single quote with double quotes in the character columns; this is the way FrontBase escapes a quote inside a string.

The data value included in each item under the dc:date tag can include both date and time or just a date. The AddItem() method uses the string value to create an integer value (Unix timestamp) for the ItemDate column in the database.

It is now time to see the script that presents the data in the browser. This script will have two modes. The first mode will list the available feeds, and the second mode will show the latest news from a selected feed.

The Code

```php
<?php
// Example 14-7-3.php
require "./rss_db.inc";
if (empty($Mode)) $Mode = "List";

$RSS = new RSSdb('localhost', 'rss', 'secret', 'rssdb');

echo "<html><body><table border=1 width=75% cellspacing=0 cellpadding=0>";

switch (strtoupper($Mode)) {
  case "LIST" :
    $feeds = $RSS->GetFeeds(false);
    foreach($feeds as $feed) {
      echo <<<FEED
<tr>
  <td><a href='$PHP_SELF?Mode=Feed&FeedId=$feed[xid]'>$feed[title]</a><td>
  <td>$feed[description]<td>
  <td>$feed[link]<td>
</tr>
FEED;
    }
    break;
  case "FEED" :
    $items = $RSS->GetItems($FeedId);
    foreach($items as $item) {
      echo <<<ITEM
<tr>
  <td><a href='$item[link]'><b>$item[title]</b></a><br>
  $item[description]<td>
</tr>
ITEM;
    }
    break;
}
echo "</table></body></html>";

?>
```

How It Works

You use the RSSdb class, defined in `rss_db.inc`, to create a list of the available feeds. Figure 14-2 shows the output.

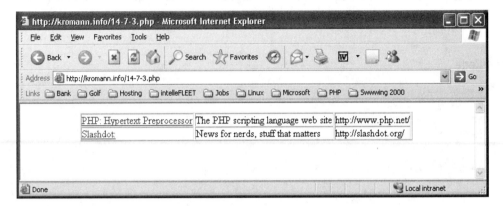

Figure 14-2. *List of available RSS feeds*

The title of each feed is a link to the ten most current items for that feed, as shown in Figure 14-3.

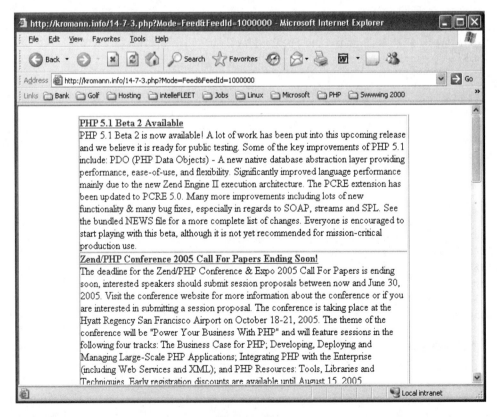

Figure 14-3. *List of items from the news feed at php.net*

14-8. Using WDDX

Web Distributed Data Exchange (WDDX) is another way to use XML documents to exchange data between applications and platforms. WDDX enables the exchange of complex data between web programming languages. This makes it possible to integrate systems written in different languages or to reuse systems written in other languages. WDDX is based on XML 1.0 and can be used with HTTP, FTP, SMTP, and POP. The communication protocol is used only to transport the XML documents from one system to another, so you can also use any other protocol that can do this.

The WDDX extension is built into Windows platforms, and you can enable it on Unix platforms with the -enable-wddx configure option. The extension does not require any external libraries. The examples in this section will work only if the WDDX extension is enabled. The WDDX extension implements six functions that enable the developer to create or parse WDDX documents (see Table 14-3).

Table 14-3. *WDDX Functions in PHP*

Name	Description
wddx_add_vars()	Adds variables to a WDDX packet with the specified ID
wddx_deserialize()	Deserializes a WDDX packet
wddx_packet_end()	Ends a WDDX packet with the specified ID
wddx_packet_start()	Starts a new WDDX packet with structure inside it
wddx_serialize_value()	Serializes a single value into a WDDX packet
wddx_serialize_vars()	Serializes variables into a WDDX packet

WDDX works as a packet format, and each document contains one packet. One packet can be a single variable or any number of simple or complex variables.

The next example shows how to create a simple WDDX document with a single variable.

The Code

```php
<?php
// Example 14-8-1.php
$var = "Creating a WDDX document with a single value.";
echo wddx_serialize_value(utf8_encode($var), "PHP Packet");
?>
```

How It Works

A string variable is declared and used as input to the wddx_serialize_value() function that creates the document. You use the utf8_encode() function to make sure any non-ASCII characters are handled correctly. The output from this script will look like this:

```
<wddxPacket version='1.0'><header><comment>PHP Packet</comment></header><data>
<string>Creating a WDDX document with a single value.</string></data></wddxPacket>
```

The next example shows how to use the previous example, with HTTP, to transfer data from one server to another.

The Code

```php
<?php
// Example 14-8-2.php
$fp = fopen("http://localhost/14-7-1.php", "rt");
if ($fp) {
  $wddx = "";
  while(!feof($fp)) {
    $wddx .= fread($fp, 4096);
  }
  fclose($fp);
  echo utf8_decode(wddx_deserialize($wddx));
}
?>
```

How It Works

First you use the fopen() and fread() functions to read the content of the file from the web server, and then you deserialize it to its original value. You use the utf8_decode() function to convert any non-ASCII characters to the correct values.

You can use the same technology to transfer more complex structures between servers/applications. The next two examples show how two arrays can be wrapped into a WDDX packet and unwrapped into the original values.

The Code

```php
<?php
// Example 14-8-3.php
$months = array(
  "January", "February", "Marts",
  "April", "May", "June",
  "July", "August", "September",
  "October", "November", "December"
);
$sales = array(
  10, 12, 15, 19, 30, 45,
  12, 50, 20, 34, 55, 70
);
$pid = wddx_packet_start("Sales 2005");
wddx_add_vars($pid, "months");
wddx_add_vars($pid, "sales");
echo wddx_packet_end($pid);
?>
```

How It Works

In this case, you embed more than one variable into a single WDDX packet. You do this by creating a packet handle called $pid with the wddx_packet_start() function. You use the packet handle each time you want to add a new variable to the packet. When you are done adding packets, you create the output with the wddx_packet_end() function.

The content of the WDDX packet can then be read from another machine with the code shown in the next example.

The Code

```php
<?php
// Example 14-9-7.php
$fp = fopen("http://localhost/14-8-7.php", "rt");
if ($fp) {
  $wddx = "";
  while(!feof($fp)) {
    $wddx .= fread($fp, 4096);
  }
  fclose($fp);
  $wddx = wddx_deserialize($wddx);
  for ($m = 0; $m < 12; $m++) {
    printf("The sale in %s was %d\n", $wddx['months'][$m], $wddx['sales'][$m]);
  }
}
?>
```

How It Works

You are reading the content of the WDDX packet from the web server and deserializing the content into the $wddx variable. This variable will be an array with all the variables as associative elements. The script will produce the following output:

```
The sale in January was 10
The sale in February was 12
The sale in Marts was 15
The sale in April was 19
The sale in May was 30
The sale in June was 45
The sale in July was 12
The sale in August was 50
The sale in September was 20
The sale in October was 34
The sale in November was 55
The sale in December was 70
```

14-9. Using SOAP

So far you have seen techniques to exchange data, where the format is simple and known to both the server and the client before the code is written and executed. It is possible to use the Simple Object Access Protocol (SOAP) to create more loosely coupled clients and servers. A SOAP message is an XML-formatted document that is usually transferred over HTTP. SOAP messages use the Web Services Description Language (WDSL) to describe locations, formats, operations, parameters, and data types for the SOAP message. This makes it possible for a SOAP client to consume a SOAP message from any web service and interpret the content correctly. The basic nature of SOAP messages is designed around a request message and a response message. The client creates a request in the form of an XML document and sends it to the server. The server then executes the request, creates a response document, and returns that to the client.

Since PHP 5.0, it is possible to enable the SOAP extension and use it to communicate with web services or even create new web services written directly in PHP. On a Unix system, you enable the SOAP extension by using the configure option –enable-soap, and on Windows systems you enable it in php.ini with the following line:

```
extension=php_soap.dll
```

You can also enable it from the script with the dl() command, if the script is executed under a nonthreaded SAPI (the type of interface between the web server and PHP). The examples in this section will work only if the SOAP extension is enabled.

Many websites (including eBay, Amazon, and PayPal) provide a SOAP API that allows other websites to reuse content and other features from their sites. Most of these services require some form of agreement and authentication to use the APIs. That is also the case for the examples shown in this section; we will use Google's search and spelling APIs to demonstrate how easy it is to write SOAP clients with the new SOAP extension in PHP.

The Google SOAP API is still under development, but developers can request an account and a key to use the API; each account is allowed 1,000 requests per day. When you request a developer account, you can download a package that includes samples on how to use the API (it does not include any PHP samples, though) and a .wsdl file that you can use to create the SOAP client. For many SOAP servers, the .wsdl file will be available online, and it can be referenced directly through HTTP.

The SoapClient() class in PHP uses the content of a .wsdl file to create the client, but you can also create the client without this file—the process is just much more complicated. The next example shows how to use one of the features included in Google's SOAP API to perform a site-specific search.

The Code

```php
<?php
// Example 14-9-1.php
if (!extension_loaded("soap")) {
  dl("php_soap.dll");
}
```

```
$client = new
    SoapClient(
    "/php/src/googleapi/GoogleSearch.wsdl"
    );

$options = array(
  "key" => "00000000000000000000000000000000",     // Replace with your own key
  "q" => "soap site:php.net",
  "start"   => 0,
  "maxResults" => 5,
  "filter" => false,
  "restrict" => "",
  "safeSearch" => false,
  "lr" => "",
  "ie" => "",
  "oe" => ""
);

$search = $client->__soapCall("doGoogleSearch", $options);
foreach($search->resultElements as $result) {
  echo $result->summary . "\n";
  echo $result->snippet . "\n";
  echo $result->URL . "\n";
}
?>
```

How It Works

First you make sure the SOAP extension is loaded, and then you create an instance of the
SoapClient() class using the GoogleSearch.wsdl file. Next, create an array with the specific
search options. Specify the options in the .wsdl file as follows:

```
<message name="doGoogleSearch">
  <part name="key"          type="xsd:string"/>
  <part name="q"            type="xsd:string"/>
  <part name="start"        type="xsd:int"/>
  <part name="maxResults"   type="xsd:int"/>
  <part name="filter"       type="xsd:boolean"/>
  <part name="restrict"     type="xsd:string"/>
  <part name="safeSearch"   type="xsd:boolean"/>
  <part name="lr"           type="xsd:string"/>
  <part name="ie"           type="xsd:string"/>
  <part name="oe"           type="xsd:string"/>
</message>
```

The SoapClient() class has a method called __soapCall() that you can use to create and send the request to the server. The result from the call is an object that includes the response document. The __soapCall() method takes two parameters, where the first is the name of the function to call and the second is an array with the arguments to that function. The search performed by this script is included in the q option and contains the string soap site:php.net. This will restrict the search on the keyword soap to one website. The output from this script will look like this:

```
<b>SOAP</b> Client/Server for PHP, PHP License. ?? Current Release. 0.9.1 (beta)
was<br>  released on 2005-05-31 <b>...</b> Implementation of <b>SOAP</b> protocol
and services <b>...</b>
http://pear.php.net/package/SOAP

The <b>SOAP</b> extension can be used to write <b>SOAP</b> Servers and Clients.
<b>...</b> Sets the<br>  directory name where the <b>SOAP</b> extension will put
cache files. <b>...</b>
http://www.php.net/soap
This is a <b>soap</b> integration for PHP (pear package).
This is a <b>soap</b> integration for PHP (pear package).
http://pear.php.net/package-info.php?pacid=87

<b>SOAP</b> Client/Server for PHP, PHP License. ?? Current Release. 0.9.1 (beta)
was<br>  released on 2005-05-31 <b>...</b> Implementation of <b>SOAP</b> protocol
and services <b>...</b>
http://pear.php.net/SOAP

PHP <b>SOAP</b> list for the <b>SOAP</b> developers, no, n/a, yes http, n/a.
Non-English<br>  language mailing lists, Moderated, Archive, Newsgroup, Normal,
Digest <b>...</b>
http://www.php.net/mailing-lists.php
```

You can also use the Google SOAP API to perform spell checking. This request is even simpler, as it takes only the developer key and a string as options; it returns a string with the suggested spelling for the string.

The Code

```php
<?php
// Example 14-9-2.php
if (!extension_loaded("soap")) {
  dl("php_soap.dll");
}

$client = new
    SoapClient(
    "/php/src/googleapi/GoogleSearch.wsdl"
    );
```

```php
$options = array(
  "key" => "0000000000000000000000000000000000",    // Replace with your own key
  "phrase" => "This bok is about PHP 5 features"
);

$search = $client->__soapCall("doSpellingSuggestion", $options);
echo "The correct spelling is: \"$spellcheck\"\n";
?>
```

How It Works

This script uses the same structure as the previous example but with a much shorter options list:

```
<message name="doSpellingSuggestion">
  <part name="key"                type="xsd:string"/>
  <part name="phrase"             type="xsd:string"/>
</message>
```

The output, with *book* spelled correct, will look like this:

```
The correct spelling is: "This book is about PHP 5 features"
```

When the SoapClient() is created, it will actually create methods for all the functions or operations defined in the .wsdl file. So, instead of calling the __soapCall() method, you can call the doSpellingSuggestion() method directly, as shown in the next example:

```php
<?php
// Example 14-9-3.php
if (!extension_loaded("soap")) {
  dl("php_soap.dll");
}

$client = new
    SoapClient(
    "/php/src/googleapi/GoogleSearch.wsdl"
    );

$key = "0000000000000000000000000000000000";    // Replace with your own key
$phrase = "This bok is about PHP 5 features";

$spellcheck = $client->doSpellingSuggestion($key, $phrase);
echo "The correct spelling is: \"$spellcheck\"\n";
?>
```

This gives shorter and slightly more readable code.

The SOAP extension in PHP also makes it easy to create your own SOAP services on your web server. The first step to do this is to create a .wsdl document. This is an XML document that describes data types, request and response documents, and other parameters for the service. Once the document is created, you can use it for both the server and the clients who want to consume the service. A simple .wsdl document that defines one method looks like this:

```
<?xml version="1.0"?>
<!-- Example books.wsdl -->
<definitions name="MyBookSearch"
             targetNamespace="urn:MyBookSearch"
             xmlns:typens="urn:MyBookSearch"
             xmlns:xsd="http://www.w3.org/2001/XMLSchema"
             xmlns:soap="http://schemas.xmlsoap.org/wsdl/soap/"
             xmlns:soapenc="http://schemas.xmlsoap.org/soap/encoding/"
             xmlns:wsdl="http://schemas.xmlsoap.org/wsdl/"
             xmlns="http://schemas.xmlsoap.org/wsdl/">

   <types>
     <xsd:schema xmlns="http://www.w3.org/2001/XMLSchema"
                 targetNamespace="urn:MyBookSearch">

       <xsd:complexType name="MyBookSearchResponse">
         <xsd:all>
           <xsd:element name="bookTitle"              type="xsd:string"/>
           <xsd:element name="bookYear"               type="xsd:int"/>
           <xsd:element name="bookAuthor"             type="xsd:string"/>
         </xsd:all>
       </xsd:complexType>

     </xsd:schema>
   </types>

   <message name="doMyBookSearch">
     <part name="bookTitle"        type="xsd:string"/>
   </message>

   <message name="doMyBookSearchResponse">
     <part name="return"        type="typens:MyBookSearchResponse"/>
   </message>

   <portType name="MyBookSearchPort">
     <operation name="doMyBookSearch">
       <input message="typens:doMyBookSearch"/>
       <output message="typens:doMyBookSearchResponse"/>
     </operation>
   </portType>

   <binding name="MyBookSearchBinding" type="typens:MyBookSearchPort">
     <soap:binding style="rpc"
                   transport="http://schemas.xmlsoap.org/soap/http"/>
```

```
    <operation name="doMyBookSearch">
      <soap:operation soapAction="urn:MyBookSearchAction"/>
      <input>
        <soap:body use="encoded"
                   namespace="urn:MyBookSearch"
                   encodingStyle="http://schemas.xmlsoap.org/soap/encoding/"/>
      </input>
      <output>
        <soap:body use="encoded"
                   namespace="urn:MyBookSearch"
                   encodingStyle="http://schemas.xmlsoap.org/soap/encoding/"/>
      </output>
    </operation>
  </binding>

  <service name="MyBookSearchService">
    <port name="MyBookSearchPort" binding="typens:MyBookSearchBinding">
      <soap:address location="http://localhost/php5/14-8-4.php"/>
    </port>
  </service>
</definitions>
```

This document defines a complete data type used by the response document to return more than one value; it defines the request and response messages, and it defines the operation implemented by the service. You can use this document to implement a simple web service with PHP, as shown in the next example.

The Code

```php
<?php
// Example 14-9-4.php
if (!extension_loaded("soap")) {
  dl("php_soap.dll");
}

ini_set("soap.wsdl_cache_enabled", "0");
$server = new SoapServer("books.wsdl");

function doMyBookSearch($bookTitle) {
  return array(
    "bookTitle" => "MyBook",
    "bookYear" => 2005,
    "bookAuthor" => "sdfkhsdkfjsdk"
  );
}

$server->AddFunction("doMyBookSearch");
$server->handle();
?>
```

How It Works

After making sure the extension is loaded, you use the ini_set() function to disable the caching of the .wsdl documents. These files are usually cached for 24 hours (also a setting in php.ini), so without this change to the cache, it would not be possible to make changes to the definitions. The server is then created from the SoapServer() class, and you assume that the .wsdl file is located in the same directory as the service. The function that you want executed each time the client requests a book is defined and added to the server. In this case, the functions do not use the input value; however, it is passed to the function, and you could use it in a database query to find the book for which you are looking.

You can now create a client for this web service.

The Code

```php
<?php
// Example 14-9-5.php
if (!extension_loaded("soap")) {
  dl("php_soap.dll");
}

ini_set("soap.wsdl_cache_enabled", "0");
$client = new SoapClient("http://localhost/php5/books.wsdl");

$search = $client->doMyBookSearch("Test");
var_dump($search);
?>
```

How It Works

You reuse the same .wsdl file from the server, but this time it is loaded via an HTTP request. When the client is created, you call the doMyBookSearch() method to request a book, and you dump the value of the search result.

```
object(stdClass)#2 (3) {
  ["bookTitle"]=>
  string(6) "MyBook"
  ["bookYear"]=>
  int(2005)
  ["bookAuthor"]=>
  string(13) "sdfkhsdkfjsdk"
}
```

Summary

In this chapter you looked at ways to generate or use documents with a high level of structure. You saw how markup can generate HTML and XML documents and how the DOM extension can make creating XML documents much easier. We also touched on the new SimpleXML extension that can read and parse XML documents from the local hard drive or a remote server.

In addition, you tackled more advanced services and how to use XML with them. You looked at a common format for site syndication, RSS. This format is widely used to create news feeds, and we showed how you can build a simple web-based reader. After RSS you learned about WDDX and how you can use it to exchange complex data between servers or applications. Finally, you learned about SOAP and its ability to provide both data and a data definition, allowing the client to consume web services without prior knowledge about the service.

Looking Ahead

The next chapter covers how to use PHP scripts to access data in a MySQL database.

CHAPTER 15

■ ■ ■

Using MySQL Databases in PHP 5

An important aspect of web development is being able to collect, store, and retrieve many different forms of data. In the past, different methods have been created to handle such features. Flat files, which are essentially text-based informational files, were the standard for many years.

After many problems with portability, speed, and functionality, flat files were generally phased out in favor of true database applications. Many database solutions are available on the Internet, including Microsoft Access, SQL Server, Oracle, and a few others.

Out of the pack of available options, however, one piece of database software has proven repeatedly to be a robust, affordable solution. MySQL is the database of choice in the open-source community because of its powerful infrastructure, fast querying, large data storage capabilities, and robust features.

Basic Database Concepts

This chapter presents a few examples of powerful PHP and MySQL-based technology. You will learn how to connect to a database, store information in a database, and retrieve information from a database; you will also learn how to put that information to good use. PHP 5 has the ability to connect to MySQL using some advanced options that have been released with the latest build of MySQL. Dubbed the mysqli extension, you will learn how to make your querying faster and more efficient. In a world where collecting information is critical, MySQL and PHP 5 make a strong couple.

15-1. Connecting to a MySQL Database

To do any work with a MySQL database, you must first open a link to the database and connect to it. Performing such functionality in PHP is quick and efficient. You can use the function mysql_connect() to connect to a database and then close the link when you are finished with it. The mysql_connect() function requires some proper login information to be passed to it in order for it to work properly, and it is important that you take the time to validate an improper login. The prototype for mysql_connect() is as follows.

```
resource mysql_connect ( [string server [, string username [, string password➥
 [, bool new_link [, int client_flags]]]]] )
```

The Code

```php
<?php

  //sample15_1.php

  //Attempt to open a connection to MySQL.
  try {
    //You must provide the host.
    $mysqlhost = "localhost";
    //The username.
    $mysqluser = "apress";
    //And the password.
    $mysqlpass = "testing";
    //And then supply them to the mysql_connect() function.
    if ($db = mysql_connect ($mysqlhost,$mysqluser,$mysqlpass)){
      //Now, you have an open connection with $db as its handler.
      echo "Successfully connected to the database.";
      //When you finish, you have to close the connection.
      mysql_close ($db);
    } else {
      throw new exception ("Sorry, could not connect to mysql.");
    }
  } catch (exception $e) {
    echo $e->getmessage ();
  }
?>
```

If you have a successful connection, you should get a proper result, as shown here:

```
Successfully connected to the database.
```

How It Works

Basically, you invoke the mysql_connect() method and pass it the connection information. This gives you access to any databases that are assigned to the apress user. If you were to supply an invalid login set, you would generate an error, and the exception handling would allow the application to die gracefully. Note also that as the good programmer that you are, you must take care of your memory usage and clean up at the end by closing the connection to the database. The mysql_close() function takes care of this handily and can receive the resource handler that was assigned with the mysql_connect() function as an argument to close. The prototype for mysql_close() is as follows:

```
bool mysql_close ( [resource link_identifier] )
```

15-2. Querying the Database

Naturally, once you have a connection to the database, you will query the database. Queries come in many shapes and forms and can have a wide variety of arguments to pass to them. MySQL makes sufficient use of Structured Query Language (SQL) and can perform functionality based upon SQL that is passed to it.

SQL allows you to perform common functionality such as insert, which allows you to enter data into a row; alter, which allows you to change the format of a table; select, which allows you to return a row set from a table in the database; and delete, which allows you to remove a row in the database. Naturally, you can perform many different queries, but the purpose of this chapter is not to give you a wide understanding of relational databases or the structure of SQL statements but to provide you with real-world examples to get your code working well in the MySQL environment.

Therefore, to perform a query in PHP, you can use the function mysql_query(). It allows you to perform a myriad of SQL functions and is quite simple to use. The prototype for mysql_query() is as follows:

resource **mysql_query** (string query [, resource link_identifier])

For this example, and the majority of examples in this chapter, assume you have a database set up called cds that contains a table called cd with the following structure:

```
cdid INT AUTO_INCREMENT PRIMARY KEY
title TINYTEXT
artist TINYTEXT
```

You will uniquely identify each record using the cdid field, name it with the title field, and provide the artist for the CD in the artist field. This table has three records, as follows:

```
1 Chuck Sum 41
2 Meteora Linkin Park
3 Mezmerize System of a Down
```

The Code

```php
<?php

//sample15_2.php

//A function to open a connection to MySQL.
function opendatabase ($host,$user,$pass) {
  //Attempt to open a connection to MySQL.
  try {
    //And then supply them to the mysql_connect() function.
    if ($db = mysql_connect ($host,$user,$pass)){
      //Return the identifier.
      return $db;
    } else {
```

```
          throw new exception ("Sorry, could not connect to mysql.");
        }
      } catch (exception $e) {
        echo $e->getmessage ();
      }
    }

    //A function to close the connection to MySQL.
    function closedatabase ($db){
      //When you finish up, you have to close the connection.
      mysql_close ($db);
    }

    //First, open a connection to the database.
    $db = opendatabase ("localhost","apress","testing");

    //The next thing you must do is select a database.
    try {
      if (!mysql_select_db ("cds",$db)){
        throw new exception ("Sorry, database could not be opened.");
      }
    } catch (exception $e) {
      echo $e->getmessage();
    }

    //Create a query that will, in this case, insert a new row.
    $myquery = "INSERT INTO cd (cdid,title,artist) VALUES➥
    ('0','Greyest of Blue Skies','Finger Eleven')";

    //Then process the query.
    try {
      if (mysql_query ($myquery, $db)){
        echo "We were successful.";
      } else {
        throw new exception (mysql_error());
      }
    } catch (exception $e) {
      echo $e->getmessage();
    }

    //Then close the database.
    closedatabase ($db);

?>
```

We were successful.

How It Works

As you can see, you have put the opening and closing of a valid connection into two different functions. You should note the opening of the connection to MySQL. Without that link, you cannot proceed any further. Now, to perform a query on a database table, you must first specify which database (that is assigned to the current user) you want to perform an action on. In this case, the function mysql_select_db() takes care of business for you.

Once you have a selected database, it is simply a matter of creating a query and executing it using the mysql_query() function. If the query succeeds, you will receive a successful message. It is important, however, to consider that the query could potentially fail (because of a syntax error or some other problem), and you take care of that in the code. The prototype for mysql_select_db() is as follows:

```
bool mysql_select_db ( string database_name [, resource link_identifier] )
```

15-3. Retrieving and Displaying Results

Naturally, alongside the ability to store information in a database, you will quite often want to be able to display information you have retrieved from the database. With the power of MySQL and PHP working together, this form of functionality is no problem. In PHP, the most common method to retrieve a row in the database is with the mysql_fetch_array() function, which puts the results garnered from a row set into an array for ease of use. Its prototype is as follows:

```
array mysql_fetch_array ( resource result [, int result_type] )
```

The following example outputs the results of the current database table.

The Code

```php
<?php

  //sample15_3.php

  //A function to open a connection to MySQL.
  function opendatabase ($host,$user,$pass) {
    //Attempt to open a connection to MySQL.
    try {
      //And then supply them to the mysql_connect() function.
      if ($db = mysql_connect ($host,$user,$pass)){
        //Return the identifier.
        return $db;
      } else {
        throw new exception ("Sorry, could not connect to mysql.");
      }
    } catch (exception $e) {
      echo $e->getmessage ();
    }
  }

function selectdb ($whichdb, $db){
```

```php
//The next thing you must do is select a database.
  try {
    if (!mysql_select_db ($whichdb,$db)){
      throw new exception ("Sorry, database could not be opened.");
    }
  } catch (exception $e) {
    echo $e->getmessage();
  }
}

//A function to close the connection to MySQL.
function closedatabase ($db){
  //When you finish up, you have to close the connection.
  mysql_close ($db);
}

//First, open a connection to the database.
$db = opendatabase ("localhost","apress","testing");

//Then select a database.
selectdb ("cds",$db);

//Now, let's create a script to output the information found within the table.
if ($aquery = mysql_query ("SELECT * FROM cd ORDER BY cdid ASC")){
  //You can loop through the rows in the table, outputting as you go.
  while ($adata = mysql_fetch_array ($aquery)){
    echo "ID: " . $adata['cdid'] . "<br />";
    echo "Title: " . stripslashes ($adata['title']) . "<br />";
    echo "Artist: " . stripslashes ($adata['artist']) . "<br />";
    echo "-------------------------------<br />";
  }
} else {
  echo mysql_error();
}

//Then close the database.
closedatabase ($db);

?>
```

```
ID: 1
Title: Chuck
Artist: Sum 41
-------------------------------
ID: 2
Title: Meteora
Artist: Linkin Park
```

```
----------------------------------
ID: 3
Title: Mezmerize
Artist: System of a Down
----------------------------------
ID: 4
Title: Greyest of Blue Skies
Artist: Finger Eleven
----------------------------------
```

How It Works

The major difference between this code sample and the previous one is that you have placed the selection of a database into a function for portability. Past that, you simply check if the query is valid (and if not, echo the error) and then loop through all the resulting rows that are returned from the mysql_fetch_array() function. As you loop through the different rows, you can output the value of the row in the array by referencing the name of the field in the database. By doing this, as you can see from the results, you can succeed in outputting the entire contents of the cd table.

15-4. Modifying Data

Obviously, database functionality would be pretty useless if the data stored in the database itself could only remain static. Luckily, MySQL provides you with a means to modify certain data. The general method for modifying a set of data is to reference a unique record ID number and then change the row if it matches the ID argument. Let's say, for instance, you want to change the information contained within the record for the Linkin Park album currently in the database. By looking at the previous results, the Linkin Park dataset looks as follows:

```
ID: 2
Title: Meteora
Artist: Linkin Park
```

Since you know that the ID number for that particular row is 2, you can easily modify the record based on that argument, as shown in the following example.

The Code

```php
<?php

//sample15_4.php

//A function to open a connection to MySQL.
function opendatabase ($host,$user,$pass) {
  //Attempt to open a connection to MySQL.
  try {
```

```php
      //And then supply them to the mysql_connect() function.
      if ($db = mysql_connect ($host,$user,$pass)){
        //Return the identifier.
        return $db;
      } else {
        throw new exception ("Sorry, could not connect to mysql.");
      }
    } catch (exception $e) {
      echo $e->getmessage ();
    }
  }

  function selectdb ($whichdb, $db){
  //The next thing you must do is select a database.
    try {
      if (!mysql_select_db ($whichdb,$db)){
        throw new exception ("Sorry, database could not be opened.");
      }
    } catch (exception $e) {
      echo $e->getmessage();
    }
  }

  //A function to close the connection to MySQL.
  function closedatabase ($db){
    //When you finish up, you have to close the connection.
    mysql_close ($db);
  }

  //First, open a connection to the database.
  $db = opendatabase ("localhost","apress","testing");

  //Then select a database.
  selectdb ("cds",$db);

  //Create a query to modify the Linkin Park record.
  $updatequery = "UPDATE cd SET title='Hybrid Theory' WHERE cdid='2'";

  //Then attempt to perform the query.
  try {
    if (mysql_query ($updatequery, $db)){
      echo "Your record has been updated.";
      //Now, let's output the record to see the changes.
      if ($aquery = mysql_query ("SELECT * FROM cd WHERE cdid='2'")){
        $adata = mysql_fetch_array ($aquery);
        echo "<br />Title: " . stripslashes ($adata['title']);
      } else {
```

```
      echo mysql_error();
    }
  } else {
    throw new exception (mysql_error());
  }
} catch (exception $e) {
  echo $e->getmessage();
}

//Then close the database.
closedatabase ($db);

?>
```

Naturally, you can test to ensure the change is valid. The results of a successful transaction are as follows:

```
Your record has been updated.
Title: Hybrid Theory
```

How It Works

As you can see, by performing a query that will update the record (with the ID as the defining attribute of the row), you can quickly and efficiently change a record at your whim. In this case, you merely changed the title of the album to another album and then outputted the change. Note that when you displayed the changed result, you specified which row you wanted to see, again via the ID number.

15-5. Deleting Data

Removing data is largely the same as updating data. You will definitely want to specify which record you are attempting to remove, as you can quite easily lose an entire table if you are not careful. The following example enables you to remove a record from your table. Should you want to remove an entire table's contents, simply leave out the where clause in the SQL code.

The Code

```php
<?php

//sample15_5.php

//A function to open a connection to MySQL.
function opendatabase ($host,$user,$pass) {
  //Attempt to open a connection to MySQL.
  try {
    //And then supply them to the mysql_connect() function.
    if ($db = mysql_connect ($host,$user,$pass)){
```

```
            //Return the identifier.
            return $db;
        } else {
            throw new exception ("Sorry, could not connect to mysql.");
        }
    } catch (exception $e) {
        echo $e->getmessage ();
    }
}

function selectdb ($whichdb, $db){
    //The next thing you must do is select a database.
    try {
        if (!mysql_select_db ($whichdb,$db)){
            throw new exception ("Sorry, database could not be opened.");
        }
    } catch (exception $e) {
        echo $e->getmessage();
    }
}

//A function to close the connection to MySQL.
function closedatabase ($db){
    //When you finish up, you have to close the connection.
    mysql_close ($db);
}

//First, open a connection to the database.
$db = opendatabase ("localhost","apress","testing");

//Then select a database.
selectdb ("cds",$db);

//Create a query to remove the recently modified Linkin Park record.
$updatequery = "DELETE FROM cd WHERE cdid='2'";

//Then attempt to perform the query.
try {
    if (mysql_query ($updatequery, $db)){
        echo "Your record has been removed.";
        //Now, let's output the record to see the changes.
        if ($aquery = mysql_query ("SELECT * FROM cd WHERE cdid='2'")){
            //You will notice that the record has been removed.
            echo "<br />" . mysql_num_rows ($aquery); //Should output a 0.
        } else {
            echo mysql_error();
        }
```

```
  } else {
    throw new exception (mysql_error());
  }
} catch (exception $e) {
  echo $e->getmessage();
}

//Then close the database.
closedatabase ($db);

?>
```

If everything goes well, you should receive a response to the screen that looks something like this:

```
Your record has been removed.
0
```

How It Works

As you can see, the vast majority of the work that went into modifying this piece of code from the previous example was in the SQL statement. Rather than using the update statement, you use the delete statement and specify the record you want to remove. To prove that the record is indeed gone, you can use the mysql_num_rows() function, which specifies the number of rows that has been returned from a select statement. Be careful when using the delete statement, as data removed in this way cannot be returned. The prototype for mysql_num_rows() is as follows:

```
int mysql_num_rows ( resource result )
```

15-6. Building Queries on the Fly

You will have plenty of opportunities to build a query on the fly. A fairly common example is receiving data from a form that will allow you to log into your account. While the functionality behind this is useful and rather powerful, it is also the preferred method for crackers to gain entry into your system. By using a technique known as *SQL injection*, malicious users can insert potentially dangerous code into your dynamic queries that could, in turn, allow them to damage your data, pull all the information from your database, or destroy the database in its entirety. Therefore, it is important that, when building dynamic queries, you take the necessary efforts to ensure all received data is stripped of potentially hazardous characters. The following example will receive posted values (from a form) and log them in accordingly if they have the right username and password.

For this particular recipe, set up a new table in the cds database called userlogin. The userlogin table structure is as follows:

```
userloginid INT AUTO_INCREMENT PRIMARY KEY
username TINYTEXT
password TINYTEXT
```

This table has one row with the following information:

```
1 apress testing
```

The Code

```php
<?php

//sample15_6.php

//A function to open a connection to MySQL.
function opendatabase ($host,$user,$pass) {
  //Attempt to open a connection to MySQL.
  try {
    //And then supply them to the mysql_connect() function.
    if ($db = mysql_connect ($host,$user,$pass)){
      //Return the identifier.
      return $db;
    } else {
      throw new exception ("Sorry, could not connect to mysql.");
    }
  } catch (exception $e) {
    echo $e->getmessage ();
  }
}

function selectdb ($whichdb, $db){
  //The next thing you must do is select a database.
  try {
    if (!mysql_select_db ($whichdb,$db)){
      throw new exception ("Sorry, database could not be opened.");
    }
  } catch (exception $e) {
    echo $e->getmessage();
  }
}

//A function to close the connection to MySQL.
function closedatabase ($db){
  //When you finish up, you have to close the connection.
  mysql_close ($db);
}
```

```php
//First, open a connection to the database.
$db = opendatabase ("localhost","apress","testing");

//Then select a database.
selectdb ("cds",$db);

//Now, assume you received these values from a posted form.
$_POST['user'] = "apress";
$_POST['pass'] = "testing";

function validatelogin ($user,$pass){
  //First, remove any potentially dangerous characters.
  mysql_real_escape_string ($user);
  mysql_real_escape_string ($pass);
  //Next, check the user and pass against the database.
  $thequery = "SELECT * FROM userlogin WHERE➥
username='$user' AND password='$pass'";
  //Now, run the query.
  if ($aquery = mysql_query ($thequery)){
    //Now, you can check for a valid match using the➥
mysql_num_rows() function.
    if (mysql_num_rows ($aquery) > 0){
      return true;
    } else {
      return false;
    }
  } else {
    echo mysql_error();
  }
}

//Now, let's attempt to validate the login.
if (validatelogin ($_POST['user'],$_POST['pass'])){
  echo "You have successfully logged in.";
} else {
  echo "Sorry, you have an incorrect username and/or password.";
}

//Then close the database.
closedatabase ($db);

?>
```

How It Works

As you can see, building a dynamic query is not all that difficult. The most important aspect when building the query is to remember to validate the data submitted in the query. The function mysql_real_escape_string() is necessary when dealing with string type values (as in this case), and the function intval() can help you when dealing with numerical values by ensuring a valid numerical response. Apart from that, you can treat a dynamic query just as you would treat a string. By using string functionality, you can dynamically build the query of your choice.

The mysqli Extension vs. the PHP 4 MySQL Extension

Over time, the mysql extension contained with PHP has performed, generally, quite well. However, certain features began to get implemented into newer versions of MySQL that began to showcase a few flaws with the mysql extension. Now, with the advent of PHP 5, a few problems have occurred (mostly with default and automatic connections). To combat these issues and bring the mysql library into the PHP 5 way of thinking (which is object-oriented), a new extension has been established, the mysqli extension.

The mysqli extension (developed by Georg Richter), which is an object-oriented version of the mysql extension, can use the new MySQL 4.1+ functionality to improve the speed, diversity, and functionality of PHP's connection with MySQL. To make the mysqli extension work in PHP, you must add the following line to the extensions area of the php.ini file:

```
extension=php_mysqli.dll
```

Now, you have to make sure you are using MySQL 4.1 or higher to implement the new extension. From there it is simply a matter of getting familiar with some new syntaxes and concepts, which will be explained as you go through this chapter.

15-7. Using the mysqli Object-Oriented API

Using the new object-oriented application programming interface (API) in the mysqli extension is really no big deal for those familiar with using objects. Basically, you create an instance of a mysqli object and use its methods rather than simply using the mysql extension's functions. The syntax is naturally a little different, but the concept behind it is easy to understand. The following example guides you through several new syntaxes and a couple of the new algorithms you can perform with the mysqli extension.

The Code

```php
<?php

//sample15_7.php

//The first thing you need to do, like any other time is➥
connect to the mysql server.
//You can do so by creating a new mysqli instance.
```

```php
$mysqli = new mysqli ("localhost","apress","testing","cds");
try {
  if (mysqli_connect_errno()){
    throw new exception ("Error: " . mysqli_connect_errno() . " - "➥
. mysqli_connect_error());
  } else {
    //Now, you can perform a myriad of functions.
    //For instance, let's output the contents of the cd table.
    if ($cdquery = $mysqli->query ("SELECT * FROM cd ORDER BY cdid ASC")){
      while ($cddata = $cdquery->fetch_array ()){
        echo "ID: " . $cddata['cdid'] . "<br />";
        echo "Title: " . stripslashes ($cddata['title']) . "<br />";
        echo "Artist: " . stripslashes ($cddata['artist']) . "<br />";
        echo "----------------------------<br />";
      }
      //Clean up.
      $cdquery->close();
    } else {
      echo $mysqli->errno . " - " . $mysqli->error;
    }

    //A new feature: using prepared statements.
    //First you prepare a statement using ? where➥
you want to use literal data.
    $prep = $mysqli->prepare ("INSERT INTO cd (cdid,title,artist)➥
VALUES ('0',?,?)");
    //Now, you can bind some parameters.
    $prep->bind_param ('ss',$title,$artist);

    //The new album to be inserted.
    $title = "Californication";
    $artist = "Red Hot Chili Peppers";

    //Then you can execute the query:
    $prep->execute();

    //And see how you did:
    echo $prep->affected_rows . " row(s) affected.";

    //Clean up.
    $prep->close();

    //Now, you can also bind results:
    if ($result = $mysqli->prepare ("SELECT title, artist FROM➥
cd WHERE cdid > '2'")){
        $result->execute ();
```

```
        //Bind the results.
        $result->bind_result ($title,$artist);

        //Then go through and echo the bound results.
        while ($result->fetch ()){
           echo "Title: " . stripslashes ($title) . "<br />";
           echo "Artist: " . stripslashes ($artist) . "<br />";
           echo "----------------------------<br />";
        }

        //Clean up.
        $result->close ();
      } else {
        echo $mysqli->errno . " - " . $mysqli->error;
      }

      //Closing the connection is simple.
      $mysqli->close();
    }
  } catch (exception $e) {
    echo $e->getmessage();
  }

?>
```

The code execution will look something like this:

```
ID: 1
Title: Chuck
Artist: Sum 41
----------------------------
ID: 2
Title: Meteora
Artist: Linkin Park
----------------------------
ID: 3
Title: Mezmerize
Artist: System of a Down
----------------------------
ID: 4
Title: Greyest of Blue Skies
Artist: Finger Eleven
----------------------------
1 row(s) affected.
Title: Mezmerize
Artist: System of a Down
----------------------------
```

```
Title: Greyest of Blue Skies
Artist: Finger Eleven
-----------------------------
Title: Californication
Artist: Red Hot Chili Peppers
-----------------------------
```

How It Works

As you can see, the API is object-oriented. The first matter of business is instantiating a `mysqli` instance. From there you can perform the different methods available to the object such as running queries and closing the connection. The list of methods available to the object is long; feel free to peruse the PHP manual for more information (although this example does introduce the basics). You can find the relevant PHP manual section at `http://www.php.net/manual/en/ref.mysqli.php`

Also included in this example is something new to the `mysqli` extension—the concept of prepared statements. Basically, you can set up a statement that you will use repeatedly with the `prepare` method on the `mysqli` object and then bind either parameters or results to it. In this recipe, you can see how to bind parameters to an `insert` statement. Every time you want to run that statement, you can simply bind new parameters to it and use the `execute()` method. The syntax for the characters you want to be able to bind is the ampersand (&) symbol for the bind-able arguments, and you can specify the data type of the argument to be bound by referring to Table 15-1.

Table 15-1. *Bind Types*

Bind Type	Column Type
i	Integer types
d	Double or floating-point types
b	BLOB (Binary Large OBject) types
s	Any other data type

The syntax for binding results is a little different. For binding results, you first run the query you want to execute in the `prepare` statement, execute it, and then bind the result to a set of variables. (Be careful, though, because you must match the amount of variables to the number of returned values.) Once the setup is complete, you can simply run the `fetch()` method to quickly and efficiently recover the bound values.

15-8. Using Exceptions to Handle Database Errors

One of the aspects that separate the great coders from the rookies is not just making usable or working code but taking care of unforeseen eventualities. When working with more than one process (PHP and MySQL), sometimes unforeseen incompatibilities or server hiccups can cause an unwanted problem. To ensure the integrity of your web applications, it is important that, if such a problem occurs, the web application dies gracefully and provides a means for the developer to track the error.

Luckily, with the inclusion of exception handling in PHP 5, you can now create custom web applications that take care of their own errors. The following class uses exception handling to perform its error handling.

The Code

```php
<?php

  //sample15_8.php

  class mydb {

    private $user;
    private $pass;
    private $host;
    private $db;

    //Constructor function.
    public function __construct (){
      $num_args = func_num_args();

      if($num_args > 0){
        $args = func_get_args();
        $this->host = $args[0];
        $this->user = $args[1];
        $this->pass = $args[2];

        $this->connect();
      }
    }

    //Function to connect to the database.
    private function connect (){
      try {
        if (!$this->db = mysql_connect ($this->host,$this->user,$this->pass)){
          $exceptionstring = "Error connection to database: <br />";
          $exceptionstring .= mysql_errno() . ": " . mysql_error();
          throw new exception ($exceptionstring);
        }
      } catch (exception $e) {
        echo $e->getmessage();
      }
    }

    //Function to select a database.
    public function selectdb ($thedb){
      try {
        if (!mysql_select_db ($thedb, $this->db)){
```

```php
        $exceptionstring = "Error opening database: $thedb: <br />";
        $exceptionstring .= mysql_errno() . ": " . mysql_error();
        throw new exception ($exceptionstring);
      }
    } catch (exception $e) {
      echo $e->getmessage();
    }
  }


  //Function to perform a query.
  public function execute ($thequery){
    try {
      if (!mysql_query ($thequery, $this->db)){
        $exceptionstring = "Error performing query: $thequery: <br />";
        $exceptionstring .= mysql_errno() . ": " . mysql_error();
        throw new exception ($exceptionstring);
      } else {
        echo "Query performed correctly: " . mysql_affected_rows ()➡
. " rows affected.<br />";
      }
    } catch (exception $e) {
      echo $e->getmessage();
    }
  }


  //Function to return a row set.
  public function getrows ($thequery){
    try {
      if (!$aquery = mysql_query ($thequery)){
        $exceptionstring = "Error performing query: $thequery: <br />";
        $exceptionstring .= mysql_errno() . ": " . mysql_error();
        throw new exception ($exceptionstring);
      } else {
        $returnarr = array ();
        while ($adata = mysql_fetch_array ($aquery)){
          $returnarr = array_merge ($returnarr,$adata);
        }
        return $returnarr;
      }
    } catch (exception $e) {
      echo $e->getmessage();
    }
  }


  //Function to close the database link.
  public function __destruct() {
    try {
```

```
      if (!mysql_close ($this->db)){
        $exceptionstring = "Error closing connection: <br />";
        $exceptionstring .= mysql_errno() . ": " . mysql_error();
        throw new exception ($exceptionstring);
      }
    } catch (exception $e) {
      echo $e->getmessage();
    }
  }


}

//Now, let's create an instance of mydb.
$mydb = new mydb ("localhost","apress","testing");

//Now, you specify a database to use.
$mydb->selectdb ("cds");

//Now, let's perform an action.
$adata = $mydb->execute ("UPDATE cd SET title='Hybrid Theory' WHERE cdid='2'");

//Then, let's try to return a row set.
$adata = $mydb->getrows ("SELECT * FROM cd ORDER BY cdid ASC");
for ($i = 0; $i < count ($adata); $i++){
  echo $adata[$i] . "<br />";
}
?>
```

```
Query performed correctly: 1 row(s) affected.
1
Chuck
Sum 41
2
Hybrid Theory
Linkin Park
3
Mezmerize
System of a Down
4
Greyest of Blue Skies
Finger Eleven
```

How It Works

As you can see, this database class (`mydb`) is completely validated by exception handling. Should anything go wrong when working with the database, the system will immediately run its exception handling capabilities and output a detailed error to help debug the situation. In the real world, you may want to consider showing users a polite message that says the website is down for maintenance (or something of the like) to alleviate any fears they may have. In a debug environment, however, this sort of code works rather well.

Note the `mysql_error()` function and the `mysql_errno()` function in this class; they will return the most recently generated error and error number (respectively) from the MySQL server. Using this sort of error handling can make debugging an application much more convenient.

15-9. Project: Displaying Linked Search Results

Linking tables makes databases powerful. By linking similar information between tables, you create a much more organized set of data and keep certain pieces of information properly separated from others. Let's build on the concept of the `cds` database. Say, perhaps, that your web application allows members of your site to log in (via the `userlogin` table) and then post reviews of their favorite albums (via a new table you are about to design, the `review` table). To keep an eye on who is posting a review, as well as which album a particular review is associated with, you must link the tables.

Linking tables generally takes place through foreign keys. A particular table can contain a linked ID to another table and contain the respective table's unique (primary) ID. The field name should be the same (for semantics), and the link itself can be performed in the query. For this example to work, you must first create the `review` table as follows:

```
reviewid INT AUTO_INCREMENT PRIMARY KEY
userloginid INT
cdid INT
rtitle TINYTEXT
review TEXT
```

You will also add two fields to the current `userlogin` table so that you can output who wrote the review and their e-mail address. The two fields look like this:

```
name TINYTEXT
email TINYTEXT
```

The following example first puts a review into the system, outputs all reviews for each album, and then displays who wrote them.

The Code

```php
<?php

  //sample15_9.php

  //A function to open a connection to MySQL.
  function opendatabase ($host,$user,$pass) {
```

```
    //Attempt to open a connection to MySQL.
    try {
      //And then supply them to the mysql_connect() function.
      if ($db = mysql_connect ($host,$user,$pass)){
        //Return the identifier.
        return $db;
      } else {
        throw new exception ("Sorry, could not connect to mysql.");
      }
    } catch (exception $e) {
      echo $e->getmessage ();
    }
  }

function selectdb ($whichdb, $db){
  //The next thing you must do is select a database.
  try {
    if (!mysql_select_db ($whichdb,$db)){
      throw new exception ("Sorry, database could not be opened.");
    }
  } catch (exception $e) {
    echo $e->getmessage();
  }
}

//A function to close the connection to MySQL.
function closedatabase ($db){
  //When you finish up, you have to close the connection.
  mysql_close ($db);
}

//First, open a connection to the database.
$db = opendatabase ("localhost","apress","testing");

//Then select a database.
selectdb ("cds",$db);

//First, add the review table.
$addquery = "CREATE TABLE IF NOT EXISTS review (";
$addquery .= "reviewid INT NOT NULL AUTO_INCREMENT, PRIMARY KEY (reviewid), ";
$addquery .= "userloginid INT, cdid INT, rtitle TINYTEXT, review TEXT)➥
TYPE=MyISAM";
try {
  if (!mysql_query ($addquery, $db)){
    throw new exception (mysql_error());
  }
} catch (exception $e) {
```

```php
    echo $e->getmessage ();
  }
  //Check the fields in the table.
  $curfields = mysql_list_fields("cds", "userlogin");
  //Run through the current fields and see if you already➡
have the name and email field.
  $columns = mysql_num_fields($curfields);
  $nameexists = false;
  $emailexists = false;
  for ($i = 0; $i < $columns; $i++){
    if (mysql_field_name ($curfields, $i) == "name"){
      $nameexists = true;
    }
    if (mysql_field_name ($curfields, $i) == "email"){
      $emailexists = true;
    }
  }
  //If the name field does not exist, create it.
  if (!$nameexists){
    $twonewquery = "ALTER TABLE userlogin ADD (name TINYTEXT)";
    try {
      if (!mysql_query ($twonewquery, $db)){
        throw new exception (mysql_error());
      }
    } catch (exception $e) {
      echo $e->getmessage ();
    }
  }
  //If the e-mail field does not exist, create it.
  if (!$emailexists){
    $twonewquery = "ALTER TABLE userlogin ADD (email TINYTEXT)";
    try {
      if (!mysql_query ($twonewquery, $db)){
        throw new exception (mysql_error());
      }
    } catch (exception $e) {
      echo $e->getmessage ();
    }
  }
  //Then, you insert a name and e-mail into the existing userlogin account, apress.
  $upquery = "UPDATE userlogin SET name='Lee Babin',➡
email='lee@babinplanet.ca' WHERE userloginid='1'";
  try {
    if (!mysql_query ($upquery, $db)){
      throw new exception (mysql_error());
    }
  } catch (exception $e) {
```

```
    echo $e->getmessage ();
  }
  //Now, you can insert a review for, let's say, Linkin Park.
  $title = "My Review";
  $body = "Wow, what a great album!";
  $insquery = "INSERT INTO review (reviewid,userloginid,cdid,rtitle,review)➥
VALUES ('0','1','2','$title','$body')";
  try {
    if (!mysql_query ($insquery, $db)){
      throw new exception (mysql_error());
    }
  } catch (exception $e) {
    echo $e->getmessage ();
  }
  //Go through all albums first.
  if ($alquery = mysql_query ("SELECT * FROM cd ORDER BY cdid ASC")){
    while ($aldata = mysql_fetch_array ($alquery)){
      echo stripslashes ($aldata['title']) . " by: " . ➥
stripslashes ($aldata['artist']) . "<br />";
      //Now, search for a review for this title.
      $jquery = "SELECT DISTINCT a.rtitle,a.review,b.name,b.email FROM ";
      $jquery .= "review a, userlogin b WHERE➥
a.userloginid=b.userloginid AND a.cdid='" . $aldata['cdid'] . "' ";
      $jquery .= "ORDER BY a.reviewid ASC";
      if ($revquery = mysql_query ($jquery)){
        //Check if there are any reviews.
        if (mysql_num_rows ($revquery) > 0){
          //Then output all reviews.
          ?><p>Reviews</p><?php
          //Count the review number.
          $revcounter = 0;
          while ($revdata = mysql_fetch_array ($revquery)){
            //Increment the counter.
            $revcounter++;
            ?><p style="font-weight: bold;">➥
<?php echo stripslashes ($revdata['rtitle']); ?></p><?php
            ?><p><?php echo stripslashes (nl2br ($revdata['review'])); ?></p><?php
            ?><p>By: <a href="mailto:<?php echo stripslashes ➥
($revdata['email']); ?>"><?php echo stripslashes (➥
$revdata['name']); ?></a></p><?php
            //Now, show the break only if you have more reviews.
            if (mysql_num_rows ($revquery) != $revcounter){
              echo "----------------------------------<br />";
            }
          }
        } else {
          ?><p>No reviews for this album.</p><?php
```

```
      }
    } else {
      echo mysql_error();
    }
    echo "----------------------------------<br />";
  }
} else {
  echo mysql_error();
}
?>
```

A proper execution of this script should look something like this:

```
Chuck by: Sum 41
No reviews for this album.
Meteora by: Linkin Park
Reviews
My Review
Wow, what a great album!
By: Lee Babin
Mezmerize by: System of a Down
No reviews for this album.
Greyest of Blue Skies by: Finger Eleven
No reviews for this album.
------------------------------------
```

How It Works

This block of code has several mechanisms, which are in place to demonstrate a few key concepts of maintaining a database through PHP. First, you will probably notice that you insert a new table through the actual PHP code. Doing so is merely a matter of creating the SQL necessary (in this case with the create command) and then executing the query. The same can be said for modifying the structure of an existing table through the alter command. Both commands are processed via the SQL code and can be processed in PHP just as you would any other query. (Therefore, you still need validation in case of a SQL failure.)

Second, displaying linked results works largely the same as displaying nonlinked results; you merely have to take a little more caution when building the SQL query. You can link a table in SQL in more than one way, but we prefer the alias method. Basically, when you input the tables within the from element of the SQL query, you designate an alias to reference the table. Therefore, the SQL looks a little bit cleaner, as you can link the required columns via the alias (as in a.userloginid=b.userloginid) rather than through the full table names (review.userloginid=userlogin.userloginid). It is also important that you designate the distinct argument in the SQL, because failure to do so can result in duplicate rows being returned.

Finally, you must specify which data you want returned from the query rather than using the all-inclusive *. The reason for this is that there will be values returned that have the same name, so if you reference the array via the name of the column, the array will not know which value you are really looking for. (For example, it would not know which userloginid to return since there will be two of them returned.) It is better in this respect to specify the actual fields you want to return from the query via their table's alias (for example, a.review).

15-10. Displaying Results in a Form

Many great PHP-based database maintenance software packages are on the market (phpMyAdmin is our personal favorite), so you have to wonder—how do they do it? Well, maintaining a database through a form is not really that big of an issue. Huge software applications such as phpMyAdmin may have more functionality than you can shake a stick at, but they all began with the basics.

A common piece of functionality you will be required to make into legitimate web code is the ability to edit the contents of a row in the database. Doing so is not a particularly grueling endeavor, but it is an important matter and should be done right. In that regard, those interested in developing for the future will surely want to start porting their applications over to the mysqli extension. The following example allows you to modify the information contained within the userlogin table of the cds database through mysqli and a web form.

The Code

```
<!DOCTYPE html PUBLIC "-//W3C//DTD XHTML 1.0 Transitional//EN"➥
 "http://www.w3.org/TR/xhtml1/DTD/xhtml1-transitional.dtd">
<html xmlns="http://www.w3.org/1999/xhtml">
<head>
<title>Sample 15.10</title>
<meta http-equiv="Content-Type" content="text/html; charset=iso-8859-1" />
</head>
<body>
  <?php
    //Get the current info.
    $mysqli = new mysqli ("localhost","apress","testing","cds");
    //Attempt to connect.
    try {
      if (mysqli_connect_errno()){
        throw new exception ("Error: " . mysqli_connect_errno() . " - "➥
 . mysqli_connect_error());
      }
    } catch (exception $e){
      echo $e->getmessage();
    }

    //Let's prepare the edit statement.
    $prep = $mysqli->prepare ("UPDATE userlogin SET name=?, email=?,➥
 username=?, password=?");
    $prep->bind_param ('ssss',$_POST['name'],$_POST['email'],$_POST['user'],➥
 $_POST['pass']);
```

```php
    //Then bind the result statement.
    if ($result = $mysqli->prepare ("SELECT name,email,username,password➥
FROM userlogin")){
    } else {
      echo $mysqli->errno . " - " . $mysqli->error;
    }

    if ($_POST['submitted'] == "yes"){
      //You simply execute the prep statement.
      $prep->execute();
      //And output the result.
      echo "Update successfully completed: " . $prep->affected_rows . "➥
row(s) affected.";
      ?><p><a href="sample15_10.php">Update again?</a></p><?php
    } else {
      //Execute the result.
      $result->execute ();
      //Bind the results.
      $result->bind_result ($name,$email,$username,$password);
      //Then fetch the row.
      result->fetch();
      ?>
      <form action="sample15_10.php" method="post">
      <p>Please fill out the form to change your login information.</p>
      <div style="width: 250px;">
        <div style="width: 30%; float: left;">
          Name:
        </div>
        <div style="width: 59%; float: right;">
          <input type="text" name="name"➥
value="<?php echo stripslashes ($name); ?>" />
        </div>
        <br style="clear: both;" />
      </div>
      <div style="width: 250px; margin-top: 10px;">
        <div style="width: 30%; float: left;">
          Email:
        </div>
        <div style="width: 59%; float: right;">
          <input type="text" name="email"➥
value="<?php echo stripslashes ($email); ?>" />
        </div>
        <br style="clear: both;" />
    </div>
      <div style="width: 250px; margin-top: 10px;">
        <div style="width: 30%; float: left;">
```

```
              Username:
          </div>
          <div style="width: 59%; float: right;">
              <input type="text" name="user"➥
  value="<?php echo stripslashes ($username); ?>" />
          </div>
          <br style="clear: both;" />
      </div>
      <div style="width: 250px; margin-top: 10px;">
          <div style="width: 30%; float: left;">
          Password:
          </div>
          <div style="width: 59%; float: right;">
              <input type="text" name="pass"➥
  value="<?php echo stripslashes ($password); ?>" />
          </div>
          <br style="clear: both;" />
      </div>
      <br />
      <input type="hidden" name="submitted" value="yes" />
      <input type="submit" value="Edit" />
      </form>
      <?php
  }
  //Close the connection.
  $mysqli->close();

    ?>
  </body>
  </html>
```

How It Works

The majority of this code is simply laying out the form in the manner you prefer. We recommend that if you actually implement this code in a web application, make sure to do your validation; for the scope of this example, though, this will work fine.

This example prepares both an update statement and the results for the form. You will note that both statements are prepared and then executed at the appropriate time. Beyond that, simply note the new mysqli usage; it works nicely in cases such as this, as you can monitor your query in one spot and execute it wherever you want. In cases where you have multiple userlogin rows in the database, it is simple to modify this code to allow the update statement to contain a dynamic where clause.

Project: Bridging the Gap Between mysql and mysqli

Like it or not, millions of solid PHP applications are running on the Internet that still use the mysql extension. Also, more web servers are still running PHP 4 than have been upgraded to PHP 5. (And, of course, the same can be said for older versions of MySQL.) It is therefore imperative to be able to realize exactly what type of database engine a particular script can use. To better accommodate a variety of scenarios, the next two examples will guide you through creating a database class that will be usable on any MySQL-enabled PHP installation (the code is written for PHP 4 and up, however).

15-11. Discovering Which Extension Is Being Used

The methodology for figuring out which extension is currently in use for MySQL is rather simple. The following code gives you a concise understanding of what extensions are available for your use.

The Code

```php
<?php

  //sample15_11.php

  //Function to determine which extensions are installed.
  //First, the basic mysql extension.
  function mysqlinstalled (){
    //You can do a quick check to see if mysql is installed➥
by determining if a mysql
    //function exists.
    if (function_exists ("mysql_connect")){
      return true;
    } else {
      return false;
    }
  }
  //And the mysqli extension next.
  function mysqliinstalled (){
    //You do this entirely the same way you did the previous function.
    if (function_exists ("mysqli_connect")){
      return true;
    } else {
      return false;
    }
  }

  //Now, you check if the mysql functionality is available.
  if (mysqlinstalled()){
    echo "<p>The mysql extension is installed.</p>";
  } else {
```

```php
     echo "<p>The mysql extension is not installed.</p>";
   }
   //And ditto for the mysqli extension.
   if (mysqliinstalled()){
     echo "<p>The mysqli extension is installed.</p>";
   } else {
     echo "<p>The mysqli extension is not installed.</p>";
   }
?>
```

In this case, the results are as follows:

```
The mysql extension is installed.
The mysqli extension is installed.
```

How It Works

The way this little sample works is quite easy. PHP checks, using the function_exists()
method, whether a particular mysql or mysqli function (which is part of the extension) exists.
If the function actually exists, then the related extension must be installed. This may seem like
a rather mundane task to accomplish, but you will use these functions in the next example.
Specifically, you will write a custom database class (based largely on the class you built in
recipe 15-8) that handles mysqli if it is available and mysql if not.

15-12. Writing a Wrapper Class to Bridge the Gap

Building code that will work on almost any platform can be difficult. You can, however, make
it slightly easier by building code that will work for you depending on differing circumstances.
In a world where you are never sure what server your code will need to be ported to, it is
important to keep all eventualities in mind. The different MySQL extensions are the same.
Keeping the goal of portability in mind, consider the following wrapper class; it allows you to
run with the cleaner, more efficient mysqli code if the extension is in place and will default to
the mysql extension should the need arise.

The Code

```php
<?php

  //sample15_12.php

  class mydb {

    private $user;
    private $pass;
    private $host;
    private $db;
```

```
//Constructor function.
public function __construct (){
  $num_args = func_num_args();

  if($num_args > 0){
    $args = func_get_args();
    $this->host = $args[0];
    $this->user = $args[1];
    $this->pass = $args[2];

    $this->connect();
  }
}

//Function to tell us if mysqli is installed.
private function mysqliinstalled (){
  if (function_exists ("mysqli_connect")){
    return true;
  } else {
    return false;
  }
}

//Function to connect to the database.
private function connect (){
  try {
    //Mysqli functionality.
    if ($this->mysqliinstalled()){
      if (!$this->db = new mysqli ($this->host,$this->user,$this->pass)){
        $exceptionstring = "Error connection to database: <br />";
        $exceptionstring .= mysqli_connect_errno() . ": "➥
. mysqli_connect_error();
        throw new exception ($exceptionstring);
      }
      //Mysql functionality.
    } else {
      if (!$this->db = mysql_connect ($this->host,$this->user,$this->pass)){
        $exceptionstring = "Error connection to database: <br />";
        $exceptionstring .= mysql_errno() . ": " . mysql_error();
        throw new exception ($exceptionstring);
      }
    }
  } catch (exception $e) {
    echo $e->getmessage();
  }
}
```

```php
//Function to select a database.
public function selectdb ($thedb){
  try {
    //Mysqli functionality.
    if ($this->mysqliinstalled()){
      if (!$this->db->select_db ($thedb)){
        $exceptionstring = "Error opening database: $thedb: <br />";
        $exceptionstring .= $this->db->errno . ": " . $this->db->error;
        throw new exception ($exceptionstring);
      }
    //Mysql functionality.
    } else {
      if (!mysql_select_db ($thedb, $this->db)){
        $exceptionstring = "Error opening database: $thedb: <br />";
        $exceptionstring .= mysql_errno() . ": " . mysql_error();
        throw new exception ($exceptionstring);
      }
    }
  } catch (exception $e) {
    echo $e->getmessage();
  }
}

//Function to perform a query.
public function execute ($thequery){
  try {
    //Mysqli functionality.
    if ($this->mysqliinstalled()){
      if (!$this->db->query ($thequery)){
        $exceptionstring = "Error performing query: $thequery: <br />";
        $exceptionstring .= $this->db->errno . ": " . $this->db->error;
        throw new exception ($exceptionstring);
      } else {
        echo "Query performed correctly: " . $this->db->affected_rows . "➡
row(s) affected.<br />";
      }
    //Mysql functionality.
    } else {
      if (!mysql_query ($thequery, $this->db)){
        $exceptionstring = "Error performing query: $thequery: <br />";
        $exceptionstring .= mysql_errno() . ": " . mysql_error();
        throw new exception ($exceptionstring);
      } else {
        echo "Query performed correctly: " . mysql_affected_rows () . "➡
row(s) affected.<br />";
      }
    }
```

```
    } catch (exception $e) {
      echo $e->getmessage();
    }
  }


  //Function to return a row set.
  public function getrows ($thequery){
    try {
      //Mysqli functionality.
      if ($this->mysqliinstalled()){
        if ($result = $this->db->query ($thequery)){
          $returnarr = array ();
          while ($adata = $result->fetch_array ()){
            $returnarr = array_merge ($returnarr,$adata);
          }
          return $returnarr;
        } else {
          $exceptionstring = "Error performing query: $thequery: <br />";
          $exceptionstring .= $this->db->errno . ": " . $this->db->error;
          throw new exception ($exceptionstring);
        }
      //Mysql functionality.
      } else {
        if (!$aquery = mysql_query ($thequery)){
          $exceptionstring = "Error performing query: $thequery: <br />";
          $exceptionstring .= mysql_errno() . ": " . mysql_error();
          throw new exception ($exceptionstring);
        } else {
          $returnarr = array ();
          while ($adata = mysql_fetch_array ($aquery)){
            $returnarr = array_merge ($returnarr,$adata);
          }
          return $returnarr;
        }
      }
    } catch (exception $e) {
      echo $e->getmessage();
    }
  }


  //Function to close the database link.
  public function __destruct() {
    try {
      //Mysqli functionality.
      if ($this->mysqliinstalled()){
        if (!$this->db->close()){
          $exceptionstring = "Error closing connection: <br />";
```

```
          $exceptionstring .= $this->db->errno . ": " . $this->db->error;
          throw new exception ($exceptionstring);
        }
      //Mysql functionality.
      } else {
        if (!mysql_close ($this->db)){
          $exceptionstring = "Error closing connection: <br />";
          $exceptionstring .= mysql_errno() . ": " . mysql_error();
          throw new exception ($exceptionstring);
        }
      }
    } catch (exception $e) {
      echo $e->getmessage();
    }
  }

}

//Now, let's create an instance of mydb.
$mydb = new mydb ("localhost","apress","testing");

//Select a database to use.
$mydb->selectdb ("cds");

//Now, let's perform an action.
$adata = $mydb->execute ("UPDATE cd SET title='Hybrid Theory' WHERE cdid='2'");

//Then, let's try to return a row set.
$adata = $mydb->getrows ("SELECT * FROM cd ORDER BY cdid ASC");
for ($i = 0; $i < count ($adata); $i++){
  echo $adata[$i] . "<br />";
}
?>
```

A run-through of this code with no errors will display the following result, whether the mysqli extension is installed or not:

```
Query performed correctly: 1 row(s) affected.
1
Chuck
Sum 41
2
Hybrid Theory
Linkin Park
3
Mezmerize
System of a Down
```

4
Greyest of Blue Skies
Finger Eleven

How It Works

As you can see, the code for this class is similar to the class you wrote in recipe 15-8 with one
major difference. Every time the code goes to execute a method, it first checks to see if the
mysqli extension is installed. If it is indeed installed, it goes about its business. If the mysqli
extension is not installed, no problems are had; the code will execute the same but with all
the mysql extension's functions. Through the use of a wrapper class here, you made this code
portable.

15-13. Project: Going from MySQL to XML and from XML to MySQL

The current standard for portable data is Extensible Markup Language (XML). XML is completely portable and can be read by almost every major software release available. In the past,
different data storage systems have handled information in a myriad of ways, often leading to
hard-to-export and hard-to-import data. With the advent of XML, however, information has
become quite a bit easier to share.

PHP 5 is no exception. One of the more valuable uses of PHP 5 is the ability to scan through
a MySQL database and output XML (or the ability to take in an XML file and convert it into a format that can be read by MySQL). In the next example, we will show how to create a simple class
whose purpose will be either to read and convert XML or to perform the opposite.

Keep in mind that in order for this script to work properly, the file you are writing the XML
to must be writable. The script will attempt to create the file, but only if the folder has the
proper permissions. For ease of use, ensure that you create the file first and CHMOD it to 777.

It is also extremely important to note that this example will create an XML backup and
then drop the database that was specified. Please ensure that you either create a new database
to play around with or run this example only on a database you do not mind losing (although
the script will re-create the database for you). The dropdb() method is in charge of actually
dropping the database, so you could simply comment out the call to that method if you are
concerned.

The Code

```php
<?php

  //sample15_13.php

  //Class to convert MySQL into XML and back.
  class xmlconverter {

    private $user;
    private $pass;
```

```php
    private $host;
    private $db;

    //Constructor function.
    public function __construct (){
      $num_args = func_num_args();

      if($num_args > 0){
        $args = func_get_args();
        $this->host = $args[0];
        $this->user = $args[1];
        $this->pass = $args[2];

        $this->connect();
      }
    }

    //Function to connect to the database.
    private function connect (){
      try {
        if (!$this->db = mysql_connect ($this->host,$this->user,$this->pass)){
          $exceptionstring = "Error connection to database: <br />";
          $exceptionstring .= mysql_errno() . ": " . mysql_error();
          throw new exception ($exceptionstring);
        }
      } catch (exception $e) {
        echo $e->getmessage();
      }
    }

    //Function to select a database.
    public function selectdb ($thedb){
      try {
        if (!mysql_select_db ($thedb, $this->db)){
          $exceptionstring = "Error opening database: $thedb: <br />";
          $exceptionstring .= mysql_errno() . ": " . mysql_error();
          throw new exception ($exceptionstring);
        }
      } catch (exception $e) {
        echo $e->getmessage();
      }
    }

    //Function to convert XML to MySQL.
    public function xmltomysql ($outputfile) {
      //First, attempt to open the database.
      $db = $this->connect ();
```

```php
//Now, attempt to open the xml for reading.
try {
  if ($file = fopen ($outputfile,"r")){
    $xml = simplexml_load_file ($outputfile);
    //First, create the db.
    try {
      if (mysql_query ("CREATE DATABASE IF NOT EXISTS " . $xml->dbname . "")){
        //Now, select the database you want to export.
        $this->selectdb ($xml->dbname,$db);
        //Then, start going through the tables and creating them.
        foreach ($xml->table as $table){
          //Attempt to create the table.
          $ctable = "CREATE TABLE IF NOT EXISTS " . $table->tname . " (";
          $colcount = 0;
          $totcolcount = 0;
          //Now, you need to know how many columns are in this table.
          foreach ($table->tstructure->tcolumn as $totcol){
            $totcolcount++;
          }
          foreach ($table->tstructure->tcolumn as $col){
            $colcount++;
            $ctable .= $col->Field." ";
            //Deal with Nulls.
            $ctable .= $col->Type." ";
            if ($col->Null == "YES"){
              $ctable .= "NULL ";
            } else {
              $ctable .= "NOT NULL ";
            }
            //Deal with the default value.
            if ($col->Default != ""){
              $ctable .= "DEFAULT ".$col->Default." ";
            }
            //Deal with Auto_Increment
            if ($col->Extra != ""){
              $ctable .= "AUTO_INCREMENT ";
            }
            //And lastly deal with primary keys.
            if ($colcount != $totcolcount){
              if ($col->Key == "PRI"){
                $ctable .= ",PRIMARY KEY(".$col->Field."), ";
              } else {
                $ctable .= ", ";
              }
            } else {
              if ($col->Key == "PRI"){
                $ctable .= ",PRIMARY KEY(".$col->Field.") ";
```

```php
        }
      }
    }
    $ctable .= ")";
    //Attempt to create the table.
    try {
      if (mysql_query ($ctable)){
        //Now you need to insert the data.
        foreach ($table->tdata->trow as $row){
          $insquery = "INSERT INTO ".$table->tname." (";
          //Find the number of rows.
          $totrow = 0;
          foreach ($row->children() as $totchild){
            $totrow++;
          }
          //First, set up the names of the values.
          $currow = 0;
          foreach ($row->children() as $name=>$node){
            $currow++;
            if ($currow != $totrow){
              $insquery .= $name.", ";
            } else {
              $insquery .= $name;
            }
          }
          $insquery .= ") VALUES (";
          //And then the data for insertion.
          $currow = 0;
          foreach ($row->children() as $childrendata){
            $currow++;
            if ($currow != $totrow){
              $insquery .= "'".$childrendata."', ";
            } else {
              $insquery .= "'".$childrendata."'";
            }
          }
          $insquery .= ")";
          //Now, attempt to do the insertion.
          try {
            if (!mysql_query ($insquery)){
              throw new exception (mysql_error());
            }
          } catch (exception $e) {
            echo $e->getmessage ();
          }
        }
      } else {
```

```
                 throw new exception (mysql_error()."<br />");
               }
            } catch (exception $e) {
              echo $e->getmessage ();
            }
          }
        } else {
          throw new exception (mysql_error());
        }
      } catch (exception $e) {
        echo $e->getmessage ();
      }

    } else {
      throw new exception ("Sorry, xml file could not be opened.");
    }
  } catch (exception $e) {
    echo $e->getmessage ();
  }


}

//Function to convert mysql to xml.
public function mysqltoxml ($database,$inputfile) {
  //First, attempt to connect to the database.
  $db = $this->connect ();
  //Now, select the database you want to export.
  $this->selectdb ($database,$db);
  //Now, attempt to open the xml file for writing.
  try {
    if ($file = fopen ($inputfile,"w")){
      //Output the version number.
      fwrite ($file, "<?xml version=\"1.0\"?>\n");
      //Now, first output the database as the main xml tab.
      fwrite ($file,"<db>\n");
      //Output the name of the database.
      fwrite ($file,"\t<dbname>".$database."</dbname>\n");
      //Now, go through the database and grab all table names.
      if ($tquery = mysql_query ("SHOW TABLES FROM $database")){
        if (mysql_num_rows ($tquery) > 0){
          while ($tdata = mysql_fetch_array ($tquery)){
            fwrite ($file,"\t<table>\n");
            fwrite ($file,"\t\t<tname>".$tdata[0]."</tname>\n");
            //Then, grab all fields in this table.
            if ($fquery = mysql_query ("SHOW COLUMNS FROM ".$tdata[0]."")){
              if (mysql_num_rows ($fquery) > 0){
                //First show the structure.
```

```
                          fwrite ($file,"\t\t<tstructure>\n");
                          //Start an array of names.
                          $narr = array ();
                          while ($fdata = mysql_fetch_assoc ($fquery)){
                            $narr[] = $fdata['Field'];
                            fwrite ($file,"\t\t\t<tcolumn>\n");
                            fwrite ($file,"\t\t\t\t<Field>".$fdata['Field']."</Field>\n");
                            fwrite ($file,"\t\t\t\t<Type>".$fdata['Type']."</Type>\n");
                            fwrite ($file,"\t\t\t\t<Null>".$fdata['Null']."</Null>\n");
                            fwrite ($file,"\t\t\t\t<Key>".$fdata['Key']."</Key>\n");
                            fwrite ($file,"\t\t\t\t<Default>".$fdata['Default'].➥
"</Default>\n");

                            fwrite ($file,"\t\t\t\t<Extra>".$fdata['Extra']."</Extra>\n");
                            fwrite ($file,"\t\t\t</tcolumn>\n");
                          }
                          fwrite ($file,"\t\t</tstructure>\n");
                          //Now, show the data.
                          if ($dquery = mysql_query ("SELECT * FROM ".$tdata[0]."")){
                            if (mysql_num_rows ($dquery) > 0 ){
                              fwrite ($file,"\t\t<tdata>\n");
                              //Start a counter.
                              while ($ddata = mysql_fetch_assoc ($dquery)){
                                fwrite ($file,"\t\t\t<trow>\n");
                                $fcounter = 0;
                                while ($ele = each ($ddata)){
                                  fwrite ($file,"\t\t\t\t\t<".$narr[$fcounter]➥
. ">".$ele['value']."</".$narr[$fcounter].">\n");
                                  $fcounter++;
                                }
                                fwrite ($file,"\t\t\t</trow>\n");
                              }
                              fwrite ($file,"\t\t</tdata>\n");
                            }
                          } else {
                            echo mysql_error();
                          }

                        }
                      } else {
                        echo mysql_error();
                      }
                      fwrite ($file,"\t</table>\n");
                  }
                }
              } else {
                echo mysql_error();
              }
```

```php
        fwrite ($file,"</db>");
      } else {
        throw new exception ("Sorry, could not open the file for writing.");
      }
    } catch (exception $e) {
      echo $e->getmessage();
    }


  }

  //Function to drop a database, be careful with this one ;).
  public function dropdb ($thedb){
    try {
      if (!mysql_query ("DROP DATABASE $thedb", $this->db)){
        $exceptionstring = "Error dropping database: $thedb: <br />";
        $exceptionstring .= mysql_errno() . ": " . mysql_error();
        throw new exception ($exceptionstring);
      }
    } catch (exception $e) {
      echo $e->getmessage();
    }
  }

  //Function to close the database link.
  public function __destruct() {
    try {
      if (!mysql_close ($this->db)){
        $exceptionstring = "Error closing connection: <br />";
        $exceptionstring .= mysql_errno() . ": " . mysql_error();
        throw new exception ($exceptionstring);
      }
    } catch (exception $e) {
      echo $e->getmessage();
    }
  }
}
//Create a new instance of the class.
$myconverter = new xmlconverter ("localhost","apress","testing");
//Then convert the database into XML.
$myconverter->mysqltoxml ("cds","test.xml");
//Then drop the database to prove it works.
$myconverter->dropdb ("cds");
//Now completely recreate the db.
$myconverter->xmltomysql ("test.xml");
?>
```

Here is what the final XML file for the cds database looks like:

```
<?xml version="1.0"?>
<db>
  <dbname>cds</dbname>
  <table>
    <tname>cd</tname>
    <tstructure>
      <tcolumn>
        <Field>cdid</Field>
        <Type>int(11)</Type>
        <Null></Null>
        <Key>PRI</Key>
        <Default></Default>
        <Extra>auto_increment</Extra>
      </tcolumn>
      <tcolumn>
        <Field>title</Field>
        <Type>tinytext</Type>
        <Null></Null>
        <Key></Key>
        <Default></Default>
        <Extra></Extra>
      </tcolumn>
      <tcolumn>
        <Field>artist</Field>
        <Type>tinytext</Type>
        <Null></Null>
        <Key></Key>
        <Default></Default>
        <Extra></Extra>
      </tcolumn>
    </tstructure>
    <tdata>
      <trow>
        <cdid>1</cdid>
        <title>Chuck</title>
        <artist>Sum 41</artist>
        </trow>
        <trow>
        <cdid>2</cdid>
        <title>Meteora</title>
        <artist>Linkin Park</artist>
        </trow>
        <trow>
        <cdid>3</cdid>
        <title>Mezmerize</title>
```

```
      <artist>System of a Down</artist>
    </trow>
    <trow>
      <cdid>4</cdid>
      <title>Greyest of Blue Skies</title>
      <artist>Finger Eleven</artist>
    </trow>
  </tdata>
</table>
<table>
  <tname>review</tname>
  <tstructure>
    <tcolumn>
      <Field>reviewid</Field>
      <Type>int(11)</Type>
      <Null></Null>
      <Key>PRI</Key>
      <Default></Default>
      <Extra>auto_increment</Extra>
    </tcolumn>
    <tcolumn>
      <Field>userloginid</Field>
      <Type>int(11)</Type>
      <Null>YES</Null>
      <Key></Key>
      <Default></Default>
      <Extra></Extra>
    </tcolumn>
    <tcolumn>
      <Field>cdid</Field>
      <Type>int(11)</Type>
      <Null>YES</Null>
      <Key></Key>
      <Default></Default>
      <Extra></Extra>
    </tcolumn>
    <tcolumn>
      <Field>rtitle</Field>
      <Type>tinytext</Type>
      <Null>YES</Null>
      <Key></Key>
      <Default></Default>
      <Extra></Extra>
    </tcolumn>
    <tcolumn>
      <Field>review</Field>
      <Type>text</Type>
```

```
        <Null>YES</Null>
        <Key></Key>
        <Default></Default>
        <Extra></Extra>
      </tcolumn>
    </tstructure>
    <tdata>
      <trow>
        <reviewid>1</reviewid>
        <userloginid>1</userloginid>
        <cdid>2</cdid>
        <rtitle>My Review</rtitle>
        <review>Wow, what a great album!</review>
      </trow>
    </tdata>
  </table>
  <table>
    <tname>userlogin</tname>
    <tstructure>
      <tcolumn>
        <Field>userloginid</Field>
        <Type>int(11)</Type>
        <Null></Null>
        <Key>PRI</Key>
        <Default></Default>
        <Extra>auto_increment</Extra>
      </tcolumn>
      <tcolumn>
        <Field>username</Field>
        <Type>tinytext</Type>
        <Null></Null>
        <Key></Key>
        <Default></Default>
        <Extra></Extra>
      </tcolumn>
     <tcolumn>
        <Field>password</Field>
        <Type>tinytext</Type>
        <Null></Null>
        <Key></Key>
        <Default></Default>
        <Extra></Extra>
      </tcolumn>
      <tcolumn>
        <Field>name</Field>
        <Type>tinytext</Type>
        <Null>YES</Null>
```

```
          <Key></Key>
          <Default></Default>
          <Extra></Extra>
        </tcolumn>
        <tcolumn>
          <Field>email</Field>
          <Type>tinytext</Type>
          <Null>YES</Null>
          <Key></Key>
          <Default></Default>
          <Extra></Extra>
        </tcolumn>
      </tstructure>
      <tdata>
        <trow>
          <userloginid>1</userloginid>
          <username>apress</username>
          <password>testing</password>
          <name>Lee Babin</name>
          <email>lee@babinplanet.ca</email>
        </trow>
      </tdata>
    </table>
  </db>
```

How It Works

This is a rather complicated class. Understanding this class requires a couple of core competencies. First, you should have a basic understanding of what XML is and how to use it. We recommend the highly competent tutorial available at W3Schools:

`http://www.w3schools.com/xml/default.asp`

Second, you are using a new set of functions available by default in the current PHP 5 compilation, Simple XML. We recommend visiting the PHP manual at `http://www.php.net/simplexml` for gaining extended knowledge on Simple XML (but, as its name implies, it is actually rather simple to figure out!).

Now that you have the core prerequisites out of the way, let's delve into this class here. You will note that most of the MySQL connecting and disconnecting functionality has been ported over from recipe 15-8, so if you have a good understanding of that, you should not have too much trouble with this.

The first new method, the `mysqltoxml()` method, takes in, as an argument, the file location you want to write the XML to. Should the file not exist or not have the proper permissions to write to, the method will return an error. If, however, the file is ready to go, the script will scan through every table in the specified database and write the equivalent XML to the specified XML file. Now, the structure for the XML is entirely up to you. In fact, it may have been more prudent to go with attributes for certain tags rather than new tags, but we were looking for ease of reading in this case.

For this XML schema, we chose the db tag as the all-inclusive dataset and structured inward from there. In this schema, you will see every table in the database (the table tag), then each column for each table structure (every tcolumn for each tstructure), and then a dynamically created dataset (within dynamically created tags in the trow element).

The mysql_fetch_assoc() function works largely like the mysql_fetch_array() function, but it uses an associative array to store the information garnered from a row. From there it is merely a matter of structuring your database queries properly (selecting from tables and showing queries) to obtain a working XML record of the entire database.

The next method, xmltomysql(), is slightly more complicated, but if you understand the core structure of the XML, you will see that it is merely a matter of reversing what you have just done with the mysqltoxml() method. Basically, the script reads the entire XML file using the simplexml_load_file() method, which creates a SIMPLEXMLElement object (an object that contains XML-related methods). From there, you can perform a rather large amount of functionality.

Using Simple XML to parse through first the database and then the tables in the database, you gradually create the database and move onto each table. Since the XML that gets created for the individual row setup does not port straight across into a valid query, a little bit of finessing was required to get the table creation queries just right. The same could be said for the data insertion, but less manipulation is required.

All in all, with the power of Simple XML and MySQL, moving between the two can be rather painless and incredibly powerful.

Summary

As the Web and the applications that are built for it progress, data and information storage is becoming more important. While many different methods exist for storing information, the MySQL solution is tried, tested, and extremely functional. As MySQL continues to evolve, so too does the PHP required to handle it. The new mysqli extension proves that MySQL and PHP listen to their users, continue to make improvements, and implement solutions to issues that developers may have.

Through carefully created and properly designed data storage, a database can be a developer's best friend. With the new, heavily object-oriented PHP 5 model, it has become easier to write code that can be used in a variety of situations and can take care of a wealth of the work for you.

To conclude, MySQL continues to be the developer's choice for a fully functional, robust, and affordable database solution. As the code written into PHP 5 continues to evolve, so too will the wondrous applications in which you can put it to use.

Looking Ahead

In the next, and final, chapter, Frank M. Kromann will provide an in-depth look at some of the services PHP 5 can provide. Expect to see a ton of strong, effective code to help you with your mail, Domain Name System (DNS), and File Transfer Protocol (FTP) issues and algorithms. All this and more are to be had in Chapter 16.

CHAPTER 16

■■■

Communicating with Internet Services

When you use PHP to build dynamic web applications, you need to communicate with other Internet services. This can be as simple as sending an e-mail with the content of a user-submitted form or as advanced as a full-featured mail client that allows the user to send and receive e-mails. PHP has several ways of communicating with Internet services. The most basic form is socket communication, where all the protocol features must be implemented in the PHP script. More advanced features for reading remote files are implemented as wrapper functions for the normal file handling functions, and some services are implemented with a function set that makes it easy to write complex applications without having to know all the details of socket-level communication.

16-1. Sending Internet Mail

You can send mail from a PHP script in at least two ways. The first way is to use one of the built-in mail functions: `mail()` or `imap_mail()`. These two functions build on the same internal mail routine, but they have a different set of arguments, and the `imap_mail()` function is available only when the Internet Message Access Protocol (IMAP) extension is loaded. The PHP Extension and Application Repository (PEAR) also provides a `mail` class. This is basically an object-oriented wrapper for the built-in `mail()` function.

The second way requires using the socket extension to create a direct connection to a Simple Mail Transfer Protocol (SMTP) mail server. This method requires knowledge of how SMTP mail servers work.

■Note Access to SMTP servers is normally restricted to specific Internet Protocol (IP) addresses or requires some form of authentication. This blocks someone from hijacking the SMTP server to send spam and viruses.

The prototypes for the two built-in mail functions are as follows. Note that the first four parameters are the same.

```
bool mail ( string to, string subject, string message➡
  [, string additional_headers [, string additional_parameters]] )
bool imap_mail ( string to, string subject, string message➡
  [, string additional_headers [, string cc [, string bcc [, string rpath]]]] )
```

To use the built-in mail functions, you must configure a few settings in php.ini. On a Unix system, you must specify the sendmail_path setting to point to where sendmail is located and add parameters. The default value is "sendmail -t -i". On a Windows system, there are three values: SMTP, smtp_port, and sendmail_from. SMTP is the hostname or IP address of the SMTP server. This can be localhost if you have an SMTP server running on the same server. For most SMTP servers, smtp_port should be 25, but in some cases you might want to change that. The sendmail_from value specifies the From: header, unless it is included in the additional headers string on all outgoing mails.

The following example shows how to send an e-mail from a PHP script.

The Code

```php
<?php
// Example 16-1-1.php
$to = "sam@somedomain.com";
$from = "joe@anotherdomain.com";
$cc = $from;
$subject = "Sending e-mails from PHP";
$body = <<< BODY
Hi Sam,

This e-mail is generated from a PHP script.

- Joe
BODY;

mail($to, $subject, $body, "From: $from\r\nCc: $cc");
?>
```

How It Works

This example defines a number of variables used as parameters to the mail() function. The $body variable is created with the HEREDOC notation, and the value is defined as everything between <<< BODY and BODY;. This notation makes it easy to include linefeeds in a variable. The additional headers form the last parameter to the mail() function. These are formed as variables embedded in a string.

16-2. Project: Sending an E-mail with a Mail Class

Using a mail class such as PEAR::Mail has a few advantages over using the plain mail() function. One of the advantages is the built-in check for valid mail addresses before sending a mail. To get the PEAR::Mail class on your system, you must run the command pear install mail. This requires that PEAR is already installed on your system.

The Code

```php
<?php
// Example 16-2-1.php
require "Mail.php";

$to = array("sam@somedomain.com");
$headers = array(
  'From' => "joe@anotherdomain.com",
  'Cc' => "joe@anotherdomain.com",
  'Subject' => "Sending e-mails from PEAR::Mail"
);

$body = <<< BODY
Hi Sam,

This e-mail is generated from a PHP script with the PEAR::Mail class.

- Joe
BODY;

$mail = Mail::factory('mail');
$mail->send($to, $headers, $body);
?>
```

How It Works

This uses the built-in mail() function to send the e-mail as plain text. The PEAR::Mail class has multiple factories to choose from (mail, sendmail, and smtp). Object-oriented programming uses factories to load/implement different technologies with the same application programming interfaces (APIs). So, in the case of the Mail() class, you can load the class elements needed to communicate with the mail server when the Mail object is created. The mail factory uses the built-in mail() function, sendmail communicates directly with the sendmail program, and the smtp factory uses sockets to connect directly to the server. The smtp factory supports authentication, allowing you to use a more secure SMTP server.

In addition to the basic Mail() class, PEAR also provides a Multipurpose Internet Mail Extensions (MIME) class that allows you to build more complex e-mails with Hypertext Markup Language (HTML), embedded images, and attachments. This class is called PEAR::Mail_mime, and the following example shows how to use this class with the Mail() class to send a message that contains plain text and an HTML body. You can install the Mail_mime class with the command pear install Mail_mime.

The Code

```php
<?php
// Example 16-2-2.php
require "Mail.php";
require "Mail/mime.php";

$to = array("sam@somedomain.com");
$headers = array(
  'From' => "joe@anotherdomain.com",
  'Cc' => "joe@anotherdomain.com",
  'Subject' => "Sending e-mails from PEAR::Mail"
);

$mime = new Mail_mime();

$txtBody = <<< BODY
Hi Sam,

This e-mail is generated from a PHP script with the PEAR::Mail class.

- Joe
BODY;

$mime->setTXTBody($txtBody);

$htmlBody = <<< BODY
<html><body>
<h1>Hi Sam,</h1><br>
This e-mail is generated from a PHP script with the PEAR::Mail class.<br>
- Joe<br>
</body></html>
BODY;

$mime->setHTMLBody($htmlBody);

$body = $mime->get();
$headers = $mime->headers($headers);

$mail = Mail::factory('mail');
$mail->send($to, $headers, $body);
?>
```

How It Works

This example uses the same basic structure as the previous example, but it also uses a class to handle the different elements of a MIME message. A MIME message has several parts, and in this case you define a plain-text version and an HTML version of the body and then add these to the MIME message. When all parts have been added to the MIME object, you extract the body and headers, and these are used to send the message.

The calls to $mime->get() and $mime->headers() must be executed in this order, because the get() method generates the necessary headers. Getting the body value first will work.

```
$body = $mime->get();
$mail->send($to, $mime->headers($headers),  $body);
```

Writing everything in a single line will not work, because PHP will execute the call to $mime->headers() first, and the header defining the mail as a multipart message will not be included in the mail. The result will be one plain-text message.

```
$mail->send($to, $mime->headers($headers),  $body = $mime->get());
```

■Note Not all mail clients can render HTML bodies. Make sure you always send a plain-text body when you send an HTML body. This makes it possible for non-HTML mail clients to display the message.

You can also use PEAR::Mail_mime to embed images into an HTML body or attach files to the message. You can choose to embed images or reference images that are available online. An embedded image will increase the size of the mail, but a reference to an online image requires the client to be online when the mail is viewed.

The following example shows how to use the PEAR::Mail and PEAR::Mail_mime classes to create and send an e-mail with an HTML body that has an embedded image.

The Code

```php
<?php
// Example 16-2-3.php
require "Mail.php";
require "Mail/mime.php";

$to = array("sam@somedomain.com");
$headers = array(
  'From' => "joe@anotherdomain.com",
  'Cc' => "joe@anotherdomain.com",
  'Subject' => "Sending e-mails from PEAR::Mail"
);
```

```
$mime = new Mail_mime();

$txtBody = "Please read the HTML part of this message"

$mime->setTXTBody($txtBody);

$htmlBody = <<< BODY
<html><body>
<h1>Hi Sam,</h1><br>
This e-mail is generated from a PHP script with the PEAR::Mail class.<br>
<img src='image.jpg'><br>
- Joe<br>
</body></html>
BODY;

$mime->setHTMLBody($htmlBody);
$mime->addHTMLImage('image.jpg', 'image/jpeg', 'image.jpg', true);

$body = $mime->get();
$headers = $mime->headers($headers);

$mail = Mail::factory('mail');
$mail->send($to, $headers, $body);
?>
```

How It Works

In this example you use the method addHTMLImage() to include a JPG image in the MIME structure. The name of the image is also used as the src property of the image tag in the HTML part of the message. When the body is generated, the image tag will be modified to reference the embedded image.

If the image is available online, you should replace the image source with the full Uniform Resource Locator (URL) to the image, and you should not include the image in the mail with the addHTMLImage() method.

16-3. Reading Mail with IMAP or POP3

You can read e-mails from a mail account with the IMAP extension. This extension supports IMAP, Post Office Protocol 3 (POP3), and Network News Transport Protocol (NNTP) services, and you can use it to read and parse messages from these systems. As mentioned in the previous section, the extension also has a function for sending mail messages, but this is not the primary purpose of the extension. The IMAP extension implements a large number of functions to maintain mailboxes, to convert data between different encodings, and so on. This section describes how to use functions that check and retrieve mail from a mailbox using IMAP and POP3.

The imap_open() function creates a connection to a mailbox, and on success it will return a handle to the mailbox that can be used when calling other imap_* functions to access additional information.

The next example shows a small class that can access IMAP, POP3, and NNTP servers to list the contents of a specific mailbox on the server. This first version of the class does not contain functions to retrieve the body of the messages, but you will add this to the class later in this section. Table 16-1 lists the methods of this class.

Table 16-1. GetMail *Methods*

Name	Description
__construct()	Class constructor. This will create the connection to the mailbox.
__destruct()	Cleans up when the object is destroyed.
num_msg()	Gets the number of messages in the mailbox.
num_recent()	Gets the number of recent messages in the mailbox.
headers()	Returns headers for all (or selected) messages in the mailbox.
format_address()	Returns an RFC-822–formatted address from an address object.
format_address_list()	Returns RFC-822–formatted addresses for an array of objects.

The Code

```php
<?php
// Example getmail.incif
(!extension_loaded("imap")) {
  dl("php_imap.dll");
}

class GetMail {
  private $host;
  private $user;
  private $pass;
  private $type;
  private $mbox;
  private $port;
  private $mh = null;

  function __construct($host, $user, $pass,
    $type = 'imap', $mbox = 'INBOX', $port = null) {
    $this->host = $host;
    $this->user = $user;
    $this->pass = $pass;
    $this->type = strtolower($type);
    if (is_null($port)) {
      switch($this->type) {
        case 'imap' :
          $this->port = 143;
          break;
        case 'pop3' :
          $this->port = 110;
          break;
```

```
      case 'nntp' :
        $this->port = 119;
        break;
      }
    }
    else {
      $this->port = $port;
    }
    $this->mbox = $mbox;
    $mailbox = "$this->host:$this->port/$this->type";
    $this->mh = imap_open("{" . $mailbox . "}$this->mbox",
      $this->user, $this->pass, 16);
  }

  function __destruct() {
    if ($this->mh) {
      imap_close($this->mh);
    }
  }

  function num_msg() {
    return imap_num_msg($this->mh);
  }

  function num_recent() {
    return imap_num_recent($this->mh);
  }

  function headers($offset = 1, $max = 0) {
    $msg_from = $offset;
    if ($max > 0) {
      $msg_to = min($max + $offset, $this->num_msg());
    }
    else {
      $msg_to = $this->num_msg();
    }
    $headers = array();
    for ($i = $msg_from; $i <= $msg_to; $i++) {
      $headers[] = imap_headerinfo($this->mh, $i);
    }
    return $headers;
  }

  function format_address($obj) {
    if (isset($obj->personal)) {
      return imap_rfc822_write_address($obj->mailbox, $obj->host, $obj->personal);
    }
```

```
    else {
      return imap_rfc822_write_address($obj->mailbox, $obj->host, '');
    }
  }

  function format_address_list($array, $sep = ", ") {
    $list = array();
    foreach($array as $obj) {
      $list[] = $this->format_address($obj);
    }
    return implode($sep, $list);
  }
}
?>
```

The GetMail class is stored in a file called getmail.inc, and you can use it to fetch the message headers in an IMAP or POP3 mail account:

```php
<?php
// Example 16-3-1.php
require "getmail.inc";

$mail = new GetMail("mail.somedomain.com", "user", "password", "pop3");

$msg = $mail->num_msg();
echo "Messages = $msg\n";
if ($msg > 0) {
  $headers = $mail->headers();
  foreach ($headers as $header) {
    echo "Subject: " . $header->subject . "\n";
    echo "\tFrom: " . $mail->format_address($header->from[0]) . "\n";
    echo "\tto: " . $mail->format_address($header->to[0]) . "\n";
  }
}
?>
```

How it Works

The getmain.inc file is included as the first file. This file will perform a check for the IMAP extension and load it if it's not already loaded. The GetMail() class is also defined in this file. For each message returned, the script will print a line with the subject, the From: address, and the To: address.

Make sure you set the correct domain, user ID, and password before you use this example.

You can use the same class to get the headers from messages stored in a news server (NNTP). The server/mailbox used in the next example holds more than 1,200 messages, so to speed things up and reduce the size of the output, the headers() function is called with two optional arguments, called $offset and $max. The first argument tells the function where to start, and the second argument tells the function how many headers to return.

The Code

```php
<?php
// Example 16-3-2.php
require "getmail.inc";

$mail = new GetMail("news.php.net", "", "", "nntp", "php.gtk.dev");
$msg = $mail->num_msg();

echo <<< HTML
<html><body><table width=100% border=1>
  <tr>
     <td>UID</td>
     <td>Date</td>
     <td>Subject</td>
  </tr>
HTML;

if ($msg > 0) {
   $headers = $mail->headers($msg - 5, 5);
   foreach ($headers as $uid=>$header) {
      echo "<tr><td>$uid</td>" .
           "<td>" . $header->date . "</td>" .
           "<td>" . $header->subject . "</td>" .
           "</tr>";
   }
}
echo <<< HTML
</table></body></html>
HTML;
?>
```

How It Works

The basic elements in this example are the same as the previous example. You use NNTP to connect to the new server, and you use an additional parameter to specify the newsgroup you want to list. When the headers() method is called, you specify the offset and the count to limit the number of messages returned. Figure 16-1 shows the output from the code, listing the five latest entries to the newsgroup.

The next step is to add functions to retrieve the content of the message body. This can either be plain text or a combination of plain text, HTML, embedded files, and attachments. This implementation will deal with only plain text, HTML, and images. The IMAP extension provides three functions to retrieve the message body. The imap_body() function will return the full body string and leave it to the client to parse the content. The imap_fetchstructure() function analyzes the structure, and imap_fetchbody() fetches the content of a single part.

You can fetch the body of a message formatted as plain text by calling imap_body(). The returned result might need some decoding of quoted printable strings before it can be used.

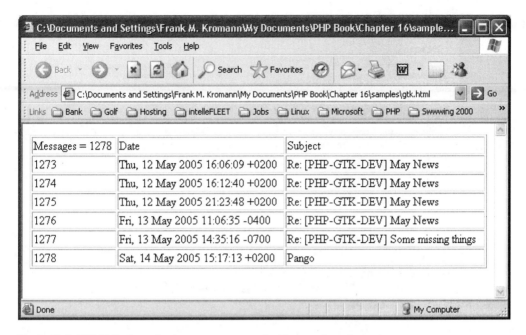

Figure 16-1. *HTML listing of a newsgroup created with* imap *functions*

More advanced message structures require a recursive function to loop through the message structure and extract each body part. The modifications to the GetMail class will allow the return of the body section as an array, as shown in the next sample.

The Code

```php
<?php
// Example getmail1.inc
if (!extension_loaded("imap")) {
  dl("php_imap.dll");
}

class GetMail {
  private $host;
  private $user;
  private $pass;
  private $type;
  private $mbox;
  private $port;
  private $mh = null;

  function __construct($host, $user, $pass, $type = 'imap',
    $mbox = 'INBOX', $port = null) {
    $this->host = $host;
    $this->user = $user;
    $this->pass = $pass;
    $this->type = strtolower($type);
```

```php
        if (is_null($port)) {
          switch($this->type) {
            case 'imap' :
              $this->port = 143;
              break;
            case 'pop3' :
              $this->port = 110;
              break;
            case 'nntp' :
              $this->port = 119;
              break;
          }
        }
        else {
          $this->port = $port;
        }
        $this->mbox = $mbox;
        $mailbox = "$this->host:$this->port/$this->type";
        $this->mh = imap_open("{" . $mailbox . "}$this->mbox",
          $this->user, $this->pass, 16);
      }

      function __destruct() {
        if ($this->mh) {
          imap_close($this->mh);
        }
      }

      function num_msg() {
        return imap_num_msg($this->mh);
      }

      function num_recent() {
        return imap_num_recent($this->mh);
      }

      function headers($offset = 1, $max = 0) {
        $msg_from = $offset;
        if ($max > 0) {
          $msg_to = min($max + $offset, $this->num_msg());
        }
        else {
          $msg_to = $this->num_msg();
        }
        $headers = array();
        for ($i = $msg_from; $i <= $msg_to; $i++) {
          $headers[imap_uid($this->mh, $i)] = imap_headerinfo($this->mh, $i);
        }
        return $headers;
      }
```

```php
function format_address($obj) {
  if (isset($obj->personal)) {
    return imap_rfc822_write_address($obj->mailbox, $obj->host, $obj->personal);
  }
  else {
    return imap_rfc822_write_address($obj->mailbox, $obj->host, '');
  }
}

function format_address_list($array, $sep = ", ") {
  $list = array();
  foreach($array as $obj) {
    $list[] = $this->format_address($obj);
  }
  return implode($sep, $list);
}

private function _decode_body($encoding, $part) {
  switch($encoding) {
    case 3: // Base64
      $strPart = imap_base64($part);
      break;
    case 4: // Quoted printable
      $strPart = imap_qprint($part);
      break;
    case 0: // 7bit
    case 1: // 8bit
    case 2: // Binary
    case 5: // Other
    default:
      break;
  }
  return $part;
}

private function _mimetype($structure) {
  $mime_type = array("TEXT", "MULTIPART", "MESSAGE",
      "APPLICATION", "AUDIO", "IMAGE", "VIDEO", "OTHER");
  if($structure->subtype) {
    return $mime_type[(int) $structure->type] . '/' . $structure->subtype;
  }
  return "TEXT/PLAIN";
}

private function _get_mime_parts($struct, $msg, &$parts,
  $options=0, $part_number=false) {
  switch ($struct->type) {
    case 0 :  // TEXT
    case 2 :  // MESSAGE
    case 3 :  // APPLICATION
    case 4 :  // AUDIO
```

```
    case 5 :  // IMAGE
    case 6 :  // VIDEO
    case 7 :  // OTHER
      if(!$part_number) {
        $part_number = "1";
      }
      $data = imap_fetchbody($this->mh, $msg, $options, $part_number);
      $parts[] = array(
        "DATA" => $this->_decode_body($struct->encoding, $data),
        "MIMETYPE" => $this->_mimetype($struct)
      );
      break;
    case 1 :  // MULTIPART
      $prefix = "";
      while(list($index, $sub_struct) = each($struct->parts)) {
        if($part_number) {
          $prefix = $part_number . '.';
        }
        $this->_get_mime_parts($sub_struct, $msg, $parts,
          $options, $prefix . ($index + 1));
      }
      break;
    }
  }

  function body($msg, $options = 0) {
    $parts = array();
    $struct = imap_fetchstructure($this->mh, $msg, $options);
    $this->_get_mime_parts($struct, $msg, $parts, $options);
    return $parts;
  }
}
?>
```

The code needed to use this class and present the result is as follows:

```
<?php
// Example 16-3-3.php
require "getmail1.inc";

$mail = new GetMail("news.php.net", "", "", "nntp", "php.gtk.dev");
$msg = $mail->num_msg();

echo <<< HTML
<html><body><table width=100% border=1>
HTML;
if ($msg > 0) {
  $headers = $mail->headers($msg);
  foreach ($headers as $uid=>$header) {
    echo "<tr><td>UID</td><td>$uid</td></tr>" .
      "<tr><td>Date</td><td>" . $header->date . "</td></td>" .
      "<tr><td>Subject</td><td>" . $header->subject . "</td></td>" .
      "<tr><td>Body</td><td>";
```

```
    foreach ($mail->body($uid, FT_UID) as $i=>$part) {
      if ($part['MIMETYPE'] == "TEXT/PLAIN") {
        echo "<pre>" . $part['DATA'] . "</pre>";
      }
    }
    echo "</td></td></tr>";
  }
}
echo <<< HTML
</table></body></html>
HTML;
?>
```

How It Works

You use the same news server as in the previous example, but now you retrieve the headers only for the last message in the newsgroup. The message ID for this message then calls the body() method to get all the parts, and for all the parts where the MIME type is text/plain, you print the actual data, as shown in Figure 16-2.

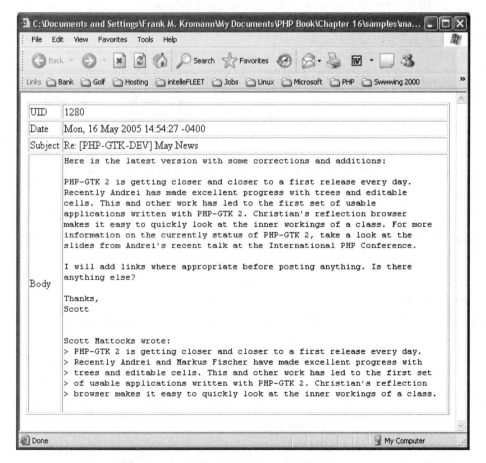

Figure 16-2. *The complete message retrieved from a newsgroup*

The modified GetMail class has four new methods, as listed in Table 16-2. Three of these are defined as private, so they can be called only from within the object.

Table 16-2. *New* GetMail *Methods*

Name	Description
_decode_body()	Converts encoded elements to readable text
_mimetype()	Finds the MIME type for a part
_get_mime_parts()	Extracts all parts of the body
body()	The public function that returns the parts

You can delete the messages in a mailbox after they are fetched or stored on the server for additional use. Deleting messages requires a call to imap_delete() for each message and one call to imap_expunge() before the session is closed. This will delete all messages marked for deletion.

If the server is an IMAP server, it's also possible to store a read/unread flag. This will allow multiple mail clients access to the same mailbox to keep track of new messages.

Table 16-3 lists the functions implemented in the IMAP extension.

Table 16-3. *Functions in the IMAP Extension*

Name	Description
imap_8bit()	Converts an 8-bit string to a quoted-printable string.
imap_alerts()	Returns all IMAP alert messages (if any) that have occurred during this page request or since the alert stack was reset.
imap_append()	Appends a string message to a specified mailbox.
imap_base64()	Decodes base 64–encoded text.
imap_binary()	Converts an 8-bit string to a base 64 string.
imap_body()	Reads the message body.
imap_bodystruct()	Reads the structure of a specified body section of a specific message.
imap_check()	Checks the current mailbox.
imap_clearflag_full()	Clears flags on messages.
imap_close()	Closes an IMAP stream.
imap_createmailbox()	Creates a new mailbox.
imap_delete()	Marks a message for deletion from the current mailbox.
imap_deletemailbox()	Deletes a mailbox.
imap_errors()	Returns all the IMAP errors (if any) that have occurred during this page request or since the error stack was reset.
imap_expunge()	Deletes all messages marked for deletion.
imap_fetch_overview()	Reads an overview of the information in the headers of the given message.
imap_fetchbody()	Fetches a particular section of the body of the message.
imap_fetchheader()	Returns the header for a message.

Name	Description
imap_fetchstructure()	Reads the structure of a particular message.
imap_get_quota()	Retrieves the quota-level settings and usage statistics per mailbox.
imap_get_quotaroot()	Retrieves the quota settings per user.
imap_getacl()	Gets the access control list (ACL) for a given mailbox.
imap_getmailboxes()	Reads the list of mailboxes, returning detailed information on each one.
imap_getsubscribed()	Lists all the subscribed mailboxes.
imap_header()	Alias of imap_headerinfo().
imap_headerinfo()	Reads the header of the message.
imap_headers()	Returns headers for all messages in a mailbox.
imap_last_error()	Returns the last IMAP error (if any) that occurred during this page request.
imap_list()	Reads the list of mailboxes.
imap_listmailbox()	Alias of imap_list().
imap_listscan()	Reads the list of mailboxes and takes a string to search for in the text of the mailbox.
imap_listsubscribed()	Alias of imap_lsub().
imap_lsub()	Lists all the subscribed mailboxes.
imap_mail_compose()	Creates a MIME message based on given envelope and body sections.
imap_mail_copy()	Copies specified messages to a mailbox.
imap_mail_move()	Moves specified messages to a mailbox.
imap_mail()	Sends an e-mail message.
imap_mailboxmsginfo()	Gets information about the current mailbox.
imap_mime_header_decode()	Decodes MIME header elements.
imap_msgno()	Returns the message sequence number for the given unique identifier (UID).
imap_num_msg()	Gives the number of messages in the current mailbox.
imap_num_recent()	Gives the number of recent messages in the current mailbox.
imap_open()	Opens an IMAP stream to a mailbox.
imap_ping()	Checks if the IMAP stream is still active.
imap_qprint()	Converts a quoted-printable string to an 8-bit string.
imap_renamemailbox()	Renames an old mailbox to a new mailbox.
imap_reopen()	Reopens IMAP stream to new mailbox.
imap_rfc822_parse_adrlist()	Parses an address string.
imap_rfc822_parse_headers()	Parses mail headers from a string.
imap_rfc822_write_address()	Returns a properly formatted e-mail address given the mailbox, host, and personal information.
imap_scanmailbox()	Alias of imap_listscan().

Continued

Table 16-3. *Continued*

Name	Description
imap_search()	Returns an array of messages matching the given search criteria.
imap_set_quota()	Sets a quota for a given mailbox.
imap_setacl()	Sets the ACL for a given mailbox.
imap_setflag_full()	Sets flags on messages.
imap_sort()	Sorts an array of message headers.
imap_status()	Returns status information on a mailbox other than the current one.
imap_subscribe()	Subscribes to a mailbox.
imap_thread()	Returns a tree of threaded message.
imap_timeout()	Sets or fetches IMAP timeout.
imap_uid()	Returns the UID for the given message sequence number.
imap_undelete()	Unmarks the message that is marked to be deleted.
imap_unsubscribe()	Unsubscribes from a mailbox.
imap_utf7_decode()	Decodes a modified UTF-7 encoded string.
imap_utf7_encode()	Converts an ISO-8859-1 string to modified UTF-7 text.
imap_utf8()	Converts MIME-encoded text to UTF-8 text.

16-4. Getting and Putting Files with FTP

Getting a file from a File Transfer Protocol (FTP) server can be as simple as getting a file from the local hard drive. You can use the same functions for file access to read files from File Transfer Protocol (FTP) sites and web servers. The following example shows how to get a file from a local hard drive.

The Code

```php
<?php
// Example 16-4-1.php
$file_name = 'somefile.ext';
$fp = fopen($file_name, 'rb');
if ($fp) {
  $data = fread($fp, filesize($file_name));
  fclose($fp);
}
?>
```

How It Works

This script uses the fopen(), fread(), and fclose() functions to open a file on a local hard drive and read its content into a variable. The filesize() function gets the size of the file so you can read the entire file in one chunk.

PHP allows the filename to be written as a URL, so you can use the same code to fetch a file from a web or an FTP server just by changing the filename to a full URL.

The Code

```php
<?php
// Example 16-4-2.php
$file_name = 'http://php.net/index.php';
$fp = fopen($file_name, 'r');
if ($fp) {
  $data = '';
  while (!feof($fp)) {
    $data .= fread($fp, 4096);
  }
  fclose($fp);
}
echo $data;
?>
```

How It Works

In the first example, the function filesize() gets the length of the file. This is not possible with remote URLs, as the server does not always include the content length in the headers, especially if the content is generated dynamically. So, in this case, you read the file in small chunks of 4,096 bytes and keep reading until the stream reports the end of the file. The eof() function checks the stream for each block you read.

If the file on the remote server is protected from anonymous access, it's possible to include a username and password in the URL like this:

```php
$file_name = 'ftp://user:pass@somedomain.com/subdir/file.txt';
```

▮**Note** The username and password will be transferred to the server as plain text.

You can use this method to write files to an FTP server with the right permissions. Some web (HTTP) servers allow writing to the server, but the fopen_wrapper for HTTP in PHP does not implement this. The next example shows how you can read a file from the local hard drive and write it to an FTP server using the fopen_wrapper for FTP.

The Code

```php
<?php
// Example 16-4-3.php
$file_name = "16.3.2.php";
$fp = fopen($file_name, 'r');
if ($fp) {
  $data = fread($fp, filesize($file_name));
  fclose($fp);

  $file_name = "ftp://user:pass@ftp.somedomain.com/home/user/$file_name";
  $fp = fopen($file_name, 'wt');
  if ($fp) {
    echo 'writing data';
    fwrite($fp, $data);
    fclose($fp);
  }
}
?>
```

How It Works

First you read a file from the local hard drive. The file is then written to a location that is specified by the full URL, with the protocol, the username, the password, and the full path to where the file is going to be stored. This will require that the FTP server is configured to allow the user to write to this location.

Using the fopen functions to access remote data makes it easy to integrate simple tasks, and it's a good method for reading remote content in text or Extensible Markup Language (XML) format, but it does not give full access to the files on the remote system. This is where the built-in FTP functions come in handy. The FTP functions let you do most of the stuff you can do from a normal FTP client program. Table 16-4 lists all the implemented FTP functions.

Table 16-4. *FTP Functions*

Name	Description
ftp_alloc()	Allocates space for a file to be uploaded
ftp_cdup()	Changes to the parent directory
ftp_chdir()	Changes the current directory on an FTP server
ftp_chmod()	Sets permissions on a file via FTP
ftp_close()	Closes an FTP connection
ftp_connect()	Opens an FTP connection
ftp_delete()	Deletes a file on the FTP server
ftp_exec()	Requests execution of a program on the FTP server
ftp_fget()	Downloads a file from the FTP server and saves to an open file
ftp_fput()	Uploads from an open file to the FTP server
ftp_get_option()	Retrieves various runtime behaviors of the current FTP stream

Name	Description
ftp_get()	Downloads a file from the FTP server
ftp_login()	Logs into an FTP connection
ftp_mdtm()	Returns the last modified time of the given file
ftp_mkdir()	Creates a directory
ftp_nb_continue()	Continues retrieving/sending a file (nonblocking)
ftp_nb_fget()	Retrieves a file from the FTP server and writes it to an open file (nonblocking)
ftp_nb_fput()	Stores a file from an open file to the FTP server (nonblocking)
ftp_nb_get()	Retrieves a file from the FTP server and writes it to a local file (nonblocking)
ftp_nb_put()	Stores a file on the FTP server (nonblocking)
ftp_nlist()	Returns a list of files in the given directory
ftp_pasv()	Turns passive mode on or off
ftp_put()	Uploads a file to the FTP server
ftp_pwd()	Returns the current directory name
ftp_quit()	Alias of ftp_close()
ftp_raw()	Sends an arbitrary command to an FTP server
ftp_rawlist()	Returns a detailed list of files in the given directory
ftp_rename()	Renames a file or a directory on the FTP server
ftp_rmdir()	Removes a directory
ftp_set_option()	Sets miscellaneous runtime FTP options
ftp_site()	Sends a SITE command to the server
ftp_size()	Returns the size of the given file
ftp_ssl_connect()	Opens a secure SSL-FTP connection
ftp_systype()	Returns the system type identifier of the remote FTP server

The FTP functions make it possible to make secure (SSL) or nonsecure connections to a remote FTP server. Creating a secure connection requires that the remote server supports that form of connection. The only difference between a secure and a nonsecure connection is the function used to create the connection. Switching between the two is a matter of choosing the right connect function. Both ftp_connect() and ftp_ssl_connect() will return a connection handle that will be passed to the other functions, so it will be transparent to use an SSL connection.

The next example shows how you can use the ftp_* functions to upload a single file to an FTP server.

The Code

```php
<?php
// Example 16-4-4.php
$conn = ftp_connect("ftp.somedomain.com");
if ($conn) {
  $session = ftp_login($conn, "user", "pass");
```

```
    if ($session) {
      if (ftp_chdir($conn, "somedir")) {
        ftp_put($conn, "remote.txt", "local.txt", FTP_ASCII);
      }
    }
    ftp_close($conn);
  }
?>
```

How It Works

The first step when using the FTP functions is to establish a connection to the server. You can then use the handle returned from ftp_connect() to create a session, change to a directory, and upload the file.

The next example shows how you can use these FTP functions to create an application that will connect to an FTP server, get all files with their file sizes from a folder, and use that data to create a list. Each filename will be presented as a link, allowing the user to download the files directly from the FTP server.

The Code

```php
<?php
// Example 16-4-5.php
function GetContent($host, $user, $pass, $folder) {
  $content = array();
  $conn = ftp_connect($host);
  if ($conn) {
    $session = ftp_login($conn, $user, $pass);
    if ($session) {
      if (empty($folder) || ftp_chdir($conn, $folder)) {
        $files = ftp_nlist($conn, ".");
        if (is_array($files)) {
          foreach($files as $file) {
            $size = ftp_size($conn, $file);
            if ($size > 0) {
              $content[] = array(
                "name" => $file,
                "url" => "ftp://$user:$pass@$host/$folder/$file",
                "size" => $size
              );
            }
          }
        }
      }
    }
    ftp_close($conn);
  }
  return $content;
}
```

```php
$files = GetContent("ftp.somedomain.com", "user", "pass", "/somedir");
echo "<html><body><table width=100% border=0>" .
    "<tr><td>Name</td><td align=right>Size</td></tr>";
foreach ($files as $file) {
  echo "<tr><td><a href='$file[url]'>$file[name]</a></td>
  <td align=right>$file[size]</td></tr>";
}
echo "</table></body></html>";
?>
```

How It Works

The function GetContent() takes four parameters that specify the hostname, user ID, password, and folder. This function will create an FTP connection, use the user ID and password to log onto the server, and change the current directory to the specified folder. A list of files for the directory is created with the ftp_nlist() function. For each file in the list, you check the size and create an entry in the array. If the file size is 0, you assume that it's a folder and do not add it to the array. When the list of files is complete, it is returned and used to generate an HTML table.

Note that the username and password for the FTP server will be exposed in the link, creating a potential security problem. To avoid this problem, you can modify the script to have two modes. The first mode gets a list of files on the FTP server, and the second mode downloads a specific file. This way the username and password will be hidden from the user. The downside of this method is the added network traffic, as the file is now transferred from the FTP server to the web server before it's transferred to the user.

The Code

```php
<?php
// Example 16-4-6.php
function GetContent($host, $user, $pass, $folder) {
  $content = array();
  $conn = ftp_connect($host);
  if ($conn) {
    $session = ftp_login($conn, $user, $pass);
    if ($session) {
      if (empty($folder) || ftp_chdir($conn, $folder)) {
        $files = ftp_nlist($conn, ".");
        if (is_array($files)) {
          foreach($files as $file) {
            $size = ftp_size($conn, $file);
            if ($size > 0) {
              $content[] = array(
                "name" => $file,
                "url" => $GLOBALS['PHP_SELF'] . "?mode=get&file=" .
                urlencode($file),
                "size" => $size
              );
```

```
            }
          }
        }
      }
    }
    ftp_close($conn);
  }
  return $content;
}

function GetFile($host, $user, $pass, $folder, $file) {
  $ret = false;
  $conn - ftp_connect($host);
  if ($conn) {
    $session = ftp_login($conn, $user, $pass);
    if ($session) {
      if (empty($folder) || ftp_chdir($conn, $folder)) {
        $local_file = tempnam(".", "ftp");
        if (ftp_get($conn, $local_file, $file, FTP_BINARY)) {
          $ret = $local_file;

        }
      }
      ftp_close($conn);
    }
    return $ret;
}

if (empty($mode)) $mode = "list";

$host = "ftp.somedomain.com";
$user = "user";
$pass = "pass";
$folder = "/somedir";

switch($mode) {
  case "list" :
    $files = GetContent($host, $user, $pass, $folder);
    echo "<html><body><table width=100% border=0>" .
        "<tr><td>Name</td><td align=right>Size</td></tr>";
    foreach ($files as $file) {
      echo "<tr><td><a href='$file[url]'>$file[name]</a></td>
        <td align=right>$file[size]</td></tr>";
    }
    echo "</table></body></html>";
    break;
```

```
  case "get" :
    $local_file = GetFile($host, $user, $pass, $folder, $file);
    if ($local_file) {
      header("Content-Type: application/octetstream");
      header("Content-Disposition: attachment; filename=\"$file\"");
      readfile($local_file);
      unlink($local_file);
    }
    else {
      echo "<html><body><h1>Error:
        </h1>Could not download $folder/$file from $host</body></html>";
    }
}
?>
```

How It Works

In the "get" section of this script, the file is downloaded from the FTP server and stored in the current working directory with a unique temporary name. When the file is downloaded to the client, the name is changed with the `header("Content-Disposition: attachment; filename=\"$file\"");` command. When the file is downloaded, it is removed from the web server. In this example, the temporary file is created in the same directory as the script, but it is better programming practice to create this file in the system's `temp` folder.

16-5. Performing DNS Lookups

Converting hostnames to IP addresses can be useful in applications that perform many connections to the same host. By using the IP address, the system will not have to perform the Domain Name System (DNS) lookup on each request. PHP has three functions that can do DNS lookups, as shown in Table 16-5.

Table 16-5. *DNS Lookup Functions*

Name	Description
gethostbyname()	Gets IP address corresponding to the hostname
gethostbyname1()	Gets list of IP addresses corresponding to the hostname
gethostbyaddr()	Gets hostname corresponding to an IP address

All these functions use the DNS servers defined on the system to resolve hostnames and IP addresses. It is not possible to communicate with other DNS servers unless you use the `PEAR::DNS` class. Unfortunately, this class does not work with PHP 5 at this time.

The first function, `gethostbyname()`, will return the IP address of the hostname (or the hostname if it was impossible to resolve it to an IP address).

The following example shows how to use these three functions.

The Code

```php
<?php
// Example 16-5-1.php
$ip = gethostbyname("www.example.com");
echo "IP = $ip\n";
$host = gethostbyaddr("192.0.34.166");
echo "Host = $host\n";
$ip = gethostbynamel("yahoo.com");
print_r($ip);
?>
```

This example produces the following output:

```
IP = 192.0.34.166
Host = www.example.com
Array
(
    [0] => 216.109.112.135
    [1] => 66.94.234.13
)
```

In addition to these simple lookup functions, it's also possible to query for a more detailed DNS record. These functions are available only on Unix systems and are listed in Table 16-6.

Table 16-6. *Additional DNS Functions*

Name	Description
getmxrr()	Fetches the mail exchange (MX) record associated with a hostname
dns_get_mx()	Alias for getmxrr()
checkdnsrr()	Checks for the existence of DNS records for a hostname
dns_check_record()	Alias for checkdnsrr()
dns_get_record()	Fetches DNS records associated with a hostname

You can use these functions to check the existence of a specific record type or to fetch a specific record from the DNS server associated with a hostname. You can check the existence of a DNS entry for a hostname, validate the existence of a mail server for an e-mail address, or read special text messages stored in DNS servers.

The next example shows how to use dns_get_record() to get the DNS information associated with the hostname www.php.net.

The Code

```php
<?php
// Example 16-5-2.php
$record = dns_get_record("www.php.net");
print_r($record);
?>
```

This example produces the following output:

```
Array
(
    [0] => Array
        (
            [host] => www.php.net
            [type] => CNAME
            [target] => php.net
            [class] => IN
            [ttl] => 80876
        )

)
```

This tells you that www.php.net is a canonical name for php.net.

16-6. Checking Whether a Host Is Alive

Troubleshooting communication with services on other hosts sometimes requires knowledge about the status of a remote server. You can get this information with the ping program. The ping program is a small network utility that sends a special Internet Control Message Protocol (ICMP) package to the remote host. If the host is configured to respond to this package type, it will send back a response. The response time will depend on the packet size as well as available bandwidth and other network factors.

When a server has disabled the response to ping packets, it is not possible to use this method to verify that the server is alive. Servers might also be located inside a firewall/router with network address translation (NAT). That makes it impossible to know the real IP address of the server, and the ability to ping the public address simply means that the router is alive.

The PEAR repository provides a class called Net_Ping that is implemented as a wrapper around the system's ping function. You can use this class to check whether a host is alive, as shown in the next example.

The Code

```php
<?php
// Example 16-6-1.php
require_once 'Net/Ping.php' ;
$ping = new Net_Ping('C:\WINDOWS\system32\ping.exe', 'windows');
$ping->setArgs(
```

```
  array(
     "count" => 5,
     "size"  => 32,
     "ttl"   => 128
  )
);
var_dump($ping->ping("yahoo.com"));
?>
```

How It Works

This example requires that PEAR::Net_Ping is installed on the system and the user has access to the ping command. This example is designed to run on a Windows system but can run on Unix systems if you change the location of the ping command and the system parameter.

When the class is instantiated, you can define some additional parameters for the ping command. In this case, you define count = 5 to indicate that you want five packages transmitted. You set the packet size to 32 bytes and the maximum time to live to 128. The result is returned as a string or a PEAR Error object.

The user account used by the web server to execute the PHP scripts might not have access to this function, or it might not have any execute rights. It is still possible to create a ping function, but it requires using socket functions and requires low-level knowledge about the ICMP packet structure. ICMP packets are used to send information about unreachable hosts, perform trace routes, and send ping requests.

An ICMP echo request packet must be at least 8 bytes long and have the following elements:

- Byte 0 = Packet type (0x08 = echo request)

- Byte 1 = Packet code (0x00 for the echo request)

- Byte 2–3 = Checksum

- Byte 4–5 = Packet ID

- Byte 6–7 = Packet sequence

- Byte 8–xx = Optional data

The data is returned in the echo package from the server and can check the quality of the line. The code in the next example shows how to build a Ping() class that will allow the script to test the connection to a host. The code is based on the code contributed to PHP's online documentation pages, but it has been modified to allow multiple requests and return additional information about the packets.

The Code

```php
<?php
// Example 16-6-2.php
if (!extension_loaded("sockets")) {
  dl("php_sockets.dll");
}
```

```php
class Ping {
  public $icmp_socket;
  public $request;
  public $request_len;
  pubic $reply;
  public $errstr;
  public $timer_start_time;

  function __construct() {
    $this->icmp_socket = socket_create(AF_INET, SOCK_RAW, 1);
    socket_set_block($this->icmp_socket);
  }

  function ip_checksum($data) {
    $sum = 0;
    for($i=0; $i<strlen($data); $i += 2) {
      if ($data[$i+1])
        $bits = unpack('n*',$data[$i].$data[$i+1]);
      else
        $bits = unpack('C*',$data[$i]);
      $sum += $bits[1];
      }

    while ($sum>>16) $sum = ($sum & 0xffff) + ($sum >> 16);
    $checksum = pack('n1',~$sum);
    return $checksum;
  }

  function start_time()  {
    $this->timer_start_time = microtime();
  }

  function get_time($precission=2) {
    // format start time
    $start_time = explode(" ", $this->timer_start_time);
    $start_time = $start_time[1] + $start_time[0];
    // get and format end time
    $end_time = explode (" ", microtime());
    $end_time = $end_time[1] + $end_time[0];
    return number_format($end_time - $start_time, $precission);
  }

  function Build_Packet($request, $size) {
    $type = "\x08";
    $code = "\x00";
    $chksm = "\x00\x00";
    $id = "\x00\x00";
```

```php
        $sqn = pack("n", $request);
        $data = "";
        for ($i = 0; $i < $size; $i++) $data .= chr(mt_rand(0,255));
        $data = "abcd";

        // now we need to change the checksum to the real checksum
        $chksm = $this->ip_checksum($type.$code.$chksm.$id.$sqn.$data);

        // now lets build the actual icmp packet
        $this->request = $type.$code.$chksm.$id.$sqn.$data;
        $this->request_len = strlen($this->request);
    }

    function Ping($dst_addr, $requests=4, $size=32, $timeout=5, $percision=3) {
        $result = array();

        // set the timeout
        socket_set_option($this->icmp_socket,
            SOL_SOCKET,  // socket level
            SO_RCVTIMEO, // timeout option
            array(
                "sec"=>$timeout,
                "usec"=>0
            )
        );

        if ($dst_addr) {
            for($r = 0; $r < $requests; $r++) {
                $dst_ip = gethostbyname($dst_addr);
                if (!socket_connect($this->icmp_socket, $dst_addr, NULL)) {
                    $this->errstr = "Unable to connect to $dst_addr";
                    return false;
                }
                $this->Build_Packet($r, $size);
                $this->start_time();
                socket_write($this->icmp_socket, $this->request, $this->request_len);
                if (@socket_recv($this->icmp_socket, &$this->reply, 256, 0)) {
                    $bytes = strlen($this->reply);
                    $time = $this->get_time($percision);
                    $ttl = ord($this->reply{7})*256 + ord($this->reply{8});
                    $result[] = "Reply from $dst_ip: bytes=$bytes seq=$r time=$time ttl=$ttl";
                }
                else {
                    $result[] = "Request timed out";
                }
            }
        }
```

```
    else {
      $this->errstr = "Destination address not specified";
      return false;
    }
    return $result;
  }
}

$ping = new Ping;
$response = $ping->ping("php.net");

if (is_array($response)) {
  foreach($response as $res) {
    echo "$res\n";
  }
}
else {
  echo $ping->errstr;
}
?>
```

How It Works

This example defines a Ping() class that uses the socket functions to communicate with the remote host. The socket functions are not built into PHP by default, so you need to load the extension or recompile PHP with the extension loaded. When the class is instantiated, you can call the ping method with a hostname as the first parameter, and it will return an array with the results of each request, like this:

```
Reply from 64.246.30.37: bytes=32 seq=0 time=0.056 ttl=50
Reply from 64.246.30.37: bytes=32 seq=1 time=0.049 ttl=50
Reply from 64.246.30.37: bytes=32 seq=2 time=0.050 ttl=50
Reply from 64.246.30.37: bytes=32 seq=3 time=0.050 ttl=50
```

16-7. Getting Information About a Domain Name

When you see a domain name as part of a URL or an e-mail address, you do not get much information about the owner of the domain. Opening a browser and navigating to the site might give you a clue, but it will not always tell you any details about who is behind the site or domain. This information is available to some degree in Whois databases. These databases are maintained by domain registrars and can give you information about the owners of a domain. However, the data for a given domain might not be available if the owner has blocked it. In addition, people can register domains under pseudonyms or with a contact person from the registrar, so you should use the information with caution.

PEAR has a nice little class that makes it possible to query a Whois database to get a string of information.

The following example shows how you can use the Net_Whois class to query information about a domain name.

The Code

```php
<?php
// Example 16-7-1.php
require_once "Net/Whois.php";

$server = "whois.networksolutions.com";
$query  = "networksolutions.com";

$whois = new Net_Whois;
$data = $whois->query($query, $server);
var_dump($data);
?>
```

The output from this code will include a disclaimer from Network Solutions and the following information:

```
NOTICE AND TERMS OF USE: You are not authorized to access or query our WHOIS
database through the use of high-volume, automated, electronic processes. The
Data in Network Solutions' WHOIS database is provided by Network Solutions for
information purposes only, and to assist persons in obtaining information about or
related to a domain name registration record. Network Solutions does not guarantee
its accuracy. By submitting a WHOIS query, you agree to abide by the following terms
of use: You agree that you may use this Data only for lawful purposes and that under
no circumstances will you use this Data to: (1) allow, enable, or otherwise support
the transmission of mass unsolicited, commercial advertising or solicitations
via e-mail, telephone, or facsimile; or (2) enable high volume, automated,
electronic processes that apply to Network Solutions (or its computer systems). The
compilation, repackaging, dissemination or other use of this Data is expressly
prohibited without the prior written consent of Network Solutions. You agree not to
use high-volume, automated, electronic processes to access or query the WHOIS
database. Network Solutions reserves the right to terminate your access to the WHOIS
database in its sole discretion, including without limitation, for excessive
querying of the WHOIS database or for failure to otherwise abide by this policy.
Network Solutions reserves the right to modify these terms at any time.

Registrant:
Network Solutions, LLC
    Network Solutions LLC
    13200 WOODLAND PARK DR
    HERNDON, VA 20171
    US

    Domain Name: NETWORKSOLUTIONS.COM
```

```
Administrative Contact, Technical Contact:
    Network Solutions, LLC          nocsupervisor@networksolutions.com
    Network Solutions LLC
    13200 WOODLAND PARK DR
    HERNDON, VA 20171
    US
    570-708-8788 fax: 703-668-5817

Record expires on 27-Apr-2015.
Record created on 27-Apr-1998.
Database last updated on 17-May-2005 01:20:59 EDT.

Domain servers in listed order:

NS1.NETSOL.COM              216.168.229.228
NS2.NETSOL.COM              216.168.229.229
NS3.NETSOL.COM              216.168.229.229
```

Summary

PHP was designed as a tool to embed business logic into HTML documents, but it has since advanced to be a complex scripting language with many extensions that allow a script developer to integrate with external web services. In this chapter, we discussed how you can use PHP to send mail and read messages from mail and news servers. You can create advanced, web-based mail clients or news readers, and you can send automated messages from a server when you need to do so.

Finally, we discussed low-level services that can get information about other servers and domains.

Index